WALTHER EICHRODT

THEOLOGY OF THE OLD TESTAMENT

VOLUME TWO

THE OLD TESTAMENT LIBRARY

General Editors

G. Ernest Wright, The Divinity School, Harvard University
John Bright, Union Theological Seminary, Richmond, Virginia
James Barr, University of Manchester
Peter Ackroyd, University of London

WALTHER EICHRODT

THEOLOGY
OF THE
OLD TESTAMENT

VOLUME TWO

Translated by
J. A. BAKER

The Westminster Press
Philadelphia

© SCM Press, Ltd. 1967
Translated by John Baker from the German
Theologie des Alten Testaments, Teil 2 /3
(fifth edition, 1964, published by
Ehrenfried Klotz Verlag, Stuttgart,
in association with
Vandenhoeck & Ruprecht, Göttingen)

Library of Congress Catalog Card No. 61–11867

Published by The Westminster Press®
Philadelphia, Pennsylvania

PRINTED IN THE UNITED STATES OF AMERICA
Fifth Printing, 1975

CONTENTS

5

PREFACE TO VOLUME TWO

T H I S second volume of my *Theology of the Old Testament* is appearing rather
a long time after the first volume, which was published in 1961. Such a long
gap was not originally intended and was the result of circumstances over
which the author had no control. Of course, he was responsible in an
indirect way; the treatments in Part Three of man's relationship with God,
Old Testament morality, the problem of sin and forgiveness, and immortality, presented the translator with particularly difficult problems in
providing English renderings of complex German formulations. It is
thanks to the inexhaustible care and dedication of the Reverend John
Baker and his theological acumen that in spite of these problems the
English version is almost an advance on the German original in clarity
and comprehensibility. He is due the author's special gratitude. The
publishers are also to be thanked for overcoming all the difficulties which
have stood in the way of the completion of this work. It is only to be
hoped that this second volume fully lives up to the expectations aroused
by the first.

Münchenstein bei Basel
November 1966   W A L T H E R   E I C H R O D T

TRANSLATOR'S PREFACE

W I T H the publication of this second volume I come to the end of a task
which has been my constant company for ten years. It might be thought
that one would reach such a goal with relief; but the outstanding feeling
is that of gratitude for the privilege of having been allowed to create the
English version of a theological classic, and after that, of something akin
to sadness at parting from an intimate friend.

I wish to record my heartfelt thanks to Professor Eichrodt for the care
with which he scrutinized every word of the typescript, thereby placing

9

both myself and every reader still further in his debt, and for the honour of his kind appreciation and encouragement; also to David Edwards, John Bowden, and the staff of the SCM Press for their immense patience and helpfulness at every stage.

Two things I may perhaps be allowed to say briefly to the reader. First, this work has deservedly attained an international reputation; but one criticism has been voiced which, it seems to me, is based very largely on a misconception. This is the objection that the 'covenant', though a major OT theme, is in fact no more than any other concept universal or normative for the OT material, and therefore constitutes a framework just as artificial and arbitrary as those of other Theologies of the OT. But the focus of these volumes is not any one concept, but only God; and the covenant occupies the place it does in the presentation not because it dominates the thought of every OT writer—this is plainly not so—but because every OT writer, even the ones who never mention the covenant, is unable to escape from the kind of God of whose dealings with the world and men the covenant is the archetypal symbol. Believe in him, wrestle with him, react against him—whatever they do, it is this kind of God, and not some other, with whom they are involved, the transcendent Lord who 'spake and it was done', who gives life and the way of life to every creature, who enters into fellowship with Man, seeking his free response, and who guides all to its goal by his unconditioned and sovereign will. To Israel this kind of God was first revealed as Lord of the Covenant; and whatever their words, whatever the widening and deepening, or narrowing and distorting, of their thoughts about him, this kind he remained. That historical fact is the ultimate justification for something which makes no claim to be a conceptual scheme (an approach quite alien anyway to the OT, as the author has himself frequently stressed), but simply the most adequate 'way in' to the complex reality of God as revealed in the OT.

Secondly, and lastly, it is this fact which makes the present work far more than a classic of OT study. For the greatest issue within Christianity today is nothing other than this: are we to go on believing in this kind of God, or not? What it means to believe in him, and what, therefore, to believe in his Son, our Saviour, has rarely, I believe, been more profoundly set forth than in the pages which follow.

Corpus Christi College, Oxford   JOHN BAKER
Christmas 1966

ABBREVIATIONS

ANEP	J. B. Pritchard, *The Ancient Near East in Pictures*, 1954
ANET	J. B. Pritchard, *Ancient Near Eastern Texts relating to the Old Testament*,[2] 1955
AO	*Der Alte Orient*
AOB	H. Gressmann, *Altorientalische Bilder zum AT*[2], 1927
AOT	H. Gressmann, *Altorientalische Texte zum AT*[2], 1926
ARW	*Archiv für Religionswissenschaft*
ATAO	A. Jeremias, *Das alte Testament im Lichte des Alten Orients*[4], 1930
ATANT	Abhandlungen zur Theologie des Alten und Neuen Testaments
ATD	Das Alte Testament Deutsch
BAT	Die Botschaft des Alten Testaments
BBB	Bonner Biblische Beiträge
BKAT	Biblischer Kommentar, Altes Testament
BWANT	Beiträge zur Wissenschaft vom Alten und Neuen Testament
BZAW	Beihefte zur Zeitschrift für die alttestamentliche Wissenschaft
EAT	Erläuterungen zum Alten Testament
EvTh	*Evangelische Theologie*
HAT	Handbuch zum Alten Testament
HRE	J. J. Herzog, *Realenzyklopädie für protestantische Theologie und Kirche*[3], ed. A. Hauck
JBL	*Journal of Biblical Literature*
KF	*Kleinasiatische Forschungen*
LVT	*Lexicon in Veteris Testamenti Libros*, ed. L. Köhler and W. Baumgartner
MVAG	Mitteilungen der Vorderasiatischen und Aegyptischen Gesellschaft
NKZ	*Neue Kirchliche Zeitschrift*
OLZ	*Orientalistische Literaturzeitung*
PEQ	*Palestine Exploration Quarterly*
RB	*Revue Biblique*

RGG	*Die Religion in Geschichte und Gegenwart*[3]
RGV	Religionsgeschichtliche Volksbücher
RHR	*Revue de l'Histoire des Religions*
RLA	*Reallexikon der Assyriologie*
SVT	*Supplements to Vetus Testamentum*
TLZ	*Theologische Literaturzeitung*
TR	*Theologische Rundschau*
TWNT	*Theologisches Wörterbuch zum Neuen Testament*
TZ	*Theologische Zeitschrift*
VT	*Vetus Testamentum*
ZAW	*Zeitschrift für die alttestamentliche Wissenschaft*
ZDMG	*Zeitschrift der Deutschen Morgenländischen Gesellschaft*
ZDPV	*Zeitschrift des Deutschen Palästinavereins*
ZTK	*Zeitschrift für Theologie und Kirche*

PART TWO

GOD AND THE WORLD

XII

THE FORMS OF GOD'S SELF-
MANIFESTATION

O N T H E S U B J E C T O F God's relations with the world Israel inherited from her pre-Mosaic past all kinds of conceptions on a
par with those of her kinsfolk in the heathen nations. However,
in accordance with the fundamental character of the Mosaic gospel[1]
these conceptions were not eradicated by any systematic purification
of dogma; it was only gradually that they underwent transformation
and reform as a result of Israel's experience of the covenant God and
his nature. It is therefore hardly surprising that in this particular context we find an erratic variety of terms and concepts, and many
elements common to the thought of the whole ancient Near East.
Nevertheless it is precisely this kaleidoscopic quality which renders all
the more impressive the single thread running through the whole—
the determination to subordinate the whole world and everything in
it to the one God of Sinai; and this dominating theme, by injecting
the old modes of speech, developed on polytheistic assumptions, with
new content, changes them into instruments suitable for proclaiming
the universal sovereignty of Yahweh.

All this applies with especial force to Old Testament statements
about the forms of God's self-manifestation. In this context men's
basic attitude to God's relationship with the world is bound to find
expression in very concrete imagery, fashioned in many cases from
the stuff of direct personal experience. Hence it is here that the influence of the Old Testament experience of God on the traditional
views of God's connection with the world can be most clearly observed, and the process studied by which as a result of that influence
this connection is defined in a quite distinctive way.

[1] Cf. vol. I, ch. II.1 (a), pp. 37f.

I. MANIFESTATIONS OF GOD IN THE REALMS OF NATURE AND OF MAN

That God can without detriment to his majesty give visible evidence of his presence on earth is a conviction taken as much for granted by Israel as by other nations. Their sharing the common view on this point is shown by the fact that they regard it as perfectly possible for the deity to manifest himself both in the forces of Nature and in human form.

1. The Israelite view is, however, distinctive in this respect. In marked contrast to the Canaanite and Babylonian conceptions it is not those natural phenomena which are directly familiar to Man and welcomed by him as beneficent, such as sun and moon, springs and rivers, trees and woods, which are regarded as the visible expressions of the Godhead, but the natural forces which break out with startling suddeness to terrify men and to threaten them with destruction, such as the lightning-flash, the dark thunder-cloud or the raging storm— all of which are combined in *the majestic phenomenon of the thunderstorm.* Hence from the earliest to the latest times the God who hastens both to judgment and to succour is envisaged in the thunderstorm,[1] riding upon the storm-clouds as if in a chariot or on a charger,[2] causing his voice to resound in the thunder,[3] hurling the lightning as his arrows or spears,[4] shooting forth fire from heaven as his burning breath or tongue of flame.[5] In the snorting of his anger he sends down the lashing rain;[6] with his fist he smites in the hail or the shattering storm.[7] The best instance of the extremely concrete way in which this vision of the divine majesty was experienced is to be found in the description of the Sinai theophany.[8] It is, moreover, only natural that the other fire-phenomena of a sinister or terrifying kind, such as volcanic eruptions,[9] subterranean fire,[10] and so on, should also be understood

[1] Cf. Ex. 19.9ff.; 20.18ff.; 24.12ff.; Deut. 5.21ff.; 33.2; Judg. 5.4ff.; Pss. 18.8ff.; 68.8ff.; 77.17ff.; 97.2ff.

[2] Cf. Pss. 18.11; 104.3; Isa. 19.1; 66.15; Hab. 3.8.

[3] Ex. 19.19; 20.18f.; I Sam. 7.10; Amos 1.2; Isa. 30.27; Ps. 29.3ff.; Job 37.5. Cf. *nātan (bᵉ)ḳōl* meaning 'to thunder', Ps. 18.4; 46.7; Jer. 25.30.

[4] Ps. 18.15; 77.18; Hab. 3.9f., 14; Zech. 9.14.

[5] Ps. 18.9; Isa. 30.27.

[6] Isa. 30.28.

[7] Amos 9.5; Isa. 2.10, 19; 9.9, 11; 10.33; 18.5; 28.2; 30.30.

[8] Ex. 19.16ff.; 20.18f.

[9] Unambiguous instances of these are few, cf. e.g., Isa. 30.33. In the case of Ex. 19.16ff. individual details from the description of a volcanic eruption may have been interpolated into the account of a storm-theophany. Isa. 29.6; Hab. 3.6ff.;

as visible evidence of the presence of God; nevertheless being less relevant to conditions in Palestine they recede markedly in importance.

Neither the ordinary storm, whatever havoc it might work, nor the terrible earthquake ever acquired a significance equal to that of the thunderstorm as the favoured medium of the theophany, for the simple reason that their destructive force remained invisible. Hence they are more often found as accompaniments and reinforcements of the thunderstorm, though numerous passages suggest that at one time they may have played a more independent role as vehicles of the divine presence.[1] By contrast, from the earliest times, the stars remain Yahweh's subordinate servants, engaging in battle, for example, as his helpers (Judg. 5.21), or exciting men's wonder and astonishment by their mysterious life and movement (Pss. 19.1ff.; 8.4), but always subject to the majesty and power of their ruler, who dwells in darkness (Ps. 19.2, 5b; I Kings 8.12 LXX). Even when the seductive power of the Canaanite fertility cults was at its height, the manner in which the God of Israel manifested himself was always quite distinct from that of the local vegetation deities.

Because of this close relation between Yahweh and the elemental power of fire attempts have been made to explain him as originally a fire-demon, and therefore a nature deity like the rest.[2] Such a conclusion, however, is only possible if individual texts are taken in false isolation without reference to the total picture of the covenant God as presented in the sources. Even though care must be taken not to overlook such ancient strands of tradition as those deriving from the Midianite conception of God, or from the attitude toward Nature of the steppe-dweller,[3] nevertheless much greater importance must

---

Jud. 5.4f.; Pss. 29 and 77.18ff. refer not to volcanic phenomena but to a combination of thunderstorm and earth-tremors, the latter being especially frequent in Palestine, the classic country for structural seismic disturbances: cf. *ZDPV* 50 (1927), pp. 290ff.; 51 (1929), pp. 124f.

[10] Ex. 3.2ff.; 13.21; 14.19ff.; Num. 11.1f.; 14.14.

[1] In Ps. 18.8ff. the combination of thunderstorm, storm and earthquake is particularly striking; cf. further the passages cited in n. 1, p. 16, and n. 9, p. 16, above. For the independent significance of storm and earthquake cf. I Sam. 14.15, and especially I Kings 19.10ff.

[2] E.g. by E. Meyer, *Die Israeliten*, 1906, p. 70; G. Hölscher, *Geschichte der isr.-jüd. Religion*, 1922, p. 67.

[3] Cf. B. D. Eerdmans, *De Godsdienst van Israel* I, 1930, pp. 35ff.; H. H. Rowley, *From Joseph to Joshua*, 1950, pp. 149ff. The worship of the storm-god Hadad by Israel's tribal kinsfolk, the Aramaeans, may be adduced in this connection; cf. vol. I, p. 201.

be attached to the patent fact that at all periods the manifestation of the divine in fire was felt to be especially congenial to the concept of Yahweh. What happened was not that the fire-nature of an originally demonic being imported the notion of the revelation of the deity in fire into the Israelite conception of God as a fortuitous characteristic, but that men's experience of the unapproachable holiness and terrifying power of the covenant God caused them to see as the appropriate symbol and speaking likeness of the divine nature that element distinguished above all others for the suddenness of its outbreaks and for the mockery which it makes of all human defences. It was therefore only to be expected that it should be the thunderstorm, that mighty spectacle of Nature so impressive both to ear and eye, together with the inexplicable and menacing phenomena of the volcano and of subterranean fire, which by their eruptions so suddenly and terrifyingly transform the hitherto familiar world, which were given prominent and particular significance. It was equally natural that it should be fire in its elemental force, so overwhelmingly superior to puny Man, and not the still flame of hearth or altar,[1] which was accorded this special status, and that it should be storm and earthquake which were indicated as its appropriate companions.

This concept of the divine fire may have been reinforced, and at the same time given a more interior meaning, by visionary experience, one of the most frequent elements in which is the sensation of dazzling light or fire.[2] Here nature-symbolism not only received compelling confirmation from personal life, but also underwent farreaching reinterpretation as the mode of God's irruption into the psychic life of Man.[3] Furthermore this more decidedly metaphorical role of the fire-element inevitably went hand in hand with new insights into the way in which God might be conceived as present in it.

For it is clear enough that originally this was understood in the thought-forms of Nature mythology. That is why it is a waste of time to argue whether the Israelite believed that he was really seeing God himself in such natural phenomena, or whether he thought of it as a figurative appearance, as the perception of God in a kind of picture. In general, popular thought makes no such fine-drawn theological distinctions, and in Israel it certainly took the vision of God in a very

[1] Exceptions to this rule are possibly to be seen in Judg. 6.21; 13.19; I Kings 18.24, 31.
[2] II Kings 2.11; Isa. 6.1; Hab. 3.4; Ezek. 1.28; Dan. 7.9; 10.6; cf. also Rev. 1.14ff.
[3] Isa. 33.14f.; 6.6f.; Ezek. 2.1ff.; 3.12ff.

realistic sense. This is quite clear from the Yahwist's account of the covenant meal on Sinai;[1] Moses and the seventy elders of the people were allowed to see the God of Israel without being exposed to the normal death-dealing effect of such a vision. It is true that even here there is an awareness of the fact that the divine majesty can be only imperfectly grasped by human sense; all detailed description of Yahweh's appearance is lacking, and he is characterized simply as gleaming light. It can, however, hardly be disputed that the original narrative is concerned with an actual vision of God.

Nevertheless as the phenomenon of fire became linked with the visionary experience in which the prophet experienced within himself the domination of the divine Lord in judgment and renewal, so fire, like storm and earthquake, acquired a predominantly symbolic significance as a representation of God's intervention in history and in the destiny of the individual, and its function as a means of making the invisible God concretely visible diminished in importance. The memorable story of Elijah's encounter with God at Horeb[2] provides the first clear indication of a changed attitude. Here it is expressly stated that Yahweh was not in the storm, nor in the earthquake, nor in the fire. The soft, gentle breeze which declares his presence to Elijah, and out of which Yahweh speaks to him, is nothing if not a descriptive symbol for whispered speech, heard by the prophet as the voice of someone talking to him in the very closest proximity.[3] The manifestation of God in fire had already betrayed a sense that the lineaments of the divine were not confined to any fixed forms, but were inconceivable by Man. Now they have passed completely into the invisible, out of which the divine word sounds forth as the only element of the divine nature which human senses can grasp. The elemental forces are no longer the means by which God is made

[1] Ex. 24.9–11.

[2] I Kings 19.10ff. The constant attempts to interpret this narrative in terms of a changed conception of God's *nature* (so most recently J. Hempel, *Gott und Mensch im AT*, 1926, pp. 43f.) are unsupported by the context, and contradicted by the whole prophetic conception of God. What is here portrayed is not the God who works silently, but the personal and spiritual God of the prophets revealing himself in the whispered word.

[3] Cf. God's speaking b^e '$\bar{o}zen$, 'in the ear' of the one whom he sends: Isa. 5.9; 22.14; Ezek. 3.10; 9.1, 5; Isa. 50.4f., and also I Sam. 9.15; II Sam. 7.27; Job 33.16. If the nearness of Yahweh in the soft breeze is the nature-symbol for his communication of himself in his word, then this conception is fundamentally different from the Egyptian conception of Amon as god of the air, despite the superficial similarity which has been stressed by K. Sethe, *Amun und die acht Urgötter von Hermopolis*, 1929, pp. 119f. Cf. also E. Sellin, *Isr.-jüd. Religionsgeschichte*, 1933, p. 17.

visible, but have become phenomena accompanying the divine activity,[1] his 'garment',[2] his glory (*kābōd*),[3] his messenger.[4] The activity of Yahweh in the prophetic word and in the testimony of the divine spirit, as Israel experienced it with such thrilling force in the emergence of prophecy, deprived the thought-patterns of Nature mythology of their power, and suffered the forms in which they had found expression to persist only as figurative illustrations of God's dealings with the world.[5]

II. An ancient belief at first sight more difficult to integrate into the Israelite experience of God is that of *Yahweh's becoming visible in human form*. It is true that not too much weight should be laid on the intercourse of Man with God in Gen. 2f., where God is described as walking in the Garden of Eden, for this particular story assumes a situation before the dawn of Time or History, and thus tells us nothing about present reality. Indeed, the conclusion to be drawn is the exact opposite; what was possible in Paradise will normally be impossible now that Paradise has been lost. Appearances in dreams are also better left out of account in this connection, for in such cases there is no question of literally seeing God.[6] On the other hand the old folk-sagas are able to tell of encounters with the deity in human form, and both Gen. 18f. and 32.24ff. are marked by a descriptive realism which cannot but recall the well-known pagan stories of the gods. Moreover, even the Moses narrative, which has been subjected to prophetic influence, sees a special pre-eminence of the founder of the religion in a direct intercourse with Yahweh 'face to face' which included a physical beholding of his 'form',[7] even though the notion of a God who shares as a guest in a meal, or who wrestles with the patriarch, has already been modified by a more spiritual way of thinking.

[1] This is clearly true of the prophetic thunderstorm theophanies, Isa. 30.27ff.; 19.1, etc.

[2] Ps. 104.1

[3] E.g. Ex. 24.17; 33.18; Ezek. 1.28; 3.13.

[4] Ps. 104.4

[5] Cf. below chs. XIII and XIV: The Spirit and the Word of God.

[6] Cf., e.g., Gen. 28.10ff.; I Sam. 3.10; and on the subject in general, E. L. Ehrlich, *Der Traum im AT* (BZAW 73), 1953.

[7] Num. 12.8; Ex. 33.23; Deut. 34.10. Even though it must be admitted that the expression 'face to face' is frequently to be taken not literally but metaphorically, as conveying the intimacy of an association (so König, *Theologie*, ch. 41.1), nevertheless the realistic significance of passages such as Gen. 32.31; Judg. 6.22; Num. 12.8, to which may also be added Ex. 4.24ff. and 24.9ff., is incontestable. Cf. in this connection F. Michaeli, *Dieu à l'image de l'homme*, 1950, pp. 63ff.

It is not permissible to evade the force of such passages by playing off against them others according to which Israel indeed heard the voice of God at Horeb, but did not see any form.[1] Such a procedure would be valid only on the historically untenable assumption that the total of statements in the Old Testament must provide a unified 'corpus of doctrine'. On the contrary one thing of which we can be sure is that at different periods Israel produced differing statements about the nature of God's relationship with the world, and that there was therefore unquestionably an advance to a deeper knowledge of God. The thing which is really remarkable, and of the greatest significance for the Old Testament conception of God, is rather that the naïve notion of a God endowed with human corporeity should have played so small a part, and that even in the few places where it does occur without qualification it should so little prejudice the absolute superiority of the divine being. A sense of direct confrontation with the living Lord stifles any thought of unworthy familiarity, or any tendency to drag the deity down to human and earthly limitations.[2]

It is a striking fact that in prophetic visions too the human manifestation of Yahweh frequently recurs, even if, with greater reticence, it is rather suggested than described;[3] and the same anthropomorphism persists in eschatological word-pictures.[4] In the latter case, it is true, we may have to reckon with the influence of recently infiltrated foreign conceptions,[5] but this provides no explanation of the prophetic instances. It will be better to revert to an observation made earlier,[6] namely that the immediate proximity and reality of God, which for us are all too easily obscured by spiritualizing concepts, are outstanding features of the Old Testament revelation, and compel men to clothe the divine presence in human form. That such language is not meant to be taken as an adequate description of the divine nature can be seen from the way in which, by blurring the details rather than presenting them with precision, the account stresses the parabolic character of the appearance, the $d^e m\bar{u}t$ $k^e mar'\bar{e}h$ $'\bar{a}d\bar{a}m$ (Ezek. 1.26).

[1] Deut. 4.12, 15–18. Cf. on this point E. König, *Theologie* 3, 4, 1923, ch. 42.1.d, and A. Dillmann, *Handbuch der AT Theologie*, 1895, p. 229.
[2] On the vividness of this sense of God's personal authority cf. what was said on God as spiritual, vol. I, ch. 6, pp. 210ff.
[3] I Kings 22.19; Amos 9.1; Isa. 6.1; Ezek. 1.26f.
[4] Zech. 14.4; Dan. 7.9.
[5] Thus Kittel derives the distinctive picture of the 'Ancient of Days' from representations of χρόνος ἀγήραος: cf. *Die hellenistische Mysterienreligion und das AT*, 1924.
[6] Cf. vol. I, pp. 211f.

iii. In view of the concrete realism which characterizes the Israelite conceptions of God's appearance in Nature it is a striking and noteworthy fact that *there is an absolute bar on the idea of his becoming visible in animal form*. This is all the more remarkable when it is remembered how widespread was the incidence of animal-worship in neighbouring kingdoms, particularly in Egypt. The attempts which have been made from time to time to read an original animal cult into the Old Testament accounts of the worship of the bull-image or of the brazen serpent must be considered to have failed.[1] More general approval has been forthcoming for the theory that totemism formed the basis of Israelite religion.[2] A more thorough investigation of primitive peoples, however, has since shown that the idea that totemism is a necessary phase in the development of all religions was mistaken. Consequently the theory has lost most of its interest, especially as the detailed arguments advanced in its support were always recognized as being inconclusive.[3] In fact neither the animal names used in Israel as personal names,[4] nor the animal sacrifices,[5] nor the distinction between clean and unclean animals,[6] nor the presence of the matriarchal principle,[7] can be shown to have resulted

---

[1] Cf. Stade, *Biblische Theologie des AT*, 1905, pp. 39, 51. The bull-images of Ex. 32.4ff.; I Kings 12.28 have nothing to do with the Egyptian bull-cult (Hitzig, *Geschichte des Volkes Israel*, 1869, p. 169), which was directed to the living animal, but represent a favourite divine symbol of Western Asia; cf. vol. I, ch. IV, p. 117. On the brazen serpent cf. vol. I, ch. IV, pp. 112f. The Serpent-stone of Jerusalem (*'eben hazzōhelet*: I Kings 1.9) may have derived from a Canaanite sanctuary, but it is not possible to say whether or how far the practices of such a sanctuary had been adopted in Israel.

[2] The most successful presentation of this view was that of W. Robertson Smith, *Animal worship and Animal Tribes among the Arabs and in the OT*, 1880, and *The Religion of the Semites²*, 1894. Among those who adopted it was B. Stade, *Theologie*, p. 142, and it was later championed by G. Hölscher, *Geschichte der isr.-jüd. Religion*, 1922, chs. 3 and 9.

[3] The strongest statement of the case is to be found in V. Zapletal, *Der Totemismus und die Religion Israels*, 1901.

[4] An argument adduced in particular by G. Kerber, *Die religionsgeschichtliche Bedeutung der hebräischen Eigennamen des AT*, 1897, but already criticized by Th. Nöldeke, *ZDMG* 1886, pp. 156ff. On the prophylactic use of such names cf. J. Wellhausen, *Reste arabischen Heidentums*, 1887, p. 200, and A. Bertholet, 'Über den Ursprung des Totemismus', *Festgabe für J.Kaftan*, 1920, pp. 8ff.

[5] It has already been explained (vol. I, ch. IV, pp. 141ff.) that a variety of motives underlies animal sacrifice, and that it is impossible to arrange them in a temporal sequence.

[6] For the various motives contributing to this phenomenon cf. vol. I, ch. IV, pp. 133ff.

[7] Even the most sympathetic exegesis can only find uncomprehended relics of this institution in the OT: cf. J. Benzinger, *Hebräische Archäologie³*, 1927, pp. 113f.

from an earlier belief according to which Israelite tribes regarded themselves as kinsfolk of particular species of animals with whom they stood in a mystical life-relationship. By the same token it follows that the divinization of the animal world exerted no influence on the relation conceived to exist between Yahweh and Nature.

2. THE SPIRITUALIZATION OF THE THEOPHANY

Alongside these naïve conceptions, however, there existed from the very first a sense that it is impossible to speak of actually seeing God; and this sense not only made itself felt in the spiritual leaders, but also played a part in popular thought. Hence spring the various attempts to characterize the theophany as an indirect, weakened appearance, distinct from the true essence of the godhead. We shall classify these attempts in ascending order of the spiritualization they evince, beginning with that which is closest to naïve popular belief.

1. *The* mal'āk *of Yahweh*

The 'angel' of Yahweh or of God, to use the customary though perhaps not wholly correct translation of the Hebrew word,[1] occupies a special place among the heavenly beings[2] who belong to the court of the great God (cf. ch. XVIII. 2.1). What was originally a foreign loan-word adopted by Israel,[3] and denoting primarily an emissary, by the addition of the divine name or in similar ways comes to denote the heavenly messenger of Yahweh, and thence is extended to cover various roles which partly obscure its original messenger connotation. Thus the angel may operate quite generally as the guide and protector of those who fear God, and in particular of the prophets (Gen.

Hence even Stade rejects this particular pillar of the totemism hypothesis (*Theologie*, p. 40).

[1] Occurring mostly in the phrase *mal'ak yhwh*: cf. Gen. 16.7, 9–11; 22.11, 15; Ex. 3.2, etc. In a few, chiefly Elohistic, passages *mal'ak hā'elōhīm*: Gen. 31.11; Ex. 14.19; Judg. 6.20; 13.6, 9; II Sam. 14.17, 20; 19.28. In two places *mal'ak 'elōhīm*: Gen. 21.17; I Sam. 29.9.
[2] For the plural form cf. Gen. 19.1, 15; 28.12; 32.2; Pss. 78.49; 91.11; 103.20; 104.4; 148.2; Job 4.18. For the angel of Yahweh or of God as a messenger cf. Gen. 24.7, 40; Num. 20.16; I Sam. 29.9; II Sam. 14.17, 20; 19.28; 24.16; I Kings 19.7; II Kings 1.3, 15; 19.35, etc.
[3] W. Baumgartner (*Schweiz. Theol. Umschau* 14, 1944, p. 98) has drawn special attention to the fact that the underlying verb *l-'-k*, 'send', is found only in Arabic, Ethiopic and Ugaritic.

24.7, 40; I Kings 19.5ff.; II Kings 1.3, 15), or in the role of assassin
bring plague and destruction as a punishment from the heavenly
King (II Sam. 24.26f.; II Kings 19.35f.), or himself be conceived of
as a heavenly judge (II Sam. 14.7, 20; 19.28; Zech. 3.1ff.). As Yahweh's emissary he appears as the special helper of Israel during the
Wilderness wanderings (Ex. 14.19; 23.20, 23; 32.34; 33.2; Num.
20.16). It is not stated that the same angel is meant in all these
passages. It may be that we ought to think of different spheres of
activity which were originally ascribed to particular divine beings,
and were then transferred to the *mal'ak yhwh*. This is especially likely
in the case of his destructive or judicial functions.[1] Thus the term
came to provide a common designation for a variety of heavenly
powers, which none the less are united not simply by an external
label, but also by an inner homogeneity, inasmuch as the *mal'āk* in
almost every case appears as a beneficent power, commissioned by
Yahweh to stand beside his people and succour them.

Among the narratives relating to the angel one particular group
stands out because it describes an emissary of Yahweh who is no
longer clearly distinguishable from his master, but in his appearing
and speaking clothes himself with Yahweh's own appearance and
speech. Thus the story of Hagar's flight (Gen. 16) makes the *mal'ak
yhwh* appear at the spring in the wilderness and proclaim to the
fugitive the destiny of her son. After the angel has vanished, however,
Hagar realizes and states explicitly that she has seen Yahweh himself (16.13).[2] Similarly in Gen. 31.11, 13 the *mal'ak hā'elōhim* can say
to Jacob: 'I am the God of Bethel', thus identifying himself with God.
Consequently, when the words of the *mal'āk* in Gen. 21.18 and 22.11
make use of the divine 'I', this is not to be regarded as a naïve self-
identification on the part of the emissary with the one who has given
him his orders,[3] but as a sign of the presence of God in the angel
phenomenon. The same conclusions may be drawn from a detailed

---

[1] F. Stier (*Gott und sein Engel im AT*, 1934) draws special attention to the ancient
Eastern conception of the heavenly vizier, associated in Babylonia and Egypt with
particular deities: cf. ch. XVIII, p. 197, below.

[2] To weaken the force of the word 'see' here, and to explain it as a figurative
'vision of God' in the sense of an experience of his succour—a usage of which a fair
number of examples can be found in the Psalter (cf. F. Stier, *op. cit.*, p. 38)—is to
fail to do justice to the character of the narrative.

[3] So E. König, *Theologie des Alten Testaments*[3, 4], pp. 191ff. The passages in
Homer (*Iliad* IV.204) and the prophets (Jer. 13.18ff.) are only remotely similar,
and do not affect the crucial point, namely the oscillation between the *mal'āk* and
Yahweh within the narrative.

examination of a series of passages belonging to the folk-saga transmitted by J and E and to the ancient core of the book of Judges;[1] and these may therefore provide a faithful reflection of Israelite popular belief. From the period of the monarchy onwards we hear no more of this close relationship between Yahweh and the *mal'āk*. Even in stories of the intervention of a divine emissary, such as are to be found in the books of Kings and in the post-exilic writings, it is clearly a matter of a servant of Yahweh quite distinct from his master.

Various attempts have been made to deny any particular theological relevance to the facts here described, and to explain them in terms of other processes known to us; but without any really striking success. Thus the *mal'āk* has been explained as a later substitute for Yahweh himself; and in certain cases this is demonstrably correct, as, for instance, Ex. 12.23, where at one time it is Yahweh and at another the angel who smites the Egyptian firstborn, or in the double account of David's census, when according to II Sam. 24.1 it was Yahweh, but according to I Chron. 21.1 the Satan who tempted the king to his disastrous scheme. On this view our narratives would represent the second phase of a religious development. The writers now no longer dare to relate the appearance of God himself in human form, as had been done at an earlier stage, but substitute for him a subordinate being from the celestial world. A third phase is reached when it becomes impossible to think of God as acting in the world at all except through intermediaries.[2] Now it is certainly true that we are dealing with a case of 'development actually present within the Israelite and Jewish religion' (Baumgartner). Nevertheless the incontrovertible evidences for it are scattered among different narratives and strata often separated from one another by centuries. By contrast it strikes one as quite extraordinary, and far from immediately credible, that the first two phases of this process should both be found in an otherwise intact narrative by a single author. Such a thesis could only be maintained, if it could be shown that in these narratives the *mal'āk* represented a secondary insertion, and if in

[1] Gen. 21.17f.; 22.11f.; 48.15f.; Ex. 3.2f., 4a, 5, 7 (J); Num. 22.22–35; Judg. 6.11–24. In Judg. 13.22, however, it is possible that, with Stier, we ought to interpret 'seeing *'elōhīm*' in a more general sense as meaning 'seeing the *mal'āk*, who is like a divine being'.

[2] So B. Stade, *Biblische Theologie des AT*, 1905, pp. 96ff.; K. Budde, *Das Buch der Richter*, 1897, p. 53; H. Gunkel, *Genesis³*, 1910, pp. 186ff.; and more recently W. Baumgartner, 'Zum Problem des "Jahve-Engels" ', *Schweiz. Theolog. Umschau* 14, 1944, pp. 97ff.

addition there were good reasons for thinking that it was mere care-lessness which had prevented the interpolation from being made consistently throughout. Such a demonstration, however, has never been successfully made; even Gunkel admits that the *mal'āk* is an integral part of the text. Moreover, an appeal to the inconsistency of the redactor, or even of the narrator himself, is hardly an appropriate method of explaining the present state of narratives which derive from more than one author. Again, a short hymn like Gen. 48.15f. exhibits the same oscillation between God and his angel in three parallel statements about God's protective activity, where the most powerful saving intervention is precisely that ascribed to the angel.[1] It would be absurd to lay the blame for this particular case on an only half-completed correction of the text.

Nor does it affect the real question to appeal to the pre-Israelite form of the saga, which may in many cases have spoken of an El, a divine being, for whom in the Israelite version the angel of Yahweh or even Yahweh himself was substituted. For even if one were pre-pared to pursue the oscillation between Yahweh and his angel back into the stage of oral transmission (which we are hardly in a position to do), nevertheless the responsibility for the alternation as it stands in the present form of the saga must be laid at the door of the last narrator, and the question therefore remains what he himself meant by it. The argument that he was compelled to represent God as speaking directly to men because of the person- and place-names aetiologically connected with many stories (cf. *yhwh šālōm*, Judg. 6.24; Ishmael, Gen. 16.11) in any case hardly applies to all the fore-going examples of subject-alternation; and in view of the freedom with which the narrator of Gen. 16 explains the name Ishmael as '*Yahweh* hears', it might be as well not to rate too highly the pressure of such considerations upon him.

Only limited significance attaches to the attempt to explain the angel's speaking in the first person in the name of Yahweh by appeal to a stylistic peculiarity, namely the Old Testament messenger style. In this the emissary delivered the words of the sender with the 'I' which the latter had originally used, after introducing him with a special formula, for example, 'Thus saith A.B.'—to which we may compare the prophetic messenger-formula, 'Thus saith Yahweh'.[2]

---

[1] G. von Rad (*Old Testament Theology* I, ET, 1962, p. 287) has rightly drawn attention to this passage.
[2] So F. Stier, *op. cit.*, pp. 9ff.

If by a kind of ellipsis the messenger formula is omitted, then the 'I' of the deity appears directly in the words of the heavenly messenger. Even if, however, in individual cases such as Gen. 21.18 or Num. 22.35 this process may be thought to have occurred, yet it can hardly be made a general principle of explanation. Quite apart from anything else, it takes no account of a change in grammatical subject outside the actual words of the message.

If then full value is to be accorded to the evidence of the ancient narrators, they saw in the *mal'ak yhwh* in certain cases the operation of God himself, and that in a manner more direct than could be achieved through any other heavenly being. Yet this operation was not so direct that the Lord of heaven could be said to have come down to earth in person; it was more as if he were making use of a mask or dummy by means of which he could have direct intercourse with his chosen servants. It is a question, therefore, of a form of Yahweh's self-manifestation which expressly safeguards his transcendent nature, and associates with this immediate but concealed form of his presence only those special activities which he undertakes among men for the accomplishment of his saving will. In the quasi-human form of the messenger he can temporarily incarnate himself in order to assure his own that he is indeed immediately at hand.

Great weight is attached to this fact by a type of explanation which seeks to elucidate the ancient Israelite conception of angels by means of animistic concepts.[1] According to this view angels are to be understood as 'powers proceeding from God' (van der Leeuw) analogous to the psychic forces which primitive man thinks of as released from his own soul to operate effectively in his environment without, however, losing their connection with his own nature. If the *mal'āk* is understood as the 'external soul' of the deity (Lods), then both its distinction from Yahweh and its identification with him become comprehensible. In so far as this attempt at explanation draws attention to the lack of a sharp dividing-line in primitive thought between the ego and the environment it may perhaps make it easier for us to understand the facility with which the Israelite made the mental switch from the *mal'āk* to God himself. Nevertheless its derivation of the divine messenger from energies which have detached themselves from the divine power comes to grief on the previous history of

[1] Cf. van der Leeuw, 'Zielen en Engelen', *Theol. Tijdschrift* (new series) 11, 1919, and *Phänomenologie der Religion*, 1933, pp. 123ff.; A. Lods, 'L'ange de Jahvé et l'âme extérieure', BZAW 27, 1914.

the word *mal'āk*, a term which from the very first presupposes the figure of the commissioned messenger, and does not arrive at this meaning by way of a gradual divergence from the concept of the soul. Hence it is quite natural that the *mal'ak yhwh* should also speak of Yahweh in the third person.

The origin, therefore, of this distinctive way of describing a theophany is to be found neither in the adoption from foreign sources of a figure from the celestial order, nor in the animistic conception of the soul, but in Israel's special experience of God, in which the transcendent majesty of the covenant Lord was combined with the immanent energy of his operation. It was for this reason that the Israelite, even in the very earliest period, experienced a difficulty in establishing a connection between the God who is beyond Man's grasp and the God who truly and actually reveals himself in the world of phenomena; and he sought to resolve this difficulty with the help of the *mal'ak yhwh*. His appearance served to make possible the direct entry of Yahweh into the field of human vision, and to make speech uttered in the divine first person audible (only in Ex. 3.4a, 5 and Judg. 6.14, 16, 23 is Yahweh himself named as the speaker), while at the same time referring the divine 'act of will, effective even from afar,'[1] the hearkening, the watchful eye, and the rescue directly to Yahweh.

In the Christian Church, from the time of the Early Fathers down to the nineteenth century, there was always a temptation to expand this distinctive expression of the divine saving activity along speculative lines, and, after the manner of Philo, to see in the angel of God the pre-existent Logos.[2] Nevertheless this interpretation has rightly been abandoned on all sides, since the God who reveals himself in the *mal'āk* is in no sense present in a human body or as a permanent personal being, but appears only during a limited period of history, namely the era of early Israel, and in a variety of forms, now in a flame, now in human lineaments, now in a dream, now in auditory experiences. On the other hand, it is as little tenable to see in the appearance of God in the form of the *mal'āk* a 'primal form of revelation' specifically characteristic of the patriarchal period,[3] for this medium of revelation still plays a part in the post-Mosaic period.

[1] E. Kautzsch, *Biblische Theologie des AT*, 1911, p. 84.

[2] E. W. Hengstenberg, *Christologie des AT*[2], 1854, vol. I, pp. 219ff.; G. F. Oehler, *Theologie des AT*[3], 1891, pp. 208ff.

[3] So O. Procksch, 'Christus im AT', *NKZ* 1933, p. 61, and *Theologie des AT*, 1950, pp. 421ff.

Furthermore, side by side with the *mal'āk* in this capacity is found from time immemorial the *mal'āk* as a creaturely messenger. Indeed, the borderline between the *mal'āk* as a specific medium of divine revelation and as the created messenger of God cannot always be sharply drawn[1] the outlines flow together, and have not set into a clearly formed dogmatic conception. That is why it was possible for other forms of Yahweh's self-manifestation to emerge without any attempt being made to equate them. Moreover, the overwhelming irruption of the experience of the spirit, which dominated the earlier prophetic movement and made Yahweh's mighty presence felt in an entirely new way, is the obvious reason why his special self-communication in the *mal'āk* fell into oblivion.

Nevertheless in this imperfect concept, which still betrays here and there an uncertain groping, sound in sentiment but unclear in its mental images, the faith of Israel very early on asserted one vital interest of its certainty of God, one which was in truth related to a major concern of the Christian Logos-doctrine. In the Nature religions the gulf which was felt to exist between the High God, exalted far above all earthly affairs, and the necessity of his real intervention in the problems of earthly life was bridged with the aid of myth-forming fantasy by introducing a new divine figure as the bearer of revelation. In Babylonia, Marduk is the one 'sent' by his Father Ea, endowed in full with his essential nature, and therefore called to men's side as their helper by means of the invocation of Ea. In Phoenicia, Astarte or Tanit is invoked as mediatrix between Baal and his worshippers.[2] In Israel, however, theological thinking successfully averted a fragmentation of the divine unity, and in so doing reflected men's living experience of the one God who had declared himself to his people as the will establishing and controlling their whole existence.

II. *The* kābōd *(the glory) of Yahweh*[3]

The concept of Yahweh's *kābōd* is as closely bound up with naïve

---

[1] Very close to the former is the angel sent to the help of Israel during the Exodus and Wilderness wanderings: Ex. 14.19; 23.20, 23; 32.34; 33.2f.; Num. 20.16. On the connection of the angel with the Name of God in Ex. 23.20f., cf. p. 43 below.

[2] Cf. in this connection the Ancient Eastern conceptions of the heavenly vizier in F. Stier, *op. cit.*, pp. 134ff., and below pp. 39 and 44.

[3] On this topic cf. W. Caspari, *Studien zur Lehre von der Herrlichkeit Gottes im AT*, 1907, and *Die Bedeutung der Wortsippe k-b-d im Hebräischen*, 1908; J. Schneider, *Δόξα* 1932; B. Stein, *Der Begriff Kebod Jahweh und seine Bedeutung für die alttestamentliche Gotteserkenntnis*, 1939.

imagery for God's appearance as that of his *mal'āk*. *Kābōd* denotes that which is 'heavy', 'weight'; and when used of something 'weighty', that which distinguishes a man and wins him respect, primarily suggests the outwardly visible, whether it be wealth, for which *kābōd* can actually be used as a synonym,[1] or an outward position of honour, power and success.[2] Hence even God's *kābōd*, his glory or majesty, includes an element of appearance, of that which catches the eye. This is especially noticeable when the *kābōd* is presented as the real content of the theophany, as the writers like to do, for example, in the case of the thunderstorm.[3] In this connection, in addition to many of the Psalms,[4] the various descriptions of the Sinai revelation are especially characteristic (Ex. 24.15ff. [P] cf. 20.16–19 [JE] and Deut. 5.22ff.). In the Exodus account the *kābōd* appearing on Sinai is pictured in the following terms: 'The glory of the LORD settled on Mount Sinai, and the cloud covered it six days; and on the seventh day he called to Moses out of the midst of the cloud. Now the appearance of the glory of the LORD was like a devouring fire on the top of the mountain in the sight of the people of Israel' (24.16f.). The connection between the *kābōd* and the storm-cloud is also indicated by the fire which issues from the latter and consumes the offerings made by Aaron,[5] or annihilates the sacrilegious,[6] and indeed is not really possible to distinguish from lightning. Hence in these passages (and originally perhaps in all[7]) the *kābōd* is 'the striking radiance which proceeds from Yahweh'[8] whenever he appears in the thunderstorm, the blinding light which proclaims the approach of God in the fire, and compels men to cast down their eyes.

Here, too, it is hardly possible to ask how close or how distant was the relation between this fiery radiance and the transcendent majesty of Yahweh. The simple man of the people will naturally have thought

---

[1] Gen. 31.1; Isa. 10.3; 66.12; Ps. 49.17.

[2] Gen. 45.13; I Kings 3.13; Prov. 21.21, etc. Hence the LXX rendering of the word by δόξα (with its connotation of 'appearance' as opposed to 'reality') throws into bold relief an element constantly present in the Hebrew.

[3] Cf. p. 16 above.

[4] Cf. esp. the thunderstorm-psalm 29, with its praise of the *'ēl hakkābōd*, and the manifestation of the divine glory in Ps. 97.1–6.

[5] Lev. 9.6, 23f.

[6] Num. 16.19, 35.

[7] So A. von Gall, *Die Herrlichkeit Gottes*, 1900, pp. 23ff. Whether Ex. 33.18ff. and Ps. 19.2 are exceptions to this, as von Rad assumes ('*kābōd* im AT', *TWNT* II, pp. 242f.), is questionable.

[8] Kautzsch, *HRE* XIX, p. 666.

differently on this subject from the educated.[1] But even with a concept of this type the sense that Yahweh's majesty was exalted far above all created things gradually asserted itself. This came about in various ways; either by stressing *the absolute transcendence of the kābōd*, so that mortal man had always to be kept apart from it, or by reducing it to a spatially and temporally limited medium of Yahweh's self-manifestation, a means by which the transcendent God made his personal presence visible to his own. An example of the former tendency is the request which, according to the Elohist, Moses made to Yahweh to be allowed to see his *kābōd* as a pledge of the divine favour (Ex. 33.18). The deadly effect of such a vision means that this petition cannot possibly be granted; it is by a special gift of God's favour that Moses is finally allowed to see the divine glory pass before his veiled eyes, at any rate from behind, that is to say, at its extreme edge and outskirts. This conception, which regards the *kābōd* as the divine majesty unapproachable by human sight, later gives rise to the hope that in the future, when God calls the new world into being, even his *kābōd* will be visible, and that not only in Israel but throughout the whole world. This thought finds wonderful expression in Isaiah, when in their song of praise the seraphim anticipate the act of salvation as if it had already in very truth been fulfilled: 'the whole earth is full of his glory' (6.3). That which the inhabitants of earth can only yearn and supplicate to gain the inhabitants of heaven may already behold —a magnificent image for that goal of divine world-dominion of which faith is so confident. The prophet, however, who made use of this terminology as appropriate to his own most personal thoughts and hopes was Deutero-Isaiah. For him, knowing himself to be standing on the threshold of a new age, the revelation of the *kābōd* of Yahweh throughout the whole world is equated with the reconcilia-

---

[1] The extreme realism which originally attached to ideas connected with the *kābōd* may be seen in the tradition of its reflection on the face of Moses: Ex. 34.29ff. To attempt to interpret the *kābōd* as a purely spiritual entity—for example, as the sum of the attributes peculiar to God's nature (Dillmann, *Alttestamentliche Theologie*, p. 283), as the distinctive majesty of his nature when revealed (H. Schultz, *Alttestamentliche Theologie*[5], 1896, p. 440), or as the purity of the Holy One, Yahweh's holy will of love (R. Krämer, 'Bausteine zum Begriff: Die Herrlichkeit Jahwes', *Aus Theologie und Geschichte der reformierten Kirche* [*Festgabe für E. F. K. Müller*], 1933, pp. 7ff.)—ignores the essential element of visible appearance connected with the word *kābōd*, and also overlooks shifts in its meaning. B. Stein (*Der Begriff Kebod Jahweh*) would like to assume that the *kābōd* was originally experienced in the sphere of God's redemptive activity, and was only secondarily extended to the world of Nature; but convincing support for this hypothesis is lacking.

tion of God and Man by means of which Paradise, and with it life in the presence of God, is restored.[1] Similarly the poet of Ps. 57 prays that the *kābōd* may soon be revealed, that is, for the victory of the kingdom of God. Other passages, too, comprehend the hope of salvation within this concept.[2]

This shift in meaning, which may be termed 'prophetic', stands in contrast to a different development which was of a priestly character. In this the *kābōd* becomes *the reflected splendour of the transcendent God*, a token of the divine glory, by means of which Yahweh declares his gracious presence. It is at the 'Tent of Meeting'[3] that Yahweh confronts his people, because it is there that his *kābōd* descends, girded with the cloud,[4] and reveals his will. After the building of the Temple Yahweh himself consecrates it as the preferred place of his revelation by the way in which the cloud fills the sanctuary as once it filled the tent-dwelling (I Kings 8.10f.; II Chron. 7.1). Because the *kābōd*, in the likeness of a mass of fire veiled in cloud, is here understood as a special *form in which God appears for the purposes of revelation*, it becomes possible for priestly thought to speak of a real entry of the transcendent God into the realm of the visible without, however, thereby prejudicing his transcendence. The description of the *kābōd* in Ezekiel (1.28) suggests that, as with the Tabernacle and the Temple, the idea is present of a copy of a heavenly prototype.[5]

In sharp contrast to the priestly conception, however, the prophet portrays the *kābōd* seen by him in his vision not as a formless brightness of light, but as a lavishly proportioned throne, gleaming with marvellous colours, with the Lord of the Universe seated upon it.[6] Here, however, it should be borne in mind that what Ezekiel sees ought to be described rather as a reflection of the heavenly glory of

---

[1] Isa. 40.5; also 59.19; 60.1f.; 66.18f.
[2] Num. 14.21; Hab. 2.14; Ps. 72.19. The transcendent *kābōd* in highest heaven is referred to in Ps. 19.2.
[3] Cf. vol. I, pp. 109ff.
[4] Ex. 16.10; 29.43; 40.34f.; Lev. 9.6, 23f.; Num. 14.10; 17.7; 20.6. The pillar of cloud and of fire which guides the people should not be confused with this.
[5] Cf. vol. I, pp. 423f.
[6] The magnificent description of the vision in Ezek. 1 has, however, been worked up in a manner which can also be detected in ch. 10, because of the impetus given by the Ark and its chariot to the development of *merkābā* speculation. 1.15–21, 23f. and smaller elements of the preceding section are therefore to be regarded as secondary, as S. Sprank (*Ezechielstudien* [BWANT III.4], 1926) was the first to attempt to prove. Elsewhere, too, however, traces of later elaboration can be established: cf. W. Eichrodt, *Der Prophet Hesekiel* (ATD 22.1), 1959, pp. 51ff.

Yahweh than as that glory itself.[1] In the language of ancient Near Eastern symbolism it illustrates the transcendence of the Ruler of the world who sits enthroned, gleaming with dazzling fire, in inaccessible holiness above the clouds of heaven and indeed the entire universe, symbolized by its corner pillars, the four Cherubim. The *kābōd* appears to the prophet as ἀπαύγασμα τῆς δόξης αὐτοῦ (Heb. 1.3), something quite distinct from the eternal primal form of the godhead,[2] in order to assure him of the nearness and power of his God despite the exile into an unclean, heathen land, and despite the desecration and destruction of the Temple which is to follow. It is therefore still no more than a form in which the transcendent God can appear whenever he wills to make a particular revelation of himself on earth. However drastic a departure its human likeness may be from the careful lack of definition in the usual priestly portrayal, yet this feature in no way detracts from the greatness of the picture of God here envisaged in parabolic terms. On the contrary, as against the danger of a flight into abstraction, it serves to uphold the historical realism of the revelation, as this had been attested by other prophets to whose spiritual vision the God who intervenes in history had appeared in the lineaments of Man (Isa. 6; Amos 9.1).

The *kābōd* appears once more (Ezek. 43.1–4), this time as a pledge of the eschatological fulfilment, when it takes up its dwelling in the new Temple on a Zion now exalted into the cosmic mountain.

Although, however, the prophet himself may have detached the presence of God from the Temple at Jerusalem in this way as a matter of principle, nevertheless the priestly redactors of his book adhered closely to the current conceptions of priestly thought when they portrayed the *kābōd* as the divine glory made manifest at a holy place.[3] Just as the *kābōd* honours the Holy of Holies of the Temple by its normally invisible presence there, so it abandons this its dwelling-place only with reluctance, withdrawing hesitantly first from the

---

[1] This is indicated by the frequent insertion of *dᵉmūt* and *mar'ēh*, which stress the parabolic character of what is seen; also by the symbolism of the God enthroned above the firmament: cf. on this point, O. Procksch, 'Die Berufungsvision Hesekiels', in BZAW 34, pp. 141ff., and W. Eichrodt, *op. cit.*, pp. 7f.

[2] As against the view of Kautzsch (*op. cit.*, pp. 89f.), who prefers to see in this passage the direct manifestation and form of the deity.

[3] Ezek. 8.4; 9.3; 10.4, 18f. On the secondary character of these passages cf. W. Zimmerli, *Ezechiel* (BKAT XIII.3), 1956, pp. 203f., and W. Eichrodt, *Der Prophet Hesekiel*, pp. 52ff.

Temple area and finally from the holy city.[1] Thus from the vision of the *kābōd* in Ezek. 1 this account derives a way of answering the agonizing question of the whereabouts of the Ark-Throne[2] in the Holy of Holies after the destruction of the Temple and city, a perplexity to which Jer. 3.16 also bears witness.[3]

The conception of the divine *kābōd* in *later Judaism*, on the one hand continued this priestly line of thought. Closely related to the glory of God is the *shekina*, the visible sign of the divine presence, which descends to earth from its concealment in heaven, and appears to men as a reflected radiance from the heavenly splendour, in particular to bless the pious at their prayers and study of the Law in the synagogue or the Rabbinic school.[4] On the other hand there are signs of a *merging of the priestly into the prophetic line*. God's self-manifestation, when he confronts his people as their sovereign lord in judgment and favour at the consummation of the kingdom of God in history, finally assumes human form. Indeed, the Messiah becomes a figure of divine glory, the splendour of which radiates from him. The Son of Man receives from the Ancient of Days 'dominion and glory and kingdom';[5] the Messiah sits on the 'throne of glory';[6] and then the redeemed enjoy the divine glory lost to mankind in the beginning through the Fall.[7] Moreover, in the κύριος τῆς δόξης[8] of the New Testament, who as their ἐλπὶς τῆς δόξης[9] grants to the faithful a share in his own glory. This particular line finds its fulfilment.[10]

In addition to this use of *kābōd* in the sense of the transcendent glory of God and the form of his self-manifestation, it is, of course, frequently employed to denote *honour and glory in general*, and as such often stands in conjunction with the miracles and signs by which

---

[1] The presupposition underlying this picture, namely that Yahweh's *kābōd* is a permanent dweller in the Holy of Holies, can hardly be regarded as contradicting those other priestly accounts in which it appears only on particular occasions, for in the latter it is the Tent, not the Temple which is involved, and Ezek. 43.7 must be taken as an eschatological statement (*contra* von Rad, *op. cit.*, p. 242).

[2] Cf. vol. I, pp. 107ff.

[3] Cf. W. Eichrodt, *Der Prophet Hesekiel*, p. 54.

[4] Cf. F. Weber, *Jüdische Theologie*[2], 1897, pp. 185ff.

[5] Dan. 7.14. O. Procksch ('Christus im AT', *NKZ*, 1933, pp. 8of.) has drawn attention to a connection between the appearance of the divine glory in Ezekiel and the heavenly figure of the Son of Man in Daniel.

[6] Enoch 45.3; 51.3; 55.4; 61.8, etc.

[7] Cf. on this point G. Kittel, *Δόξα*, *TWNT* II, pp. 249f.

[8] I Cor. 2.8; James 2.1.

[9] Col. 1.27.

[10] Cf. G. Kittel, *op. cit.*, pp. 251ff.

Yahweh demonstrates his power.[1] This usage, which should be distinguished from the important theological expressions which have been discussed in this section, need not detain us further.

III. *The* pānīm *(the face) of God*

In this expression, too, we are presented with a term for God's self-manifestation which was originally thought of in a completely naïve and concrete way. In paganism it was possible to speak of the face with absolute realism, since in the Temple the face of the statue of the god was always there in front of one. Hence such phrases as to 'behold', or 'soothe', or 'seek' the face of God[2] were without doubt originally associated with such concrete ideas. A more spiritual conception was, however, also possible even in paganism,[3] if the worshipper were not entirely limited to the notion that in the statue he had the god actually in front of him, but could understand the image as a representation of the invisible sovereign god, whose gaze he knew to be fixed on him even outside the temple, and for the help and guidance of whose hand he made supplication.[4] This abstract use of the word *pānīm* to denote the gracious attention and presence of the deity was bound to spread all the more in a society which, like Israel, had completely rejected any plastic representation of the godhead.[5]

(*a*) It is true that *a concrete conception of the pānīm* is also found in the popular tales of ancient Israel. Thus Jacob was astounded that he should have escaped with his life in spite of having seen the divine being, with whom he had been wrestling, face to face, and he called

---

[1] Num. 14.22; Pss. 24.8; 66.2; 79.9; 96.3; Isa. 42.8; 48.11, etc.

[2] *rā'āh 'et-p°nē yhwh*: Ex. 23.15, 17; 34.20, 23f.; Deut. 16.16; 31.11; Isa. 1.12; Ps. 42.3 (the Massoretic pointing of the verb as niphal, adopted for dogmatic reasons, should in all cases be altered to the qal). *ḥillāh ('et-)p°nē yhwh*: Ex. 32.11; I Sam. 13.12, etc.; cf. p. 36 below, n. 8. *biḳḳēš ('et-) p°nē yhwh*: Ps. 27.8f., etc.; cf. p. 36 below, n. 7.

[3] This is true, for example, in Babylonia even of so realistic an expression as 'to grasp the garment of the god', which signifies urgent prayer. Cf. F. Nötscher, '*Das Angesicht Gottes schauen*' *nach biblischer und babylonischer Auffassung*, 1924, p. 66.

[4] Hence the frequent prayer to the deity to take the hand of the one who comes to him for succour (Nötscher, *op. cit.*, pp. 70ff.).

[5] On the meaning of the phrase 'to see the face of God', and of related concepts, cf. W. W. Baudissin, ' "Gott schauen" in der alttestamentlichen Religion', *ARW* 1915, pp. 173ff.; J. Böhmer, *Gottes Angesicht* (Beiträge zur Förderung christl. Theologie, XII.4); P. Dhorme, 'L'emploi métaphorique des noms de parties du corps en hébreu et en accadien. III. Le visage', *RB* 1921, pp. 374ff.; F. Nötscher, *op. cit.*

the scene of his adventure Peniel (Face of God).[1] The same idea is present in Judg. 6.22. It was not long, however, before objections were raised to this naïve view; according to Ex. 33.20 no one, not even such an elect man of God as Moses, can in any circumstances look upon the *pānīm* of God.

(*b*) There could, however, of course be no objection to speaking of seeing the face of Yahweh *in a metaphorical sense*—hence the extremely frequent use of the expression to mean 'enter the sanctuary'.[2] This particular application of the phrase, despite there being no visible image of God in the Israelite cult, was made all the easier by the fact that in secular life admittance to an audience with a superior was described as 'seeing the countenance' of the person in question,[3] a usage exactly paralleled in Babylonian.[4] With this went a refinement of the phrase to imply that the purpose of the encounter was to testify to one's own subordinate position, and to ask for help; and this makes it entirely understandable that there should have been no scruples about adopting the expression into the religious vocabulary.[5] In this way the thought of God's gracious presence and succour is readily associated with the cultic term, and may indeed so predominate that 'seeing Yahweh' becomes a synonym for the experience of his help or for life in his presence, quite independently of any reference to the cultic centre. 'I shall behold thy face in righteousness' prays the singer of the seventeenth Psalm, referring to the experience of the divine lovingkindness in that inward communion with his God which by its consoling power raises him above all the pain and deprivation of his life.[6]

There is a similar recession of the cultic reference when the phrase, 'to seek the face of Yahweh',[7] is primarily thought of as a turning to the deity in time of trouble, either to ask for his help or in penitence. Likewise Man's 'soothing' the face of God,[8] or God's lifting up the

---

[1] Gen. 32.31.
[2] Ex. 23.15, 17; 34.20, 23f.; Deut. 16.16; 31.11; Isa. 1.12; Ps. 42.3.
[3] Gen. 32.21; 43.3, 5; 44.23, 26; Ex. 10.28f.; II Sam. 14.24, 28, 32.
[4] Found as early as the Amarna letters; cf. Nötscher, *op. cit.*, pp. 77ff.
[5] For another factor which made this process easier cf. below.
[6] Ps. 17.15; similarly Ps. 11.7; Job 33.25f.; cf. also Ps. 27.13, 'see the goodness of the LORD'; Ps. 140.14, 'dwell in thy presence'; Isa. 38.11, 'see the LORD'. Cf. J. Lindblom, 'Bemerkungen zu den Psalmen', *ZAW* 58, 1942–3, pp. 11f.
[7] In a cultic sense: Ps. 24.6; I Chron. 21.30; in a metaphorical sense: II Sam. 21.1; Pss. 27.8; 105.4b; Hos. 5.15; II Chron. 7.14.
[8] Ex. 32.11; I Sam. 13.12; I Kings 13.6; II Kings 13.14; Jer. 26.19; Zech. 7.2; 8.21f.; Mal. 1.9; Ps. 119.58; II Chron. 33.12; Dan. 9.13.

light of his countenance,[1] are standard expressions for the restoration of a relationship of favour between God and Man, and in no way imply the idea of a visible form. Even Babylonian prayers speak in a similarly metaphorical way of the face or the eyes of the deity.[2] Hence nothing more than a heightened metaphor is involved when it is said of Moses that God used to speak with him 'face to face';[3] the meaning is quite superfluously elucidated by the insertion of the comment, 'as a man speaks to his friend' (Ex. 33.11). It is the direct personal meeting and speaking with the invisible God which is described as speaking 'face to face'.[4] In this sense, too, Ezekiel proclaims that Yahweh will enter into judgment with Israel face to face (20.35ff.).

The same is true of those passages in which *pānīm* is used to bring out the personal involvement of the one concerned, to stress his direct intervention. Just as the personal presence of Absalom with the army is described as his 'face' going into battle,[5] so the Psalmist pictures the omnipresence of God as the nearness of his face, from which there is no escape in flight.[6]

(c) Many would understand that remarkable passage, Ex. 33.14f., in which Yahweh promises Moses that his *pānīm* will go with him, in the same sense. Nevertheless, even if, taken absolutely literally, the text is susceptible of such an interpretation, it fails to do justice to the distinctive emphasis on the *pānīm* in these verses. The point at issue here is how the people are to be led through the Wilderness, a question which is answered in different ways by the various strata. Thus in E it is the angel of God who undertakes the task,[7] in J₁ Yahweh himself is prayed to go with them,[8] but in J₂ by contrast he causes his

---

[1] Num. 6.25f.; Pss. 4.7; 31.7; 67.2; 80.4, 8, 20; 119.135; Dan. 9.17.
[2] Cf., e.g., the blessing-formula: 'May Ea rejoice over thee! May Damkina, the queen of the deep, lighten thee with her countenance! May Marduk, the great overseer of the Igigi, lift up thy head!' (A. Jeremias, *ATAO*, pp. 443, and in addition Nötscher, *op. cit.*, pp. 142ff.).
[3] Ex. 33.11; Deut. 34.10. Similarly of Israel, Deut. 5.4; Ezek. 20.35f.; cf. 'mouth to mouth', Num. 12.8.
[4] Explicitly stated Deut. 4.12; cf. 5.4.
[5] II Sam. 17.11.
[6] Ps. 139.7. Nevertheless, as against the view of Nötscher (*op. cit.*, p. 52), *pānīm* is not to be characterized as a substitute for the personal pronoun, for in such passages as Gen. 32.21; Ezek. 6.9; Prov. 7.15, etc., the physical imagery of the face still plays some part in the thought of propitiation, confrontation or shame.
[7] Ex. 33.2.
[8] Ex. 33.16f.

pānīm to attend them[1] as the means whereby he is to lead his people. No doubt when compared with J₁ this does represent a weakening of the language, but it still implies a closer relationship between God and his people than does the sending of the angel in E. It is almost impossible not to conclude that we have here another *form of self-manifestation of the transcendent God*, by means of which his presence is at the same time made tolerable to men and guaranteed to them. It is quite possible that this particular form of manifestation was originally more closely associated with a material medium, namely the Ark of Yahweh. The Yahwistic account of its construction has been lost; nevertheless Num. 10.29ff. shows that its function was the same as that of the *pānīm*, to guide the people through the Wilderness. When one remembers the character of the Ark as this may be deduced from other traditions, namely that of an empty divine throne guaranteeing God's presence in the midst of his people,[2] then it becomes even more probable that the Yahwist is interpreting this presence in terms of the *pānīm*. At the same time the belief that the *pānīm* of Yahweh was present in the Ark could assist the naturalization of the religious language which described a visit to the sanctuary as a vision of the face of God.

Indeed, the metaphorical use of *pānīm*, which in this way came to predominate, may at an early stage have repressed its independent value as a form of the divine self-manifestation, and caused it to fall into oblivion. Only in relatively few passages is it still discernible.[3] The disappearance of the Ark into the cella of the Temple, and its consequent withdrawal from the worshipping life of the nation, must have assisted this process. With the *kābōd* at any rate the *pānīm* had no connection; the two concepts derive from different roots, and were never combined with one another.[4]

---

[1] Ex. 33.14f. *pānay yēlēkū* should be completed by the addition of *lᵉpāneykā*, and the pointing *hᵃniḥōtī* changed to *hinḥētī*, rendering: 'My *pānīm* shall go before you, and thus will I lead you.' H. Middendorf, too, has argued for the distinctive character of the phraseology here, in which he sees an expression of the special guidance of God (*'Gott sieht'. Eine terminologische Studie über das Schauen Gottes im AT*, Diss. Freiburg, 1935, pp. 102ff.).

[2] Cf. vol. I, pp. 107ff.

[3] Deut. 4.37; Isa. 63.9 (emend, following the LXX: *lō' sīr ūmal'āk pānāw hōšī'ūm*—'no messenger nor angel, [but] his *pānīm* succoured them'); Pss. 21.10; 80.17; Lam. 4.16. The Psalm-passages have been contested, but the suggested emendations to *'pk* or *pyk* seem unnecessary; cf. A. Weiser, *The Psalms*, ET, 1962, *ad loc.*

[4] König's assumption that the 'face of God' must have been present even when no more than the glory was perceived (*Theologie*⁴, p. 127) has no basis in the sources.

Nevertheless the theologoumenon of the *pānīm* may claim our particular attention precisely because it throws into sharp relief the distinctive pattern of thought of Israelite religious faith. Yet the face of God plays a similar role in Phoenician culture, as may be seen from the Carthaginian votive tablets to Baal and Tanit, on which the latter is regularly described as *pn b'l*, i.e. *peně ba'al*, the face of Baal.[1] She therefore acts for Baal as a manifestation of his being in which he himself draws near to men. Patently the High God is already far removed from his worshippers, and arranges for Tanit to represent him, just as an earthly king is not accessible to every subject, but directs him to his minister. And so, it is clear, the goddess became the trusted and beloved protectress, whose name always stands first in the inscriptions; whoever sees her sees the face of Baal. The best commentary on this conception is Gen. 33.10, where Jacob says to Esau: 'To see your face is like seeing the face of God, with such favour have you received me.' God's gracious countenance is therefore manifested in a man when the latter shows favour in God's stead, as it were; and in this way it comes to be an expression for God's representative.

It is true that in Israel this type of concept encountered peculiar difficulties. Whereas in pagan religions there was always another deity to undertake the role of representative, the Old Testament conception of God did not admit the possibility of introducing such a bearer of the divine countenance, with the result that the latter was itself bound to become virtually a hypostasis. As such, however, it never came to full development, but remained a peculiarly equivocal expression, speaking of God's personal activity in veiled language.[2] Whereas pagan religion overcame the underlying difficulty by means of sexual differentiation within the divine order, and thus was confirmed in its polytheistic thinking, Israel renounced the advantages of the concept as a graphic illustration in favour of loyalty to the concept of God as one. In this forceful emphasis on the unitary nature of Yahweh we can see clearly the strength of the drive to monotheism within the religion of ancient Israel.

---

[1] The relevant inscriptions have been collected in *Répertoire d'Épigraphie sémitique* II, 1907–14, p. 452.
[2] König (*op. cit.*, p. 126) attempts to paraphrase it as 'concentration on the borders of the divine spiritual sphere', a definition which can hardly be said to make the meaning any clearer.

IV. *The Name of Yahweh*

In the forms of revelation so far discussed there is a marked recession in the degree of anthropomorphism in the conception of the deity, inasmuch as neither *kābōd* nor *pānīm* necessarily imply human features, or even tend to do so. Nevertheless, as we have seen, the idea of a mode of appearance visible to human eyes still attached at least to the former, even if in the case of the *pānīm* it was already coming to be doubted. With the theologoumenon of the Name, however, any such element was wholly excluded.

(*a*) In order to understand this it is necessary to realize the vital reciprocal relationship which according to ancient ideas subsisted between the name and its owner.[1] When it is believed that the nature of a thing is comprehended in its name, then on the one hand emphasis is laid on the idea that knowledge of the name mediates a *direct relationship with the nature*, and on the other the name is regarded as to such an extent an *expression of the individual character* of its owner that it can, in fact, stand for him, become a concept interchangeable with him. The naming of the animals by Adam is not only an assertion of his sovereignty over them, it expresses their natures.[2] In the context of human names this belief finds expression in the giving of new names to vassals by their overlords, or to disciples by their masters; the new name stamps a new pattern of life, so to speak, on the recipient.[3] Similarly, with his name a man may seek to transmit something of his nature to later generations through his children and grand-children;[4] and the phrase 'to be called' is widely used to express a new way of life.[5] Conversely, the name is so closely bound up with the particularity of the person that a change in his condition calls for a new name,[6] the experience of special divine favour is described as a knowing or calling by a new name,[7] and the plural form *šēmōt* can be used to mean 'individual persons'.[8]

---

[1] On this point cf. the observations made in vol. I, ch. VI, pp. 206ff. Also G. Contenau, 'De la valeur du nom chez les Babyloniens et de quelques-unes de ses conséquences', *RHR* 81, 1920, pp. 316ff.

[2] Gen. 2.19f.

[3] II Kings 23.34; 24.17; II Sam. 12.25.

[4] Gen. 48.16; Deut. 25.6f.; Num. 27.4; Ruth 4.5, 10f.; cf. Isa. 56.5.

[5] Hos. 2.1; Isa. 1.26; 9.5; 44.5; 62.2; 65.15; cf. Rev. 2.17.

[6] Ruth 1.20f.

[7] Ex. 31.2; 33.12, 17; Isa. 45.3f.; 49.1

[8] Num. 1.2: cf. in German the old usage 'Mannsnamen', still retained in dialect, to which von Orelli has called attention (*HRE* XIII, p. 628).

(*b*) In the *use of the divine Name* the counterpart to these ideas is the *dynamic conception of the Name of Yahweh* as the guarantee of the divine presence,[1] and the use of God's name as an interchangeable term for his person. Moreover, whereas Israel never set so high a value on the *human* name as many primitive societies have done, for whom a man's name may become virtually a separate entity parallel to himself and exerting great influence on his life for good or ill,[2] yet so far as the divine name was concerned Israelite thought even reached the point of giving it a certain independence over against Yahweh himself, of bestowing on it a hypostatic character. This development grew to such a pitch that with the increasing importance of the cultic sites and of the invocation of the deity performed there the belief that it was possible to call God's presence to one by means of the Name *as occasion demanded* changed into the assumption that *God as manifested in his Name was permanently present* at the holy place. At a very early stage cultic language had described God's readiness to visit his worshippers as his 'causing his name to be remembered',[3] and Isaiah could speak of Zion as the 'place of the name of the LORD of hosts',[4] where he is to be found even by Gentile nations. In Jeremiah the designation of the central cultic site as the place where Yahweh causes his name to dwell already occurs as a stock phrase,[5] and in the Holiness Code the desecration of the Temple is intimately connected with the profanation of Yahweh's holy name.[6] The association of Yahweh's name with the sanctuary to denote the particular presence of God in that place, a usage detectable in all these examples, is distilled in Deuteronomy into the formula that Yahweh causes his name to dwell in his chosen place, or has set it there.[7] The Name, therefore, now acquires a more independent function as the *representative of the transcendent God*, by means of which he assures men of his nearness and the continuing efficacy of his power, while at the same

---

[1] Cf. vol. I, pp. 206f., and O. Grether, *Name und Wort Gottes im AT*, 1934, pp. 18ff.

[2] Cf. F. Giesebrecht, *Die alttestamentliche Schätzung des Gottesnamens und ihre religionsgeschichtliche Grundlage*, 1901, pp. 75f., 91ff.; J. G. Frazer, *The Golden Bough*, abridged edition, 1923, pp. 244ff.

[3] *hizkīr*: Ex. 20.24.

[4] Isa. 18.7.

[5] Jer. 7.12.

[6] Lev. 20.3; that this is an instance of pre-Deuteronomic usage is proved by Amos 2.7.

[7] Deut. 12.5, 11, 21; 14.23f.; 16.2, 6, 11; 26.2; I Kings 11.36; 14.21; II Kings 21.4, 7; II Chron. 6.20; Neh. 1.9.

time warning them that his exalted sovereignty will not tolerate any sort of restriction at the hands of Man's egoistic desires. In this way, by a bold development of the rudimentary ideas already available, a form of manifestation was arrived at in which Yahweh himself was active, but within the limits which he himself desired, and which could be spoken of in hypostatic language.

The theological importance of this formulation is obvious. On the one hand the danger of a materialistic conception of God, inherent in the general ancient view of the god as dwelling in the sanctuary,[1] is overcome by the sharp distinction drawn between the authority embodied in the Name at a particular place for the purposes of revelation and the transcendent fullness of the divine nature. This balancing of the dynamic conception, according to which the utterance of the Name called the deity to one's side,[2] by the static, the whole interest of which is to maintain unimpaired the permanent divine presence, safeguarded the vital concern of priestly religion, the real presence of God in the sanctuary.[3] At the same time, however, a magico-mystical conception of his immanence was avoided. The god who confronts men in prayer and sacrifice through the communication of his Name is the God who can be known as a personal Thou. In none of the pagan religions, in which also the divine Name none the less played a large part in the cult, is it possible to discover a similar attempt to safeguard the transcendence of God.

(c) A second road to the hypostatization of the divine Name started not from its dynamic use in invocation, but from the *equation of the name and the person*.[4] The main incentive to explore this path was the destruction of the Temple, as a result of which the representative of Yahweh on earth lost his dwelling-place, and the idea of the Name residing in the Temple ceased to have any relevant meaning. In such circumstances its use as an interchangeable term for Yahweh himself and as a symbol summing up his activity in revelation proved of the greatest help. Liberated from earth the Name was exalted to the side of Yahweh in heaven as the recipient of cultic worship, directed now not to the incomprehensible God in the fullness of his transcendent nature, but only to him as he presented himself to men in his Name. The extraordinarily large number of phrases linking human worship

[1] Cf. vol. I, ch. IV, pp. 102f.
[2] On the development of this conception in Ex. 23.21 and Isa. 30.27 cf. § (c) below.
[3] Cf. vol. I, ch. IX, pp. 422ff.
[4] Cf. O. Grether, *op. cit.*, pp. 26ff., 35ff.

in the forms of thanksgiving, praise, blessing, reverence and love, with the divine Name[1] thus betrays a heightened feeling for the un-approachability of the deity, a feeling which was then bound to lead to an even greater stress on the fact that this transcendent God had revealed himself in his Name, in order to assure men of the reality of their intercourse with him. This line of thought finds its clearest expression when, even though there is no intention of uttering it, *the Name of God is made the subject of an action or attitude*: 'I will give thanks to thy name, O LORD, for it is good, for it has delivered me from every trouble.'[2] Moreover, many other passages, which designate the Name of Yahweh as the *medium of his operation*, come under this head—for example, the prayer: 'Save me, O God, by thy name, and vindicate me by thy might!'[3] Even though it may not always be possible to draw the dividing-line with precision, nevertheless there can be no doubt that what is happening here is a transition from the Name as an interchangeable term for the divine person to its use as a designation for the divine power, a hypostatic entity through which Yahweh guides the course of the world without leaving his transcendent glory.

In contrast to the cultic hypostatization of Yahweh's Name the superiority of this second hypostasis may be seen in the fact that it is not locally restricted, but can radiate divine help and power to any quarter of the earth. In this respect it is analogous to the *mal'ak yhwh*, and it is conceivable that it was linked with this form of divine manifestation. This would explain why a theologian of the Deutero-nomic school based the authority of the angelic commander whom Yahweh, according to E, sent with his people through the Wilderness on the fact that God's Name was in him.[4] Here we see the revival of a half-dead recollection that there had been something quite dis-tinctive and particular about the angel of Yahweh; but this special significance is explained by the statement that he was the bearer of the divine Name, and had thus made real the hidden presence of the covenant God himself.

As happened in this case with the *mal'āk*, so a later writer (Isa. 30.27ff.) explained the famous thunderstorm theophany, with its

---

[1] E.g. I Kings 8.33; Pss. 148.5; 118.26; 86.9; 5.12, etc. Further passages are cited in Grether, *op. cit.*, pp. 37f., 47f.
[2] Ps. 54.8f. (So MT: RSV, presumably following LXX, reads, 'Thou hast delivered me', thus obliterating the point. Tr.) Cf. also Pss. 20.2; 75.2; 89.25; 124.8; Prov. 18.10.
[3] Ps. 54.3: cf. Pss. 89.25; 44.6; 118.10–12.
[4] Ex. 23.20f.

vivid portrayal of the manifestation of Yahweh's wrath, by ascribing it not to Yahweh himself, but to his 'Name'.[1] While Isaiah himself, as may be seen from another passage, has no scruple about making Yahweh intervene in person,[2] for Judaism, with its belief in a transcendent God, such immediacy was only acceptable on condition that mention was made of the form in which the supramundane majesty of the deity was manifested.

In the case of this theologoumenon of the Name there is a *religio-historical parallel* which strikingly illuminates the distinctive character of the Israelite belief. According to the Eshmuna inscription (*c.* 450 BC),[3] a temple was dedicated in Sidon to the goddess Astarte in which she was given the epithet *šēm ba ʿal*, Name of Baal. This is clearly to designate her as the favourite representative of the High God, who himself withdraws from direct dealings with his worshippers. Because the Name of Baal has been made over to her, she is in a position to bring his nature effectively to bear, just as a plenipotentiary royal minister is allowed to make decrees over the royal seal, and to use the king's signature, in order to legitimate his own commands as the royal will. What here, as a result of the objective thinking of polytheism, is presented in the guise of two divine persons, in Israel finds expression in the distinction between the transcendent God and the form in which he manifests himself on earth; and this hypostatization of the Name is so completely dependent for its existence on the divine act of revelation that it never constitutes a danger to the unity of God.

It is only in *later Judaism* that the revelatory function of the divine Name becomes less prominent. It is now transformed into a mysterious *divine essence*, the mediatory activities of which serve only to make men more aware of the separation of God from the world. No longer is it God himself who acts through the medium of his Name, but the Name is a substitute for the self-manifesting God. Hence the use of the Name in the Mishnah and in the Similitudes of Enoch, despite the many points of contact between these writings and Old Testament usage, has already acquired a quite different meaning. Belief in magic also seized on the idea of the power inherent in the divine Name, and sought to enlist its forces in its own service.[4] How de-

---

[1] Possibly all that was necessary to achieve this was the repointing of an original *šām* ('there'), a reading which is perfectly conceivable in view of the vividness with which the divine entry is here described: so Grätz.

[2] Isa. 9.7ff.

[3] Cf. *AOT*, pp. 446f.

[4] Cf. vol. I, pp. 219f.

cisively the Name had by now changed from a concept concerned with God's revelation in history to an ontological one may be seen from the fact that now the names of the Son of Man and of the pious in general were credited with an independent existence in heaven even before their owners had come into being on earth, thus investing the latter with a kind of pre-existence.[1]

Only in the New Testament does the divine Name recover its old revelatory significance. The redemptive work of Jesus can be summed up by saying that he revealed the Name of God to Man,[2] and in the glorification of the divine Name he himself saw the purpose of his life.[3] Moreover, because this revelation of the divine Name came to pass not simply through his words but through his whole life's work, it finds its most concise expression in the name of Jesus, to which the Apostle can transfer the Old Testament promise that the nations shall confess the One God.[4] At the same time, however, because the name of Jesus always confronts men's consciousness with a sharply delineated historical person, it is in the person of Jesus that the function of the Name of Yahweh as a form of the divine self-manifestation finds its fulfilment.

[1] Enoch 48.2f.; 69.26; 43.4; 70.1, 2. On this subject cf. W. Bousset–H. Gressmann, *Die Religion des Judentums im späthellenistischen Zeitalter*[3], 1926, pp. 349f.
[2] John 17.6, 26.
[3] John 12.28.
[4] Phil. 2.9ff.; cf. Isa. 45.23.

XIII

THE COSMIC POWERS OF GOD

O N THE SUBJECT OF the manner and method in which God accomplishes his will in the world the Old Testament contains ideas of various kinds. In addition to the sort of simple statement which will always be the first to occur to unreflective faith, as that God created, effected or sent this or that, acting in a quasi-human way, there are more complicated conceptions of the fulfilment of the divine intention. These result from the attempts of more developed thought to give some account of the distinctive quality of the various processes involved, in the course of which it is partially influenced by elements from all kinds of ancient ideas. Among these media of the divine activity an outstanding part is played by the idea of the *rūaḥ*, the spirit.

A. THE SPIRIT OF GOD

Our understanding of this concept is made much easier by the fact that we are still in a position to determine the literal meaning underlying the word. *Rūaḥ* has retained at all times—and in this it is akin to the Greek πνεῦμα—the meaning 'wind', denoting the movement of air both outside Man in Nature, and inside him, his own breath.[1] Just as, in ancient popular belief, the wind was regarded as something mysterious, the bringer of life and fertility, so at an early stage primitive Man observed that breath also was an indispensable bearer of life, the origin of which he could not explain. No wonder, then, that in the blowing of the wind and the rhythm of human respiration ancient Man detected a divine mystery, and saw in this element in Nature, at once so near to him and yet so incomprehensible, a symbol of the mysterious nearness and activity of the divine. As the bearer of

[1] Ps. 135.17; Job 9.18; 19.17.

life, therefore, the wind tends to become in the theistic religions the breath of life, proceeding from God, and both animating Nature and bestowing life on Man. The living breath in each human being may, then, be regarded as an effect of the divine breath of life, as, for example, in Egypt, where exactly as in Israel the deity breathes the life-breath into Man, and thus calls him into living existence. On the other hand, the divine breath of life may be thought of as bestowing vital powers surpassing the normal capacity of men, in particular long life, the power of healing the sick, or supernatural knowledge giving one command of omens and oracles. This was the direction taken above all by Babylonian ideas.[1]

I. THE SPIRIT OF GOD AS THE PRINCIPLE OF LIFE

In Israel both these conceptions of a breath of life in a narrower and wider sense, recalling as they do corresponding ideas of *mana* among primitive peoples, were combined, so that we cannot say whether originally only the Babylonian conception was known, and then in Canaan was enlarged by the Egyptian, or whether the whole conceptual complex developed along quite different lines. Just as Man only comes to life in the first place because God breathes into him his own breath of life,[2] so in order for him to succeed during life the *rūaḥ* must not be impaired or dwindle away,[3] or, if it does vanish, it must return to him.[4] Moreover, even the animal kingdom is called into existence by the same vital principle.[5] Hence every living thing

[1] Cf. K. Sethe, *Amun und die acht Urgötter von Hermopolis* (Abhandlungen des Preuss. Akademie der Wissenschaften, 1929, Philos.-hist. Klasse no. 4), pp. 9off.; J. Hehn, 'Zum Problem des Geistes im Alten Orient und im AT', *ZAW* 1925, pp. 210ff. The omission of this religio-historical background to the OT concept has spoilt the otherwise distinguished study by A. R. Johnson (*The Vitality of the Individual in the Thought of Ancient Israel*, 1949, pp. 26ff.) by causing him at times to lose sight of the sheer superiority in potency of the spirit.

[2] Gen. 2.7; Job 33.4. The *nišmat ḥayyīm* of the former passage plays the same part in J as the *rūaḥ ḥayyīm* in P (cf. Gen. 7.22 with 6.17 and 7.15), and must be the older and more popular expression for the breath of life; hence the Job passage is justified in using both in synonymous parallelism. Instances of *rūaḥ* for 'breath' may also be found at Isa. 42.5; Lam. 4.20; Job 9.18; 19.17; 27.3, and possibly also I Kings 10.5; for God's anger, Ex. 15.8; Isa. 30.28; Ps. 18.16; Job 4.9. For a good survey of all the evidence cf. F. Baumgärtel, 'Geist im AT', *TWNT* VI, pp. 357ff.

[3] Josh. 5.1; II Sam. 13.39 (LXX of Lucian); Isa. 65.14; Pss. 143.7; 146.4; Job 17.1; Prov. 15.4.

[4] Gen. 45.27; Judg. 15.19; I Sam. 30.12.

[5] Gen. 6.17; 7.15, 22; Eccles 3.19, 21. Whether Gen. 1.2 refers to the spirit of God moving over the waters seems doubtful. Such an idea certainly does not fit

in the world is dependent on God's constantly letting his breath of life go forth to renew the created order;[1] and when its vital spirit from God is withdrawn every creature must sink down in death.[2] Thus *rūaḥ* is at all times plainly superior to Man, a divine power within his mortal body, subject to the rule of God alone.[3]

Comprised in the word 'spirit', therefore, is the mystery of life, life in the myriad forms of abundant Nature constantly overcoming death, life calling the new generations of mankind into being, life bringing back the individual from sickness or mortal peril to new and vigorous existence. It will at once be obvious what importance this belief in the divine breath of life, a belief which Israel shared with other peoples, was bound to acquire once it was associated with the covenant God, conceived as jealous and utterly personal. As soon as the swarm of gods had fallen away, the idea of the spirit of life made it infinitively easier to maintain a unitary conception of the cosmos. Where the pagan saw a multitude of different vital and spiritual powers, to the Israelites was revealed the universal power of the one God, who by virtue of his living breath made the multiplicity of the world both dependent upon and related to himself, without thereby depriving it of the diversity of its life or debasing it to the level of an inanimate machine. In this way they were enabled to *reject the polytheistic world-view*, while at the same time avoiding a deviation into rigid deism. At the other extreme, however, their sense of Yahweh as the personal and mighty sovereign kept them from misusing the concept of the spirit to *explain the world on pantheistic and mystical lines*, presuming on the basis of the creature's share in the divine life-spirit to construct a natural unity of Creator and created. That such a divinization of Nature did not come about was due to the fact that

---

very well into the general pattern of thought of the Priestly account of creation. If *rūaḥ ʾelōhîm* is translated 'storm of God' in the sense of 'mighty storm', then the writer's intention will become clear. Cf. p. 105 below.

[1] Ps. 104.30; cf. also Num. 16.22; 27.16 (P); Gen. 45.27; Ezek. 37.14; Job 10.12; 17.1.
[2] Gen. 6.3; Ps. 104.29; Job 34.14; Eccles 3.19, 21; 12.7.
[3] Ezek. 2.2; 3.14; 11.5a; 37.1, 5f., 8–10; Zech. 12.1; Job 12.10. This life-giving spirit of God, transcending the individual, must be sharply distinguished from the individual human spirit, also denoted occasionally by the word *rūaḥ*. The latter as an organ of psychic life forms the focal centre of thoughts, decisions and moods, and thus constitutes a psychological concept as opposed to the cosmological one of the breath of life: cf., e.g., Isa. 57.16; Ps. 31.6; Num. 14.24; Judg. 8.3; Ex. 6.9, etc. On the whole subject cf. ch. XVI, pp. 131ff., below.

the Israelite view of Nature, like their other beliefs, was determined by their historical experience of Yahweh's sovereignty, which called for a corresponding absolute divine authority over the spirit of life as a demonstration that at every moment the creature was dependent upon the Creator.[1] The classic text for this attitude is the story of the sons of God and the daughters of men,[2] in which an ancient pagan myth is used as a vehicle for Yahweh's sentence of judgment, in order to make clear once for all that the creature's share in the *rūaḥ* is a gift of grace, which can at any time be revoked, from the one who is the living Lord over the spirit of life. In contrast to the thought of heathenism, with its endless traditions about the generations of heroes, the same material is here used to indicate unmistakably the unbridgeable gulf which separates the creature from the eternal God.[3]

Similarly the association of the spirit of life with the creative word was another way of asserting the sovereignty of the divine Lord over the dominant forces in Nature. The inner homogeneity of the two concepts was already suggested by the primary concrete meaning of the idiom which enabled the same expression to be used to designate both the spirit of God as the breath of life going forth from him and the word of God as the breath of his mouth.[4] Thus it was that, even though it had long been possible in paganism to describe the speech of the deity as the breath of life,[5] this primal association only became effective when God made himself known not as a force of Nature but as a personal will. This truth the Psalmist, in patent dependence on the priestly account of creation, was able to formulate in the brief statement of faith, 'By the word of the LORD the heavens were made, and all their host by the breath of his mouth.'[6] It is, therefore, as the possessor of the spirit of life that God utters the creative word. Like-

---

[1] This shaping of the Israelite view of Nature by their idea of the divine sovereignty will have to occupy us again when we come to discuss the biblical idea of the Creator. Cf. ch. XV below.

[2] Gen. 6.1–4. In spite of the broken and fragmentary state of the text, and the difficulty of establishing a definite meaning for *yādōn*, the import of the passage in the context of the whole Yahwistic work can hardly be in doubt.

[3] This is all the more remarkable, since *rūaḥ* here comes very close to denoting the divine nature itself, and thus brings perilously near the idea of the divinization of the creature: cf. P. Volz, *Der Geist Gottes*, 1910, p. 70.

[4] *rūaḥ śᵉpātāw*, Isa. 11.4; *rūaḥ pîw*, Ps. 33.6.

[5] The Egyptians said of Isis: 'Her speech is the breath of life—her words drive away sickness.' The Babylonians could praise Marduk with the words: 'The opening of thy mouth (i.e. thy word) is the breath of a good wind, the life of the land.' Cf. J. Hehn, *op. cit.*, pp. 218f.

[6] Ps. 33.6.

wise it is only in the power of the divine spirit, which has endowed his frail body with supernatural strength for the performance of his prophetic ministry,[1] that the prophet Ezekiel, as the one commissioned by God, speaks the word of command which mediates the divine life-giving breath, and causes the dry bones to rise again as living men.

2. THE SPIRIT OF GOD AS THE INSTRUMENT OF THE SALVATION HISTORY

It can be seen from the examples so far cited that Israel's general picture of God resulted in a characteristic deviation from the common oriental conception of the spirit; but the OT conception only attains its proper significance from its connection with historical experience. God's activity in history, aimed at the creation of a consecrated people of God, was discerned not only in isolated marvellous events, but also in the emergence of specially equipped men and women whose leadership in word and deed, by wars of liberation without and by the establishment of the will of God in the social and moral order within, dragged the dull mass of the people with them, again and again smashing and sweeping away all the obstacles which the incursion of heathen morals and ways of thought raised against them. In the activity of these mediators and instruments of the divine covenant purpose of salvation the Israelite people recognized afresh the irruption of God's transcendent life into the paltry patchwork of this world; and they could find no other way of grasping the astounding force which radiated from these leaders, and gave them the capacity for their task, than to designate it the living breath or spirit of God— an identification to which acquaintance with the corresponding Babylonian language may have predisposed them.[2] Here again the most striking feature was the *mysterious nature of the divine life*. In the fact that at the mortal crises of the nation's history men hitherto

---

[1] Ezekiel is in this respect in line with the pre-exilic writing prophets, that it is not the spirit which endues him with the gift of prophecy (cf. p. 56 below). However, in his case the spirit plays a part unknown in the records of the other prophets. It is the mediator of divine vital power for God's messenger, who is broken down and physically crippled by his experiences; it is also the force that transports him (2.2; 3.12, 14; 8.3; 11.1, 24; 37.1; 43.5), and enables him to utter the word of power which is instantaneous in its reviving or death-dealing effect. There can be no doubt that here we can see the continuing influence of ancient Israelite conceptions of the divine breath of life.

[2] Cf. p. 47 above.

completely unknown and unimportant, such as Gideon[1] or Jephthah,[2] could carry the dejected people with them to inspired military
achievements; that the Nazirite Samson[3] could display the strength
of a giant; that a diffident youth like Saul[4] could compel the people
to accept his leadership, and decisively defeat the insolent king of the
Ammonites, men acknowledged the bestowal of the divine life-giving
power. They discerned it also in the ecstasy of the prophetic bands,
when forgetful of self in the praise of the God of Israel in song and
dance all who took part were plunged in rapture,[5] when the outward
eye was closed in the night of unconsciousness and in its place an
inner eye opened to behold the mysteries of the divine realm and to
make them known in oracles,[6] when astonishing miraculous powers
burst forth to heal the sick, to satisfy the hungry, and to recall the
dead to life.[7] Among other incidents ascribed to the marvellous
power of the spirit were a sudden disappearance, a miraculous parting of the Jordan, and a startling dream-interpretation.[8] The unifying
factors behind all these varied phenomena were first, that in them
men saw the radiance of a higher kind of life, translating Man into
direct contact with the divine world, and secondly, that they all
occurred in the service of the establishment of the kingdom of God in
Israel. It would therefore be an importation of an alien point of view
to try to assume a different concept of the spirit according to the
political or religious nature of the effects ascribed to it.[9] Certainly the
influence of nabism on the concept of the spirit is not to be underestimated;[10] but in the heroic spirit and the prophetic alike the *rūaḥ* is

[1] Judg. 6.34.
[2] Judg. 11.29.
[3] Judg. 13.25; 14.6, 19; 15.14.
[4] I Sam. 10.6; 11.6.
[5] Cf. vol. I, pp. 309–12.
[6] Num. 24.3ff., 15ff.; II Sam. 23.2ff.
[7] II Kings 5; I Kings 17.14ff.; II Kings 4.1ff., 38ff., 42ff.; 7.1ff.; I Kings
17.17ff.; II Kings 4.18ff.; 13.21. It is, however, noticeable that these miracles are
not ascribed directly to the spirit, but always to the men who are acknowledged
elsewhere to be the mediators of the spirit.
[8] I Kings 18.12; II Kings 2.16; II Kings 2.9ff.; Gen. 41.38. On the first two
passages mentioned cf. also the remarks on the activity of the spirit for evil,
pp. 56f. below.
[9] So A. Jepsen, *Nabi*, 1934, pp. 19ff. His derivation of the spirit of nabism from
the evil spirit at work in the insane depends too strongly on externals (e.g. frenzy
both in certain mad people and in the *nᵉbī'īm*), and disregards the fact that the
spirit of prophecy is never looked upon as an evil spirit, but always exhibits
positive characteristics.
[10] Cf. p. 53 below.

primarily nothing other than the supra-sensible causality of the miraculous. This agrees with the fact that the power of the spirit emerges like a volcanic eruption, now here now there, sudden and unmediated, and then disappears again according as God calls his own to particular deeds. This trait is also reflected in the expressions used to describe the coming of the spirit, as when it is spoken of as pushing, rushing upon, or pulling someone.[1] The way in which in many accounts the *rūaḥ* acquires almost personal characteristics, and appears as an independent agent, to the detriment even of the man whom Yahweh has commissioned,[2] may on occasion savour of the demonic; though this does not entitle us to deduce an original demonistic stage of the concept of the spirit from this vivid, personifying type of narrative.[3] In such instances the alien, compulsive element is all the more clearly recognizable. The spirit appears as an intermittent divine force, absolutely outside the control of Man, and suddenly overpowering him. It is, however, precisely because of this characteristic that in the face of such events men feel themselves directly confronted by the divine Lord, whose majesty evokes in Man not only bliss but also fear and trembling.

Once this is grasped it also becomes easier to understand why after the rise of the monarchy the connection of the *rūaḥ* with the exercise of political power comes to an end. To the extent that the monarchy buttressed itself as a permanent institution with, wherever possible, a fixed hereditary succession it lost the charismatic character which had been such a feature of the older leadership, and stepped out of the sphere of the inexplicable and miraculous, which is the proper domain of the *rūaḥ*'s operation.[4] No wonder, then, that to the religious charismatics the period of the Judges appeared the ideal time of direct divine guidance, and that they ascribed the victories won by a young and unestablished people to the breaking through of the wonder-working divine spirit of life. The portentous shift of political power under the monarchy[5] is here expressed in religious terms, which Isaiah also adopted, when he contrasted the kingdom of his own day

---

[1] *pāʿam*, Judg. 13.25; *ṣālaḥ*, I Sam. 10.6; 11.6; *lābēš*, Judg. 6.34.
[2] I Kings 22.21f.; II Kings 2.16; I Sam. 16.14f.
[3] So P. Volz, *Der Geist Gottes*, pp. 2ff. This is not to deny that the *rūaḥ* may on occasion take over functions which in other religions are carried out by demons. On the reasons for this cf. p. 55 below.
[4] Cf. vol. I, pp. 308f., 441f.
[5] Cf. vol. I, pp. 442ff.

with the God-sent redeemer on whom Yahweh's spirit in its fullness was to rest.[1]

The effect of the concept of the spirit on religious thought was all the more lasting as a result of the way in which it was shaped by the experience of the spirit's power in the early prophetic movement. The impact with which group ecstasy broke into the life of the people, and gave a mighty impetus to the struggle for Israel and Yahweh, made the direct working of God through the spirit a self-evident certainty for thousands. Such a development, however, rendered the older ideas on the forms of God's self-manifestation superfluous, at any rate in so far as they had not already been strongly spiritualized. If Yahweh was present everywhere in his living breath, and could thereby engage his power at any point, then the stories of his walking on earth were no longer indispensable to the religious concern with his presence. In this way, therefore, faith in the invisible nearness of God acquired an ally whose importance can hardly be overestimated, and one which effectively combated the tendency to local limitation inherent in a vivid and concrete conception of the divine personhood. God's transcendence became clearer without his immanence thereby being called in question.

This more formal clarification of the Yahwistic faith was, however, greatly assisted by the fact that in the marvellous world of the *rūaḥ* by far the most prominent feature was the *spiritual and personal operation of the covenant God*, with his call to commitment and decision. For among all the wonders of the spirit the proclamation of the word of Yahweh came more and more to take the central place. That the 'men of the spirit'[2] were at the same time the mediators of the word,[3] and that not simply in cases where a divine oracle was explicitly ascribed to the spirit,[4] explains the profound influence both on individuals and on the nation at large which enabled them to determine decisively the pattern of religious thought. It was indeed only because of this that the wondrous works of spiritual power were interpreted as signs that the covenant God was ready and strong to succour. Certainly the tendency to misuse the marvellous powers of the prophets to satisfy the popular craving for miracle, and thus to relegate the working of the spirit one-sidedly to the category of external

[1] Isa. 11.2.
[2] Hos. 9.7.
[3] Cf. the detailed discussion in vol. I, pp. 312, 321ff.
[4] Num. 24.2ff.; II Sam. 23.2; I Kings 22.24; cf. Gen. 41.38.

supernatural aid, was ever present in Israel, and many prophetic circles were only too prepared to meet the demand.[1] That the prophets were not, in fact, dragged down into the murky atmosphere of magic and thaumaturgy was due first and foremost to the fact that the word of God again and again made itself heard in the men who were driven by his spirit.

Because it was for the office of messenger and spokesman of Yahweh that the spirit primarily equipped men, the *man of the spirit was marked out* not so much by his translation into the divine realm as *by his particular function*, in his exercise of which he was constantly reminded of his dependence on the God who had sent him by the sudden coming and going of the spirit. It is true that scattered statements begin to speak of a permanent association with the spirit, but it is precisely the fact that this kind of thing is said of Moses and Elijah,[2] men whose uniqueness is emphasized elsewhere,[3] which shows that in general the erratic incidence of the spirit continued to be the norm. Furthermore it was impossible to bequeath or transfer the spirit, and so pass on its marvellous power.[4]

The significance of all this can be made clear by a brief consideration of the ecstatic experiences of heathen nations. These, too, regarded ecstasy as the release of divine powers,[5] but because they did not see behind the phenomenon the one unapproachable divine Lord it was possible for the ecstatic to be thought of as possessed or filled by a god, and thus for man to become divinized.[6] This removal of the barriers between God and Man naturally resulted in a belief on men's part that they could take the very power of the divine into their own service, and exercise control over it, the more so because phenomena of possession could be evoked by the use of all kinds of external

---

[1] II Kings 2.23ff.; 4.1ff., 38ff.; 5.8ff.; 6.1ff.; and cf. vol. I, pp. 320, 325f.

[2] Num. 11.17, 25; II Kings 2.9, 15.

[3] Num. 12.6ff.; II Kings 2.11.

[4] Num. 11.14ff. speaks of a distribution by Yahweh of the spirit resting on Moses. This conception of the *rūaḥ* as a spirit connected with an office betrays the later stratum within E; in the golden age political leaders also had to be men of the spirit (contrast Ex. 18.13ff.). This is a link with the priestly idea of the *rūaḥ* as something which is bound up with an office, and therefore becomes effective when that office is transferred, for example, by imposition of hands or anointing: cf. Deut. 34.9; I Sam. 16.13. It would be a methodological error to argue from these late passages to the original conceptions of endowment with the spirit (cf. Jepsen, *Nabi*, p. 23).

[5] For Babylonia cf. J. Hehn, *op. cit.*, pp. 223f.; for Phoenicia, the story of Wen-Amon, *ANET*, pp. 25ff.

[6] Cf. vol. I, pp. 317ff.

methods, such as narcotics, and managed as required. Israel remained protected from this labyrinthine enchanted garden of occult forces and powers, because it recognized in ecstasy the spirit of the living God, who did not organize spectacular marvels to satisfy human curiosity, nor tolerate indulgence in a sorcerer's sense of power, but sought by his signs to enlist men in his service and to equip them for the joyful performance of his will.

In addition, however, to the reverence and holy awe which were called forth in Israel by the operation of the spirit there was another element which at first sight strikes us as strange, namely *the power of the spirit for evil*. This is not so much a question of those instances in which the noun *rūaḥ* is qualified by the epithet 'evil' (*rāʿā*),[1] or where a more particular description, such as 'spirit of harlotry',[2] of deep sleep',[3] of 'jealousy',[4] or of 'drunkenness',[5] characterizes the spiritual force as destructive. The use of *rūaḥ* in this sense is exactly paralleled in Babylonia, where the good wind has as its counterpart the evil wind,[6] which brings sickness and is personified as a demon.[7] Nevertheless the Old Testament view is distinguished from that of paganism by the fact that the evil spiritual power is subordinated to the punishing God,[8] and does not appear as an unpredictable demonic being, operating independently.

What is harder to understand is that even the spirit of prophecy may feature as a lying spirit (*rūaḥ šeḳer*), as it is portrayed in the vision of Micaiah ben Imlah.[9] It is the shattering experience of false prophecy in the name of the holy God which finds expression in the statement that that which is essentially the breath of life has been sent by God for the express purpose of destruction.[10] Here, struggling to

---

[1] I Sam. 16.14f.; 18.10; 19.9; Judg. 9.23.
[2] Hos. 4.12; 5.4.
[3] Isa. 29.10.
[4] Num. 5.14.
[5] Isa. 19.14: RSV 'confusion'.
[6] Cf. Isa. 40.7.
[7] Cf. J. Hehn, *op. cit.*, p. 221.
[8] Made explicit in all passages except those in Hosea and Num. 5.14, where presumably, unless one ought to postulate a variant view, the question is not considered. Cf. also Isa. 40.7.
[9] I Kings 22.21ff.
[10] It is hardly permissible to use the personification of the prophetic spirit in this remarkable account of a vision as proof of the originally demonic character of the *rūaḥ*. It is much more likely to be an instance of the pictorial use of the ancient oriental idea of the court of the heavenly king, which would explain why in v. 23 the action is ascribed to Yahweh alone.

find words, is a profound recognition that the good power of God may act upon the deceitful as poison or a cup of reeling, or that, as Ps. 18.27 has it, the same God who to the pure shows himself pure with the crooked deals perversely. For it is definitely not stated that the four hundred prophets of Ahab at all times showed themselves false prophets. In its destructive as in its other workings the *rūaḥ* is something given for the occasion, and then vanishing once more; and in this one case it works for disaster, because Yahweh wills to dupe Ahab, and engineer his ruin.[1] Nevertheless it cannot be gainsaid that what underlies the story of the lying spirit is the severe disappointment experienced at a failure of prophetism[2] in a crucial hour, as a result of which confidence in the spirit of prophecy was badly shaken. It is not contested that the *rūaḥ* can also reveal what is true and right, but it is now clear that the only prophet who is completely to be trusted is the one who had been admitted directly into Yahweh's company.

On this premise it becomes possible to understand the astonishing fact that in the line of divine messengers from Amos onwards there is absolutely no mention of the *rūaḥ* as the power that equips and legitimates the prophet.[3] They know themselves called, enlightened and commissioned by Yahweh in person,[4] and make use, when they wish to describe the overwhelming effect of God upon them in the state of ecstasy, of the phrase 'the hand of Yahweh' (*yad yhwh*), occasional instances of which are found earlier,[5] and which better fits the immediacy of their experience of God than the term *rūaḥ*.[6] This is not to say that they now make the *rūaḥ* a bone of contention, or seek to defame it as a destructive force.[7] On the con-

---

[1] Nevertheless the remark that Ahab had a long-standing aversion from Micaiah because of his prophecies of misfortune suggests that the court prophets, who normally gave the king favourable oracles, had already ceased to be pure vessels of the spirit.

[2] On the degeneration of nabism and its causes, cf. vol. I, pp. 332–8.

[3] In Micah 3.8 the phrase *'et-rūaḥ yhwh* is recognized to be an interpolation, probably in reminiscence of Isa. 11.2. In Hos. 9.7 the description of the prophet as *'iš hārūaḥ* is put into the mouth of the people. Isa. 30.1 does not link *rūaḥ* with the prophet's authority. The only exception is Ezekiel, on whom cf. p. 50, n. 1, above.

[4] Cf. especially the accounts of the prophet's call in Isa. 6; Amos 7; and Jer. 1.

[5] Isa. 8.11; Jer. 15.17; Ezek. 1.3; 3.14, 22; 8.1; 33.22; 37.1; 40.1. Cf. on this point Volz, *op. cit.*, p. 70, n. 1.

[6] I Kings 18.46; II Kings 3.15.

[7] The exegesis by which Jepsen tries to find this idea in Isa. 29.10; Micah 2.11; and Jer. 5.13 is untenable. The first passage is not addressed purely to the prophets; and in the last two the meaning of *rūaḥ* is 'wind', 'nothingness'.

trary it is striking that in their fiercest controversies with the guild-prophets spirit-possession plays no part. Hence it is clear that they avoid this concept only so far as they personally are concerned, because having been discredited by their opponents it can only complicate their dispute with them. How little it occurred to the true prophets to adopt a purely negative attitude to the living power of the *rūaḥ* may best be seen from the part which the concept plays in the thought of Isaiah and Ezekiel.

3. THE SPIRIT OF GOD AS THE CONSUMMATING POWER OF THE NEW AGE

The more relentlessly the prophets of the eighth and seventh centuries proclaimed the imminent storm of annihilation hanging over a world ripe for judgment, and the irruption of the divine in a new and more real form, the more drastically as a result of this new vision of God were the traditional statements of faith about the divine order transformed and filled with new content. As we have already seen happen many times with regard to the concept of the covenant, and the picture of God in prophetism,[1] so, too, the concept of the spirit is melted down and cast in a new form. To begin with, indeed, the spirit of God withdraws, so to speak, nearer to God himself, being more profoundly understood as *the power of the divine nature*, and not just as a force proceeding from him. Isaiah goes further than anyone else in this direction when, in a polemical utterance against the Egyptianizing policy of Judah in the time of Sennacherib, he characterizes the opposition of such political intrigues to Yahweh as enmity toward his spirit:

> Woe to the rebellious children, says the LORD,
> who carry out a plan, but not mine;
> and who make a league, but not of my spirit,
> that they may add sin to sin.[2]

That which is here seen as opposition to the spirit of God is the mendacity and self-aggrandizement of the rulers of Judah, which went hand in hand with unscrupulous exploitation of the people. Hence in this context the spirit must refer to the spiritual power of truth, purity and righteousness in which the holy God reveals

[1] Cf. vol. I, pp. 58ff., 224ff., 237ff., 244ff., 250ff., 267f., 278ff.
[2] Isa. 30.1.

himself.[1] The imperishable divine life, which is Yahweh's to command, and which in another passage[2] Isaiah again terms *rūaḥ*, contrasting it with *bāśār*, that is to say, the limitations of earthly being, is here linked as closely as possible with God's moral exaltedness, thus introducing the majesty of the ethical norm as a controlling principle into the marvellous realm of the spirit. Again, in the promise to the remnant of the nation (Isa. 28.5f.), the spirit of righteousness is inseparably associated with the divine glory as the moral power in which God himself draws near to his people.[3]

This direct association of the spirit with the holy personal will of the universal God is obviously connected with the intense immediacy with which in general the prophets see God at work, and is just one aspect of that colossal concentration of the concept of God which they achieved in their preaching, and the echoes of which can still be detected in Deutero-Isaiah and the Psalter.[4] Another consequence, however, was that men were able to speak in a new and more comprehensive way of *the workings of the spirit*. They no longer ascribed to the spirit merely the exceptional, those actions effected by miraculous power; now it was only as a fruit of the spirit, that is to say, as a product of a new and deeper communion with God, that they dared to hope for the right performance of God's will in religious humility and moral obedience. It was precisely in the struggle against the self-will of their compatriots that the profound insight of the prophets discerned in increasing measure Man's incapacity to live in the presence of God, and to translate his commands into action. Hence they saw no assurance of faithfulness in belief and conduct save in a divine transformation of men's hearts, or through entry into the sphere of the spirit's working;[5] and the pinnacle of their hopes was

[1] The interpretation of *rūaḥ* as here referring to the spirit of prophecy is exegetically impossible, since the relevant member of the verse stands in synonymous parallelism with the preceding one, and is separated so far from v. 2 that the asking counsel of Yahweh mentioned there cannot be adduced in explanation. Furthermore such an exegesis would run contrary to the silence of the prophet elsewhere on the subject of endowment with the *rūaḥ*.

[2] Isa. 31.3.

[3] To describe the *rūaḥ* as the 'divinity' or 'eternity' of Yahweh (so Volz, *op. cit.*, p. 73) will not do, and obliterates the dividing-line between this concept and those of the *kābōd* and the *ḳōdeš*. What is here involved is a power of God at work in the world, but one that is at the same time the power of his moral majesty. The *rūaḥ* is, so to speak, the force exerted by God's holiness (*ḳōdeš*).

[4] Isa. 40.13f.; Ps. 139.7.

[5] The purport of Jer. 31.31ff., even though it does not speak of the spirit, is in effect no different from that of Isa. 32.15ff.; 11.9 or Ezek. 36.26ff., namely a new

the emergence of a new cosmos out of the chaos of the present, made possible by such a divine intervention. To a growing extent, therefore, the activity of the spirit was shifted to the communication of religious and moral power. This first becomes apparent with regard to the messianic king, who is portrayed as the favoured bearer of the spirit,[1] and draws from its living fountain not only superhuman wisdom and strength, but also knowledge and fear of God. Deutero-Isaiah pictures the Servant of God in similar terms.[2] But if there is to be a real renewal, then not only the one who leads the people to salvation, but also those who are led, must receive a share in God's spirit. With increasing certainty the promise of an inner relationship with the spirit of God is extended to the citizens of the messianic kingdom, whether it is to be poured out upon them,[3] or whether God will set it in men's inward parts, and so change their stony heart into a heart of flesh.[4] In this way there is an advance from a picture of power working externally to one involving the innermost foundations of the personal life; Man's relationship with God is no longer left to his own efforts, but is given him by the spirit. Because, however, all this is seen as *the central miracle of the new age*, the spirit as the living power of the new creation finds its proper place in eschatology.

By a parallel development the spirit's operation is no longer regarded as something occurring in fits and starts in isolated individual events, only to disappear once more. Because the new life is a life in God's presence, so, too, the power of the divine nature, the spirit, exerts *a permanent influence on Man*. It rests on God's chosen instruments, or is set within their hearts, or penetrates them as the rain penetrates the earth, creating in them a constant association with God, and therewith the power to fashion their lives according to his will.

For classical prophecy, in accordance with its judgment on the total alienation from God of its own time, the spirit of God is removed from the picture of the present—of which the most that can be said is that the contempt in which the spirit is held merely serves to confirm

---

possibility, created by God himself, of realizing the will of God in human life. Zech. 12.10; Joel 2.18ff.; 3.1f. also point in this direction: cf. p. 67 below, n. 1.

[1] Isa. 11.2. Cf. R. Koch, *Geist und Messias, Beitrag zur bibl. Theologie des AT*, 1950, pp. 71ff.
[2] Isa. 42.1, with which cf. 61.1, possibly a fragment of the Servant Songs.
[3] Isa. 32.15; 44.3; Ezek. 39.29.
[4] Ezek. 11.19; 36.26f.

the ripeness of this world for judgment—and unfolds its living power only in the new age,[1] where it makes possible a full communion of Man with the holy God. This prophetic preaching, however, was not only readily adopted in early Judaism, but in combination with men's other experiences of the spirit in the past underwent an extremely momentous refashioning.

4. GOD'S SPIRIT AS THE POWER BEHIND THE LIFE OF THE PEOPLE OF GOD

It almost seems as if in Judaism everything which earlier generations had learned and enunciated about the working of the spirit of God came alive more than ever before, and exerted a direct influence on the conduct of daily life. Even if many other valuable legacies of the prophetic teaching fell into the background and lingered on disregarded, either half understood or completely forgotten, insight into the meaning of the spirit was enlarged and deepened in the most undreamed-of way.

This may be seen first of all in the development by which the spirit of God is made markedly independent, so that it can now be portrayed as a so-called *hypostasis*, that is to say, a separate entity which acts of its own motion, and is of itself concerned with human affairs.[2] This does not mean that the spirit is once again becoming divorced from God; on the contrary, its substantiality always remains in the shadow of the covenant God, and exists only as a form of his revelation. However, by becoming a personal subject it applies the essentially divine power within it to particular effect, acquiring a kind of mediatory position between God and Man. In this way, too, it now obtains a share in the holiness, that is, the unapproachable majesty, of God; it becomes God's holy spirit.[3] A man's attitude toward it determines his attitude to God; disobedience to the holy spirit grieves it, and causes it to withdraw, with the result that the flow of divine life is cut off.

Corresponding to this heightened importance of the spirit in the

---

[1] F. Baumgärtel has expressed doubts about this (*TWNT* VI, p. 363), but cites no passage attributing judgment in the present or divine activity in the past to the operation of the spirit. In Isa. 31.3 and 30.1 what is meant is clearly the destruction of the faithless for their resistance to Yahweh's spirit-nature; there is no suggestion that the spirit is the power which actively executes the punishment.

[2] Cf. H. Ringgren, *Word and Wisdom*, 1947, pp. 165ff.

[3] Isa. 63.10f.; Ps. 51.13.

picture of God is a very *considerable extension of the sphere of its dominion.* No longer are its operations seen only in the great saving acts of the men of God in the past; no longer is it only in the age of salvation to come that the spirit is expected to consummate God's rule by the inner transformation of men's hearts. Instead it is the spirit which, in past, present and future, is the true governor of Israel, and in which the transcendent God, dwelling in light unapproachable, in very truth draws near to his people. Hence a quite new awareness of the spirit's leading sounds through the national lament, Isa. 63.11ff.: 'I remember the days of old, of Moses and his people. Where is he who brought them up out of the sea with the shepherds of his flock? Where is he who put in the midst of them his holy Spirit, who caused his glorious arm to go at the right hand of Moses . . . who led them through the floods, like a horse through the desert, without stumbling? As cattle go down into the valley, the Spirit of the LORD gave them rest! . . . But they rebelled and grieved his holy Spirit; therefore he turned to be their enemy, and himself fought against them.'

Here, as in other passages,[1] the spirit is the medium through which God's presence in the midst of his people becomes a reality, and in which all the divine gifts and powers which work within that people are combined. It is clear from several passages that the gifts and achievements of the prophets are particularly thought of in this regard;[2] but the efficacy of the *rūaḥ* goes far beyond this, and includes all the marvellous powers which have maintained the national life of Israel in the course of her history.

What is completely new, however, is that this spirit is also experienced as the nation's *guide and protector in the present.* Even though the period of the post-exilic community was a day of small things, when many high-flown hopes had to be laid to rest, and when men were shown that they must continue to wait for that realization of the prophetic promises which they had supposed to be so near at hand, one thing, in respect of which they were assured by the words of the prophets that the ancient predictions were indeed about to be fulfilled, the returning exiles did not suffer to be taken from them, and that was the presence as their true governor and guide of the spirit of

[1] Ps. 106.33; Zech. 7.12; Isa. 34.16; Hag. 2.5. (The rendering of Isa. 63.11ff. here given varies in certain details from that of the RSV. Tr.)
[2] Zech. 7.12; Neh. 9.30; II Chron. 15.1; the gloss *'et-rūaḥ yhwh* at Micah 3.8; II Chron. 20.14; 24.20.

God. Indeed, their experience of the spirit's leading became for the Jewish community virtually a pledge that they were standing on the very threshold of the age of salvation, and that all the wretchedness and poverty of their external situation were but the curtain behind which the glorious inheritance destined by God for his people was hidden. So Haggai stirred up the hearts of his contemporaries, when they became discouraged in their Temple-building, with the words: 'Take courage, all you people of the land, and work, for I am with you, says the LORD of hosts . . . My Spirit abides among you; fear not!'[1] So, too, the governor Zerubbabel, who had neither troops nor allies at his disposal with which to resist his enemies, was encouraged by the prophet Zechariah: 'Not by might, nor by power, but by my Spirit, says the LORD of hosts.'[2] Moreover, in the last of his night-visions, in the imagery of the heavenly chariots going forth to the four winds, the prophet sees the living power of the spirit of God bringing its creative work to fulfilment even in the Gentile world, even indeed in Babylonia, generally accounted the most obdurate enemy of God, in order that the congregation drawn from the heathen may be joined to the people of God in Judaea.[3] Like the whole series, this final night-vision indicates the tension with which the post-exilic community connected the whole consummation of world-history with their own present condition, seeing in both the operation of that spirit whom they knew to be at work there and then in their midst. Hence the spirit is also the sign of the everlasting covenant which Yahweh has made with Israel;[4] and as the spirit of judgment and destruction it prepares the redeemed in Israel for the visible dwelling of God among them.[5]

As well as the community, however, *the individual receives comfort*

----

[1] Hag. 2.4f. V. 5a, 'according to the word that I gave you when you came out of Egypt', is missing from the LXX, and is certainly a corruption of the text, introduced as a gloss on *rūḥî*. For conjectural emendation cf. O. Procksch, *Die kleinen prophetischen Schriften nach dem Exil*, 1916, p. 19, and K. Elliger, *Das Buch der zwölf kleinen Propheten* II (ATD 25)³, 1956, p. 91.

[2] Zech. 4.6b.

[3] Zech. 6.1–8. The interpretation of this vision is not undisputed. Sellin, Elliger and Horst adopt the view of Rothstein (*Die Nachtgesichte des Sacharja*, 1910), according to which the vision is concerned with the gathering together of the Diaspora. This in itself attractive explanation is not, however, convincing, because the special emphasis on the chariot going to the North would then imply a sudden narrowing of the universal outlook of v. 7 (as Horst rightly points out); also 2.14ff. and 8.20ff. lead one to expect a vision of world-wide salvation.

[4] Isa. 59.21.

[5] Isa. 4.4.

from the spirit's help and support. When, deeply disturbed by his sin, a man prays for a new heart and, as it were, a new spirit, he adds the petition: 'Take not thy holy Spirit from me!'[1] When commending his future to God's guidance he pleads: 'Let thy good spirit lead me on a level path!'[2] Now, too, the individualistically orientated teaching of the wisdom schools becomes open to the new assurance of the spirit's guidance in the congregation. The sage, for whom indeed the fear of God is the beginning and fulfilment of true wisdom,[3] is aware that right training in such wisdom is only to be had through the spirit. Because it is the breath of the Almighty which gives men understanding, Elihu can dispute authoritatively even with the old men in the certainty that he is enlightened by the spirit.[4] Finally the personified Wisdom is ready to shed forth her spirit on all who hearken to her.[5]

Hand in hand with this experience of the spirit's guidance in the present goes *the effort to bring greater and greater areas of life within the scope of its dominion.* Thus political activity,[6] and the whole field of art, whether it be inspired poetry[7] or the many varieties of craftsmanship,[8] are subsumed under the operation of the spirit, and any skill in these directions is thankfully venerated as given by it. Here are the very definite beginnings of a systematic understanding of the *whole* of life as proceeding from the power of the spirit, the aim of which is to actualize the will of God in all the forms of human existence. To achieve the major goal of becoming a holy people every power and every gift must experience the renewing influence of the spirit. It is no mere coincidence that it should be the priestly writers in whom these tendencies are discernible. Into their total vision of the realization of the eternal kingdom of God on earth the proposition that the spirit was the power of God in the present fitted extremely well, and enriched the fundamentally static character of their view of history with

---

[1] Ps. 51.11.

[2] Ps. 143.10.

[3] Prov. 1.7; 9.10; 14.27; 15.33; Ecclus 1.16, 18.

[4] Job 32.8ff., 18. Daniel, too, should be mentioned here, in so far as he is described as a wise man: cf. Dan. 4.5f., 15; 5.11f. The connection of wisdom with the spirit of God is strongly represented in the extra-canonical wisdom literature: cf., e.g., Ecclus 16.25; 39.6ff.; Wisd. 7.7; 9.17; also frequent instances in Philo.

[5] Prov. 1.23. It is true that the translation of *rūaḥ* here by 'anger' can be defended; yet the very juxtaposition of spirit and word may be an argument for our interpretation: cf. the following paragraphs.

[6] Deut. 34.9 (cf. Num. 27.18); I Chron. 12.19.

[7] II Chron. 25.1–3.

[8] Ex. 23.3; 31.2; 35.31 (late stratum in P).

a dynamic element which brought home to them the essentially supernatural and marvellous quality of God's sovereignty.

In spite of this surprising readiness to come to terms with the power of the spirit present at all times and in every situation the danger, which could so easily attend such a view, of a heightened subjectivity and of the practice of a mystical piety never became acute. Even though in Hellenistic Judaism an intrusive mysticism may here and there have seized upon the concept of the spirit, yet figures such as Philo, or communities like those of the Therapeutae, were very much the exception, and in no way reacted upon the Judaism of Palestine. The reason for this is to be found in *the close association of spirit and word*, which now came to life in a new form, and accorded well with the overall orientation of religious life toward the Law. For it was at this period that with joy and gratitude men recognized the Word of God in the Law and the Prophets, those writings which through all disasters had been preserved as a priceless legacy. And while the present felt itself less and less able to utter the living word of God by direct inspiration, it saw none the less in the written testimony of the great acts of God in the past a standard and directive for its own situation. The effect of the spirit was to make the word from the past live, and to bring it into contact with the present in binding immediacy. Hence in those passages in which the Jewish community is shown the permanent foundations on which its life is to be built, and on the basis of which it is to progress with joy to new forms of living, word and spirit are mentioned together. Side by side with the spirit which God causes to rest upon his people the words which he has put into their mouth form the content of the everlasting covenant linking Israel with its God.[1] Zechariah associates the fulfilment, whether for evil or for good, of the words of the earlier prophets, to which he constantly appeals, and in which the Law is included (1.6), with the operation of the spirit within the community.[2] The penitential prayer of Nehemiah speaks of the instruction given by the spirit through the word of the Law and the Prophets,[3] and the gloss on

[1] Isa. 59.21. The echo of Deut. 30.14 is unmistakable.

[2] Zech. 1.6; 4.6; 7.12. It was the spirit which gave rise to the word of God uttered in times past and now of normative significance in the present, and which is at the same time the power giving life to the community. If the vision of the olive trees (4.11ff.) is meant to designate the governor and the High Priest as the mediators of the divine spirit (so Sellin, *ad loc.*), then it is through them as the guarantors of the authority of the word that the link between word and spirit is firmly established.

[3] Neh. 9.20, 30.

Hag. 2.5 connects the presence of the spirit in the congregation with the word given by Yahweh to Israel when they came out of Egypt.[1] Through the working of the spirit, therefore, in which the community can rejoice and take comfort, the same God speaks to them who once chose the small, rebellious and disobedient people of Israel, who led them through the centuries, and now links his revelation to that history and its tradition. Experience of the spirit does not open up a way to direct mystical contact with God, in treading which Man can forget his own sin and God's majesty, but it leads him again and again to learn obediently from the word about God's judgment and mercy; and under his guidance the word becomes the means by which God acts in living power, preparing his congregation to be his instrument.

Thus in the religious life of the Jewish community the spirit of God acquires a very real existential significance, for it is through the spirit that the history of revelation becomes a living force, and the foundation of an existence based on faith. In possessing it men had the ἀῤῥαβὼν τῆς κληρονομίας,[2] the pledge of the inheritance, for the full possession of which Israel had still to wait, while in the form of a servant she lived as a wanderer among the nations.

Later Judaism[3] retained this deposit of faith, developing it in many directions, but also weakening it here and there. As the spirit of prophecy the *rūaḥ* plays an especially large role, and the Targums like to interpolate it under this name (*rūaḥ nᵉbū'ā*) into the ancient narratives, even when some other meaning is actually intended by the original text.[4] Its efficacy is also extended to cover the process by which the sacred Scriptures came into being, and is understood in the sense of the inspiration of the biblical writers[5]—indeed, it is even claimed for the translators of the LXX. Quotations from the Scriptures can now be introduced with the formula, 'the (holy) spirit says . . .',[6] thus making the link between word and spirit even closer, though at the same time more external. Particular words of Scripture are to be regarded as direct utterances of the holy Spirit.[7] Even

---

[1] Cf. also the obvious coupling of spirit and word in Prov. 1.23.
[2] Eph. 1.14.
[3] On this subject cf. the detailed presentation in Volz, *Der Geist Gottes*, pp. 78ff.
[4] E.g. Gen. 45.27; Judg. 3.10; I Sam. 16.13; Ex. 35.31.
[5] Cf. Volz, *op. cit.*, pp. 83f.
[6] So Ps. 119.165 in Ber. rab. 44.17; Deb. rab. 23a; Ps. 31.19 in Shem. rab. 39.33: cf. Heb. 3.7; I Clem. 13.1.
[7] Cf. Volz, *op. cit.*, p. 167.

though rabbinic theory restricted itself in this regard to the canon, the apocalyptists went further, and appealed to the authority of the spirit to authenticate their visions.[1]

The spirit also appears as the effective power of life present in the community and the individual; but it is significant that it is pre-eminently in the cult, where the congregation is seized by the rapturous enthusiasm of the divine praises, that it becomes conscious of the spirit, and furthermore thinks of the chief person of the cult, the High Priest, as impregnated with its power.[2] The spirit's guidance of the individual is seen above all in the sage, whose wisdom as knowledge and service of God has a religious character, and as popular instruction continues the function of the prophet;[3] but the spirit as the power behind all good deeds, and as guidance in moral decision, is thought of as present in all the pious.[4] On the other hand, the expansion of the concept to denote a world-controlling moral force, which as a cosmic element of pantheistic type helps to maintain the fabric of the universe, clearly betrays Stoic influences, paving the way for a rationalistic and idealist interpretation of the cosmos.[5] A development more strictly in accordance with the Old Testament conception of the spirit is that by which the cosmic function of the spirit comes to be regarded as that of architect of the universe;[6] and it is in this connection that the resurrection of the dead, that indispensable preliminary to the creation of a new world, is also thought of as his work.[7]

The older views, however, are not only developed in these various ways; now and then they are weakened. Thus, as the consideration of the wonderful works of the spirit is directed more and more to the external and visible, men are no longer content to accept its silent and hidden operation within the community as a sufficient pledge, and they tend to identify great teachers, distinguished by prophecies and miracles, as the men of the spirit, and to glorify them in countless legends.[8] In the process the danger of distorting the reverential

---

[1] Enoch 71.5, 11; 91.1; II(4) Esd. 5.22.
[2] Cf. Volz, op. cit., pp. 136f., 133ff.
[3] Cf. p. 63 above, n. 5.
[4] Cf. esp. the Testaments of the Twelve Patriarchs and Philo.
[5] As in the Wisdom of Solomon and Philo.
[6] Judith 16.15; Bar. 21.4; 23.5 (Syr. vers.): cf. Enoch 60.12ff.
[7] Sotah IX, 15: cf. Sanh. X, 3.
[8] Taan. III, 8. Cf. F. Weber, *Jüd. Theologie*[2], p. 125. On the communication of the spirit by the laying on of hands by the Rabbis cf. *ibid.*, pp. 126f. Further dis-

humility proper to a willing instrument in presence of the spirit into an arrogant control over its marvellous power is not always avoided. Even in earlier times the assurance of standing on the threshold of the new age, and of possessing the firstfruits of the spirit, was sometimes suffocated by the oppressive sense of one's own spiritual poverty, and replaced by a yearning and watching for the day when the spirit would be poured out as the first stage of the final salvation.[1] Furthermore, the frequent understanding of the spirit as the effective cause of piety of life was often balanced by an equally widespread notion of the activity of evil spirits, which to an increasing extent were held responsible for all evil thoughts and deeds. In such circumstances talk of the spirit of God is more an expression of speculative thought than of genuine religious experience.

Since there can be little doubt that the extensive spread of belief in spirits within Judaism was due in part to the intrusion of popular Persian superstitions,[2] one may easily be inclined to ascribe the growing importance of the concept of *the* Spirit in later Judaism likewise to the *influence of corresponding religious ideas in Zoroastrianism.* Even in the earliest religious poems of the Persian reformer, the Gathas, a good deal is already said about the holy and divine Spirit, Spenta Mainyu, and functions are ascribed to him similar to those with which the Jews credited the *rūaḥ.* In Zoroastrianism, too, we find the same oscillation between the spirit as the divine principle of life and as an independent being within the divine realm. In either case, however, it is associated as closely as possible with the good God, Ahura Mazdah, much more closely indeed than any of the other hypostases, of whom the most notable are the seven Amesha Spentas. The latter ought rather to be described as partial manifestations of the powers and resources of the divine order, but Spenta Mainyu is the mediator of God's own activity, as such himself a part of the divine nature, co-operating both in the creation of the world and in its winding-up at the end of time. Moreover, by virtue of his opposition to the evil spirit, Spenta Mainyu is almost an ethical cosmic principle, in accordance with which good men are empowered and rewarded, and the wicked are delivered up to judgment; hence

---

cussion in A. Schlatter, *Geschichte Israels*[3], 1925, p. 312; Strack-Billerbeck, *Kommentar zum NT aus Talmud und Midrasch* II, 1924, pp. 128f., 133f.

[1] Joel 3.1ff.; Zech. 12.10.
[2] Cf. p. 209 below.

he himself is never invoked in prayer as a divine person. Belief in this good spirit seems to be fundamentally associated with the dualistic world-view as a whole, and not to have been incorporated into the monotheistic faith in the one good God, Ahura Mazdah, until Zoroaster himself.

The possibility that these ideas may have exercised some influence on Jewish belief in the Spirit certainly deserves the most serious consideration.[1] It is quite conceivable that on the Jewish side, perhaps, in an effort to reach a mutual understanding with their Persian overlords, some may have spoken of the work of the Spirit with as much deliberation as they used in referring to Yahweh as the God of Heaven. Nevertheless on reflection the balance of probability is against such an assumption; for the Spirit-hypostasis does not become naturalized in popular thinking until the Hellenistic period, so that, apart from the Babylonian Diaspora, there was no longer any great incentive for Judaism to accommodate itself to the ideas of Persian religion. Furthermore, within the wider development of that religion the Spirit-hypostasis of Zoroaster's own preaching steadily declined in importance, and was finally absorbed in Ahura Mazdah.[2] The history of the concept in Zoroastrianism, therefore, is precisely the reverse of the development of the Jewish conception, and this must be a constant warning against the tendency to find a causal relation between Persian and Jewish ideas of the Spirit. Finally, such caution commends itself all the more in that an internal motivation for the growth of the Jewish view of the Spirit of God is clearly discernible, and that therefore it is possible that its development was purely internal to Judaism.

---

[1] H. Ringgren considers that at the very least the probability is that the hypostatization of the spirit was accelerated and intensified as a result of Iranian influence (*Word and Wisdom*, 1947, p. 171).

[2] Cf. P. Volz, 'Der heilige Geist in den Gathas des Sarathuschtra', *Eucharisterion Gunkel dargebracht*, 1923, pp. 339f.

XIV

THE COSMIC POWERS OF GOD
(*continued*)

B. THE WORD OF GOD

I. THE SIGNIFICANCE OF THE WORD IN THE COMPARATIVE STUDY OF RELIGIONS

IN DISCUSSING THE SUBJECT both of sacred rites and of the name of God and its meaning we had occasion to remark that for ancient Man the spoken word possessed an importance quite different from that which it enjoys today.[1] It makes no difference whether this fact is the result of a *mana*-type concept or of belief in spirits; in either case throughout ancient times the word is regarded as the medium of powers which effectively influence events. This is not, of course, true of simply any word, but it certainly applies to words spoken with great emphasis and firm intention, of which the supreme examples are the curse and the blessing.[2] The whole wide field of magical spells is evidence of this. Naturally, too, the invocation of the deity imbues the word with special efficacy, and the curse and the blessing thus become weapons in the hand of the poor and helpless before which even the strongest may quail. In popular belief such words have what is virtually a life of their own; they are like independent beings waiting their opportunity to invade reality. And even when this is denied them they remain dangerous for a long time, like a long-forgotten mine in the sea, or a grenade buried in a ploughed field. The most striking Israelite instance of this belief occurs in the story of David. The curse of Shimei hangs like a threatening thunder-cloud over the

---

[1] Cf. vol. I, pp. 173f., 207f.
[2] Cf. J. Hempel, 'Die israelitischen Anschauungen von Segen und Fluch', *ZDMG*, 1925, pp. 20ff.

head of the king, and its deadly lightning, if it does not strike him in his lifetime, may still harm his descendants. It may also, however, recoil on the head of the man who uttered it, and thus be rendered harmless; the mine is then, so to speak, exploded, even though it has not injured the man for whom it was intended. This explains the point of David's infamous testament to Solomon.[1] Or the curse may be disarmed by a blessing, as was expected of the Gibeonites.[2]

If therefore even a word of Man can be so potent, a word of God must possess the same characteristics to a still higher degree. Thus Babylonian religion has a lively sense of the power of the divine word, which is celebrated in special hymns, the so-called Enem-hymns.[3] These portray primarily the destructive power of the word over Nature and humanity, emphasizing in particular the fact that neither its inner meaning nor its external identity can be detected; it catches its victim like a concealed net, its nature being in every respect that of a powerful spell, hidden from Man. Hence it has no soothsayer nor seer to communicate it; or, if it is revealed to such a one, there is nothing for him to do but tremble and lament, for it utterly overwhelms him and destroys his strength. All this is in keeping with the part played by the divine word in the strange episode from the fourth tablet of the Babylonian Creation epic, *enuma eliš*. In this account of the trial of strength by which Marduk proves his ability to make use of the power transferred to him by the gods for the purpose of his fight with Chaos, it is related that his word was able to annihilate a robe, and then create it again, whereupon the gods pay him homage.[4] The divine word displays beneficent effects in a hymn to the moon-god Sin,[5] in which it is credited not merely with bestowing food and drink, flocks and herds and the increase of living creatures, but also with his reigning in truth and righteousness. Because it is the god's function as ruler that is here being extolled, the word, as the declara-

---

[1] I Kings 2.8f.

[2] II Sam. 21.3: cf. Judg. 17.1f.

[3] Cf. S. Langdon, *Sumerian and Babylonian Psalms*, 1909, pp. xixf., and nos. I, II, III, IV, VIII, and IX; M. Jastrow, *Die Religion Babyloniens und Assyriens* II, 1904, pp. 24ff.; H. Zimmern, *Babylonische Hymnen und Gebete. 2. Auswahl* (Der alte Orient XIII.1), 1911, pp. 21ff.

[4] ANET, p. 66.

[5] *AOT*, p. 242. On the basis of these and similar descriptions of the word L. Dürr (*Die Wertung des göttlichen Wortes im AT und im alten Orient* [MVAG 42, 1], 1938) and, in agreement with him, H. Ringgren (*Word and Wisdom. Studies in the Hypostatization of divine Qualities and Functions in the Ancient Near East*, 1947, pp. 65ff.) have concluded that we already have here an example of a divine hypostasis; but it is questionable whether the extant material will justify such an assumption.

tion of the royal will, transcends the limits of the merely magical, and acquires a moral quality. Yet there is nothing more than this one isolated instance; of conscious understanding of the moral function of the divine word there is none. Similarly in Egypt the word is designated as the instrument by which Thoth creates the world; but here again it is a potent medium of magic, a word within which the power of the divine enchanter is concealed.[1] The word of the priestly ministers in the recitation of the ritual and the prayers also possesses a thoroughly magical character.[2]

2. THE WORD OF GOD IN ISRAEL

I. In Israel, too, the word was understood as the cosmic power of the Creator God, but there is no instance of its being conceived as a medium of magic, concealed from Man. On the contrary it is a clear declaration of the will of the divine sovereign. The classic source on this subject is the Priestly account of creation, with its description of the cosmos as a wonderfully organized structure proceeding from the word of divine command, an expression of the free self-direction of a will conscious of its goal. The same conception is found in the hymns of Deutero-Isaiah,[3] and in those Psalms which extol God's glory in the creation;[4] and it is wholly in keeping with it that the heavens should declare the glory of God, and the babbling of children become a testimony to his greatness.[5]

II. This clear insight into the significance of the divine word as an expression of God's sovereignty, which is so characteristic of the Old Testament documents, is ultimately based, however, on the *experience of the divine word in history*, to which it owes its force and conciseness. Israel's special relationship with her God rests from the first on the word of that God. The basic law of the Sinai covenant, the Decalogue, is given the name *ʿaśeret haddᵉbārîm*, 'the ten words',[6] as the

---

[1] Cf. H. O. Lange, 'Die Ägypter', *Lehrbuch der Religionsgeschichte*[4], ed. Chantepie de la Saussaye, 1925, I, p. 483. The same is true of the utterance of the universal Lord in the creation saga, which we possess only in a late version: 'Manifold were the creations which came forth out of my mouth' (cf. Lehmann-Haas, *Textbuch zur Religionsgeschichte*[2], p. 254).

[2] For the religio-historical analogies cf. further J. Szeruda, *Das Wort Jahves* (Diss. Basel), 1921, pp. 45ff.

[3] Isa. 40.26; 44.24; 48.13; 50.2f.

[4] Pss. 33.6, 9; 104.7; 147.4f., 15ff.; 148.5f.

[5] Pss. 19.2ff.; 8.3.

[6] Ex. 20.1; 34.1, 27f.; Deut. 4.10, 13, 36; 5.5, 19; 9.10; 10.2, 4.

mighty proclamation of the divine will by which the people's way of life is determined, and the foundation laid for all future legislation. When, in Deuteronomy, the term *dᵉbārîm* is extended to cover every kind of legal material,[1] the 'word', as the comprehensive designation for the nation's law, acquires a heightened significance, and of itself bestows on this law a share in the revelatory status of the law of Sinai. Thus the whole life of God's people is based on the word of God, in which is summed up the clear and unambiguous will of their sovereign Lord. The inner potency which gives this word its effectiveness derives entirely from the shattering majesty of the one who utters it. Even the threats and promises which form the framework of the law,[2] and which, according to the behaviour of Man, attach to it an automatic effect comparable to that of cursing and blessing utterances, leave one in no doubt that their dynamism is rooted in the personal will of the lawgiver, and that they have therefore nothing in common with the coercive character of natural forces or magical spells.

Side by side with this divine word in the law, with its validity for all occasions, we find the particular proclamation of the divine will for particular situations, the *prophetic word of God*, or *dᵉbar yhwh*. The prophetic word achieves its effect not in opposition to the legal *dābār*, but on the basis of it, and in order to implement its true purpose in the teeth of every kind of misinterpretation and misunderstanding. By suppressing and subordinating to itself first the mechanical oracle (Urim and Thummim, ephod) and then also the psychically extraordinary forms of prophecy (dream, vision, audition) it reveals with especial clarity and impressiveness the spiritual and personal nature of God's self-communication, and his absolute superiority to all mantic and magical arts. In his intercourse with his people God holds the initiative, and all human autonomy whether in the prophetic recipient or in his hearers must surrender to the might of the divine word. At the same time, however, the prophets to whom the word is entrusted find a power put into their hands which proves itself superior to all political and military force. Moreover, this can be seen not merely from those individual marvellous events in which a miracle or a punitive judgment follows their word, as is so strikingly described, for example, in the Elijah stories, but from the whole

---

[1] Deut. 1.18; 12.28; 15.15; 24.18, 22; 28.14; 30.14; Ex. 12.24.
[2] Deut. 28; Lev. 26; described as *dᵉbārîm*, Deut. 4.30; 30.1; Josh. 21.45; 23.15; I Kings 8.56.

direction and development of the history both of their own nation and of other nations. Isaiah sees his God hurl a word against Israel like a weapon; it falls, and strikes home in Jacob, calling forth destructive effects which, in the form of a steadily intensifying series of divine acts of punishment, smash the disobedient people to pieces.[1] Jeremiah is called to be a prophet over the nations by God's putting his word into his mouth, so that he now has power not only to plant and to build, but also to pluck up and to break down.[2] By eating the word in the form of a scroll Ezekiel learns that a power existing objectively over against him is now effective within him to kill and to make anew, in order that the 'rebellious house' may be fashioned into a people of God.[3] Deutero-Isaiah sees the word of God going forth like a swift messenger to establish the divine will with full authority, and then to return to God again.[4] As a cosmic power of God, therefore, the word takes very much the place for these men which in popular thinking was occupied by the *rūaḥ*, and enables them to discern God's direct control of history.

It was on this basis of the value attached to the word by the prophets that the *Deuteronomic view of history* was constructed, the authors of which sought to present the destiny of the nation systematically as the product of the word of Yahweh. At the more external level the continuous operation of God's word in Israel's history was ensured by the promise of an unbroken line of prophets from Moses onwards.[5] The more inward aspect is represented by the efforts, apparent both in the introduction to the law-book[6] and in the Deuteronomic redaction of the historical works, to explain every event in terms of willing performance or disobedient disregard of the divine commands. At the same time the divine words of blessing and promise, whether in the pledge that Israel shall possess the land of Canaan[7] or in the assurance of an everlasting line to the Davidic dynasty,[8] are invested

---

[1] Isa. 9.7ff.; cf. Hos. 6.5. In the case of Isaiah the word is the prophetic doom-oracle of earlier times, not a word of indefinite content (cf. H. Grether, *Name und Wort Gottes im AT*, 1934, pp. 104f.).

[2] Jer. 1.5, 9f.

[3] Ezek. 2.4ff.; 3.1ff.

[4] Isa. 55.10f.

[5] Deut. 18.15, 18.

[6] Deut. 1–3.

[7] Deut. 7.8; 8,18; 9.5; 9.5; Josh. 21.44f.; 23.14; I Kings 8.56. From a later period, Ps. 105.8f., 42ff.

[8] I Kings 2.4; 8.20; 11.12f., 32, 36; 15.4; II Kings 8.19; II Chron. 21.7; 23.3; Pss. 89.2ff., 25ff.; 132.10ff.

with a power quite independent of Man which is decisive for the whole pattern of history, and which embodies God's sovereign control of all historical forces. In all these ways the word proves itself the guiding force of history. Because, moreover, the will of God, whose purposes never change, is present in the individual prophetic word, the latter can be combined with the word of the law in a unitary entity; the portrayal of Moses and his work in terms of the prophetic ministry[1] expresses this connection clearly enough. *The word thus becomes an expression of God's saving will and universal design exalted over history*, at one moment in the static and unalterable form of law, at another in the dynamic movement of the word of prophecy, making history into the organic process in which God's cosmic purposes are hammered out. It is in this sense that the warning at the end of Deuteronomy[2] impresses on men the immediate presence and life-creating power of the divine word in which the God of revelation himself draws near to his people and conducts his dealings with them.

III. This importance of the word for God's revelatory activity within his own *people* explains why the statements about his *relation to the world*, which first appear in the seventh century and in which also the word is the intermediary, exhibit that clarity and force which so markedly distinguishes them from similar statements in paganism.[3] For now *the processes of Nature also fall into the category of the free moral activity of a purposeful will*, and are thereby lifted out of the sphere of naturalistic determinism or magical caprice, and linked as closely as possible with history. It is no accident that the Israelite account of the genesis of the world at the behest of the divine creative word forms the opening of an historical work which with unprecedented stringency and consistency makes the absolute superiority of God over Nature the basis of its statements about him. God's activity in Nature, creating the setting for Man's natural existence, is seen by the Deuteronomist as the utterance of that divine command on which both Nature and history alike depend: 'Man lives by every-thing that proceeds out of the mouth of the LORD.'[4] When Deutero-

---

[1] Cf. Deut. 18,15, 18, and the description of the proclamation of the law as a communication of the *debārīm*: Deut. 1.18; 4.2; 6.6; 12.28; 13.1; 15.15; 24.18, 22; 28.14; 30.1; 32.46.

[2] Deut. 30.11ff.

[3] Cf. pp. 70f. above.

[4] Deut. 8.3.

Isaiah speaks of Yahweh's counting the host of heaven, leading them forth and calling them by name,[1] or praises the Mighty One who calls earth and heaven, and they stand forth together,[2] then this utterance of the Creator God falls within the same vast perspective of the establishment and consummation of his kingdom as does his word published through the prophets. Indeed, the prophet can quite deliberately set both side by side as terms in a series, the unifying principle of which is the redemptive will of the Holy One of Israel.[3]

It is not unimportant to observe in this connection how the ancient *dynamic of the prophetic word* is extended to the word as a cosmic power. God says to the deep, 'Be dried up!'—he calls to earth and heaven, his rebuke makes the sea dry, and even the motion of the stars in their courses, a phenomenon universally regarded as the most impressive example of a self-contained, once for all established system, is transformed into the obedient sortie of an army which Yahweh sets in motion by his word of command.[4] The effects of this view may be seen also in the Psalms, where, partly in dependence on Deutero-Isaiah,[5] partly by independent formulation,[6] the processes of Nature are portrayed as the movement of living forces released by a specific word from Yahweh. By contrast the *priestly description of the creative word* is already tending toward the static conception of *a system which*, after its once for all promulgation in the past, *continues with absolute regularity for ever*, entrusting to the earth forces working in accordance with fixed laws,[7] assigning to the heavenly bodies the rule over day and night,[8] and by the blessing pronounced upon the animals and Man[9] liberating a power which from henceforward works automatically, and by which the whole of the future is already predetermined in a particular direction. It is clearly the divine word of the Law, given in the past, which leads these writers in their contemplation of God's creative work to this static conception of the natural order, by which everything is compelled to pass under the yoke of the

[1] Isa. 40.26.
[2] Isa. 48.13.
[3] Isa. 44.24ff.; 50.2.
[4] Isa. 44.25; 48.13; 50.2; 40.26.
[5] Pss. 104.7; 147.4.
[6] Pss. 147.15ff.; 148.8.
[7] Gen. 1.11, 24.
[8] Gen. 1.16ff.
[9] Gen. 1.22, 28.

divine lawgiver. The effect of this conception can be detected not only in many Psalms, which extol the command given once for all by the Creator as a perpetual ordinance,[1] but also in echoes in Deutero-Isaiah, when he contrasts the eternally enduring word of God with the transience of all human things.[2] In the same way he can see the divine word by which history is controlled as anchored in the promise made once to David but valid for all time.[3]

IV. This priestly conception of the word of God was considerably reinforced by the growing practice of *restricting the word of God in the law to the sacred Scripture*. As early as Deuteronomy the term *dābār* was frequently used to refer to the law as it existed in written form;[4] but in the post-exilic period this way of speaking increased significantly,[5] until finally even the technical term for the word of prophecy, *dᵉbar yhwh*, was applied to the Law.[6] Moreover, the prophetic word, too, became increasingly something codified in writing. The literary activity of the prophets had already helped to create, side by side with the unpredictable word uttered for the specific historical moment, the word eternally fixed and of uniform validity for all moments; and now the collection of the prophetic words in books under the superscription: *dᵉbar yhwh 'ᵃšer hāyāh 'el—*, 'the word of Yahweh which came to . . .' brought the authority of the written prophetic word to full flower.[7] The more during the Exile men were compelled to make reading from the sacred Scriptures the focus of divine worship, the more natural it became to look for the word as a fixed entity in a sacred book. The post-exilic prophets point explicitly to the words of their predecessors, accessible to all, as a valid norm[8] by means of which the contemporary situation can be given direction and purpose; and thus the prophetic writings,[9] or even the Law and the Prophets, are cited as *dābār*.[10] Here we arrive at the consummation of the priestly view, for which the word is equated with the eternally

---

[1] Pss. 33.6, 9; 148.5f.

[2] Isa. 40.8.

[3] Isa. 55.3.

[4] Deut. 4.2; 30.14; 32.47.

[5] Isa. 66.2, 5; Pss. 12.7; 50.17; 119.9, 17, 57, 101, 161; 147.19; Prov. 16.20; 30.5; Job. 23.12; Ezra 9.4; II Chron. 34.21.

[6] Num. 15.31; I Chron. 15.15; II Chron. 30.12; 34.21; 35.6.

[7] Hos. 1.1; Joel 1.1; Micah 1.1; Zeph. 1.1; Hag. 1.1; Zech. 1.1.

[8] Ezek. 38.17; 39.8 (the words of a post-exilic prophet); Zech. 1.6; 7.7, 12—cf. Hag. 2.5. Cf. p. 64 above.

[9] Pss. 12.16; 147.19.

[10] Ps. 51.6 (reading *bidbārekā*); Isa. 59.21.

valid institution of the divine lawgiver, subjecting to his will both Nature and human life alike.

v. It cannot be denied that implicit in this substitution of the static concept of the Law for the dynamic one of the Word was the threat of a deistic removal of God far from the events of this world. The fact that isolated instances of older ideas of the word, which treasured it as a medium of revelation to be experienced in the present,[1] or contemplated it in its creative power,[2] still occurred would have made no difference. More important was the linking of the Word with the Spirit of God,[3] which preserved its living dynamic, and kept it from petrifying in an impersonal world order. Even more effective, however, was the steady process by which *the Word was hypostatized,* so confirming and intensifying its function as a divine cosmic power.[4] For the significance of this development was by no means merely negative, a method of linking the transcendent God to the world through the mediatory services of a hypostasis; it witnesses just as much to the experience of the Word as a living and present reality, the effects of which men could discern from day to day, and in them be confronted by the operation of the living God himself. The presuppositions necessary for treating the Word as an independent entity of this kind were already present in the strong emphasis in the prophets on the objectivity of the Word, the strange power of which, subjecting to itself all human thought, and acting entirely of its own motion, they portrayed in such striking images and analogies[5] that from time to time some have wished to see an hypostasis of the Word even at this stage. The line of poetic personification, however, was crossed only at a much later period, when independent effectiveness was ascribed to the Word without its being given a particular content or connected with a person commissioned

---

[1] Job 4.12; 15.11.

[2] Enoch 5.3; Apoc.Bar. 21.4.

[3] Cf. pp. 64f. above.

[4] Cf. L. Dürr, *Die Wertung des göttlichen Wortes,* 1938, pp. 122ff.; H. Grether, *Name und Wort Gottes im AT,* pp. 150ff.; H. Ringgren, *Word and Wisdom,* 1947, pp. 157ff.

[5] For the Word as a weapon hurled by God, Isa. 9.7; as a blazing fire, Jer. 20.9; as a crushing hammer, Jer. 23.29; as a swift messenger, Isa. 55.10f.; as an independent being giving orders, I Kings 13.9, 17, 32; 20.35; II Kings 20.4; Jer. 39.16. The stock phrase, 'the word of the LORD came to . . .', instead of 'the LORD spoke to . . .', should also be included among the expressions which had this objectifying effect. It will not do, however, to regard such passages as already evincing a hypostatization of the word, as Ringgren suggests (cf. previous note).

to communicate it. Thus it can be said that Yahweh sends his word, and it heals the sick;[1] that it runs upon earth, scattering snow and ice, but also brings the melting warmth.[2] Above all, however, it was God's intervention in the history of his people which later Judaism attributed to the Word as an independently active force. Neither herb nor plaster healed the Israelites who had been bitten by serpents, but 'thy word, O Lord, which heals all things'.[3] Like a savage warrior the almighty Word leaps down from heaven, where it has been resting in the royal throne, into the midst of the land of Egypt, which has been dedicated to destruction, in order to smite its firstborn.[4] In the nature of the case the word of inspiration also plays a special part in this development. When Abraham is inspired, the voice of a Strong One falls from heaven, speaking and calling in a fiery cloudburst,[5] and similarly with Enoch and Baruch.[6] The Targums like to replace God in the sacred text by the Word, here called *mēmrā'* or *dibbūrā*, and conceived as an independent divine power; thus at the Sinai revelation Moses brings the people near to the Word of God, the Word of God guides Israel through the Wilderness, and the Word can even be provoked.[7]

In all these statements the predominant concern is that of the salvation history, namely the presence of the transcendent God in the destinies of his people; but in the development of the concept of the Word in Philo the emphasis is on speculative interests, and under the influence of Greek, and in particular Stoic philosophy the Logos becomes the cosmic mind, and historical revelation recedes in importance.

---

[1] Ps. 107.20. Hoping and waiting for the *dābār* (as in Pss. 119.81, 114, 147; 130.5), and praising it (Ps. 56.5, 11), without further defining its content, also suggest that it is regarded as the representative of God's power in history, to which the speaker is looking for help.

[2] Ps. 147.15ff.

[3] Wisd. 16.12.

[4] Wisd. 18.15. According to a gloss at Bar. 4.37; 5.5, the children of Israel are gathered together to Jerusalem by the Word of the Holy One.

[5] *Die Apokalypse Abrahams* (Studien zur Geschichte der Theologie und Kirche I), ed. Bonwetsch, 1897, IX, p. 20, XIX.5, p. 30; Jub. 12.17, cf. 5.7.

[6] Enoch 91.1; Apoc. Bar. 1.1; 10.1: cf. the inspiration of the Sibyl, Or. Sib. III. 162, 297, 491.

[7] Targ. Onk. at Ex. 19.17 and Deut. 1.30; Targ. Jon. at II Kings 19.28. For further examples of this use of *mēmrā'* and *dibbūrā* cf. H. Ringgren, *op. cit.*, pp. 161ff. On the whole subject cf. Bousset, *Die Religion des Judentums*[3], p. 347; Szeruda, *op. cit.*, pp. 66ff.; F. Weber, *Jüdische Theologie*[2], pp. 180ff.

3. SPIRIT AND WORD

The process described above, by which inspiration, the control of history, and creation were all included in the activity of the Word, made it inevitable that statements about the Word should in many cases overlap with those about the Spirit. Indeed, Jewish thought was never able to make a precise delimitation between them. One might possibly say that at any given time there are different angles from which men speak of the operation of one hypostasis or the other; if the idea of the spirit is connected with that of divine life in the world, then the idea of the Word has to do with that of the revelation of the God who controls history and of his will. The determining principles are those of animating power and expressed thought and will respectively. In particular cases, however, it is clear that this distinction is no longer present to the consciousness of the writers.[1]

The thought of the New Testament reverts all the more strongly to the original essential characteristics of Word and Spirit. The Word regains its proper function as the means by which the divine will is revealed. This is not confined to the way in which the good news of the divine redemption, endued with its own special dynamic, demonstrates its power, spreads abroad, runs, cannot be bound, and as the judge of the thoughts and intents of the heart confronts each individual with the need for decision.[2] It holds good more than ever when, as a result of being *equated with Jesus*, the Word becomes an independent person, and thus enters on a mode of existence apparently at variance with traditional beliefs. The designation of Christ as the Logos in John 1 is just as firmly connected with the Old Testament conception of the Word as it is sharply opposed to the Hellenistic concept of the Logos; for it knows nothing either of a cosmic mind in the pantheistic, or of a redemptive idea in the idealistic and mystical

---

[1] An attempt at equating the two may be observed in the remarkable postulate of the *bat ḳōl*, the voice of God, by means of which, according to Jewish belief, on special occasions brief words or sentences of a revelatory character are communicated. If the supernatural illumination of God's instruments, by which they were given continuous and coherent instruction, could be attributed to the Holy Spirit, then it was the task of the Word, which proceeded from the divine voice, to guide them to decisions, to strengthen them, and to grant them revelations in particular instances. Hence the Word can be mentioned in combination with the Spirit as, so to speak, complementary to the latter (cf. F. Weber, *Jüdische Theologie*[2], pp. 194f.). Nevertheless the role of the hypostatized Word does not seem to have undergone any obvious limitation as a result of this.

[2] Acts 19.20; 6.7; 12.24; II Thess. 3.1; II Tim. 2.9; Heb. 4.12f.

sense, but sees the universal and sovereign will of the personal God incarnate in all its dynamic momentum in the life of a human person. To sum up the fundamental features of the biblical revelation in *one* Word was a complex requirement. On the one hand this Word must reveal the divine will in a way which would confirm the personal and spiritual nature of God's dealings with men as opposed to any idea of physical divinization or mystical union, yet at the same time safeguard the hiddenness of the divine majesty. On the other it must also comprehend within the scope of its one revelation both creation and redemption, the valid permanent order and the new act of God, the static and the dynamic, the present and the future. All this was only possible by applying the absolute fullness of the Old Testament concept of the Word of God to the person of the Redeemer; and that is why this New Testament development can only be understood on the basis of the Old.

Furthermore, it was the *association of Spirit and Word*, as this in its various forms determined the Old Testament conception of the Spirit, which was incomparably fulfilled in the New Testament belief in the Holy Spirit, through whose power Jesus accomplished his prophetic mission, and in the Paraclete sent by him, who continually renews his work in the community, and gives to the members of the Body of Christ a share in a life of divine power. Both in their manifold congruencies and in their distinguishing characteristics Word and Spirit are now given an internal rationale in the relationship of λόγος and πνεῦμα as Persons of the Trinity, in whom, emerging from the transcendent divine glory, the One God condescends to men, and becomes conceivable to them, without in any way surrendering his absolute otherness. Something, therefore, which in the Old Covenant was indeed recognized as significant for salvation history and eschatology, but which nevertheless was often felt to involve conflict and unresolvable tension, in the New Covenant is experienced as the unimaginable richness of the divine nature, and thereby understood in its ultimate unity.

C. THE WISDOM OF GOD

For a long time the wisdom of God made virtually no contribution to Israel's religious understanding. Clearly God was the possessor of the highest wisdom, just as he surpassed men in every other respect. Otherwise the skill of the farmer, the ability of the king or the judge, and the talent of the artist would not have been ascribed to his instruction.[1] For Israel's central concerns, however, the fullness of divine life, and the divine self-communication in spirit and word were far more important than wisdom.

I. WISDOM AS SAVOIR FAIRE

When Israel does begin to concern herself more closely with wisdom, it has a strongly secular flavour, and is only loosely connected with religious faith. The practice of gnomic wisdom in Solomonic circles[2] was concerned first and foremost with skill in practical affairs, as well as with all kinds of riddles and fables dealing with the worlds of animals and plants, and not with abstract investigation into wisdom or philosophic contemplation of the universe. It turned its keen interest on the rich complexity of human circumstances, and tried to establish rules for success in daily life.[3]

In this instruction in practical matters, however, Israel was trespassing on a domain which had long been cultivated by her neighbours.[4] The Egyptians in particular were keen practitioners of proverbial wisdom, and their collections, from as far back as the third millennium BC, at the same time witness finely to a pious and reverent mind. When in the Solomonic period Israel was opened up to foreign cultures, and a close link was established with Egypt by the king's marriage, it is easy to understand that grateful use was made of the productions of this foreign wisdom teaching,[5] just as the proverbial wisdom of the Edomites and Arabs was also highly valued.[6] The very fact of this historical situation makes it plain that Israelite wisdom literature could not give a central place to the national Yahweh

---

[1] Isa. 28.23ff.; II Sam. 14.17, 20; I Kings 3.9, 12, 28; 5.9ff.; Ex. 28.3; 35.31—cf. Isa. 31.2; 40.13f.

[2] I Kings 5.9ff.; 10.1.

[3] G. von Rad gives a witty account of this type of wisdom as an 'elementary form of instruction in how to get on in life' by 'rational elucidation and organization' of the world—cf. the § 'Israel's Wisdom deriving from experience' in his *Old Testament Theology* I, pp. 418ff.

[4] Cf. J. J. A. van Dijk, *La sagesse suméro-accadienne. Recherches sur les genres littéraires des textes sapientiaux*, 1953.

[5] The most striking example of the adoption of Egyptian proverbial wisdom is afforded by a comparison of Prov. 22.17–23.11 with the Sayings of Amen-em-ope, dating from *c.* 1000 BC. Cf. H. Gressmann, 'Die neugefundene Lehre des Amenemope und die vorexilische Spruchdichtung Israels', *ZAW*, 1924, pp. 272ff. On the whole subject cf. further P. Humbert, *Recherches sur les sources égyptiennes de la littérature sapientiale d'Israel*, 1929.

[6] I Kings 5.11; Prov. 30f.

religion with its cultus and its messianic hopes, but was bound instead to begin from the outlook of mankind in general. Furthermore the mediators of the international wisdom literature belonged to a particular class, that of the scribes or higher officials, ministers and officers, whose worldly wisdom was naturally strongly imprinted with the interests and experiences of their own group, and no longer possessed any marked sense of national solidarity. But in the nature of the case such a decline in national awareness was inevitable. Concern with the direction of individual life will always take more account of what is common to humanity at large in respect of character, disposition and circumstances; for, so far as possible, it has to lay down universally valid axioms for the guidance of practical affairs, and therefore cannot enter very closely into the supra-individual aims of a nation's history. This, of course, does not exclude the possibility that the latter may indirectly determine the content and orientation of this practical lore, as in the event did happen, though only in the closing stages of the study of wisdom in later Judaism. In earlier times it still remained strongly dependent on foreign models,[1] and unaware of the necessary differences between the basis of morals in Israel and in other nations.

The result was an unprejudiced borrowing of foreign wisdom; and even if in the process morally inferior motives were introduced, nevertheless the value of this participation in the general mental stock of civilized Man is not to be underestimated. For one thing it awakened a lively realization that other nations had a share in the deposit of truth, and this prevented a premature exclusion of the outside world, with its concomitants of chauvinistic narrowness and ossification. In the common possession of wisdom the people of God knew themselves to be at one with many non-Israelites.

Such an attitude was, it is true, made more difficult, if not entirely crushed, by Israel's political fortunes. The arduous political and religious struggles in which men fought to maintain the supreme values of the national life were hardly a favourable time for the practice of international wisdom, though in periods of relative quiet there was a revival of the study, as the work of the 'men of Hezekiah' mentioned in Prov. 25.1 suggests. It was, however, only when Israel had renounced a political life of its own, and organized itself into an

---

[1] A very cautious account of this gradual transformation of Israelite wisdom is given by J. Fichtner, *Die altorientalische Weisheit in ihrer israelitisch-jüdischen Ausprägung. Eine Studie zur Nationalisierung der Weisheit in Israel*, 1933. Cf. further J. C. Rylaarsdam, *Revelation in Jewish Wisdom Literature*, 1946.

ecclesiastical state under the suzerainty of Persia, and when not a few of its citizens had attained high positions in government service—and even more when, with the advent of Hellenism, a new and freer air began to blow, disseminating knowledge among the nations—that this stunted twig of the spiritual life also began to bloom again. Once more learning from foreign models was resumed, but this time with a more conscious selection of those elements in keeping with Israel's own nature. For as a result of a long history of suffering all Israelites had now become consciously proud of their own inheritance, and had no wish to surrender any part of it. The evidence for this new flowering of wisdom is to be found in the first part of the book of Proverbs (1–9), the book of Job, Ecclesiastes, and such apocryphal writings as Ecclesiasticus, Baruch and the Wisdom of Solomon.

2. WISDOM AS THE PRINCIPLE OF COSMIC ORDER, AND AS HYPOSTASIS

The first point to strike one on reading this literature is the way in which *the concept of wisdom has been radically expanded.* Not only the old skill in practical affairs but also *the purpose and order discernible in the cosmos* are now regarded as effects of wisdom. The hymn in praise of wisdom in Job 28 particularly emphasizes this aspect when it connects wisdom closely with the work of creation:

> God understands the way to it,
>   and he knows its place.
> When he gave to the wind its weight,
>   and meted out the waters by measure;
> when he made a decree for the rain,
>   and a way for the lightning of the thunder;
> then he saw it and declared it;
>   he established it, and searched it out.[1]

In these noble verses the poet links the mystery of Nature with the divine wisdom, which stood before the face of God as a pattern of that which was to be created, and so determined the natural order. An earlier writer had already declared that the world had been made in

---

[1] Job 28.23, 25–27. The text is not undisputed, but the exposition of Budde seems to be the best. (Budde's translation from his commentary on Job is the one quoted in the German edition; the RSV rendering has been used here, since it corresponds exactly to that of Budde. Tr.). For a similar interpretation cf. H. Ringgren, *op. cit.*, pp. 91ff.

wisdom,[1] but here *ḥokmā* is presented with distinctive emphasis as being in its original essence a cosmic principle. The writer of Prov. 8 also speaks of this divine cosmic principle in very much the same way. If wisdom here commends herself as a teacher, yet she bases her authority on her coming into existence *before* all created things, and on the relationship with the Creator God which she is privileged to enjoy:

> The LORD created me as the first revelation of his power,[2]
> the first of his acts of old.
> Ages ago I was set up,
> at the first, before the beginning of the earth.
> When there were no depths I was brought forth,
> when there were no springs abounding with water.
> Before the mountains had been planted,
> before the hills, I was brought forth;
> before he had made the earth with its fields,
> and the mass of the clods of the world.
> When he established the heavens, I was there,
> when he drew a circle on the face of the deep,
> when he made huge the clouds above,
> when he established the fountains of the deep,
> when he assigned to the sea its limit,
> so that the waters might not transgress their shore,
> when he made strong the foundations of the earth . . .
> then was I beside him, like a master workman,
> playing before him at all times,
> sporting with his inhabited world
> and delighting in the sons of men.[3]

---

[1] Ps. 104.24.

[2] This translation has been proposed by J. B. Bauer (*VT* VIII, 1958, pp. 91f.), who draws attention to the sense of *drkt* = 'sovereignty, power' in the Ugaritic texts.

[3] Prov. 8.22–31. For the translation and its justification cf. C. Steuernagel in Kautzsch-Bertholet, *Die heilige Schrift des AT*. (The RSV has been retained wherever it gives substantially the same sense as the German rendering; in lines 1, 7, 10, 13, 16, 17, 20 and 21 direct translation has been made from the German version, but the departures from the RSV which this involves are of detailed significance only. Tr.) In the text of v. 30, however, the word *'āmōn* ought not to be translated 'little child', but denotes an 'overseer', even though elsewhere the form is vocalized differently (*'ommān*, So of S. 7.2; *'ūmmān* in the Mishnah). Against this rendering appeal is made principally to the expressions in vv. 30f., which speak of wisdom as 'playing' or 'sporting', ideas seemingly incompatible with the conception of the cosmic architect. This is, however, simply to overlook the fact that a poetic description, which may in any case have been influenced by mythological portrayals of a divine child, does not usually stop to ask whether its imagery will serve to illumine a sober and considered understanding. The statements in v. 25 were still too close for the poet to be able to speak of her as a mature adult. In addition it

Here too, therefore, wisdom is the cosmic thought, proceeding from God, creatively organizing and acting, and an objective reality even to God himself. Henceforward this connection with the creation and sustaining of all things was inseparable from wisdom, as the literature of later Judaism bears witness.[1]

If it is asked why the *ḥokmā*, which hitherto had been primarily the method of instruction in right living, should now be understood so emphatically as creative wisdom, the answer is to be thought of less in terms of influence from Babylonian, Egyptian or Persian mythology[2] than of contact with the philosophical schools of Hellenism. Jewish scholars of the third century BC, such as the famous Aristobulus of Alexandria, reveal what a strong impression the natural philosophy of Aristotle in particular had made on Jewish thought; but even before the time of these theologians Jews must have found their point of contact with Hellenism in the sense of wonder which they shared in their contemplation of the cosmos, and have managed to incorporate this into their concept of wisdom.

---

should be remembered that the picture of the child at play is, in fact, a matchless illustration of the effortlessness with which God or his wisdom masters the mighty task of creation. The contrast is definitely not disturbing, but heightens the poetic effect. Since Job 28 proves that the mediatory status of wisdom at the creation was a current idea at this time, there can be no reason for excising it here. In the same way Wisd. 7.22 speaks of the πάντων τεχνῖτις. H. Ringgren also supports this translation of 'āmōn (*op. cit.*, pp. 99ff.).

[1] Ecclus. 1.2–6; 24.5f.; Slavonic Enoch 30.8; Wisd. 7.12, 17ff., 21f.; 8.1, 4f.; 9.9; similarly in Philo, cf. W. Schencke, *Die Chokma (Sophia) in der jüdischen Hypostasenspekulation*, 1913, p. 69.

[2] That behind the Wisdom hypostasis lies an actual myth of a goddess of creation and revelation, as Schencke and also Bultmann ('Der religionsgeschichtliche Hintergrund des Prologs zum Johannesevangelium', *Eucharisterion, Gunkel darg.*, 1923, pp. 1ff.) have argued, seems to me unprovable. In Babylonia it is primarily the description of the wisdom of the cosmic creator Marduk, and of his relations with his father Ea, which exhibits many startling similarities with Israelite ways of thought, but without making direct influence probable (cf. Heinisch, *Die persönliche Weisheit des AT in religionsgeschichtlicher Beleuchtung*, 1923, pp. 47ff.). Much more remote are the analogies with the Egyptian gods Ptah and Thoth, and with the Persian conceptions of the two Amesha Spentas, Vohu Maneh (Good Mind) and Armaiti (Humility), of whom the former, in the manner of a Logos, was Ahura's instrument in the creation of the earth, while the latter, as Ahura's wife and daughter, became the mother of the first Man, and through him of all mankind. One ought, however, to take the influence of Persian religion more positively into account when considering the increased tendency to hypostasis speculations in general.

Not only was the sphere of wisdom's operation thus enlarged, the concept was further enriched by being *exalted into a hypostasis*. Because of the peculiar character of oriental poetic diction it is easy to understand that there should often be considerable doubt whether anything more is involved than poetic personification, implying no kind of dogmatic statement.[1] An appeal to the personification of wickedness and folly in Proverbs[2] would seem to support this view. However, the most that these last examples prove is that this stylistic form had been in use for a very long time, and was, in fact, still used when, in the case of Wisdom, personification had already passed over into hypostatization. Moreover, even if one was not prepared to see the descriptions in Job 28 and Proverbs 8 as anything more than mere imagery—though even at this stage God's will and thought are clearly enough considered as personal, independent power proceeding from God—the picture drawn in the Apocrypha would provide a decisive argument to the contrary, for here there can be no doubt whatever of the separate existence of Wisdom. In these texts Wisdom proceeds out of the mouth of the Most High,[3] she is a breath of the power of God, an effluence of the glory of the Almighty, a reflection from eternal light, an image of the goodness of God,[4] and she partakes of God's holiness, majesty and love. She is granted a dwelling among the angels in heaven,[5] yea, she sits on the throne of God,[6] and chooses his works.[7] It is to her that God gave the command to make Man.[8] In view of all this the hypostatic character of Wisdom in the earlier descriptions must also be acknowledged, and its emergence explained not merely in terms of the logical separation between the transcendent God and the immanent world-process, but also as a result of the value set upon themselves by the wisdom teachers, who wished to rate their own authority no less highly than that enjoyed by the prophets, who appealed to the Word and Spirit of God. Indeed, Wisdom has as much power to reward and punish as Yahweh himself.[9]

This development of the concept of Wisdom gained in importance,

[1] Cf. E. König, *Theologie* [3,4], p. 187; J. Fichtner, *op. cit.*, p. 119; W. Frankenberg, *Die Sprüche* (Göttingen Handkommentar zum AT II.3), 1898, pp. 6of., *et al.*
[2] Prov. 7.10ff.; 9.13ff.
[3] Ecclus 24.3.
[4] Wisd. 7.25f.
[5] Enoch 42.1f.
[6] Wisd. 9.4, cf. 8.3.
[7] Wisd. 8.4.
[8] Slavonic Enoch 30.8.
[9] Prov. 1.22ff.; 3.16f., cf. 3.6, 11f.; also 1.28, cf. Amos 8.12; Isa. 55.6; 65.1.

because it afforded the possibility of acknowledging truths possessed by foreign nations by describing them as participation in the divine *hokmā*. For since Wisdom is already made known in the creation, she is naturally accessible to all peoples. Her connection with the ancient conception of practical shrewdness could be accommodated by making the latter the gift and endowment of Wisdom. As the creator of Man she loves him,[1] and seeks to make him happy. She invites him into her house,[2] and encourages him to make a covenant with her. She it is who bestows sovereignty and skill in government on the kings and nobles of the earth.[3] 'Every voice that exhorts to good, is her voice. Every perception of truth and every practice of virtue comes under her influence, and is her work. Whoever rejects her, forfeits life; whoever possesses her, has found life.'[4] In this way a wide sector was opened up within which it was possible to come to terms with foreign practical wisdom, and to make its much-admired insights one's own. Knowledge of Nature, and the moulding of the individual life, formed a bridge between Israel and the pagan world. In so doing men had no thought of imperilling Israel's own inheritance, but believed themselves capable of loyally holding fast to Yahweh.

Yet this assimilation to alien truth did indeed conceal dangers. The more important the divine Wisdom discernible in Nature became, the easier it was to suppose that from that starting-point one could arrive at a rational understanding of God accessible even to the heathen. And the greater the confidence that wisdom could achieve this goal, the more quickly were men ready to expect from her a solution to the rest of life's riddles as well. If the former error is more apparent in the Jewish theology of Alexandria with its rationalization of revealed knowledge,[5] and in apocryphal writings like the Wisdom of Solomon,[6] the latter became acute in the Palestinian community, when in its struggle for certitude concerning God's sovereignty living piety was threatened by a dogmatic explanation of the world quite

---

[1] Prov. 8.17, 31b.

[2] Prov. 8.1ff.; 1.20ff.

[3] Prov. 8.15f.

[4] A. Dillmann, *Handbuch der alttestamentlichen Theologie,*, p. 347. G. von Rad (*Old Testament Theology* I, p. 443) rightly emphasizes that with this imploring invitation of Wisdom, which brings the offer of salvation with special urgency directly to the individual, something new comes into the life of Judaism.

[5] Cf. A. Schlatter, *Geschichte Israels von Alexander dem Grossen bis Hadrian*[3], 1925, pp. 77ff.

[6] Wisd. 7.17ff.

divorced from reality.[1] Hence it was of decisive importance for wisdom teaching that from its own ranks there should arise a resolute rejection of all attempts to assimilate it to paganism or bring it down to that level, and an energetic reconsideration of its own understanding of the world along the lines laid down in the religion of Israel. Thus it is precisely the cosmic significance of Wisdom which the author of Job 28 plans to use in order to prove that, although indeed the traces of Wisdom are to be found everywhere, yet nowhere on earth is she herself to be found. The underworld, too, and the kingdom of the dead, say: 'We have heard the rumour of her!' But God alone knows and possesses her, for at the creation he brought her forth from himself as, so to speak, the cosmic idea or the model of the cosmic structure, and he penetrated into all her mysteries and searched them out.[2] This world-pervading and controlling Wisdom, however, he kept back from Man, granting him instead a different kind of wisdom, one appropriate to him: 'Behold, the fear of the Lord, that is wisdom; and to depart from evil is understanding'.[3] This fierce polemic by the poet of Job against the presumptuous way in which men fancy themselves to have sat in God's council is clearly intended as a protest against the current wisdom teaching with its self-conceit, as this is represented by Job's friends.[4] In opposition to them the poet stresses that God's wisdom is not placed in its entirety within Man's grasp for him to read off from the works of creation alone. Because Man can discover only traces of Wisdom, but never Wisdom herself, therefore there remain riddles in the course of the universe which Man cannot plumb, but can only accept in awe and adoration before the all-wise Creator. The speeches of God himself[5] express even more powerfully the ideal of self-effacement which keeps silence before the marvels and mysteries of creation, a self-effacement which leads, however, not to slavish subjection, but, because of the gracious self-communication of the Lord of the universe, to trustful surrender. This dethroning of all autonomous wisdom is also the concern of Koheleth, when he indeed acknowledges wisdom within

---

[1] Cf. the speeches of the friends in Job, and the mechanical doctrine of retribution to be found in such passages as Prov. 1.19, 31ff.; 2.21f.; 3.33ff., etc. and Pss. 37; 39; 49; 73; 128. On this subject cf. Eichrodt, 'Vorsehungsglaube und Theodizee im AT', *Procksch-Festschrift*, 1934, pp. 62f.

[2] Job 28.27.

[3] Job 28.28.

[4] Job 5.2ff.; 8.8ff.; 15.2ff., 7ff., 17ff., etc.

[5] Job 38–42.

its limits as a high good,[1] but at the same time throws a fierce light on its 'vanity', so far as ultimate questions are concerned, by his profound meditations on the power of God in creation.[2]

3. WISDOM AS A PRINCIPLE OF REVELATION[3]

It is true that it proved impossible to carry through absolutely rigorously this clear and logical critique of the wisdom teaching. There can, however, be no doubt that it contributed to the fact that the wisdom teachers *renewed a vigorous search for a link with the Old Testament understanding of God*, and that the primary attachment of all human efforts after truth to the revelation was more clearly perceived. As early as Proverbs wisdom and the fear of Yahweh are sometimes used as interchangeable concepts,[4] and the fear of Yahweh is described as the *rē'šīt* of wisdom; that is to say, not only its beginning, but its chief ingredient, its essence, its germ[5]—though it is true that the logical conclusions from this are not always clearly drawn. In Ben Sirach we find a quite new attempt to do justice to the distinctive character of the Israelite inheritance. It is true that he continues to see that there is a deposit of truth mediated by Wisdom, and is therefore unwilling to break the links with heathen wisdom teaching. God has poured out his Wisdom over all his works; all flesh possesses as much of her as his bounty has willed to bestow.[6] Wisdom, however, is still the rationale of the cosmos, existing before all created things, and in its profundity impenetrable to Man, and reserved to God alone.[7] Hence God bestowed her in abundance only on those who feared him; indeed, she is created with the pious in the womb.[8] Israel

[1] Eccles 2.13f., 26; 4.13; 7.4f., 11f.; 9.16ff.

[2] Cf. in this connection, H. W. Hertzberg, *Der Prediger übersetzt und erklärt*, 1932, pp. 42ff. In Koheleth criticism the positive elements are on the whole too little regarded, as, for example, in A. Lauha, 'Die Krise des religiösen Glaubens bei Kohelet', *VT* Suppl. III, pp. 183ff.

[3] J. C. Rylaarsdam investigates the opposition between rationalist and theological wisdom teaching, and the changeover from one to the other: cf. p. 82, n. 1 above.

[4] Prov. 13.14 and 14.27.

[5] Prov. 1.7; 9.10; the weakening of these statements by Budde, (*Hiob*, 1913, p. 170), as though they referred only to an elementary stage of wisdom beyond which the fully qualified exponent will press on by his own efforts to complete understanding, overlooks the fact that *rē'šīt* means far more than this, and that its fuller connotation cannot be disregarded in this context.

[6] Ecclus. 1.10.

[7] Ecclus 1.2–8.

[8] Ecclus 1.10, 14.

thus has an unchallengeable advantage, which is ultimately defined as lying in a particular quarter, namely *God's revelation within Israel*. For the Creator of all things commanded Wisdom: 'Let your dwelling be in Jacob, and your inheritance in Israel!' There she served before him in the holy tabernacle, and then on Mount Zion, above all, where she took root in the honoured people.[1] In particular she was embodied in the Law of Moses, from which she caused her doctrine to shine abroad.[2] Here, therefore, we are confronted with *Wisdom in a narrower sense*, which coincides with God's revelation to Israel, which for the Jews is comprised pre-eminently in the Law.

This orientation of Wisdom toward the Law also occurs in many of the didactic poems in the Psalter[3] and in Baruch.[4] It finds its full development in the Pirke Aboth, for which the true sage is the teacher of the Torah, and the Law constitutes the unique and absolute norm.[5]

This change in the character of the wisdom teacher, which took place primarily in the Palestinian community, also had its effect in the *Diaspora*, though not, it is true, universally. Just as the Wisdom of Solomon praises the faith of the patriarchs as the true wisdom, so Philo portrays Moses as a teacher of wisdom, to whom the divine words were revealed in ecstasy, and whose laws are therefore supremely rational and universally binding. This, however, did not prevent the infiltration of a whole range of Platonic and Stoic influences, whether it be in individual philosophic ideas such as the dualistic world-view, the pre-existence of the soul, the eternal duration of matter, and the immanent world-soul, all of which play a part in the Wisdom of Solomon, or in the whole structure of ethics, as in IV Maccabees, or in the transformation of the Old Testament faith into the philosophical religion of Hellenism which Philo accomplished with the help of allegorical exegesis of the Scriptures. Despite a formal connection with the Old Testament revelation, in all these instances the wisdom of heathenism was triumphant.

Because of this enlargement of the concept of Wisdom there was inevitable *overlapping with the hypostases of Word and Spirit*, and this had a complicating effect which hampered clear exposition. In particular Wisdom and the Spirit, because of the similarity of their functions,

[1] Ecclus 24.8f.
[2] Ecclus 24.23ff.
[3] Pss. 111; 119.97ff.
[4] Bar. 4.1.
[5] Pirke Aboth I. 11f.; II.8; I.2.

easily combine to form a homogeneous concept. Sometimes they are arranged in synonymous parallelism, as in Dan. 5.11ff. or Wisd. 9.17; sometimes their functions merge, as in Philo and II(4) Esdras; sometimes they are identical, as in the Wisdom of Solomon, where Wisdom, like the Spirit, is the breath of God, representing the divine power both in the physical and in the moral order, and as a πνεῦμα φιλάνθρωπον educates mankind. Whereas in this document the Word is still clearly distinct from Wisdom, and appears as an independent angelic being,[1] in Ben Sirach Wisdom is virtually born from the Word,[2] and in Philo is presented conversely as the mother of the Logos, with God as the father. The Jewish teachers never found a method of organizing these various hypostases into a single system.

4. THE IMPORTANCE OF THE CONCEPT FOR THE PROBLEM OF TRUTH

Nevertheless *the importance of the Wisdom hypostasis* for the dialogue of the Old Testament faith with the world of Hellenistic spirituality should not be underestimated. Its significance within the congregation increased markedly as a result of its association with the Law, for this gave it new content in the form of knowledge of God to add to its practical wisdom and understanding of Nature. But this was not all. It also gave the community a platform from which they were able to answer the problem of truth posed by Hellenistic wisdom, without in the process evaporating or curtailing their faith in the revelation of God within Israel. It was possible to give an affirmative answer to the question whether divine truth was accessible also to the heathen, and to appeal in support of this answer to the co-operation of the divine Wisdom in the creation, as a result of which it had been communicated to all creatures. But the further question, how this was to be reconciled with the absolute claims made for the divine revelation within Israel, was resolved by placing alongside that *revelatio generalis* a *revelatio specialis*, the peculiar possession of Israel alone.

In this way both that which the two societies had in common and that which distinguished them were brought within the scope of a single practicable formula, thus averting the danger which must have threatened had there been a total equation of divine wisdom in Israel

---

[1] Wisd. 9.1; 16.12; 18.15f.
[2] Ecclus 1.4; 24.3.

and in the pagan world. Pagan wisdom had no right to handle the material of Israel's special revelation, and to subordinate it to its own categories, as the Jewish theologians of Alexandria sought to do. On the contrary, the divine revelation given to Israel, being the higher wisdom, was bound to reserve the right to decide what was true and what was false in pagan knowledge. The Jew had no need to investigate the 'hidden things', the 'superfluous' information, with which imagination and illusion led the restless cravings of curiosity into error.[1] In the fear of God, which showed itself in obedience to the Law, he had not only the beginning and root, but also the fulfilment and crown of Wisdom.[2] In this way a vital need of the Israelite aspiration after knowledge was satisfied.

[1] Ecclus 3.22–24.
[2] Ecclus 1.14, 16, 18, 20.

XV

COSMOLOGY AND CREATION

I. ISRAELITE COSMOLOGY

ISRAELITE COSMOLOGY EXHIBITS, AS is only to be expected, extensive agreement with the general ideas of the ancient world on the subject, without any attempt at organizing the material into a systematic unity. In the thought of ancient Man heaven was not normally conceived as something etheric or immaterial, but rather as an exceptionally massive structure, far surpassing the earth in stability. Hence it is the first thing to emerge from the watery Chaos at the creation, when it is described as *rāḳīaʻ*,[1] literally, 'that which is stamped down solid' (Gk. στερέωμα; Lat. *firmamentum*). Resting on pillars, it overarched the earth,[2] hard as a molten mirror.[3] Poetic hyperbole can compare it with a veil or tent which Yahweh has stretched over the earth.[4] Its function in creation certainly calls for the greatest possible solidity, for this is nothing less than the separation of the heavenly and earthly oceans. If the masses of water in heaven[5] and on earth were to flow together, the result would be a return to Chaos. Hence the windows and doors of the great heavenly reservoir[6] are well secured, and opened only to release the rain.[7] At the judgment of the Deluge the floods of the heavenly ocean poured

---

[1] Gen. 1.6.

[2] Job. 26.9, 11. A quartet of such pillars is suggested by the four Cherubim of Ezekiel's vision (Ezek. 1.5ff.), who bear the *rāḳīaʻ*, and represent the four corners of the earth.

[3] Job 37.18.

[4] Isa. 40.22; possibly also 42.5; 48.13; 51.13; Job 9.8. In any case the point of the comparison is to depict the transcendent ease with which God performs the act.

[5] Gen. 1.7; 7.11; Pss. 104.3; 148.4.

[6] Job 38.22.

[7] II Kings 7.2, 19; Ps. 78.23.

unhindered through them, and buried the earth beneath their waves; only the closing of the windows of heaven brought the devastation to a halt.[1] The cosmic scope of such a catastrophe is especially vividly depicted in the Babylonian account of the Flood, according to which even the heavenly world was threatened, so that the gods in their anxiety took shelter with the Father of the gods in the topmost storey of heaven.[2] Reference to this highest throne of God, rising above the heavenly ocean like a balcony set on beams, is also to be found in the Old Testament.[3] Such a picture presupposes a heavenly world consisting of a number of spheres; and in fact the Israelites, too, conceived of more than one court in heaven, since they can speak of 'heaven and the heaven of heavens', *haššāmayim ūšemē haššāmayim*,[4] and use *šemē haššāmayim* to refer to the topmost heaven.[5] The Old Testament, however, contains no information as to the number of circles in heaven. The Babylonians computed three, in the highest of which stood the throne of Anu, the father of the gods. Nevertheless they also knew of a sevenfold system of celestial spheres.[6] Similar ideas occur among other peoples. Yet it is clear that the Israelites characteristically attached no importance to such a division of heaven,[7] the reason no doubt being that in any case the whole celestial world was subject to *one* Lord. Matters were quite different for the Babylonians, for whom the various spheres were of significance as the dwellings or throne-rooms of the various gods.

As with the heaven, so with the earth, which like a well-constructed building also rests on foundations or pillars sunk into the waters below the earth,[8] and perhaps to be identified with the roots of the mountains.[9] For it rests on the lower ocean, *yammīm* or *tehōm*, which also surrounds it on all sides.[10] This explains the amazement of the

---

[1] Gen. 7.11; 8.2.

[2] Cf. ANET, p. 93.

[3] Pss. 29.3; 104.3. In Babylonia cf. Shamash enthroned above the heavenly waters (Guthe, *Kurzes Bibelwörterbuch*, 1903, p. 67). More primitive is the removal of God's heavenly dwelling-place to a high mountain (Ps. 48.3; Ezek. 28.2, 14ff.; cf. Ex. 24.9f.), which is also thought of as the location of Paradise.

[4] I Kings 8.27; Deut. 10.14; Neh. 9.6.

[5] Ps. 148.4.

[6] Cf. B. Meissner, *Babylonien und Assyrien* II, 1925, pp. 108ff.

[7] Only in later Judaism do we find mention of the threefold system of heavens (II Cor. 12.2).

[8] Prov. 8.25, 29; Job 9.6; 38.6; Pss. 18.16; 104.5.

[9] Ps. 46.3; Jonah 2.6.

[10] Pss. 139.9; 104.6ff.

Psalmist when he describes how Yahweh has firmly established the earth on the sea with its currents and whirlpools, so that it stands securely.[1] And if ever it does totter at the uproar of the elements, then Yahweh holds its pillars firm.[2] In only one passage do we come across a different, and very remarkable, idea of the earth's position, namely that it is hung up like a ball swinging over nothingness.[3]

The earth is mysteriously connected with the lower ocean by means of the springs and streams through which the latter rises up to her. Hence the ancient benediction on the tribes of Joseph wishes them the 'blessings of the deep that couches beneath'.[4] But this connection may also bring disaster, if the 'fountains of the great deep'[5] burst open, and the masses of water gush forth unhindered, as happened at the Deluge.

The Babylonians distinguished between the upper earth, the one inhabited by Man, and a middle and a lower earth, the kingdom of the water-god Ea, and the abode of the departed respectively. Only the latter of these two conceptions was shared by Israel; but that it was can be seen from the designation of the underworld as 'earth'.[6] The more usual name, $š^e$'$ōl$, of uncertain origin and meaning,[7] suggests, even in the earliest instances,[8] the idea of a subterranean area into which Man descends after death. There are references elsewhere to the depths of Sheol;[9] according to Job 26.5 it is beneath the waters, to Job 11.8 it is the farthest antipodes of heaven. Naturally it is filled with darkness,[10] and sometimes is described as a prison with gates and bars.[11] Elsewhere it is pictured as a broad land,[12] through which flow the 'brooks of Belial',[13] shut off from the sea.[14] In poetic language it also

[1] Pss. 24.2; 136.6; cf. 93.2ff.; 96.10; Isa. 42.5; 44.24; 45.18.

[2] Pss. 75.4; 46.3.

[3] Job. 26.7ff. In Babylonian thought, too, the earth is connected with the heaven by cords and pegs. A chamber in the temple of Enlil is called 'Bond of heaven and earth', and is certainly intended as a representation of the heavenly cord, the Milky Way (cf. B. Meissner, *op. cit.*, p. 111).

[4] t^ehōm rōbeṣet tāḥat, Gen. 49.25.

[5] ma'y^enōt t^ehōm rabbā, Gen. 7.11.

[6] Ps. 61.3; Jonah 2.7.

[7] Cf. ch. XIX below.

[8] Gen. 37.35; 42.38; 44.29, 31; Num. 16.30, 33.

[9] Ps. 88.7.

[10] Job 7.9f.; 10.21; 38.17; Pss. 88.13; 94.17; 143.3; Lam. 3.6.

[11] Isa. 38.10; Job 17.16; 38.17; Ps. 9.14; Jonah 2.7.

[12] Job 10.21f.; Ps. 88.13.

[13] Ps. 18.5; RSV 'torrents of perdition'.

[14] Jonah 2.6f.; Ps. 69.15ff.

occurs personified as a monster with gaping jaws, insatiable and cruel,[1] or as a hunter, casting a club or net.[2,3]

Ps. 18.5–17 presents an immense and splendid panorama of Israelite cosmology. The singer, fighting against the waters of the Underworld, that is to say, struggling in a mortal crisis, sends up his cry for help to Yahweh's heavenly place. As God sallies forth to battle, the pillars and foundations of heaven and earth shake at the weight of his footfall. Then Yahweh swoops down, riding upon the Cherub, and hurls himself on the powers of hell, so that the primal ocean shrinks back in terror, and the foundations of the earth are laid bare. Reaching down from on high, the divine redeemer draws his ward out of the waters of death, and leads him forth into a broad place. The mythological colours of this canvas are still fresh, and enable us to see clearly its relationship to the nature myths of the Babylonians and other peoples. And yet the sole purpose is to construct a picture which will display as impressively as possible both the greatness of the crisis and the omnipotence of Yahweh.

The naïvety of the cosmology, determined as it is by the limitations of ancient Man's knowledge of Nature, results in something which is to our modern way of thinking admittedly an imperfect and childlike reflection of reality. But as far as statements about the relation of God to the world are concerned, the greater or lesser perfection of the cosmology is irrelevant, since it constitutes no more than a medium for the religious judgment, which in turn is nourished from quite different sources. Indeed, it is precisely when one bears in mind how much of the external cosmological material was common to all cultures that the immense originality and independence with which Israel framed her ideas of the mystery of the genesis and dissolution of this world becomes clear.

2. THE DISTINCTIVE CHARACTER OF THE ISRAELITE BELIEF IN CREATION

Although the statements in the Old Testament about God's relation to the world are so many and various, they nevertheless show

---

[1] Isa. 5.14; Hab. 2.5; Prov. 27.20; 30.16; S. of S. 8.6.
[2] Pss. 18.6; 116.3.
[3] On conditions in the world of the dead, cf. ch. XIX.

themselves at one in this, that throughout they stress the complete dependence of the earthly order on God.[1] This outlook finds its most striking expression, however, in the statements about *God's creation of the world*. That this is an immemorial belief in Israel can no longer be disputed, despite the fact that for years it was customary to doubt it.[2] It is known not only to the accounts proper of creation in Gen. 1 and 2, the basic forms of which, as uncovered by scholarship, go back far beyond the period of the latest redaction, but also to incidental expressions in the historical books and the Psalms,[3] and to numerous allusions to the Chaos conflict in the prophets, Psalms and wisdom literature.[4] It has become all the more superfluous to doubt Israel's early acquaintance with the idea of creation, however, in that the comparative study of religions has produced more than one example of the dissemination of the idea in Israel's oriental environment. It did not even need to be the supreme God to whom such creative activity was ascribed; the Egyptians, for instance, preferred to associate the creation of Man with Khnum, one of the subordinate gods. Today the tendency is rather to try to bring down the Israelite creation beliefs to the level of those in heathen mythology, and to underestimate their religious significance.[5] It is, of course, true that there is a manifest relationship between individual features of the biblical creation narratives and similar ideas in Babylonia, Phoenicia or Egypt.[6] And yet even the most naïve of Israel's ideas of creation is from the start fundamentally different from every heathen conception of the way in which the world came into being; and the similarity of the underlying material can, in fact, serve to make this difference all the more striking.

---

[1] As the earliest evidence for this may be mentioned: Josh. 10.12; Judg. 5.20; Gen. 49.25; Ex. 15.8, 11; Num. 16.30; Deut. 33.14ff.; Ps. 29. Cf. also vol. I, pp. 228ff.

[2] With the predilection of, e.g., B. Stade (*Biblische Theologie des AT*, 1908, pp. 92f., 238f.) for denying ancient Israel any cosmological interests whatever, and for abscribing belief in creation to the adoption of Assyrian ideas during the eighth century BC at earliest, may be contrasted Gunkel's verdict: 'The creation myth belongs to the earliest elements of the Israelite saga tradition' (*Genesis*[3], 1910, p. 119).

[3] Gen. 14.19; I Kings 8.12 (LXX); Pss. 8; 19; 24; 104.

[4] Isa. 17.12–14; 27.1; 51.9f.; Jer. 5.22; Hab. 3.10; Nah. 1.4; Pss. 46; 89.11; Prov. 8.29; Job 9.13; 26.12; 38.8f., etc.

[5] So, for example, G. Hölscher, *Geschichte der israelitischen und jüdischen Religion*, 1922, pp. 41f.

[6] Cf. on this subject Gunkel, *Genesis*[3], pp. 4ff., 101ff.; W. Lotz, *Die biblische Urgeschichte*, 1907; E. Sellin, *Die biblische Urgeschichte*[2], 1913.

1. *The creation as the free institution of a spiritual and personal will*

(a) *The influence of the covenant concept*

The first point to note is that *creation does not draw the deity into the flux of the world-process*, but sets him over against it in complete independence. Even when the idea of creation is expressed in the mythical form of the Chaos conflict, so far as we can reconstruct this from later poetic allusions,[1] Yahweh is the central and uniquely powerful figure, and there is no sense that any other will could be in serious competition with his. Just as, in the present, Yahweh was experienced in the life of his people as a single divine will of incomparable strength, so to their backward gaze all created things came under his limitless authority. The concentration of faith upon the one covenant God thus invested statements about creation with a significance totally different from anything that was possible in polytheism; and this sense of a single will behind the world must have been a powerful influence in preparing the way for the idea of the unity of the world itself.

This understanding of the creation as the work of the covenant God not only clarified Israel's vision of the world, it also endued the will of the Creator from the start with the *characteristics of personal and spiritual activity*, and of moral purpose. Where Yahweh was acknowledged as Creator, it was inconceivable that the creation should be based on impulsive caprice, or the unpredictable and aimless sport of kindred or hostile divine powers; the sovereignty of God experienced in the present meant that it could only have been transcendent rationality and moral force which determined the character of the created order.

(b) *The exclusion of the theogony*

Along the lines thus sketched out in principle the explicit statements of the Old Testament on the subject of creation develop with increasing consistency. One piece of negative evidence for this is the permanent exclusion of an element important in oriental cosmogony at large, namely the emergence of the gods. As to how its God came into being Israel could say nothing whatever. Even when she had not as yet discovered the most precise formula for expressing the eternity of God—such as that, for example, which occurs in Isa. 41.4: 'I, the

---

[1] Cf. p. 97, n. 4, above.

LORD, the first, and with the last; I am He'—yet she never knew of a time when, so to speak, Yahweh had not been there. By contrast, in the religions of the ancient oriental civilizations cosmogony always involves theogony, a principle of which the introduction to the Babylonian creation epic, *enuma eliš*, may stand as the classic example.[1] The emergence of the gods from the chaotic primordial ground of the universe stamped them as deified natural forces; and even their association with the values of cultural and moral life, of which they are sometimes found as the guardians, cannot erase this character. Only the stuff of the universe, basic matter, is eternal; and the creator god can never be more than a craftsman, a Demiurge, who forms the world out of already existent chaotic materials. By their unqualified rejection of theogony the Old Testament affirmations establish the unconditional dependence of the world on God, and protect the conception of God's relation to the universe from those errors which, generally speaking, become inevitable whenever matter is given independent status over against him. The first of these errors is dualism, which, in order to explain the world, asserts a second principle in addition to God; the second is pantheism, which identifies God and the world, and makes the deity an impersonal force, pulsing everywhere, yet everywhere eluding Man's grasp. Hence in Israel the assertion that God created the world acquires a new meaning not to be found elsewhere: creation is *the free institution of a will which contains its own norm.*

(*c*) *The Creator as Lord: creation through the Word*

This imbuing of the received tradition with new meaning, however, is not merely a negative matter of excluding certain ideas basic to the ancient oriental conception; it has a positive effect on the way in which the picture of creation is presented as a whole. Though the forms in which in Gen. 2 the Yahwist describes the moulding and animating first of man, then of the animals, and finally of woman, may be childlike, almost forcing the Creator into the position of an

---

[1] 'When on high the heaven had not been named, firm ground below had not been called by name, naught but primordial Apsu, their begetter, [and] Mummu-Tiamat, she who bore them all, their waters commingling as a single body; no reed hut had been matted, no marsh land had appeared, when no gods whatever had been brought into being, uncalled by name, their destinies undetermined—then it was that the gods were formed within them . . .' (here follows a genealogy of the gods). For the translation cf. Pritchard, *ANET*, pp. 6of.

artist who achieves his purpose only after repeated attempts,[1] yet the absolute authority of Yahweh over his work, and the mystery surrounding the inconceivable power of the Creator, are carefully safeguarded. Moreover, in the primaeval history, which is inseparably connected with the story of creation, and in which the stories of Cain, of the Flood and of the Tower of Babel paint so impressive a picture of the Lord who deals with mankind in judgment and grace, care is taken to ensure that from the start the relationship of the Creator and the creature cannot be regarded as in any way naturalistic, a matter of physical kinship or congruence. Instead it points to the fact that a creature which in itself is wholly impotent, with no inherent right to life, is called to moral fellowship with its Creator. The same thought is represented in the Priestly account of creation in conceptually stronger terms; *by shifting the act of creation to the Word the origin of the creature is attributed entirely to the miracle of the transcendent creative will.* In mysterious concealment this will remain completely impenetrable, not surrendering itself to the creature as a ground of being to which he can have constant access;[2] rather does it at all times keep him aware of the difference of the 'wholly other', and opens up the way to spiritual fellowship only by the encouragement of its words of blessing and promise.

(d) The inner coherence of creation and history

Because, however, creation is understood as the free institution of the conditioned by the Unconditioned, it is not possible for the life of the creature to be an independent unfolding of its own nature under its own authority. The centre of gravity of the creature's existence is the will of the Creator, who confronts the creature as a 'Thou', and considers it worthy of dialogue. The creation is thus from the very first integrated into a spiritual process in which each individual event acquires its value from the overall meaning of the whole; that is to say,

[1] The greatly superior artistry of the narrator in shaping his material is shown by the fact that, when one reads the story, this impression is not the dominant one, but is forced into the background by other ideas such as those of the superiority of Man to the animals, the development of his spiritual powers in the naming of the other creatures, and the complementing of his ego by the woman alone, the only personal being of equal status with himself.

[2] Cf. H. W. Schmidt, 'Die ersten und die letzten Dinge', *Jahrb. der Theol. Schule Bethel*, 1930, pp. 211ff. The spiritual achievement of the Priestly narrator becomes all the more clearly recognizable when attention is paid to the methodical reshaping of the material effected by his consistent use of God's creative utterance: cf. L. Rost, 'Der Schöpfungsbericht der Priesterschrift', *Christentum und Wissenschaft*, 1934, pp. 172ff.

into history. The creature can discover its destiny only in constant interaction with the will of God, at whose hands it experiences at the same time both limitation and renewal. It is no mere accident, therefore, but very much of a piece with what has already been said, that both the Yahwist and the Priestly writers make the *creation the starting-point of a history*—a history determined on the one hand by the self-willed flight of the creature from that life-relationship with God which is essential to him, and on the other by God's activity, shaping history in an inexhaustible variety of ways in order to bring back to God those who are lost in alienation from him. In this way, then, these writers give formal expression to their conviction that as a free act the creation belongs within the sphere of history: 'In this account of creation we are concerned with a series of historical events worked out within the substratum of Nature.'[1] Causality is not the basic principle which determines the relation of the Creator to the creature; he is not 'cause' in the sense of part of a process, which can be arrived at by going back through a continuum. He is the 'source' of the cosmos in the sense of a self-sufficient norm which expresses itself in autonomous action.

(e) *Creatio ex nihilo*

The logical conclusion of thus deriving the world from the miracle of creative act is creation *ex nihilo*. Now it is certainly fair to ask whether the thought-form in which this expression is cast is not specifically Western, and cannot therefore be assumed without more ado in the thinking of the ancient East. It may be argued that even in those Old Testament passages where an original watery chaos seems to precede the creation of the universe nevertheless both theologically and psychologically the whole manner in which the subject is treated indicates that the real concern is the revelation of the absolute omnipotence of God; and that in so far as nothing equal or comparable to this power plays any part, the ultimate aim of the narrative is the same as that of our own formula of creation *ex nihilo*.[2] Equally it

---

[1] R. Hönigswald, *Erkenntnistheoretisches zur Schöpfungsgeschichte der Genesis*, 1932, p. 20.

[2] It is from this angle that P. Reymond approaches the question in his attractive study, *L'eau, sa vie et sa signification dans l'A.T.* (1958; cf. pp. 173ff.). In his opinion it is not the contrast between existence and non-existence, but that between the revelation of a person or power and the absence of such a revelation which is decisive for ancient thought. It may, however, be asked whether in taking this view he has not overlooked ancient magical beliefs as a possible source for the notion of creation *ex nihilo*, at first sight so highly theoretical and abstract (cf. pp. 70f. above).

cannot be denied that such a formula does not occur in the Old Testament, and that II Maccabees, a book written under Hellenistic influence, is the first work in which the writer dares to say: ἐξ οὐκ ὄντων ἐποίησεν αὐτὰ ὁ θεός (7.28). The object of this divine activity is defined as 'heaven and earth and all that is in them', so that the statement certainly cannot be restricted to 'the stars and things on earth',[1] but must include the entire cosmos.

Long before this, however, affirmations in the hymns and in the wisdom teaching concerning creation have an all-embracing character which betrays a natural habit of speaking as comprehensively as possible about Yahweh's creative power, even though exact conceptual analysis may disclose that the ideas are still too imprecisely defined to allow us to conclude that the existence of the basic material of creation independently of Yahweh was ruled out. Nevertheless it is striking that the watery chaos, which in the Accadian creation myths is thought of as present before any act of creation,[2] and in the Old Testament is given the name $t^e h \bar{o} m$, a word cognate to the name of the Babylonian primordial chaos, Tiamat, should be brought within the scope of creation. When Wisdom describes herself as the first of the works of Yahweh,[3] she includes among the things which were then not yet in existence the $t^e h \bar{o} m \bar{o} t$; because of the parallelism with $ma^c y^e n \bar{o} t$ this term cannot simply be taken to mean 'springs',[4] but must be interpreted as the primaeval floods from which the springs are fed.[5] In Ps. 148.3–5, moreover, not only the sun, moon, stars and heavens, but also the waters above the heavens, that is to say, the upper portion of the $t^e h \bar{o} m$, which is divided into two halves, are called upon to praise Yahweh because they were created at the word of his command. Here then, without special emphasis, but all the more

[1] So Reymond, *op. cit.*, p. 176. The considerations advanced by A. Ehrhardt ('Creatio ex nihilo', *Studia Theologica* IV, 1951–2, pp. 26f.) also seem indecisive; the same idea occurs in Jub. 2.2; 14.4; Apoc. Baruch 48.8, and the fact that it was also widespread in rabbinic Judaism makes it unconvincing to doubt its existence in the immediately preceding period.

[2] According to the Creation Epic, even the gods proceed from this chaos (cf. *ANET*, pp. 60f.); it is the embodiment of the formless emptiness preceding the beginnings of the cosmic process.

[3] Prov. 8.22; cf. p. 84 above.

[4] As Reymond has tried to maintain (*op. cit.*, pp. 61, 175).

[5] So Köhler-Baumgartner, *LVT*. Cf. Gen. 49.25; Deut. 33.13, where the $t^e h \bar{o} m$ $r \bar{o} b e \xi e t \ t \bar{a} h a t$ occurs as the source of fertility. In Deut. 8.7, too, the reference of $t^e h \bar{o} m \bar{o} t$ is to the water of the primordial ocean forming the foundations of the world, which causes the springs to rise. In Amos 7.4 the fire sent by Yahweh devours the $t^e h \bar{o} m \ rabb \bar{a}$, and thus ravages the farmlands which are watered from it.

impressively for the naturalness of the statement, we find the distinctive term for God's wondrous creation, *bārā'*—a verb which never occurs with the accusative of the material used in the creative act[1]—used to describe the origin of a major part of the primal Chaos. That the word of divine command is mentioned in this context as the medium of creation likewise serves to emphasize the peculiar independence of the Creator; and the same is true of Ps. 33.6, 9, where the word is exalted as the unique medium of power. When it is remembered that ancient thought included annihilation and new creation among the direct effects of the mighty word of the deity, it must be admitted that we are here not very far from creation *ex nihilo*—a development to which ancient magical ideas may have contributed.[2]

Less clear are the repeated statements that Yahweh 'made' the earth and the sea.[3] The imprecision of this expression, which can also be applied to the creation of the limited earthly sea by the division of the *tᵉhōm*, is a warning that too much stress should not be laid upon it, even though the hymns of praise suggest a wider rather than a narrower connotation for the phrase. Nevertheless it should be remembered that the usage of the word *yām* is also affected by the mystery of the sea, and that features associated with one who since the time of the creation has been the great primaeval enemy of Yahweh, and therefore the link with *tᵉhōm*, may easily be uppermost in such passages.[4]

It was the creation story of the Priestly writer which clarified the concepts in these affirmations of Yahweh's unique creative power, unrestricted in its operation by any hostile will. Whereas the older account by the Yahwist illustrates the state of the world in the beginning, before the Creator fashioned it, simply by enumerating the various things which were not yet in existence,[5] P expends great care not only in laying down the sequence of the works of creation,

[1] Cf. F. Böhl, '*bārā*' als Terminus der Weltschöpfung im alttestamentlichen Sprachgebrauch', *Alttest. Studien Kittel dargebr.*, 1913, pp. 42ff.; P. Humbert, 'Émploi et portée du verbe bârâ, créer, dans l'Ancien Testament', *ThZ* 3, 1947, pp. 401ff.

[2] Cf. pp. 70f. above. It seems unnecessary to assume, with E. Jacob (*Theology of the OT*, ET, 1958, p. 148, n. 2), that specifically Egyptian influence must lie behind this development, though in view of the well-known connection between Israelite wisdom literature and that of Egypt there would be nothing surprising in such an influence.

[3] Ps. 95.5; Jonah 1.9.

[4] Cf. P. Reymond, *op. cit.*, pp. 182ff.

[5] Gen. 2.4b.

but also in choosing the expressions to describe them. In the very first sentence the dominating theme of the whole is powerfully sounded, and every word witnesses to the sureness of the author in the formulation of metaphysical ideas. The use of the term *berē'šīt* fixes an absolute beginning for the creation,[1] a beginning, that is, in terms of a normative, not a causal approach to the genesis of the universe.[2] By contrast heathen mythological and philosophical thought speaks of the world as having no beginning.[3] The use of the name Elohim gathers all the divine forces into a personal unity, and thus contrasts one absolute Lord of the divine realm with the polytheistic thinking of the heathen cosmogony.[4] Moreover, to describe God's act of creation the writer selects none of the many verbs for fashioning—such as '-*s-h*, do, make; *y-s-d*, found; *y-ṣ-d*, form; *kōnēn*, establish; *ḳ-n-h*, prepare; *hōlīd*, engender—which were applied to it in more naïve usage. Aware that in all these expressions the distinctive meaning of the miracle of creation was not adequately embodied, he turned to the word *bārā'*, the technical term for that marvellous divine creativity which brings forth something new and astonishing.[5] Moreover, the object of the verb is given as *'ēt haššāmayim we'ēt hā'āreṣ*, the heaven and the earth, a phrase frequently used elsewhere to express the idea of the universe or cosmos,[6] for which there is no special word in Hebrew. Study of this carefully considered formulation makes it clear that the verse as a whole is not to be explained as an anticipation of what follows, ponderous in style and inept in

---

[1] The attempt of P. Humbert ('Trois notes sur Geènse 1', *Interpretationes ad VT pertinentes S. Mowinckel septuagenario missae*, 1955, pp. 85ff.) to show that *berē'šīt* cannot be understood as an absolute determinative of time overvalues the lexical statistics, and pays too little attention to the context of the passages adduced. In addition to Isa. 46.10 the related term *mērō'š* in Isa. 40.21 ought also to be taken into account. Cf. W. Eichrodt, 'In the Beginning', *Israel's Prophetic Heritage* (*Muilenburg-Festschrift*), New York, 1962.

[2] Cf. R. Hönigswald, *Erkenntnistheoretisches zur Schöpfungsgeschichte der Genesis*, 1932, p. 20.

[3] In the myths chaos or primal matter is already in existence in the beginning, and it is impossible to go back beyond it. For Plato and Aristotle the existence of the world from eternity is a basic presupposition.

[4] Cf. vol. I, pp. 185f.

[5] Cf. p. 103, n. 1 above. The word is used with the same signification in Ex. 34.10; Isa. 48.7; Jer. 31.22; Ps. 51.12.

[6] In any event formless chaos is certainly not meant (Wellhausen, *Prolegomena zur Geschichte Israels*[6], 1905, p. 296), an interpretation which is contradicted by the usage elsewhere, and which also ignores the fact that chaos is called *hā'āreṣ* in vv. 2, 8, 10.

matter,[1] but that it fulfils the function of a superscription of lapidary brevity and expressive force, evoking incomparably the character of the creation as an all-inclusive act.

It is no great step to argue from what are clearly the fundamental concerns of this affirmation to creation *ex nihilo* in the strict sense. The fact that this would imply a conception of the creation which cannot be demonstrated for certain elsewhere in the Old Testament is assuredly no reason for rejecting it as impossible, all the more that such a 'rising above the general level'[2] is precisely the mark of creative thinking, and at the same time would agree very well with the general direction of the thought of P. Nevertheless it may be asked whether the description to be found in v. 2 will permit of such an unambiguous definition. It has always been recognized that the words *tōhū wābōhū* in this verse expressed the formlessness of chaos. When this phrase is compared with Isa. 34.11, Jer. 4.23, and Isa. 40.17, it will be seen that the emphasis is on the annihilation of all real existence, on nothingness as opposed to all created life. Moreover, the *tᵉhōm* or primordial waters overlaid with darkness, the relationship of which to the Babylonian chaos monster Tiamat is beyond doubt, has in this context shed all vestige of mythological content. It no longer represents that which is hostile to God, that which ought not to exist, but rather serves as an image for the formlessness and life-lessness which precede the divine act of creation, without any tangible or objective quality. Finally a third element, the picture of the raging *rūaḥ 'elōhīm*, the mighty wind which rushes along without rest or purpose,[3] serves to convey the impalpable character of a situation devoid of all creative potential, and to complete the picture of 'non-existence' at which the author clearly is aiming.

How great is his capacity for abstraction, despite the fact that he is using concepts from a traditional picture of Chaos, can be seen

---

[1] The view expressed in the commentaries of Dillmann, Holzinger and Skinner, and more recently by Humbert (cf. 'Trois notes', *op. cit.*).

[2] The arguments brought against such a conjecture, not only here but in other cases, such as analysis of the Psalms, seem to be a most serious indication of a tendency to exalt the average into the norm.

[3] This rendering of *rūaḥ* in this verse was already known to the Church Fathers and the Reformers, and has in recent times been championed by P. Heinisch, B. Jakob and G. von Rad in their commentaries on Genesis. Among modern scholars J. B. Peters ('The Wind of God', *JBL*, 1914, pp. 81 ff.) was apparently the first to draw attention once again to this use of *'elōhīm* as a superlative (cf. Gen. 38.8; Ps. 36.7; 80.11). A detailed investigation has been made by Galling, 'Der Charakter der Chaosschilderung in Gen. 1.2', *ZTK*, 1950, pp. 145ff.

from the contrast between his work and that closest to it, the Phoenician tradition. The latter assumes as primary factors a dark wind, made fertile by Spirit, and a slimy, dark chaos; from the intercourse of their passionate embrace arises the chaos being, Mot, from whom the universe proceeds. Such ingredients as Gen. 1 does borrow from this myth of a primordial engendering are pointedly stripped of all capacity to create. Utterly formless nothingness, darkness, and turbulent motion are used to construct an image of that nullity which constitutes the setting of the creation. It is true that the Priestly narrator has not yet found his way through to an abstract conceptual terminology; but the way in which, with the means available, he has managed to express that notion of nothingness which he had in mind can only excite our admiration. The sensibilia which form the substratum of his thought, in particular the primordial flood or *tᵉhōm*, may indeed have involved the constant danger that his description would be misunderstood to imply a pre-existent primal matter. Yet Yahweh's irresistible creative act, independent of all earthly preconditions, and revealed in the word of creation as the supreme spiritual power and the true source of life, is so decidedly the focus of attention that the real concern behind the formula of creation *ex nihilo* is thereby satisfied.

In this way the concept of creation was thought out in Israel to its logical conclusion, and the deistic notion of God as *prima causa*, incorporated into the chain of cause and effect as one term in the process, was neutralized by the stress on the absolute freedom with which God acts. The world has its centre of gravity not in itself but in God; it possesses no independent being. Even space and time are only established at the creation, for before the first day no time can possibly be conceived.

(f) The eschatological Creator God

Whereas in the passage we have been considering priestly thought drew its conclusions from the Old Testament belief about God primarily with reference to the present world-order, and used the concept of creation to forge an effective defence against any assimilation of God and the world, prophetic thought found a quite different way of expressing God's absolute sovereignty over all created things, by daring to speak of a new heaven and a new earth.[1] For prophecy, which saw the mark of the present order much more in the rebellion

[1] Isa. 51.6; 34.4; 65.17; 66.22; Ps. 102.26–28.

of the creature against the Creator than in its unresisting submission to divine omnipotence, the contemporary existence of the world was drastically devalued, and its religious basis of much less interest than the coming of the great turning-point of world history. Indeed, by going so far as to declare the annihilation of this age and the irruption of chaos,[1] the prophetic proclamations of judgment could give the impression that the bond between God and the world had been finally severed, that God's own works were alienated from him, and that the power at enmity with God had become lord over creation. To jeopardize the divine majesty in this way, however, was utterly impossible for the prophetic view of God, and therefore attempts were constantly renewed to arrive at a deeper understanding of the co-inherence of annihilating judgment and life-creating grace.[2] The more darkly looms the immediate future, the higher rises their certainty that the establishment of God's kingdom on earth cannot be thwarted by any human opposition; and the unity which they have been seeking between the inexorable judge and the mighty redeemer is eventually discovered in the *declaration of the new creation*. Because, however, the new heaven and the new earth are not pictured as a fantastic, magical world, but are intended as the consummation of God's historically conditioned revelation, Yahweh's sovereignty over Israel and the nations,[3] continuity with the present order is maintained at the decisive point, that of absolute subordination to Yahweh's cosmic purposes. The eschatological Creator God is not the enemy but the perfecter of the first creation. Finally, the pure miracle of his new creative act, which rules out any form of gradual evolution, corresponds plainly enough to the idea of creation *ex nihilo* which the Priestly interpretation of the world had used to express the absolute freedom of the Creator.

II. *The Creator's witness to himself in his works*

(a) *The original perfection of the creation*

That the idea of creation should be thus safeguarded against the error of confusing God with the world by no means excludes the un-

---

[1] Amos 7.4; Jer. 4.23ff.; Zeph. 1.2f., 14ff.; Isa. 51.6: cf. H. Gressmann, *Ursprung der isr.-jüd. Eschatologie*, 1905.

[2] Isaiah in particular stresses the sheerly miraculous character of Yahweh's dealings in which grace and judgment are so inseparably entwined (Isa. 28.11, 16ff., 21, 23ff.; 29.14; 31.8). Cf. also vol. I, pp. 381ff., 385ff.

[3] Cf. vol. I, pp. 386f.

folding of the *wealth of content in the Creator-creature relationship* as a witness within the world itself to the wisdom and goodness of God. Rather does it give a rightful place to the religious interpretation of the universe. Hence the Israelite belief in creation is associated with a strong *conviction of the original perfection of created things*. In the Yahwist account of creation this is not asserted in so many words; it has to be read between the lines, in particular in the jubilant cry of the man, when he finds in the woman the complement exactly appropriate to him: 'This at last is bone of my bones and flesh of my flesh!' Nowhere is there any trace of a belief that imperfection was inherent in the creature from the start because by reason of its involvement in matter it was cut off from the divine life. However deeply Israelite thought was conscious of the gulf between the worlds of God and Man, it never attempted to explain this gulf in terms of the material character of Nature, as if this in and of itself gave rise to an imperfect kind of existence. Instead the Israelite conception is characterized by a marked optimism with regard to created things, at any rate in so far as they come unharmed from God's creative hand. This is made explicit for the first time in Gen. 1, where the Priestly author stresses that God's own assessment of his creative work was *ṭôb, mᵉ'ōd ṭôb*, 'Good, very good!' In every part it corresponds to the intentions of its Creator; no hostile power was able to frustrate his design.

One important factor in this evaluation of the world was undoubtedly the absence of a belief in basic matter, independent of God, as a prerequisite of creation—a marked point of contrast with the heathen cosmogonies. For it is precisely to matter that imperfection is normally ascribed. Because according to Israel's belief both matter and form proceed from God's creative power, both must be good, that is, both must correspond to his purpose. That the predicate 'good' is to be understood in this sense, and is not meant to denote a state of unlimited perfection, follows from the way in which elsewhere it is held to be self-evident that good and evil, light and darkness, are both to be ascribed to Yahweh, and therefore that any idea of an alien power in the universe is to be rejected.[1] It is precisely this conviction which makes it possible to adopt a fundamentally affirmative attitude in the face of the evil in the world. Whereas the heathen and philosophical theories of creation mostly carry at least the seed of pessimism within themselves, Israel, by virtue of its belief in creation, is able to attain to a forceful affirmation of the universe. That this is

[1] Amos 3.6; Isa. 41.23; 45.7; 54.16; Lam. 3.38; Eccles 7.14.

of the greatest moment for the whole Israelite way of life, inasmuch as piety is never forced into an antagonistic or ascetic attitude toward the blessings of creation, must always be borne in mind when trying to understand the Old Testament ideal of the devout life.[1]

(b) Teleology in the structure of the cosmos

It will already be clear that these statements about the goodness of the created order do not represent an empirical observation of experience, an inference from zestful surrender to the blessings of Nature in daily life, confirmed by the youthful sense of power of a nation daily increasing in might. If this were so one could only regard them as mere superficiality. We are, however, dealing here with something which is essentially an utterance of faith, and which because it is born out of a knowledge of the lovingkindness and faithfulness of the covenant God can say Yea to the actions of that same God in Nature. This principle applies equally to Israel's insights into *the large-scale teleology which permeates the whole creation*. This marvellous purposefulness in the structure of the cosmos is first described in terms of a system seemingly designed to lead up to Man. The Yahwist account of creation is already thinking along these lines, when it sees the animals as created for Man's sake, and describes the function of the first man as that of guarding and tending the garden of Paradise. However naïve the imagery in which these thoughts are clothed, the real concern of the narrator in what is patently an immemorial saga-form is nevertheless made clear enough, namely the superiority of Man to the animals. Only Man can provide Man with a complement at his own level; everything non-human can stand to him only in the relation of a servant.

What in this account has to be read between the lines is made explicit with absolute clarity by the author of Gen. 1. In his beautifully planned, architectonic organization of the works of creation, the definitions and classifications of which bring out the theme of unity in diversity, he achieves an impressive presentation of the purposeful arrangement of the cosmic structure. Moreover, he exhibits the inner necessity of this structure by ascribing each particular work of creation to God's word, and by allowing the older ideas of making and shaping by God's hand to recede right into the background. This word of creation, however, does not imply simply ease and effortlessness, but also systematic thought and self-conscious will, which

[1] Cf. ch. XXII below: The Effect of Piety on Conduct.

remain fundamentally distinct from all unconscious generation or quasi-instinctive emanation.[1] Furthermore, as a result of his being made in the image of God, Man acquires not only supreme value, but also the power for his work in the world, the programme of which is summed up in the divine blessing: 'Be fruitful and multiply, and fill the earth and subdue it!' In this way a tremendous motive power is implanted in human life, which inevitably drives it on to great goals, and which rules out any idea of human destiny as an aimless wandering to and fro, a random rise and fall. His duty of realizing the task laid upon him by God subordinates Man to the mighty teleological world movement, which by its own inner logic moves inexorably toward the concept of history. It is even possible that the writer already has in mind in his very first word, $b^e r\bar{e}'\check{s}\bar{\imath}t$, in the beginning, a distant goal of the world process, the $'a\dot{h}^a r\bar{\imath}t\ hayy\bar{a}m\bar{\imath}m$, the end of the days.[2]

Deutero-Isaiah evinces similar ideas, when he ascribes not only the purposefulness of the general course of world history but also the particular destiny of Israel to God's systematic action. Especially striking is the following divine utterance: 'For thus says the LORD, who created the heavens (he is God!), who formed the earth and made it (he established it; he did not create it a chaos, he formed it to be inhabited!): . . . "I did not speak in secret . . . I did not say to the offspring of Jacob, 'Seek me in chaos [that is, at random.] I the LORD speak the truth, I declare what is right." '[3] Yahweh's opposition to all the haphazard tyranny of the powers of Chaos is here made utterly plain; his idea in creation is the salvation of mankind, which he brings about by his purposeful government.

Further evidence of the sensitivity of Israelite feeling for the marvellous construction of the world is afforded by the astonished wonderment which contemplation of the skilful ordering of the cosmos produces, and which breaks out again and again in praise of the Creator that forms a part of hymnody, so it would seem, from the earliest times.[4] That heaven and earth witness to the incomparable mind of the Creator is manifestly a stock reflection of the post-exilic

---

[1] This may be compared with the Phoenician story of creation ascribed to Sanchuniathon, and preserved for us by Eusebius. Here the instinctive aspect has to be brought within the scope of the spirit's working by the laboured device of the awakening of πόθος, the sexual instinct. Cf. A. Jeremias, *ATAO*, p. 24.

[2] So O. Procksch, *Genesis* [2, 3], 1924, p. 441.

[3] Isa. 45.18f.; cf. also Isa. 45.7, 12; 50.2f.; 51.13, 15.

[4] Pss. 8; 24.1f.; 19.2–7.

period;[1] and Wisdom is even portrayed in hypostasis as herself the master workman at the foundation of the world.[2] In the late wisdom book of Koheleth, too, the mysterious order which sets everything in its right place is given eloquent expression: 'He has made everything beautiful in its time!'[3]

It is understandable enough that such ideas should occur particularly in the Wisdom literature. Yet it is not the rationalistic aspect of its thought which has here gained the upper hand, making of the marvellous structure of the world a convenient setting for Man and an agreeable field of activity for its own intellectual speculations about God's nature and governance. The basic assumption behind the biblical idea of creation, that by his free institution of created things the Creator does not surrender himself to the control of his creatures, but remains the utterly exalted, is still too deeply stamped on their consciousness. Hence at all periods a lively sense of the impenetrable mystery of creation remains alive alongside the awareness of its teleological character, and on occasion indeed turns fiercely against the profane audacity with which Man seeks to use the marvels of creation as a means of direct access to the Creator. It is not simply that there is stress on the enigmatic, stupendous and terrifying elements in Nature, as well as on its purposefulness, all of which bring home to Man his total inadequacy for understanding God's actions—as when, for example, the monstrous scale of heaven and earth, the riddles of physical phenomena, or the endless ages of the epochs of Nature are set in emphatic contrast to the smallness of Man and the brevity of his life.[4] In certain passages it is also 'explicitly that which is contrary to all reason, purpose or law'[5] in the created order which is thrown into relief, with the result that the Creator is attested as the incomprehensibly wonderful,[6] one who can never be incorporated as 'universal Mind' into a rational cosmic system, but who grants the experience of himself as Creator only to those who in faithful self-surrender lay hold on him in his indirect self-communication through his Word. The teleology of the creation in the Old Testament sense is thus sharply to be distinguished from the philosophical manipula-

---

[1] Ps. 136.5; Prov. 3.19f.; Jer. 10.12.
[2] Prov. 8.22ff.; cf. pp. 84f. above.
[3] Eccles. 3.11; 7.29.
[4] Isa. 40.12, 14; Job 38.5; 37.15ff.; 38.12ff., 22ff.; Pss. 107.27; 147.15ff.; Jer. 14.22; Ps. 90.2ff.
[5] Hempel, *Gott und Mensch im AT*, p. 71.
[6] Job 38–42; Eccles. 6.10; 9.1; cf. Ecclus 43.5, 28f.

tion of the world as a rational institution with a view to elucidating God's cosmic plan—an exercise at which the writers of many of the documents of later Judaism tend to show off rather smugly.[1] Only when qualified by the incomprehensible freedom of the Creator can the cosmos be understood as pointing to the goodness of the divine universal Lord toward all his creatures.[2]

(c) *The unity of the cosmos*

It was, however, precisely this carefully considered restriction on the use of the creation as evidence which safeguarded a different insight, one which when combined with the belief in creation became an inalienable part of the Israelite understanding of the world: their *recognition of the unity of the cosmos*. This is already present in principle in Gen. 2, despite the fact that in that chapter many individual items are enumerated, so to speak, at random, without any effort at completeness or classification. What makes it possible to feel the unity of all visible things is the relationship with God which as creatures they have in common. This idea, however, is clearly grasped for the first time only in Gen. 1. The political upheavals of the eighth and seventh centuries had led to a general widening of horizons, and at the same time the conception of God as a transcendent being exalted above the world became fully developed.[3] The combination of these two influences brought men to see the universe as a unity, organized and internally related in all its parts, and permeated as well by a single will. The view of Nature thus arrived at was the only one which could satisfy reflective thought, just as it was also the only one which matched the clarity of religious belief. It must be clear, however, that it was indebted for its inner strength essentially to men's experience of Yahweh's title to unlimited authority, and was able for this reason alone to maintain itself in face of the contradictions in the cosmic process. In this connection it was of special importance that the idea of creation gave men a bulwark against all those pseudo-religious expedients which seek to assist faith by offering a rationalistic harmonization of the universe. For this meant that the natural order, which can never be completely explained in terms of human convenience, but must always remain ambiguous, was prevented from

[1] Cf. Wisd. 7.14, 17ff.; 8.8; 9.16ff.; 13.1ff.
[2] Cf. my treatment of 'Vorsehungsglaube und Theodizee im AT' in the *Procksch-Festschrift*, 1934, pp. 65ff.
[3] Cf. vol. I, pp. 410ff.

becoming an intolerable burden to the life of faith. Instead it drove men to a more stringent consideration of those basic principles of the religious interpretation of the world in which they could find genuine support. In this way the world of Old Testament faith was preserved from the intrusion both of a mythical plurality of creative powers and of the deistic reduction of the idea of creation to an externally regulated cosmic unity.

This view of the universe as a unified entity was given its loveliest expression in the religious lyric poetry of the Old Testament. In addition to other nature psalms,[1] Ps. 104 is outstanding for the way in which its picture of the world is completely filled with the idea of the unity, the coherence, the harmonious order of the cosmos. Even when account has been taken of the stimulus which the singer received from Egyptian poetry,[2] the force with which the Yahwist faith permeates his material, and shapes it to its own sense, is unmistakable, and compels one to conclude that here Israelite feeling for the natural order found the expression best suited to the absolute claims of belief in Yahweh.[3]

III. *Comparison with the creation myth of Babylonia*

The fact that the Israelite picture of the world has many features in common with those of the ancient Near East in general, and of Babylonia in particular, raises the question of the relationship in which the Old Testament idea of creation stands to its non-Israelite counterparts. The only extensive creation epic extant comes from Babylonia—and indeed far surpasses in importance even other Babylonian accounts of creation,[4] both in its detail and in its, so to speak, official status. (It may indeed have formed the liturgical text regularly recited at the New Year Festival.) This, then, is obviously the text most deserving of serious consideration in any comparison with the biblical creation stories.

---

[1] Pss. 8; 19.1—6; 29.

[2] On this subject cf. ch. XVII, pp. 154ff. below.

[3] Cf. also the judgment of Alexander von Humboldt (*Kosmos* II, 1847, pp. 46f.): 'It might be said that within the scope of this single Psalm is set out a picture of the entire cosmos. . . . It is astonishing to see in a lyric poem of such short compass the universe, heaven and earth, portrayed in a few bold strokes.' A fine assessment will be found in O. Eissfeldt, 'Alexander von Humboldt's "Kosmos" und der 104. Psalm', *Forschungen und Fortschritte* 33, 1959, no. 4, pp. 113ff.

[4] For a collection of the extant Babylonian creation stories cf. A. Jirku, *Altorientalischer Kommentar zum AT*, 1923, pp. 1ff.; in addition cf. *AOT*, pp. 108ff., where further translations and comment are supplied.

At the very heart of the *enuma eliš* epic stands the conflict of the god Marduk with the forces of Chaos, and their defeat. The corpse of the monster Tiamat serves as material for the construction of the world. There can be no doubt that this powerful picture of the divine conflict at the beginning of the creation was also known in Israel. Occasional allusions have preserved statements about a battle of Yahweh against a sea and chaos monster called Rahab or Leviathan. Thus Isa. 51.9 reads: 'Was it not thou that didst cut Rahab in pieces, that didst pierce the dragon?'; and Ps. 89.11: 'Thou didst crush Rahab like a carcass, thou didst scatter thy enemies with thy mighty arm'.[1]

It is not impossible that Israel, too, knew of a myth of Yahweh as the warrior against Chaos, analogous to that current in Babylonia, even though no proof can be adduced for such a view. The crucial point, however, is that even if such a myth did exist it manifestly exerted no very profound influence on Israel's understanding of the world. Moreover, it should not be overlooked that the allusions mentioned, when—as in Pss. 74 and 89—they are linked with statements about the creation, have no inner coherence with the latter, but simply make use of the mythical picture as an isolated poetic ornament in order to depict Yahweh's power in the most dazzling possible colours. This applies even more forcibly when the thought is less of the act of creation than of the demonstration of Yahweh's power in the rescue of his people from Egypt, for which the Chaos conflict forms as it were the prototype[2] (Isa. 51.9f.), or when the merciless anger of Yahweh has to be exemplified (Job 7.12; 9.13). The favourite poetic personification of the sea as a monster which Yahweh by his rebuke frightens away or restrains[3]—an image which, in fact, has nothing to do with the myth—may have helped to keep the myth of the chaos conflict in particular alive, and thus may account for its occasional echoes in the prophets.[4] In these contexts, however, the

[1] Cf. also Job 9.13; 26.12; Isa. 30.7; Ps. 74.13f. (The rendering of the verse from Ps. 89 is that of RSV: the author translates: 'Thou didst crush Rahab as one that is pierced.' Tr.)

[2] This historicization of the myth was carried even further when Rahab became simply a pseudonym for Egypt (Ps. 87.4; Isa. 30.7), while Leviathan denoted Syria (Isa. 27.1).

[3] Job 7.12; Isa. 17.12–14; 50.2; Nahum 1.4; Hab. 3.10; Job 38.10f.; Pss. 18.16; 46.3f.; 77.17; 104.7; 106.9; 114.3, 5; cf. Ps. 106.9, where the Red Sea is threatened.

[4] That it should be the sea which attracted such poetic and mythic personification is understandable enough in view of the powerful impression which its surging waves make upon men. Thus on one occasion we even find it portrayed as a giant's offspring bursting forth from the womb, with clouds and darkness as its swaddling clothes (Job 38.8f.).

myth no longer has a life of its own. It is of no consequence for Israel's understanding of the world, but belongs to the treasure-house of poetry, on which poets and prophets liked to draw in order to clothe their thoughts in rich apparel.[1] How early this neutralization of the myth began it is naturally impossible to say; among other things it will not have had the same significance at one and the same time for different strata of the community. Nevertheless it is noteworthy that as early as the Yahwist no use is made of it in his account of creation. The more Israel became aware of the nature of its faith, the less room, it is clear, remained for any genuine myth of the origin of the world.

Even if the basic form of the Babylonian epic, the divine conflict, could never take root in Israel, nevertheless there was scope for agreement on certain other fundamental ideas. Many external details in the genesis of the cosmos, such as the emergence of the earth from the water, the division into the heavenly and the earthly spheres, the importance of light, and the formation of Man in the likeness of the divine nature, are common to both traditions. And even at the level of more profound thinking concerning the nature of the world there are points of contact between the Babylonian world-view and that of Israel. Thus the Babylonian poem, too, recognizes in the cosmos the work of a superior intelligence as opposed to a mindless impulse toward life, or chaotic caprice; and by seeing the authority of heavenly powers at work in the emergence as well as in the maintenance of the world, it testifies to a deep meaning in the universe, and one which also gives purpose and direction to the life of Man. Indeed, the profoundly religious conviction that the earthly order is a copy of the heavenly links the destiny of Man in the closest possible way with the divine powers, and teaches him both to conduct and to understand his life with constant reference to celestial authority.

But however little we may question the deeper spiritual and religious values of the Babylonian cosmogony, we must still keep very clearly in mind the characteristics which differentiate it from the Old Testament interpretation of the universe. These derive first and foremost from its idea of God, which in turn decisively determines its

---

[1] The same is no doubt true of the allusion in Ps. 90.2, where the earth comes forth from the travail of a mighty primal being, and the mountains are born; for the myth which lies behind this imagery no Babylonian counterpart has survived. The same application can be established for other myths; e.g. the myth of the Day Star, Isa. 14.12ff., and of the Cherub on the mountain of God, Ezek. 28, etc. Cf. M. Noth, 'Die Historisierung des Mythus', *Christentum und Wissenschaft* 4, 1928, pp. 265ff., 301ff.

attitude to Nature. Whereas Israel's covenant God makes himself known in personal and moral action, and can therefore be experienced as spiritual personality independent of Nature, the Babylonian conception of God remains bogged down in naturalism. The Babylonian epic of the origin of the universe is an explicit Nature myth, in which natural forces are personified and made to play an active part. Hence the gods are not eternal, but emerge like everything else from the chaotic primordial matter. By the same token there is also no possibility of overcoming polytheism and its religious fragmentation; the diversity of Nature has obscured the uniqueness of the Creator. Hence the creating deity must remain a Demiurge, with quasi-human features, fashioning whatever material is available. A sheer act of *de novo* institution by the divine word is outside the purview of the epic.

If Nature thus shows itself stronger than the deity, it is only natural that in the end it will also provide the organizing principle by which heaven and earth are controlled. Hence it is the law of cyclic recurrence, deduced in the first place from the course of the stars in heaven, which determines the goal and direction of all events, and also underlies the Creation Epic itself, which as a liturgical text celebrates the renewal of the cosmic lordship of Marduk, the great king of the gods, year by year. Because the pattern of ancient Eastern thought is dictated by this eternal recurrence of the same events, the idea of history as a non-recurring, purposeful process in Time, susceptible of an overall comprehensive meaning, remains closed to it; nor can the creation become the starting-point for a train of historical events, even though the city of Babylon, and the hegemony engineered for it by Hammurabi, played a decisive part in shaping the epic into a victory for the Babylonian city-god Marduk.[1]

Consequently it is precisely the essential elements in the Old Testament concept of creation which are alien to ancient Eastern thought, and which by virtue of their whole character were bound to be so alien. For in the covenant God, by whose act of election she knew herself to be destined as the people of God to a special mission, Israel had learned to know a God quite different from those of any other ancient Eastern nation; and therefore her attitude to Nature also was radically different, and could break through barriers which elsewhere had proved without exception unbreakable. So strongly did she define the freedom and sovereignty of god *vis-à-vis* the world, and at the same time the indissoluble connection of the world to God, as

[1] Rightly emphasized by A. Weiser, *Glaube und Geschichte im AT*, 1931, pp. 24ff.

opposed to all mythical, pantheistic or deistic conceptions of Nature, that even we today can find nothing of essential moment to add. Rather are we confronted here with an affirmation which is equally essential to the Christian world-view, an affirmation of normative significance not merely for the Old but also for the New Testament, and one with which to this day, we cannot dispense.

XVI

THE PLACE OF MAN IN THE CREATION

I. THE PECULIAR VALUE OF MAN AS COMPARED WITH OTHER CREATURES

I. *Indirect evidence*

AN AWARENESS THAT MAN occupies a special position *vis-à-vis* the Nature that forms his environment is to be found in Israel first of all in a conviction which she shares with other peoples. This is that there are at least certain areas of Nature that exist within an order of their own and in conformity with their own laws, which Man is required to acknowledge, and which debar him from controlling them just as he pleases. Such areas, protected in most cases by the supra-sensible power believed to stand behind them, and delimited by appropriate taboo prohibitions, have from the earliest times aroused in Man the suspicion that Nature confronts him not as something having an obvious affinity with himself but as an autonomous entity keeping him at a distance. In Israel this limitation went hand in hand with belief in a God who was the effective sovereign of Nature as well as of history. Hence those ordinances which restricted human exploitation fell within the scope of conditions laid down at the creation, and gave Man's obedient observance of them the character of submission to the personal will of a Creator. Adopted into the nation's law,[1] these became a part of the historically conditioned social order of the people of God, and through their inculcation of particular duties toward Nature led to the recognition of a natural cosmic order which Man, precisely because he is a subject of the covenant God and a member of the favoured covenant people, has

---

[1] Ex. 23.19; 34.26; Deut. 22.9ff.; Lev. 19.19; 22.24f., 27f. Cf. the prohibition of mutilation (Deut. 23.2), and the rules protecting animals (Deut. 22.6f.; Prov. 12.10).

to respect. The remoteness of Nature, its alien quality and the way in which it stands over against Man are thus all given weight and meaning by their association with God, and in his confrontation with autonomous Nature Man sees himself as having a divine vocation. This shaping of the Man-Nature relationship into a matter of personal conduct acquires its focal point in the bestowal on Israel of Canaan as the God-given land of her inheritance. By making possession of the land dependent upon faithfulness to the covenant[1] God includes Man's relation to Nature within the sphere of responsible human behaviour, and impresses upon him his distinctive position in the world of creatures. His sin means that the land is defiled,[2] and the same land will vomit forth the nation which has become untrue to its moral responsibility.[3]

Another influence working in the same direction was the concentration of faith on the one God, for this ruled out with increasing stringency the recognition, in Nature as well as elsewhere, of any independent divinity apart from that of Yahweh. As men experienced the exclusive character of Yahweh's will as revealed in his control of history, so the life of Nature also became subject to him.[4] This dedivinization of Nature not only freed Israel from the cultic practices which sought to drag her down into a mystical union with the forces of Nature through sexual licence and devotion to lifeless idols,[5] it also opened her eyes to the fact that the gulf between Man and Nature was something inherent in the very deepest level of men's spiritual and personal being. Hence it was impossible on the one hand that Man should find anywhere in Nature a being corresponding to himself, and on the other it made him joyfully certain in his relationship with God of his value as a responsible personal I. Just as God himself is not a natural force, but the living Lord who associates with men only through the fellowship of the word, so Man also sees himself

---

[1] Cf. the story of the spies (Num. 13f.), the barring of Moses from setting foot on the land (Deut. 34.4), the linking of affliction and apostasy, and the cursing of the unfaithful, in the Song of Deborah (Judg. 5.8, 23), the atmosphere of the Samuel and Saul narratives, the stress laid in Deuteronomy on the possession of the land as Yahweh's primary blessing on the righteous people of God, and the laws relating to the sabbatical and jubilee years in Lev. 25.4ff. and Ex. 23.10f.

[2] Deut. 24.4; Jer. 2.7; 3.1f., 9; 16.18; Ezek. 36.17f.; Lev. 18.25, 27; Ezra 9.11.

[3] Lev. 18.25, 28; 20.22.

[4] Cf. vol. I, p. 186.

[5] Amos 2.7; Hos. 4.14; I Kings 15.12; 22.47; Deut. 23.18, etc. In this context also belong the prohibitions of bestiality (Ex. 22.19; Deut. 27.21; Lev. 18.23; 20.15f.). For polemic against the worship of sacred objects cf. Hos. 13.2; Jer. 2.27; Isa. 44.17ff.

as set over against the multitude of natural objects and forces as different in kind, as one whose being and status find their security only in God.

ii. *Conscious formulations*

(*a*) This sense of Man's special position within the world of created things, nourished by law and history, receives conscious formulation and summary in the two accounts of Creation and in the Nature hymn of Ps. 8. The factor common to all these documents is their vision of Man as the noblest work of God's creation, and thus as the one to whom the Creator has promised the position of ruler in this world. But the explanations which they give of the essential reason for this preferential position vary. Ps. 8 and Gen. 2 are the most closely akin in the particular stress which they lay on *the difference in power between Man and the other creatures*. This is obviously the predominant approach for the ancient Israelite view in general. Of the two texts Ps. 8 exhibits it in its more naïve form, attributing Man's position simply to the sovereign will of the omnipotent God, and thus putting it beyond further discussion. Just as God is king in the heavenly realm, so Man in carrying out his commission is king of the earthly realm, crowned with glory and honour, and by virtue of his status only a little lower than the inhabitants of heaven. This confident comparison of Man to the *'elōhīm*, from whom he is distinct only in degree, is likewise ancient in character.[1] The almost defiant sense of power, and the naïve joy in what Man can achieve, as evinced in the lively description of his kingdom,[2] rings with all the self-confidence of antiquity,[3] and is given a distinctive twist only by the fact that it is combined with the most profound reverence before the almighty Lord of creation. What makes the free sovereign power of the latter impressive is precisely the fact that the one whom he clothes with royal status is a weak and insignificant creature who by himself could never be more than an eloquent testimony to the complete impotence of created things. Because it is God's inconceivably marvellous power

[1] This alone ought to warn us against expounding the Psalm as if it were dependent on Gen. 1 (Duhm, Kittel, *et al.*). Man's resemblance to the lower *'elōhīm* is not the same thing as his being made in the image of God; and the identification of the primacy which the former gives him with his dominion over the earth is more naïve than the derivation of this dominion from a special word of blessing which simply adds it *per accidens* to the state of being in God's image. Hence Gunkel, too, argues for pre-exilic provenance.

[2] Vv. 7–9.

[3] It is not without point that this description is often compared to the hymn in praise of Man's dominion in the *Antigone* of Sophocles.

which alone is the basis of human self-confidence, the contrast between Man and the glittering heavenly bodies serves to bring out in
all the more pure a form the sense of Man's special position. Ultimately therefore it is a spiritual factor which determines the value
Man sets upon himself, namely his consciousness of partnership with
God, a privilege of which no other creature is considered worthy.

(*b*) This comes out even more clearly in the Yahwist creation
story, when the author describes how Man becomes a living being.
Here he lays especial stress on the fact that life is a divine gift, bestowed directly by God through the insufflation of the *nišmat ḥayyîm*,
the breath of life.[1] It is true that the life of all other beings is also
ascribed to this divine breath of life,[2] and that even the animals are
classified with Man as *nepeš ḥayyā*.[3] However, it was clearly the
narrator's intention to mark Man out from the other creatures, since
only in his case does he relate a direct transfer of the divine breath.
Whereas the animals are produced and brought to life simply, so to
speak, by the universal divine breath blowing through the whole of
Nature, and therefore partake of life only as a class of beings, Man
receives his life by a special act of God, and is thus treated as an independent spiritual I, and accorded a closer association with God
than the animals. This is confirmed by the continuation of the
narrative, where everything is directed to showing that he occupies a
superior position *vis-à-vis* the animal world, inasmuch as he is able to
interpret the nature of the other creatures by giving them their names.
Only in one like himself does he find a complement and an equal. It
is true that the mythical form of the ancient tradition, according to
which woman was placed on the same footing as man only by a
supplementary creative act, has not been eliminated. But her position
as *'ēzer kᵉnegdō*, a help appropriate to man, is the basis of an I-Thou
relationship which raises Man essentially above the level of the animals, and offers him the proper fulfilment of his own nature only in
association with another being like himself. With a view to this fulfilment man is granted the right to subordinate the ties of blood to
those of this newly developing partnership, thus depriving of its
power the patriarchal order of the family with its strict demands of
pietas. The value thus set on the relation of the sexes is markedly different from the evaluation of woman generally obtaining in the

[1] Gen. 2.7.
[2] Cf. pp. 47ff. above.
[3] Gen. 2.19.

ancient world, which regarded her simply as an instrument of pleasure and procreation. Here woman as well as man is singled out from the rest of creation as uniquely capable of life as an individual, and set at the side of God. It is in keeping with this that Man stands at the head of created things as the one to whom the care of the paradise garden is entrusted.

(c) The affirmations of the first Creation story, that of Gen. 1, also point in the same direction. Here, however, we are already at the stage of the formulation of theological concepts; and of these the one which sums up the statements of the Priestly author about the God-given value of Man is that of the 'image of God'.[1] In the ancient Israelite account which formed the basis of his own the ṣelem'elōhīm, the image of God, may once have been conceived in a quite concrete way. This is suggested not only by the stories of God's appearing in the form of a man[2] but also by the accounts from Babylonian culture of the creation of Man, which frequently appear to have a physical similarity in mind.[3]

This is confirmed by the fact that the narrator expresses the idea of likeness to God by the term ṣelem, the meaning of which unquestionably points in this direction, as Humbert[4] and Köhler[5] have proved as clearly as anyone could desire. The word denotes a statue, that is, a plastic representation, and finally also a two-dimensional image or a drawing. If therefore Man is created beṣelem 'elōhīm, in accordance with the picture of God,[6] then it is certain that the original idea was of Man's outward form as a copy of God's; and here Man's upright posture and movement may have been a major ingredient in the likeness.[7] That this idea was, in fact, an innovation on the part of the Priestly writer himself (so Köhler) is as improbable as anything could well be; rather, like so much else in his account, it will have come down to him by way of an older tradition, the existence of which is indicated also by the Babylonian texts just mentioned. It is consonant

[1] Gen. 1.26f.

[2] Cf. pp. 20f. above.

[3] This applies particularly to the Sumerian liturgy of the goddess Nintu from Kish (cited in A. Jeremias, *Handbuch der altorientalischen Geistesgeschichte*[2], 1925, p. 88), who fashions a male being in the image of the god Asshirgi, and a female in her own image. The creation of Enkidu in the Gilgamesh Epic (I.30f.) as a being like Anu is also to be understood in this sense.

[4] *Études sur le récit du paradis et de la chute dans la Genèse*, 1940, pp. 153ff.

[5] 'Die Grundstelle der Imago-Dei-Lehre, Genesis 1.26' *TZ* 4, 1948, pp. 16ff.

[6] This is a case of normative *bēt*, not *bēt essentiae*.

[7] So Köhler, *op. cit.*, pp. 19f.

with this that he does not adopt the crucial word (*selem*) as an adequate description of the picture of Man which he has in mind, but takes care to define it more closely; *beṣalmēnū* is both limited and weakened by the addition of *kidmūtēnū*. This abstract formation from the root *dmh* signifies 'similarity' or 'likeness'; added to *ṣelem* as an explanatory qualification its only possible purpose is to exclude the idea of an actual copy of God, and to limit the concept to one of similarity. With regard to this usage of *demūt* Ezekiel, whose vocabulary in other respects also has many points of contact with that of the Priestly writings, is particularly illuminating. He uses it in ch. 1 to emphasize the purely approximate nature of the correspondence between his description of the enthroned universal Lord and the reality; in his portrayal both of the mixomorphic bearers of the throne, and of the God who appears above them, he continually inserts the word *demūt* in the sense of 'something resembling . . .' In this way everything is 'moved on to the level of that which cannot be perceived by the senses, the spiritualized, the symbolic which is at once unreal and more than real' (Köhler). In other contexts, too, the expression serves to 'weaken the degree of likeness' (Köhler).[1] This suggests that the Priestly narrator no longer had any intention of taking *ṣelem* to mean a simple copy of God's outward form, but that what was in his mind was something for which the concept 'copy' was only an inadequate description, a correspondence between God and Man which could only figuratively be characterized as the endowment of Man with God's 'image'. Hence in Gen. 5.1, where he alludes once more to the creation of Man, he can content himself with the term *demūt*, and leave out *ṣelem* altogether.

In fact, the concept of the image was perfectly susceptible of such extension. Thus in Babylonian it occurs in the senses of the form in which something is manifested, of a representative, a substitute, or an equivalent, and can itself be replaced by the concept *sikru*, meaning 'name in the sense of nature'.[2] The spiritualization which the Priestly author had in mind should be sought in a similar direction,[3] for this, in fact, accords with the whole pattern of his spirituality. It is he who

---

[1] Cf. II Kings 16.10; II Chron. 4.3; Dan. 10.16.

[2] For the evidence cf. J. Hehn, 'Zum Terminus "Bild Gottes" ', *Sachau-Festschrift*, 1915, pp. 41ff.

[3] For this reason it is impossible to follow Köhler in defining P's weakening of the old terminology as implying that men were created in the (upright) form of God, yet nevertheless not completely so, but only in the degree to which it looks as if they had this form. A clear concept cannot be combined with saving clauses of this kind.

better than any other writer knows how to convey vividly, both here and elsewhere, the absolute otherness and transcendence of the divine nature, he who eliminates all trace of anthropomorphism from his theophanies, and acknowledges no angel to mediate between God and Man because of his strict refusal to bring the divine realm down into the sphere of the creaturely. It was no longer possible for such a writer to speak without demur of a physical copy of God; he was bound to try to comprehend *ṣelem* in a wider sense, to advance from the idea of a tangible image to that of parabolic similarity.[1] Such an advance was, in fact, made easier for him by the Israelite view of human nature, which conceived the body very definitely as the form in which the psychic life was expressed. Strict separation between body and soul is here unknown; Man does not *have* a body and a soul, he *is* both of them at once.[2] This made it possible, when considering the relation of the *ṣelem 'elōhīm* to the human body, to bring to the fore as the decisive element its function as the medium of spiritual and personal life.

There are other pointers in the work of the Priestly writer, in addition to this use of *demūt*, to the shift of the *ṣelem*-concept from physical similarity to spiritual correspondence. First of all there is the choice of the plural suffix in the crucial declaration: 'Let us make man in *our* image.' It does not matter whether the fact that the divine invitation is issued in the plural is explained as an address to the heavenly court surrounding God,[3] or rather, bearing in mind that this conception is not found in P, as a plural of deliberation with oneself[4] or of reflection;[5] or again whether by thus dissolving 'I' into

[1] That commentators should disregard these facts, and prefer on the basis of purely philological conjectures to saddle P with a physical correspondence between God and Man is part of their horror of any so-called 'breakthrough', a horror which makes them sceptical in face of a creative reshaping of traditional spiritual values. The appeal to the theophanies and anthropomorphisms of the OT in order to support an exaggeratedly physical interpretation of the *ṣelem 'elōhīm* though it may certainly be appropriate for ascertaining the original meaning of the concept (cf. p. 16 above), can have no significance for the usage of P, since here such expressions are not omitted by accident, but are avoided from a clear sense of their inadequacy.

[2] Cf. section II of this chapter, pp. 131ff. below. J. J. Stamm has also recently laid emphasis on this insight: *Die Gottebenbildlichkeit des Menschen im AT* (Theol. Studien 54), 1959.

[3] So, most recently, A. Alt, 'Gedanken über das Königtum Jahves', *Kleine Schriften zur Geschichte des Volkes Israel*, 1953, p. 352.

[4] Cf. H. Holzinger *ad loc.* in Kautzsch-Bertholet, *Die heilige Schrift des AT*[4], 1922.

[5] Cf. F. Horst, 'Face to face. The biblical doctrine of the image of God', *Interpretation*, 4, 1950, pp. 259ff.

'we' the writer should be taken to imply the combination in the person of the deity of a wealth of different powers,[1] or whether he is using the vulgar idiom which substitutes 'one' or 'we' for 'I' in order to avoid a premature use of the first person.[2] In any of these cases the reference to creation as 'in our image' instead of 'in my image' is definitely aimed at avoiding an altogether too narrow connection with God's own form,[3] and at changing the naïvely materialistic conception of earlier times into a more vaguely worded correspondence between the human and divine natures.[4]

In keeping with this is the way in which the Priestly thinker speaks of the passing on of the image of God from Adam to his son Seth.[5] His stress on the fact that Seth was conceived in the likeness and after the image of his father, thus placing *demūt* first, may not be without significance. In so careful a stylist this inversion must spring from a deliberate intention of turning the reader's thoughts away from physical similarity (which indeed is found equally in the parents and young of animals, and cannot therefore be regarded as itself especially marvellous) toward a spiritual definition of the human image, summing up that which is distinctively human. This is not contradicted by the writer's explanation of the inviolability of human life compared with that of the animals.[6] Though the divine protection of Man is based on the *ṣelem 'elōhīm*, the writer is certainly not thinking primarily, or even at all, of the difference between human and animal bodies, but of the psychophysical totality of human existence, which bears the stamp of a fundamentally different kind of life, and thus has reference to its creator.

If therefore we wish to define correctly the content of the *ṣelem 'elōhīm*, we cannot be content with lexical data, but first and foremost must ask in what form the divine nature was revealed to the Priestly writer. Now, it is clear that in his account of creation everything from

---

[1] A. Dillmann, *Die Genesis*[6], 1892, *ad loc*. This conception comes closest to the old Trinitarian one, which has recently been revived in a distinctive form by K. Barth. Barth assumes that the words refer to a God who is One, yet nevertheless has within himself the distinction between I and Thou (*Church Dogmatics* III, 1, ET, 1958, p. 192).

[2] L. Köhler, *op. cit.*, p. 22.

[3] So also W. Baumgartner.

[4] This is all the more understandable in view of the fact that heathen ideas of the place of the divine pattern in the creation of Man also included the element of sexual differentiation. In the Sumerian liturgy mentioned above the male being is fashioned in the image of the god, the female in the image of the goddess.

[5] Gen. 5.3.

[6] Gen. 9.6.

the very first line is deliberately designed to portray the creator as conscious, autarkic will, revealing itself ever more clearly in resistless, purposeful creation by means of the Word. What Israel, through God's self-communication in the covenant, had experienced as the fundamental character of the divine nature, and had ever more deeply comprehended as such in her historical experience of his sovereignty, namely the personhood of the God who thus dealt with her,[1] the Priestly writer now succeeds in bringing vividly to life as the determining force behind the process of creation. In the light of the position allotted to Man within the created order the Creator is seen as a personal Thou who discloses himself for the purpose of fellowship with his noblest creature; and from this personal Thou every being that wears a human face takes its stamp. For Man to be created in the likeness of God's image can only mean that on him, too, personhood is bestowed as the definitive characteristic of his nature. He has a share in the personhood of God; and as a being capable of self-awareness and of self-determination he is open to the divine address and capable of responsible conduct. This quality of personhood shapes the totality of his psycho-physical existence; it is this which comprises the essentially human, and distinguishes him from all other creatures.

The importance of this special character of human nature is further emphasized by the fact that it is universally valid. Because man and woman emerge at the same time from the hand of the Creator, and are created in the same way after God's image, the difference between the sexes is no longer relevant to their position before God. This affirmation cuts away the ground from under the mythological fables of the old creation stories, which told of an exchange of male and female sex-characteristics, or of their fusion, in the first creatures; and in this way all ambiguity as to the relationship between the sexes is removed.[2] At the same time the verse does away

[1] Cf. the discussion in vol. I, pp. 206ff.

[2] Despite the clarity of the language employed the opinion has been expressed that Gen. 1.27 refers to a single hermaphrodite being, an androgyne (so F. Schwally, *ARW* 9, 1906, pp. 172ff.), such as seems to play a part in the Creation story of Berossus (cf. *AOT*, p. 137). However, not only is the rendering of 1.27c as 'male and female created he him' arrived at by a textual emendation ('*ōtō* for '*ōtām*) for which there is not the slightest justification, but it also ignores the meaning of *zākār* and *neḵēbā*, which occur again in the work of the Priestly writer in later passages, and denote not the adjectives 'male' and 'female' but quite concretely the male and female sections of the species: cf. Gen. 17.10ff.; Ex. 12.48; Lev. 6.11, etc. The attempt to discover remnants of myth in this verse has therefore rightly been abandoned by all commentators. The speculations of later Judaism on the androgynous character of Adam (cf. Böklen, *Adam und Kain* [Myth. Bibl. I.2, 3], 1907;

with any justification for holding the female half of the race in contempt as inferior, or in some way closer to the animals. The relationship between man and woman is placed on the same basis as that
between Man and God; their encounter as personal beings leads to a
living for each other in responsible co-operation which draws its
strength from their common encounter with God.[1]

The connection between Man's creation in the image of God and
his dominant position within the world of creatures is much less
direct. This dominance is indeed associated with the declaration of
God's intention to create Man, being mentioned as a consequence of
the especially close relationship of this creature to his Creator; but
in the detailed exposition of the divine plan it is then quite clearly
distinguished from this relationship as a separate item which has to
be promised by a special creative act of blessing.[2] Subjugation of the
earth and dominion over its creatures bestows on the human race a
common universal task, and in the execution of this task Man's special
nature is to become visibly effective in that he is hereby made the
responsible representative of the divine cosmic Lord. It has been
rightly pointed out that these few words contain a whole programme
for the cultural history of mankind;[3] and this programme is all the
more valuable by virtue of the fact that it does not exclude but includes the attaching of manifest value to work. By distributing the
activity of creation over a period of a week, concluding with a day of
rest which is now to be fixed as a permanent ordinance,[4] the writer
derives from a primal divine decree the belief that Man does not
exist merely for heedless enjoyment—as innumerable myths of the
beginnings of mankind like to relate—but is meant to find the
development of his aptitudes and powers in purposeful labour, in
which he is to possess a facsimile of the divine work of creation and its
joy. Work is not, therefore, as it is regarded elsewhere in antiquity, a

---

E. Bischoff, *Babylonisch-Astrales im Weltbild des Talmud und Midrasch*, 1907, p. 100;
E. König, *Genesis*[2, 3], *ad loc.*) have, of course, no bearing on our text.

[1] So also F. Horst, *op. cit.*, pp. 266–8, and J. J. Stamm, *op. cit.*, pp. 19f.
[2] It is therefore impossible to follow earlier exegetes (cf. H. Holzinger, *Genesis*,
1898, p. 12—and also Luther) in linking Man's likeness to God with his position of
sovereignty. In this lies the clear distinction between our present passage and Ps. 8:
cf. pp. 120f. above.
[3] H. Gunkel, *Genesis*[3], 1910, p. 113.
[4] Gen. 2.1–3.

curse or the miserable lot of slaves, but a task assigned by God. The point of the day of rest, however, is to make Man aware that he is not chained to his work in ceaseless drudgery, but like God may rejoice in his labours. Even *vis-à-vis* his work he is to remain master, and not to sink to the position of a slave.

Again clearly distinct from Man's godlikeness is the mention of the capacity for reproduction which is bestowed upon him, and by which he is to take possession of the earth. This power is given to him, as to the animals, by a special word of blessing. In this way it is exalted as a high divine gift, so leaving no room for an ascetic denigration of this faculty, and yet at the same time its divinization is made quite impossible. It is a divine gift; but it is not a sign of godlikeness by means of which Man can become aware of his kinship with God, and gain control of divine power. The intrusion of sexuality into Man's relationship with God—a deviation of the majority of agricultural religions, and one which Israel encountered in the religious world of Canaan—is thus branded as a wicked distortion of the Creator's will.[1]

On the other hand, it follows directly from the distinctive creative character accorded to all men alike, and inherited by them un-impaired,[2] that in the Old Testament the differences between various peoples and races, which for the normal outlook of antiquity are matters of fundamental importance,[3] seem inessential. The Old Testament knows nothing of races which are basically inferior and unworthy to be called human. It is true that there is a sober awareness of the way races differ in their dispositions and destinies, but this leaves no room for racial pride or arrogance, for all are equal before God their Creator, and the destiny of each is decided by their attitude to him. This in no way controverts the emphasis on the favoured position of Israel to be found in many Old Testament passages; for this position is thought of only as a matter of history, not of principle, and is attributed to the action of God, and not to peculiar advantages of nature or endowment.

From what has been said it will be clear that the image of God is not to be understood as a quality bestowed on Man, an item of equip-

---

[1] On this point cf. the pertinent observations of W. Zimmerli, *I Mos. 1–11, Die Urgeschichte* I, 1943, pp. 86ff.

[2] Cf. p. 125 above.

[3] One instance that will readily come to mind is the impenetrable wall of partition between Greeks and barbarians in Hellenism.

ment additional to the simple terms of human existence,[1] whether this endowment be defined more precisely as the gift of psychic powers, or of reason, or of the sense of the eternal, the good and the true, or of intelligence and immortality.[2] Nor can there be any question of assigning two different contents to *ṣelem* and *dᵉmūt* respectively—as, for example, the physical and the spiritual resemblance of Man to God,[3] or reason and freewill on the one hand and ethical perfection on the other.[4] The same applies to a definition which became immensely important in dogmatic theology, namely that which understood Man's having been made in the image of God as a special moral perfection or *iustitia originalis* of the first man, which was then lost as a result of the Fall. The grain of truth in this view is the reference to the power of moral judgment which is bound up with our concept of a person as such, a power which reveals itself in the sense of moral responsibility. This is, however, only a precondition of moral conduct and probation, not the thing itself. How little such a view was in the mind of the Priestly author may be seen simply enough from the fact that in his opinion the privilege bestowed on Man of being the bearer of the divine image was never lost, but for all time constitutes the basis of his special position *vis-à-vis* the animals.[5]

[1] It is difficult to understand how J. J. Stamm (*Die Gottebenbildlichkeit des Menschen im AT*, 1959, p. 8) came to misunderstand my remarks as implying this, in view of my emphasis on the body as the medium of spiritual and personal life and on the relationship of the image of God to human existence as a totality.

[2] Cf. A. Dillmann, *Die Genesis*⁶, 1892, pp. 32f.; E. König, *Theologie*³, ⁴, pp. 214ff.

[3] O. Procksch, *Die Genesis*², ³, pp. 448ff.

[4] The dogma of the Roman Catholic Church as laid down at the Council of Trent.

[5] The attempt of Karl Barth to interpret the *ṣelem 'ᵉlōhīm* (*Church Dogmatics* III/1, pp. 191ff.) has one decisive point of contact with that given here, namely in the emphasis on the fact that as bearer of the divine image Man is a being whom God 'addressed . . . as a Thou and made responsible as an I' (*op. cit.*, p. 203). When, however, basing himself on his own peculiar understanding of the plural in Gen. 1.26 (cf. p. 125, n. 1), he connects the primal divine image with the I-Thou relationship which is given form in the mutual confrontation and support of man and woman (*op. cit.*, pp. 194f.); when he takes *ṣelem* and *dᵉmūt* as meaning prototype and pattern; and when he works out an *analogia relationis* between human existence and the internal dynamic of the divine nature; then his exposition of the creation document cannot be said to have any adequate philological foundation, and is alien to the Priestly thinker's picture of God as this can be established from other passages. Cf. on this question the carefully weighed remarks of J. J. Stamm, 'Die Imago-lehre von K. Barth und die alttestamentliche Wissenschaft', *Antwort*, *Festschrift für K. Barth*, 1956, pp. 84ff., and *Die Gottebenbildlichkeit im AT*, (Theologische Studien 54), 1959.

Man's endowment with the *imago Dei* should not therefore be used as a basis for developing a dogmatic doctrine of mankind's primal condition.[1] On the other hand, the passage in question acquires all the greater importance for the problem of universal revelation. For by virtue of his pre-eminence above all other creatures Man stands as a sinner in a special relationship with God, accessible to the judging and compassionate word of the Lord whose image he wears, and called to responsibility. This is bound to have decisive consequences for our conception of sin and redemption.[2] In this connection, however, it should be noted that in addition to those New Testament passages which simply follow Gen. 1.26 in describing Man as bearing the image of God (James 3.9 and, in a wider sense, Acts 17.28) there are others which regard this image as either not yet or no longer present in the sinner, and understand redemption as its restoration.[3] This is undoubtedly bound up with the fact that Christ, in an immense deepening of the concept, is described as the direct manifestation of the image of God,[4] while the rest of mankind partake of this image only in an analogue, something similar to the original. Hence Paul's hope reaches out to our being conformed to the image of the Son of God,[5] and thus to a new glory of the redeemed as yet unknown in the Old Testament, by which they become εἰκὼν καὶ δόξα θεοῦ.[6]

It is a testimony to the importance of the Priestly thinker that no other Old Testament author reached the heights of his conception, and that nowhere is there any attempt to develop it further. Only in the Apocrypha are there instances of efforts at learned interpretation of the image of God.[7] Nevertheless it must be said that this conception does not just express the idiosyncratic opinion of a clever mind far beyond the normal run of Old Testament thought; it sums up in a most effective way those other religious judgments on the subject of

---

[1] That there are important difficulties even from the dogmatic point of view in this use of Gen. 1.26—even in its most widespread application to *iustitia originalis*—has been strongly emphasized by F. K. Schumann (*Imago Dei. Beiträge zur theologischen Anthropologie, G. Krüger dargebr.*, 1932, pp. 173f.).

[2] Cf. on this point E. Brunner, *Natur und Gnade*, 1934 (ET in *Natural Theology*, 1946); P. Althaus, 'Uroffenbarung', *Luthertum*, 1935, pp. 4ff.; and my own comments in ch. XXIII below: Sin and Evil.

[3] Col. 3.10; Eph. 4.24; Rom. 8.29.

[4] εἰκὼν τοῦ θεοῦ II Cor. 4.4; Col. 1.15: χαρακτὴρ τῆς ὑποστάσεως αὐτοῦ Heb. 1.3.

[5] Rom. 8.29; I Cor. 15.49.

[6] I Cor. 11.7.

[7] Ecclus 17.3ff.; Wisd. 2.23.

Man as God's creature which were formulated elsewhere in the Old Testament.

We must now turn to a fresh aspect of the Old Testament picture of Man, and examine its views on Man's psychic life.

2. THE COMPONENTS OF HUMAN NATURE

The distinction between an inner, spiritual aspect and a physical aspect of human nature which was to be found in both creation stories is not simply an opinion peculiar to these accounts, but a constituent element of the whole Old Testament view of Man. Quite apart from explicit statements about the two-sided character of human nature,[1] the belief is universal in the Old Testament that Man on the one hand consists of earthy matter, that he is dust and ashes,[2] and on the other that he can claim as his own a spiritual potentiality which alone makes him a conscious ego. The great variety of expressions used to designate this spiritual aspect serve to present it from a number of different angles. One of the most common of these terms is *rūaḥ*.

i. *The individual spirit of Man (rūaḥ)*

It has already been pointed out above that the spirit of the individual man designated by the term *rūaḥ* is to be distinguished sharply from the concept of the Spirit of God.[3] The new usage of the word is undoubtedly connected with the derivation of all earthly life from that supra-individual divine vital force which, as the breath of God, pervades the whole creation. But even though, in this sense, *rūaḥ* encountered Man as something far superior to him, never coming under his control, yet, if a man wished to talk of the vital energy dwelling within himself, it was possible for him to speak of 'his' *rūaḥ*, to attribute marked deteriorations in his physical or psychic state to its impairment or diminution,[4] or to explain them as an unrest, a dis-

[1] Pss. 90.3; 146.4; Job 4.19; 10.9; 33.6; 34.14f.; Eccles. 12.7.

[2] Gen. 18.27; Ps. 103.14. The derivation of *'ādām* from *'ªdāmā*, characterizing Man as the earth-born (a view still held by E. König, *Genesis*[2, 3], 1925, pp. 158f., and *Theologie*[3, 4], pp. 210f.), has now been fairly generally abandoned. A better theory is that of L. Rost ('Die Bezeichnung für Land und Volk im AT', *Procksch-Festschrift*, 1934, pp. 125ff.), who suggests a common root for both words, the basic meaning of which was the colour reddish-brown. Comparable to the description of Man as dust and ashes is the use of the term *bāśār*, flesh, which characterizes the weakness of his earthy nature: Gen. 6.3, 12; Isa. 31.3; 40.5f.; Jer. 45.5; Ps. 56.5.

[3] Cf. p. 48, n. 3, above.

[4] Cf. p. 47 above.

turbance, of a vital element proper to himself. In so doing, *rūaḥ* was still at first kept as something independent of human subjectivity, since in all such cases it was a question of strong external influences operating upon men, and overwhelming them. But when the usage was extended from physical to psychic circumstances the first steps had been taken toward using *rūaḥ* in the sense of a psychological term. A link between the physical and the spiritual aspect of life was afforded by the fact that strong psychical excitement also becomes physically visible in violent gestures, a flushed countenance, pounding of the heart, and so on. Thus the threatening anger of the Ephraimites against Gideon is described as *rūaḥ*, and the ebbing of the vital energy thus excited is vividly pictured by the verb *rāpā*, 'to become slack', 'be laid to rest'.[1] The tormenting disquiet which Pharaoh suffered on account of his dark dreams is described as a 'being pushed' of his spirit,[2] the inward agitation being attributed to a disturbance of the vital spirit within the man, so that it surges to and fro like water in a vessel. When Ahab, utterly disconcerted and distressed by the rejection of his offer to Naboth, throws himself on his couch and refuses to eat, this is explained as wilfulness and rebellion of the *rūaḥ*.[3] It is therefore primarily those emotions which overwhelm men, and make them act in a way contrary to their customary temper, which are associated with the element of *rūaḥ*.[4]

From this habit of describing movements within the psyche as manifestations of the *rūaḥ* present in Man there arose in later times, as men acquired a better understanding of the autonomy and unity of the psychic life, a development by means of a simple generalization whereby the *rūaḥ* was made responsible for *all* psychic affects, and was indeed virtually regarded as the *organ of psychic life*. Since this comprehensive use of *rūaḥ* as the dominant factor in human psychology can be observed from Ezekiel onwards, it must have emerged toward the end of the monarchy. Thus Ezekiel speaks of the *maᶜᵃlōt rūḥᵃkem*, 'that which rises in your spirits', to denote the secret plans of his opponents.[5] And when he wishes to describe the new inner

[1] Judg. 8.3; in the same sense Ps. 76.13; Prov. 16.32; 25.28; 29.11; Job 15.13; Isa. 25.4; Eccles. 10.4.

[2] *wattitpāᶜem rūḥō* Gen. 41.8: cf. Dan. 2.3.

[3] I Kings 21.5 (*s-r-h* is much better derived from *s-r-r* than from *s-w-r*).

[4] Cf. further Gen. 26.35; I Sam. 1.15; I Kings 10.5, and in the later period Isa. 54.6; 65.14; Prov. 15.4, 13; 16.18, 32; 17.22; 18.14; 25.28; 29.23; Pss. 34.19; 51.19; Ex. 6.9; Job 7.11; 17.1.

[5] Ezek. 11.5b; also *hāᶜōlā ᶜal-rūḥᵃkem* 20.32. Similarly Ezek. 13.3; Ps. 77.7 ('my spirit must search'); Prov. 1.23; 16.2; Isa. 26.9; Mal. 2.16.

condition of mankind in the messianic age, he not only pictures men as permeated with Yahweh's *rūaḥ*, but promises them the possession of a new *rūaḥ*, that is, a new spiritual habitus.[1] The word may here be translated virtually as 'mind' or 'disposition', and in this sense is a favourite term of later writers.[2] In this development it is important that the new organ of psychic life is seen first and foremost as an ethical direction of the will,[3] and so it can also be used to describe individual moral qualities.[4] Furthermore, when the reference is to the spirit of Man in the wider sense, it is concerned predominantly with the higher spiritual functions: the spirit searches out God's ways;[5] it is despondent when divine help is slow in coming;[6] David holds the plans for every detail of the Temple building in his spirit.[7] It is therefore understandable that Yahweh's direct influence on a man is aimed especially at the *rūaḥ* as the organ of higher psychic activity: he awakens or stirs it up to decisive action,[8] but he may also harden it, and so inflict punishment.[9] The more common usage in such cases, however, is to speak of the heart (cf. p. 143 below).

It is clear that the spirit is here losing the character of an independent supra-individual force, and is being completely incorporated into the psychic life of Man. Nevertheless its original nature continues to have this much effect, that it designates primarily the higher level of Man's interior life. Moreover, the fact that the same term was used to denote the *rūaḥ* both of the deity and of Man, despite there being no directly religious value attached to the human *rūaḥ*, kept men continually aware that by the terms of the creation their world was linked to the supra-sensory world of God—and this all the more when, as sometimes happens, God's inner personal nature is described as *rūaḥ* by a simple transference from the human condition.[10] On the other hand, it is unquestionable that neither here nor elsewhere is *rūaḥ* used to mean a spiritual *alter ego* in Man, which as his higher self

---

[1] Ezek. 11.19; 18.31; 36.26; 39.29.
[2] Ezek. 13.3; Job 20.3; 21.4; 32.18; Ex. 35.21; Num. 14.24; Eccles. 7.9.
[3] So also Isa. 29.24; Pss. 51.12ff.; 32.2; 78.8; Prov. 11.13.
[4] Patience Eccles. 7.8; humility, Isa. 57.15; trustworthiness, Num. 14.24; Pss. 32.2; 51.12, 14; 78.8; Prov. 11.13; arrogance, Prov. 16.18; Eccles. 7.8; Ps. 76.13; impatience, Prov. 14.29; Job 21.4; Micah 2.7; Ex. 6.9.
[5] Ps. 77.7; Isa. 26.9.
[6] Isa. 57.16; 61.3; 66.2; Ezek. 21.12; Pss. 77.4; 142.4; 143.4, 7.
[7] I Chron. 28.12, cf. Ex. 35.21.
[8] Ezra 1.1, 5; Hag. 1.14; Jer. 51.11; I Chron. 5.26; II Chron. 21.16; 36.22.
[9] Deut. 2.30.
[10] Micah 2.7.

might possess a more permanent mode of existence, superior to death. All such ideas are products of the compelling influence of the animistic theory put forward by Tylor, which today can no longer be regarded as tenable. They can only be supported by inadmissibly combining statements of a strictly psychological kind about the *rūaḥ* with others of different categories.[1]

ii. *The 'soul' (nepeš)*[2]

The view that it was possible to discover in Israelite belief conceptions corresponding to the shadow- and breath-souls of the theory of W. Wundt[3] seized on the concept of the *nepeš* even more eagerly than on that of the *rūaḥ*, especially since the unhappy rendering of the term by 'soul' opened the door from the start to the Greek beliefs concerning the soul. Fortunately, however, it is possible in the case of this word, too, to establish *the basic physical connotation*, namely first of all the 'neck', 'throat' or 'gullet',[4] and then by extension that which comes out of the throat, the 'breath' or 'breath of life'.[5] The former meaning is still clearly discernible in expressions which speak of the hunger and thirst, the ravening and greed of the *nepeš*,[6] or of its being threatened by snare, sword or flood;[7] while the second may be detected principally in the description of impatience as a 'growing short' of the *nepeš*,[8] and in the use of the same stem in the Niphla *yinnāpēš* to mean 'breathe deeply', 'recover'.[9] As the characteristic

[1] Cf., e.g., P. Torge, *Seelenglaube und Unsterblichkeitshoffnung im AT*, 1909, p. 22.

[2] The reader should consult the treatments of this subject in the following monographs: G. H. Bekker, *Het Begrip Nefesj in het Oude Testament*, 1942; A. R. Johnson, *The Vitality of the Individual in the Thought of Ancient Israel*, 1949, pp. 9–26; D. Lys, *Nephesh. Histoire de l'âme dans la révélation d'Israel au sein des religions proche-orientales*, 1959.

[3] *Völkerpsychologie III: Mythus und Religion*.

[4] This has been made absolutely clear by L. Dürr's most valuable study, 'Hebr. *nepeš* = akk. napištu = Gurgel, Kehle', *ZAW*, 1925, pp. 262ff. G. H. Bekker (*op. cit.*, pp. 120ff.) has contested this derivation, and prefers to assume 'breath' as the basic concept, but his reasons are not convincing.

[5] This meaning is found also in Assyrian, Syriac and Arabic. T. C. Vriezen (*An Outline of Old Testament Theology*, 1958), in the light of the related verbal stems *n-š-p*, *n-š-b* and *n-š-m*, prefers to find the basic concept not in the breath but in the activity of blowing or breathing, the drawing of breath.

[6] Isa. 29.8; 32.6; Prov. 10.3; Jer. 31.25; Prov. 25.25; 28.25; Isa. 5.14; Hab. 2.5, etc.

[7] Prov. 18.7; 22.25; Ps. 124.4f., etc.; Jer. 4.10, etc.; Ps. 69.2; Jonah 2.6, etc. On many passages opinions may naturally differ; there are sometimes good reasons for the renderings 'life' or 'greed'.

[8] *tiḳṣar napšī*: Num. 21.4; Judg. 10.16; 16.16; Zech. 11.8.

[9] Ex. 23.12; 31.17; II Sam. 16.14.

sign of the living both in human beings and in animals the breath may appear to be the 'extra thing which the living possess',[1] that which distinguishes them from the dead. Thus it becomes a substance which inheres in the living even apart from the breath; in short, it becomes *equated simply with 'life'*.[2] Hence it is granted to animals as well, and one can speak equally of the *nepeš bᵉhēmā* and of the *nepeš 'ādām*.[3] Whereas the parallel word *nᵉšāmā*, breath, always kept its physical connotation, in the case of *nepeš* the sense of this is almost lost, and life itself takes the place of breath as a sign of life.[4] It is important to remember, however, that this is not a case of an abstract concept, but of a substantial entity which might almost be described as the stuff of life. There is a clear affinity with the *mana* of primitive peoples, and this gives the *nepeš* a dynamic character.[5]

Even these simple observations will have shown how dangerous it must be for the understanding of Old Testament psychology to translate *nepeš* as 'soul' *tout court*. First and foremost the word means 'life', and what is more, in contradistinction to *rūaḥ*, *life bound up with a body*. Hence at death the *nepeš* ceases to exist, just as the animal body without it becomes a corpse. It may therefore be said quite simply that the *nepeš* dies;[6] at the same time it is perfectly feasible to think of it as leaving a man at death,[7] though this does not mean that one can ask where it has gone! It is enough that it has disappeared. More frequently it is described as having been taken or swept away.[8] Only

---

[1] J. Köberle, *Natur und Geist nach der Auffassung des AT*, 1901, pp. 180f.

[2] The *nepeš* is rescued from peril of death, I Sam. 19.11; II Sam. 19.6; Amos 2.14f., etc.; enemies seek it, Ex. 4.19; I Sam 20.1; they lie in wait for it, Ps. 59.4; the *nepeš* of the man who is doomed to die must be redeemed, Ex. 30.15f.; Num. 31.50; used as a pregnant expression in the phrase *bᵉnepeš*, meaning 'at the cost of', or 'in jeopardy of' one's life, II Sam. 14.7; 18.13; 23.17, etc. Cf. the extensive list of passages in J. Schwab, *Der begriff der nefeš in den hg. Schriften des AT* (Munich Dissertation), 1913.

[3] Lev. 24.18; cf. Gen. 9.4; Lev. 17.11, 14; Deut. 12.23.

[4] It is not without interest that in Homer and throughout the most ancient Greek linguistic usage we find a very similar state of affairs: there ψυχή, when it is used of living people, always means 'life', but never 'soul' in the sense of a spiritual *alter ego* in Man. Moreover, ψυχή has quite lost the meaning 'breath'; just as the Hebrews use *nᵉšāmā*, Homer uses the terms ἀυτμή and πνοίη. Cf. Walter Otto, *Die Manen*, 1923.

[5] This is especially emphasized by D. Lys (*op. cit., passim*). For the same reason Vriezen prefers to speak of 'vital motion' rather than of 'life'.

[6] Num. 23.10; Judg. 16.30.

[7] Gen. 35.18; I Kings 17.21; conversely one may speak of the return of the *nepeš* at the resuscitation of a dead person, I Kings 17.17ff. Lys detects here a residuum of the primitive conception of the external soul (*op. cit.*, p. 125).

[8] With *l-ḳ-ḥ* and *'-s-p*: I Sam. 24.12; I Kings 19.4; Jonah 4.3, etc.; Ps. 26.9.

the living possesses *nepeš*,[1] and when he has killed must therefore give his own *nepeš* for that of the other person.[2] It is easily understandable that the blood should be pre-eminently the vehicle of the *nepeš*, so that it can be stated quite categorically that the blood *is* the *nepeš*.[3] Whoever loses his blood also loses his life. It is pointless to try to evade the naïve identification of the two entities by thinking of the *nepeš* as the principle of life which is intimately connected with the blood.[4] It is the distinguishing feature of Israelite as of all other primitive thinking that it makes no difference between spiritual principle and physical manifestation, but sees life manifested as a totality in the blood, just as it can also be represented by other parts of the body (cf. the sections on Flesh, Heart, etc., below).[5] In the same way the root *nafs* in Arabic may be used simply to denote the blood.

At this point the relationship of *nepeš* to the concept of *rūaḥ* as the universal breath of life, supra-individual in character, is perfectly clear. If *nepeš* is the individual life in association with a body, *rūaḥ* is the life force present everywhere and existing independently over against the single individual.[6] We might say that the same force is considered from different points of view. The vital element considered as *principium*, effective power, is called *rūaḥ*; the same thing as realized in the creature, and active, that is as *principatum*, is called *nepeš*.[7] If *nepeš* is individual, and comes to an end with the death of the individual, *rūaḥ* is universal, and independent of the death of the creature; it does not die.[8]

[1] II Sam. 1.9.

[2] Ex. 21.23; cf. I Kings 19.2; Judg. 9.17; Josh. c.24.

[3] Deut. 12.23; Lev. 17.14. Another way of expressing this is to say, the *nepeš* is in the blood, Lev. 17.11; cf. Gen. 9.4. D. Lys would like to see a shift in the understanding of the concept in progress here, making the *nepeš* into a sacred substance in Man, the preservation of which from pollution is to be the prime concern of the pious, and which is not completely lost to him even in death, but gives him a special character there, too (*op. cit.*, pp. 163ff., 169f.). Yet in view of the total disappearance of this conception in later Judaism it must be asked whether this is not to read too much into the identification with the blood.

[4] So J. Schwab, *op. cit.*, pp. 23f.

[5] Cf. J. Pedersen, *Israel* I–II, 1926, pp. 171f.

[6] Cf. pp. 47f. above.

[7] Cf. A. Dillmann, *Handbuch der alttest. Theologie*, p. 359. Nevertheless this must not be understood without qualification, as though *nepeš* could be regarded as an effect of *rūaḥ*. Thought certainly tends to link up the two entities in this way; but the connection is nowhere explicit in the Old Testament. Rather do the two concepts stand independently side by side.

[8] Hence Lichtenstein's remark about the *nepeš* (*Das Wort nepeš in der Bibel*, 1920, p. 62): 'It is in itself imperishable, and lives for ever', in fact applies only to the *rūaḥ*, and to that precisely in so far as it possesses supra-individual character.

Nepeš undergoes a minor extension of meaning, but one implicit in the logic of the concept, when it comes to denote not just the life within the individual, but *the living individual himself*.[1] When describing the execution of the ban on conquered cities the victims of the extermination may be specified as *kol-hannepeš*, every living being.[2] In the taking of a census the persons counted were designated simply by *nepeš*, rather as we today might speak of 'seventy souls'.[3] This is especially the usage in Hebrew when referring to slaves;[4] but the individual is also described in this way in legal contexts.[5] Here the aspect of the concept which makes it the characteristic term for the individual has become so predominant that *nepeš* even comes to mean a single being without qualification, regardless of whether it is alive or not; one is simply speaking of the individual. The recollection of the original meaning has here been so completely eradicated that a special qualification is added to indicate whether the individual in question is alive or dead: *nepeš ḥayyā*, the living being, is opposed to *nepeš mēt*, the dead one, the corpse.[6] The *locus classicus* for this phase of the semantic development is Gen. 2.7, which describes how Man by insufflation of the divine breath becomes a living being, *lᵉnepeš ḥayyā*. Here *nepeš* is obviously not meant as a *tertium quid* between spirit and body, but denotes the totality which has come about through the combination of the body formed out of the earth and the divine breath breathed into it. In the same way the expression *nepeš ḥayyā* is used of the animals.[7]

---

[1] Gen. 14.21; Deut. 24.7; Jer. 2.34; 43.6; Ezek. 17.17; Prov. 28.17.

[2] Josh. 10.28, 30, 32, 35, 37, etc.

[3] Gen. 46.15, 18, 22, 25–27; Ex. 1.5; Deut. 10.22; Num. 31.35, 40; Jer. 52.29, 30.

[4] Gen. 12.5: *hannepeš ᵃšer ʿāsū bᵉhārān*, 'the souls (i.e. the slaves) that they had acquired in Haran'. Similarly Gen. 36.6; Ezek. 27.13; Lev. 22.11.

[5] Gen. 17.14; Ex. 12.15, 19; 31.14; Lev. 4.2; 5.1, 2, 4, etc.; Num. 19.13, etc. This usage occurs with striking frequency in Ezekiel and in the Priestly Code. Undoubtedly what is here particularly in mind is the individual in his responsibility toward God, possessing a God-given 'potency' which ought not to be polluted by sin.

[6] Num. 6.6; Lev. 21.11 (conj.), cf. Num. 19.13. *Nepeš* is used without qualification to denote the corpse in Lev. 19.28; 22.4; Num. 5.2; 9.6, 7, 10. The false rendering 'the soul of a dead person' can only be arrived at by disregarding the opposition of *nepeš ḥayyā* and *nepeš mēt*. In none of these passages is there any allusion to a spirit of the dead; moreover, spirits of the dead are never referred to as *nᵉpāšōt*. On this subject cf. further ch. XIX below. The coupling of *nepeš* with the masculine form *mēt* indicates that the latter is substantive in character, and is used in the sense of 'death': cf. Lys, *op. cit.*, p. 164.

[7] Gen. 1.20f., 24; 2.19; 9.10, 12, 15; Lev. 11.10, 46. The fact that P does not apply the phrase to human beings shows that he is using it with a special nuance, in which *ḥayyā* likewise appears to be employed in a substantive sense, meaning 'life': cf. A. R. Johnson, *op. cit.*, p. 23, n. 2.

This predominance of the individualistic reference in the concept comes out most sharply when *it is used in place of the personal or reflexive pronoun*. This does not mean that it has become merely a colourless pronoun; in such instances a certain solemnity or special emphasis is always in mind. Thus, although this usage is found in all the Old Testament writings, it is especially popular in the poetic books, when the singer wishes to recount his personal experiences, sufferings and triumphs,[1] or in the admonitions of prophets and lawgivers.[2] Particularly distinctive is the practice of the Psalmist in addressing himself as *napšī*, setting his whole being over against himself as a kind of higher ego (Pss. 42.6, 12; 43.5; 62.6; 103.1f., etc.). The intention of laying solemn emphasis on the person of the speaker is naturally all the more actively present when it is God who speaks of his *nepeš* or swears by it.[3]

The use of *nepeš* to mean the individual life also gives rise, however, to *a second line of semantic development*, the outcome of which is to place the whole emphasis not on the element of individuality but on that of being alive. As an expression for this fact of being alive, for vitality, *nepeš* covers *every type of wish, desire or vital urge*. Thus *nepeš* is manifested in the desire for food and drink,[4] in the reproductive impulse,[5] and in wishes of every other sort.[6] Conversely the feelings of satiation and refreshment are ascribed to it.[7] Because *nepeš* is regarded in this way as the subject of physical impulses, it may in the end itself become a designation for greed or, passively considered, for sensation. 'Man's life, his vitality, has then become as it were identical with his desire or his feeling'.[8] Hence the greedy man is described as *ba'al nepeš*[9] or *'az nepeš*,[10] the possessor of appetite or the man of strong appetite. When the Psalmist is afraid in face of his enemies' measureless hate and yearning for revenge, he asks God not to give him up to the *nepeš* of his opponent.[11] But passive excitement also may be called

[1] Gen. 49.6; Pss. 3.3; 11.1; 35.7; 88.15; 120.6; 142.5; Lam. 3.58, etc.
[2] Isa. 3.9; Jer. 3.11; 37.9; 42.20; Ezek. 4.14; Lev. 11.43f.; 20.25; Deut. 13.7; Prov. 11.17.
[3] Jer. 5.9, 29; 9.8; Amos 6.8.
[4] Deut. 12.15, 20f.; I Sam. 2.16; Micah 7.1; Prov. 10.3; 12.10; 25.25; Ps. 107.9, etc.
[5] Jer. 2.24.
[6] Deut. 14.26; 18.6; I Sam. 23.20; Prov. 21.10; Ps. 10.3, etc.
[7] Pss. 23.3; 35.17; 63.6; 107.9; Prov. 6.30; Jer. 31.14; Lam. 1.11, 16, 19.
[8] J. Köberle, *op. cit.*, p. 208.
[9] Prov. 23.2.
[10] Isa. 56.11.
[11] Pss. 27.12; 41.3; Prov. 13.2, cf. Pss. 17.9; 35.25.

nepeš, where we would speak of 'feeling', 'emotion' or 'mood'. Hannah pours out her *nepeš* before God;[1] and when the lawgiver seeks to awaken sympathy for the unprotected alien, he recalls Israel to her own experience: 'you know the *nepeš* of a stranger'.[2]

The aspect of vitality in the concept of the *nepeš* becomes still more accentuated when the term is used to refer to *feelings and emotions of a spiritual kind*. Grief and pain,[3] joy and peace,[4] longing and love,[5] hatred and scorn,[6] loathing and weariness,[7] all are felt by and expressed in terms of the *nepeš*. Where these emotions occur, that is a sign of the presence of the *nepeš*. The use of the word 'heart' in English often presents analogies to this sense of *nepeš*; and it is certainly true that when used in this way to denote the subject of psychical sensations *nepeš* has become something like *a spiritual potentiality in Man*, and has moved closer to our concept of 'soul'. Nevertheless it is still clear that the Hebrew mind, when using the term *nepeš*, was far from conceiving of a soul in the sense of a spiritual *alter ego* of the physical person. What the Hebrew sought to express was rather that the impulses and emotions in question were manifestations of the vital energy within the person, being closely bound up with the life of the individual, and only existent in it. Finally this is also true of the highest psychical expression ascribed to the *nepeš*, the longing for God. A man may lift up his soul to God;[8] the soul may wait and hope,[9] yea, thirst and be consumed with desire for God;[10] but when consoled by him it exults[11] and rests in its God.[12] Even if, in a number of these passages, no more is implied than a special emphasis on the subject who is speaking—*nepeš* thus being a substitute for the personal pronoun—nevertheless the use of *nepeš* still renders the tone of these statements more intense.

There is here very plainly a marked parallel to a similar usage of

[1] I Sam. 1.15.
[2] Ex. 23.9.
[3] Cf. the instances where *nepeš* is coupled with the root *m-r-r*, to be bitter: I Sam. 1.10; 30.6; Ezek. 27.31; Job 27.2; Prov. 31.6, etc. For the *nepeš* bowed down and anxious cf. Pss. 42.6, 7, 12; 43.5; 107.26; Prov. 21.23; Pss. 6.4; 143.12; Isa. 15.4.
[4] Pss. 86.4; 94.19; Jer. 6.16; Lam. 3.17.
[5] Ps. 63.2; Gen. 34.3; 44.30; I Sam. 20.17; S. of S. 1.7; 3.1ff.
[6] Isa. 1.14; Ps. 11.5; Jer. 15.1; Ezek. 25.15; 36.5; Isa. 49.7.
[7] Job 10.1; Jer. 6.8; Ezek. 23.17f.
[8] Pss. 25.1; 86.4; 143.8.
[9] Pss. 33.20; 130.5f.
[10] Pss. 42.2f.; 63.2; 84.3; 119.81; 143.6; Lam. 3.25.
[11] Pss. 34.3; 35.9; 103.1f., 22; 104.1, 35; 146.1; Isa. 61.10.
[12] Pss. 62.2, 6; 63.9.

rūaḥ;[1] and certainly in later times the distinction between the two concepts in such cases was no longer always clearly perceived. Nevertheless here too, if the history of the concept is carefully traced, the root idea will still be felt to be that of a strong impulse of desire or emotion, and its satisfaction, thus indicating the narrow dividing-line between the concepts of *nepeš* and *rūaḥ*, which still exists even if it may not always be possible to discern it in particular cases. Thus the affective states attributed to the *rūaḥ* evince no sort of physical or animal character; and likewise it is significant that the *rūaḥ*, even where it is presented as the power behind the life of animals, is never associated with the blood, nor does one ever speak of the individual *rūaḥ* of an animal. Moreover, in the sphere of higher psychical activity the *rūaḥ* far transcends mere desire and feeling—the proper field of the *nepeš*—and is depicted as the 'impetus and energy behind willing and acting',[2] something which actively urges to good or evil; and as the seat of ethical attitudes it comes directly under the influence of God.

However clearly the broad outlines of the semantic history of *nepeš* may be discerned, a problem nevertheless remains in arriving at a more precise definition in any particular case. This is closely connected with the fact that for the most part the various meanings cannot be distributed among different periods, but overlap and are used side by side, so that unless care is exercised one can end up by making contradictory statements. It may, however, be taken as an assured conclusion that in no instance does there underlie the use of *nepeš* that conception of an immaterial *alter ego*, the origins of which have perforce been assumed to lie in primitive observation of the breath or the shadow, or in men's experiences of dreams, visions, sickness and death. This theory is as little verifiable in the case of Israel as it has proved susceptible of confirmation for primitive peoples. Equally remote from the concept of *nepeš*, however, is the signification of a numinous substance in Man which survives death and forms the necessary presupposition of a cult of the dead such as flourished in Canaan among Israel's neighbours. The vital force connoted by *nepeš* has no independent numinous character, but is the gift of the Creator to the creature. It remains susceptible to the grip of death, and can offer no protection against this ultimate limit set to life in fellowship with God. Despite this, however, the usage of *nepeš* reflects

[1] Cf. p. 133 above.
[2] R. Smend, *Lehrbuch der alttest. Religionsgeschichte*[2], 1899, p. 441.

the glory and richness of the life bestowed upon Man, and does not result in a pessimistic attitude toward the creation. This places the question both of the pre-existence and of the immortality either of Man or of a part of him in a new light. More will have to be said on the latter subject below;[1] but even at this stage it can be stated quite definitely that there is absolutely no evidence for any *pre-existence of the nepeš* in the sense of the Platonic theory of ideas. Herder[2] and others allowed themselves to be misled into this assumption by certain poetic images; thus the praise of Yahweh as being so powerful that he could bring down to Sheol and bring up again[3] they interpreted as implying a pre-existence in the realm of the shades, whereas the poet was thinking only of rescue from mortal peril. Job's lament over the lot of mankind—'Naked I came from my mother's womb, and naked shall I return thither'[4]—does not imply by the indefinite term *šommāh* either the earth, indicated by a gesture, or his mother's womb, which would suggest either reincarnation or rebirth, but the world of the dead, the name of which is for preference never explicitly mentioned, but only hinted at. Similarly the heightening of the divine miracle of creation—'My frame was not hidden from thee, when I was being made in secret, intricately wrought in the depths of the earth'—is a poetic comparison of the womb with the dark depths of the earth, an image to which the writer may, it is true, have been stimulated by acquaintance with a myth of the origin of human life in the womb of 'Mother Earth'.[5] It is entirely in keeping with what we have so far established about the concept of the *nepeš* as a vital potentiality indissolubly connected with the body that the Old Testament should know of *nepeš* solely in combination with the body not only in the creation story but also in the case of a man conceived in the ordinary way.[6]

What it has been possible to discover so far concerning both *rūaḥ* and *nepeš* has shown that we are not dealing with strictly defined concepts in systematic psychology, but with affirmations concerning

---

[1] Cf. chs. XIX and XXIV.

[2] *Vom Geist der Hebräischen Poesie* I, 1782, pp. 64ff.

[3] I Sam. 2.6.

[4] Job. 1.21.

[5] Ps. 139.15. Cf. the commentaries of Gunkel and Kittel *ad loc.* Ecclus 40.1 also seems to be no more than a conceit on an idea of the same sort. Torge (*op. cit.*, p. 33, n. 2) also assumes that the idea of the Earth as the All-Mother may have arisen in Judaism as the result of an influx of Greek culture. On the other hand, it cannot be shown to have been prominent in ancient Israel.

[6] On the change of outlook in later Judaism cf. below.

one and the same psychical reality considered now from one point of view now from another. The same conclusion will emerge from a glance at other psychological terms used not indeed so frequently but in an extraordinarily significant way to describe psychical processes.

III. *The breath* (*neš̄āmā*)

The normal term for breath, *neš̄āmā*, occurs only rarely as a metaphor to express psychical realities. It is used as a collective term for all living creatures, in the same sense as *kol-nepeš*;[1] and on one occasion, perhaps in a deliberately recherché usage, it represents human self-consciousness in a way analogous to the use of *rūaḥ* elsewhere.[2] This use of the term is not to be taken as evidence for a fundamental semantic development, for in every other instance the distinguishing mark of this word is its thoroughgoing retention of its basic physical meaning.[3] As God's own breath it shares with *rūaḥ* the signification of God's life-giving power in creation,[4] and also of the destructive breath of the divine anger.[5] In these instances it seems to have been used originally as the concrete popular expression, and later as a poetic synonym for *rūaḥ*. As this divine breath it is *nišmat ḥayyīm*, the breath of life, a phrase used by the Yahwist in the same sense as *rūaḥ ḥayyīm* by P.[6] The equation with *nepeš*, when it is introduced as a collective term for all living creatures, is purely superficial, an idiom to which a striving after greater elegance of expression may have contributed. The word never acquired any great influence in Old Testament psychology.

IV. *The heart* (*lēb*)

The intensity of the feelings, and their influence on all inner processes, is reflected in the very far-reaching importance which the heart, *lēb*, attained as an expression of the spiritual. That strong emotion was actually physically felt in the heart, either in the slowing-down or quickening of the heart-beat, in an intermittent pulse or in direct sensations of pain, must of itself have turned attention to this organ, and accorded it an important place in the description of

---

[1] Deut. 20.16; Josh. 10.40; 11.11, 14; I Kings 15.29; Ps. 150.6; Isa. 57.16.
[2] Prov. 20.27.
[3] I Kings 17.17; Gen. 7.22; Isa. 2.22; Dan. 5.23; 10.17.
[4] Gen. 2.7; 7.22; Isa. 42.5; Job 26.4; 27.3; 32.8; 33.4; 34.14.
[5] II Sam. 22.16; Isa. 30.33; Job 4.9.
[6] Cf. Gen. 2.7; 7.22 (where *rūaḥ* should be excised) with 6.17; 7.15.

psychical conditions. In fact, every survey of the linguistic evidence has shown[1] that there is hardly a spiritual process which could not be brought into some connection with the heart. It is made the organ equally of feelings, intellectual activities, and the working of the will. The fact that Accadian shows an exactly corresponding usage for the cognate word *libbu*[2] suggests that the employment of the term forced itself on primitive Man as axiomatic. The result in Hebrew, when feelings are in question, is a marked area of contact between *lēb* and *nepeš*. As regards joy and sorrow it is possible equally well to talk of 'strengthening the heart'[3] or 'refreshing the soul', of 'pouring out the heart'[4] or 'pouring out the soul'. Similar overlapping with *rūaḥ* was unavoidable. One can speak either of a 'broken heart'[5] or of a 'broken spirit', and describe pride as a lifting up either of the heart[6] or of the spirit. Nevertheless such turns of phrase are not the really distinctive element in the usage of *lēb*. The great majority of instances of the word refer to intellectual and volitional processes,[7] and it is this which gives it its distinctive stamp in Hebrew thought. When Hosea wishes to characterize the senseless political behaviour of the Northern kingdom, he says that Ephraim has no heart, that is to say, no understanding;[8] when Jeremiah wishes to stigmatize Israel's child sacrifices as utterly contrary to the will of Yahweh, he says that Yahweh never commanded it, and that such a thing never came into his heart.[9] This indicates where the emphasis lies, even when *lēb* acts as a comprehensive term for the personality as a whole, its inner life, its character.[10] It is the conscious and deliberate spiritual activity of the self-contained human ego which is meant, and this stands in perceptible contrast both to the strongly animal and instinctive

[1] Cf. Frz. Delitzsch, *Biblische Psychologie*[2], 1861, pp. 248ff. An absolutely complete survey of the occurrence of the word in the OT, with brief exegesis and classification of the various meanings, is to be found in F. H. von Meyenfeldt, *Het hart (lēb, lēbāb) in het Oude Testament* (Diss. Free University of Amsterdam), 1950.

[2] For proof of this cf. Frd. Delitzsch, *Assyrisches Wörterbuch*, 1887–90, p. 367.

[3] *sāʿad lēb*: Gen. 18.5; Judg. 19.5, 8; Ps. 104.15; *yiṭab libbekā*: I Kings 21.7.

[4] *šāpak lēb*: Ps. 62.9; Lam. 2.19.

[5] Ps. 34.19; 51.19.

[6] Ezek. 28.2, 5, 17; Ps. 131.1; Prov. 18.12.

[7] Wheeler Robinson assigns to these categories 204 and 195 instances respectively, 166 to the emotional life, and some 280 to the sphere of personality and character ('Hebrew Psychology', *The People and the Book*, ed. A. S. Peake, 1925, pp. 353–82). Cf. also C. Tresmontant, *Essai sur la pensée hébraïque*[2], 1956, ch. III, 1, 'Le coeur de l'homme', pp. 119ff.

[8] Hos. 7.11, cf. 4.11; Job 12.3; Prov. 15.32; Jer. 5.21.

[9] Jer. 19.5; cf. I Kings 8.17; 10.2; Isa. 10.7.

[10] Isa. 10.7; Prov. 3.1; 24.17.

character of the activity of the *nepeš*, and to the *rūaḥ*, which acts under overwhelming influences, and completely dominates men. Especially linked therefore with the operation of the *lēb* is *the element of responsibility*. That which comes out of the heart is quite distinctively the property of the whole inner man, and therefore makes him, as a consciously acting ego, responsible for it. Thus Isaiah's reproach against the soulless worship of his people is summed up in the saying that their heart is far from Yahweh.[1] A vivid description of the awakening conscience is the blow with which the heart, as the seat of the sense of responsibility, smites its possessor (I Sam. 24.6; II Sam. 24.10; I Kings 8.38). The reproach of conscience is an 'offence of heart' (I Sam. 25.31); the tormenting recollection of one's own evil deeds is kept stored up in the heart (I Kings 2.44; Eccles. 7.22); and conversely the heart of the innocent is aware of no evil within itself (Gen. 20.5; Job 27.6). To make inwardly one's own the will of God as revealed in the Law calls above all for a new heart.[2] The power of resistance and the quiet confidence of a self-sufficient personality is described as a firm or fixed heart, *lēb nākōn*,[3] while a divided or underhand character is *lēb wālēb*.[4]

It is this which determines the special overtones of *lēb* in those areas where its usage has points of contact with that of *nepeš* and *rūaḥ*. Whether in the matter of feelings or of moral conduct it is the interior direction of the will which is decisive for the use of *lēb*, even though the writer may no longer have been aware of this in any particular instance. Just as one speaks of hardness of heart and not of *nepeš*,[5] so a *rūaḥ nākōn*[6] is a steadfastness effected by a higher power, while a steadfast heart stresses more the expression of a personal will.[7] Thus, too, the intellectual activity of the heart occurs in close association with understanding and will; and because of this, knowledge is never simply that of the disinterested spectator, but is conveyed by energetic inner participation and decision.[8] Here the predominance of the will, which is decisive for Hebrew psychology, and more pre-

---

[1] Isa. 29.13. Cf. also the frequent phrases with *lēb* used to denote moral qualities: *lēb ne'emān, lēb nākōn, lēb ṭāhōr, lēb yāšār, lēbāb 'ikkēš*, etc. Cf. Frz. Delitzsch, *op. cit.*, p. 250.

[2] Ezek. 11.19; 36.26.

[3] Pss. 57.8; 108.2; 112.7.

[4] Ps. 12.3; I Chron. 12.33.

[5] Deut. 2.30; Ex. 7.3; Ps. 95.8.

[6] Ps. 51.12.

[7] Hence the use of *lēb nākōn* in the sense of uprightness: Ps. 78.37.

[8] Gen. 6.5; 8.21; Deut. 29.3; Isa. 32.4; Prov. 8.5; 14.10; 24.32.

cisely of the morally controlled and responsible will, finds eloquent expression, and from this standpoint throws a distinctive light on the psychic processes.

v. *Other parts of the body as organs of psychic processes*

Frequently found in association with the heart are *the reins (kidneys)*, *kᵉlāyōt*, which, as befits their situation especially deep within the body, serve to designate certain psychic processes as issuing from the innermost being, for ever unfathomable to Man. Only God is able to search and test the heart and reins;[1] and that he does so shows that his concern is not with external performance or service, but only with the surrender of the innermost man—hence it is no accident that the expression is a favourite with Jeremiah above all.[2] Similarly the distresses which strike a man in his reins are those which are especially profound;[3] and both the instruction that comes from within, and the deep inward sense of relief from anxious care, proceed from the reins.[4]

Very similar in pattern is the usage connected with *the bowels* (*mēˤîm, raḥᵃmîm*) as the seat of those emotions which agitate one most deeply, and are on occasion intensified to the point of actual physical pain, as in the tormented scream of Jeremiah at the mighty panorama of insurgent doom.[5] Hence one speaks of the seething, fermenting or troubling of the bowels.[6] Significantly an exactly parallel use of *lēb* and *nepeš* is also possible.[7] Moreover, as in the case of *nepeš*, the name of the organ can be used to represent the emotion, so that *raḥᵃmîm* by itself signifies compassion.[8]

The related collective concept, *ḳereb, the inward parts* (poet. *beṭen*) occurs in a more general sense. Both as the seat[9] and the organ[10] of psychic processes, and when used to denote these processes them-

[1] Jer. 11.20; 17.10; 20.12; Ps. 7.10; 26.2; Prov. 17.3; 21.2.
[2] Cf. also Jer. 12.2, where mouth and reins are contrasted in the same way as lips and heart in Isa. 29.13.
[3] Ps. 73.21; Job 16.13; 19.27; Lam. 3.13.
[4] Ps. 16.7; Prov. 23.16.
[5] Jer. 4.19.
[6] Job 30.27; Lam. 1.20; 2.11; Isa. 16.11; Jer. 31.20; S. of S. 5.4. Cf. the line from Goethe's *Mignonlied*: 'Es schwindelt mir, es brennt mein Eingeweide!' (lit. 'My head swims, there is a burning in my bowels').
[7] Jer. 4.19; 49.36; Ps. 42.6, 12; 43.5.
[8] Gen. 43.14; Deut. 13.18; II Sam. 24.14, etc.; cf. vol. I, p. 250.
[9] Zech. 12.1; Isa. 26.9; Ps. 51.12; I Kings 3.28.
[10] Isa. 16.11.

selves,[1] it contrasts them with the external world as events unfolding in Man's interior life, and so draws attention to the distinctive character and independence of the spiritual realm.[2] Of much less importance is *the liver, kābēd,* which in striking contrast to its frequent employment in Accadian seems to have attracted little attention from the Hebrews. To the extant references[3] may be added cases in which *kᵉbōdī* has been substituted for an original *kᵉbēdī,* still in places attested by the LXX.[4] As a vital centre and a seat of psychic sensations the word is less a designation for sensual passion[5] than a concept parallel to *lēb* or *nepeš,* in conjunction with which it is used synonymously.[6]

It is a striking fact that *the head* is completely missing from the list of psychological terms. Only in Daniel is there mention of 'visions of the head',[7] and here the thought is less of fantasy than of the physical setting of the eyes, and therefore of the organ of vision. The centre of reflective thought is always the heart. By contrast it may seem surprising to find *the bones, ʿeṣem, ʾᵃṣāmīm, ʾᵃṣāmōt,* as an organ of psychic life. Whether as the most solid and permanent part of the body they afforded an appropriate designation for the basic element of Man's psychic nature,[8] or whether as a manifestation of solid strength they became directly an expression for psychic energy,[9] in any case they provide a particularly forcible illustration of the immediacy with which the Hebrew conceived the physical as an expression of the psychical. The kind of psychological shock particularly described in terms of the bones was that which staggered the most powerful resources of the human spirit.[10] However, they were also used as a current idiom for the inner man in general.[11]

In view of this high value set on the physical aspect of Man it is no cause for surprise that *the flesh, bāśār,* is also found as the subject of psychic activity, as when it longs after God, rejoices in God, and feels

[1] Ps. 5.10.
[2] Cf. J. Köberle, *op. cit.,* p. 192.
[3] Lam. 2.11; Prov. 7.23.
[4] Pss. 7.6; 16.9; 30.13; 57.9; 108.2; Gen. 49.6.
[5] Only Prov. 7.23 calls for consideration in this connection.
[6] With *lēb* as the self-conscious ego: Ps. 16.9; similarly 57.8f.; 108.2; with *nepeš,* in the sense of life: Ps. 7.6.
[7] Dan. 2.28; 4.2, 7, 10; 7.1, 15.
[8] So J. Köberle, *op. cit.,* p. 193.
[9] So J. Pedersen, *Israel,* p. 172.
[10] Isa. 38.13; 58.11; Jer. 23.9; Pss. 6.3; 31.11; 32.3; 51.10; 102.4; Job 4.14; 30.17, etc.
[11] Pss. 35.10; 38.4; Prov. 3.8; 16.24.

pain in the underworld.[1] Hence it comes to denote virtually the person,[2] and 'all flesh' means every living being, both human and animal.[3] *Kol-bāśār* and *kol-nepeš* are used in the same sense.[4] For the fleshy parts of the body the Hebrews used *šeʾēr*, for the corpse *gūpā*, *gᵉwiyyā* and *peger*. *Bāśār* by contrast is the living body controlled by *nepeš*. Thus, just as with the *nepeš*, one can say: 'Man *is bāśār*.' In both instances the same reality is involved, namely the living human being.

VI. *Summary assessment of Old Testament psychology*

From the wealth of idiom to express psychological events which has been quoted it ought by now to be as clear as anyone could wish that Hebrew thought was not interested in a theoretical analysis of psychical phenomena, but was dominated by the effort to describe as vividly as possible the qualitative difference between the various psychic processes, and to throw into relief the feelings connected with them. The result is a treasury of turns of phrase which interlock in the most complex manner, an abundance of psychological terms which permit of putting into words a great number of often very delicate nuances in spiritual phenomena, but which resist systematic compilation and arrangement within a single framework. All that can be deduced is certain basic principles determinative for the Hebrew concept of Man.

The first thing to strike one is that, while the Israelite view of human nature is very clearly aware of the distinctive character of the life of the psyche as contrasted with the external physical processes, so that *bāśār* can occur in a certain opposition to *rūaḥ*, *nepeš* and *lēb*, nevertheless a strict dualism, which feels that flesh and spirit, body and soul, are irreconcilable opposites, is completely unknown. Instead the living body and its individual parts are so definitely thought of as organs and media of personal life that the person in his totality can express himself and be apprehended in any part.[5] The apparently independent activity of the various psychic organs and energies should not, however, deceive one into thinking that on this view human personal life was composed merely of a number of more or

---

[1] Pss. 16.9; 84.3; 63.2; 119.20; Job 14.22.
[2] Lev. 13.18; Eccles. 4.5; 5.5; Neh. 5.5.
[3] Gen. 6.13, 17; 7.15; Ps. 136.25.
[4] Gen. 6.13, 17; 7.15, 21.
[5] 'The Hebrew idea of personality is an animated body, and not an incarnated soul' (Wheeler Robinson, *op. cit.*, p. 362); cf. p. 143 above, n. 7.

less unrelated centres, with the result that the sense of unity in this loosely federated 'United States'[1] could only assert itself rather weakly, and the concept of personality evince no solid organization. On the contrary it is precisely the distinctive characteristic of Hebrew thought that it constantly sees the whole in the individual part, and even when apparently describing isolated expressions of vitality with a law of their own still has in mind the personal life as a totality.[2]

In a formal context Israelite psychology attaches importance to distinguishing between spiritual activity and passivity. The major psychological concepts clearly develop in the direction of a perceptible contrast between instinctive activity conditioned by the animal life (*nepeš*) and conscious spiritual activity (*lēb*), and between both and domination by the impact of forces from outside (*rūaḥ*). The conscious distinction thus drawn between impulse and will in human decisions and conduct indicates how the Israelites arrived at a clear formation of ethical concepts.

At the same time another line leads from emphasis on the individual and the particular, represented by the *nepeš*, to that which occurs universally and is available to all without distinction, as characterized by the *rūaḥ*. That the majority of psychological descriptions is devoted to the depiction of the subjective and individual is simply a consequence of the fact that the Hebrew method of observation was directed to the individual event.

However clearly *nepeš* and *rūaḥ* are here confronted, it is nevertheless impossible to comprehend them as two component parts of the spiritual nature of Man. They are excellent descriptions of the differing qualities of psychical events, but they are not in any way suitable terms for special capacities or areas of the psyche. Instead they always represent the whole life of the person from a particular point of view. A trichotomistic human psychology is therefore as little to be based on the Old Testament concepts as a dualistic one.

---

[1] Wheeler Robinson, *op. cit.*, p. 354.

[2] J. Pedersen (*op. cit.*, pp. 170ff.) is right to put the strongest possible emphasis on this. Similarly A. R. Johnson (*The Vitality of the Individual in the Thought of Ancient Israel*, 1949) has attached the greatest importance to demonstrating the relationship of all the various descriptions of bodily and psychic life to a spiritual totality, a unity of the person which subordinates everything to itself. A dissolution of this personal unity into independent spiritual spheres in accordance with the slogan, 'diffusion of consciousness', introduced by Wheeler Robinson, cannot therefore be maintained.

Of the greatest consequence, however, is the realism in biblical psychology, which brings the body into organic connection with the psychic life. Here we have an affirmation of human existence in the body, with all that follows from this. For the body is not an object which we possess, but which stands outside our real being; it is not simply the natural basis and instrument to which we are assigned, but which does not belong to our essential self. It is the living form of that self, the necessary expression of our individual existence, in which the meaning of our life must find its realization. Hence the body cannot be despised as the prison of the soul, or feared as the enemy of the spirit. On the other hand, it is equally not regarded in a materialistic light as the real man, a being who can find the goal and meaning of his existence in physical events. Instead it is understood as in all its parts the medium of a spiritual and personal life,[1] which stands under divine vocation, and finds its nobility in being God's image.

The repercussions of this holistic view of human nature on the shaping both of the God-Man relationship and of Man's relations with his world can be detected at every turn. Where Man knew nothing of an immortal soul-substance, he was bound to be conscious with peculiar immediacy of his constant dependence upon God as the only source of life in every peril. Equally the high value set on earthly goods appears in a new light, when we consider their direct connection with psychic realities. Likewise it becomes plain how deeply rooted is the strong sense of solidarity which binds the individual to family, race and nation, when it is realized that kinship according to the flesh was for the Hebrew at the same time a fellowship in the realm of the soul and all its forces which possessed decisive importance for human life (cf. ch. XX below).

But the lines extend even further, affecting Israel's views on sin and redemption. For it is a consequence of their outlook on the psychic life that sin cannot be explained one-sidedly as *concupiscentia*, the desire of the flesh, but must be understood as a reality of the psyche as a whole, drawing the body into sympathy with it. Hence redemption also must be accomplished in a bodily event. True worship lays claim not only to the soul, but also to the body, and endues the whole cultus with a special character; effective divine help must embrace the whole sphere of psychic life, and that includes the body;

---

[1] 'The proposition that the soul of man is flesh is indissolubly connected with the converse, i.e. that flesh is soul' (Pedersen, *op. cit.*, p. 178).

and if hope should dare to soar even to the conquest of death, then it can envisage such a thing not in the impossible form of the immortality of a spiritual portion of Man, but only in a new mode of existence for him as a whole.

It was left to Greek philosophy in the Hellenistic period to make a breach in this closed circle of attitudes.[1] Thus for the writer of II Maccabees the *rūaḥ* as the principle of life indwelling Man disappears in favour of a dichotomistic application of the concepts of *nepeš* and *bāśār* as the two components of human nature. In the Wisdom of Solomon *nepeš-ψυχή* becomes the imperishable substance which as an indestructible principle of life guarantees Man immortality;[2] it is pre-existent, and if equipped with good qualities also receives an unspotted body as its dwelling-place.[3] This, however, is understood as the lower part of human nature, weighing down the soul and clogging the spirit.[4] This alliance between the Old Testament ways of thought and the concepts of Alexandrian-Platonic philosophy led in Philo to a complete capitulation to the Greek view of Man. Nevertheless it is precisely this invasion of an alien spirit into the world of Old Testament thought which brings out even more clearly the irreconcilable opposition between the Israelite interpretation of human nature and philosophical psychology with all its logical consequences, and may therefore itself serve to train us in an objective evaluation of the ideas of the Old Testament.

[1] Cf. on this point J. Schwab, *Der Begriff der nefeš in den heiligen Schriften des AT*, 1913, pp. 79ff.
[2] Wisd. 2.22f.; 3.1f.; 4.14; 5.16.
[3] Wisd. 8.19f.
[4] Wisd. 9.15.

XVII

THE MAINTENANCE OF THE WORLD

THE OLD TESTAMENT LEAVES no doubt on the subject: By the creation the creature is entrusted with powers and gifts in the development and use of which he is called to lead a life of his own. Just as the earth, and likewise the sea, is endowed in its own sphere with the power of bringing forth plants and even animals as a permanent capability,[1] so Man has authority over a wide sphere of activity. Here he rules in the fullness of his own power, installed as lord over the created world,[2] called by the divine blessing at creation to people the earth by virtue of his natural fertility, and equipped to overthrow all obstacles to the spread of his sovereignty.[3] As regards the relation in which this life proper to the creature, established once for all at the creation, stands to God, the creation-concept in its Old Testament form already offers certain conclusions. On the one hand, by the concept of the creature, which is inseparable from the idea of creation, it presupposes the permanent dependence of the world on God, with no room for a detachment of the created thing from him who created it;[4] and on the other it shows that a necessary consequence of the act of creation is an historical process which finds its forward motive power in the permanent life-relationship of the creature with the Creator. Similarly the self-attestation of the Creator in his work by means of the teleology visible in the structure of the cosmos points to abiding values which the creaturely life strives to actualize, and which exclude the possibility that the world-process should be governed by capricious forces.[5]

---

[1] Gen. 1.11, 20, 24. Cf. the popular view that the stable cycle of natural phenomena is a once-for-all divine decree: Gen. 8.22.

[2] Ps. 8. 6–9.

[3] Gen. 1.28.

[4] Cf. pp. 99f. above.

[5] Cf. pp. 109ff. above.

Even though all this indicates the general direction in which Israelite reflection on the further history of the created order was bound to move, nevertheless there are still varying possibilities, differing in their religious value, as to the more precise definition and development of the basic elements of belief already contained in the idea of creation. The most important points involved here are indicated by the concepts of law in Nature, of miracles, and of Providence.

I. LAW IN THE NATURAL PROCESS

1. (a) An important element in Man's experience of the life proper to Nature is his observation of the inherent regularity of its events. Yet the whole character of Israel's approach to Nature would seem to be unfavourable to the acquisition of this knowledge, since she does not confront Nature objectively, but sees it from a strongly subjective angle as involved in every event of human life, and judges it from that standpoint. This applies both to the popular outlook and to that of the earlier prophets. We have already seen how Nature imposes definite demands on Man, and so exercises a regulating effect on his conduct.[1] But Nature is closely related to him not simply as the setting in which he has to work but also as the accompaniment and reflection of his activity and experience. Just as men know her to be involved with them in the destinies of their own nation, fighting in alliance with Israel,[2] rejoicing and clapping her hands at Israel's redemption,[3] and dismayed at her apostasy,[4] so she sympathizes with the people in their rejection, and from a state of desolation achieves a renewal of paradisal abundance when the broken bond between God and his people is mended once more.[5] Indeed, in her dealings with men, refusing them her gifts or bestowing them in willing service, Nature behaves in accordance with the pattern of God's own activity.[6]

Already in this vivid sense of *Nature as a living thing*, ascribing to the non-human creation a relationship with its divine Lord analogous to that enjoyed by the people of God themselves, may be seen the marked and direct connection of natural events with God, of whose

[1] Pp. 118f. above.
[2] Judg. 5.20; Josh. 10.12f.
[3] Isa. 35.1f.; 43.20; 44.23; 49.13; 55.12; Joel 2.21f.; Pss. 96.11f.; 98.8.
[4] Isa. 1.2; Jer. 2.12; 6.19; Micah 6.1f.; Deut. 32.1.
[5] Cf. vol. I, pp. 479ff.
[6] Hosea 2.20, 23f.; Job 31.38; Ps. 65.13f.

activity in history and in the life of his people they are the accompaniment. Hence the stage is nowhere reached at which the forces of Nature are credited with a mythological life of their own, as a result of which they might be able to assert themselves as independent entities over against God. It is certain that Israel knew of such mythological conceptions, partly from her own past, and partly from neighbouring peoples. But just as she made use of the traditional material purely as poetic decoration, so her personifying view of Nature evinced no capacity for producing new ideas of this mythical kind.[1]

(b) Conversely, however, it was possible just as spontaneously and axiomatically to portray natural events, which elsewhere might have been given an anthropomorphic life of their own, as *a direct act of God*, who controls both Nature and history by the omnipotence with which he fills all things. Thus the bestowal of rain and fertility is the direct gift of Yahweh; in the rain he blesses the field,[2] causes the plants to grow, and gives the animals their food;[3] he nourishes his people with fruits of the ground,[4] and punishes her by withholding them.[5] Just as he desires to be petitioned afresh every time for the blessing of children, which he grants or refuses,[6] so he himself forms the individual human being in his mother's womb, clothes him with skin and flesh, gives him the breath of life, and summons each new generation into existence.[7] The sick man recognizes his sickness as God's visitation,[8] the shipwrecked sailor sees him stirring the sea by means of the storm wind.[9] The earthquake comes from the blow of his fist,[10] the smoking volcanoes have felt his touch.[11] After the night he brings in the morning,[12] and holds sway over the course of the stars.[13] The regular return both of the seasons of the year with their gifts of harvest and of the comforting light of day after the dark of the night spring from the

---

[1] Cf. the fragments of the Chaos conflict-myth cited on p. 114 above.
[2] Gen. 27.27; Ps. 65.7–14; Jer. 5.24; 10.13.
[3] Pss. 147.8f.; 145.15f.; Job 38.39ff.
[4] Gen. 26.12; 27.28; 49.25; Hos. 2.10ff.; Ps. 107.35ff.
[5] Amos 4.6ff.; Ps. 107.33f., etc.
[6] Gen. 15.5f.; 18.10ff.; 25.21; 30.2, 8.
[7] Pss. 22.10f.; 90.3; 139.13ff.; Job 10.8–12; 31.15; Isa. 41.4; Mal. 2.10.
[8] I Kings 17.17f.; II Kings 20.3; Ps. 6.2ff., etc.: cf. Ps. 107.17f.
[9] Ps. 107.23ff.; Jonah 1.4.
[10] Isa. 9.7f.; Nahum 1.5; Job 9.6.
[11] Pss. 144.5; 104.32.
[12] Amos 5.8.
[13] Job 9.7, 9; Isa. 40.26; Ps. 147.4.

paternal care of the Creator, who even after the judgment of the Deluge wills to preserve his creature.[1] In everything his wonders may be discerned;[2] the pious soul, overleaping all intermediate causes, sees God forming the universe at every moment. This conception is strikingly expressed in the fact that the Hebrew language has no special word for the sustaining of the universe, but for both creation and preservation uses the verb *bārā'*.[3] It is hardly going too far to describe this Old Testament view of the maintenance of the world as *creatio continua*.[4] As opposed to similar expressions in Egyptian and Babylonian hymns,[5] the Old Testament statements naturally acquire a wholly new meaning through both the emphasis with which they are related to the one Creator God and the distinctive form of their idea of the Creator. Hence they give expression not only to the popular faith of early Israel, but equally to the prophetic outlook on Nature. For it was plainly of great moment to the prophets to perceive God's operation in Nature as closely and directly as in history.

II. It is implicit in the peculiar character of this view of the natural order, which fixes wholly on the individual event and places it within the mighty interplay of divine and human action, that men should find it hard to arrive at a disinterested attitude to the life of Nature as a whole and to its basic laws. This state of affairs changes *when Nature receives attention for its own sake as a work of God's creating and ordering*, the anthropocentric outlook thus making way for a cosmic one. This shift of standpoint is most strikingly worked out in the Priestly account of creation, in which the concept of the universe stands out as the dominating element. 'In a systematically planned hierarchy the component parts of the world here fit together into the cosmic whole as so many realizations of the divine thought in creation.'[6] Man, too, fits into this cosmos as one part alongside the others—even if the most privileged part—and is given his allotted task.

[1] Gen. 8.22.

[2] Job 9.10; Ps. 107.24.

[3] Ex. 34.10; Num. 16.30; Isa. 43.1, 15; 45.7; 48.7; 54.16; 57.19; 65.18; Ezek. 21.35; Pss. 51.12; 102.19; Eccles. 12.1.

[4] As rightly suggested by G. F. Oehler, *Theologie des AT*[3], 1891, p. 188. That the old-fashioned supranaturalism was able to discern in this, generally speaking, only the indirect operation of God, shows how far it had strayed from the biblical idea of creation; cf. E. König, *Theologie*[2, 3], pp. 208f.

[5] Cf. G. Röder, *Urkunden zur Religion des alten Ägypten*, 1923, pp. 7f.; 22; 62ff.; A. Falkenstein and W. von Soden, *Sumerische und akkadische Hymnen und Gebete*, 1953, pp. 80; 241; 249f.; 254f.

[6] P. Kleinert, 'Die Naturanschauung des AT', *Theol. Studien und Kritiken*, 1898, p. 16.

(a) In accordance with what has been said earlier[1] about the religious structure of the priesthood, and in particular about its predilection for the concept of regular order, it is readily understandable that it should be precisely in these circles that attention should be paid to the independent life of the universe, and should lead to the formulation of ideas of this kind. By the same token the most important extant pieces of evidence for this view of Nature occur in hymnic poetry, which, even if not used directly for the purposes of the cultus, was nevertheless influenced by the stylistic forms there developed. Of these hymns Pss. 8, 19A and 29 ought probably to be regarded as older than Gen. 1, while Pss. 104 and 148 belong rather to a later period. All these hymns are distinguished by the fact that they regard the marvellous life of Nature in itself, quite apart from Man, as a subject meriting enthusiastic description, and thus acquire an eye for the grand totality of the natural order. It is clear that what must have impressed the writers was the element of the unfailingly permanent, that which in spite of all flux and change possesses stability in itself and recurs in accordance with a regular system. It would seem, too, that foreign patterns from the hymnody of the ancient East contributed to this development[2] by directing the attention of the Israelite poets to a theme which originally was remote from their interests. Yet they were quick to bring the new subject-matter into line with Israelite feeling, and to permeate it with the spirit of the Yahwist faith. In Ps. 29 the individuality of early Israel is brought out most forcefully in the praise of the divine glory in the thunderstorm; while the other hymns display their sense of the overwhelming greatness, order and beauty of the cosmos, so far beyond Man's power to grasp that they leave him only the response of wondering reverence, in their solemn contemplation of the regular course of the stars,[3] the marvellous music of the spheres,[4] the firm control of the forces of Nature which allows them to move only in accordance with

[1] Vol. I, pp. 402ff.
[2] In the case of Ps. 19 the model seems to have been an ancient hymn to the sun; Ps. 29 may be compared with a hymn to the Babylonian storm-god Hadad (cf. M. Jastrow, *Die Religion Babyloniens und Assyriens* I, pp. 482f.), though one ought more probably to think in terms of a Canaanite Baal hymn, such as those suggested especially by Ugaritic parallels (cf. H. J. Kraus, *Psalmen* (Bibl. Kommentar Neukirchen. XV), 1959, 'Erklärung und Literaturangaben', pp. 233ff.). In the case of Ps. 104 the influence, possibly indirect, of the famous Hymn to the Sun of Ikhnaton has been clearly established.
[3] Pss. 8.4; 19.2, 5–7; 104.19; 148.3.
[4] Ps. 19.3–5.

fixed ordinances,[1] and the mysterious treasures in the great household of the natural[2] world. In face of the immensity and power of these works of creation Man cannot but be aware of his own infinite littleness, and bow himself in the dust.[3]

This cosmic outlook combines with the ancient Israelite view of Nature the constant reference of everything to the Creator as the origin and source of universal life. This is the point at which the ancient oriental models used by the hymn-writers underwent a decisive transformation. The personal will of the transcendent God deprives even the most impressive phenomena of Nature of independent significance, and makes them witnesses to the infinite power and wisdom of the one Lord. This is true even in the case of that most magnificent of all the products of Man's contemplation of the universe in the ancient East, Ikhnaton's Hymn to the Sun. There is no disputing the compelling power of this grandly conceived panorama of a world controlled by the goodness of God, in which every life, not simply that of Man, has its own autonomous necessity and justification. But the transcendence of the divine creative will, its essential difference from all intra-mundane powers, is obscured; and there is therefore no possibility of Man's arriving at a real spiritual fellowship with this divine sustainer of the world in a relationship of moral responsibility and decision, and the ethical contrast which bursts from the singer at the end of Ps. 104[4] remains beyond its ken.

Nevertheless the relationship between God and the world envisaged in this cosmic view of Nature also exhibits a significant difference from the popular outlook as developed by the prophets, in that *it understands God's sovereignty incomparably more emphatically as something indirect*, exercised through the operation of forces established once for all and guided in predetermined courses. The vision of an articulated universe, with its multiplicity of interacting and yet systematically coherent events, inevitably opened men's eyes to the stability of great complexes, and thus made them more or less clearly conscious of the rule of definite ordinances and laws in the cosmos.

(*b*) Various passages indicate that this awakening vision of the world did not remain a matter of no importance, but extended its influence into other spheres of thought. If the text already mentioned,

[1] Pss. 104.9; 148.6.
[2] Pss. 104.2ff., 25ff.; 148.7ff.
[3] Ps. 8.5; cf. Isa. 40.15, 17; Job 38.4ff.
[4] Ps. 104.35.

the Yahwist primal history, in its account of God's fresh initiative of grace to the earth after the Flood echoes the elevated language of the hymn,[1] its scope after all extends far beyond the immediate effects of the Deluge, giving praise for the constancy of the seasons as the great fundamental ordinances of life. It is, in fact, only the insertion of this proclamation of permanent universal laws into its present context which prevents its objectivity from becoming absolute, and makes it instead an expression of the divine care for Man.[2] The eschatological covenant with the animals in Hosea,[3] which undoubtedly pre-supposes a covenant made at the beginning of Time, should be under-stood not as an attempt to explain the regularity of natural pheno-mena[4] but quite certainly at a much more primitive level as an explanation of the distinctive character of the animals.[5] By contrast, from *the time of Jeremiah* onwards, a remarkable openness to regularity in the order of Nature is discernible. It is as though amid the storms which led to the shattering of the State and brought insecurity into every situation of life reflective thought had become especially sensi-tive to the serene uniformity of the economy of Nature. Thus Jere-miah praises the *ḥukkōt ḳāṣîr*, the settled ordinances of harvest, constituted by the regular cycle of autumnal and spring rains, as a special gift of Yahweh's goodness,[6] and points the erratic and unstable people to the punctuality with which the migratory birds arrive and depart.[7] Indeed, he even compares his God's unshakable disposition of love to the eternal ordinances, *ḥūḳîm*, revealed in the courses of the stars and in the movement of the sea.[8] The prophet already sees the divine cosmic order as possessing such autonomy that not only can he apply to it the same word as was used for the statutes of the Israelite covenant order, but he even contrasts it as a self-contained totality with the standards by which the world of men is governed, and claims it as a guarantee that the divine sovereignty will also be implemented in human history. In this way the popular parallel drawn between Nature and the life of mankind is raised from the level of a naïve and arbitrary connection to that of a relationship, the necessity of which

---

[1] Gen. 8.22.

[2] Procksch (*Die Genesis*[2, 3], p. 70) would seem to feel that the thought-content of this element in the narrative is not purely that of the Yahwist.

[3] Hos. 2.18 (MT 2.20).

[4] So Gressmann, *Der Ursprung der israelitisch-jüdischen Eschatologie*, 1905, p. 206.

[5] Eichrodt, *Die Hoffnung des ewigen Friedens*, 1920, pp. 89f.

[6] Jer. 5.24.

[7] Jer. 8.7.

[8] Jer. 31.35f.

is inherent in the essential nature of two realms supported by the same sovereign will.

(c) It is no mere coincidence that Jeremiah's occasional use of the cosmic element in his preaching should be in line with that clear grasp of the cosmos as an organism with laws proper to its own life which characterizes the *Priestly account of Creation* in Gen. 1. Here not only are Nature and Man seen as endowed with permanent capacities, not only are complementarity and mutual service brought out as a law of the universe in the purposefully interacting works of creation, but a clear distinction is also made between the origin and the continuance of the world, between creation and preservation, by concluding the Creation with the day of rest.[1] This results, moreover, in the formulation of a concept of great theological importance, namely that of *the constancy of the divine creative will*. By conferring on the work of his hands a life of its own the Creator stamps it, as it were, with the seal of his own approval, and raises it above the level of a worthless and ephemeral formation to that of a permanent existence. The creation is not merely a game of caprice, something which might equally well disappear again without trace, a divine fantasy, as in the Indian conception, but possesses a God-given right to existence in itself. Thus God's creative act is confirmed as the operation of a constant, purposeful will.

Quite clearly this conception is at *the opposite pole from the heathen world-view*. In the latter the attitude of the deity to the world is always incalculable and capricious. This stands out especially sharply if we compare the biblical and Babylonian sagas of the Flood. Among the Babylonians the reason for the cataclysm is the baseless rage of a god against the creation, in face of which even the celestial world is shaken. The only thing that prevents the annihilation of the created order is the superior cunning of another god. The biblical conception, on the other hand, sees in the Deluge precisely the means by which the divine plan in creation is brought to fulfilment. There is no question of an attack on the order of the universe, the cosmos: God's judicial action is directed against Man alone.

It is equally clear, however, that any idea of a regularity in Nature such as formed the basis of the ancient belief in Fate is rejected. In this belief Fate is greater than the gods. An incomprehensible but regular mechanism directs the continued existence of the world in order finally to guide it to its dissolution. By contrast the thought of

[1] Gen. 2.1-3.

the Old Testament believer penetrates to the idea of a divine founder of the natural order, who uses it to attain his own cosmic purpose, and, of course, remains at all times superior to it.

(d) This cosmic view of Nature exercises its strongest influence in *Deutero-Isaiah*. He not only sets the glory of the work of creation before the eyes of his people as a proof of the incomparable superiority of the power of the God of Israel to that of the gods of the heathen,[1] but also sees in that work an actual source of revelation, on which faith in God's power and will to redeem can feed.[2] For the Lord from whose control none of the countless glittering stars dares withdraw itself, and before whom the human race appear as grasshoppers and the mightiest nations as a drop in a bucket is also he whose righteousness brings all creatures within the scope of his covenant grace, and ushers in the new world in which salvation is fulfilled.[3] It is this which enables the prophet to take as the subject of his hymn precisely the solid, objective reality and magnitude of the marvellous system and purpose in the events of Nature. Nevertheless Deutero-Isaiah does not abandon the old idiom which spoke of God's direct operation in the events of Nature, but here, too, shows himself the inheritor of a great past, a thinker who knows how to synthetize opposing insights.[4]

The fertilizing and liberating effect of this new world-view on religious belief is shown by the willingness of the prophets to introduce references to the natural order and its uniformity. Side by side with fragments of liturgical hymns[5] occur more stereotyped turns of phrase which in the manner of Deutero-Isaiah employ the greatness of the creation in polemical argument against the makers of idols, or use it to encourage the pious.[6] Another distinctive conception is the mention of a *berit* of Yahweh with day and night, the firmness of which promises to the covenant with David an analogous continuance.[7] In fact, the same section even speaks of *ḥukkōt šāmayim wā'āreṣ* laws embracing heaven and earth, a phrase which makes it seem that the writer had arrived at something very like our own conception of

[1] Isa. 40.15ff., 22.
[2] Isa. 40.26.
[3] Cf. vol. I, pp. 246f.
[4] Isa. 41.18ff.; 43.19f.; 44.3; 48.21; 49.10f.; 50.2. For Nature as sharing rejoicingly in Israel's redemption cf. 42.10–12; 44.23; 49.13.
[5] To this category certainly belong the three passages in Amos: 4.13; 5.8; 9.5f. Cf. F. Horst, 'Die Doxologien im Amosbuch', *ZAW* 1929, pp. 45ff.
[6] Cf. Jer. 10.12f.; 32.17.
[7] Jer. 33.20.

laws of Nature.[1] The real interest of these statements, however, lies less in their maintaining the independence of the natural order than in their total subordination of it to God's power, a relation most appropriately expressed in the idea of a law imposed upon Nature. It may therefore be said that the order of Nature is considered only as the 'expression of God's omnipotent freedom'.[2]

(e) The *wisdom literature* takes over the cosmic view of Nature, but uses it in a different way by portraying the hypostatized Wisdom as the architect of the universe.[3] It is easily understandable that in this context the wisdom teachers should have in mind an emphasis on the objective and autonomous element in the marvellous structure of the world, even though elsewhere, in the popular manner, they like to use Nature as a mirror and instructor for human life.[4] For it was precisely as mistress of the miracles and mysteries of the cosmos that Wisdom was bound to acquire status and authority, and to find willing acceptance of her teaching.[5] On the other hand, however, this emphasis on the autonomous life of Nature, incomprehensible to Man, provided a welcome weapon for all those who saw in the overweening rationalism of the wisdom teachers a growing danger to clear knowledge of God and to genuine human self-surrender to him.[6] It was with this in mind that the author of Job 28 set the nature of the divine wisdom before his contemporaries as something inaccessible to the whole earthly order, and therefore also to men; and in the speeches of God in the same book particular emphasis is placed for preference on precisely those aspects of Nature which make a mockery of human insight or utilitarian calculation. It is the latter which call in question the rule of rational law in the cosmic order; instead they point to an autonomous value in the life of the universe, independent of Man, and so are able to bring men inward conviction of the ineffable glory of the Creator as the miracle transcending all other miracles.[7] By making precisely this profound sense of the alien character of the cosmic structure the point at which the call of the universal God to men is heard the writer points to the *absolute* quality

---

[1] Jer. 33.25.
[2] H. Schultz, *Alttestamentliche Theologie*[5], p. 453.
[3] Cf. Job 28.23ff.; Prov. 8.22ff. and pp. 83ff. above.
[4] Prov. 6.6ff.; 11.22; 16.24; 17.12; 19.12; 20.2.
[5] Wisd. 6.22; 7.17ff.; 8.3f.
[6] Cf. pp. 87ff. above.
[7] A more detailed discussion will be found in my paper on 'Vorsehungsglaube und Theodizee im AT', *Procksch-Festschrift*, pp. 65ff.

of the miracle of creation. Even the preservation of the world can be inwardly accepted as a witness to the Creator only by the man who comprehends it from within the covenant relationship, and is able to affirm it in the act of faith.

(*f*) The change in the evaluation of the autonomy of Nature which was accomplished in the work of Deutero-Isaiah received its most refined expression in the book of Ecclesiastes. Here *the alien and incomprehensible quality of the cosmos* has become so intensified that the regularity of its ordinances is no longer presented as an occasion for joy and wonder, but for 'weariness', profound disillusionment and dejection. It seems no more than the running of a soulless piece of precision mechanism having no understandable purpose, nor any share in the sufferings and desires, the torments and hopes of man-kind.[1] This is the 'vanity' of a natural reading of the cosmic riddle. Thus the very uniformity of the natural process is used to demonstrate that for all self-sufficient wisdom it must always remain ambiguous; and this ensures the effectiveness of a resistance already implicit in the Old Testament concept of creation to any attempt to transform it into that of a rational cosmic Mind. In this way Koheleth, as none before him, completes the de-personalization of the natural order, and so comes closest to the modern conception of the laws of Nature—except that he sees this not indeed as a triumph but as a limitation of the human spirit thrown back on its own resources.[2]

III. It is a significant fact about the Old Testament view of Nature that it succeeded in *combining both the basic types of outlook*. It was able to press its recognition of the autonomy of Nature to the point at which the natural order became totally alien to human understand-ing without, however, surrendering anything of God's direct opera-tion in natural events. It thus escaped the dangers that arise when either of these types is developed in isolation into a self-contained view of the universe—namely on the one hand, when God is extern-ally divorced from the world as in Deism, which knows only of a God who 'gives a push from outside' and then leaves the cosmos to its own laws, and on the other, when an enthusiastic mythologizing of Nature breaks down its regularity into arbitrary divine acts, and no longer sees any revelatory value in the great uniformities of creation. The former involves the surrender of the vital religious interest in God's

---

[1] Eccles 1.4ff.
[2] On the attitude of later Judaism to the cosmos cf. A. Bertholet, *Bibl. Theologie des AT* II, 1911, p. 406.

dealings with his creatures; the latter contains the threat of an emotional transgression of the limits implicit in the created order between God, who even in his revelation never delivers himself up to the desires of men, and the creature, who is meant to reverence the mystery of the divine majesty by keeping his place within his own order.[1] Once again we are pointed to a divine reality transcending human thought, this time by the combination of the priestly-static and prophetic-dynamic views of Nature which, though not, it is true, conceptually harmonized, are nevertheless pragmatically united as *the inseparable and mutually indispensable aspects of a religious interpretation of Nature based on the revelation of the covenant God.* Here, too, therefore, we find a state of affairs similar to that already encountered earlier in other contexts as a distinctive characteristic of the faith of the Old Testament.[2]

2. MIRACLE

I. The independent attitude which the faith of Israel maintained toward the laws of Nature also marks its approach to miracle. Throughout the Old Testament the miraculous is conceived in the widest possible terms. Even the course of Nature itself counts as a miracle.[3] This association of the miraculous with the activity of the Creator God is characteristic of the term *beri'ā*, lit. 'creation', that is, something resulting from the activity of the Creator.[4] Other terms for the miraculous characterize it as a manifestation of God's supreme power in extraordinary events. Thus it is called *pele'* or *niplā'ā*, in so far as it awakens astonishment,[5] *nōrā'* as it evokes terror,[6] *gebūrā* as a work of power,[7] and, by an analogous formation, *gedōlā* as a great act.[8] Frequently the miraculous is simply termed a 'deed', *'alīlā, ma'alāl,* or *ma'aśeh.*[9] Other designations common throughout the Old Testament

---

[1] On the subject of these dangers cf. my remarks on the priestly and prophetic types, vol. I, pp. 389ff. and 434ff.

[2] Cf. especially vol. I, pp. 286f., 387ff. and 433ff.

[3] Pss. 89.6; 106.2; 139.14; Job 5.9f.

[4] Num. 16.30; Ex. 34.10; Jer. 31.22; Isa. 48.7.

[5] Ex. 15.11; Isa. 25.1, and Ex. 3.20; 34.10; Josh. 3.5; Judg. 6.13; Pss. 71.17; 75.2, etc.

[6] Ex. 34.10; II Sam. 7.23.

[7] Deut. 3.24; Pss. 20.7; 106.2; 150.2.

[8] II Sam. 7.23; II Kings 8.4; Pss. 71.19; 136.4; Job 5.9; 9.10.

[9] Deut. 3.24; Ps. 86.8; Isa. 12.4; Pss. 9.12; 77.13, etc.

are *mōpēt* and *'ōt*, in the sense of the portentous or miraculous sign which points to an invisible power.[1]

11. It is precisely the terms last mentioned which indicate most strikingly *wherein lies the real importance of the miraculous for faith*—not in its material factuality, but in its *evidential character*. Indeed it is nowhere stated how a miracle is to be recognized, except that men find it new and surprising. God's marvellous activity is recognized even in ordinary everyday events, such as the blowing of the east wind at the right moment, so that the waves of the Red Sea are held back, or in the little incidents of life—the friendliness of a young girl, the folly of a disloyal son of the king, the unexpected overthrow of one's enemies.[2] Hence it is not, generally speaking, the especially abnormal character of the event which makes it a miracle; what strikes men forcibly is a clear impression of God's care or retribution within it. Least of all does it occur to the devout Old Testament believer to make a breach of the laws of Nature a *condicio sine qua non* of the miraculous character of an event, though marvellous occurrences in this sense are not unknown.[3] In contrast to our own scientific outlook, however, the Israelite does not think in terms of an unbreakable natural order such as would restrict even God's operation. For him the sun's standing still, or going back on its course, is on the same plane as the retreat of the Red Sea because of the God-sent east wind, or as the hailstorm which smites the fleeing Philistines. As a result a naïve and imperfect idea of the forces and laws of the cosmos may on occasion lead to misunderstandings and incorrect explanations of events experienced by the writer or handed down in tradition;[4] nevertheless the Israelite rightly sees in God's sovereign control of Nature, as manifested also in his miracles, proof that the created order is totally dependent on the will of him who called it into being. And he is in no doubt at all that there is no law of Nature which can

---

[1] Isa. 8.18; 20.3; Deut. 13.2; Ex. 4.21; 7.3, 9; 11.10; 12.13; 13.9; Judg. 6.17, 36ff.; Pss. 105.5; 135.9, etc.

[2] Gen. 24.12ff.; II Sam. 17.14; Ex. 14.21; I Sam. 7.10f.; 14.23, 45.

[3] Num. 16.30; Josh. 10.10ff.; II Kings 20.10.

[4] Thus the celebrated sun-miracle of Josh. 10 ought to be attributed to a literal interpretation of the purely poetic description preserved in an ancient song-fragment (vv. 12–14); and an eclipse of the sun probably underlies Isaiah's sign in II Kings 20.8–11. It is well known that in the case of other miracles, such as the plagues of Egypt, the passage of the Red Sea, the feeding with the manna, etc., simple natural phenomena have been elaborated in various ways in the oral tradition. Nevertheless this secondary elaboration of the miracle-stories does not affect their real point. The defective knowledge of Nature which has crept in in such cases should not be confused with defective religious judgment.

hinder God from enlisting the forces of Nature in his service. For the deity there are absolutely no limits to his power—hence the question: 'Is anything too hard for the LORD?'[1]

If, however, the real significance of the miraculous is that, like an outstretched finger, it points to God's invisible power, and so reveals God as ever near and controlling all things, then it is understandable that faith has at all times experienced miracles, and continues to experience them, while those who are alienated from God look for them everywhere in vain, and complain that such things are nowhere to be found. The man who knows God hears his step in the tramp of daily events, discerns him near at hand to help, and hears his answer to the appeal of prayer in a hundred happenings outwardly small and insignificant, where another man can talk only of remarkable coincidence, amazing accident, or a peculiar turn of events. That is why periods when the life of faith is strong, and men have enthusiastically surrendered themselves to God, have also always been times rich in miracles, even though there have been no world-shaking occurrences to record, whereas those epochs in which the strength of the religious life has diminished, so that God has become either a power far removed from the world in unapproachable majesty or an empty concept, are insatiable in their desire to experience miracles, and yet remain unsatisfied even when the most wonderful things are going on all around them.

With such an assurance of God's nearness it is understandable that the devout Israelite did not prescribe to his God how a miracle should be performed in order to count as a real miracle, but recognized the true value of the miraculous in its character as a σημεῖον. He was furthermore protected from an incessant hankering after the sensational by the conviction that something surprising and intriguing might very well proceed from forces other than God, and prove to be the work of sorcerers, or of other 'elōhīm-type powers.[2] Indeed, God might even allow a dangerous man to succeed in working a miracle once in a way, in order that God's worshippers might be put to the proof, to see whether they would remain loyal to his commands in all circumstances, or would allow themselves to be led astray.[3] Hence it is explicitly stated in the Law[4] that a miracle is not, and by itself

---

[1] Gen. 18.14; Deut. 8.3f.
[2] Ex. 7.11, 22; 8.7, 18; 9.11; II Kings 3.27.
[3] Deut. 13.2–4.
[4] Cf. previous note.

never can be, a sufficient proof that God has sent a man. Instead this evidence must be verified by its agreement with the nature of Yahweh as known from other sources. In this way the miraculous is co-ordinated with the divine holiness, the divine nature proper to Yahweh.[1]

III. Both these factors, the distinction between miracles worked by Yahweh and those called forth by powers at enmity with God, and the extension of the category of the miraculous to cover every event in which Yahweh's power is made manifest, preserve Israelite belief in miracles from a crude addiction to the marvellous and from the miracle without meaning or value. The crucial characteristic of the miraculous is that it is firmly connected with God's redemptive activity, as this is known from his words. It fits into the complex of God-directed history, so that it never occurs in isolation simply for its own sake, but as *a part contributing to a greater whole*.[2] Where God seeks to further the advance of his kingdom in the teeth of accumulated obstacles, to awaken faith, and to bring men to safety through hard times, there we see the miraculous become prominent in Israelite religion. Thus it plays a more decided and visible role in the critical periods of the kingdom of God—in the Exodus from Egypt, in Israel's unification to be a nation devoted to Yahweh's service, in the struggle of Elijah and Elisha against the seductions of the worship of the Tyrian Baal, flaunting itself in all the magic and glamour of cosmopolitan civilization, and in the threat to Jerusalem by the world-ruler Sennacherib.

At the same time it is precisely these events outside the ordinary run which make it clear that God does not work miracles either to satisfy curiosity or to back up human convenience or to protect his own from suffering in all circumstances, but rather to educate them in an unconditional trust which will then be secure in hard times even without special miraculous help. One might almost sum it up in a paradox: God works miracles in order to free his followers from the desire for miracles. And where God does not attain this goal the miracle burdens those who experience it with grievous responsibility, and constitutes a judgment upon them. It is noticeably the very miracles of the days of Moses, Elijah and Isaiah which are followed

---

[1] I Sam 6.20; II Sam. 6.6f.; Ex. 15.11; Ps. 77.14f.; Lev. 10.1ff.

[2] The same state of affairs comes to light when a general examination is made of the Old Testament concept of the power of God, and the way in which that concept develops: cf. Grundmann, *TWNT* II, 1934, pp. 292ff.

by the outpouring of God's judgment on their contemporaries, who wished to celebrate such wondrous events merely by merrymaking and to make use of them to gratify their own pride, while frivolously disregarding their real meaning, which was to lead men to God himself.

iv. Thus the miraculous fits *into the Israelite view of Nature* as an important, indeed *indispensable ingredient*. It confirms the complete dependence of the created order on its Creator without prejudicing that autonomous life which Nature leads as the possessor of divine powers. Moreover, it safeguards and guarantees to men a direct link with God which no elemental force or law of Nature can obstruct. In this way it speaks a language which every man can understand, which requires no esoteric knowledge for its interpretation, and is independent of subjective conviction.

On the other hand, Israelite faith successfully averted the *dangers* which threatened it because of this very belief in the miraculous. It did not allow it to lead to an abandonment of belief in the regularity of Nature, or to contempt for the will of the Creator as expressed in the natural order, or to the setting aside of the laws of Nature as something inferior and unworthy of God. What enabled them to avoid these errors was, of course, the fact that in addition to extraordinary events they also prized and lovingly studied the daily phenomena of the course of Nature and of human life as witnesses to the divine activity. Nature does not hide God, so that he can be observed only in happenings which are either outside Nature or contrary to it; it glorifies him. Equally, however, the other danger present in a belief in miracle was avoided, namely that Man would claim an exceptional position in the natural order, and set God's power over Nature constantly in motion in the interests of his own convenience or his own shrinking from pain. Here a strong defence was provided by the realization that the miraculous primarily serves the purposes of God's kingdom and of training men up to faith, and thus involves a serious responsibility for all those on whom it is bestowed.

This clear line was seldom overstepped in the Old Testament. Only a few miracle-stories show themselves inadequately accredited by the standards obtaining within the Old Testament itself, as, for example, I Kings 13 or many of the miracles in the history of Elisha,[1] in which the influence of the craving for wonders in nabistic circles

[1] E.g. II Kings 4.1ff., 38ff.; 6.1ff.

may be detected. It is, however, characteristic that a real addiction to the miraculous is found only with a slackening of religious strength. The apocryphal literature[1] and to some extent also the Chronicler[2] reveal the way in which, in the belief that the age of revelation has come to an end, miracles are required as a proof of every direct manifestation of God. Because contact with the divine realm has been lost in daily life, men think that they can find God only in the supernatural and magical. Judaism in the time of Jesus affords the clearest possible confirmation both of this and at the same time of the fact that this lust for miracles can never be satisfied. Given experience of the miraculous, 'the appetite' merely 'grows by what it feeds on'.[3, 4]

3. PROVIDENCE

The contemplation of God's working in Nature, particularly when prominence is given to the purposiveness of his ordinances, leads men to a concept which has always played a large part in theology, namely

[1] II Macc. 1.19ff.; 3.23ff.; 10.28ff.; III Macc. 2.21ff.; I Enoch 106; Vit. Ad. 46; the additions to Daniel. esp. Song of the Three Children, vv. 24ff., and Bel 31ff.; 36ff.; II(4) Esd. 13.44, 47.

[2] II Chron. 13.15; 14.12; 20.22ff.; 25.10ff.; 32.20f.

[3] Matt. 12.38f.; 16.1; Luke 11.16; John 4.48.

[4] It is really superfluous to emphasize that this assessment of the theological content of the Old Testament belief in miracles presupposes the necessary historical and critical work on the tradition of the miracle-stories, since the same is true of every chapter in this book. Nevertheless in this particular context a few remarks on this subject may save us the discussion of many detailed problems. Anyone who is aware, as a result of comparing parallel passages, of the gradual growth and elaboration of miracle-stories will adduce neither the sun-miracle at the time of Hezekiah's sickness (II Kings 20.8–11 and Isa. 38.7f.) nor the miracle-stories of Chronicles and Daniel as typical for Old Testament belief in the miraculous, nor in general will he make his overall assessment on the basis of the individual miracle-story and its external authentication. The decisive factor in any evaluation of the miraculous elements in the so-called primal history of Gen. 1–11 is the recognition that in this series of narratives we are not dealing with historical tradition, properly speaking, at all, but with a prophetic interpretation of history, which has made out of the material of ancient myths something entirely new and not to be found in any other nation, namely a magnificent survey of the basic presuppositions of human history, presuppositions which themselves rest on decisions transcending the historical. Hence the aspects of these stories which deal with the natural order are removed from the scope of historical evaluation. Because, however, they partake of the general deficiencies of the knowledge of Nature in the ancient world, it is possible for them to relate certain things without any special sense that they are abnormal, whereas a more mature knowledge appreciates their impossibility—as, for example, in the matter of the more detailed circumstances of the Flood story, etc.

that of divine Providence. Nevertheless, even though this concept may sometimes be applied to the whole world-sustaining activity of God, it will be more practical here to restrict it to God's guiding of human destinies.

1. *The development of belief in Providence*

(*a*) As a conceptual formulation divine Providence occurs in only one passage in the Old Testament, namely Job 10.12, which speaks of the *pᵉkuddā* of God; that is to say, his superintendence or care by which creatures are preserved.[1] Yet it is with this subject as with many others: the words are not found, but the substance is there. And certainly it was *from the history of his own nation* that the Old Testament believer *first grasped* what God's Providence was about.[2] For the exodus from Egypt, the wandering in the wilderness, and the conquest of Canaan constituted from of old the great fundamental facts of Israel's faith, in which were illustrated not only God's victorious power but also his care for his people, a care which extended even to the individual, and on which confidence in his further help and guidance was founded. It was from these basic experiences of the community that all later historical developments acquired their meaning as acts of Yahweh directed to the establishment of his sovereignty. Hence through all the narratives of Israel's history there blows a religious spirit; and even where considerations of religious edification are as decidedly in the background as they are, for example, in the greater part of the David story (II Sam. 9–20), nevertheless a reverential wonder in face of the exalted power of God can be clearly detected in the narrative as a whole. But it was particularly in the stories of the Patriarchs that the Israelite story-tellers loved to provide their people with illustrations of divine Providence. They were never tired of relating how in the destinies of these favourite figures of popular saga even the evil in life, indeed men's very sins and perversities, were guided to a good end. The history of the Fathers is full of such examples; there is no need to recall more than the abduction of Sarah (Gen. 12, and the parallels in chs. 20 and 26), the whole Jacob saga, with its themes of testing, purifying and blessing, and the story of Joseph. In individual passages, it is true, the level

[1] In the Apocrypha occur the terms πρόνοια and προνοεῖν: Wisd. 6.7; 14.3; 17.2.

[2] This section adheres closely to my earlier remarks on this subject in the essay, 'Vorsehungsglaube und Theodizee im AT', *Procksch-Festschrift*, 1934, pp. 45ff. Cf. also F. Nötscher, *Gotteswege und Menschenwege in der Bibel und in Qumran* (BBB 15), 1958.

may vary. Sometimes in the Abraham and Jacob narratives, as told by the Yahwist, the moral element is in the background, and simple joy at the triumph of the friend of God predominates; but the Joseph story in particular is the classic expression of a morally profound belief in Providence: 'As for you, you meant evil against me; but God meant it for good, to bring it about that many people should be kept alive, as they are today' (Gen. 50.20). What holds good in every case, however, is that it is the agent of God's plan in history who is seen to be safe under the special protection of the God from whom he has received his commission. It is not just any favourite of the deity, but the man who is entrusted with a great historical mission who stands under the *providentia specialis* of Yahweh. If the Yahwist narrator deliberately sets out to portray the story of Abraham as a series of surprises, in which Yahweh is constantly bringing human hopes and expectations to nought in order thereafter to grant his own salvation in ways men had never hoped for, he does so because he wishes to illustrate clearly God's purposeful dealing with the agent of his saving counsels. The same applies to the youth of Moses (Ex. 2) or of Samuel (I Sam. 1), to the description of Saul's enmity against David, and so on. Certainly the great leaders and protagonists of the nation's future are generally also the moral characters, but the main stress is laid not on this but on the purposeful dealings of God in the execution of his designs.

(*b*) This belief in Providence, which grew out of the experience of Yahweh's historical dealings with his people, inevitably affected also Israel's *view of the Gentile world*. It is true that they did not at once extend to their consideration of the fortunes of foreign nations that which they had experienced in their own destiny, and draw the logical conclusion of God's unified government of the world. Generally speaking, Yahweh's guidance of the destinies of these other peoples only entered the sphere of faith in proportion to Israel's direct contact with them. Nevertheless within this framework all their statements about Yahweh's control over the nation are, in fact, shaped by their own experience of his direction of history. Because Israel has been promised Canaan as her dwelling-place, the Canaanites must experience Yahweh's overwhelming power, and endure punishment for their godlessness.[1] Because Pharaoh opposes Israel's departure, he is humbled by Yahweh.[2] Here and there, too, the view is found that the

[1] Gen. 15.16; Deut. 9.5.
[2] Ex. 7.14ff., 23; 8.4ff., 24ff., etc.

nations are bound in the sight of God by a universal moral law which brings them all within the sphere of Yahweh's operation, as when the expulsion of the Canaanites is explained in terms of their sin,[1] or when the cry of the iniquity of the Sodomites comes up to Yahweh, and induces him to intervene.[2] Undoubtedly this sense of a moral obligation binding on all peoples introduced a very important element which effectively prepared the way for a comprehensive understanding of the destinies of the nations. A pointer in the same direction is the unreflecting extension of Yahweh's judicial authority to the whole earth in the primal history stories of the Deluge and the Tower of Babel; and again the conviction of the common origin of all peoples, in virtue of which they really form one great family, which has led to the one and only attempt known to us from antiquity to demonstrate this, the Table of the Nations in Gen. 10. For the most part, however, this goes no further than isolated instances of a rather haphazard application of these convictions to the fortunes of Israel's neighbours. The level which other ancient peoples with their belief in certain basic and universal divine laws also attained was not in practice surpassed.

This atomistic view of God's judgment on the nations, simply in accordance with whichever of them was the adversary of the moment but without reference to the totality of their destinies either in the past or in the future, was significantly surpassed in only one context, namely that of reflection on the goal of history. It is true that even here the relationship of Yahweh to the Gentiles remains sometimes a rather negative one. The ancient oracles of blessing in Num. 23 and 24 know only of their overthrow, and the Psalms which celebrate the king as divine redeemer and bringer of the age of salvation speak less of a positive guidance of the nations' destinies by Yahweh than of their humbling themselves before Yahweh's representative on earth as a condition of escaping judgment.[3] But side by side with these ideas we find from the first that of the bestowal of blessing on the Gentiles, a prospect strongly emphasized in the terms of God's blessing on the patriarchs,[4] and known also to the Messianic hope in the strict sense of that term.[5] In other words, precisely at the point where Israel's faith in the special divine direction of her history found its

[1] Gen. 9.22; Lev. 18.24ff.; Deut. 12.29ff.; 18.12; 20.18.
[2] Gen. 18.20f.
[3] Pss. 2.9ff.; 21.10f.; 45.6; 110.5ff.
[4] Gen. 12.2f. and parallels.
[5] Gen. 49.10.

boldest expression the destiny of the other groups of mankind was stoutly grappled to her own by the belief that they, too, at any rate in the end-event of their history, would be seen to be equally the objects of divine Providence. For the present, however, God lets the nations go their own way; as one passage puts it,[1] he has given them the stars to be their gods, and abandoned them to the hosts of heaven.

It was prophetism which first taught Israel that Yahweh takes the nations into his service in the present as well. The way to this realization was certainly prepared by the closer alliance with the Syrian group of states which from the days of Omri and Ahab onwards determined Israel's foreign policy. The internationalist tendency of the time not only resulted in increasing economic and cultural exchange, but also opened the way to religious influences and re-actions,[2] and could also make the positive value of foreign national characteristics appear in a new light. The decisive factor, however, was the prophetic recognition that Israel was not fulfilling her mission as the agent of Yahweh's sovereignty, charged with realizing the divine plan for the world, and that therefore God would call other nations into his service. The circles of Elijah and Elisha had already ceased to regard the Arameans simply as national enemies, and acknowledged them as Yahweh's rods of correction prepared for his degenerate people;[3] and they were followed by Amos, who put Israel's history in the setting of the history of other nations, and pointed out emphatically that they were guided by Yahweh's will in a similar way. Not only was Israel on a par with the heathen as regards the divine word of judgment, inasmuch as both were to meet with punishment (Amos 1 and 2), but the heathen had equal value with the Israelites as objects of Yahweh's care: ' "Are you not like the Ethiopians to me, O people of Israel?" says the LORD. "Did I not bring up Israel from the land of Egypt, and the Philistines from Caphtor and the Syrians from Kir?" ' (Amos 9.7).

It was Isaiah, however, standing as he did on a watch-tower too high for other men to scale, who had a vision of the divine Providence in its full universality. At that moment of world-history when the dominant power of Assyria was breaking up the old fabric of the Near Eastern states in order to build her own empire it was given to

[1] Deut. 4.19, cf. 32.8f.

[2] Thus side by side with the invasion of Israel by the Tyrian Baal there is the extension of prophetic influence to Phoenicia and Damascus: I Kings 17.8ff.; II Kings 5; 8.7ff.

[3] I Kings 19.15ff.; II Kings 8.10ff.

this prophet to perceive in the fearful work of destruction the far-seeing and constructive plan of his God, who willed to lead the nations not into the house of bondage of the Assyrian overseer but into the Father's house of the divine world-ruler. It was not Israel alone who had her special task; Assyria, too, had been furnished with a particular commission which assigned her her place in the great οἰκονομία τοῦ κόσμου (Isa. 10.5ff.). Each refused her allotted service. But the wisdom of God proceeded to make use of even the rebellious and resistant as instruments to attain its goals.[1] Thus that which confronted the prophet in concrete individual events was revealed to him as the meaning of the whole world process; it was penetrated by a systematic movement, incorporating all nations in order to construct the βασιλεία θεοῦ, the kingdom of peace and righteousness,[2] as described in the noble vision of Isa. 2.2–4. In this world-wide refashioning of things, however, Jerusalem has her importance only as the place where the foundation of the great structure is laid; for here the faithful community forms the precious cornerstone, supporting the work which Yahweh has established. In this vision Israelite belief in Providence is filled with universal content, and a positive evaluation of history becomes possible, with the help of which even grievous disasters can be not only endured but treated as constructive factors in world-events.

Isaiah's successors, too, see God's direction of history within this grand perspective. Jeremiah was able to proclaim the ruin of his people in terms of Yahweh's charging his servant, Nebuchadrezzar, with the destruction of Jerusalem (Jer. 25.9; 27.6; 43.10). The heathen monarch is given the honorific title ʿebed, which elsewhere was used of the Israelite king as God's intimate and Yahweh's minister plenipotentiary. Ezekiel in his vision sees the advancing foreign peoples as angels of Yahweh who at his command invade the holy city with their weapons of destruction (Ezek. 9.1ff.); and the great panorama of final judgment (Ezek. 38f.)[3] takes up an image used by Isaiah,[4] and describes Gog of the land of Magog as a wild beast led by Yahweh at his bridle. The anti-God world-power can by its enterprises achieve nothing but the setting forward of the kingdom of God. So, too, Deutero-Isaiah sees the Holy One of Israel directing

[1] Isa. 29.15f.; 10.15ff., 23; 37.28f.; 9.3ff.
[2] Isa. 10.12; 14.26; 18.7; 22.11; 28.16ff., 22, 23–29.
[3] The provenance of Ezekiel is, of course, open to justifiable doubts.
[4] Ezek. 38.4; cf. Isa. 37.29.

world-history to his own ends by causing Cyrus to shine in the international sky like a meteor, so that by his unprecedented string of victories the fame of Yahweh may be spread to the farthest islands, and the fall of the Babylonian empire may open to the exiled Israelites the highway into the new age.[1]

The unexampled boldness of this belief in Providence underwent an important modification in Daniel and the apocalyptists by the incorporation of the doctrine of world epochs.[2] It is not known under what influences this modification was adopted.[3] It is in any case clear that an element in the world-view of antiquity, the understanding of history as a sequence of periods which come to an end at regular intervals, has here invaded the prophetic conception, and been amalgamated with it. The really important matter, however, is not the provenance of these elements but the way in which they were united with the traditional stock of Israelite ideas. Indeed, at the decisive point the apocalyptists completely transform the ancient periodic system. When after the passing of the iron age the golden ought to return, and the cycle begin afresh, something entirely new is introduced, the eternal kingdom which comes down from heaven, bringing with it the final conclusion of earthly history. This conception remains true to the fundamental outlook of the prophets while enriching it from the experience of centuries. Whereas for the prophets, who saw themselves standing immediately on the threshold of the new age, the old order had no intrinsic interest, for the apocalyptists the old order was given greater significance by a detailed presentation of the course of its history. It became more definitely apparent that there was a need for a special history of the earthly order, cast in a distinctive mould; this world also had to complete its formation, and come to maturity, before God could bring in his consummation.

In addition to this type of belief in Providence, which was the product of prophecy, and drew its strength from the assurance that this age was hastening to its end and from the revelation of the God who was to come, confidence in God's direction of human history created for itself in Israel yet *another form*, the distinctive character of

[1] Isa. 41.25; 43.14; 44.28; 45.1–7; 46.10f.
[2] Dan. 2.31ff.; 7; 8.
[3] It is debated whether this development was the effect of Chaldean-Iranian stellar religion, Egyptian gnosis and aeon-mysticism, or Greek philosophical ideas: cf. H. Gressmann, *Die hellenistische Gestirnreligion*, 1925; W. Baumgartner, *Das Buch Daniel*, 1926, p. 18ff.

which has for the most part been too little regarded—that, namely, which was *based on the Priestly world-view*. It is, of course, true that this form did not develop in entire independence of the prophetic preaching; but it displays at all times its distinctive character, and turns every stimulus received from prophecy to the service of its own consciously maintained particular approach.[1] The foundation of this view was that all relations between God and the world were regulated through the Law, which brought about the subordination of all existing things to the sovereign governing will of the transcendent God. In the nature of the Law as the ordinance established once for all by God, who is exalted above the world, lies the explanation of the immense stress placed on the unalterable validity of the universal constitution therein set up. No historical event can shatter this framework. Rather is everything that happens conceivable only within it as an unfolding of basic conditions laid down once for all. This is possible only because the wise prevision of the Creator and Lawgiver has arranged everything with marvellous appropriateness, and has allotted Man a place as the image of God and lord over the creatures in which he can fulfil the meaning of his life by carrying out the task appointed for him. Hence God's relationship with Israel and with the nations also displays the character of an eternally valid order of life, expressed in the form of the Noachic covenant, which is binding on all men, and of the covenant with Abraham, which is binding on Israel alone. In such a context the goal of the divine governance of the world can only appear as the maintenance of the eternal ordinances, and their restoration when they are attacked by a human race alienated from God. It is not the irruption of the kingdom of God into a world which is hostile to him, and which has to be laid at the feet of the only Lord of the universe at the cost of fearful struggle; it is not the vision of a future age of perfect divine sovereignty, the organic growth of which constitutes the hidden meaning of the present age, itself condemned to be done away; it is not these which provide the form in which the rule of divine Providence is expressed. Instead it is the continual execution of Yahweh's judgment, by which he holds firm the pillars of the earth (Ps. 75), and again and again pierces the obscurity of events to show himself Lord of his eternal realm and King of the universe.[2] The meaning of history is therefore to be found in the regular sequence of sin and punishment, and in the restoration thus

---

[1] Cf. vol. I, pp. 410ff. and 424ff.

[2] Pss. 9.12f.; 48.3, 5ff.; 68; 74.18ff.; 85.5–8; 96.3ff.; 136.23f.; 145.11ff;. 147.13.

effected of the state of affairs willed by God; and it is this which the Priestly history-writing attempts to exhibit.[1] Man's response to God's activity is to consist in grateful obeisance before this divine cosmic Lord, who grants access to himself here and now both to Israel and to the Gentiles, and in the fulfilment of men's allotted tasks provides them with the means of rejoicing in his government.[2]

(c) The Old Testament belief in Providence was slower to incorporate into its scheme *the fate of the individual* than the destiny of the Gentile world. Its basic starting-point in the divine rule over Israel meant that for a long time the all-dominating interest in the fortunes of the nation pushed the personal concerns of the individual member of that nation into the background. In any case in the early period with its strong sense of solidarity it was taken for granted that personal interests should take second place to the claims of the people as a whole. With all the unbroken force of primitive vitality men felt their individual lives to be embedded in the great organism of the life of the whole community, without which the individual existence was a nullity, a leaf blown about by the wind, while in the prosperity of the community, on the other hand, the individual could alone find his own fulfilment. His devotion to the great whole was therefore the natural thing, his being bound to the destinies of the totality an axiomatic process of life. This is seen most clearly in the assertion of collective retribution, which feels it to be a completely just ordinance that the individual should be involved in the guilt of the community, and conversely that the action of the individual should react upon the fate of the group.[3]

This should not, of course, be misunderstood, as it has sometimes been,[4] to mean that until the age of prophetism it was impossible to speak of personal trust in Yahweh by the individual Israelite. Even in the earliest laws the demands of God call the individual 'Thou' to account; and conversely the individual is certain that he may expect from Yahweh the protection of his justice.[5] Very common personal names, such as Jonathan ('Yahweh has given'), Joiada ('Yahweh

[1] Cf. I Sam. 4–6; II Sam. 6; II Kings 12; 22; II Chron. 15.8–18; 17.7ff.; 19.4ff.; 29ff.; 34f.

[2] Pss. 9.5, 8f.; 57; 65.6, 9; 66; 93; 96; 97; 99; 113.3f; 145 11–13; 148 11, 13

[3] Ex 20.5; 34.7; Num. 14.18; Deut. 5.9; Josh. 7.1; I Sam. 14; II Kings 9.26, etc.

[4] Cf., e.g., R. Smend, *Alttestamentliche Religionsgeschichte*, 1899, p. 103; similarly B. Stade, *Biblische Theologie des AT*, 1905, p. 194.

[5] Cf. Gen. 16.5; 20.3ff.; 31.7, 50; I Sam. 24.13ff.; 25.39; II Sam. 18.31; 16.12; Ex. 22.20, 26, etc.

has regarded'), and others, express the confidence that the fortunes of the individual also come under God's direction. Furthermore the vivid images of the 'bundle of life', the 'book of life' and the 'wings of God'[1] show that it was precisely popular thought which loved to describe God's care for the individual member of the nation.[2]

This belief in Providence—which certainly has its occasional parallels even in heathenism—derived its unshakeable firmness and unique energy from the practice of explaining every event without exception in terms of God's action, a course which involved excluding any seeming accident, and ascribing even evil to the will of God. When once in a way there is unreflecting mention of a *mikreh*, an accident,[3] this is nevertheless more in the sense of there being no human intention involved, though God's guiding hand is still thought of as active. Indeed, this is seen as controlling even the unfortunate act of the individual who is guilty of manslaughter, and who is therefore granted the protection of asylum.[4]

This example reminds us that misfortune and evil of all kinds are reckoned as God's doing, effected and sent by him.[5] The jealous exclusiveness and the absolute sovereign power of Yahweh leave no room either for an independent hostile divine will or for the capricious activity of demons, who play such a large part in the religions of the neighbouring heathen peoples. Hence for every event there was but *one* divine causality; and the frank derivation of even the dark and enigmatic side of the cosmic process from the one divine Lord—a derivation which was given concise and striking formulation in the well-known prophetic sayings of Amos 3.5f. and Isa. 45.7[6]—made it clear beyond all question that no limits could confine the Providence of God.

Early Israelite belief in Providence was thus distinguished by a deep-rooted inner stability. Nevertheless it was in general satisfied to detect God's care primarily in the single event, and did not as yet think to discover in the course of each individual life the embodiment of a divine plan linking beginning and end in an artistically shaped

---

[1] I Sam. 25.29; Ex. 32.32f.; Isa. 4.3; Mal. 3.16; Pss. 69.29; 139.16; Dan. 12.1; Pss. 17.8; 36.8; 57.2; 63.8; 91.4.
[2] Cf. on this point the remarks in ch. XX: The Individual and the Community in the Old Testament God-Man Relationship.
[3] I Sam. 6.9; Ruth 2.3, cf. v. 20.
[4] Ex. 21.13.
[5] Cf. J. Scharbert, *Der Schmerz im AT* (BBB 8), 1955, pp. 194ff.
[6] Cf. in addition Isa. 54.16; Lam. 3.37f.; Eccles. 7.14.

whole. What might be conceivable in the case of the great leaders of the nation it was not yet open to each individual Israelite to claim for himself. Not until Jeremiah do we encounter direct evidence of belief in a comprehensive incorporation of the individual life into God's design.[1] And indeed it was only at that period, when with the breaking up of the old national order the individual found himself thrown back more and more on his own resources, that the presuppositions could be created for arriving at a new understanding of himself on the basis of the belief in Providence. Hence in more than one passage we now come across the marvelling contemplation of God's care which orders great things and small alike.[2] This attainment of a new inwardness in the God-Man relationship finds expression in the way in which men now dare to apply the father-son relationship to God's attitude to the pious individual.[3] With this went a new evaluation of suffering as fatherly correction, which enabled it to be seen as the healing work of the physician, and virtually a mark of divine favour.[4] The extension of the power and direction of the divine spirit to the life of the individual also indicates a new certainty of God's immediate nearness and guidance.[5]

Belief in Providence was therefore able in this way to incorporate all the phenomena of life, evil included, within its scope.[6] As a result the conceptions of God's world-sustaining activity were clothed in a form which enabled the absolute sovereignty of God over the world, as expressed in principle in the idea of creation, to be applied consistently to the practical business of living.

II. *Providence and freedom*

Where belief in Providence grew, as it did in Israel, out of the sense of a divine reality determining the whole life of the nation, it is understandable enough that it should pay no attention to the problem raised for individual psychology. Indeed, it seems as if it were under some compulsive necessity to clash head-on with the freedom of

---

[1] Jer. 1.5: cf. Isa. 49.2.

[2] Prov. 20.24; Job 5.19–27; 14.5; Pss. 16.5ff.; 37.5, 18, 23; 73.23f.; 139.16. In later Judaism, e.g., Jub. 16.3; 32.21ff.; II Enoch 53.2.

[3] Prov. 3.12; Pss. 68.6; 103.13; Wisd. 2.16ff.; 5.5.

[4] Prov. 3.12; Job 36.5ff.; Pss. 66.10; 118.18; 119.67, 71; Lam. 3.27. Cf. E. F. Sutcliffe, *Providence and Suffering in the Old and New Testament*, 1955.

[5] Cf. pp. 61f. above.

[6] On sin and evil in the life of the individual, and the particular formation which these gave to the attitude of faith cf. ch. XXIII below.

human personal life, the more unhesitatingly it subordinated every event to the systematic action of God. From the very beginning Israel's belief in God's power in history and individual life went far beyond that large-scale fulfilment of his decrees which made use even of human refractoriness for its own ends, and implemented its royal dominion in the teeth of all external opposition. Even the innermost life of Man was subjected to the all-pervading divine energy. It is not simply that God allows a man to think thus and not otherwise; he is himself also at work within these acts of personal freedom. He causes Absalom to reject the good counsel of Ahitophel, in order to bring evil upon him;[1] he inspires Rehoboam to reject the petitions of the people;[2] he stirs up David to begin the disastrous census.[3] He seems to goad Saul into his unappeasable hostility toward David;[4] he hardens the hearts of Pharaoh,[5] of Sihon,[6] and also of the Canaanites as a whole.[7] Indeed, he even sends out his prophets with the explicit command: 'Make the heart of this people fat, and their ears heavy, and shut their eyes; lest they see with their eyes, and hear with their ears, and understand with their hearts, and turn and be healed.'[8] He pours out upon his people a spirit of deep sleep,[9] and hardens their heart.[10]

One will never do justice to the profound grasp of the reality of God which is evinced in these statements by trying to explain them in terms of God's permissive will. This theological dilution both fails in what it sets out to achieve and at the same time stands in danger of making an everyday commonplace out of a distinctive historical phenomenon. In the cases mentioned what is involved is a real act of God, in whose hand men are as clay in the hand of the potter.[11] The conviction of the poet of Proverbs—'The king's heart is a stream of water in the hand of the LORD; he turns it wherever he will'[12]—is equally applicable to the early Israelite period. The remarkable

[1] II Sam. 17.14.
[2] I Kings 12.15.
[3] II Sam. 24.1.
[4] I Sam. 26.19.
[5] Ex. 4.21; 7.3; 10.1, 27; 14.4, 8.
[6] Deut. 2.30.
[7] Josh. 11.20.
[8] Isa. 6.10.
[9] Isa. 29.10.
[10] Isa. 63.17.
[11] Jer. 18.6.
[12] Prov. 21.1: cf. Ps. 33.15; Zech. 12.1.

thing, however, is that this never led to a flat determinism, depriving Man of the responsibility for his actions. At all times the capacity for self-determination is insistently retained. The whole ethical exhortation of the prophets is based on the conviction that decision is placed in the hands of men. But the Law, too, setting before Man the choice of life or death, rests on this presupposition.[1] The fundamental postulate of moral freedom is thus found in equal force alongside the religious conviction of God's effective action in all things; and no attempt is made to create a harmonizing adjustment between them. It is testimony to the compelling power of the Old Testament experience of God that it was able to affirm both realities at once, and to endure the tension between them, without discounting anything of their unconditional validity.

This state of affairs may, nevertheless, become somewhat easier to understand if we scrutinize more closely the precise instances in which a divine causality is especially emphasized. If we do, we find first of all that it frequently implies no more than *the power of evil to grow and spread*, whereby it becomes ripe for judgment. The all-sustaining energy of God's power operates also within the evil which has been begun by the perversion of the creature's will. This is certainly in mind in the case of Pharaoh's obduracy, where his own guilt is also acknowledged by repeated statements that he himself hardened his heart,[2] and even, on certain occasions, acknowledged that he was in the wrong. A similar interpretation would be correct for the passage from Isaiah mentioned above and in the case of Absalom.[3]

But it is not always possible to manage with this explanation. More than once an unbiased exegesis is unable to discover any fault on the part of men which could have decided Yahweh on his action (cf. especially I Sam. 16.14ff.; 26.19; II Sam. 24.1). Here there can be no doubt that the Israelite sees the reality more impartially for what it is than any theory of retribution can tolerate. For him the evil human action brought about by Yahweh comes under the heading of misfortune sent by God, something which cannot be explained on a rational basis, but must simply be reserved to God's majesty. Nevertheless it is a significant fact, which should on no account be overlooked, that in all these instances an extraordinary event is involved.[4]

[1] Cf. Ex. 20.12; Lev. 26; Deut. 20.13f.
[2] Ex. 8.28; 9.7, 34; 9.27; 10.16.
[3] The same applies to Judg. 9.23f.; I Kings 12.15; 22.21.
[4] Cf. on this point the remarks in vol. I, pp. 262f.

'If a man in incomprehensible blindness became untrue to himself, so that his action finally resulted in misfortune for himself and for the people of God, then this too was God's work. For otherwise how was it to be explained? Ancient Israel knew nothing of a world of evil spirits (in the moral sense) which as tempters apart from God affected men's actions; yet in such behaviour men saw conduct that was not free, that had been supernaturally conditioned. There was no other way of expressing the uncanny, overpowering, "demonic" character of the power of sin, than by seeing this too as a work of Yahweh, even if one executed in anger.'[1]

The candour of this world-view of the early period, which was still capable of acknowledging instances that could not be brought within the category of guilt and punishment, *was no longer displayed by Judaism*. This indicates an undeniable narrowing of the horizon. The metaphysical relationship between divine causality and human freedom could even now be left undisturbed; but where the problem touched the question of guilt it pricked and tormented. The individual, who after the break-up of the nation found himself thrown back on his own resources and compelled to struggle for new foundations for his faith, longed with an intensity quite different from that of earlier times for proof of God's government of the world precisely within the sphere of his own life, and therefore seized on the doctrine of individual retribution as the reasonable schema for explaining the world, the one which promised to protect his personal assurance of God against all doubts. In such circumstances it was easy for any individual case which could not be fitted as it stood into the dogma of retribution to be experienced as a threat to faith; and the relationship between divine and human causality, between God's effective action in everything and Man's behaviour, seemed therefore to be rightly determined only where there was an exact correlation in accordance with the principle of reward and punishment. The continual gainsaying of reality into which men were driven by this theory led, however, to that deformation of religious thinking of which the poet of Job was able to present a typical picture in the speeches of the friends, and which occurs also in many Psalms.[2] In later Judaism the development of angelology and demonology made it possible to have recourse to a non-human evil power, as was done,

[1] J. Köberle, *Sünde und Gnade im religiösen Leben des Volkes Israel bis auf Christum*, 1905, pp. 51f.
[2] Pss. 7.4ff.; 35.11, 19; 41.7f.; 69.5, 22; 70.3f.

for example, by the Chronicler in his alteration to the David story;[1] but this afforded only slight easement. Hence the challenge to faith, breaking out again and again at this point, was able to provide the impetus of a powerful inner movement which drove Jewish religious belief away from the theoretical mastering of the riddle implicit in human freedom, and guided it to a deeper grasp of the mutuality of divine and human action, rooted ultimately in God's sovereign power as Creator and Redeemer. The revived awareness of the prophetic message of the God who comes, of the marvel of that fellowship with God which can be personally experienced here in the present, and of the mystery of creation, which opens up an inner connection between Creator and creature, led to joyful affirmation of the divine freedom, which is quite another thing from caprice, and which reveals itself to those who trust in God rather as succour and grace.[2] Here the way was opened to an understanding of a theonomy of human action leading far beyond all autonomy and heteronomy, and such as Paul, consistently with his Old Testament starting-points, was able to proclaim as the ἔννομος χριστοῦ.[3]

III. *The development of the picture of God on the basis of belief in Providence*

The more consistently belief in Providence was built up in all its aspects, the stronger was its effect on the conceptual clarification and enlargement of the picture of God; and it played a not unimportant part in removing the last hindrances to universalization of the idea of God both in thought and speech. Ever clearer theoretical formulations were now arrived at for that which, even without adequate expression, had hitherto been an established part of the concerns of practical belief; and in this way the content of that which we are accustomed to term *the metaphysical attributes of God* was appositely described.

Thus it is certain that the faith of early Israel was unable to speak of the *omnipotence of God*; and even the prophets coined no word for this concept. Yet it is true that at no time was the devout Israelite capable of supposing that there was anything God could not do; it was simply that it satisfied his practical concerns to think of God as more powerful than all his opponents. We have already shown what

---

[1] Cf. I Chron. 21.1 with II Sam. 24.1.
[2] A more detailed examination of a subject which in this context can of necessity be only briefly indicated will be found in ch. XXIII: Sin and Forgiveness.
[3] I Cor. 9.21.

part confidence in God's power played both for Israel's historical awareness and for her attitude to Nature.[1] A kind of confession of the unlimited character of God's power was afforded by the names with which men designated the divine helper as supreme, such as *'elyōn* or *šadday*.[2] To a lesser degree the same purpose was fulfilled by the more general terms for the exalted or mighty God, such as *rām, niśśā', niśgāb, gā'ōn, 'ªbīr yaʿªḳōb*, etc.,[3] which acquired stronger content only as a result of the statements linked with them. It is also well known that popular speech in its description of Yahweh's power frequently remained bogged down in anthropomorphic limitations without facing clearly their real significance.[4] Only when the experience of God's care had come to embrace every quarter of the world, and had recognized not only in every detail of history but also in the events of Nature the one divine Lord[5] who directs according to his will both the sum of things and the smallest human life, could those classic propositions be arrived at which concisely and appositely sum up God's almighty operation: 'For he spoke, and it came to be; he commanded, and it stood forth' (Ps. 33.9); 'Whatever the LORD pleases he does, in heaven and on earth' (Ps. 135.6; cf. 115.3); 'I know that thou canst do all things' (Job 42.2).[6]

The same is true of the sense of *God's omnipresence*. The pious Israelite never doubted that his God was present in every place where men turned to him in believing prayer.[7] This was in no way contradicted by the fact that the cultic worship of God could not be carried on at any spot one chose, but only at particular sites chosen by Yahweh himself; for this did not imply any idea of the deity's being locally limited to these sites, but simply of the sovereign freedom of his self-revelation,[8] for which, moreover, a distinctive expression had been worked out in the dogma of the dwelling of the divine Name at the cultic centres.[9] Furthermore unreflecting references to Yahweh's

[1] Cf. vol. I, pp. 228ff.
[2] Cf. vol. I, pp. 181f.
[3] Isa. 2.11; 57.15; Pss. 99.2; 113.4; Ex. 15.7; Job 37.4; 40.10; Amos 8.7; Gen. 49.24; Isa. 1.24; 49.26; 60.16; Ps. 132.2, 5.
[4] Cf. Gen. 2.20; 7.16; 32.27; Ex. 17.11f.; Judg. 11.24; II Kings 3.27; Hos.5.12; 13.7f.; Isa. 42.13f.
[5] In this connection especial stress should be laid on Gen. 1; Ps. 104; Job 38ff. and the conjunction of creation and history in Deutero-Isaiah: cf. vol. I, p. 226.
[6] Cf. in addition Gen. 18.14; Zech. 8.6; Isa. 43.13.
[7] Gen. 24.12; Judg. 16.28; I Sam. 26.23f.; 30.6ff., 23, 26; II Sam. 15.8.
[8] Cf. vol. I, pp. 102f.
[9] Cf. pp. 41f. above.

abode on Sinai or to his dwelling-place in heaven, which are found side by side with these cultic statements,[1] kept alive the awareness that the dynamic presence of Yahweh was not identical with his connection with any particular place. Nevertheless all these ways of speaking were marked by a certain inadequacy, and it was possible under the influence of Canaanite religion for their misunderstanding in the sense of local limitation to become here and there an acute danger. It was therefore an increase in spiritual clarity when men's enlarged vision of the world and their experience of God's working as exalted above space and time, both of which were constantly intensified by the prophets,[2] also broke the bonds of the traditional terminology, and defined Yahweh's presence in every place in the clearest terms: 'Behold, heaven and the highest heaven cannot contain thee' (I Kings 8.27); 'Heaven is my throne and the earth is my footstool' (Isa. 66.1); 'Am I a God at hand, says the LORD, and not a God afar off? . . . Do I not fill heaven and earth?' (Jer. 23.23f.). So, too, the poet of Ps. 139 can describe this continual nearness of God as the incomprehensible and inconceivable miracle which at every moment sets Man under the penetrating eye of the great divine Thou.[3]

It also looks like a crude contradiction of Yahweh's *omniscience* that he should have to convince himself personally of the truth of a report.[4] And yet this did not hinder men from believing that everything was open to him, that nothing could be hidden from him. To him both past and future were laid bare; and it was on this that belief in prophecy and in decision by lot was based. The prophets were never tired of impressing on men that everything that was to come was bound to be shaped according to Yahweh's plan and decree;[5] the Creator knew his creature right to the very depths of his being.[6] This belief was only carried to its logical conclusion when from the time of Jeremiah onwards it was emphasized with especial force that to the eyes of God even the most secret things lay bare, that he knew the abyss and the realm of the dead and also the heart of Man.[7]

[1] Cf. pp. 186ff. below.

[2] Amos 9.2–4; Isa. 6.3; Zeph. 1.12; Isa. 43.2; Zech. 4.10.

[3] On the comparison of this Psalm with a hymn to Varuna in the Indian Atharva-Veda, cf. E. Sellin, *Theologie des AT*, 1933, p. 26.

[4] Gen. 11.5; 18.21.

[5] Isa. 5.19; 14.26; 19.17; 28.29; Micah 4.12; Jer. 27.1ff.; 49.20; 50.45.

[6] Isa. 29.16.

[7] Prov. 15.11; Job 26.6; I Kings 8.39; Jer. 11.20; 17.10; 20.12; Pss. 139.1–4; 11.4; 33.15; 51.8; 94.11.

Again it was Deutero-Isaiah who formulated outstandingly powerful expressions for the divine knowledge that embraces everything without exception.[1]

It will be clear from what has been said earlier[2] how greatly men's eyes for the divine *wisdom*, in the sense of the systematic ordering of all events, must have been opened by the prophetic interpretation of history. When the early period spoke of God's wisdom it did so more in the sense of miraculous knowledge, as when the angel of Yahweh is mentioned as the quintessence of wisdom.[3] The comprehensive vision of the world-process as a wondrous structure fashioned by the divine wisdom, which allots to every man his place and makes 'everything beautiful in its time', was first put into clear words by the prophets. Thus Isaiah is able to illustrate the wise dispensation of his God in the parables of seedtime and harvest,[4] and Deutero-Isaiah never wearies of contrasting the superior insight and unsearchable wisdom of the God of Israel with the helplessness of the idols and the folly of their worshippers.[5] The efforts of the wisdom teachers to understand the divine wisdom moved, as we have seen,[6] along quite different lines. Not history but Nature was for them the field of its activity, with the result that its greatness, ultimately inaccessible to Man, and mystery were the qualities that received most attention. In human life, however, they saw its operation more in the equipping of the individual to lead a life pleasing to God. When history does come within their purview it is the static ordering of the nation's life by the Law, not the dynamic guidance of the movement of history to a distant goal, which is praised as the revelation of wisdom. It was precisely in this way, moreover, that as a hypostatic entity it became the means of absorbing the truths possessed by the heathen nations into the revelation of the one God.

In all this conceptual clarification of the picture of God the dominant element is less the effort to achieve a speculative grasp of God's nature and to describe it than the need to confirm faith in him. 'Piety did not strive after the concept of the absolute, but after the effectual power of the divine personhood. . . . That to which men

[1] Isa. 41.22–24; 43.10–13; 44.6–8; cf. Zech. 4.10; Job 28.24.
[2] Cf. pp. 171f. above.
[3] II Sam. 14.17.
[4] Isa. 28.23ff.; cf. 14.24ff.; 22.11; 29.14; 31.2; 37.26.
[5] Isa. 40.12ff., 28; 41.4ff., 22ff.; 42.5f.; 43.9ff.; 44.6ff., 24ff.; 45.7, 9ff., 18ff.; 46.10; 55.8f., etc.
[6] Cf. pp. 83ff. above.

clung was the personal freedom of God *vis-à-vis* Time, Space and things created, which assured the believer that he was the absolutely reliable covenant God of his people, impeded by no restrictions.'[1] His omnipotence is the guarantee that for God nothing is impossible; his omniscience is directed to the most secret attitudes of men; by virtue of his omnipresence God is near to the pious; and his eternity is closely connected with his unchangeableness and faithfulness. In other words the metaphysical attributes of God are only conceptualized on the basis of men's experience of his personal action in judgment and forgiveness, and from this they derive their distinctive form.

[1] H. Schultz, *Theologie*[4], 1889, p. 533.

XVIII

THE CELESTIAL WORLD

I. YAHWEH'S DWELLING-PLACE IN HEAVEN

THE RELIGIO-HISTORICAL OUTLOOK of the Wellhausen school for a long time accepted more or less without question the proposition that only in the time of Ezekiel did Israel's God Yahweh, as the result of a fusion of ancient Israelite and Babylonian ideas, 'grow to heavenly stature'.[1] Before that it was impossible to speak of Yahweh as a sky-god.

Today this conception has already received one severe blow simply from our increased knowledge of the Baal religion, in which Baal plays the part of a sky-god—a fact all the more crucial, the more strongly had the thesis been elaborated that Israelite religion after the Conquest was extensively assimilated to that of the land of Canaan.

But neither could such a view be maintained on the basis of the Old Testament evidence. Its strongest line of argument was the collation of all those texts which speak of Yahweh's dwelling or presence in a particular place on earth. And indeed these statements do at first sight seem to betray a very restricted conception of Yahweh's relation to the spatial order. In particular there are two series of statements which in their mutual relationship seem to be based on quite primitive ideas, the first being the accounts of Yahweh's appearances on Sinai (especially Ex. 19 and I Kings 19.11), and the second the references to his presence in the sanctuaries of Canaan.[2] From this starting-point attempts have been made to demonstrate a development from lower to higher along the following lines. Sinai was the ancient mountain of the gods, and as such Yahweh's natural dwelling-place; but as a result of the invasion and settlement of Canaan his abode was

---

[1] B. Stade, *Biblische Theologie des AT*, 1905, p. 291.
[2] Ex. 23.15; 34.20; II Sam. 15.25; II Kings 17.33; Deut. 16.16.

detached from Sinai, and transferred to Canaan, where by a fusion of Yahweh with the Baals it became identified with the sanctuaries of the Canaanite countryside. Thus the organic connection of Yahweh with the land became so close that without it he was no longer thinkable, and the whole relationship of Israel to him was bound up with her occupation of his land in a way which meant a total assimilation to the popular Canaanite religion. The only serious setback to this heathen way of thinking resulted from the conflict between the prophets and the people. In order to deprive the people of the soft pillow of their belief that for his own sake Yahweh was bound to protect the land which was his dwelling-place the prophets returned to the old conception of Yahweh's dwelling on Sinai—as, for example, did Elijah—and indeed enlarged the idea to imply that Yahweh never had come with his people into the land, but had remained on Sinai all the time.[1]

But however skilfully this line of development is drawn, it will not bear closer examination. In the first place there is no valid proof which can be adduced to show that in the earliest period Sinai as the mountain of the gods was regarded as the true dwelling-place of Yahweh. Even if the designation *har hā'elōhîm*, mountain of God, does suggest that the mountain already had a sacred character in earlier times, this still tells us nothing about the nature of the divine revelation given to Moses. At the same time the Yahwist stratum— not to mention the Elohist[2]—knows only of a coming of Yahweh to Sinai or a descent upon it, and says nothing of his permanent abiding there.[3] Since this conception accords with the use of nomadic shrines in the Mosaic period,[4] it is methodologically inadmissible on the one hand to disregard the testimony of the documents in the desire to reconstruct an underlying stage of thought for which the only adducible evidence is the analogy of certain heathen customs,[5] while on the other studiously ignoring the fact that the unique effects of the Mosaic revelation point to a special quality in its source. Furthermore there is no mention in later times of any kind of pilgrimage to Yahweh's alleged dwelling-place, which on this showing one would

---

[1] I Kings 19.8ff.; Ex. 33.1–5.
[2] On the mode of Yahweh's self-manifestation in E cf. vol. I, pp. 109ff.
[3] Ex. 3.7ff.; 19.11, 18, 20; 34.5.
[4] Cf. vol. I, pp. 108f.
[5] That points of contact with other conceptions already existed in ancient Near Eastern thought in general has been mentioned earlier: cf. vol. I, p. 104. n.3.

expect to find in those groups within the nation influenced by the prophets.[1]

Moreover, if the prophets had, in fact, contrasted the theologoumenon of Yahweh's dwelling on Sinai with the popular conception of his presence at the country sanctuaries, one would have expected to hear something of their polemic on this point! In fact, neither Elijah nor any of the later prophets inveigh against such a popular conception. On the contrary it is precisely in the writing prophets that we find repeated pronouncements about Canaan as Yahweh's dwelling-place;[2] and clearly they are aware neither of propagating something new nor of reviving an older idea. Instead the two conceptions, of Yahweh's particular association with Sinai and with the cult sites of Canaan, are at all times found side by side, and indeed often in the same writers. Once again therefore the beautifully constructed developmental theory comes to pieces in one's hands.

It may, however, be asked whether these ideas do not, in fact, restrict Yahweh's power within very narrow spatial limitations. The temptation to do so was certainly always present; and where in particular any considerable amalgamation with the Canaanites took place, men no doubt succumbed to it. This may have occurred especially in the form of a fission of the unitary conception of God, so that Yahweh now took different forms at different centres, just as Baal in each town bore his local character.[3] Thus one could speak of the Yahweh of Shiloh, for example, to whom Elkanah according to I Sam. 1.3 went up year by year to pay homage and to sacrifice; or again, of the Yahweh of Hebron, to whom according to II Sam. 15.7 Absalom had made a vow which clearly could be paid only at the Hebron sanctuary. Hence the widely accepted interpretation of Deut. 6.4 as a protest against the disintegration of Yahweh into various local deities, the verse in this case being rendered: 'Yahweh our God is a single Yahweh!'

The striking point, however, is that there is no sign of this disintegration of the deity in the thought of the leading spirits of Israel. It can be clearly proved that an assertion that Yahweh dwelt and manifested himself at a particular place involved absolutely no idea of *limiting* God to the place in question. In one of the oldest hymns,

[1] Elijah's journey to Horeb cannot be included in this category, since its purpose is precisely to portray the unique position of Elijah by placing him on a level with Moses.

[2] Cf. Hos. 8.1ff.; 9.3, 15; Isa. 6; 8.18.

[3] Cf. on this subject vol. I, pp. 103ff.

Judg. 5, Yahweh comes from Sinai to the help of his people fighting in Canaan, thus testifying that even in the earliest period men did not think of Yahweh as spatially restricted to the mountain of God in the south, but believed that he heard and granted the prayer of his people in the Promised Land. According to I Kings 19.11 Elijah received his revelation as the Lord *passed by*; God here, too, therefore appearing as the One who comes, and not as bound to his *māḵōm*. Moreover, that this view was a living reality to everyone even before the time of Elijah may be seen from the Yahwist narrative in Ex. 33.12–23 and 34.8ff., where Yahweh reveals himself to Moses on Sinai in a very similar way, and promises to go with him into the land of Canaan.

Just as little did belief in the particular presence of Yahweh at the cult sites of Canaan restrict the sphere of the divine power and existence virtually to the borders of the land. Judg. 16.28 shows Samson calling on Yahweh, and his act of vengeance, in Philistia; Gen. 24.12 relates how Eliezer's prayer was answered in Aram. According to I Sam. 30.6ff., 23, 26, David remained a true Yahweh-worshipper in Philistia, just as Absalom did in Geshur (II Sam. 15.8). Even if, generally speaking, a regular cultus was impracticable—though here, too, as in the case of Naaman (II Kings 5.17ff.), there is evidence of exceptions—yet in foreign lands men were still sure of the effective presence of Yahweh. Otherwise one would have to assume that when Hosea describes the heathen land as unclean and as a place where cultic worship cannot be offered[1] he is denying the existence of Yahweh outside Canaan. In general, however, in order to see how completely untenable is the assertion that Yahweh's effectiveness was restricted[2] it is only necessary to bear in mind the whole early historical narrative, in which it is taken for granted that Yahweh has shown himself superior to all alien gods and peoples not only in Egypt and in the Wilderness, but also against the Amalekites and Moabites, the Philistines, Arameans and Edomites, in Damascus and in Phoenicia. Thus it is that a narrative which quite certainly goes back behind the Yahwist stratum can declare with magnificent assurance of faith (I Sam. 14.6) that for God nothing is impossible: 'for nothing can hinder the LORD from saving by many or by few'.

[1] Hos. 9.4, cf. 3.4; Deut. 28.36; Jer. 16.13.
[2] Even passages such as Gen. 11.7; 18.21 are not evidence to the contrary. They may in part indicate echoes of the original form of the myth, and in part result from a striving after more vivid description.

If therefore the two series of conceptions, of the revelation of Yahweh on Sinai and of his dwelling at the cult sites of Canaan, neither contradict one another nor necessarily confine the deity within spatial limits,[1] then *the fact that they exist side by side becomes of the greatest importance for the permanent distinction of Yahweh from the other ancient Semitic gods.* For this implies the confession that there was a time when Yahweh exercised his sovereignty over Israel *even without possessing Canaan,* and only later bestowed on them the Land of Promise in particular historical acts (cf. Judg. 1.4, 19, 22). In this way his existence was elevated into a certainty in no sense dependent upon the land which was now designated as his particular inheritance; and the close association with Canaan was understood as his own free act. Consequently the description of the land as the house and inheritance of Yahweh acquired a wholly different significance in Israel from that which the same terminology had, for example, in Moab. When Moab is called the land of Chemosh, this is in the sense of a naturalistic bond between the country and the god; the Moabites venerated their Chemosh as the god connected with the land from of old. By contrast Canaan is called the house of Yahweh in the sense that he has established himself there for the purpose of his revelation. Thus the statements about Yahweh's dwelling-place do not imply a physically limited, bodily presence, but *dynamic presence,* his presence in revelation. Even though in early times men had no dogma of the omnipresence of Yahweh, they were nevertheless sure of his nearness wherever they had need of him; that is to say, that the revelation of Yahweh as a god near at hand took the place in its practical application of the formula of a metaphysical attribute.

Another influence resisting any narrow interpretation of the concept of Yahweh's dwelling-place on earth was that of *a third conception of his abiding-place,* namely *belief in his residing in heaven.* Since we have already concluded from the divine names that Yahweh was known as the Most High and the Creator, and also that as Elohim he summed up the pantheon in his own person,[2] belief in his dwelling in heaven can only be regarded as the natural complement to this. Explicit evidence for the time of the Judges and the early monarchy is afforded by the following passages: Gen. 11.5; 19.24; 21.17; 22.11; 24.7; 28.12; Pss. 2.4; 18.7; Ex. 19.18; I Kings 8.12.[3]

[1] Cf. vol. I, pp. 102ff.
[2] Cf. vol. I, pp. 181ff.
[3] The exegetical devices by which scholars of an earlier generation tried to

In the prophetic period the widening of men's vision of the world and the deepening of their grasp of Yahweh's universal power gave them a special sensitivity to his exaltedness, with the result that the texts which speak of heaven as the true dwelling-place of Yahweh are multiplied. On Sinai he had spoken with the people from heaven;[1] now it is in heaven that he sits enthroned in his palace as king of the universe.[2] Thence—as Solomon's prayer in the Temple expressed it[3] —he answers the supplications of his people, when they spread out their hands toward heaven. In the Persian period preference is given more than ever to the description of Yahweh as the God of Heaven,[4] because, as the name Elyon had done,[5] it allowed of a link with the elements of truth in the heathen concept of God.

The decisive factor with regard to this localization of Yahweh, however, is not a metaphysical and speculative but a religious concern; Yahweh's exalted position above the earth illustrates the fact that he sees everything, and that neither the iniquity nor the piety of men remains hidden from him.[6] And as with his omniscience this is also the favourite illustration of his omnipotence; Isa. 40.22 describes men as grasshoppers in the presence of him who sits upon the circle of the earth.

When it is noted that assertions of Yahweh's dwelling in heaven often occur in the selfsame authors as those of his revelation at places on earth,[7] it becomes completely beyond question that such ex-

---

deny the value of these pieces of evidence strike us today as curious. Thus, for example, Stade's opinion that Gen. 11 can tell us nothing of the faith of early Israel because it is a 'foreign myth' rests on the naïve idea that no 'foreign myths' were taken over by Israel until the Assyrian-Babylonian period, but that they adopted them *en masse* all at once! One good result of the study of the sagas has been to give us different notions of the migration of saga material and of its very gradual assimilation into alien systems of thought. If, then, Gen. 11 is foreign narrative material, it must have circulated in Israel long before the time of the Yahwist. Modern exegesis normally rejects the arbitrary excision of the phrase *min-haššāmayim* in passages such as Gen. 19.24; 21.17 and 22.11 simply because it cannot be fitted into the theory.

[1] Ex. 20.22; Deut. 4.36.
[2] Isa. 31.4; Micah 1.2; Deut. 26.15; I Kings 8.30; Hab. 2.20; Ps. 11.4.
[3] I Kings 8.22, 32, 34. Cf. also what has been said about the Temple as the dwelling-place of Yahweh's Name: vol. I, pp. 106f., and pp. 41f. above.
[4] II Chron. 36.23; Ezra 1.2; 5.12; 6.9f.; 7.12, 21, 23; Neh. 1.4f.; 2.4, 20; Dan. 2.18f., 28, 37, 44.
[5] Cf. vol. I, pp. 181f.
[6] Pss. 11.4; 14.2; 33.13ff.; 102.20f.; 113.5–7; 138.6; Isa. 57.15; Job 28.24.
[7] Cf. Isa. 6.1; 8.18; 31.4; 18.4; Jer. 7.14 and 23.24; Ps. 20.3 and 7.

pressions do not imply an interest in any particular localization of Yahweh. In every case it is rather the religious need which is the criterion, now calling for the portrayal of a God near at hand or the recollection of the privilege of his self-revelation in the midst of his people, now preferring to set before men's eyes the remote, exalted God, in order to educate them in reverence and trust. That even the conception of God as the God of heaven was not in itself an infallible protection against dragging him down to the human level is shown by Job 22.13–14, where the godless attempt to comfort themselves with the words: 'What does God know? Can he judge through the deep darkness? Thick clouds enwrap him, so that he does not see, and he walks on the vault of heaven.' But the same idea could be equally dangerous to living piety when God's heavenly dwelling was taken to imply his separation from earth in a deistic sense, with the result that the feeling for the immediate nearness of God was lost. Such errors arouse frequent protests. In the present context it is interesting to note that none of this ever led to an assertion of Yahweh's nature as purely spiritual,[1] involving as this does an abstraction which it is always difficult for human thinking to make, but that men were content with the negative statement that Yahweh was too exalted even for heaven to contain him (I Kings 8.27). Or the two great domains are set on a par side by side as Yahweh's realm: to Yahweh 'belong heaven and the heaven of heavens, the earth with all that is in it' (Deut. 10.14); he alone 'is God in heaven above and on the earth beneath' (Deut. 4.39; Josh. 2.11); yea, he fills heaven and earth (Jer. 23.24).

The religious significance of these expressions is not, of course, lessened by the fact that Israel's conception of the cosmos and of the place of heaven within it displays some decidedly naïve features, and is very largely in agreement with the cosmological conceptions of non-Israelite peoples.[2] That this should be so throws as little doubt on the primacy of the dynamic over the localized idea of Yahweh's presence as on the distinctive character of the Israelite creation belief. And the effectiveness of this primacy may be seen in the control which it exercises over even the loftier statements about Yahweh's dwelling and in the refusal to allow mythopoeic imagination to play arbitrarily about the figure of the Lord enthroned in heaven. The concept most frequently associated with Yahweh's dwelling in heaven is that of the

[1] Cf. vol. I, pp. 210ff.
[2] Cf. the remarks on pp. 93ff. above.

sovereign and king; evidence for this is to be found in both earlier and later presentations, even those in which the title *melek* is not used. Of prime importance in this connection is Isa. 6. Here before the eyes of the prophet waiting in the Temple the earthly sanctuary opens up into the heavenly throne-room wherein Yahweh holds council as king in the midst of his celestial courtiers. That this was a visionary experience, in which, as is well known, traditional imagery plays a large part, does not exclude the possibility that particular elements in the vision, and especially that of Yahweh's kingship, were already present beforehand in the prophet's consciousness. Confirmation of this is afforded both by I Kings 22.19, in which Yahweh as king of heaven takes counsel with the entire heavenly host, standing beside him to right and left, how best to deceive Ahab, and by the old folk-tale of Job 1 and 2 with its very similar picture. Ex. 24.10 may also be adduced, where the theophany to the elders of Israel is described in the words: 'there was under his feet as it were a pavement of sapphire stone, like the very heaven for clearness.' The same association of royal sovereignty with heavenly grandeur occurs in many cultic poems.[1] The earthly counterpart of the heavenly throne, however, is the Ark of Yahweh with the cherubim. This sacred object belongs to the class of empty divine thrones, and as the God of the Ark Yahweh acquires the epithet *yōšēb hakkerūbīm*, he who is enthroned upon the cherubim.[2] The nature of the cosmic conceptions associated with Yahweh's enthronement in heaven is instructively indicated by the call-vision of Ezekiel (Ezek. 1). Here again ancient traditions from the world-view of priestly circles take on new life in the visionary experience. In the cherub-throne memory patently returns to Yahweh enthroned upon the Ark; but the form has been changed. The plat-form of the throne, called *rākīa*, is the reflection of the heavenly *rākīa*, the dome of the sky, and like that contains within its hollow lightnings and flames. The one enthroned upon this *rākīa* is a *demūt* or *mar'eh*, a likeness of Yahweh who sits enthroned above the summit of the dome of the sky; and in this way striking expression is given to God's transcendence, his supramundane character.[3] The cosmic significance of the whole is confirmed by the four cherubim, who as the corner-pillars of the vault of heaven represent the four corners of

[1] E.g. Pss. 29.10; 48.3; 68.25; 74.12.
[2] I Sam. 4.4; II Sam. 6.2; II Kings 19.15; Ps. 80.2, etc.
[3] Cf. O. Procksch, 'Die Berufungsvision Hesekiels', *Budde-Festschrift*, 1920, pp. 141ff.

the world—in astronomical terms, Taurus, Leo, Scorpio and Aquarius.

What is new and distinctive in the prophet's picture is not that he possesses such conceptions of Yahweh's cosmic throne but that they play so large a part in his thought. This is bound up with the fact that for the priest who has had to live through the destruction of the Temple the transcendence of God is an anchor for his faith, without which it would inevitably have suffered shipwreck. At the same time, however, this king of heaven is for him the one who acts in the present moment, who calls his messengers to himself even in the unclean land of exile and carries on his work. Here again the particular turns of phrase are determined not by theological speculation but by the concern for God's presence in self-revelation. Only in later Judaism did the theoretic-constructive element invade the prophetic vision, and systematize the picture of the *kābōd* in accordance with the needs of the Jewish concept of holiness by inventing a heavenly Ark-shrine to take the place of the earthly one which had been destroyed.[1] Yet even here it was still a question of giving expression to the practical ideas of faith, and not of a completely unrelated fantasy-formation.

2. THE HEAVENLY POWERS AS SERVANTS OF YAHWEH

1. *The angels*

With the conception of Yahweh as the God of heaven all kinds of figures of the suprasensible world are inseparably connected, which may be subsumed under the general heading of *angels*. The Hebrew name is *mal'ākīm*, but also *benē hā'elōhīm*. In addition they are also referred to as: *kedōšīm*, Ps. 89.6, 8; Job. 5.1; 15.15; Zech. 14.5; Dan. 4.14; *benē 'elyōn*, Ps. 82.6; *'abbīrīm*, Ps. 78.25; *rāmīm*, Job 21.22; *gibbōrīm*, Ps. 103.20; Joel 4.11. Collectively their multitude is termed *ṣebā' yhwh*, I Kings 22.19; II Chron. 18.18; Ps. 148.2; *maḥaneh*, Gen. 32.2f. or *kehal* or *sōd kedōšīm*, Ps. 89.6, 8, and *'adat 'ēl*, Ps. 82.1. There can be no doubt that these beings derive from pre-Mosaic popular belief. This may be seen most clearly from Gen. 6.1–4, where

---

[1] This was done by elaborating Ezek. 10, which had already provided the source from which vv. 15–21 of ch. 1 derive. Cf. the study by S. Sprank, *Ezechielstudien* (BWANT III.4), 1926. Similarly W. Zimmerli, *Ezechiel* (BK XIII.1), *ad loc.*, who, however, regards 1.15ff. as primary.

the connection between the *beṉē 'elōhīm* and pagan mythology can still be plainly traced. According to Job 1.6; 2.1; 38.7, they are identical with the *mal'ākīm*. These 'heavenly' or 'divine' beings belong to the great host of nameless divine spirits which in all religions are active intermediaries between the great gods and mankind, and owe their origin partly to the need to create a picture of God's power by equipping him with a heavenly court, and partly to the ubiquitous undercurrent of animistic belief in spirits. It would be strange indeed if such figures had not also found a home in pre-Mosaic Israel.[1]

It is therefore completely unnecessary to suspect that behind these angelic beings stand the gods of an earlier time, who were stripped of their sovereign status and degraded to the level of servants of Yahweh only as a result of Mosaism. If so, then Israel's forefathers must have had a monstrous number of gods! Furthermore it becomes increasingly apparent that it is mistaken to picture the foundation of a religion as necessarily involving the absorption of the deities that had preceded it by, so to speak, taking them on the domestic staff and giving them sinecure positions. This may be true of many culture religions, the slow modifications of which make it possible for the ancient principal gods to be imperceptibly retired; but it does not apply to those religions which owe their existence to a founder, and which only establish themselves with a violent struggle. Thus whereas Bousset, for instance, regarded the Amesha Spentas of the Zoroastrian religion as a textbook example of the process by which concrete divine beings could be evaporated into abstract figures,[2] it is now recognized that the development ran, in fact, in the opposite direction, that is, from the personification of abstract concepts to concrete protecting spirits, while the ancient Persian gods were the objects of Zoroaster's fierce attack.[3]

As little valid is the view, revived by E. König, that the line of development is from the conception of the 'angel of Yahweh', an almost hypostatic form of Yahweh's manifestation, to that of numerous angels.[4] This reconstruction fails to do justice to Israel's participation in the ideas of the ancient world. Rather different is the

---

[1] Cf. G. W. Heidt, *Angelology of the Old Testament*, 1949.

[2] *Kyrios Christos*[2], 1926, p. 306.

[3] Demonstrated by B. Geiger, *Die Amesha Spentas. Ihr Wesen und ihre ursprüngliche Bedeutung* (Sitzungsberichte der Akademie der Wissenschaften in Wien: Phil.-hist. Klasse 176.7), 1916; also more recently R. C. Zaehner, *Dawn and Twilight of Zoroastrianism*, 1961.

[4] *Theologie des AT*[3, 4], p. 196.

question whether the plural *mal'ākīm* may not be a secondary formation from the singular *mal'āk*, which originally represented the
abstract 'sending'. This is, however, improbable;[1] and in any case the
derivation of the word still tells us nothing about the origin of the
thing, especially since there are also other designations for it.

Furthermore, if the living conception of divine messengers in
paganism is borne in mind, it will from the start prove impossible
to accept the rationalistic explanation that angels are merely personified natural forces. Even though here and there a striking natural
phenomenon may instinctively be personified (e.g. the pillar of cloud
and of fire), nevertheless the angels are nowhere thought of as mere
natural phenomena or mere forces, but as personal beings of a supernatural kind.[2]

It is nearer the mark to derive the concept of angels from the
starry heaven. Job 38.7 places the *kōkebē bōķer* in parallelism with the
benē hā'elōhīm. Like the angels the stars and the astral deities are
frequently described as *(kol-)sebā' haššāmayim*,[3] particularly as the
objects of heathen worship.[4] Indeed, in view of such passages as
Judg. 5.20 ('From heaven fought the stars . . .'), Josh. 5.14f. (*sar
sebā' yhwh*), Isa. 24.21 (the punishment of the *sebā hammārōm*), and
Isa. 40.26,[5] the question may be asked whether we ought not to
distinguish the *benē 'elōhīm* from the *mal'ākīm*, interpreting the former
as the stars thought of as living beings. The immemorial connection
of the Hebrew tribes with Mesopotamia, where stellar worship had
been domesticated from of old, could be adduced in support of this
view. These supraterrestrial beings would then be described as
mal'ākīm from the standpoint of the Yahwist faith, thus becoming the
ones who are sent, subordinated to the one God and deprived of
independent significance. Moreover, the incorporation of deities of
Canaanite origin into Yahweh's court cannot be excluded, especially

---

[1] On the derivation of *mal'āk* cf. p. 23, n. 3, above.

[2] A favourite verse cited in this connection, Ps. 104.4, can easily mislead if incorrectly translated. It does not mean: 'He makes his angels winds and his servants
flames of fire', but 'he makes winds his messengers and flaming fire his servants'—
'*ōseh mal'ākāw rūḥōt mesāretāw 'ešlōhēṭ*—i.e. he takes the forces of Nature into his
service, *as if they were* his angels.

[3] Isa. 40.26; 45.12; Jer. 33.22; Ps. 33.6; Neh. 9.6.

[4] Deut. 4.19; 17.3; II Kings 17.16; 21.3, 5, etc.

[5] An echo of such conceptions may also occur in Gen. 1.16, if sun and moon are
there to be regarded as vested with sovereignty. Also passages such as Deut. 32.8;
4.19; 29.35, according to which Yahweh himself has placed the heathen nations
under the dominion of the star-gods, would be relevant. Isa. 24.21–23 shows
Yahweh as passing judgment on these gods. Cf. pp. 199f. below.

when we remember the council of the gods in Ps. 82.1, a feature known also from the Ugaritic texts, except that there the president is El, the Father of the gods.

We are therefore confronted with a conception which came to Yahwism from the traditions of the nation's past, and was incorporated by it. But this also implies that *the angel concept is a complex entity* to which various tendencies have contributed. On the one hand there is the influence of pagan ideas which Yahwism has been unable completely to assimilate. Thus we come across angels who go in to the daughters of men (Gen. 6.1–4), or who accept hospitality from Abraham at Mamre and from Lot in Sodom, and eat earthly food (Gen. 18.8; 19.3). The star angels mentioned in Job 38.7 and Isa. 14.12ff. reflect respectively the age-old stellar worship and the myth of the glorious star *hēlāl*. However, it is not only this intrusion of the physical into the divine realm which betrays the origin of the angelic beings as foreign to the faith of Yahweh but also the threat which they present of obscuring the uniqueness of the God of Israel. In II Kings 18.4 we hear quite incidentally of a *neḥuštān*, a bronze serpent, which probably belonged to the category of angels, and to which incense was burned in Jerusalem until Hezekiah destroyed it.[1]

In fact, however, no great danger to faith seems to have developed in this quarter; but the same cannot be said of the ancient oriental *concept of the heavenly vizier*, who as the representative of the supreme God carries out his will on earth. This figure of the heavenly court, best known from the concrete instances of Nebo in Babylonia and Thoth in Egypt, seems also to have been not unknown in Israel,[2] as isolated mentions of an angel invested with similar authority allow us to conjecture.[3] Nevertheless, while this heavenly vizier plays an

---

[1] On the serpent-staff of Moses cf. vol. I, pp. 112f. Serpents as protecting spirits and *genii locorum* in the service of the deity seem to have been popular in Palestine, as the excavations at Gezer and Beth-Shan indicate: cf. *AOB*, figs. 398, 672f., and Alan Rowe, *The Topography and History of Beth-Shan* (Publications of the Palestine section of the Museum of the University of Pennsylvania, vol. I), 1930, p. 1, n. 5, and pp. 10ff. Among the discoveries at Hazor there is a cultic standard which bears the picture of a goddess flanked by two serpents: cf. *The Holy Land. New Light on the Prehistory and Early History of Israel* (Antiquity and Survival II.2–3), 1957, p. 167 and fig. 10.

[2] F. Stier (*Gott und sein Engel im AT*, 1934) has performed the great service of developing this hypothesis systematically, and investing it with a high degree of probability, even if his demonstration is not tenable in every detail.

[3] It is chiefly the statements of Josh. 5.13; Ex. 23.20ff. and Judg. 5.23 which, when compared with Ezek. 9.2 (the angel with the writing instrument) and Mal. 3.1 (the angel of the covenant), enable one to deduce the existence of the concept

important role in the later period,[1] he does not make himself fully
felt in the historical narratives of early Israel, since the mighty
activity of the divine Lord of the covenant left no room for such a
parallel and competitive being. It seems indeed as if the penchant for
this figure which existed in many circles may have been consciously
played down by the great historians. The reluctance not only of the
prophets but also of the Priestly writer to admit such mediators is
well known. Hence the heavenly intermediaries, however popular
they may have been with ordinary folk, were nevertheless unable to
secure honour in the cult, and their existence remained shadowy.
They re-emerge only in the epigones of the prophetic movement, and
then in later Judaism very speedily acquire importance. Thus in
Ezekiel we encounter the figure of a heavenly scribe[2] who together
with six other celestial beings carries out God's sentence of judgment
and who in his outward features strongly recalls Nebo, though without indeed attaining any greater significance. In Zechariah an angel
makes intercession for the nation whose punishment has lasted so
long, and receives an assurance that Yahweh will soon have compassion.[3] The acquittal of the High Priest before the heavenly court
is also attributed to an angel as president of the court.[4] In Malachi
the angel of the covenant takes a similar part in the prophet's
expectation of the final judgment; the judicial act is committed to
him as the representative of the heavenly king, and it is he who is to
purge out a new covenant people. The link here established between
the angel and the divine covenant already calls to mind the attribu-
tion of the Sinai covenant to the mediation of angels which we find
in the apocryphal writings and in the New Testament.[5] Considerable
light is also thrown on the figure of the special protective spirit and
champion of Israel in Daniel, where under the name of Michael he

---

of a heavenly vizier. If this line of argument is correct, then other passages such as
Ex. 14.19; 32.34; 33.2; Num. 20.16 fall into place of themselves. It has already
been suggested (cf. pp. 191ff. above) that the idea of the heavenly ruler was bound
to provide suitable points of contact for the figure of such a celestial plenipotentiary.
In addition there was the undeniable tendency of nabism to stress the gulf between
the heavenly Lord and his people; and this explains why most of our examples
come from the Elohist writer, who was close to these circles.

[1] Dan. 12.1ff.; Test. Dan 5f.; Test. Levi 5; Ass. Mos. 10.1ff., etc.
[2] Ezek. 9.2.
[3] Zech. 1.12
[4] Zech. 3.1–8.
[5] Jub. 6.19, 22; 14.20; Gal. 3.19; Acts 7.53; Heb. 2.2.

takes a pre-eminent part in the redemption of the nation at the end of time.[1] In the rest of apocalyptic literature he is even more prominent,[2] and is perhaps to be identified with the 'One like a man' or the 'Son of Man' in Daniel and in the Similitudes of Enoch.[3]

A very similar role was played in Israelite popular belief by the concept of *the angels of the nations*.[4] Originally in all probability national deities, after their degradation to the rank of angelic beings, they serve to universalize the faith of Yahweh by illustrating the unbounded world sovereignty of the God of Israel even in the present age. Yahweh, who has himself assigned them their spheres of dominion,[5] calls them to account for their evil rule, and finally carries out sentence of death upon them.[6] It is likely that this imagery was fostered by analogy with the Great King, who ruled the various parts of his empire through his viceroys. Whereas, however, the whole conception remained more or less peripheral in the early Israelite and prophetic periods because it was paralysed by belief in the direct and mighty operation of the God near at hand,[7] in the Persian and Hellenistic eras it came to full flower. It attained its most alien development in Daniel, where the decree of the 'Watchers' and the sentence of the 'Holy Ones' plays so great a part in the punishment of Nebuchadrezzar[8] that the real government of the world seems to have been transferred to them. They recall the seven princes round the throne of the Great King of Persia[9]—in Dan. 10.13, 20 they even bear the same title, *śārīm*—or the seven Amesha Spentas who attend Ahura Mazda. As an indication that in Israel, too, they were seven in number may be mentioned, in addition to Ezek. 9.2ff., Zech. 3.9; 4.10, where there are references to the seven eyes of God which pass through the whole earth.[10] In the Apocalypse of the Beasts in Enoch there are seventy shepherds who under the supervision of Michael

---

[1] Dan. 10.13, 21; 12.1ff.

[2] Cf. p. 198 n. 1 above.

[3] So Bertholet, *Daniel und die griechische Gefahr* (RGV 11.17), 1907, pp. 51f., and F. Stier, *op. cit.*, pp. 96ff. On the *mal'ak yhwh* in the special sense of the term cf. pp. 23f. above.

[4] Cf. Bertholet, 'Der Schutzengel Persiens' in *Oriental Studies in honour of Dasturji Saheb C.E.P.*, 1934, pp. 34ff.

[5] Deut. 4.19; 32.8f.; Ps. 89.6.

[6] Pss. 58; 82; Isa. 24.21.

[7] Cf. what was said above (pp. 168ff.) on belief in Providence.

[8] Dan. 4.14.

[9] Esth. 1.14.

[10] For the number seven cf. also Test. Levi 8; Tobit 12.15 and Rev. 1.4, 16, 20; 2.1; 3.1 (seven spirits and seven stars).

carry out the government of the nations. In the literature of later Judaism the exercise of world sovereignty by the angelic princes is a very common conception.[1] It is plain that with the ever-increasing emphasis on the divine transcendence an angelology is proliferating which definitely involves an obscuring of the idea of God.

The same applies to *the intrusion of a mediating angel into the relationship between the individual believer and his God.* This *mal'āk mēlīṣ* makes intercession to God for the sick person, who then receives grace and deliverance.[2] According to other passages it is the seven highest angels who bring the prayers of the saints before God, and have access to him.[3] Just as the guardian angel shelters each human being in life,[4] so after death the soul is escorted by an angel.[5] Here, too, there is undoubtedly the influence of heathen ideas.[6]

It is merely one of the outward signs of the excessive importance attached to the angelic world that it is now richly furnished with names, whereas in earlier times angels were nameless; Dan. 8.16 records the name of Gabriel, and Tobit 3.17 Raphael, while Enoch and II(4) Esdras are full of the proper names of angels as well as describing their position in the hierarchy. Indeed, among the Essenes and the Christian Gnostics mentioned in the New Testament we find actual worship of angels, their genealogical organization, and speculations about their influence on the course of secular and sacred history.[7]

It is clear that such a complex entity, retaining as it did its heathen ingredients, was able to find employment only as *an ancillary conception* in any Yahwist faith aware of its own nature, and never acquired central importance. As such an ancillary conception it served in the first place *to illustrate the exaltedness of Yahweh.* Under this head we may

---

[1] Cf. Strack-Billerbeck, *Kommentar zum NT aus Talmud und Midrasch* II, p. 360; III, p. 48, and Bousset-Gressmann, *Die Religion des Judentums im späthellenistischen Zeitalter*[3], pp. 322ff.

[2] Job 5.1; 33.19-23.

[3] Tobit 12.15; 3.16 cf. 12.12; also Test. Dan 6; Jub. 30.20.

[4] Test. Jos. 6; Targ. Ps.-Jon. on Gen. 33.10; 48.16; Acts 12.13f.; Matt. 18.10.

[5] Test. Asher 6; Test. Levi 5.

[6] In Babylonia intermediary deities, whether inferior gods or guardian spirits especially sent by the chief god, play a great part. Cf. B. Meissner, *Babylonien und Assyrien* II, 1925, pp. 79 and 136; also the designs on the cylinder-seals: *AOB*, fig. 323; O. Weber, *Altorientalische Siegelbilder* (Der Alte Orient 17/18), 1920.

[7] For the Essenes cf. K. Schubert, *Die Gemeinde vom Toten Meer*, 1958, pp. 57ff.; Millar Burrows, *More Light on the Dead Sea Scrolls*, 1958, pp. 280ff. In the New Testament cf. Col. 2; Jude 8.

include everything that has been said above concerning the court of the heavenly king. Here, too, belong the choirs which praise the majesty of God in his heavenly palace (Pss. 29; 103.20f.; 148.1ff.), and which escort him in his theophanies (Job 38.7; Deut. 33.3; Zech. 14.5; Ps. 68.18; Dan. 7.10). As partakers in the celestial glory a kind of fire and light nature is proper to them (II Kings 2.11; 6.17). Job 15.15 compares them with the sky for purity and brightness. A distinctive characteristic is that in contrast to the cherubim they are always thought of in anthropomorphic terms, and therefore also as wingless (cf. Gen. 28). Another feature which serves to highlight the divine exaltedness is that the angels far surpass men in intellectual power; it is proverbial to say of a clever man: 'He has wisdom like the wisdom of the angel of God to know all things that are on the earth' (II Sam. 14.20; 19.28). At the same time, however, the gulf between them and God is strictly maintained, and in this way, too, the exaltation of the deity is emphasized: 'Behold, God puts no trust in his holy ones, and the heavens are not clean in his sight' (Job 15.15).

In addition to the divine exaltedness it is his *succouring power* in which men rejoice when they consider the angels. As early as Judg. 5.20 we find them intervening as Yahweh's warriors to help in the battle against the Canaanites. According to Ex. 23.20–23; 14.19, Israel was escorted by an angel on its journey from Egypt to Canaan —though these passages may have in mind the *mal'āk yhwh*. The individual, too, put his trust in angelic protection, as did Eliezer, for example, on his journey to Aram (Gen. 24.7).[1] In prayer the nearness of God's protection is associated with angels.[2]

Finally, the concept of angels also mediates a *lively sense of Yahweh's power to punish*. In Ex. 12.23 an angel carries out the annihilation of the Egyptian firstborn; in II Sam. 24.16; I Chron. 21.25 the angel of pestilence smites the Israelites on account of David's census; in II Kings 19.35 the great mortality in the camp of Sennacherib is ascribed to an angel. In contexts such as these the angelic being sometimes bears the name *mašḥīt*, 'destroyer'; Prov. 16.14 and Job 33.22 speak of the *memītīm*, the 'death-bringers', and Ps. 78.49 of *mal'akē rā'īm*; that is, 'angels of disaster'. This should not, however, be understood to imply a special class of angels, a sort of Satanic powers;

---

[1] Cf. I Kings 19.5; II Kings 1.15 (Elijah); I Kings 13.18 (a prophet); Dan. 3.25; 6.22.
[2] Pss. 34.8; 91.11f.

just as Yahweh himself sends both good and evil, so, too, the *mašḥit* may at another time bring blessing.

Generally speaking, wherever belief in angels retains the character of an ancillary concept it constitutes no danger to the purity of the idea of God, but can on the contrary make the conviction of his providence and power clearer and more distinct. The assurance of a heavenly world over against the earthly will not, after all, be able to dispense with the concept of angels, if it wishes to give a vivid impression of the richness and complexity of that world. The New Testament affords the best illustration of this. Jesus' conviction that the celestial order is fully involved in what he is achieving on earth takes over the angel concept of his contemporaries. Yet we nowhere find him referring to a particular angel or using the name of an angel to authenticate his mission or to strengthen confidence in his word. In this context faith must always remain alive to the danger of slipping into a world of mythological fantasy.

ii. *Cherubim and seraphim*

With the *cherubim and seraphim* we encounter an angel-concept painted in more strongly mythological colours, which calls for a brief notice. The very fact of the mixed form, half human, half animal, in which they appear points to their origin in mythological thought. One of the most important sources of information about the cherubim is the descriptions in Ezek. 1 and 10, which certainly reproduce ancient ideas. According to these passages they are mixomorphs which, while certainly deriving from mankind their upright posture, face and hands, are nevertheless connected with the animals by virtue of their four wings, their animal faces, and their feet. There is ample evidence of similar hybrid beings in Babylonian representations which have come to light as the result of excavation. Phoenician art played a large part in mediating the Babylonian conception to Canaan, as may be seen from Phoenician seals and ivories which have been discovered.[1] That the biblical conception in its turn developed under the influence of Phoenician art is clear from the Palestinian ivories found at Megiddo and Samaria (cf. especially the work of A. Jirku

---

[1] For the Babylonian imagery cf. *AOB*, figs. 378–82; 390f.; J. B. Pritchard, *ANEP*, pp. 212–17; for the Phoenician art-objects cf. H. Frankfort, *Cylinder Seals*, 1939, pp. 256ff.; W. F. Albright, *Archaeology and the Religion of Israel*[2], 1946, pl. IV; A. Jirku, *Die Welt der Bibel*, 1957, pls. 63 and 98.

cited p. 202, n. 1). The function of these living creatures, as distinct from that of the angels, is not to serve as messengers but as sentinels at the throne of the holy God. This can be seen not only from Ezekiel's description, but also from the use of these mixomorphs as emblems in the furnishing of the sanctuary, where statues of cherubim stood above the Ark of the Covenant, and their pictures were woven into coverings and curtains, and incised on the leaves of doors and on walls.[1] The guarding of Paradise (Gen. 3.24) also comes under this head, inasmuch as this, too, is thought of as a dwelling-place of God.

Another function ascribed to the cherubim seems at first sight incompatible with this, namely their service as Yahweh's chariot. Not only does the *rāķia'* of Ezekiel's description, which bears the throne of God, rest on the cherubim, but Yahweh also goes or rides on a cherub in the picture in Ps. 18.11, which sounds genuinely ancient.

The association of these two forms of service with one and the same creature cannot be explained from the *name*. It is not possible to derive this from either the Hebrew or the Arabic, and the probability is that it is a loan-word from the Babylonian term for such beings, *kuribu*.[2] A connection with the Indo-Germanic *gryphus* is problematic. These winged mixomorphs were also well known in Babylonia as spirits of wind or storm.

This, and the Old Testament descriptions of their travelling through the air, have led to the conjecture that the cherub in origin represents nothing other than the personified storm-cloud. In the context of Ps. 18 this is extraordinarily illuminating; for the mighty phenomena of the storm are directly linked with Yahweh's riding upon the cherub: 'He made darkness his covering around him, his canopy thick clouds dark with water. Out of the brightness before him there broke through his clouds hailstones and coals of fire' (vv. 11f.). With this may be compared parallel expressions such as Ps. 104.3: 'who makest the clouds thy chariot', Isa. 19.1: 'Yahweh is riding on a swift cloud and comes to Egypt', and similarly Deut. 33.26. In keeping with this is the fact that in the book of Ezekiel the noise of the wings is compared to thunder, and that in the space

---

[1] I Kings 6.23ff.; 8.6ff.; Ex. 25.18ff.; 26.31; Ezek. 41.18ff. The finest illustration of a cherub-throne is to be found on the sarcophagus of Ahiram, king of Byblos: cf. A. Jirku, *op. cit.*, pl. 22. G. E. Wright (*Biblical Archaeology*, 1957) attempts a reconstruction of the cherubim in the Temple.

[2] Cf. Meissner, *OLZ* 1911, pp. 476f., and *Babylonien und Assyrien* II, 1925, p. 50.

between the four cherubim flashing fire is visible.[1] This picture of the storm-cloud pierced by lightning accords even more closely with Gen. 3.24, where the garden of God on the summit of the cosmic mountain is guarded against the invasion of men by the cherub with the 'flaming sword which turned every way', that is, by the storm-cloud hanging low over the peak. Finally, the water-tanks (RSV: 'lavers') of the Solomonic Temple, which represent nothing other than rain-clouds, and which are decorated with cherubim (I Kings 7.29, 36), point to the same nature imagery.[2] That this nature symbol was borrowed by Israel from her Canaanite environment is indicated by the Ugaritic epithet for Baal, 'Rider on the Clouds', which may be compared with Pss. 18.11 and 68.5.[3]

That such a nature symbol should turn into a guardian of the deity is easily understandable precisely because Yahweh's dwelling is in heaven. So, too, is the fact that all kinds of other mythological material, possibly of Phoenician provenance, attached itself to this fabulous being. One instance is preserved in Ezek. 28.14ff., in which the king of Tyre is compared to the cherub who walked upon the mountain of the gods and, seduced into arrogancy by his own wisdom, was hurled down from his high estate.[4] Here 'the enigmatic figure of these fantasy-formations corresponds to the mystery and unsearchableness of God; divine nearness and divine inaccessibility are by them given living actuality'.[5]

Similar considerations apply to the *seraphim*. Though they are mentioned only once, in Isa. 6.2f., it is as something perfectly well known. As heavenly ministers they stand by the enthroned God in deep reverence, covering faces and feet with their wings. In possessing human voices and hands they resemble the cherubim, but differ from them in having a serpent's body—at any rate the *śārāp meʿōpēp*, which in Isa. 14.29; 30.6 is mentioned alongside other serpents of the wilderness, points to this and cannot imply an animal of a totally different kind. The *nāḥāš śārāp*, the saraph-serpents of Num. 21.6, which are sent among the Israelites as a punishment on their journey

---

[1] Ezek. 1.24; 10.5 and 1.13; 10.6f.; except for 1.13 all these passages display secondary elaboration: cf. W. Eichrodt, *Der Prophet Hesekiel* (ATD 22.1), 1959, *ad loc.*

[2] Cf. R. Kittel, *Studien zur hebr. Archäologie und Religionsgeschichte*, 1908, pp. 236ff.

[3] Cf. G. R. Driver, *Canaanite Myths and Legends*, 1956, pp. 81f. III* A.

[4] Cf. O. Eissfeldt, *Baal Zaphon*, 1932, pp. 14, 18ff., and G. Fohrer, *Ezechiel*, 1955, *ad loc.*

[5] H. Schultz, *Alttestamentliche Theologie*[5], 1896, pp. 488f.

through the wilderness, come in the same category.[1] It may therefore be conjectured that in ancient Israelite popular belief demonic serpent beings played a part as guardians of the deity. In Isaiah these creatures are basically no more than symbols of the consuming holiness and universally effective power of Yahweh.

III. *Satan*

The demons are not to be included in Yahweh's heavenly court. They do indeed play a part in popular belief, but they are not associated with the Lord of heaven, and therefore call for consideration at a different point.

This does not, however, apply to the figure of the *Satan*. He belongs in Yahweh's heavenly court as a fully-qualified member, and by nature has nothing to do with demons.[2]

Originally, indeed, *haśśāṭān* designates an angel of Yahweh entrusted with a particular task. He is the Public Prosecutor or District Attorney, who brings men's guilt to God's remembrance. Hence in the LXX he is also called κατήγωρ or διάβολος, the 'adversary', 'persecutor' or 'accuser'. That such an occupation does not necessarily presuppose an evil character is clear from the fact that men of God are also expected to uncover human guilt, *yazkīrū ʿāwōn* (Elijah: I Kings 17.18). When therefore the Satan or Accuser attacks the High Priest Joshua (Zech. 3.1–5),[3] who as his polluted garments indicate is by no means free from guilt, or when (Job 1.6–12; 2.1–7), while attending the heavenly council as one of the *bᵉnē ʾelōhīm*, he describes the piety of Job as very much in need of testing, he is only doing his duty, and comes in the same class as the *malʾāk mašḥīt*.[4] If

---

[1] It is interesting that certain mixomorphic creatures which have been discovered in a grave of the Twelfth Dynasty at Beni Hassan are called in Demotic, the secular dialect of Egypt, *serref*.

[2] An instructive critique of earlier views may be found in R. R. Schärf, *Die Gestalt des Satans im AT* (Diss. Zürich, 1948).

[3] It will not do to explain the High Priest's predicament as that of the representative of an unclean community, for acquittal brings him a purely personal privilege; moreover, the guilt of the people is treated in the sixth vision (Zech. 5.1ff.).

[4] It is quite impossible to say, as Dillmann does (*Alttest. Theologie*, p. 338), that the accusation against the High Priest in Zech. 3 is contrary to God's plans; he is simply doing his duty, but is rebuked because God wishes to show grace rather than justice. It would be easier to find a certain element of malice in the enthusiasm of the Accuser in the Job story; occupation easily corrupts character. But it is only necessary to remember that we are dealing with the illustrative detail of a folk-story to reject any theological evaluation of this particular trait.

an allusion to the role of the public prosecutor at the courts of the Asiatic kings, apparently echoed in the *mazkīr 'āwōn* of Ezek. 21.28; 29.16, is justified, then we would have to see in the Satan, as in the heavenly vizier, an official of the celestial court modelled on the pattern of earthly empires. This derivation is more probable than one from the *bel dababi*, the 'accuser' who in Babylonia attended each human being and who was the counterpart of the individual protective deity.[1]

Not only the fact that this description is in entire conformity with the Hebrew conception of angels but also the good Hebrew root of the name *śāṭān* argues against the borrowing of this figure from foreign sources. Both the verb *śāṭan*, to 'persecute', 'make war upon', and so to 'attack with accusations', to 'accuse', and the noun *śāṭān*, 'adversary', 'opponent', are also used of human beings.[2] In addition the angel of Yahweh who according to Num. 22.22, 32 opposes Balaam does so as a Satan: *lᵉśāṭān*, that is, as an adversary. That this genuinely Hebraic conception of the Satan is fairly ancient may be deduced from the fact that the prologue to the Book of Job is based on an older popular story.

Even if, however, no qualitatively new element is introduced into the general conception of angels, it remains noteworthy that it should be the popular religion which imports the figure of the Satan into the literature, and that prophecy makes use of it only in its later phase. One feels that in earlier times the spiritual leaders of Israel found it unnecessary to speak of this figure—a sign that it is not yet of central importance.

I Chron. 21.1 introduces a slight change into the narrative inasmuch as here the tempting of David to number the people is ascribed not to God, as in the parallel passage in II Sam. 24.1, but to Satan. This is remarkable in two ways. First, the accuser is now given a proper name, *śāṭān*, and is no longer *haśśāṭān*. This shows that by the fourth century in Israel the concept of a supernatural adversary had solidified into a quite definite, sharply delineated figure.[3] Secondly, temptation to evil is now associated with this

---

[1] E. Schrader, *Die Keilinschriften und das AT*³, 1903, pp. 461, 463. According to B. Landsberger this refers to a man: cf. G. von Rad, *TWNT* II, p. 74, n. 16. It is quite untenable to explain the Satan psychologically as the personified voice of a bad conscience (so K. Marti, *Geschichte der isr. Religion*⁴, 1903, p. 249).

[2] For the former cf. Pss. 38.21; 109.4; for the latter I Sam. 29.4; I Kings 5.18; Ps. 109.6, etc.

[3] Kaupel (*Die Dämonen im AT*, 1930, pp. 104ff.), in dependence on F. H. Kugler, attempted without success to deny the importance of this passage by reference to I Kings 5.18 and Ps. 109.6.

being. The faith of the earlier period felt compelled to think of God's activity in as comprehensive terms as possible, and therefore ascribed evil to him as well. Now this part of the divine operations is to a certain extent detached from God and made into an independent hypostasis.[1] In this way the preconditions were established for introducing into religious thought an evil spirit, the originator of evil, as a superhuman focus of all sin.

It is not, however, possible to say more on this point solely on the basis of the passage just cited. The elaboration and dogmatic formulation of the idea took place, strictly speaking, not within the Old Testament but in the apocrypha and pseudepigrapha.[2] It is true nevertheless that one can point to certain passages in the Old Testament where there are glimmerings of the idea of a superhuman being hostile to God. Such is Gen. 3, where, while it is true that to the mind of the narrator the serpent cannot have been more than one of the beasts of the field, endowed merely with special cunning, yet there is a hint of a demonic character. For in the present form of the story the serpent's awareness of the effect of the tree of knowledge, and its bitter enmity against God, remain unexplained, and involuntarily recall the demons in serpent form who figure in the mythology of almost all peoples. To this extent the writer of the Wisdom of Solomon is not so very far wrong when he expounds Gen. 3 in the sense that in the serpent the διάβολος was at work (Wisd. 2.24); and on the basis of Rev. 12.1 and 20.2 the Church has sided with him.

Another passage on which the faith of the Church has fastened, and not altogether without justification, is Gen. 6.1–4, which has already been mentioned. However impermissible it may be to look here for a theory of the origin of evil, and even though it is plain that the story is fragmentary and intentionally unclear, nevertheless we are not entitled to say that no ethical standard at all is applied to the action of the *benē* *'elōhīm*. The incident is undoubtedly felt to be an outrage against God; and as soon as the development of the concept of Satan led men to the idea that the origin of evil was to be sought

[1] Cf. pp. 177f. above. For this reason R. R. Schärf (*op. cit.*, p. 60) describes the Satan not unjustifiably as 'a personified function of God which gradually develops into something outside the divine personality and breaks loose from it'. Her attempt at a psychological explanation of the Satan figure on the basis of C. G. Jung's theory of archetypes does not call for comment here.

[2] Cf. Wisd. Sol. 2.23f.; Test. Dan 5; Test. Napht. 3; Test. Asher 3; Jub. 19.28; Martyrdom of Isaiah 2.2, 7. On this subject cf. H. Bietenhard, *Die himmlische Welt im Urchristentum und Spätjudentum*, 1951, pp. 113ff.; W. Förster, 'Die spätjüdische Satansauffassung', *TWNT* II, pp. 74ff.

in the angelic order, then inevitably they turned to this narrative. It is true that in so doing they were going beyond the intention of the ancient narrator, but they had not incorrectly sensed the original meaning of his story, which he had, in fact, suppressed.

Finally, mention must be made of the *hēlāl* of Isa. 14.12, the bright star and son of the dawn, who wished to take heaven by storm in order to set up his throne higher than the stars of God. This figure of a Titanic assailant of heaven was undoubtedly used by Isaiah only as a poetic simile for the outrageous self-aggrandizement of the earthly world-ruler. But behind it stands a myth, stemming indeed from paganism, of the rebellion of an angelic being against the most high God, which ended in his being thrown down into the underworld. When this bright star was named in the Latin translation Lucifer, and interpreted by Tertullian and Gregory the Great through association with Luke 10.18 as Satan, once again the influence of the pre-Israelite view came to life.

The conception of a supernatural power of evil would seem to be more strongly spiritualized in the genuinely Israelite *rūaḥ ḥaṭṭum'ā* (Zech. 13.2). This is related to the *rūaḥ zᵉnūnîm* of Hos. 4.12; 5.4, which appears as an evil spiritual power of independent operation, and in some sense anticipates the substance of the Satan concept. As the antithesis of the *rūaḥ* hypostasis by which fullness of life and moral strength are communicated to the congregation of God it holds sway among men as a permanent power of impurity, to be extirpated only by Yahweh in the age of salvation. The people cannot of themselves do away with it, for it is supernatural in character. Related to this is the vision of Zech. 5.7ff., where iniquity appears as a woman who by the power of the angels is removed from the people of the age of salvation. Strangely enough these two conceptions exerted no influence on future developments.

The spiritual process which led to the dogmatic formulation of the idea of Satan may therefore be characterized by saying that concepts suppressed in the Old Testament awake to new life in later Judaism. I Enoch 15f. provides an explicit description of the fall of the angels and their subsequent punishment.[1]

---

[1] Cf. H. Bietenhard, *Die himmlische Welt im Urchristentum und Spätjudentum*, 1951, pp. 205, 211; L. Jung, *Fallen Angels in Jewish, Christian and Mohammedan Literature*, 1926. On the role of Satan as the Angel of Darkness in the writings of the Qumran community cf. F. Nötscher, 'Geist und Geister in den Texten von Qumran', *Mélanges Bibliques A. Robert*, 1955, pp. 305ff.; H. W. Huppenbauer, 'Der Mensch

The suggestion that the influence of Persian religion, in which the evil spirit Angrya Mainyu played so great a part, also affected this process is not to be dismissed out of hand. At least the Book of Tobit shows unquestionable influence of Persian demonological beliefs; it is the Persian name Aeshma Daeva which is modified into that of the evil spirit Asmodeus. Hence the possibility cannot be ruled out that stimuli from this quarter may have affected developments in the Hellenistic period, when the individual figure of Satan was surrounded by a kingdom of ministering spirits which gradually grew into a counterpart of the transcendent divine world, and in which all the forces of evil upon earth found their real support and source of power.[1] But the dualism which the Persian religion never overcame, and which is implicit in the eternity of the evil as well as the good spirit, at no time became proper to the concept of Satan. Isa. 45.7 et al. seem indeed to be direct polemic against such an idea.[2]

It is obvious that the use of the Satan concept in this way to anchor the ethical opposition between good and evil in the metaphysical order was not only a genuine interpretation of Old Testament statements, but also increased the force and profundity of that opposition and gave an immense impetus to men's sense of responsibility. It is here and not in any explanation of the problems of the world that the value of this vision of the realm of evil—a value recognized in the New Testament also—is to be found. Speculation about the fall of the angels must, on the other hand, be rejected on the basis of the Old Testament itself as unbiblical.

---

zwischen zwei Welten. Der Dualismus der Texte von Qumran (Höhle I) und der Damaskusfragmente. Ein Beitrag zur Vorgeschichte des Evangeliums', *ATANT* 34, 1959.

[1] Cf. vol. I, pp. 471, 487ff.
[2] An exhaustive discussion of the possibility of Persian influence may be found in E. Langton, *Essentials of Demonology*, 1949, pp. 61ff.

THE UNDERWORLD

I N ADDITION TO THE worlds of heaven and earth the Israelites knew also of an Underworld. Whereas, however, the concepts of the first two, despite clear affinities with the corresponding ideas in heathenism, were strongly influenced by Israel's distinctive spirituality, the same cannot be said of the Underworld—at any rate in so far as its presentation independently of belief in redemption is concerned. The links with Babylonian conceptions are particularly close.[1] But ample parallels can also be adduced from the belief of primitive peoples, proving that even the religion of the great civilizations cannot in this respect exactly boast of great achievements.

I. SHEOL

Like most nations, Israel knows of a place of the dead, which from the fact that one has to go down to reach it (the standard term is *yārad*) appears to have been a kind of underworld. This is the *še'ōl*. The word seems to be of immemorial antiquity; it is one of those concepts which no longer require the article, and thus have virtually become proper names. The etymology is in dispute.[2] The earliest

[1] Cf. A. Jeremias, *Die babylonisch-assyrischen Vorstellungen vom Leben nach dem Tode*, 1887; *Hölle und Paradies bei den Babyloniern*[2], 1903.

[2] The derivation from a root *š-ʿ-l*, 'to be hollow', has been universally abandoned as linguistically impossible. L. Köhler (*TZ* II, 1946, pp. 71ff.) has put forward an explanation of the word on the basis of the Hebrew root *š-ʾ-h*, 'to be desolate', strengthened by the addition of the formative element *l*, thus giving the sense 'the desolate realm' or the 'un-world'. W. Baumgartner (*TZ* II, 1946, pp. 233ff.), while admitting the possibility of this, prefers as more probable the derivation proposed as early as 1926 by W. F. A. Albright from the Babylonian *shuʾara*. Originally this word denoted the sojourn of Tammuz in the underworld, and then came to designate the underworld itself. There are frequent instances in Semitic languages of the substitution of *l* for *r*, and the fact that *še'ōl* takes no article, which gives it the appearance of a proper name, fits well with an adoption from Babylonian mythology.

mentions occur in Gen. 37.35; 42.38; 44.29, 31; Num. 16.30, 33. From these passages we can derive the idea of a place under the earth to which one descends, but in which there is no community of the dead one with another and consequently no hope of seeing again those who have gone before. This agrees completely with later statements on the subject, so that it is permissible to assume a fairly unchanging picture of Sheol through the centuries.[1]

Generally speaking, existence in Sheol is a faithful, if shadowy, copy of existence on earth. There, too, kings sit on their thrones (Isa. 14.9ff.) and the prophet wears his mantle (I Sam. 28.14), and therefore rank and calling continue. But it is a place of silence and stillness where the impotence of the shadow beings makes the boisterous vigour of real life quite impossible. Indeed, the shades themselves bear the name $r^e p\bar{a}'\bar{\imath}m$, the 'weak' or 'powerless' ones. That is why even those spirits of the dead which are conjured up can do no more than chirp (Isa. 8.19; 29.4). Going down into the underworld is characterized as becoming weak, $hull\bar{a}h$, (Isa. 14.10), and the state of the dead is compared to that of men who sleep (Nahum 3.18). The picture in Isa. 14 of the excitement throughout the realm of the dead when the oppressor of the nations, who kept the whole world in suspense, also arrives below as a powerless shade is a poetic description which, in fact, confirms by contrast the customary state of silence. As a rule the dead know nothing of events in the world above; cf. Job 14.21: 'his sons come to honour, and he does not know it'; Eccles 9.5f.: 'the dead know nothing'.

We can see something of the radical affinity between these ideas and those of Babylonia from the pictures of the world of the dead in the myth of Ishtar's Descent into the Underworld and in the Gilgamesh Epic.[2] According to these documents the underworld is a domain enclosed by walls and gates, with its entrance in the far West, and accessible only by crossing the river of the underworld. It is described as the dark land, the dwelling which no man leaves who enters it, whose inhabitants lack the light, and have earth for their miserable nourishment and clay for their food. Clothed like birds with a coat of feathers, they live in gloom, while dust lies thick on door and bolt. In this house of dust dwell the high priest and the acolyte, the exorcist and the interpreter of dreams and the priest who

---

[1] On the physical features of Sheol cf. pp. 95f. above.
[2] Cf. A. Ungnad, *Die Religion der Babylonier und Assyrer*, 1921, pp. 142 and 118; *AOT*, pp. 206ff. and 185f.

anoints the great gods, as well as Etana and other sages of ancient times. The distinctions of earthly life are therefore retained. But existence there below is without peace or joy, so that, as Gilgamesh's friend Enkidu says, the man who experiences the order of the underworld must sit and weep the whole day through.

These descriptions are manifestly the product of an imagination which on the one hand has brought together all that is sorrowful and ugly, and yet on the other has been compelled to make use for the purpose of illustration of the conditions of earthly life. Moreover, life beneath the earth is influenced by events above to the extent that there is a relation between the treatment of the corpse of the dead person and his condition in the underworld. According to the Gilgamesh Epic the man who has been slain in battle is allowed to lie on a couch and to drink pure water so long as his relatives take trouble on his behalf. But if a man has found no grave his dead spirit knows no rest; he wanders about as a vagrant, and has to eat the leavings in the pot and the bits thrown out on the street.

This connection between the absence or inadequacy of burial and a worse lot in the underworld seems to have played some part in Israel also. In Isa. 14 the refusal of honourable interment (vv. 19f.) results in the dishonouring of the tyrant in the underworld (v. 11). Similarly in Ezek. 32.23 the Assyrian is banished to the farthest corner of Sheol. This is why the Israelite attaches such value to regular burial (cf. Gen. 23 and the care taken over the interment of the patriarchs), and feels the prophets' predictions of the desecration of graves and of the scattering of the bones of the dead as such an appalling threat: cf. II Kings 9.10 Jer. 8.1; 16.4; 22.19.[1]

2. THE GRAVE AND SURVIVAL IN THE GRAVE

Consequently the survival of the dead person depends to a certain extent on the fate of his corpse. This is somewhat surprising in association with a belief in distant Sheol and its shadowy images; but it would at once become understandable if it were the grave which had

---

[1] Cf. also I Sam. 17.44, 46, and A. Bertholet, *Die israelitischen Vorstellungen vom Zustande nach dem Tode*, 1899; G. Beer, 'Der biblische Hades' (*Theol. Abhandlungen zu Ehren H. J. Holtzmanns*, 1902); Aubrey R. Johnson, *The Vitality of the Individual in the Thought of Ancient Israel*, 1949, pp. 88ff.; E. Ebeling, *Tod und Leben nach den Vorstellungen der Babylonier* I, 1931; A. Heidel, *The Gilgamesh Epic and OT Parallels*, 1945. On the subject of the judgment of the dead cf. ch. XXIV below.

originally counted as the dwelling-place of the dead. In fact, side by side with the Sheol conception we do find another—and to all appearance older—view, according to which the dead dwell in the grave. Not only is the grave called the habitation of the dead (Isa. 22.16), but great importance is attached to being buried alongside the members of one's family (cf. II Sam. 17.23; 19.38, Gen. 47.30; 50.25). This explains why to bury someone among the common people, as Jehoiakim did the prophet Uriah, is to dishonour him (Jer. 26.23). This, too, is the origin of the fairly common expressions 'to be gathered to one's fathers' and 'to go to or sleep with one's fathers': *ne'esap 'el-'ammāw; šākab 'im-'abōtāw*.[1] To see one of the bench-type graves, which were the sort in most common use in ancient Israel, is to realize that such phrases are to be taken literally. The family dead were simply laid on rock shelves extending along the walls in the burial cave; later the bones were collected in an artificial cavity. Thus even in death the family remained united. As a natural result the phraseology became generalized, and could be used in cases where there was no question of an ancestral grave, as with Abraham, Moses and Aaron.

This concern to be united with one's fathers and the other members of the family clearly derives from a belief that the dead still survive in some way or other in the grave. This is, in fact, the oldest form of belief in survival, being found even among primitive peoples. Strictly understood it is incompatible with the idea of Sheol, the general gathering-place of the dead; but it is perverse to seek to iron out this contradiction by assuming a line of development: one grave—many graves—great burial cave—underworld. For the same contradiction is found among primitives. The idea of Sheol, deriving as it does from the exercise of the imagination, was manifestly never able to efface entirely belief in the presence of the dead in the grave, and this for the quite simple reason that the latter had appearances on its side. The custom of giving food to the dead, which even though taboo continued in Israel down to the very latest period (cf. Deut. 26.14; Ecclus 30.18; Tobit 4.17), indicates the toughness of this belief. To this day little pans of water can be seen on Muslim graves, placed there for the dead to drink from, though people do not like to talk about the practice. And something of the same kind underlies the custom still carried on in Europe today of placing little Christmas trees on the graves of children. In this last-named instance no one

[1] Gen. 25.8; 35.29; 49.49, 33; Deut. 32.50; Judg. 2.10; I Kings 2.10.

would, of course, speak of a cult of the dead; and the term is equally inappropriate to the leaving of food for the dead in ancient Israel.

That, however, which lives on in the grave is not a soul which had once been present in the living person but the whole man. Hence the dead are called neither *nepeš* nor *nᵉpāšōt* nor *rūaḥ* but *mētîm* or *rᵉpā'îm*, the 'dead' or the 'weak'.[1] Israel fully shared the primitive belief that a shadowy image of the dead person detached itself from him and continued to eke out a bare existence; and we only confuse this idea if we mix it up with our own concept of the soul. For death results from God's withdrawing the breath of life, the *rūaḥ*, whereupon Man expires and once more becomes dust, that is, inanimate matter (Gen. 3.19; Job 34.14f.; Eccles. 12.7). In this respect Man is like the animals (Ps. 104.29); hence the Preacher asks despairingly (Eccles. 3.18–21) whether after death there is any difference between the two. Equally the *nepeš*, the life or individual existence, comes to an end. If it is sometimes said that the *nepeš* goes down into Sheol, or is rescued from it, this does not refer to actual death, but is poetic diction for mortal danger, *nepeš* signifying either the life which already seemed to have succumbed to death, or simply standing for the personal pronoun: 'my soul' = 'I' (cf. Pss. 16.10; 30.4; 49.16; 86.13; 89.49; Prov. 23.14). What survives, therefore, is not a *part* of the living man but a shadowy image of the *whole* man. There is no need here to discuss the

---

[1] This translation explains the word in terms of the root *r-p-h*, 'to become slack'. In Late Phoenician inscriptions the word is used to mean 'shades' or 'spirits'. The problem of the Old Testament usage lies in the fact that the same word concurrently denotes a people of the primal age (Gen. 14.5; Deut. 2.11, 20; 3.11, 13; Josh. 12.4; 13.12; 17.15), but that we cannot assume two different roots for the two meanings (as L. Köhler does, *LVT*). The interpretation is still further complicated by the presence of the word in the Ugaritic texts, where it denotes a group of (7 or 8?) servants either of the sun-goddess Shepesh or of the dying and rising Baal. They are also called *'lnm*, probably 'the divine ones', so that explanations oscillate between genuine divine beings (so Ch. Virolleaud, 'Les Rephaim: fragments der poèmes de Ras Shamra', *Syria* XXII, 1941, pp. 1–30; Dussaud, *et al.*) and human cultic officials who as attendants of the god-king possessed divine authority for carrying out the fertility rites (so esp. J. Gray, 'The Rephaim', *Palestine Expl. Quarterly* 21, 1949, pp. 27ff., and *The Legacy of Canaan*, 1957, pp. 153f.). The signification of the word might in both cases be 'healers' or 'possessors of healing powers'; but other interpretations are also possible: cf. the list in G. R. Driver, *Canaanite Myths and Legends*, 1956, p. 155, cf. pp. 9f. How from this starting-point the word could come to denote both the spirits of the dead (possibly originally chthonic deities who would be related both to the world of the dead and to the fertility of the earth) and peoples of the primal age (here the favoured explanation is in terms of an euhemeristic deviation) is as yet completely unclear. I am indebted to Walter Baumgartner for several references; for further information the reader is directed to his provisional account in *TR* 13, 1941, p. 89.

origins of this remarkable belief; in all probability it has something to do with the experience, in itself inexplicable, of the *revenant*.

Among non-Israelite peoples this belief often exerted a strong influence on their religious life. That the potential for such a development was also present in Israel may be seen from the designation of the dead as *'elōhīm*, divine beings (I Sam. 28.13), to whom a knowledge of the future is attributed. There are also necromancers, *yiddᵉ'ōnī*, that is, 'knowing ones'[1] (Isa. 8.19; Lev. 19.31; 20.6; Deut. 18.11; I Sam. 28.3, 9, etc.), who understand the art of causing the dead to appear and speak. The dead person in this case is termed an *'ōb* (Lev. 19.31; 20.6, 27; Deut. 18.11), a word which may simply mean a *revenant* (cf. the Arabic root *'-w-b*, to return; Sabaean *y-'-b*). According to Lev. 20.27 the dead may also enter a man or woman, take possession of them and speak through them. This is an animistic elaboration of belief in the returning dead.

Furthermore, the mourning customs practised in Israel, partly forbidden, partly tolerated by the Law, point in some degree to an influence of the dead upon the living and vice versa. When as a sign of mourning people tear their clothes, sit in ashes, scatter earth upon their heads, and wear sackcloth in place of their ordinary clothing, the origin of this custom, agreeing as it does with the practice of primitive peoples, can hardly be interpreted as anything other than an attempt to make oneself unrecognizable to the dead from fear of their envy or malice. The legal prescription (Num. 19.15) that every open vessel which does not have a covering secured with a cord becomes unclean as a result of the proximity of a dead body must likewise derive from the fear that the spirit of the dead may try to hide itself in the house in order to avoid having to enter the grave with the corpse. Among the Batak of Sumatra it is the custom for this reason to make a loud clamour at the interment, and also for preference to remove the body through a hole broken in the wall of the hut rather than through the door, in order that the spirit of the dead may not find its way back again.

This is not, of course, to say that the original meaning of these various practices was at all periods consciously present to the

[1] Many also see in this word a term for the actual spirit of the dead. The attractive explanation of both expressions as referring to certain implements with which the interrogation of the dead spirit was carried out, namely the bull-roarer, well known from primitive religion, a view which has been put forward by H. Schmidt (*Marti-Festschrift*, BZAW 41, 1925, pp. 253ff.), will not bear closer examination (cf. K. Budde, *Jesajas Erleben*, 1928, p. 92, n. 2, and *ZAW* 46, pp. 75f.).

Israelites. Instead in most cases the same process will have taken place as may be observed with many of our own customs, namely that the original meaning is quite forgotten. Hence such practices are not properly of interest either for religion or for biblical theology, but only for the archaeologist.[1]

3. THE PROBLEM OF ANCESTOR WORSHIP

It would, however, be quite a different matter if on the basis of these customs the existence of ancestor worship could be proved, as in particular J. C. Matthes[2] and Fr. Schwally[3] believed. In that case the practice, for example, of wounding oneself by incisions, of cutting off and tearing out the hair of the head and the beard respectively, and of veiling the head or at least the lower part of the face, would be a ritual of dedication to the service of the dead by which one declared oneself a slave of the ancestral spirit now venerated as a god. It is, however, precisely the comparison with primitive ideas which shows this interpretation to be in error. For the incisions that draw blood and the offering of the hair do not originally have a sacrificial significance, but are methods of resuscitation applied to those who have just died in an attempt to transfer to them the life-force present in these things.[4] This interpretation is supported by the evidence of the practice of sprinkling the sick with blood in order to endue them with fresh strength. It was, moreover, precisely these mourning customs which Israelite law strictly forbade,[5] not indeed so much because they had been tenaciously rooted from earlier times as because they were constantly trying to force their way in from the Canaanites and other neighbouring peoples.

---

[1] Rightly stressed by E. Kautzsch, *Bibl. Theologie des AT*, p. 13.

[2] 'Rouw en doodenvereering in Israel', *Theol. Tijdschr.* 1900, pp. 97ff., 193ff.

[3] *Das Leben nach dem Tode nach den Vorstellungen des alten Israel und des Judentums*, 1892. Cf. also J. Lippert, *Der Seelenkult in seinen Beziehungen zur althebräischen Religion*, 1881; P. Torge, *Seelenglauben und Unsterblichkeitshoffnung im AT*, 1909.

[4] Less probable is the explanation in terms of a prophylactic rite designed to make the mourner unrecognizable to the spirit of the dead person. The earlier overvaluation of animism as a principle of interpretation has today been overcome by the recognition that belief in *mana* represents a more original and much more comprehensive element in the world of primitive ideas: cf., e.g., N. Söderblom, *Das Werden des Gottesglaubens*[2], 1926; K. Beth, *Religion und Magie bei den Naturvölkern*[2], 1927; C. H. Ratschow, *Magie und Religion*, 1947; G. van der Leeuw, *Phänomenologie der Religion*[2], 1956.

[5] Deut. 14.1f.; Lev. 19.27f.; 21.5.

It is for the same reason that the Law draws so sharp a line of separation between the dead and the religion of Yahweh. Any contact with, even indeed the mere proximity of, a corpse is enough to render one unclean.[1] The lawgiver was plainly aware of the danger which, in view of the persistent influence of the religious environment, any suggestion of tolerance toward these widespread mourning customs was bound to bring with it. But we have no right whatever to derive the pollution proclaimed in the Law from some special holiness attaching to the worship of the dead in ancient Israel.

Just as little has the custom of leaving food for the dead[2] anything to do with a sacrificial meal in honour of the divinized ancestors; nor is there any evidence to be found elsewhere in the Old Testament which can be adduced in support of such a supposition. Ps. 106.28 mentions *zibḥē mētīm*, which were eaten in connection with the cult of Baal Peor, and were therefore a foreign importation. The custom of handing the mourner food and a cup of consolation, with which he may end his fast, is, of course, something entirely different from a sacrificial meal, and implies no more than a simple expression of sympathy with one's friend.

If any circumstance at all can be pressed into service to provide some sort of effective proof of the existence of ancestor worship, then the only one worthy of real consideration is the strikingly high regard in which the ancestral graves were held. Genesis in particular is absolutely full of traditions about the graves of the patriarchs and their families, and attaches palpable importance to the fact that all the forebears of the nation found their last resting-place in Canaan, and that their graves are still known right down to the writer's own time. Thus we are given a most circumstantial account of the way in which Abraham purchased the cave of Machpelah near Hebron (Gen. 23), and how by Sarah's side he himself (25.9), and later Isaac and Rebekah (35.29; 49.31) and Jacob and Leah (49.29ff.; 50.12f.), were buried there. In addition we know of the grave of Rachel on the road from Bethel to Ephrata (35.19), and that of Deborah, Rebekah's nurse, by the oak of Bethel (35.8). Tradition has also handed down to us the burial-places of Aaron (Deut. 10.6), Miriam (Num. 20.1), Joseph (Josh. 24.32), Joshua (Josh. 24.30), Gideon (Judg. 8.32), Jephthah (Judg. 12.7), Samson (Judg. 16.31) and the so-called Minor Judges, though the first two in this list are admittedly outside Canaan.

[1] Lev. 21; Num. 5.2; 19.11ff., 14ff.
[2] Cf. p. 213 above.

It is, however, a striking fact that precisely in the case of the graves of the patriarchs the source which gives such detailed information about them should be the latest, namely the Priestly stratum, the clear and sober monotheism of which must from the outset protect it against any suspicion that it wished to show reverence for the sites of an ancient cult of the dead. Only as regards the graves of Rachel and Deborah does our information come from an older source, the Elohist; but these are just the instances in which ancestor-worship is as good as excluded. For if normally only male ancestors have a claim to adoration, then this certainly rules out the nurse of the tribal mother! Attempts have indeed been made to educe from the Priestly narrative a polemic against the cult of the dead, and to say that the writer, precisely because he makes no mention of any kind of cult at the graves, is seeking to bring out the absurdity of the grave cultus: a grave is a grave—and nothing more! But such a method of polemic, consisting of a detailed account of the purchase of the graves, is so ineffectual as to be simply unbelievable. If this had been his intention, P is much more likely to have followed the example of the older sources, and said nothing at all about the ancestral burial-places. Far more probably he had a positive interest in them, related to rights of possession. Either he was particularly interested in the change of the legal position of Abraham in Canaan when by his purchase of real estate his status was raised from that of a client without legal rights to that of a landowner of equal standing with the native-born, or it is a question of the right to ownership of Hebron after the Edomites had settled there in the sixth century. In either case, of course, Gen. 23 and the passages dependent upon it would have to be regarded as a later side interest in the Priestly historical narrative.

The problem is more complicated in the case of the graves of the Judges, which are mentioned in the older sources and especially in the Elohistic. Here certainly there can be no question of simple ancestor-worship, but there is a suggestion of a hero-cult. Now Wundt[1] has drawn attention to the fact that those heroes who stand half-way between gods and men have, as a result of the fusion of ancestors venerated as divine with local nature deities, acquired their character partly because the ancestral line was traced back to God as its originator or because a political leader proclaimed himself directly as a god, leaving out the generations in between. The nature myth

---

[1] W. Wundt, *Völkerpsychologie* 4.1, pp. 452ff.

then absorbs the elements of ancestor-worship by anthropomorphiz-ing its own divine figures, and turning them into bringers of culture and founders of states. This modification was given its classical expression among the Greeks. Now, if these conditions for the emergence of a hero-cult are borne in mind, then on the basis of our knowledge of both the Canaanite and the Israelite religions it must be said that in Canaan such a cult is extremely unlikely. Not only are the local nature deities there already closely bound up with the Baal as the sky-god, a relationship which is bound to obstruct their demotion to the status of human bringers of culture, but a prime requisite for this religious development is lacking, namely that of ancestor-worship.

Two last arguments for the existence of ancestor-worship must be mentioned—the cultic importance of the family unit, and the institu-tion of levirate marriage. Both, however, are very weak, and affect nothing of what has already been established. Certainly it is notice-able that in Israel right up to a late period the family forms not just a social but also a cultic group. Thus David, according to I Sam. 20.6, 29, has his absence from the royal court excused on the grounds that he has had to go to an annual sacrificial feast of his clan at Bethlehem. But we also find the same kind of *zebaḥ hayyāmīm* being offered by a family at prominent sanctuaries such as Shiloh (cf. I Sam. 1.21; 2.19), with the implication that the family as a cultic group was felt to be the normal unit in the Yahweh cultus. To assert that this custom could only have arisen as a result of an earlier veneration of common ancestors, and could not be based on the importance of the family as the primary social group, is pure *petitio principii*.

Finally, the institution of levirate marriage is much better explained in terms of ancient belief in *mana* than of ancestor-worship. Deut. 25.7ff. requires that the brother of a husband who has died childless should marry his widow, and then have the first son of this marriage entered in the family records as the son of the dead man. Gen. 38 affords evidence that this custom is ancient. Now, there is no need to deny that it is in many ways attractive to explain levirate marriage in terms of the desire to guarantee the dead man the cultus that is his due, all the more so as this marriage with the brother-in-law occurs precisely among those people with whom ancestor-worship is indi-genous, namely Indians, Persians, Afghans and others. Nevertheless too much should not be built on this fact. If one is not prepared to regard as original the motive given in the Israelite Law, namely the retention of the inheritance of the dead for the family and the tribe, there is yet another to be taken into account, that is, that the name of the one who has died childless should not be rooted out of Israel. This explanation is supported by Absalom's action in setting up a memorial to himself during his lifetime, because he wished to prevent his name falling into oblivion as a result of his childlessness (II Sam. 18.18). Patently there can be no question of ancestor-worship here, for it is impossible to imagine how the memorial could be a substitute for the cult of the dead. The most probable explanation of the belief here mentioned is the primitive one that a man survives in his progeny, and that his name forms a kind of *alter ego* which in relative independence of the man who bears it, and yet not without influence on his fortunes, leads an existence of its own. According to the most recent investigations, this belief is more probably to be included under the general head of belief in *mana*; for the conception is dominated less by the survival of the soul than by the retention of vital power within the family. In course of time this primitive basis could, of course, be spiritualized, so that in retaining the name there was more thought of keeping in remembrance the person in question. At the same time, however, the association of a firm right of inheritance with the institution of marrying the brother-in-law gave the custom permanent stability even after the original content had evaporated.

The extant evidence therefore provides only a shaky foundation for assuming that there was originally ancestor-worship in Israel; while on the other hand there is a positive counter-indication, often too little taken into account, and that is the silence of the religious law on the subject of this cult.[1] While all other kinds of religious abuses are condemned, ancestor-worship receives no mention whatever. For even the prohibition against *enquiring* of the dead has nothing to do with ancestor-*worship*, nor indeed with the *worship* of any of the dead. If, however, ancestor-worship had really flourished among the Hebrew tribes in the pre-Mosaic period, one would have expected a totally different attitude toward it on the part of the Yahwist religion from that indicated by the evidence.[2]

[1] Particularly emphasized by E. König, *Theologie*[3, 4], p. 31.

[2] The following writers have come out against the existence of ancestor worship in early Israel: J. Frey, *Tod, Seelenglaube und Seelenkult im alten Israel*, 1898; K. Grüneisen, *Der Ahnenkultus und die Urreligion Israels*, 1899; P. Heinisch, *Die Trauergebräuche bei den Israeliten*, 1931. The theory is still maintained by G. Hölscher, *Geschichte der isr. und jüd. Religion*, 1922, pp. 30f., 37ff. R. Martin-Achard (*De la mort à la résurrection d'après l'Ancien Testament*, 1956, pp. 21ff.) reserves judgment.

4. THE IMPORTANCE FOR ISRAELITE RELIGION
OF ISRAEL'S BELIEFS ABOUT THE DEAD

All the indications we have collected relating in one way or another to those Israelite practices concerned with life after death prove one thing at least clearly enough: there were growth-points in plenty in the world of Israelite ideas from which a genuine cult of the dead could have become firmly established, or from which the life of the dead could at least have developed into an unhealthy encumbrance to religious life and thought. Isa. 65.4 shows that it was precisely in times of external collapse that religious malformations of this kind ventured into the light: 'A people who provoke Yahweh . . . who sit in tombs and spend the night in the sepulchres (RSV: secret places).' All the more remarkable is it that Israelite religion succeeded in overcoming, almost without trace, the danger which threatened it from this direction. The unimportance of the dead for the normal life of the Israelite is an incontrovertible fact, paralleled in only one other instance in the history of ancient religion, that of Homer's Greece. The two situations are, however, quite different. In the feudal society of the Homeric period there was an unbridled will to live which in combination with especially propitious outward circumstances fashioned a social religion that utterly refused the dead access into the present world, and confined them to Hades. Greek popular religion, however, was never freed from the spell cast by beliefs about the dead.

In Israel by contrast it was the shattering experience of God's will to rule which shut the gates of the kingdom of the dead, and proscribed any dealings with the departed. Yahweh's claim to exclusive lordship covered not only alien gods but also those subterranean powers which might offer their help to men. In this way his sovereignty was deliberately concentrated on this world; it was on this earth that God's kingdom was to be set up. The direction of all his forces to this end gave a man's life its whole content and value. Hence Yahweh claimed the living for himself, and united them to his people; the dead had no further relationship with him.

This is not to say that the realm of the dead is anywhere thought of as something independent of Yahweh, as so to speak standing under its own sovereign. Even if Amos 9.2 is the first explicit mention of Yahweh's power over Sheol, yet this could hardly have been doubted even before that time. There was simply no occasion to speak of it,

since Yahweh himself did not bother about the dead. Sheol was the
land of oblivion (Ps. 88.6, 11ff.), where one was cut off from God's
wonderful acts. It is true that it was not doubted that Yahweh could
even raise men from the dead; the miracles of Elijah and Elisha, as
well as Isaiah's offer to Ahaz to give him a sign from Sheol (Isa. 7.11),
bear witness to this. Moreover, in the stories of Enoch and Elijah,
whom Yahweh had snatched away to himself to enlist them as
warriors in his heavenly hosts, we see a premonition of immortality.
All this, however, remained the exception which only made death
seem to the average Israelite all the more definitely a separation from
Yahweh. Thus the Mosaic religion hermetically sealed the gate of
Sheol. When therefore the Israelite prayed to Yahweh for mercy in
sickness or in peril of death, he liked to remind him that by death he
would lose his worshipper, and thus the praise which the redeemed
would lavish upon him would be denied to him (Pss. 6.6; 30.10;
88.10–13; 115.17; Isa. 38.18).

Hence the Sheol conception was of value to the Yahweh religion
inasmuch as it was well adapted to break down any relations between
the individual and the dead. By shifting survival from the grave to a
distant shadow kingdom it made it easier to establish the gulf between
this world and the one beyond. That such a purely negative attitude
to the world of the dead should be in general tolerable to the religious
consciousness is certainly to be explained in terms of the strongly
developed national and community sense in which the Israelite was
brought up. The value of the individual lagged far behind the
problem of the nation's destiny in significance. Yahweh was the God
of the people and of history; and when the people had lost their
national independence it was the close-knit group of the family which
ensured a certain consolation for the individual. In the family,
indeed, he found a kind of survival, a sort of participation in the
destinies of the greater whole, because it reproduced his name. In
reality, however, we should not estimate too highly the loss which
Israel's religious sense had to bear as a result of the decisive rejection
of the world of the dead. What the heathen religions here possessed
was more of a burden than an enrichment, and brought more torment
and fear than deliverance. Hence the Mosaic religion's explicit lack
of interest often had the effect of a liberation.

The positive value of such an attitude consisted in this. First, it
made it possible for belief in the God near at hand and in his retribution in this world to become deeply rooted; and at the same time it

enabled the individual to be trained not to thrust his own little ego selfishly into the foreground, but to feel the cause of God's sovereignty and of the people of God as axiomatically of greater importance. This meant that Yahwism renounced the opportunity of appropriating those mystical ideas which in, for example, the Adonis or Osiris cults held out the prospect of victory over death. That such ideas were known in Israel follows virtually without saying from the nation's close association with Phoenicia; but there is also explicit evidence in such prophetic passages as Hos. 6.2; Isa. 17.10; 10.4. Because the Yahweh religion persisted throughout, despite many affinities in thought, in rejecting such elements, it averted any invasion of Nature mysticism in this sphere, and prepared the way for the attempt—and indeed the successful attempt—to resolve the riddle of death in exclusively moral terms.

5. THE DEMONS

Despite the fact that the demons are not in general associated with the dead, Israel's *ideas of the demonic* are best treated in conjunction with the realm of the dead, for the simple reason that they cannot be included in the worlds of heaven and earth. This is also in keeping with their very minor significance in Israel's religious life. It is, in fact, more a question either of an undeveloped inheritance from the heathen past or of a variety of superstitions intruded at a late date.[1]

The truth of this assertion can be seen right from the start in the fact that the demons are not associated in any way either with Yahweh or with the angelic powers. The doctrine of a fall of the spiritual world, as a result of which Satanic forces were released, is foreign to the Old Testament. The mention of *mal'ᵃkē rāʿim* in Ps. 78.49 refers not to evil angels but to angels of misfortune.[2] Popular belief, however, knew of all kinds of hobgoblins, among which the *śeʿirim* seem to have played a large part. The etymology (*śeʿir* = he-goat) suggests that we are probably concerned here with a goat-shaped being, a kind of devil of the fields recalling the Greek satyr

[1] An exhaustive treatment of the idea of demons may be found in E. Langton, *Essentials of Demonology. A Study of Jewish and Christian Doctrine, its Origin and Development*, 1949.

[2] Cf. p. 201 above. Similar figures are the angels of death in Job 33.22, with which cf. II Sam. 24.16; II Kings 19.35; Ex. 12.23. The interpretation of Prov. 16.14 remains uncertain. On the subject of the *rūaḥ rāʿā*, sometimes wrongly understood as demonic, cf. pp. 52 and 55f. above. The term *rūḥin*, 'spirits', to denote demonic beings occurs first in the midrashic literature of later Judaism.

and considered as a genius of fertility. Hence sacrifices are offered to them, especially in the syncretistic period of Manasseh (cf. II Kings 23.8). Lev. 17.7 condemns such sacrifices as a type of idolatry already practised in the Wilderness; II Chron. 11.15 reproaches Jeroboam with having offered them. In other passages the *śeᶜîrîm* figure as denizens of desolate ruins (Isa. 13.21; 34.14); here the term appears to have already become a collective name for demons of all kinds.

In the last-named passage a female night-phantom, *lîlît*, is mentioned in conjunction with them. This figure plainly derives from Babylonia, where a rich selection of such fiends was available. Under the same name, Lilith, she appears there as a storm demon, dwelling in the wilderness, from which she bursts forth to attack men. The *ᶜalûḳā* of Prov. 30.15 seems to be a spectre of a similar kind; as a monster of the vampire type[1] it belongs to the same class of beings as the *lamia* of the Romans or the ghoul of the Arabs. It is not impossible that the *meᵓārebîm*, or 'liers in wait', who according to II Chron. 20.22 at the prayer of the Israelites caused discord in the host of the allied Ammonites, Moabites and Edomites, also represent demonic beings of this kind.

A special place in this class of fiends should be accorded to the *šēdim*, mentioned in Deut. 32.17 and Ps. 106.37.[2] Certain demons of the same name are found in Babylonia, where they act partly as protective deities, partly as hostile spirits. From the fact that there are hints of sacrifices to these demons on the part of the Israelites it might be conjectured that they were originally gods, who featured to some extent in syncretistic periods, and were later degraded to the level of evil spirits. The child-sacrifices mentioned in this context suggest in particular Milcom or the Baal-type nature deities of Canaan.[3]

While the worship of these demons was in part directly combated, in part disapproved of in silence, with the result that they played no great part for the religiously vital section of the people, one of their number achieved a firm place in religious practice, namely the *ᶜazāᵓzēl* of Lev. 16. At the annual Atonement Festival the High Priest had to determine by lot which of the two he-goats intended as sin-offerings for the people was to be 'for Yahweh', *lyhwh*, and which 'for

---

[1] In Arabic the same root provides the term for a leech.

[2] Slight textual emendation would also yield the name in Hos. 12.12 and Ps. 91.6: cf. Wellhausen, *Die kleinen Propheten*³, 1898, p. 131, and B. Duhm, *Die Psalmen*², 1922, p. 345.

[3] C. Steuernagel (*Deuteronomium*, 1900, p. 117) and H. Kaupel (*Die Dämonen im Alten Testament*, 1930, pp. 12ff.) prefer to understand the passages of true demons.

Azazel', $la^{\zeta a}z\bar{a}$'$z\bar{e}l$. The latter then had to be taken to a remote place in the desert, while the other was to be prepared as a sin-offering for Yahweh. It is clear that this practice was not merely one first devised in the Exile, but must represent an age-old element. But precisely for this reason the question has to be asked whether it is still possible to establish the original meaning of the rite, which at the time the Law was recorded had perhaps already been forgotten. Many conjectures have been made on the subject of the name Azazel without arriving at any generally accepted result. At all events it must be a proper name, and not any kind of appellative, since in Lev. 16.8 it can only designate a being opposed to Yahweh.[1] The symbolic meaning of the action carried out with the goat is still fairly clear; he is burdened with the sin of the congregation (v. 21), and has to carry it away into a remote region ('$eres\ g^{e}z\bar{e}r\bar{a}$: v. 22) from which he never finds his way back. This presents a concrete performance, comparable to the vision in Zech. 5.5–11, the freeing of the community from the burden of sin, conceived in a quite material way.[2] It would seem therefore that there must have been the conception of a land where everything that was opposed to God had its home, and which was demonic in character. How it comes about that in this instance the particular demon Azazel plays the principal role we do not know. Certainly an ancient superstition of the nomadic tribes dwelling in the steppe is involved—Kadesh in particular comes to mind; to the oasis-dweller the inhospitable desert appears as the place of demons. That Azazel is an embodiment of Satan is, in view of what has already been noted about the latter, quite out of the question.[3] Even in this context his part is in no way an active one; each year he merely has, as it were, his bare living expenses thrown to him. Only in later Judaism was his name attached to the leader of the fallen angels, and his punishment modelled on the account of the killing of the scapegoat in the Mishna.[4]

---

[1] The word was interpreted as an appellative by Luther, who, following the Vulgate version, *caper emissarius*, rendered it as 'lediger Bock' (lit. 'freegoat' = Eng. 'scapegoat'). E. König (*Theologie*[3, 4], p. 230) and H. Grimme (*ARW*, 1911, pp. 130ff.) also attempt appellative interpretations. R. R. Schärf (*op. cit.*, p. 138, n. 74) agrees with the older derivation from '-z-z and '$\bar{e}l$, meaning 'The Mighty One of God'.

[2] Cf. also Lev. 14.1–9, 49ff., and vol. I, pp. 164f.

[3] It is therefore going far too far to call him 'God's adversary, a figure corresponding to Satan' (Galling, *RGG*[2] II, p. 964; similarly Kaupel, *op. cit.*, pp. 91, 123f.).

[4] Cf. I Enoch 10.4ff. Cf. also C. L. Feinberg, 'The Scapegoat of Lev. 16', *Bibliotheca Sacra* 115, 1958, pp. 320–33; L. Rost, *ZDPV* 67, 1943, pp. 212ff.

This systematizing of divergent views makes the almost forgotten demon into an explicit anti-God principle.

It will have been noticed that in the case of these few named demons we are given no detailed information, but only very faint and indefinite outlines of figures mentioned entirely incidentally. Even after every effort has been made to wring more particulars from hints elsewhere in the Old Testament, this result is not essentially altered. It is true that many cultic practices,[1] and food and purity laws,[2] conceal what were originally apotropaic rites against demons; but the lawgiver was no longer aware of their original meaning, and their incorporation into the worship of Yahweh proves only how decisively the covenant God had driven out all other powers, and concentrated every cultic activity on himself. Thus the demons were even to all intents and purposes dispossessed from their most characteristic activity, the causation of illness; it is Yahweh who sends sickness, and also heals it.[3] Even though the notion of demons of sickness may still occur from time to time,[4] the situation is in no sense comparable to that in Babylonia, where every illness at once suggested the work of demonic forces.[5] The tremendous energy with which the divine Lord of the nation focused the whole of its life and thought upon himself robbed the demons of their significance, and thus burst for Israel one of the most dangerous bonds which trammelled the religious life of

---

[1] Cf., e.g., Ex. 28.33–35, and the comments of Wellhausen, *Skizzen und Vorarbeiten* III, *Prolegomena*[3], 1886, p. 144; also A. Jirku, *Die Dämonen und ihre Abwehr im AT*, 1912, pp. 82, 85; H. Duhm, *Die bösen Geister im AT*, 1904, p. 7.

[2] One may think, for example, of the food laws of Lev. 11 compared with Isa. 65.4, of the hostile attitude to sexual processes in Lev. 12 and 15 (S. of S. 3.8 may refer to demons as disturbers of the wedding-night), or of the water of purification made with the ashes of the red heifer (Num. 19.1–10). On this subject cf. J. Döller, *Die Reinheits- und Speisegesetze des AT in religionsgeschichtlicher Beleuchtung*, 1917, pp. 116f., 269ff., or N. Peters, *Die Religion des AT*, 1912, pp. 639ff.; cf. also the observations on the Passover—vol. I, p. 163.

[3] Cf. Lev. 26.16 and the idiom of the 'blow of Yahweh', vol. I, p. 259, n. 2.

[4] So perhaps Job 18.13; 19.12; Ps. 91.5f. Yet here the concept of demons serves rather as a poetic personification of plague and disease. These powers, too, figured prominently as Yahweh's servants: cf. Hab. 3.5, where in addition to the personified figure of the plague the Canaanite god of death, Resheph, also follows in Yahweh's train.

[5] The attempts of S. Mowinckel (*Psalmenstudien* I, 1921) and M. Nicolsky (*Spuren magischer Formeln in den Psalmen*, 1927) to demonstrate extensive reference to demons in the regular cultus have not been successful; A. Lods is nearer to the truth ('Les idées des Israélites sur la maladie, ses causes et ses remèdes', *Marti-Festschrift*, BZAW 41, pp. 181ff.). Cf. also Kaupel, *op. cit.*, pp. 36ff., and my own comments in *Theologie der Gegenwart*, 1928, p. 242.

heathenism.[1] Hence the Israelite cultus contains neither prayers nor ceremonies for warding off demons; nor does the Israelite in his prayer think of contrasting the power of Yahweh with that of the demons as the reason for the assurance of his faith, as happens, for example, in Babylonian prayers and exorcisms in the case of the principal gods. The Yahwist faith also maintained with success an inflexible attitude of rejection, which it expressed in prohibition and reproof, toward the constant threat to import ideas of this kind from foreign sources.[2] And when in post-exilic Judaism, because of the weakening of men's sense of the immediate nearness of God, belief in demons as well as belief in angels awoke to more vigorous life,[3] the concept of Yahweh as the Creator of the world, which by that time had become deeply ingrained, sufficed to provide a sure defence against any ascription to the demons of independent significance—as an Aramaic cursing formula against star-demons, which has by chance been preserved, affords eloquent testimony.[4] Hence it has been said: 'One could imagine every trace of kakodaemonistic conceptions removed from the Old Testament without feeling that this would essentially alter the character of even the ancient popular religion, to say nothing of the prophetic.'[5]

Only in later Judaism, under the influence of a radical change in men's feelings about the world, did a new demonological realism invade the realm of faith. It is characteristic of this period that the demons, which hitherto had been associated only with physical evil, that is to say, misfortune, are now made responsible for ethical evil, or sin. At the same time this only made the gulf between the service of God and of the demons quite impossible to cross. For now there could be no question, as there had been in earlier times, of contingent subordinate powers additional to Yahweh. Their ethical opposition to God and his kingdom had turned the demons into devils, and placed dealings with them under the severest imaginable ban. Even though Jewish apocryphal literature and the Talmud now liked to give full play to the imagination in describing the demonic realm,

---

[1] On the importance of the *rūah*-concept for the idea of Yahweh's all-embracing power cf. pp. 53f. above; also vol. I, pp. 261ff., and on the whole subject, P. Volz, *Das Dämonische in Jahve*, 1924.

[2] Deut. 18.9ff.; Num. 23.23; Hos. 4.12; Isa. 2.6; 17.10f.; Mal. 3.5.

[3] Cf. W. Bousset-H. Gressmann, *Die Religion des Judentums im späthellenistischen Zeitalter*[3], pp. 331ff.

[4] Cf. Jer. 10.11 and *ad loc*. B. Duhm, *Das Buch Jeremia erklärt*, 1901, pp. 101f.

[5] H. Duhm, *op. cit.*, p. 65.

arranging the demons in various classes and groups and finally in a kingdom of their own,[1] there was no longer any danger that this would prejudice the exclusive worship of Yahweh; and even dualism, with its inevitable consequence of the obscuring of monotheistic awareness, was permanently averted. Nevertheless it cannot be denied that there was a considerable darkening of life's horizons. In this situation only a *new* assurance of the nearness of the redeeming covenant God could lead to freedom and that religious confidence, capable of overcoming the world, which had been characteristic of the prophetic period. Hence even this line of development in the Old Testament's understanding of its faith points beyond itself to the age of the New Covenant.

[1] Cf. on this point vol. I, pp. 227 and 471.

PART THREE

GOD AND MAN

XX

THE INDIVIDUAL AND THE COMMUNITY IN THE OLD TESTAMENT GOD-MAN RELATIONSHIP

ONE OF THE REPROACHES frequently levelled at Old Testament piety is that it never overcomes its fixation on the collective, but remains stationary at that stage of ancient man's development which rated the value of the individual human being inferior to that of the nation; and that it is therefore possible for God to be venerated and worshipped only as the national God, never as the God of the individual. From this point of view attachment to the community is felt to be merely a limitation, and the criterion by which piety is evaluated is its greater or lesser consonance with a fundamentally individualistic attitude to life. When this is combined with an assessment of the New Testament as the realization of a God-Man relationship that is supposedly purely individualistic, then all the emphasis, even in a sympathetic consideration of Old Testament piety, is shifted to demonstrating the victory of individualistic thinking over all community-oriented attitudes as the goal and climax of its development.[1]

An examination of this question is made extremely difficult from the start by the ill-defined and inadequate delimitation of the concepts 'collectivism' and 'individualism'. For the most part collectivism is understood as an impersonal attitude to the holy, guided by mass-instincts or sacred traditions, and ruling out any individual shaping of thought and action.[2] By contrast, individualism is defined as that

[1] This is still the position adopted in a work remarkable for its serious and exhaustive treatment, F. Baumgärtel, *Die Eigenart der alttestamentlichen Frömmigkeit*, 1932. A different view is taken in J. Hempel, *Das Ethos des AT*, 1938, pp. 32ff.

[2] Thus R. Smend, *Lehrbuch der alttestamentlichen Religionsgeschichte²*, 1899, p. 103, writes: 'The affairs of the individual were not brought before Yahweh with the

spiritual state which affirms its own existence without regard for any collective ties of nation or cult community, and seeks to develop its own attitude to God and the world. The practice of drawing a distinction between these two patterns of living and then playing them off one against the other was, however, something that grew up in the soil of philosophical idealism; and to transfer it to the conditions of ancient society can lead only to misunderstanding. Even the attempt to refine the differentiation of these patterns by introducing the concepts of personalism and impersonalism[1] can do no more than mitigate their immense oversimplification of the shape of life in the ancient world without, in fact, doing justice to it.

Instead of employing such conceptual categories it is better to keep firmly in mind the striking fundamental characteristic of all forms of community in the ancient world, and in particular of those of Israel, namely the strength of their sense of solidarity—a sense which adjusts itself in a variety of ways to changes in the shape of society, but is always the essential determinant of its distinctive quality. In interplay with this solidarity thinking we find a living individuality which, as distinct from individualism, is to be understood as the capacity for personal responsibility and for shaping one's own life. This does not stand in mutually exclusive opposition to, but in fruitful tension with, the duty of solidarity, and as such affects the individual and motivates his conduct.[2]

I. SOLIDARITY THINKING IN ISRAEL'S ENVIRONMENT

The sense of solidarity in the peoples of the ancient East is expressed

---

same confidence as were those of the nation. They were too trifling for that.' Similarly B. Stade, *Biblische Theologie*, 1905, pp. 191ff.: 'In the religion of Israel we are dealing with a relationship not between the individual Israelite (much less the human being) and God, but between the nation Israel and Yahweh. . . . The religious unit is the nation and not the individual. . . . We are a long way from any developed feeling for the individual; the sense of community is predominant. . . . Even less than the nation can the individual expect to experience Yahweh's help at all times. . . . At any moment Yahweh may become a man's enemy; and the pious must then resign himself to this situation just as if it were a decree of Fate.'

[1] So A. V. Ström: cf. J. Scharbert, *Solidarität in Segen und Fluch im AT und in seiner Umwelt*, 1958, pp. 6f.

[2] Cf. also C. Ryder Smith, *The Bible Doctrine of Man*, 1951; E. Wright, *The Biblical Doctrine of Man in Society*, 1954; H. H. Rowley, *The Faith of Israel*, 1956, pp. 99–123; J. de Fraine, *Adam et son lignage* (Museum Lossianum, Section Biblique 2), 1959; R. de Vaux, *Ancient Israel*, ET, 1961, pp. 3–212.

in very different forms according as it is fashioned in the circumstances of nomadic life or springs up in the settled existence of the peasantry of the civilized states.[1] For the nomadic way of life it is clan-thinking which is characteristic. The clan as a closely integrated unit not only determines the external structures of society, but ensures that the common life of the members of the clan is founded on a spiritual and psychical unity in which each individual is a representative of the whole, and in turn has his entire private attitude to life shaped by the whole. This distinctive sense of belonging together is rooted in the structure of patriarchal society, where the father of the tribe moulds the life of his great family both externally and internally, and occupies a place of decisive importance for the tribal destiny. By their descent from him the members of the tribe are incorporated as kinsmen in a family community, and welded into a social unit outside which there can be no meaningful life for the individual, since he would be abandoned to every kind of danger without the protection of law.

This close association of the individual and the community means that among the fundamental principles of the concept of law are the collective liability of the tribe for the trespasses of its members, and equally the championing by the tribe of any member injured by an outsider. The laws of blood-vengeance and guest-friendship, which can retain their inviolable character only in such circumstances, constitute the most striking expressions of this social structure. Equally important, however, is the *patria potestas* of the tribal father, which forms the foundation of all justice and the fountainhead of legal tradition. It is as a legacy from the father of the tribe that the tribal order is unassailable and binding on every member; but at the same time it also bestows well-being and peace on all who belong to the community. The preservation of the ancestral grave as a sacred place by means of pilgrimages and monuments keeps alive the personal link with the forefather. By virtue of this link men hope that the power of life and blessing inherent in the tribal patriarch will be effective in their own life.

The influence of the forefather of the tribe is at its most profound

---

[1] J. Scharbert (*Solidarität in Segen und Fluch im AT und in seiner Umwelt* [BBB 14], 1958) has rightly drawn attention to this fact, and directed the study of the sense of solidarity in the ancient East along new paths by his extensive investigations. My own comments in this chapter are indebted to him both for a valuable wealth of detail and for welcome confirmation of the basic lines of thought. Cf. also S. Nyström, *Beduinentum und Jahvismus*, 1946.

where he is also the founder of its established religion, as having been the first worshipper of the tribal god.[1] Clan thinking, however, also plays a part in men's understanding of the world and of history, when the group system of the tribes and their basic kinship-structure are projected on to the history and the mutual relationship of the nations.[2]

Nevertheless, however strong may be the dominating influence of the community on the life of the individual in such circumstances, we cannot speak of collectivism in the old sense (cf. p. 231, n. 2, above). Within the bonds of customary law the head of the household can determine the shaping of his own life and of the life of his family at his discretion without acknowledging any judge higher than himself. It is even open to him to detach himself from his own tribal association and to join an alien one. The freedom of those members of a family who are subject to *patria potestas* lies under stricter limitations, though law and custom give them a protection against arbitrary tyranny and a direct interest in the prosperity of the tribe. Such conditions naturally rule out any individualistic attitudes; but the sense of the spiritual unity of all members of the tribe leads to a vigilant responsibility on the part of each individual member, and to willing commitment to the welfare of the whole.

The feeling of solidarity in the settled civilizations develops in a way that is clearly distinct from this.[3] Here the closed system of the clan dissolves, and in place of tribes and clans spring up local communities—the village, the town, the nation. These are constructed out of individual families and it is to the family that the sense of solidarity is now diverted. In law this is expressed by the prohibition of blood-revenge. In its place we find in the Code of Hammurabi and in the Old Assyrian laws the legal talion, which, generally speaking, makes the lawbreaker himself answerable for his crime. Where retribution extends beyond the person of the culprit, and exacts the penalty for his offence from one of his family or of his servants,[4] this is done for the practical purpose of drawing upon the property of the guilty to provide reparation. Only the immediate family can be penalized in this way, and it is therefore possible to speak of 'father-

---

[1] Cf. A. Alt, 'Der Gott der Väter', *Kleine Schriften* I, 1953, pp. 1ff., esp. pp. 31ff.
[2] Cf. Gen. 9.24–27; 10.1–32, and the way in which the Yahwistic writer in the Pentateuch organizes the peoples of the Davidic kingdom in a genealogical system.
[3] Cf. J. Scharbert, *op. cit.*, pp. 24ff.
[4] This may occur in cases of murder as well as in those relating to property or commerce: cf. the clauses enacting indirect talion in the Code of Hammurabi (cf.

punishment'.[1] In such contexts the continuing effects of nomadic law may be detected at many points; but clan liability in the true sense no longer plays any part.

Clan liability is, however, more prominent in the practice *of the Hittites*, in particular in the sacral law, and in that relating to manslaughter and to offences against the king.[2] Nevertheless there is a definite tendency toward mitigation of this collective responsibility, and in the course of a fairly long period individual punishment seems first to have been introduced alongside it, and gradually to have replaced it altogether.

Where the deity is expected to take punitive action, it is not uncommon for the criminal's punishment to include the extermination of his family. But this is less a genuine instance of collective responsibility than of retribution against the paterfamilias who in this way is touched in the loss of his family and so of his posterity. A permanent organic connection between the descendants and the father of the family, by virtue of which they partake of his special powers or suffer as a result of his guilt, is unknown.[3]

It is clear that in the highly civilized states the sense of solidarity is

---

vol. I, pp. 77f.) and in the Old Assyrian Laws (§§ 49, 50, 54, 55). In such cases, however, the way in which the penalty reacts upon the guilty person himself should be noted; this is the prevailing note in § 49. The fact that kings, when punishing rebels, also execute their families (cf. G. Furlani, *RLA* III, 1957, pp. 16f.) may be due to the more serious view taken of high treason than of other crimes, since this is placed on a level with sacrilege, and therefore punished with especial severity. In Israel this conception would seem to be confirmed by Ex. 22.20, 28 (MT 22.19, 27), cf. 21.17. This also explains why especial stress is laid on the relaxation of the penalty under Amaziah (II Kings 14.6): cf. vol. I, p. 78, n. 3.

[1] Cf. D. Daube, *Studies in Biblical Law*, 1947, pp. 154–89, for the distinction between 'ruler-punishment' and 'father-punishment': also J. Scharbert, *op. cit.*, pp. 20f.
[2] Cf. G. Furlani, *RLA* III, 1957, pp. 18f.; J. Friedrich, 'Hethitische Gesetze' *AO* 23/2, 1922, §§ 1–4, 44, 173, 174; Pritchard, *ANET* 208a, 209c, 210bc.
[3] This does not prevent men from seeking the roots of a particular crisis in some guilt of their forebears, as when, for example in the Accadian exorcism texts or in the Hittite prayers for use in time of plague (A. Götze, 'Die Pestgebete des Muršiliš', *KF* I, 1929, pp. 204–35; Pritchard, *ANET*, pp. 394–6), some means is being sought of lifting the curse which rests on the suppliant. Behind this lies the tabuistic conception of sin and of its contagious power. The link with kinsfolk or with previous generations remains entirely external and fortuitous. Benedictions on one's descendants in prayers of dedicatory inscriptions do not presuppose a mystical organic unity between the generations, but simply testify to the expression in religious form of the concern of the paterfamilias for his own, or even to his wish for the continuance of his own name beyond death.

restricted to the immediate family, where it is taken for granted that each member is a representative of the family, and in particular of the father of the household, and that the sin of the head of the family exerts an influence on the destiny of all. Nevertheless true collective responsibility is definitely receding in importance, and when it comes to reckoning guilt individual responsibility is by far the weightier principle. Objective guilt—even in a case of subjective innocence—is a conception closely bound up with the family, and is therefore felt not as unjust but as a natural consequence of family collectivism—though as a result of a tabooistic understanding of sin it plays a larger part in the religious than in the legal sphere.

2. FREEDOM AND BONDAGE OF THE INDIVIDUAL IN ISRAEL

1. The Old Testament evidence leaves no doubt that the structure of society in ancient Israel was determined by *the salient features of clan thinking*. Clearly prominent are a strong tribal sense and a resistance to any serious limitation of tribal independence. There is widespread evidence that the way of life of the tribe is shaped by the tradition concerning the tribal ancestor and the ordinances established by him, even as regards the distinctive character of their religion. Israel therefore shares the community sense typical of a nomadic culture corresponding to the way of life of the wandering tribes in the early period. Because of this the individual in Israel can see his existence only in terms of his membership of the tribe, and outside that circle knows no viable way of life.[1] Where the life of the individual is so inseparably bound up with that of society as a whole that it can have no claim to independent validity, there thought and conduct also are to a very large extent determined by the community. What are the custom and practice of the community? What is to its advantage or disadvantage? These are for the most part the criteria of decisive significance. The individual citizen cannot arrange his life independently at his own discretion, for then he would place himself outside the national community, and cut through the roots of his existence. Through thick and thin it is tribe-centred thinking which exerts the decisive influence

[1] So also J. Scharbert, *op. cit.*, p. 78. J. de Fraine ('Individu et société dans la religion de l'Ancien Testament', *Biblica* 33, 1952, p. 326) apparently wishes to question this social conditioning; but his otherwise valuable study leaves out of account the historical background of the Mosaic gospel, which is not helpful to an understanding of its effect.

upon him. 'That is not done in Israel!'—that is to say, in the tribal federation of that name—is a guiding principle of private conduct.[1] It is obvious that in such circumstances every new piece of legislation which corrected the traditional views of right and wrong in any important particular was bound to have a hard time contending with tribal and national custom. On the other hand, by proclaiming a fresh sphere of authority of the covenant God, such laws were plainly well adapted to break down tribal egoism, and to awaken the sense of a higher court of appeal than tribal tradition in the shaping of daily life.

Nevertheless no legal ordinance could simply put an end to the powerful *influence of tribal thinking*. Thus we find *blood-revenge*, that most intense expression of the vital unity of the clan, recognized as a legitimate measure down into the monarchical period,[2] even though strictly speaking it ran counter to the ethos of the centralized state and its systematized legal practice. In tribal thinking not only the individual criminal but the whole community to which he belongs is held responsible for his action. Hence the individual is also ready in his dealings with his clan to nominate the members of his own family as a pledge for the fulfilment of his obligations.[3] How seriously the resistance of the tribe to superior authority could jeopardize obedience to the commands of the covenant God is shown by the solidarity of Benjamin with the lawbreakers of Gibeah,[4] the result of which was to subject the whole tribe to the coercive measures decreed by the sacral league, because the group is regarded as responsible for the crime of its members. Clan solidarity is also shown by the sparing of a whole family for the deserts of one of its members.[5] The ambition of the original leading tribe, Reuben, when the primacy was transferred to Joseph, jeopardized the tribal coalition,[6] and it is similarly imperilled by the bloody deeds of Levi and Simeon, intended to revenge the disrespect shown to their family honour.[7] And even when the sacral confederation of the tribes carries out its obligation to

---

[1] Gen. 34.7; for an example of the continuing influence of the principle in the life of the nation-state cf. II Sam. 13.12.

[2] Cf. E. Merz, *Die Blutrache bei den Israeliten*, 1916; and Gen. 4.23f.; 9.6, 34; I Sam. 25.33; Ex. 21.14.

[3] Gen. 42.37f.

[4] Judg. 20.13f.; cf. 15.9–13.

[5] Judg. 1.24f.; Josh. 6.22–25.

[6] Num. 16.

[7] Gen. 49.5–7 and 34.

provide the protection of the law in internal affairs, yet acts of violence against aliens seem to be permitted where they can be practised without prejudice to the interests of the league.[1]

But though the effects of tribe-centred thinking might in these ways restrict and endanger the institution of the covenant, they could also work to its positive advantage; and by it the tribal structure of society could in turn be strengthened. For the solidarity-relationship of the members of the covenant was able to build on the solidarity association of the clan, and to be understood as an organic extension of the latter. Just as in secular life the ties formed by blood-relationship could be extended by means of connubium, of treaty, or of adoption in the sense of a fictitious consanguinity, so the unification of the tribes into the people of Yahweh brought about an enlargement of the circle of those linked by solidarity, creating a new physical and psychical whole within which an inward bond of a higher sort held the members of the covenant together with the firmness of a clan community. Here the solidarity thinking which derived from a common experience of divine redemption and covenant-making was underpinned genealogically by the fact that in the patriarchal history all Israelites were seen as brothers deriving from one father. The stress laid in Deuteronomy on describing all members of the covenant as brothers is therefore more than a formula of religious association; it is nourished by the strength of that habit of thinking in terms of genealogical relationship by which Israel made her own coherence vivid to herself. Because *the community felt itself to be a genealogical unity* it was furnished with the necessary precondition for learning *to regard itself as a constant entity* even through successive generations, just as the community of the clan passes on its organic form and its spiritual character from one generation to another, and maintains itself by virtue of this common inheritance. But together with the covenant relationship, which determines its spiritual form, *the element of responsibility* now becomes part of the self-understanding of the nation with a force hitherto unknown, in that genealogical thinking enters into an alliance with the principle of divine retribution, thus preparing the way for the conception of corporate guilt, which opens up new insights into God's dealings with the community.[2]

[1] Judg. 18.14ff.; Gen. 12.12; 19.4ff.; 49.17, 27.
[2] Cf. vol. I, pp. 39f. and 462ff. Hence the importance of the patriarchal narratives for the common historical experience of all succeeding generations: 'The Israelitic narratives of the fathers is the condensed history of many generations' J. Pedersen, *Israel* I–II, p. 476).

The fellowship with God communicated to the individual in the covenant fits without difficulty into this understanding of the people of God. For that which forms the foundation of a man's relationship with God is not his own limited personal experience but the experience of the national community which bears him. As a member of the nation to which God has revealed himself and given his promises he dares to believe in the relevance of God's power, wisdom and goodness to his own life also. In this way therefore solidarity provides free scope for a thoroughly personal relationship with God. Incorporated into the cultic community of the amphictyony the Israelite experiences in the cultic action the real self-communication of his God through the priestly proclamation of his holy ordinances, and rejoices in the covenant favour and the covenant promises. In the festivals carried out at the sanctuary according to the prescribed forms he expresses his thanksgiving and petition, his vows and confessions of sin, and in union with the congregation acquires that feeling of being religiously at home which enables him to place his own little life trustfully in God's hand. Collective cohesion proves itself a reinforcement of the individual's power to shape his own life.

Supported by a world sustained and interpenetrated by cultic ordinances the individual does not experience personal misfortune and unanswered prayer as any real assault on his assurance of God. Even though the distress and pain of life were strongly felt in ancient Israel, it nevertheless could not occur to the pious to desire that the reality and nearness of God should be demonstrated specifically in his own individual life. Since he is only a leaf on the tree of the nation, what matter if the leaf wither provided that the tree remains? So, too, the individual does not think of feeling mutinous against his involvement in the distress or affliction of the nation, tribe or family as against an unjust divine Providence. That the sins of the fathers should be visited on the children is to him an obvious expression of God's righteousness,[1] and the limited duration of such visitations when contrasted with the unlimited blessings bestowed on the pious is regarded as a particular proof of the divine mercy. Only when the nation is overwhelmed with misfortune, perishing under the tyranny of vaunting enemies, or decimated by famine and disease, does the cry go up: Has Yahweh abandoned us? Has his arm become short, so that it cannot save? In such circumstances, when the framework of

[1] Ex. 20.5; Num. 14.18; Deut. 5.9. For particular historical instances cf. Num. 16; I Kings 14.10; I Sam. 2.31; II Sam. 12.10, 14; Amos 7.17, etc.

men's lives, the community called to be God's people, is in mortal peril, the assurance of God can be sorely tried, and even collapse in unbelief in the conclusion that God has given up his people, or that he is impotent in face of the gods of the enemy.

II. Settlement in Canaan brought about *a significant revision* of this type of solidarity dependent upon clan-thinking. More and more the clan is replaced by the local community of the village and district, and urban culture dissolves the old social ties. The equality that obtained between those bound in the same kin-group is prejudiced by the inequality of possessions, and economic dependence threatens the poor with the loss of his freedom. The kinsman's duty of redemption, the *ge'ullā*, loses the character of an unconditional obligation, and even the Deuteronomic law cannot check its dissolution.[1] The widow, who formerly could return to her father's house, now as a result of the removal of this resource often falls into severe hardship,[2] if she has no property of her own at her disposal.[3] In place of the clan the local court takes over the protection of the individual; and even the king may intervene in his favour.[4] But the constant complaints about discrimination against the orphan and widow make it clear that this protection was inadequate; and behind the large number of ruined lives from which David recruited his troop of brigands[5] stands not only the Philistine crisis, but also the decline of the collective security afforded by the clan.

The result of these developments for the position of the individual in the community was that the sense of solidarity was transferred from the clan to the family; and within this smaller group the individuality of each member of the family was able to make itself more strongly felt. One consequence is that collective responsibility plays no more part in legal life. The Book of the Covenant knows nothing of the punishment even of the sons of the guilty; the murderer, adulterer, and so on, is called to account only in his own person; his family are not touched. The far-reaching clan responsibility found among the Hittites is unknown in Israel; and the liability of one member of a family for another, which still plays a part in cases of indirect talion even in the highest neighbouring civilizations, is

[1] Deut. 25.5–10.
[2] Ex. 22.22–24; Deut. 16.11, 14; 24.17, 19–21; Isa. 1.17; Jer. 7.6.
[3] Judg. 17.2; II Kings 8.1–6; Ruth 4.3. II Sam. 14.5ff. shows her living with her sons.
[4] II Sam. 14.5ff.; II Kings 8.6; 4.13.
[5] I Sam. 22.2; 23.13.

categorically rejected.[1] The involvement of the family in the punishment of the guilty is retained only in very serious cases of a breach of sacral law, and in the crime of high treason;[2] and here the reasons are partly a tabooistic conception of the pollution of the family through its head,[3] and partly the likely presumption that the members of the family were accessories.[4] But even in such cases the tendency to restrict the punishment to the person who is really guilty emerges quite early on.[5] Similarly blood-revenge is limited by the right of sanctuary.[6] In civil law certainly, just as in ancient Eastern law elsewhere, it is customary for a debtor's place to be taken by members of his family, and for their labour to be applied to paying off the debt;[7] yet the claim of the creditor on the debtor's demise to make good his loss from the children is felt to be unjust,[8] and other expedients are used in an effort to secure a release, either by the law of the seventh year or by special remission of the debt.[9] All in all there is an unmistakable heightening of the value of the individual.

III. Unquestionably the recollection of the Lord of the Covenant and of his beneficent purpose toward all members of the covenant community was a powerful stimulus in the task of providing increased legal protection for the individual endangered by the breakdown of clan solidarity. If special attention is given even in the very earliest laws to the afflicted and the economically weak, and warnings are given against oppressing them, this is because such conduct calls forth Yahweh's vengeance. This succour given by the covenant God to the individual through the processes of law is, however, only the result of a much more comprehensive protection of solidarity as such at the time when the nation settled in the midst of civilization; for at the time when the bond of the clan was breaking down the religious order of life maintained that close association of the members of the covenant which had grown out of clan-thinking. The binding

---

[1] Cf. vol. I, pp. 77ff. and 78, n. 3.

[2] Josh. 7.24ff.; I Sam. 22.12ff.; II Kings 9.26. In II Sam. 21.6ff. the principle of blood-revenge still plays some part.

[3] This seems to be assumed in Deut. 22.8; cf. also II Sam. 20.14, 21.

[4] This consideration is decisive in Deut. 13.7ff.

[5] II Kings 14.6.

[6] Ex. 21.12–14; Num. 35.13–29; Deut. 4.14–43; Josh. 20: cf. A. Alt, 'Die Ursprünge des israelitischen Rechts', *Kleine Schriften* I, pp. 308–12.

[7] Cf. the Code of Hammurabi, §§ 115–17; Old Assyrian Laws, § 48; Nimrud Tablets 3433, 3441 (cf. D. J. Wiseman, 'Nimrud Tablets', *Iraq* 15, 1953, nos. 135–60, pp. 136, 142f.); Lev. 25.41; Neh. 5.2–5.

[8] II Kings 4.1; Micah 2.8f.

[9] Ex. 21.2; Lev. 25.39ff.; Deut. 15.12ff.; Isa. 34.8ff., 14.

together of the whole people in one great family, imbued with the patriarchal blessing in which each individual received a share, uniting all generations in a common attitude of responsibility before God, and keeping their sense of unity alive through the years, proved itself a strong barrier against the break-up of the tribal confederation into locally distinct parts determined by their various special interests, and going their own ways—a development which came about in the period of the Judges with the drawing apart of the inhabitants of the Judaean massif, those settled in the centre of the land, and the tribes living in Galilee and east of the Jordan. The fragmentation which then threatened as a result of the geography of the land could be checked only because obligation toward the covenant God raised the archaic cohesion of the clan to a higher level, where it remained independent of tribal thinking, and thus rendered ineffective the centrifugal forces which such thinking involved. The collective relationship, based on the divine revelation, and described in the covenant formula: 'You shall be my people, and I will be your God', united the multitude of individuals, regardless of their tribal affilia-tions, as representatives of a common religious task, and placed them directly under the command of God. Indeed, this people of Yahweh time and again absorbed foreign elements who were willing to fit into the law of Israel's life. In this way the dangerous effects of clan-thinking, which favoured the development of a ruthless tribal egoism, were effectively checked. Moreover, in addition to the blessing of the tribal patriarchs, which highlighted the loyalty of God to his people, there was the blessing flowing from the covenant-making on Sinai, in which the whole nation was united as the legitimate heir of the divine promise. Because this blessing reached out beyond the ties of blood (Jethro, Ex. 18.10ff.; Hobab, Num. 10.29ff.), it caused men to recognize that, even where ties of blood were present, the constitutive element was community of sentiment, and as such made it clear that association with the God who gave the blessing meant, in fact, com-mitment to a task that was constantly being presented in new forms.

3. THE SPECIAL STAMP GIVEN TO SOLIDARITY THINKING IN THE MONARCHICAL PERIOD

1. As a result of the foundation and consolidation of the state by David and Solomon this vital expression of individual life in a tribal league that was predominantly collective in character underwent

a remarkable reshaping. The story of the succession in II Samuel, and the whole Yahwist historical narrative which is closely linked with it, by their high degree of emancipation from the sacral conception of life which had marked the earliest period of Israel's history, and by their liberal evaluation of rationalistic expediency in the exercise of kingly power, reveal a new mood for which Man stands at the centre of events, and is appreciated in his distinctive personal quality. In conjunction with this development the operations of the deity move out of the sphere of the miraculous and of the immediacy of the cult very largely into the hiddenness of an indirect guidance of history.[1] And yet at the same time the Yahwist writer can bring the superiority of the divine governance, a superiority so great as to be miraculous, vividly to life, by showing that it attains its goal of salvation by the purposeful use of independent human decision—the wide scope given to which in no way relaxes men's strict responsibility in face of the divine will, but gives it its full importance. Hence this new orientation of the understanding of history, which is sometimes described as Solomonic humanism, is no shallow rationalistic creed. The collective relationship of the divine covenant, which placed the whole existence of the nation at the service of God's plan, also exercised its influence on this latest spiritual adaptation, and blocked every attempt to secularize the will of Yahweh, or to change the concept of the nation from sacred to profane. It was at this point that David's lust for power was halted,[2] it was this idea which dominated the struggle of Elijah and his successors to beat back the intrusion of a secularized monarchy into the law of Israel's innermost life.[3] The Deuteronomic lawgiver built on the same foundation, when he gave to the idea of the covenant that strongly personalist stamp which determined both his paraenetic method of teaching the Law and his theocratic conception of the State.[4] The hypertrophied cultus of the later monarchy might suppress the sense of personal vocation in popular piety; the monarchy itself might tend to subordinate the moral demands of God to nationalistic egomania, and so substitute the commandment of national solidarity for the personal sense of responsibility; but again

---

[1] G. von Rad is the first to have pointed this out with proper emphasis (*Das formgeschichtliche Problem des Hexateuchs*, 1938, pp. 62ff.—ET in *The Problem of the Hexateuch and other Essays*, 1966, pp. 68ff.).

[2] II Sam. 24.1ff.

[3] I Kings 19.18. 7,000 was a large enough number to represent the true people of Yahweh!

[4] Cf. vol. I, pp. 55f., 90ff.

and again the hold of the collective was restrained by the spiritual leaders, who stood unrelentingly for the control of the nation by Yahweh's decree, and so summoned the individual to selfless commitment to the cause of the sovereignty of God.

How this awakening and strengthening of individuality also affected the formation of popular piety has already been described.[1] All that need be pointed out here is that the same influence is manifest in ethical behaviour, and necessitated the taking of a higher view of the relationship of man to man than was customary in common popular morality.[2]

At the same time, none the less, *the genealogical conception remains fundamental for the understanding of history*, and is able to exert a decisive influence by making clear that the power of community to determine destiny is an essential factor in the historical drama. Hence the Yahwistic narrative is permeated by the conviction that the genealogical cohesion of the nations and of humanity is expressed in a mental solidarity by virtue of which opposition to God is a basic attitude of the human race. In the primal history of Gen. 1–11 the major fundamental factors in the destiny of mankind become visible in the way in which the curse or blessing proceeding from the ancestors determines the fortunes of their descendants, and subjects them to the same fate. Similarly Israel's history is from the very beginning controlled by the decisions of the tribal patriarchs, and falls under the blessing promised to them. This blessing assigns to the nation, united with its ancestors in a physical and psychical totality, the special path it has to tread. This does not indeed do away with the importance of personal decision for the individual citizen. History is not fixed by a collective determinism, but leaves room for obedient or disobedient attitudes on the part of men to the divine decree. Nevertheless, inasmuch as the types of right and wrong attitudes to God are already to be seen in the fathers of the tribe, this sets the pattern for the interpretation of the succeeding history, and through the indissoluble union of the generations gives rise to a continual effort to realize afresh the goal originally set them. Thus the genealogical conception results in a view of history the cohesive force of which also provides later writers, such as the Deuteronomic and Priestly historians, with the possibility of combining past and present in a vast spiritual history which is a true unity.

[1] Cf. vol. I, pp. 136ff.
[2] A fuller discussion of this point will be found below, pp. 321f.

11. That which, in spite of the sensible limitations of a self-conscious nationalism, was thus already alive in ancient Israel received reinforcement and development of the utmost consequence from *the work of the great prophets*. The social fragmentation of the people, and the impact of international civilization, which took place just at this time, had already shaken any idea that the unrestricted sway of morality and custom could be taken for granted. The unity of the nation was imperilled by the struggle between the privileged and the oppressed classes; and the simultaneous abandonment of the old patriarchal morality and of a peasant economy shattered the solidity of the common way of life.[1] But the effects of this slackening of the old, established standards were only fully felt as a result of *the divine demand for conversion*, proclaimed with unprecedented vehemence and harshness by the prophets; for this demand, even though directed to the nation as a whole, yet made its appeal to the individual's capacity for decision, calling him to a conscious grasp of his obligation as an individual, even if this involved him in breaking with hallowed tradition.[2] By conversion the prophets understood not a forcible re-establishment of the ancient, primitive conditions, but the bringing of every department of life under the sovereign claims of the holy God. Moreover, this God, who had encountered them in their own lives with consuming immediacy, and had bound them to his will as their one guiding principle, they now set over against any form of autocratic national self-will as the sovereign will compelling men to ultimate personal decision. This meant that at one and the same moment the spiritual independence of the individual was summoned to the most extreme exertions and set upon the unshakeable ground of the divine promise. The resultant conflict and division within the people of Yahweh was bound to place *the significance of the individual for the formation of the God-Man relationship* in a new light, and to express *the great fundamental ideas of divine revelation in precise personal terms*. Just as, with regard to God's marvellous nature, the newly comprehended mystery of his personal being led men far beyond all magical or juristic categories, and made them recognize even his

---

[1] The Canaanite city constitution, with its aristocratic form of government by the *baʿᵃlē hāʿîr*, and the extension of the city's domain over the surrounding country-side, which led to the growth of *latifundia* and thus came into conflict with the ancient Israelite concept of the peasant proprietor, must also be taken into account as an important factor in the social and spiritual revolution (L. Rost in a letter to the author).

[2] Cf. pp. 467ff. below.

holiness as life of a personal kind,[1] so the person of Man, as a Thou called by God, acquired a unique value;[2] and this in turn gave the sphere of ultimate personal decision, namely the moral, that quite distinctive majesty from which derive both the dignity and the limitation alike of cultus and of law.[3] And because even the nation's sin springs in the last analysis from roots in personal life, the judgment, redemption and renewal of the individual—in short, the reshaping of the whole relationship between the individual and his God becomes the indispensable means to the redemption of God's people. In the re-creation of the individual, and nowhere else, God achieves the re-creating of his congregation.[4] Even so, the solidarity of the nation in responsibility is still maintained, and the 'house of Israel' designated as the entity, unchanged since the day of its election, in which God is bringing his design of salvation to its goal.

4. POLITICAL COLLAPSE
AND THE RESHAPING OF INDIVIDUAL LIFE

1. In the seventh century this new definition of the relationship between the individual and the community proved to be the salvation of the mission entrusted to Israel. For at this time, when under Manasseh's despotic rule Near Eastern culture and religion flooded over Judah, and sought to uproot and sweep away all that was indigenous and genuinely Israelite in character, there was an inner disruption of national unity. The catastrophic end of the State's existence, which followed almost at once, then robbed of their outward home a people who had already become inwardly homeless. The result of these disasters was *to emancipate the individual from the ancient sacred ties of community*; but this emancipation could no longer bring about a strengthening of spiritual independence, but only the unrestricted licence of a self-destructive individualism. The lower strata of society sank more and more, now that the spiritual prop of

---

[1] Cf. vol. I, pp. 280f.
[2] Cf. vol. I, pp. 356ff.
[3] Cf. vol. I, pp. 360ff.
[4] Cf. pp. 457f., 465ff., below It is important not to allow the fact that the prophetic preaching is normally addressed to the nation to blind one to this increasing concentration upon the individual. Decisive in this respect is the fact that throughout everything is seen in terms of the person. In addition the description of Israel as *benē yiśro'ēl* instead of just *yiśro'ēl* or *'iś yiśro'ēl*, a usage which from the time of Amos onwards becomes more and more popular, seems equally to point to a relaxation of the old collective consciousness.

their ancestral faith had been taken away from them, into ugly superstition and crude Nature worship. The ruling classes sought salvation in a characterless cosmopolitanism, which took pains to have the gods of the current ruling power as their helpers in time of need, but at the same time continued to show reverence to Yahweh. At bottom, however, they properly trusted no god, and regarded the religious enthusiasm of the people with a sceptical smile, thinking themselves far above such a limited outlook, and seeing no social order to hinder them any longer from cunningly exploiting these lower classes in the interests of their own well-being.[1] Once the bond of nation and State, which till then had enclosed and safeguarded the life of the individual, had been completely smashed by the deportations of the Exile, and at the same time an end had been made of the community of the Temple worship, which had constantly drawn the individual within its sphere of influence, and given him the feeling of being at home in things religious, there seemed to be no longer any barrier to total loss of self-control.

In this situation everything depended on whether Israel's faith in God could endure the collapse of all the natural supports which it had hitherto possessed in the form of the old patriarchal morality, the sense of nationhood, the State, the monarchy, and the structures of cultic life, and fashion *a new life-relationship between the community and the individual*, or whether it itself would be sucked down into the process of dissolution. The answer to this question was given in the life, work, sufferings and struggles of two men, in whom the personalism of the prophetic preaching reached its definitive form, and led to the shaping of an individuality which was to be the indestructible kernel of a new community—*Jeremiah and Ezekiel*.

How in the life of the former the false pretensions of personality advanced by the spiritual attitude of his times were broken, and a new personal nature awakened to life through repentance and forgiveness, can be seen supremely in his Confessions[2] and in the narratives of his friend and disciple Baruch. To this great experience of the prophet, however, was added another, namely that this personal I, which was delivered up to death by God's hand, but also sustained and restored by him, was granted a new relationship with God which even the withdrawal—as a result of his excommunication

---

[1] Cf. the sombre picture in Micah 6f. and Zeph. 1.
[2] Jer. 15.10ff.; 17.9ff.; 20.7ff.

—of the collective guarantees of God's nearness, the national community and the Temple congregation, could not destroy. His God is near even to the ostracized, causing him to know the power of the divine fellowship, and thus making him a pillar of iron and a wall of brass. But this new worship in which he as an individual now becomes assured of his God means purity of heart and the prayer of the heart— purity of heart which, however clear the conscience, is nevertheless deeply imbued with the awareness that only God himself can overcome the innermost resistance of the human heart toward him, and create a clean heart. Thus even Jeremiah is forced to lament: 'The heart is unfathomably deep, and desperately corrupt; who can understand it?' And the answer which he receives is: 'I the LORD search the heart and try the reins!' It is because of this that he can go on to pray with confidence: 'Heal me, O LORD, and I shall be healed; save me, and I shall be saved; for thou alone art my hope.'[1]

This which had been given him he was able, once the deportation of the year 598 had freed him from his fiercest enemies, and palpably vindicated him, to pass on to his people. In the letter which, on the occasion of an embassy from King Zedekiah to Babylon, he sent to those in exile[2] he was able to hold out the prospect not only that the people would grow and flourish there but also that they would be able to have regular intercourse with God, legitimated by Yahweh himself through the visible proofs of his favour. In the heathen land, which Hosea and Amos had characterized as unclean, which polluted even the food obtained from it,[3] *prayer and obedience* were wholly adequate as *the central expressions of faith.*

The power of the new worship is shown, moreover, by the fact that it could dare *to bridge the gulf between Jew and Gentile*—something which under the dominance of collectivism was impossible. That to which the prophet summons them is prayer for the heathen land—'the one place in the Old Testament where intercession for enemies and unbelievers is commanded'.[4] Even though the motive of self-interest is expressly mentioned in the context, yet the way in which both the personal longing for revenge and the national desire for retribution are overcome is remarkable, culminating as it does in the formation of a new fellowship with the heathen through intercession.

[1] Jer. 17.9, 10, 14.
[2] Jer. 29.
[3] Hos. 9.1ff.; Amos 7.17.
[4] P. Volz, *Jeremia*[2], 1921, *ad loc.*

II. Unquestionably we have here the first steps toward providing the individual element in the God-Man relationship with a new basis and an access of strength which were to prove an effective counter to the cosmopolitan individualism of the sceptic and the hedonist,[1] because they showed the individual the way to a personal and independent fellowship with God. It was the work of the prophet of the Exile, Ezekiel, to supply him in addition with the support of a community, thus guaranteeing him a future. To this man was given authority to proclaim, in the presence of the wreckage of the nation vegetating in careless stupidity or baffled doubt, a divine offer of favour, opening up the way to a new people of God. This—and not a doctrine of retribution—is what chapter 18 of his book is about, when in the solemn language of the Temple *tōrā* he announces the removal of the collective fellowship of guilt by which the sons had to do penance for the sins of the fathers. The individual called by God's word is shown the way into a new 'house of Israel', which is to realize the old covenant community in a new form. The God who 'has no pleasure in the death of the wicked, but rather that he should turn from his way and live'[2] wishes to give each member of his guilt-laden people free scope to be able to enter into a relationship of personal service and loyalty to the God of the fathers, rid of the shackles of inherited guilt.

From those religious and social demands of the Law which could be fulfilled in Exile[3] resulted the direct appeal to the conscience and voluntary decision of the individual for a new solidarity with his fellow men. No solid legal system guaranteed by the State any longer existed to stand behind the citizen; but out of the old covenant law was erected a moral and social standard for human life which led to inward liberation in union with the moral will of God, and established a new community of faith and purpose in a foreign land.[4] Out of the profound convictions and decisions of individuals a common pattern of conduct is arrived at, having no further connection with the ideal of a national community, but leading to the creation of a congregation of God's people such as had in earlier times formed the living core of

---

[1] The importance of Jeremiah in this respect has been well summed up by A. C. Knudson in the following words: 'Here we have, it is true, no formal doctrine of individualism, but we have individualism in concrete living expression' (*The religious teaching of the Old Testament*, 1926, pp. 342f.).

[2] Ezek. 18.23, 32.

[3] As set out, e.g., in Ezek. 18.5-8, 10-13, 15-17.

[4] Cf. W. Eichrodt, *Der Prophet Hesekiel*, 1959, pp. 148ff.

the nation,[1] but now with a vocation to develop as and by itself. Here the confrontation of collectivism and individualism is transcended, and the individual ego discovers an encounter with God which is identical with incorporation into a new relationship to his fellow men.

This congregation cannot, however, seek the purpose of its existence within itself, but only in the consummation promised by God, for it knows itself to have been established with an eye to the coming of this consummation.[2] The imperative of striving after renewal is bound up with the indicative of the divine gift of renewal.[3] Hence the prophetic promise calls upon men to set forth, leaving behind them all the consolations of a paltry, legalist uprightness, in order to give their whole attention to that ultimate decisive change in their situation in which the new fellowship with God, experienced in the present, is to find its fulfilment. The thoroughgoing personalism of the new fellowship transforms the ancient hope of Israel into something new, in that it understands the spiritual rebirth of the individual member of the nation as the central gift and endowment of the age of salvation.

Under the influence of this prophetic preaching there grew up in Babylonia, at the very moment when the ancient city of God, Jerusalem, was facing destruction, the beginnings of a community life in which Ezekiel's summons was translated into action. Indeed, it is as good as certain that, quite apart from the activity of the prophet himself, gatherings for worship took place spontaneously at places of prayer by the water or in the houses of scribes, and that at these gatherings many of the songs of Zion were sung (Ps. 137.1f.), and the misfortunes of the nation were brought before God with fasting, penitential lament, and tearful petition. It is also extremely probable that they included the giving of priestly instruction on how to live in the impure land and how to preserve their ancient customs. Yet in all this there was no advance beyond the practice and retention of the old traditional deposit in a very impoverished form; and on the whole the dominant note was the hope of a speedy return to the homeland. In such a situation to transmit new impulses was impossible.

But things were very different whenever the excitement of the prophetic message was able to make itself felt in such assemblies, and

---

[1] Cf. H. Wheeler Robinson, 'The Hebrew Conception of Corporate Personality', BZAW 66, 1936, pp. 54f.

[2] Ezek. 34–37.

[3] Cf. 18.31 with 36.26.

to take charge of them. Hence it was an important development when a new focus of community life arose in the house of the prophet himself, where the elders and other members of the Babylonian colony forgathered to hear a word from Yahweh, and to ask for counsel in all manner of problems.[1] Here the individual was constantly being summoned to take decisions which were bound to change his whole life and to guide it in a new direction. In spite of the originally intractable quality of his hearers Ezekiel must in time have found adherents who spread his message abroad, and thus imported into the gatherings of those who held fast to the faith of their fathers a ferment which effectively changed their character. In the light of Ezek. 33.1ff. it can be assumed without question that Ezekiel himself, especially after his threats of doom had been confirmed by events, worked as a teacher in these meetings for worship. About the course of events in detail, however, we know nothing;[2] how far the prophetic teaching was able to overcome the opposition which undoubtedly arose and to seize control, or whether it met with only limited agreement and had to submit to an assimilation to other tendencies, we have no reliable information. On such questions only more, or less, probable conclusions can be drawn.

III. What is certain is that the period of the Exile became for the exiled community an extremely fruitful time of reflection and of the laying of new foundations for the spiritual life. It can be established that these years saw a purposeful collection and revision of Israel's spiritual heritage in the form of records of laws, historical works, prophetic oracles and books of poetry, which were intended not for enthusiastic readers, but for hearers who were attentive and desirous to learn. Here we can observe the continuing influence of prophetic ideas, transmitted through complex refraction in the Deuteronomic literature, side by side with a priestly school in the narrower sense which was directed strictly toward legal standardization of the community life.[3] These movements, reaching far down into the post-exilic period, justify the conclusion that the pattern of spiritual reconstruction in Exile was determined by their confrontation, just as

---

[1] Cf. Ezek. 8.1; 12.9; 14.1; 20.1; 24.19; 33.30f.

[2] It is going much too far to conclude, as A. Menes ('Tempel und Synagoge', *ZAW* 50, 1932, pp. 268ff.) wishes to do on the basis of Ezek. 11.16; Josh. 22 and the Talmudic tradition, that the rise of the synagogue in Babylonia belongs to this period.

[3] It is precisely in the collection of the records of Ezekiel and of his utterances that these two competing streams of material can be very clearly distinguished.

their exponents were the outstanding leaders of the exiled community. We may therefore assume an awakening, under Ezekiel's influence, of readiness for responsibility, and education for religious adulthood in a worship based essentially on the presentation and exposition of the Word. The sermon-type instruction in Deuteronomy, the practice of which had certainly not yet been completely discontinued, and the Levitical preaching which we find interspersed in the books of Chronicles,[1] and which must have developed long before the time of the Chronicler himself, as well as the Deuteronomic paraeneses in the historical books, throw light on the homiletic exegesis of the written word in the community assembly as early as the time of the Exile, and show how the sacred traditions of the community were used in order to mediate the central content of faith. Here it was possible even for the layman to achieve a high degree of religious formation, which he then had opportunity to employ in the practical details of life in his dealings with heathen, apostates and proselytes.

All this was not necessarily in opposition to the high value placed on the outward regulation of life according to the prescriptions of the Law as championed above all from the priestly side. Ezekiel, too, was fully conversant with this.[2] Furthermore men learned to see the Law with new eyes as the means of protecting themselves in a heathen environment against the contagion of superstitious practices, and of developing a way of life truly their own in character. The sabbath, circumcision and purity laws now acquired topical importance, and fitted into the worship of God as serviceable means to an end.[3] At the same time, in the keeping of the Law men became aware of a fellowship which united individuals in a bond so firm as to be unbreakable precisely because they had entered into it by their own personal decision and not from custom or tradition, and which afforded them the means of putting their faith into action.

This was all the more so when the priestly practice of the Law did not ignore the effect of the prophetic preaching. Even though in many ways it strengthened collective ties by the introduction of new institutions and rules, yet at the same time it spread throughout Israel an

---

[1] G. von Rad has drawn attention to this in the *Procksch-Festschrift*, pp. 118ff.

[2] Ezek. 4.14; 18.6; 20.7, 25f., 28, 30f., 40f., etc. On the other hand, the passages in ch. 20 relating to the hallowing of the Sabbath are the work of a later hand.

[3] Cf. the deeply thought-out interpretations of the two first-named institutions in the Priestly narrative: Gen. 2.2f.; 17.9ff. Also E. Jenni, *Die theologische Begründung des Sabbathgebotes im AT* (Theologische Studien, ed. K. Barth, no. 46), 1956.

understanding of the personal character of the divine will, and taught men to comprehend the Law as an expression of personal sovereignty. This may be seen from the way in which the multiplicity of regulations in the cultic law is linked throughout to the demands of the will of the covenant God, and thus forged into a spiritual unity. The consequences of this development for our evaluation of sacrificial worship, of purity rites, of sacred places and seasons, as well as of the practice of prayer, have already been emphasized elsewhere.[1] In addition we must mention the energy with which it was impressed upon the people precisely by the priestly practice of the Law that piety was a matter to be verified by moral conduct.[2] The very fact that it was possible within the priestly legal tradition to derive the social law from love as the highest force in personal and moral life,[3] and that in priestly historical writing the idea of Man in the image of God was used as a key to the interpretation of human history, shows how profound was the influence exerted on priestly thinking by the personal nature of the holy covenant God.

5. THE INDIVIDUAL IN THE COMMUNITY OF THE LAW

I. The transformation of the historical situation, by which the community recovered their homeland and Temple, confronted them with new problems and decisions. It is true that there was no sense of a disturbing contradiction between all that had been acquired for the first time in the hard school of the Exile and the reconstruction of a Jewish community in Jerusalem—indeed, what had been gained was understood precisely as a right preparation and transition to this rebuilding. Neither Ezekiel nor Jeremiah had left any doubt that the renewed showing of God's favour, for which they commanded men to wait in faith, would bring with it the full restoration of the people in their own land.[4] Hence, too, their work for the establishing of the community in exile had absolutely nothing to do with any idea of creating a substitute for the way of life which had hitherto been that of the nation, but was carried on with an eye to the emergence of a new nation through God's miraculous power. None the less, this new

[1] Cf. vol. I, pp. 98ff.
[2] Cf. vol. I, pp. 415f.
[3] Lev. 19.18; cf. vol. I, pp. 93f.
[4] Jer. 31; Ezek. 37.

people and realm proved, in fact, to be something different from the old nation-state, however unsuspectingly the colours and outlines of the latter may have been used to describe it. For *the concept of the nation had now moved into the light of eschatology*, and had thereby been projected on to another plane. No longer could a simple restoration of earlier conditions adequately fulfil the prophetic promise, but only a nation supplied with all the marvels of God's world, rejoicing with their messianic king in direct fellowship with their divine Lord in the paradise land, surrounded by the Gentile nations now likewise renewed and united in the service of Yahweh. But with this vision of the future nation as a part of God's new order,[1] finding its meaning in the fulfilment of God's moral plan for the world, the limited popular conception of the God-Man relationship is freed from the restrictions of nationalism, and set wholly within obedience to God's creative and revelatory will. Because the God of judgment and redemption is the Creator, the hope of a great turning-point in human affairs is also inevitably fixed on a new incarnation of the nation, in which all the strivings of history are to attain their goal.[2]

Because the concept of the nation was in this way detached from the empirical present, and made into an element in the hope of salvation, *it exerted a distinctive effect on the formation of the community*. On the one hand it meant that the congregation in exile were never able to regard themselves as the exclusive form of the people of God in history, but only as *the point of transition to a new national existence, a prediction of the coming fulfilment*. The recovery of the holy land confirmed, as it were, only that theirs was a genuine intermediate form, preserving through every metamorphosis the continuity of God's historical action. By the fact that nowhere else than in Jerusalem was it permissible for the new Temple as a sign of the return of divine favour to be built it was once again impressed upon men that revelation is election, election within the historical reality of space and time.

[1] Cf. especially in this connection the glowing pictures painted by the prophet of the Exile, Deutero-Isaiah.

[2] Cf. vol. I, pp. 490f. We may see from this how little the 'breaking down of attachment to the nation and people' is to be used as a valid criterion for evaluating Israelite faith in God. Taking the OT hope as a whole the restoration of the nation almost always signifies something other than plain, unabashed 'nationalism', even though the latter may obtrude itself here and there. The goal of a faith which is alive to God's creative action can never be redemption *from* nationhood, as a one-sidedly individualistic understanding of faith might assume, but redemption *of* both the nation and the nations through a new creative act of God.

On the other hand, the community called to such a task is *from the outset intolerant of any arbitrary restoration of the nation-state by taking advantage of a favourable whim of destiny*. The goal toward which she knew herself to be led no earthly political skill could attain, but only endanger. However warmly prophecy might pin its hopes on the vocation of Zerubbabel to be the messianic saviour-king, it yet waited as decidedly upon Yahweh's shaking of heaven and earth,[1] and warned against overhasty measures of self-help.[2] Indeed, by its intervention it rendered impossible an attempt at union with the Samaritans which had seemed to place within men's grasp the recovery of a stronger national community, and so ensured that a place in the land could not be taken to imply a place in the people of God.[3] Conversely it opened the doors of entry into the community with an astonishing universalism on the sole condition that a guarantee of 'holding fast the covenant' (Isa. 56.4, 6) were given; that is, wherever there was a willingness to be incorporated into the community built on the Law. The narrow bounds of membership of a common race[4] are here abolished in favour of a unity in faith, and the result is a marked influx of proselytes from heathenism.[5] There could be no clearer assertion that not everyone who has Israelite blood in his veins belongs to the people of the promise, but only the man who appropriates the spiritual inheritance with which Israel is entrusted and proves its worth in his life. Even 'the born Jew must now make himself into a Jew'.[6]

After the failure of Zerubbabel, however, Zechariah accepted the rule of the priesthood, and the continued existence of the community through this means, as the order willed by God. Nevertheless he indicated that its noblest significance was as a surrogate for the Messiah and a prophetic pointer to his coming.[7] After a protracted period of wavering, during which the secular authorities and the High Priests inclined more strongly to the rationalistic solutions of

---

[1] Hag. 2.6f., 21f.; Zech. 1.11f.; 2.17.

[2] Zech. 2.5ff.; for opposition to the building of the walls cf. 4.6.

[3] Hag. 2.10–14, according to the most probable exegesis. A similar rejection of an impure mixed nation occurs in Isa. 57 and 65. The same exclusion naturally applied also to those unreliable elements within Judah itself which had been receptive to the influences of their heathen environment.

[4] Deut. 23.4, 8f. Cf. J. Jeremias, *Jerusalem zur Zeit Jesu* II, 1929, pp. 103, 111.

[5] Cf. Ezra 6.21; Neh. 10.29f.

[6] J. Wellhausen, *Israelitische und jüdische Geschichte*[7], 1914, p. 200.

[7] Zech. 3.8–10; 6.9ff. Cf. W. Eichrodt, 'Vom Symbol zum Typos. Ein Beitrag zur Sacharja-Exegese', *TZ* 13, 1957, pp. 509ff.

natural political skill,[1] the decision of prophecy, enforced by the authority of Ezra and Nehemiah, became finally definitive for the community. With the rejection of all messianic dreams[2] it was acknowledged that the State must be renounced until God himself should create the new Israel; and *the shaping of life in accordance with the standard of the Law* was resolutely grasped *as the task appointed by God*, the Law being now understood as the formative principle of history, uniting past and present.[3] From now on the settled ordinances of community life were developed with ever-increasing logical consistency, making the community both an unshakeable bulwark against the tides of heathenism surging in from every side, a thorough-going educator of its members, and a spiritual home for the far-flung Diaspora and for a constantly growing circle of proselytes.

II. In this way the form of the community was stabilized, being built on the foundation of the independence and responsibility of its members, because it heard full and clear in the call of God to his people a call also to the individual. But the life of the community in the succeeding centuries showed that a constant struggle was necessary to keep the powerful reciprocal influence of individual and society from unbalancing to one side or the other. That in all these struggles it proved possible to avert the enslavement of the individual by the community as effectively as the excessive growth of an unbridled individualism, demonstrates the stability of the foundations on which the Jewish community was built.

There was one threat that individuality would be endangered, when the hope of a new kind of existence for the nation was lost in nationalistic trains of thought, and the new people of God was envisaged as a political entity with a stubborn claim to sovereignty.[4] Here the individual was no longer able to take his belonging to God seriously as a decision of faith, but made it an external matter of membership of the nation. It was therefore all the more important that those voices should not be silenced which proclaimed, along with the consummation of Israel, the simultaneous redemption of the nations, and their incorporation among the members of God's

---

[1] On the interplay of political forces in this period cf. the study by A. Alt, 'Die Rolle Samarias bei der Entstehung des Judentums', *Procksch-Festschrift*, pp. 5ff.

[2] Neh. 6.10ff.

[3] Cf. H. H. Schäder, *Esra der Schreiber* (Beiträge zur historischen Theologie, no. 5), 1930.

[4] Cf. Obadiah; Isa. 34f.; Zech. 9.13ff.; 10.3ff.; 14.12ff.; Joel 4; Ps. 149; Esther; also vol. I, pp. 467ff.

kingdom, and which even in the present welcomed the heathen to a share in the salvation of Israel and in the divine mercy.[1] This universalistic attitude reveals a conviction of the primacy of the individual decision for or against God over all collective ties, and a corresponding belief in one saving counsel of God, transcending all national boundaries, and opening to each individual the way to himself.

Manifest resistance also developed to the temptation which threatened *from the cultic aspect of community life*, namely to rest content with the atoning power of the Temple worship, guaranteed by the Law and the hierarchy. Thus fasting, as a pious performance substituted for a personal and responsible involvement in the life of society, is clearly and sharply condemned on principle;[2] and where external correctness in devout observance takes the place of interior surrender, it is consciously rejected.[3]

That the whole community should be filled with this spirit was, however, too much to hope for. In fact, it was resistance to this claim of God's order to the whole man which brought the like-minded together in pugnacious factions, and thus split the community into hostile camps. It is true that this development freed those who were loyal to the Law from the ever-present temptation to regard all those united in the external framework of the community unquestioningly as the new Israel; the interim character of the community was safeguarded. But once they had become a party the champions of the community ideal were unable to protect themselves against the awakening in their own midst of the conventicle mentality, for which outward conformity to convention became the criterion of piety. Here the concern of the pious for his own good reputation threatened to substitute the fear of men for independence of action.[4]

Nevertheless it was these circles, plunged into strife and suffering, which in the great questions of faith helped forward the victory of an assurance personally arrived at and personally communicated. The prophetic conception of sin as the real hindrance to God's gracious work was here still a living reality,[5] and here, too, therefore forgive-

---

[1] Zech. 2.14f.; 6.1–8; 8.20ff.; Mal. 1.11; Isa. 24–27; Pss. 93; 96: 97; 99; and the narratives of Jonah and Ruth, in which the heathen figure as models of faith and trust in God.

[2] Cf. the great utterance on fasting in Isa. 58, and Zechariah's criticism: Zech. 7.5–10.

[3] Cf. Pss. 50; 139.23f.; I Chron. 29.17.

[4] Prov. 10.7; 22.1; 5.14.

[5] Pss. 25.11; 32; 51; 65.4; 130.

ness was hymned as a miraculous liberation of the whole personal life by God's unfathomable mercy, in praise that was ever new because it sprang from the depths of personal experience.[1] In such circumstances indeed it was possible for the absolution which took place in the innermost sanctuary of the heart to be praised as an event proceeding from God's sovereign decision, and essentially independent of the whole statutory apparatus of sacrificial worship.[2] Thus, too, it came about that the profoundest of all the prophetic interpretations of suffering, namely that which saw it as a vicarious act for the redemption of sinners, and a supremely effective means to the building of the kingdom of God, now found new voices to expound and proclaim it.[3] And it is precisely those documents which give us an unqualified insight into the shadow-side of the conventicle character, the Psalms, which at the same time testify to an individual prayer-life full of force and ardour, in which the individual seeks direct fellowship with his God, and is thereby summoned to self-examination and reflection.[4] It is expressive of this that we now find the praying person addressing himself as 'my soul', and thus as a believer setting his own being over against himself in his responsibility before God.[5] In this striving after new forms of expression for the God-Man relationship concepts from cultic life may indeed serve as images of the individual's relation to God.[6] That all this did not produce a situation in which the individual was divorced from the communal pattern of piety is shown by the far-reaching standardization of the language of lyric poetry, which only rarely expresses the unrepeatable and unique, but tends instead toward the formation of an ideal picture of the pious.[7] Personal experience does not burst out of the community context in order to make itself the object of attention, but fuses its new content into the language of the community, thus at the same time fertilizing the latter in a most effective way.[8]

The community thus striving to preserve and purify its faith opened its doors wide to the God-fearers from heathenism who wished to

---

[1] Pss. 25.8ff.; 32.1f., 11; 86.5, 15; 103.3; Micah 7.18–20.
[2] Pss. 40.10f.; 50.14, 23; 51.17f.; 141.2.
[3] Zech. 11–13; Ps. 22.
[4] Pss. 139.23f.; 73.21f.; 19.13f.; 62.11, etc.
[5] Cf. p. 138 above.
[6] Pss. 16.1; 61.5; 141.2 cf. Deut. 10.16; 30.6; Jer. 4.4.
[7] Recent study of the Psalter has rightly drawn attention to this.
[8] How little one should see this as an impoverishment or stunting of potential growth is clear from the similar case of the poetry of the Christian Church.

attach themselves to it.[1] Missionary ideas were stirring which envisaged an expansion of the community by winning individuals regardless of whether or not they belonged to the nation.[2] But the most striking witness to the vitality of this individual life of faith is the certainty which now breaks through that even death cannot put an end to the fellowship between God and those who believe in him. The way in which, on the basis of the personal assurance of salvation, the conviction grew that even in death one was covered by God's hand, indeed, that one was taken away to glory[3]—a conviction which gradually took on the form of a belief in resurrection[4]—is perhaps the most remarkable and consequential enlargement which a vital individualism bestowed on the world of faith.

III. In the instances we have been considering, the individual is, generally speaking, supported by a strong community life, and nourished by the resources of his people's salvation-history. This bond was, however, strikingly loosened in the case of one influential section of the community, namely the exponents of the wisdom teaching. Their radical links with international wisdom literature resulted from the very first, as we saw earlier,[5] in a recession of the distinctively Israelite elements in the religious faith of these circles. In the discussion of the practical direction of life, as also in the knowledge of Nature made possible by Wisdom,[6] the most prominent viewpoints were those universal to mankind. In his confidence that along these lines even the most difficult problems of life could be resolved the wisdom teacher dared to give pre-eminence to that which was rationally discernible about the world and Man over the knowledge that came by faith. Moreover, because God was conceived no longer as the director of salvation-history, but only as Creator, giving goal and purpose to human life, the individual saw himself set as a creature in a cosmos within which he was compelled to make good his right to life, and the purpose of his life, in ominous isolation. From the beginning scepticism hung on the heels of his optimistic self-

[1] Pss. 115.11–13; 118.4; 135.20.
[2] Ps. 145.12; Ecclus. 10.19; 15.20; 24.19. In Pharisaism, too, there was a strong trend toward the conversion of the heathen. Among its exponents were Hillel and Simon ben Gamaliel. Cf. the thirteenth petition of the Eighteen Benedictions, and the criticism of this missionary zeal in Matt. 23.15.
[3] Pss. 16; 49; 73.
[4] Cf. ch. XXIV below.
[5] Cf. p. 82 above.
[6] Cf. pp. 83ff. above.

confidence[1] that the riddle of this cosmos could be plumbed, and Man shown his place within it, a scepticism which had long been at home in ancient Eastern wisdom. In Israel it led inevitably to a profound religious crisis, because here the will of God hidden behind the created order was taken seriously as the only universal power. Hence the problem of God's righteous retribution in the life of the individual, which had also been broached in Egyptian and Babylonian wisdom, acquired an urgency unknown in these other quarters. The attempt to master this question, so tormenting for faith, along rationalist lines, and thereby to subdue the dark reality of God to the force of individual thought, now grown to independence, was therefore pursued with a logic that was at once desperate and daunted by nothing, even though in the process the picture of the gracious God became strange and threatening. The isolation of the individual in answering the problem of God proved itself the beginning of a road which was to lead through deeper reflection to despair, as with unsparing frankness the book of Job makes clear. The fact that the solution there attempted holds fast to an orientation toward the Creator God betrays clearly enough that this particular wisdom teacher was finally compelled to return in his thinking to the dimension of revelation in order to indicate a way of escape to the individual lost in his loneliness. Koheleth then went on with total radicalism to pillory the utter inadequacy of human wisdom teaching as a means of comprehending the counsels of God.

Nevertheless in various forms the attempt at theodicy formed a continuing accompaniment to the interior history of Judaism, casting its shadow across the picture of God, the understanding of history, the life of prayer, and the eschatological hope.[2] Indeed, one cannot ignore the existence here and there of attempts at imposing an individual pattern on life which has nothing more to do with the community tradition. The poem of Job, revolutionary in form as well as in content, points to a personality of astonishing spiritual power and independence who, in wrestling with the central problem of life, dared to blaze new trails far divergent from the average thinking of the community in his search for the divine righteousness.[3] And the

---

[1] We meet this self-confidence as the invisible opponent against whom all the argumentation in Job 28 and Ecclesiastes is directed.

[2] A detailed discussion of all these points will be found on pp. 486ff. below.

[3] Cf. the fine characterization of the book by P. Humbert ('Le modernisme de Job', *Wisdom in Israel and in the Ancient Near East: presented to H. H. Rowley*, 1955, pp. 150ff.), in which, however, the links with a genuinely Israelite piety are given too little importance.

author of Koheleth, in a manner which has caused great offence to many, adopted a position so far outside the scope of the Jewish community that he could be taken for an agnostic sceptic who had completely broken with the faith of his nation.

But even if we disregard these outstanding individual figures the whole general tendency of the wisdom teaching favoured a self-sufficient subjectivism. For its exponents promised to show each pious soul the way to wisdom, that is, to the practical mastery of life; and in so far as this set up an ethical ideal for human living, and held it out as a goal attainable by persevering effort,[1] it gave rise to a subjectivism turned in upon the self, and needing no other being for its fulfilment. This self-sufficiency is even more marked in the fact that such men are able to give to others of their superfluity, and to become their guides and models. Ever greater esteem is bestowed upon the scribe who is able, because his own experience has verified his teaching, to show others the way to life, and to prove more than a match for his opponents in disputation.[2] The wise man, as the international hero of romance, enjoyed great popularity even among Jewish readers.[3] Reputation, a central necessity for any individualistic view of life, was gladly conferred on these scribes, most of whom came from lay families, and could not therefore be assured of any honourable status by inherited office, and equally gladly accepted by them.[4] The influence of Greek ideals of human life, and of the Greek concept of personality, now begin to be noticeable. Furthermore, where such crucial value was attached to learning and education, only the instructed individual could hope to attain the goal of life; all the rest were bound to fall behind. Consequently admiration for the scribe reached fantastic heights; he became a kind of superman who could work miracles and compel God by his prayers, and was

[1] An instructive summary of this ideal is to be found in Job 31.

[2] Cf. the behaviour of the friends in the book of Job, especially the self-confidence of Elihu; but n.b. also Ps. 119.99. Later Hillel and Shammai, as the perfect models for fulfilling the Law, were to provide the ideal for all succeeding generations.

[3] The Story of Ahikar, the discovery of which at Elephantine testifies to its wide dissemination in Jewish circles, glorifies the supremacy of the wise in the whole Aramaic-speaking world, and beyond. It is also not irrelevant that the Law is now referred to as the Law of Moses instead of, as hitherto, the Law of God.

[4] Cf. Dan. 12.3; the praise of the scribe in Ben Sira; and later the stories of Simeon ben Shatah (A. Schlatter, *Geschichte Israels*[3], 1925, pp. 153ff.), and the contempt for the unlearned in Pirke Aboth II.5.

honoured even after death by memorial offerings.[1] It is worth noting, however, that there is in addition another type of scribe, who remains much more strongly linked with the prophetic tradition, and who finds a loyal following as a preacher of the truth who has been tested and proved by suffering. The 'Teacher of Righteousness', who plays such a large part in the Qumran texts as the inspired man to whom God has revealed the true meaning of the Holy Scriptures, and who finds his mission in the inculcation of the Law, is a representative example of this type.

iv. An extension of the same trend was to result, both in the Jewish and the Hellenistic milieu, in *the growth of sects*, which represented the final triumph of the strivings of the individual for deliverance from the authority of the community. The Essenes, who emerged shortly after the Maccabean period, developed into a kind of monastic order, the heart of whose way of life was the high value they attached to the Law and to sacramental purifications and common meals; with this, however, they combined rejection of the Temple cult and sacrifices, a rule of celibacy, the exclusion of all those not consecrated in accordance with their secret rules, and an ascetic ethic. This information, which derives from Josephus, Philo and Pliny the Elder, has been startlingly confirmed by the discovery of the authentic remains of this community, or at least of one closely related to it, at Qumran in the Wilderness of Judaea.[2] These discoveries have supplemented our knowledge of sectarian piety at important points, revealing a rigid predestinarianism and a strict dualism of God and Devil, flesh and spirit, as well as a claim to be the genuine covenant people. These doctrines, which indeed derive partly from foreign sources, combine with those already mentioned to create a way of life irreconcilably opposed to the Jewish community, its sacred traditions, its cultic fellowship, its professional ethic, in short its whole normative way of life. This opposition is only thinly concealed by their participation in national duties such as wall-

[1] Thus Philo speaks of 'divine men', when he is quoting learned exegetes. In Aboth IV.12 reverence for the scribe is placed on a par with reverence for God. Josephus and the Mishna record stories of the renowned man of prayer, Onias. Veneration of the graves of scribes continued right down to modern times at Tiberias and Safed. Cf. further J. Jeremias, *Jerusalem zur Zeit Jesu* II, pp. 101ff., and R. Mach, *Der Zaddik in Talmud und Midrasch*, 1957.

[2] For an introduction to the subject cf. Millar Burrows, *The Dead Sea Scrolls*[7], 1956, and *More Light on the Dead Sea Scrolls*, 1958; also H. Bardtke, *Die Handschriftenfunde am Toten Meer*, vol. I, 1953; vol. II, *Die Sekte von Qumran*, 1958; vol. III, *Die Handschriftenfunde in der Wüste Juda*, 1962.

building and defence. Here the community of the people of God, standing above the judgment of the individual, is shattered in favour of a self-chosen way to the establishment of the holy congregation destined for perfection. While the people were inclined to tolerate, indeed to admire these separatists, Pharisaism saw clearly that their place was outside the community, and acted accordingly by refusing to recognize them. Nevertheless, even in this exclusive order we may still discern a combination of authoritative leadership on the part of the overseers with co-operation by the whole community in administration and legal decisions which makes it impossible to speak of subjective caprice as its governing principle. Instead there is an organically articulated unity with a graduated system of rank, in which the decisions of the individual are imbedded in the overarching order of the community.[1]

In a similar way, though manifestly not with the same systematic solidity, baptist sects—Hemerobaptists, Masbotheans, and possibly still others[2]—championed a sacramental ideal of holiness, in which purity guaranteed by lustrations was combined with fantastic salvation doctrines of all kinds. The striving of the Therapeutae for holiness strikes one as even more subjectivist. This group, according to Philo's description,[3] led an ascetic life of meditation and pious practices as a society of hermits in the neighbourhood of Alexandria. The rejection of particular external means of sanctification in favour of a concentrated absorption in the Holy Scriptures as the key to all knowledge suggests a marked affinity to Hellenistic wisdom teaching, which set such a high value on γνῶσις as the way to redemption.

Of itself the extreme individualism of these sects was not strong enough to shake the firm fundamental principles of the community, because these were embodied not in a dogmatic system but in a practical approach to life, the norm of which was not open to discussion. Except where men, with the help of alien forces, were moving toward a deliberate breakaway from this basis, the wave of individualism broke against the rock of the strict demand that the whole of life be related to the will of the divine Lord of the covenant, whose declaration in the Law dethroned all human autonomy, and com-

---

[1] This has been clearly brought out by Bo Reicke ('Die Verfassung der Urgemeinde im Lichte jüdischer Dokumente', *TZ* 10, 1954, pp. 95ff.).

[2] On the information handed down by the Church Fathers concerning these sects cf. W. Bousset-H. Gressmann, *Die Religion des Judentums im späthellenistischen Zeitalter*[3], p. 461, n. 1, and p. 464.

[3] *De Vita Contemplativa*.

pelled the individual striving after his own perfection to bow to the sovereign authority of a heavenly king who had no need of any human arguments designed to prove or to justify him. And because there is the closest possible link between the proclamation of the Law and reference to the mystery of creation, which allowed men to understand the world only as a simple exercise of God's creative will, a firm barrier was set up against those tendencies to rationalization and subjectivist analysis of the traditional system of faith which customarily went hand in hand with an intensified individualism.

In all these developments we can see how the rooting of the individual in the community constantly liberates forces which are adequate to meet the dangers of subjectivism, and justify the faith of the community that it is guided by God's word and spirit. Yet the struggle never completely succeeded in rendering the opponent harmless; for the latter derived his strength from the tension which bore so heavily on the community, between the ideal of human life as set out in the Law with its static world-view and the hope of the coming consummation with its unlimited dynamic. Pharisaism indeed safeguarded the spiritual inheritance of the community by warding off every attack on the Law of God. Standing between the nationalistically minded Sadducees and the individualistic orientation of the Essenes it preserved the supranational significance of the Law, even at the risk of thereby having to split the community of the nation, and closed its ranks against the particularist narrowness which wished to use the Law solely as a means to maintain the national entity. But it was unable to show men a way out of the inner tension which dominated the life of the community. Indeed, by finally making obedience to the Law the appointed method of bringing in the final salvation it laid upon the community a task so impossible of fulfilment that it continually nourished men's doubts as to the justice of God's governance of the world, and provided a specious justification for attempts to find a solution along the lines of theodicy.

Only a revolutionary act of God, which by a final resolution of the problem of guilt should open up new possibilities for the life of the individual, and at the same time, with 'the perfect law of liberty' (James 1.25), grant the community the means of overcoming its inner tensions through the gift of the Spirit, could bring to full effect that which was premised in the old covenant. Moreover, because of the fact that the work of the messianic king was already complete, there was no longer any need to reckon on human performance in order to bring in the consummation still to come. Instead, the time of waiting for this consummation to break through in bodily and visible form could be understood as the time of God's patience and preservation of the faithful, uniting within itself both dynamic movement and assured rest because of the knowledge that all is in the hand of God, who guides history to its goal at the right moment.

6. THE RELATION OF OLD TESTAMENT PIETY
TO INDIVIDUALISM

From the overall picture now arrived at of the development of individuality in Old Testament piety it is possible to answer fairly easily the problem of its relationship to genuine individualism. The religious faith of the Old Testament helped religious individuality to come to life in a context of strong collective ties, because it understood God's demands to the nation as at the same time a call to the individual, imposing upon him an obligation of unconditional loyalty even when the call ran counter to the natural bonds of community. This fundamental conception of the covenant relationship is seen in its full power in the formation of the congregation after the destruction of the nation-state. But Old Testament faith knows nothing, in any situation or at any time, of a religious individualism which grants a man a private relationship with God unconnected with the community either in its roots, its realization or its goal. Just as it is the formation of a divine *society* which gives meaning to the divine demand that summons the individual and enlists him in its service, so it is in serving his brethren that the obedience of the one who is called is proved, it is in the common cultic festivals that his religious life finds its natural expression, and it is toward a perfected people of God that his hope is directed.

Nevertheless it has been thought that at least at certain 'high points' of Old Testament belief we can detect a breakthrough to individualism. Indications of this seemed to be present above all in prophecy. It was possible, for example, to point to the fact that one result of the prophetic preaching of punitive judgment was that belief was no longer subject to nationalistic ties and limitations, and that this had averted an infringement of God's freedom by the covenant concept. Eschatological universalism, too, which is closely bound up with moral renewal, could be used to illustrate the breaking down of the limitations of collective thinking, in that emphasis was

now laid on the very opposite of the nationalist and cultic future hope
as cherished in certain popular circles. And yet it would be a complete
misunderstanding of the prophetic preaching to seek to interpret or
conceive their individualizing effect in the sense of a religious
individualism which throws aside all collective ties as inessential for
the relation of the individual to God. The only result of such an interpretation would be to make each allusion to the new creation of the
people under the messianic saviour prince on an earth restored to its
paradisal state—a consummation which the prophets certainly
promised—a constant perplexity. This leaves two possibilities, each
of them untenable. Either the prophets must be set down as by nature
inwardly unclear and full of contradictions, because they are still
caught up in the restrictions of popular thinking, or these prophetic
promises must be explained as unauthentic, which is possible only if
the issue is very definitely prejudged. The crucial mistake is to confuse
involvement in the nation with the collective tie as such, and to
explain the prophets' emancipation from all particularistic narrowness on the grounds of their supposed individualistic thinking. On the
contrary, it must surely be clear that the struggle against limiting the
covenant relationship to the nation was carried on not with an eye to
the religious situation of the individual but to safeguard the honour
of God. Hence it could perfectly well go hand in hand with hope
for a rebirth of the nation and labour for a new people of God. If in
the process the future nation imperceptibly takes on the features of a
religious community, this is certainly an expression of the way in
which the individual factor in religious thought has been powerfully
intensified. But we are still far from individualism in the true sense.
Just as it is the personal decision of the individual which ultimately
determines the life of the community, so for its part the community
remains the mother of the religious life of the individual. For it is the
community which provides the context within which revelation,
whether past or present, or as yet in the future, must take place. It is
the continuity of God's activity in history for the setting up of the kingdom
of God which, for prophetic thinking, guarantees the continued
existence of the community; and therefore it is God himself who
brings about the individual's attachment to this particular people,
and prevents his relapse into the natural categories of a national
religion, whatever their kind. Moreover, eschatological universalism
never implies a flight from the hope for the nation's future into an
individualistic ideal world, but affirms that it is precisely the national

ties which provide the framework within which the divine community of the future is to be realized.[1] Prophetic thought does not see community and individual in mutually exclusive opposition, but in fruitful interaction.

The same is true of the post-exilic community with its somewhat highly strung and forceful individuality. Here, too, one is easily apt to detect the rudiments of a purely individualistic piety, whether it be with reference to the emphatic rejection of sacrificial offerings or to the certainty of the conquest of death in the Psalms, or by appealing to the subjectivism of Job or Koheleth. But the abandonment of the nation as a plank in their platform in the debates of these wisdom teachers is determined much more by the fact that they enter into the type of teaching given by their opponents, and then use *reductio ad absurdum* to destroy it with its own arguments. In the process the appeal to the Creator God and to his self-communication in the word awakens the deepest insights Israel was ever to receive in her knowledge of revelation. Furthermore, the writers of the Psalms are so conscious of standing within the community of the pious that it is from her that they derive their highest powers.[2] And coming as they do from the circles of the faithful they recognize in the mercy shown to them the duty of proclaiming the salvation they have experienced to their compatriots.[3] Here again therefore the individual experience of faith, which results in an unimagined enlargement of the traditional deposit of belief, ultimately flows back into the service of the community, and supplies new resources to those circles where religion was a living reality, and on whom fell the burden of the struggle for the faith of the fathers.

[1] The OT never speaks of a destruction of the nations with a view to the setting up of a fellowship of believing individuals: cf., e.g., the classic passages Isa. 2.2f.; Zeph. 3.9f.; Isa. 19.23; Zech. 8.22.
[2] Pss. 16.3; 40.4, 17; 73.15.
[3] Pss. 40.10f.; 49.2ff.; 50.5; 51.15, 17.

XXI

THE FUNDAMENTAL FORMS OF MAN'S PERSONAL RELATIONSHIP WITH GOD

I F THE PRECEDING CHAPTER has given us any insight at all into the living growth of individuality even in the earliest period of Israel's history, then it will also be apparent that a personal relationship with God was already possible in Israel, and in fact existed, before the emergence of the explicitly individual thinking of the prophets. Moreover, leaving aside the marked differentiations which were to be made in later epochs, the early stage exhibits *one fundamental feature in common* with all the later forms in which piety found expression, namely *the demands made upon the will far above all else, and the strong sense of the permanent gulf between God and Man.*[1] In view of the discussion already given in vol. I, there is no need to do more than mention that the decisive reason for this consistent note in Old Testament piety lies in something which is true of all periods— the awe-inspiring grandeur and the jealous exclusiveness of the will of God as revealed.

I. THE FEAR OF GOD

1. This predominant trait in the personal relationship of Man with God in the Old Testament is given linguistic expression in the habit of describing the whole religious relationship as *the fear of God* or *of Yahweh, yir'at 'elōhīm* or *yir'at yhwh*, and likewise, right religious conduct is termed God- or Yahweh-fearing, *yerē' 'elōhīm (yhwh)*, a usage which persists with remarkable regularity from the earliest to the latest times.[2] There can be no doubt that this shows the sense of the gap between God and Man to be the dominant element in Old

[1] Cf. J. Hempel, *Gott und Mensch im AT*, 1926, ²1935.
[2] Gen. 20.11; 22.12; 42.18; Ex. 18.21; II Kings 4.1; Isa. 11.2; 29.13; 50.10; Deut. 4.10; 25.18; Ps. 90.11; Prov. 2.5; Job 1.1, 8; II Chron. 6.33; Eccles. 7.18, etc.

Testament piety, and the temptation is never very far distant to take this fact as justifying a depreciatory assessment of such piety as servility and decadent self-surrender. A moment's consideration, however, of *the universal importance of fear in all religions* may be sufficient warning against such a step. Indeed, when this distinctive phenomenon is investigated, it becomes plain that religious fear is not simply a matter of a naked feeling of terror, putting one to flight, but of an *oscillation between repulsion and attraction*, between *mysterium tremendum* and *fascinans*.[1] Certainly in many primitive cults of the dead or of demons the feeling of terror may predominate, and, in fact, come to exercise almost complete control. But this limiting case, in which the pendulum of inner emotion has swung far to one side, should not be allowed to obscure the fact that religious fear is bi-polar or ambivalent, and conceals within itself at the same time both anxiety and trust. The focus of the interior emotion is therefore just as capable of shifting to the other pole, causing fear to be all but forgotten in trustful love. Even here, however, some element of anxiety, however slight, remains, so that the true mid-point of this basic religious feeling may be described as 'awe'.[2]

II. There can be no doubt that *in the Old Testament statements about the fear of God the inward agitation produced by the mysterium tremendum* emerges with extraordinary emphasis. Trembling in face of the divine presence, and fear of the flaming wrath of the avenger of all faithlessness, not only mark the Moses narratives, but are similarly found throughout the accounts both of the early Israelite and of the prophetic period. In full accord with what was said earlier about the nature of God[3] this implies *an attitude in the human psyche exactly corresponding to the divine self-communication*. This is made clear particularly in demonstrations of God's holiness, for fear is, in fact, in all cases the human correlate of this divine attribute.[4] Not only is *nōrā'*, 'terrifying', used as the correlative concept to *ḳādōš*, 'holy',[5] but holiness as

[1] Cf. R. Otto, *The Idea of the Holy*; S. Kierkegaard, *The Concept of Dread*; G. van der Leeuw, *Phänomenologie der Religion*[2], 1956, pp. 527ff.

[2] So R. Otto (the original German term is 'Scheu'). The word 'reverence' ('Ehrfurcht') preferred by Hänel (*Religion der Heiligkeit*) may well be too refined to keep one aware of the intended element of inward terror.

[3] Cf. vol. I, pp. 228f.

[4] Rightly pointed out by H. A. Brongers, 'La crainte du Seigneur', *Oudtestamentische Studien* V, 1948, pp. 151ff.

[5] Cf. Gen. 28.17 with Ex. 3.5f., and Ps. 139.14 (emended text as adopted in RSV) with the praise of the Holy One in I Sam. 2.2; n.b. also the praise of the terrible God in Ex. 15.11; Pss. 99.3; 111.9.

the unapproachable majesty of the divine, convincing every creature of its own nothingness by the exercise of supramundane miraculous power, evokes that most profound of all forms of terror, which cannot be further explained or derived, and which yet as an overwhelming primal feeling seizes the whole of life and shakes it to its foundations.[1]

The pre-eminence of this feeling in the psychical attitude of the Old Testament believer is *ensured by two factors*: first, that all magical practices, by means of which a man might be able to exert pressure on the deity, and escape from his claims, are excluded from the Yahweh cult;[2] secondly, that any transference of religious fear on to divine beings other than Yahweh is ruled out by the withdrawal of demonic powers from the religious picture of the world.[3] Consequently *the encounter with the one Lord of the divine realm*, in whom all the saving and destructive effects of higher powers were combined, *constituted an absolute imperilling of human existence*, against which there was no protection. The fear of God is here deepened to a basic attitude affecting the whole man.

This makes it all the more remarkable that alongside this profound awareness of the destructive and therefore terrifying otherness of the divine nature we find, *as equally indispensable elements in the fear of God, confidence and trust in the help of this very same Being*. The religious feeling of terror does not have the character of panic, nor even that of servile anxiety, but contains a mysterious power of attraction which is converted into wonder, obedience, self-surrender, and enthusiasm. This is expressed not only in hymns of praise evoked by God's mighty acts —which, in any case, being confessions of the faith of the community, cannot be taken just as they stand as evidence for the fundamental mood of the individual—but in the unreflecting joy in Yahweh's presence, and the confidence in his protection and succouring justice, shown by the very people who are gripped with terror at the sudden outbreak of God's anger. Thus the Ark as the locus of God's presence is not only an object of fear in face of the devastating divine holiness, but also of joy in the divine power and in the promise of his being near at hand to aid.[4] Jacob's fear of the mysterious divine world

---

[1] I Sam. 6.20; Ex. 15.11; I Sam. 2.2; Lev. 10.2f.; 20.3; 22.2f., 32; Num. 16; Amos. 2.7; 4.2; Isa. 6.3ff.

[2] Cf. vol. I, pp. 173ff., 207f. On the revival of magic in later Judaism, cf. vol. I, pp. 219f., and the Mishna, Tract. Sabb. VI.2.

[3] Cf. pp. 223ff. above.

[4] For the former cf. I Sam. 6.19ff.; II Sam. 6.9; for the latter I Sam. 6.13, 19 (LXX); II Sam. 6.15. 21f.

manifested to him at Bethel does not stop him from seizing on the promise of this God, and placing himself permanently under his protection.[1] Nor does recoil from the mortal peril inherent in seeing God prevent men from counting this vision as the supreme blessing.[2] Clearly it is the very fact that men survive the deadly effect of God's entry into human life which results in their feeling an exuberant sense of liberation when they experience his turning to them as something hidden in the heart of apparent rejection; and this sense finds its natural expression only in thankfulness and joy. The intensity with which, in the right sort of fear of God, men are aware of this attracting and binding force in God's self-communication, and feel it as a counterpoise to the sense of sheer terror, is perhaps most strikingly summed up in the words of Moses addressed to the people on Sinai, when they were filled with consuming anxiety: '*Do not fear!* for God has come to prove you, and *that the fear of him may be before your eyes, that you may not sin.*'[3]

That which made it possible, however, for the fear of God to take this special form was the deity's distinctive self-communication as a covenant God. Here the terrifyingly unapproachable God reveals himself as at the same time a leader and protector of his people, one who has bound up his gift of life with fixed ordinances governing the way in which that life is to be lived by the nation. The transformation of religious feeling which this induced, from a sense of numinous terror to a reverential awe in which trust already predominates, may be seen at its finest in *the writings of the Yahwist narrator.* For here age-old stories, only slightly retouched, and still testifying to the most archaic emotions of the people, are combined with passages wholly permeated by the spirit of the Yahweh religion. Thus something of the shriek of numinous horror still sounds through the story of Yahweh's attack on Moses by night;[4] it breaks out, too, in the accounts of Gideon[5] and Manoah[6] in their encounters with God. This inner trembling also plays a part in

---

[1] Gen. 28.17, 20ff.; 35.3.

[2] Cf. on the one hand Ex. 19.21; 33.20, on the other Ex. 24.11; 33.18; also Gen. 16.13. Elsewhere the richer meaning of *y-r-'* occurs even in secular usage: cf. Josh. 4.14, where Kautzsch-Bertholet (*Die heilige Schrift des AT*[4]) renders 'hold in honour'('hochhalten').

[3] Ex. 20.20.

[4] Ex. 4.24ff.

[5] Judg. 6.22.

[6] Judg. 13.6. The angel of Yahweh is described as *nōrā' me'ōd*; cf. the fear of death expressed in 13.22.

the story of God's making a covenant with Abraham,[1] though on that occasion it is directly overcome by the promise of the covenant God. Thus, generally speaking, fear takes on a different character when it expresses the mental attitude of a servant in the presence of his lord, a relation in which the patriarchal history portrays its heroes with inimitable understanding. Unshakeable confidence and willing obedience, humble renunciation of one's own way and unconditional adherence to the goal of God's leading, are all here described in such a way as to reveal with deep feeling that turning of the individual to God which is such a vital element in the fear of God.

Even at this stage the Old Testament fear of God shows itself characteristically different from the attitude to the deity which lies at the root of neighbouring religions. There, even when men know full well the numinous terribleness of the power of God, and bear eloquent testimony to it,[2] it is unable to release effects similar to those in Israel, because the impression made does not produce in men the certainty that they have been totally abandoned. The juxtaposition of diverse and to some extent rival gods, the derogation from the power of the gods by the demons, and the eagerness with which men had recourse to prophylactic magic, prevented that abolition of all safeguards in face of the terrifying nature of the divine which is the typical mark of the Old Testament evidence. Conversely, the confident trust which constantly prevails as the basic note in Israel's fear of God has no parallel in the other religions of the ancient Near East. The will of these nature gods is too little reliable and too ambiguous for men to be able to credit them with a coherent total purpose; and they are themselves too strongly exposed to the evil power of the demons for their promises to be able to banish anxiety. Certain beautiful expressions of trust in individual prayers[3] cannot blind us to the fact that the confidence which lives in them was unable to embrace and dominate the whole of Man's relation to God. Anxiety remains 'one of the basic elements in Babylonian piety'.[4]

---

[1] Gen. 15.12; similarly also Gen. 28.17; Ex. 3.6; Job 4.12ff.

[2] Cf. e.g., the descriptions of Ninib and Nergal in M. Jastrow, *Die Religion Babyloniens und Assyriens* I, 1904, pp. 455 and 474ff., or that of the frightful effects of the divine word in the Enem hymns (pp. 40f.).

[3] In addition to many Babylonian prayers the Egyptian lay prayers from the New Kingdom deserve especial mention in this context. Erman was the first to draw attention to them, and Gunkel devoted a whole essay to them alone (*Reden und Aufsätze*, pp. 141ff.). Cf. also *AOT*, p. 32.

[4] So H. Seeger in his first-class treatment of the problem of piety: *Die Triebkräfte des religiösen Lebens in Israel und Babylon*, 1923, p. 17.

Above all, however, there was lacking that which gave the Old Testament fear of God its distinctive character, namely its connection with the sense of obligation toward the will of God, whether this was thought of as the original source of the settled ordinances of cosmic life, or as something which invades history in living self-demonstration. Consequently *the fear of God is mentioned again and again as the basis of respect for the divine norms.* Men shrink from injustice in view of the majesty of the divine lawgiver, who alone is to be feared; and that not only in Israel[1]—a similar attitude to the holiness of the law is assumed to exist also among the pious heathen.[2] Hence the fear of God is an indispensable virtue of the judge,[3] and part of the necessary equipment of the king.[4] There is a very close, almost stereotyped connection, in admonitions to observe the law, between the fear of God and walking in his ways;[5] indeed, the word by which God reveals his will is seen as the best guidance to a right fear of God.[6] The wisdom teachers, too, group together the fear of God and the avoidance of evil.[7]

What is happening is clear enough. Because the fear of God is understood as a relationship with the sovereign divine will, the irrational element in that fear, the numinous feeling of terror in face of a divine power which is unknown and which may break forth abruptly at any time, is being repressed in favour of an attitude of reverence, learned by human mediation, for divine ordinances which can certainly be known and which remain permanently present. *The fear of God is thus filled with a complex rational content, with the result that predominance is given to the positive element in the God-Man relationship.* Because the will of God is known primarily as something consistent and perspicuously clear, and is accepted into the fabric of life, *quiet confidence in the manifest God* gets the upper hand over terror in the presence of the hidden one. Moreover, this confidence acquires a sure foundation in men's constantly renewed experience of the goodness of the lawgiver as this allows itself to be discerned in the practical direction of life at the hand of the law. For with the commandment is bound up also the promise of divine mercy and forgiveness, con-

---

[1] Gen. 39.9; Ex. 1.17, 21.
[2] Gen. 20.8, 11; 42.18.
[3] Ex. 18.21.
[4] II Sam. 23.3; Isa. 11.2.
[5] Deut. 10.12, 20; Josh. 24.14, cf. Ps. 86.11.
[6] Deut. 4.10; 17.19; 31.13.
[7] Prov. 3.7; 8.13; 14.2; 16.6; Job 1.8.

stantly proclaimed to the penitent in the cult, and assuring him of life and peace as Yahweh's beneficent will. It is true that this close association of the fear of God with the Law also has its dangers. It may happen that external legal observance covers itself with the name of the fear of God, when it no longer has any living relationship with him, and so can be justly stigmatized by the prophetic critique as a mechanical commandment of men.[1] Yet here, too, the way is prepared for a striving after inner unity with the will of God which develops the God-Man relationship to an entirely new level of intensity

This help which the Law gives men in overcoming by trust their anxiety in the face of God has no counterpart in the other religions of the ancient Near East. The Babylonians indeed knew of many divine commands which they had to keep, both cultic and moral, but no unified law, because they knew of no unified divine will. Hence the discovery of the will of God remained quite literally an endless task, the fulfilment of which was a goal which could never be attained with certainty.

In addition, however, to the static supremacy and grandeur with which the divine majesty confronted the Israelite in the ordinances of the Law, there was also God's mighty intervention in history to present him with *the dynamic of an unknown and impenetrable will*, and to direct his fear along *the path of adventurous trust*. Thus it is the very shrinking, awe and alarm of the elders of the people in face of the wonder-working God which leads them to recognize Moses as his messenger and to accept in faith the liberation promised by him.[2] Whereas the Egyptians refuse to fear before Yahweh, and therefore despise the one whom he has sent,[3] in Israel the experience of his marvellous acts confirms the fear of God, and awakens trust in him and in his servants for the future as well.[4] If Yahweh is worshipped through the centuries as 'majestic in holiness, terrible in glorious deeds' (Ex. 15.11), this is linked with the strong hope that he will triumph over all resistance and achieve his goal in history, the blessing of mankind through his chosen people (Gen. 12.1–3). Thus fear, transformed into daring trust, lays the foundation for the eschatological hope. Only by hardening their heart against the terrifying

[1] Isa. 29.13.
[2] Ex. 4.1ff., 31.
[3] Ex. 9.20f., 30.
[4] Ex. 14.31; 19.9.

working of Yahweh's power can the people, in the course of their journey through the wilderness, fall into that irreverent derision of and contempt for God which refuses to believe his promises, and through its disobedience conjures up his judgment.[1] Elsewhere, too, we find this fear of the God who summons men to obedience by the agency of his messengers, compelling them to submit to his will in trust, and only then allowing them to count on his protection against threatening dangers.[2] This self-commitment, which is ready for the most extreme demands, and which bestows on the true fear of God the character of unconditional trust even in face of his enigmatic and uncomprehended will, is grasped most profoundly in the Elohist's narrative of Abraham's sacrifice of Isaac.[3]

Outside Israel there is at most a number of individual oracles, such as those which conveyed to Assyrian and Egyptian kings the consent of the gods to their undertakings, and the promise of their help,[4] which can be cited as expressions of a divine authority in history calling for the response of faith. There is no question that such divine messages were capable of arousing powerful confidence in the help of the gods, as the prayers of kings testify.[5] Nevertheless this spiritual condition was unable to determine men's total attitude to life. This was not due only to the effect of those obstacles already mentioned, polytheism and the fear of demons. Above all, there could be no comprehension of a clear moral saving will, guiding the whole of history, because neither was there a clear concept of history to hand,[6] nor was there any understanding of how the will of God might be considered from universal angles which would take in his whole providential government of the world. In Israel, however, it was precisely this

---

[1] Num. 14.11, 22, 24.

[2] I Sam. 11.7; 16.4; I Kings 18.12ff.

[3] Gen. 22.

[4] Cf. the oracles of Ishtar to Esarhaddon (O. Weber, *Die Literatur der Babylonier und Assyrer*, 1907, pp. 181ff.; *AOT*, pp. 281f.; *ANET*, pp. 449f.); also the enquiries made to the sun-god (Weber, pp. 177ff.), and the oracle of the moon-god Sin to the same king (A. Jeremias, *ATAO*, p. 738). Cf. also M. Jastrow, *op. cit.*, vol. I, pp. 443f.; II, p. 152. Also, the answer of the god Nebo to the supplication of Assurbanipal (H. Zimmern, *Babylonische Hymnen und Gebete* II, 1911, pp. 20f. = A.Ungnad, *Die Religion der Babylonier und Assyrer*, 1921, pp. 180ff.), the oracle of Ninlil to the same king (*ANET*, pp. 450f.), and the encouraging call of the god Re to Rameses II in the battle of Kadesh (A. Erman, *Literatur der Ägypter*, 1923, pp. 329f.) should be mentioned.

[5] Cf. the prayer on the memorial of the king of Cutha, cited in O. Weber, *op. cit.*, p. 203, and the prayers of Assurbanipal to Nebo connected with the above-mentioned Nebo oracle.

[6] Cf. vol. I, pp. 41f.

view of history, already impressed on the people by the old story-tellers, which provided the basis on which fear of God could develop into faithful obedience to One who through his messengers called men to discipleship.

For where the fear of God was spoken of in this way the concept proved itself large enough to make room for yet another aspect of the God-Man relationship. Because men had experienced God as still active even in his hiddenness, they pressed on to *a deliberate affirmation of the divine mystery*, and thus replaced the panic-like character of fear with a positive relationship. In several passages the word *he'emīn*, 'to consider firm, trustworthy, to find reliability in', is used to describe this relationship;[1] and it does indeed very happily strike the exact note of the adventurous attitude toward God.[2] It is a question of affirming that the hidden God is active, even when one cannot see the whole course of this activity or know what its goal may be. However, when the trustworthiness which has till now been experienced in God's other dealings is credited to this activity also, then clearly men have achieved *an adherence to God which is carried through whatever appearances may suggest*—and for this *a strong individual vitality* is essential. This is why one can do no more than give a very sketchy account of the concept of the fear of God. The immediate emotional reflex which is its predominant feature is replaced by deliberate decision between opposed possibilities. The fact that, despite all this, the fear of God did manage to remain for a long time the supraordinate concept simply proves, when looked at in another way, that it long ago out-grew its original content. It needed only a deepening of individual responsibility to enable the independent importance of the act of

---

[1] Ex. 14.31; Num. 14.11; for belief in God as also belief in his messengers cf. Ex. 4.1ff., 31; 19.9.

[2] Since the basic meaning of the root '-m-n in Arabic is 'to be secure, out of danger', there is also the possibility that *he'emīn* should be rendered 'to regard as assured', 'to find security in'. The root would then be semantically closer to *b-ṭ-ḥ* and *ḥ-s-h*. This, however, makes no essential difference to the theological content of the word. On the basis of an exhaustive analysis of OT usage A. Weiser would like to reaffirm the view already put forward by him on an earlier occasion ('Glauben im AT', *Festschrift für G. Beer*, 1935, pp. 88ff.), and see in the root '-m-n a formal relational concept, the content of which is determined in each instance by the particular subject to which it is grammatically related; thus the verb describes the specific individual character of the subject as real (*TWNT* VI, pp. 184ff.). Nevertheless I feel that the variety of usage of the root does not imply that we must give up any idea of a concrete basic meaning, but rather that the diversity can in every case be derived from the meaning mentioned above. T. C. Vriezen explains '-m-n as 'holding' or 'bearing', in order to provide a starting-point from which to derive the meanings of other instances (*Geloven en Vertrouwen*, 1959, pp. 12ff.).

faith in men's personal relationship with God to come to the fore. To this development, however, there are no parallels outside Israel; the basis for it lay in the points already explained.

2. FAITH IN GOD

1. The struggle carried on by Elijah and Elisha created deep divisions within the nation. As a result of their *call to decision* against the government's religio-political programme it was no longer possible for the individual to fall in as a matter of course with the activities of the group. The bond of national solidarity, hitherto all-embracing, proved breakable in the religious tug-of-war; and the guarantees of Israel's well-being embodied in the monarchy were called in question as a result of the ruthless critique on the part of the prophetic leaders. Those who acknowledged that the prophetic zealots were right, and so accepted the possibility that Israel's political position was in the utmost peril, by so doing *left behind the security of collective thinking and action*, and gave up all earthly assurances of the nation's future. The tension between this break-up of the givenness of the nation and the unqualified conviction that Israel had a divine commission *vis-à-vis* the Gentile world was only supportable where the individual's relationship with God was concentrated with unprecedented intensity on the will of the covenant God, and so became capable of the adventure of understanding that, whatever the jeopardy in which external institutions were placed, the setting up of God's kingdom as a religious reality was unassailable. In other words, *the attitude of faith had to emerge as of decisive significance for the God-Man relationship*.

It is therefore no coincidence that *the Elohist historian*, whose work in other respects also fits into the background of the Elijah period, should have been the one to make *the word of faith the outstanding theme of his patriarchal history*.[1] What he in his historical situation had experienced as a crucial expression of the individual's relationship with God, he recognized as also the key to the piety in the life of the father of the nation. In *Abraham* therefore he presented his contemporaries with *the type of the faithful*, the man who takes his stand on the

---

[1] Gen. 15.6. Cf. H. W. Heidland, *Die Anrechnung des Glaubens zur Gerechtigkeit*, 1936. The view of Gen. 15.6 as a redactional insertion linking the two parts of ch. 15 (T. C. Vriezen, *Geloven en Vertrouwen*, p. 16) seems to me to fail to do justice to the importance of this statement.

promises of God, and who lives by his assurance of God's will, whatever appearances may suggest to the contrary. In the writer's powerful symbolism the silent starry heaven points to the illimitable power
of the hidden God who manifests himself only in his word, and who
in this way elicits the venture of personal trust in which Man gives
himself wholly into God's hand.

As the foregoing survey of the rich content of the term 'fear of God'
will have shown, there was no need for the Elohist to import any
foreign element into Abraham's relationship with God in order to
arrive at this interpretation. He simply deepens the exposition of the
received tradition by emphasizing as an independent function, of
decisive importance for piety, an ingredient in the personal God-Man
relationship which other writers had regarded as of no more than
subordinate significance. The greatness of the inconceivable God, the
marvellous otherness of his nature, is taken just as seriously as it is in
the context of the fear of God; but here the affirmation of this greatness in a lively movement of the heart includes *a voluntary surrender of
the ego in full awareness of the implications of this decision*, thus bringing to
maturity that personal attitude *vis-à-vis* the dynamic of the divine
will which was already very much a living reality in the fear of God.

To see in this impressive picture of the decision of faith, as it lays
hold of the promise of God, and thus becomes assured of a new way
into an unknown land, only adherence to and perseverance in an
essential relationship of trust already existing is manifestly to under-
rate its importance.[1] The very use of the distinctive perfect with *waw
copulativum* to introduce the movement of faith draws attention to the
fact that here a new element is emerging for the first time,[2] one which
cannot be incorporated into a continuum; and the clear connection
of faith with God's word of promise, which Abraham encounters at
the very point where he is seeking to deviate from the true meaning
of his life, gives the conduct of the patriarch still more the character
of a decisive turning-point in his story. Here a new understanding of
God's activity and of his own position is opened up to him. To speak
in this context of nothing more than the reinforcement of an earlier
faith of Abraham is clearly to mistake the significance of this element

[1] So M. Buber, *Zwei Glaubensweisen*, 1950.
[2] Cf. the similar passages Josh. 9.12; Judg. 5.26; I Kings 24.14; Isa. 22.14;
Gen. 21.25, and on the whole question G. Schrenk, 'Martin Bubers Beurteilung
des Paulus in seiner Schrift "Zwei Glaubensweisen" ', *Judaica* VIII, 1952, pp. 1ff.,
and T. C. Vriezen, *Geloven en Vertrouwen*, 1959.

in the thematic structure of the historian's work. Abraham makes his decision for affirming the new condition offered him in the promise, and for basing his whole future life on this foundation.

This is a crucial step toward the opening up of a new dimension for individual piety, as becomes plain in the equation of faith with *ṣᵉdāḳā*; that is, with right conduct toward the God-given community. Justification at the mouth of the priest, who in Yahweh's name declares the one who has fulfilled a cultic duty to be pleasing to God,[1] is taken out of its rigidly cultic setting and transferred to the intimate inward relationship between Man and his God. It is this which is now *acknowledged as conduct in accordance with the covenant*, and that not by any human representative, but by Yahweh himself. It is not (as has been wrongly maintained) that God pays a reward for faithful performance[2]—whether Abraham experiences anything of God's award or not is plainly of no interest to the narrator—but that the faith-relationship in itself is expounded as the righteous fulfilment of the covenant fellowship on Man's part. Thus the covenant which was bestowed upon the people of Israel in fulfilment of the promise to Abraham acquires its inner vitality not from the cultic event but from the conscious spiritual and psychical attitude of the member of the covenant community toward the promise of the one who establishes the covenant. In this way the cultic formulas of justification become forms for giving expression to a spiritual event.

It is nevertheless far from the Elohist's intention to substitute faith for the fear of God, even though it is clear that for him the element of adventurous trust is operative even within human fear, as Gen. 22 in particular proves. Faith, as conduct directed toward an object, still plainly bears *the character of an individual act* by means of which a man actualizes his relationship with God in a particular situation; and it does not yet include, as does the fear of God, Man's permanent attitude toward God. Here the ultimate step was first taken by *the prophecy of Isaiah*.

II. It was, of course, in no way alien to Isaiah to use the concept of fear to describe a right relationship with God. He can depict the right

---

[1] G. von Rad ('Die Anrechnung des Glaubens zur Gerechtigkeit', *TLZ*, 1951, pp. 129ff.—ET in *The Problem of the Hexateuch*, 1966, pp. 125ff.) has drawn especial attention to this point in the light of the priestly formulas of acceptance in Leviticus (cf. on this subject R. Rendtorff, *Die Gesetze in der Priesterschrift*, 1954) and of Ezek. 18.

[2] Cf. H. Holzinger, *Genesis*, 1898, *ad loc.*

attitude to God both for himself,[1] for the nation,[2] and for the Saviour-King[3] of the future, as fear and trembling. The dominant traits in his picture of God, surpassing greatness and consuming holiness, are, after all, particularly favourable to an emphasis on fear as the sense of one's own nothingness, and on pride as its sinful inversion. But those impulses, both external and internal, which explain the Elohist's special position are even more prominently discernible in the case of Isaiah, and lead him to a *new formulation of Man's total attitude to God.* The disintegration of the national community, which had already begun a hundred years before, had been carried a stage further as a result of the prophetic preaching, with a corresponding intensification of the responsibility of the individual. At the same time, however, there were already signs in the political field of that constellation of forces which was to make the Syrian states the shuttlecock of the world powers, with the result that Israel's religiously based claim to be of special account in the world seemed bound to succumb before the brute force of the great empires. In such circumstances *the problem of God's control of world-history* inevitably became a burning issue, and, in view of the threatening world situation, a matter of how men were to be assured of the power and purpose of a God who was apparently inactive and far withdrawn from his people. Isaiah's firm conviction from the very start of his mission that there would be a merciless judgment on both nation and state turned this problem into an insoluble riddle. To break out of the brazen ring of annihilation which God had thrown round his people was beyond any possibility open to mere men. Hence the call to faith which the prophet uttered in this situation is not to be equated with the soothing commonplace that things were not so bad as all that, and that if only men would act prudently and without panic, and not lose their faith in the future, matters would still work out reasonably well. For at every period of his ministry he held fast unshakeably to his conviction of approaching disaster. If in such circumstances hopeful behaviour was to be possible at all, then it was bound to imply the paradox that the God of judgment was also the God of redemption, that the God who kills also

---

[1] Isa. 6.5; 8.12f.

[2] Isa. 29.13; 32.11. Cf. also the way in which the prophet censures as a perversion of the proper fear of God the brazen attitude of contempt which is described as rejection of counsel, blaspheming the word of God, refusal to regard Yahweh's work, arrogantly turning one's back on him, and so on: 5.12, 24; 9.8, 12; 22.11; 28.9, 14; 30.9.

[3] 11.2.

makes alive, and that he who takes down to the depths also brings up again. It is only possible to grasp this paradox, however, where God himself provides the firm ground underfoot on which a man may stand while doing so. Isaiah was granted this firm foothold when, in the hour of his call, he experienced simultaneously both pardon and mortal dread. In this moment he understood that the holy God comes forth from his unapproachable exaltedness, and condescends to lost Man, in order to absolve him and to take him into his service. *The antinomy which is beyond the comprehension of human thought, namely that the implacably just, holy and pure gives life and pardon in and through the execution of his judgment—indeed, that there is no other way to him than along the way of death—this antinomy is an element which can never be removed from the revelation of God to Isaiah.* And it was on this basis that there grew up that which the prophet calls faith: trusting self-commitment to the hand which is stretched out against Man over the abyss of death. *In every passage where Isaiah summons men to faith he is aware of both himself and his hearers as confronted by the reality of the wrathful and yet gracious God*, the God who by his concrete promise breaks through the total darkness of the historical situation sufficiently for men to lay hold on him, and by an act of profound inward assent to say a free Yes to his offer. Thus King Ahaz is offered the promise of the destruction of his enemies, and, when this apparently does not satisfy him, a miraculous sign from heaven or from the underworld, as a jumping-off point for a courageous confession of Yahweh.[1] Similarly the divine disclosure of the future in clear intimations of judgment or salvation both for the prophet himself[2] and for King Hezekiah and the leading states-men with whom Isaiah is in conflict over the right political decision[3] is one of God-proffered help, by which the courage needed for the adventure of faith both can and should be kindled. It is no use having recourse to previous guarantees of men's relationship with God, as provided by the dogma of election and its presentation in the cult; instead the individual is called to abandon this protective framework in order to affirm by free self-surrender the new and unexpected will of God in his particular historical situation.[4] *Only the conviction of being called and sustained by God himself makes it at all possible for men to transcend*

---

[1] Isa. 7.4ff., 11.
[2] Isa. 8.1f., 17.
[3] Isa. 28–31; 37.6, 21ff.
[4] Here once again Buber's attempt to understand the Old Testament faith, in contrast to that of the New, as an existential condition proves impossible.

the limits of all merely human potential in order to walk with the enigmatic God of the universe along the giddy paths by which he strides through history.

It is this sense of being caught up in God's prevenient action which gives to faith that *distinctive interplay of activity and passivity* which to the inspection of reason must continually seem incomprehensible and contradictory. For on the one hand the response of faith to God's offer undoubtedly involves entering in some sense into a passive state, implicit in which is the confession of one's own impotence, and the renunciation of any self-help by means of one's own strength and cleverness. Not for nothing is the demand for faith always followed closely by the exhortation to be still,[1] and to afford rest to the weary, that is, to the oppressed and exploited classes of the nation.[2] On the other hand, faith also implies intense spiritual activity, and audacious risks. It is not simply that faith, as personal decision for the proffered revelation, and conscious resistance to the counter-arguments of reason and to the menace of the actual situation, involves considerable strain on men's inner resources. The renunciation of external political busy-ness, which is demanded of Ahaz and Hezekiah, and the remaining on the defensive without allies, requires courage which is adequate even to the ultimate self-sacrifice in an apparently hopeless predicament, and is intimately related to recognition of the social demands of Yahweh, which is, of course, unthinkable without sacrifice and the surrender of selfish advantage. This activity is most effectively illustrated by the conduct of the prophet himself, who as he waits in faith has indeed to forget any idea of acting in his own power,[3] but has at the same time to demonstrate the obedience of faith by his continual championship and struggle for the cause of his God. Because faith springs not from any subjective good disposition in Man, but from the fact of being laid claim to by God, it involves partnership with God and growth in obedience to him all along the line.

The same truth is also very clearly expressed in the fact that faith involves *condemning the hitherto perverted direction of one's life*. Not for nothing does Isaiah contrast trust in God with false confidence in earthly and visible realities. This distorted attitude comes for him

---

[1] *haškēṭ* Isa. 7.4; cf. also *naḥat* Isa. 30.15. Cf. also Isa. 8.13–15, where the prophet himself is warned against any restless meddling.
[2] Isa. 28.12.
[3] Isa. 8.11ff.; 16ff.

under the head of an opposition that takes in the whole of life, that of flesh and spirit, the divine and eternal life-force and the human and transitory one.[1] Thus right confidence has as its inseparable companion *conversion*,[2] and it is precisely this fact which distinguishes it from all emotional euphoria. The energy with which Isaiah acknowledges and proclaims Yahweh as the Holy One of Israel introduces *the element of penitent humility* into any faith directed toward this God. Faith does not ignore the facts of sin and judgment, but takes in both their reality and the overcoming of that reality by God himself. To this extent it clearly points the way to the justification belief of the New Testament.

Thus, by surrendering to the judging and redeeming reality of God all right to a life of one's own, faith achieves *in practice the acknowledgment by the individual of the sole sovereignty of Yahweh*, and thus actualizes the basic demand of Yahwism—a demand which hitherto had found its strongest support in the fear of God springing from the sense of solidarity of the people of God—from the side of personal decision. The deliberate way in which Isaiah uses *faith as a comprehensive term for the total God-Man relationship* is most clearly seen in the absolute use of the word *he'emīn* without object in 7.9 and 28.16, passages to which the neologism *biṭḥā* (30.15), used in an equally absolute manner, forms a noteworthy parallel. That the relationship with God conveyed by these words possesses absolutely decisive importance for human existence is shown by the famous play on words in 7.9, which by expressing 'believing' and 'being established' in forms of the same root, '-m-n, links them as terms for the same reality. Similarly in 30.15 *gebūrā* in the general sense of the power to assert onself in the vortex of world events is equated with trust. Hence just as the act of faith clearly requires to be put into practice over and over again, so, too, *he'emīn* expresses *a total spiritual attitude* which is absolutely determinative for the relationship of the individual with

[1] Isa. 30.12; 31.1, 3.

[2] Isa. 30.15. Cf. on this point E. K. Dietrich, *Die Umkehr im AT und im Judentum*, 1936, pp. 64ff. It is true, nevertheless, that the significance of the word *šūb* for Isaiah in this connection has been greatly overestimated. Apart from the instance just quoted only 9.12 can definitely be attributed to him, and here *šūb*, as a synonym for enquiring from God, means to make an initial act of turning to him, to pay attention to him for the very first time, and so does not imply conversion in the full sense. In 6.10 the translation is doubtful; unless one is prepared to render with the adverb 'again', the reference is to turning away from previous contempt for Yahweh, and the sense is therefore predominantly negative.

God.[1] It might be described as *the fighting-line for Man in relationship with God*, the only place where, in the midst of the great cosmic catastrophe, when the head-on collision of God and the world erupts with annihilating force, Man both in attack and defence can preserve his link with the eternal world.

This comprehensive conception of faith also leaves its stamp on *the other terms used by Isaiah for the God-Man relationship*.[2] Thus *bāṭaḥ*, from being a description of the state of security, comes to be used of the relationship with God created by trusting in and building on his promise, surrendering in a renunciation of all self-assurance to the guidance of the One who alone is powerful, and therein finding superhuman resources.[3] *ḥāsāh*, 'to seek refuge', also becomes deepened into the venture of free trust.[4] Similarly *ḳiwwāh*[5] becomes an extraordinarily vivid expression not only as elsewhere for the *condition* of waiting in tension, but also for ὑπομονή, that steadfast endurance which, whatever the burden laid upon it, is sure that the promises will be fulfilled, and which enables faith to utter its daring 'Nevertheless . . .', however hopeless the outlook. In these ways the relationship of faith as a thing of dynamic movement dominates the bond between the believer and his God.

III. The way toward an assurance of God thus indicated to the individual proved itself again and again capable of solving the pressing problems and doubts which beset men amid the uncertainties of the struggle of world-history in which Israel's destiny was involved, and continually led to the discovery of *new and distinctive forms of expression*, which caught in words the personal experience here realized in practice. In the following century, during which the Assyrian empire reached the pinnacle of its power, the spiritual leaders set up the faith-relationship with God as a solid bulwark against the world of appearance. Herein lay the strength to overcome the challenge which was bound to press upon them in view of the nation's external vassalage and internal disintegration. Certainly the arrogant self-assertion of brute force in international affairs, which

---

[1] Weiser gives the following attractive description: 'Faith is for Isaiah the form of existence specific to the man who is attached to God' ('Glauben im AT', *Beer-Festschrift*, p. 93, n. 40). It may, however, be asked whether in this definition the dynamic element in faith is not underplayed at the expense of the ontic.

[2] This has been strikingly demonstrated by Weiser in the works cited above.

[3] Isa. 30.15.

[4] Isa. 14.32.

[5] Isa. 8.17, where it is used in conjunction with *ḥikkāh*.

seemed to give the lie to Isaiah's hope for the world sovereignty of Israel's God, made divine Providence a riddle to *Habakkuk*, and wrung from him the tormenting questions 'How long?' and 'Why?'[1] But the divine answer which was given to him,[2] and which treats the inexorably approaching end of all human self-aggrandisement as an imminent prospect, ends with a word of exhortation directing the questioner to *'emūnā*, 'steadfastness', as the source of an indestructible life; and in this particular context steadfastness can only mean the religious attitude of unshakeable trust, that is, faith:[3] 'Endure in patience! It (sc. the revelation) is surely coming to pass, it is not delaying. See! the man who is puffed up is unable to hold on to his life,[4] but the righteous will have life through his faith!' This passage indicates the profoundly *existential meaning of the attitude of faith* as contrasted with all those attitudes which rely on appearances, and which despise faith as a hopeless waiting for something which will never come. Because it takes the word of divine revelation seriously, and so creates a real link with the Lord of all life, faith can prove itself an inexhaustible source of vital power. For the God by whose claim to sole sovereignty over the world and time faith allows itself to be taken captive recognizes this attitude for his part as righteous, that is, in accordance with the covenant relationship. Thus Habakkuk combines in his understanding of faith the witness of the Elohist with that of Isaiah: *the right interior attitude to the divine order, arrived at by faith, is the only basis for the true life of the covenant people*, for amid the collapse of all human power and greatness this attitude becomes aware that a transcendent life has been bestowed upon it.

Jeremiah seems to give the same word more of an ethical connotation; he sets the striving after *'emūnā* in parallel with upright conduct (5.1), and in opposition to hypocritical mendacity (5.2f.),[5] so that the best rendering would seem to be 'sincerity' or 'truthfulness'. Yet it is remarkable in how comprehensive a sense the word is used both here and in 7.28; it can serve to sum up the right attitude to God, lack of which is sufficient to justify the sentence of final rejection. This may be influenced by the absolute use of the word in Isaiah. The reason why in his own use of the word Jeremiah inclines more strongly to

---

[1] Hab. 1.2f., 13.
[2] Hab. 2.2–4.
[3] So also T. C. Vriezen, *Geloven en Vertrouwen*, p. 16.
[4] This rendering adopts the conjecture of E. Sellin, *Das Zwölfprophetenbuch*[2, 3], 1930, *ad loc.*
[5] On the text cf. B. Duhm, *Jeremia, ad loc.*

the Niphal of the verb will be considered in connection with his total conception of the God-Man relationship.[1] Jeremiah also adopts the use of *b-ṭ-ḥ* in the sense of faithful trust in order to characterize the overall relationship of the believer to Yahweh (39.18).

By contrast *Zephaniah* formulates the right attitude toward God, both in its positive and negative aspects, as believing trust. Jerusalem's sin is summed up in the fact that she does not trust in Yahweh, nor does she draw near to her God. On the other hand, the humble and insignificant people to whom Yahweh shows his favour will be those who have sought refuge in Yahweh's name and who have learned not to glory in their own strength.[2] For Zephaniah therefore faith includes the humble conversion which turns away from all earthly powers and which honours Yahweh alone as the Mighty One.[3] In addition, however, there is a close connection with moral purity as expressed in obedience to God's command, thus indicating faith as also the decisive force behind the moral life.[4] Here the effects of the attitude of faith embrace the whole of life—a feature also found in Isaiah—and are clearly and deliberately *related to ethical renewal*; and in this new unity with the will of God faith forms the only genuine basis for the nation's life.

Deutero-Isaiah in his turn takes up the word of faith as a battle-cry of his programme, characteristically, however, using a form of the root *ḳ-w-h*,[5] stressing the element of *steadfast waiting in tension which marks the venture of faith*. For the situation of the nation in exile is that of a community oppressed by the burden of severe disappointments, and this is threatening to lead many astray into doubting God's faithfulness: 'My way is hid from the LORD, and my right is disregarded by my God' (40.27). Even here, however, God reaches out his helping hand to his own in the promise of the liberation that is to come with Cyrus, in order to encourage them to a bold act of faith and thus to make them witnesses to Yahweh's mighty acts and to the power of succour which is his alone.[6] Because this waiting in faith is focused on the God who is 'supremely mighty and rich in power', it is precisely under the heavy pressure of adversity that it can release unsuspected forces which carry men beyond the hopelessness of the

---

[1] Cf. p. 295 below.
[2] Zeph. 3.2; 3.11f.
[3] Cf. also Zeph. 2.3.
[4] Zeph. 3.2a, 3ff., 13.
[5] *ḳōwē yhwh*, 'they who wait for Yahweh', Isa. 40.31; 49.23.
[6] Isa. 42.18ff.; 43.10ff.; 44.21f.; 48.1ff.; 49.23; 50.10; cf. 51.5.

moment. The metaphor of the eagles' wings enters religious language as a most beautiful symbol of the power of faith to bear men up to God, and agrees with the earlier evidence which we have considered in bringing out the fundamental difference between the confident expectation which builds on God's promise and the tension which is the product of feverish impatience. But the most convincing demonstration of the truth of this lofty teaching is that given by the prophet himself. For it was at the very moment when, after the overthrow of Babylon by the Persians, the delay in permission to return home seemed to falsify his prediction, and subjected the exiles to a severe test, that he gave his people that canticle of blessed confidence in the all-conquering love of God which has been preserved in Isa. 49–55. What is more, even for the Gentile nations a right relationship with God which can be confident of his revelation is expressed in waiting upon God himself.[1] In his footsteps one of his disciples exhorts men to follow the example of the servant of God by seeking firm ground amid the general upheaval in unqualified trust in the God of judgment.[2] Again the watchword of 57.13, promising possession of the land to those who seek refuge in Yahweh,[3] that is, to the exiles who return in faith as opposed to the claims of the inhabitants of the land of Judah who have been corrupted by the heathen, is linked in spirit with the Prophet of the Exile, and once again sets before the eyes of the feeble group of returning Jews the source from which their life can draw invincible strength.

IV. Almost more strongly, however, than in these individual passages the force of Isaiah's preaching of faith continues to make itself felt where it determines men's total attitude, even though the actual cry of 'faith' is not taken up. Thus *Ezekiel's invitation* to the doubting pious of his day to take advantage of the gracious offer of their God, and to move onward to a new offering of their lives in response to the God who gives life,[4] is as little to be separated from the attitude of trustful faith as the same prophet's unbending refusal to countenance a Temple building in a foreign land because for him the continuation of the salvation-history was firmly rooted in Jerusalem.[5] In his vision of the spirit of God restoring the dead bones to

---

[1] Isa. 42.4 *y-ḥ-l*; 51.5 combined with *ḳ-w-h*.

[2] Isa. 50.10, where *b-ṭ-ḥ* is even further intensified by *s-m-k*, 'support oneself upon', and is intimately bound up with the fear of God.

[3] Here *ḥ-s-h* replaces *h-'-m-n*.

[4] Ezek. 18; cf. p. 249 above and ch. XXIII, pp. 485ff. below.

[5] Ezek. 20.40ff.

life[1] he has left an impressive memorial to the faith which depends entirely upon God, and can therefore set no limits to his redeeming power. Ultimately, therefore, the work of this mighty preacher of repentance, whose call to the individual is summed up more in the concept of conversion, *šūb*, than in that of faith, rests on that supremely personal attitude of responsibility which takes the divine promise seriously. And it was this for which Isaiah with his call to faith had sought to prepare the way.

Nor are *the view of history and the law-teaching of the Priestly school* uninfluenced by this concept, however little its predominant concern with the practical obedience of keeping the law might at first lead one to think so. The reshaping of the covenant concept, which replaces the legal relationship with one of pure grace, finding the beginning of this in the making of the covenant with Abraham, evinces an overall attitude to the Law which is far removed from any idea that the God-Man relationship can be actualized by the pious works of men.[2] In this outline of history the proper function of the Law consists in enabling the whole people to make the Abraham covenant their own, and to give outward reality to the covenant promise by which Yahweh declares himself Israel's God. The Law is thus permanently subordinated to the *berīt*; and the transposing of the Sinai covenant to the covenant with Abraham brings out with unmistakable clarity God's intention of establishing a truly personal fellowship between himself and Man. For the great covenant promises, on which the real content of the covenant rests, and which receive no more than reinforcement through the covenant sign of circumcision, can only be accepted and appropriated by faith in the hidden God who is revealed in his word. In the little touch by which Abraham at first doubts the possibility of Sarah's bearing a son, even though this is the one thing toward which the whole covenant-making is directed, and endangers the *berīt* by his desire to transfer it to Ishmael,[3] there is an emphatic indication that the content of the covenant cannot be actualized except by the complete self-commitment of Man to God in personal trust. *Hence the obedient performance of the rite of circumcision takes on the character of an act of faith,* by which Abraham in the teeth of all arguments from reason and appearance affirms the divine institu-

[1] Ezek. 37.
[2] Cf. vol. I, pp. 56f.
[3] Gen. 17.16f.

tion in the form in which it is offered to him.[1] The same theme, which in the original form of P may have been reinforced at this point by God's command to Abraham to migrate, is also found at an earlier stage in the establishment of the covenant with Noah. The command which attaches to the promise in this covenant-making, namely to go on board the ark with his wife and children,[2] demands faith and obedience as a necessary precondition of the b*erit*. The same thought plays its part later on in the appropriation of the Abraham covenant to Israel; for the realization of the covenant promise in the liberation from Egypt, the miraculous leading through the wilderness, the construction of God's own dwelling in the midst of the people, and the taking possession of the Promised Land—in all of which Yahweh reveals himself as the God of Israel—again and again relies upon the faithful concurrence of the people. Refusal on their part does not indeed make the covenant invalid, for this rests solely on God's sovereign appointment, but it does call down the divine punishment both on the congregation and on their leaders, Moses and Aaron, and excludes from enjoyment of the promised blessings of salvation.[3] Thus *the whole process by which salvation is realized in covenant and Law is comprehended in the dialectic of the faith-relationship*. The sovereign institution of the order of salvation by the exalted God is not the exercise of a tyrant's power, to which men's inner agreement is a matter of indifference, but an act of self-attestation aimed at eliciting a living personal fellowship, on the part of one who is eternally faithful, and in whose majestic purpose human salvation is rooted.

It is entirely in keeping with this that even in *the teaching of the Law* the Priestly Code does not give the central place to external legality, but to the obedience which flows from an inward consent to God's order of salvation. This is attested by two facts: first, by the whole way in which the Law brings conduct toward one's neighbour under the norm of the concept of love;[4] secondly, by the cultus, the central concern of which, the procuring of atonement, summons men from all confidence in their own performance, and directs them toward an attitude of personal trust in their God, because it is wholly dependent upon the unconditioned authority of the God who has instituted the atonement.[5]

[1] Cf. the corresponding emphasis on the faithfulness of Abraham in Neh. 9.8.
[2] Gen. 6.18.
[3] Ex. 6.9, 12; Num. 13f.; 20.12.
[4] Cf. vol. I, pp. 94ff.
[5] Cf. vol. I, pp. 163ff.

Thus both in the Priestly outline of history and in the practical teaching of the Law the whole corpus of tradition is distinctively transformed and attuned to the prophetic understanding of faith. This is indeed frequently concealed by the continued use of archaic formulations which stress the fear of God as the motive for keeping the Law,[1] and which are also in keeping with the marked prominence of holiness in the priestly picture of God. For all this, however, it is no longer fear but the faith-relationship which has become normative for the personal relation of Man to God in obedient subjection to the Law. Yet this only serves to bring to light what is at bottom the inner dynamic of the whole Priestly interpretation of the world and of history. This interpretation is not built on rationalistic deductions from some empirical datum, be it the worship of the Temple or the order of Nature. It rests entirely on an understanding of reality through faith, an understanding which draws from the confident affirmation of God's self-communication to his people strength to hold fast to the gospel of Yahweh's unlimited sovereignty, though the whole world gainsay it, and to champion this without fear. Hence, even if the starting-point for faith in the case of the priest is different from that of the prophet, namely the covenant promise of the divine king, which has become a present reality in the shape of the Law, as opposed to the word of promise of the hidden director of history, which points to the future, nevertheless the inner movement of the heart, affirming the claim made in either form, remains essentially the same. In both instances it is a matter of assurance of that hidden God for whom the Priestly Code as exclusively as Isaiah reserves the title of the Holy One.

3. LOVE FOR GOD

Almost at the same time as the personal God-Man relationship was being reshaped by the battle-cry of faith *the concept of fear was transformed in yet another way by the preaching of love for God*, the work of three sharply etched personalities, Hosea, Jeremiah, and the author of Deuteronomy. Here again it was the vitality of direct personal relationship with God on the part of individuals which of its own inner necessity burst the bounds of the traditional concept of the fear of God, once the latter had reached the stage where it could no longer expand to make room for the new forms developing from it.[2]

[1] Lev. 19.14, 30, 32; 25.17, 36, 43; 26.2; Num. 4.18–20; 17.27f.
[2] Cf. C. Wiéner, *Recherches sur l'amour pour Dieu dans l'Ancien Testament. Étude d'une racine*, 1957.

The way was *inwardly prepared* for this emergence of the new form of the God-Man relationship by the distinctive link between the fear of God and the authority of his ordinances for human life. In this context the deity allows the mystery of his numinous otherness, worshipped in fear, to recede into the background behind the proclamation of his faithful concern for the life of the covenant people, and thus awakens trust in his goodness.[1] Terrifying holiness now manifests itself as jealousy, *ḳin'ā*, which permits the object of its choice no relations with other powers, because its incomparable majesty cannot suffer its influence to be shared with any rivals whatever. Here, then, *attention is focused on the visible proof of God's purpose of fellowship*, and it is this which brings to life within the fear of God joy at receiving his benefits, gratitude at being undeservingly favoured, and pride in unmerited privilege.

The moment, however, when all these impulses blaze up together in one single emotion of shattering inward effect comes with the recognition of the divine election and covenant-making as revealing a supernatural and wholly miraculous power of life, in which God stoops down in a way incomprehensible to human thinking, and opens to the lost and to those who have incurred his wrath the way back into fellowship with himself. Thus *Hosea*, who is the first to perceive the unwearying love of his God at work in the history of the nation, can also describe the right relationship with God from the human side as *the manifestation in practice of the direct sense of inward mutual belonging*, an awareness which dominates the whole being, and drives it far beyond all those requirements of duty which arise from rational reflection, into unreserved surrender. It is worth noting that in this context the prophet does not choose the root *'-h-b*, which is used of human love, and which he uses instead to denote the perversion of the search for God, the expending of the natural religious instinct in the unbridled impurities of the high places tainted by the cult of Baal.[2] In its place he prefers to speak of *the knowledge of God*, by which indeed he means no merely theoretical knowledge of God's nature and will but the practical application of a relationship of love and trust, as this is seen at its loveliest in the association of a true wife and her husband. This does not mean that in every passage where he speaks of the knowledge of God Hosea must have the marriage bond in mind. This knowledge,

---

[1] Cf. pp. 273f. above.
[2] Hos. 3.1b; 4.18; 8.9; 9.1; the local deities are described as *mᵉ'ahᵃbîm* in the pejorative sense of paramours: 2.7, 9, 12, 14f.; 9.10.

the lack of which the prophet mentions as the major reason for the
coming judgment, is also the experience and recognition of God's
succouring acts, which ought to lead to obedience and trust, and as
such bears a strongly noetic character, and can describe the process
of getting to know someone through acquaintance and experience, a
sense in which it is used with regard to the things of everyday life.[1] At
all events it does not denote the contemplative knowledge of the wise,
but a perceiving which at the same time always includes an interior
relation to the one known. In the case of Man's knowledge of God
this is a relation of surrender and obedience, in that of God's knowledge of Man one of care and election. It thus corresponds to the
usage of *y-d-ʿ* as this can be established from other passages, where it
denotes a link between persons whose lives are closely involved one
with another.[2] As regards Hosea, however, it cannot be overlooked
that the highly significant story of his marriage, which stands at the
beginning of his message, and was the means by which Yahweh gave
him a new understanding of God's relationship with Israel, also
gives the word *y-d-ʿ* the warmer tone of inward intimacy, even where
the marriage bond is not explicitly mentioned.[3] Clearly, when used of
the God-Man relationship, the word will describe not the capricious
instinctual affect but the *responsive love and trustful surrender* awakened
by the unmerited love of God. Because God 'knows' his people, that
is to say, he has introduced them into a permanent relationship of the
closest mutual belonging, that same people for their part have both

---

[1] This is the justified element in the protest of H. W. Wolff (*EvTh* 12, 1952,
pp. 533ff.) against allowing the meaning of *y-d-ʿ* to slip into the realm of the purely
affective. Nevertheless his own interpretation of the knowledge of God as coming
down to the priest via the cult tradition, and being passed on by him to the people,
fails to do justice to the deep interior dynamic which links this knowing to its
object, and because of which it attains its full content only when it is knowledge
which has become concrete in action. On this point cf. the extensive study by
W. Zimmerli, *Erkenntnis Gottes nach dem Buch Ezechiel* (ATANT 27), 1954.

[2] Cf. E. Baumann, '*y-d-ʿ* und seine Derivate', *ZAW*, 1908, pp. 22ff., 110ff.
Largely in agreement is G. J. Botterweck, '*Gott erkennen*' *im Sprachgebrauch des AT*
(BBB 2), 1951. The latter, however, in his emphasis on the 'practical knowledge of
God' and 'religious fellowship with God' is occasionally driven to equate this
knowledge with the 'fulfilment of religious and moral duties' (p. 45), where a more
precise distinction of concepts would seem to be called for. He also rejects any connection with the marriage relationship in his explanation of the concept.

[3] The refusal to accept the existence of this connection (H. W. Wolff, *op. cit.*,
pp. 537f.) means closing one's eyes to the penetrating influence of this basic
experience of the prophet, and cannot be maintained. However, especially with
so sensitive a man, we must, of course, reckon with the fact that the stress laid on
this particular element will vary within the prophet's message.

the ability and the obligation to embrace him in 'knowledge'; that is, in a loving affection which results in the permanent demonstration of loyalty and kindness. The command to the people, *tēdaʿ*, 'thou shalt know', is rooted in the previous experience of *ᵃnī yᵉdaʿtīkā*, 'I have known thee' (13.4f.).[1] No other expression could more strongly recall the covenant established by God,[2] which rests on God's prevenient love, and at the same time remove the concept from any association with juristic thinking and incorporate it into the context of moral trust. It is therefore entirely appropriate that more than once in this connection prominence should be given to *remembering and despising Yahweh's law*.[3] It is in the law that Yahweh's election, by which he claims Israel for himself alone, finds expression; and if men are to affirm this election from inward affection, then this must show itself in their taking this claim of ownership seriously, in the qualities of covenant-love and faithfulness, *ḥesed* and *ᵉmūnā*, which Hosea likes to couple with the knowledge of God,[4] not as extras to supply something lacking in the latter, but as the outward demonstration of the complete inward mutual belonging which it represents. The opposite of this is the forgetting of Yahweh,[5] which Hosea spotlights throughout the history of his people, both past and present. To forget, here, does not imply that some previously existing knowledge has been extinguished. It means to let a fact which is still perfectly well known go down the wind, to jettison a life-relationship, the demands of which are felt to be burdensome, and which men in their arrogance imagine they can disregard. But the liberation striven for in this way proves in the end to be enslavement to the unbridled love-instinct, fornication with the Baalim. In a complete misapprehension of this bondage the nation can fancy that the possibility of turning and renewing the original relationship of trust is still open,[6] whereas, in fact, the inner alienation of the spirit of whoredom makes it impossible for her any longer to arrive at a true knowledge of Yahweh.[7] This merciless diagnosis of the inner condition of Israel completes the picture of the right God-Man relationship as one of a covenant of love in which

---

[1] This reciprocity of the process of knowing is rightly emphasized by S. Mowinckel, *Die Erkenntnis Gottes bei den alttestamentlichen Propheten*, 1941, pp. 6ff.

[2] Cf. the earlier use of the word by Amos (3.2).

[3] Hos. 4.6; 6.5–7; 8.1, 12.

[4] Hos. 2.21f.; 4.1; 6.6: cf. vol. I, pp. 232ff.

[5] Hos. 4.6; 13.6.

[6] Hos. 6.3.

[7] Hos. 5.4.

everything depends on the motion of the heart and soul, and the slightest unfaithfulness, the smallest breach of trust, causes irreparable damage. The worship of Yahweh exclusively is here given the most compelling of all motivations as being an indispensable element in that relationship of trust which binds the lover unbreakably to the beloved.

This derivation of all worship from an inner openness to God's activity was also upheld by *Jeremiah* at every stage of his lifelong struggle. He characterizes the essential unnaturalness of apostasy to Baal by portraying it as the baseless abandonment of a covenant of love from which nothing but salvation and blessing of every kind had flowed over the nation (2.2ff.). The folly of such conduct is, however, intimately bound up with the fact that Israel no longer 'knows' Yahweh, and has allowed herself to be deluded into stepping outside the inward relationship of trust and surrender (4.22). The way in which the prophet sees the relationship of God and people as a direct, natural bond is impressively indicated by his adoption of the word '-h-b, with its immediacy of emotional force, to describe the once untroubled association of love between Yahweh and Israel, an association which he illustrates even more tenderly than Hosea by his use of the imagery of the time of betrothal. *hesed*, when taken in conjunction with these ideas, shifts its meaning, as on occasion it already does in Hosea, from dutiful conduct more decisively into the sphere of direct inclination, of love. In the abandonment of Israel's unique status her leaders, especially the priests, have shown the people the way by their bad example (2.8). They, who prided themselves on knowing God's law, were in reality alienated from his will, because they had not surrendered themselves inwardly in true knowledge of him. From this change in the interior attitude toward God springs the moral anarchy which substitutes lies and faithlessness for truth and faith in dealings between man and man as well (9.1–5). By contrast, the man who lives in 'serious and genuine intimacy with Yahweh'[1] in unqualified surrender can do no other than show God's kind of goodness also to his fellow men—which is why Jeremiah holds up King Josiah to his unkingly successor as a classic example (22.16). This was the true glory, because it was the privilege granted to no other nation beside Israel (9.23). In this context, however, where the dominant idea is one of joyful acceptance of the divine demonstration of love,

[1] E. Baumann, *op. cit.*, p. 133.

'*emūnā*[1] cannot bear the sense of faithful steadfastness despite the concealment of God's plan. Instead, in accordance with the meaning of the Niphal of the verb, it must denote the trustworthiness which shows itself toward God and Man in purity of heart and faithful maintenance of the love relationship. A return to this profoundly inward fellowship of love and trust with God, which then determines life in its totality, is only possible, however, to the man who is ready for interior conversion; it has nothing to do with indulging oneself in pious feelings.[2] But because the inner compulsion to evil is so strong that those who have gone astray deliberately shut themselves off from knowledge of Yahweh,[3] the prophet cannot hope for any change as a result of his own teaching, but only through the creative intervention of Yahweh himself. For he alone can transform the heart of the infatuated, so that they open themselves to his love, and through the forgiveness of sin remove the most serious obstacle to untroubled intimacy with him.[4] But in the people of the age of salvation a new spirit of dedication will animate every individual without exception; and through this spirit the new covenant, bringing the profoundest content of the old to fulfilment, will become a reality. The law, on which men have hitherto made shipwreck (2.8; 11.1ff.; cf. 8.7f.), it will now be possible genuinely to fulfil as a result of inward communion with the lawgiver. In this way, through an inner surrender to the God of revelation, we arrive once again at the human response to God's demonstration of love; and it is this which finally brings to pass the goal of election, the separating from the nations of the world of a people wholly and exclusively belonging to Yahweh.

In the thought of both prophets there is a close association between the individual's relationship with God and the restoration of the covenant relationship of the whole people, for they see the latter as achieved when men understand that love for God is the inwardly necessary response to the overwhelming gift of election. This insight had powerful consequential effects in *the preaching of Deuteronomy*. For the problem with which this writer is most deeply concerned is none

---

[1] Cf. p. 285 above.

[2] Jer. 9.4f. (following the reading of the LXX; cf. *Biblia Hebraica* and W. Rudolph, *Jeremia*, 1947, *ad loc.*); 24.7.

[3] Jer. 9.5; cf. 5.22f., where instead of the knowledge of Yahweh, but with the same meaning, we find fear in the presence of divine omnipotence used in order to characterize the rebellious mentality of the people even more strongly; and with both passages cf. 13.23.

[4] Jer. 24.7; 31.33f.

other than the restoration of the covenant people to its God-willed form at a time when the disastrous inroads of heathen thought and morals had plunged Israel into a serious crisis, dangerously under-mining her only proper foundation, the clear understanding of her religious position and task. The complete dissolution of a unified national will, devoted without reserve to the goals of the divine covenant, made it hopeless from the start to appeal to predominantly collective ties and motivations, unless one could also succeed in impressing these afresh on the heart and conscience of the individual as immediately comprehensible and binding demands. The reduction of the God-Man relationship to the primary emotional force of love, embracing the whole nature of Man, as this had been worked out by Hosea and Jeremiah, inevitably acquired concrete importance when it was a question of finding the way to the nation's heart, and not simply of maintaining an external legal system with the help of the power of the State. The Deuteronomist knows how to give his preach-ing of the Law, *by means of the command to love*, both *inner unity and at the same time that direct impact in pastoral exhortation and education* which continually brings men back from all the various forms of externalism to the most inward decision of conscience. It is this which gives his preaching an importance for the development of the individual God-Man relationship such as hardly any other document was ever to attain again.

This insistence on love for God takes its right place in the whole complex of the God-Man relationship from the start, because it always involves *recollection of God's prevenient act of love*.[1] The Deutero-nomist attempts to illuminate the whole history of the nation with the light of God's love by expounding its basic revelation in the in-conceivable election of tiny Israel above all the nations, an election which became a living reality in the three covenant makings.[2] Furthermore he reminds his hearers of God's faithful care for his people as attested in the guiding of the patriarchs and in the leading through the wilderness. The central manifestation of the love of God, however, consists in this, that he bestows on Israel his word—whether this be the word of the Law on the tablets in the Ark of the Covenant, or the word of prophecy—which guarantees that his guidance will be constantly present in all the situations of history. In this word he as a

---

[1] On the subject-matter of this paragraph cf. the outstanding treatment by H. Breit, *Die Predigt des Deuteronomisten*, 1933, pp. 111ff.

[2] Cf. vol. I, pp. 53f.

person encounters his people, and establishes a direct link with them. Even Yahweh's acts of judgment are subordinate to the purposes of his love; indeed, at bottom they spring from this love, which as *ḳin'ā*, jealousy, is bound to bring to nought with fearful punishment any attempt to seduce the object of its choice.[1] Hence the cultus, especially the Sabbath and the feast of the Passover,[2] forms a continual remembrance of God's act of love, and is meant to lead to the expression of grateful joy.

There can be no doubt that this interpretation of history on the basis of the concept of love implies *a certain 'rationalization' of the God-Man relationship*. The subordination of woe to weal does not indeed altogether eliminate the demonic aspect of God, but it does present it as the negative side of the love with which he cares for men, with the result that God's nature loses the sinister and alien quality which repels them. One indication of this which cannot be overlooked is the complete absence of the designation of God as *ḳādōš*, holy, the term which so powerfully expresses the divine otherness.

To such a God, who so fully discloses his inmost self, and goes so far to adapt himself to the weakness of men in order that they may be able to approach him with confidence,[3] and that their weak faith may be protected in face of temptation,[4] Man can only respond in trustful love. Like Jeremiah, but now without any restrictions whatever, the Deuteronomist uses the root *'-h-b* to denote this love, *spontaneous and direct, a force that fills Man's whole being*. He also likes to use characteristic phrases to emphasize the way in which this ardent love involves every part of Man: 'with all your heart, and with all your soul, and with all your might'.[5] His use of the root *d-b-ḳ*, to hold fast to,[6] denoting unreserved surrender, serves the same purpose. The attitude here implied is not, however, to be confused with an erotic devotion to God; and care is taken to ensure this by *the close link between love and the demand for obedience and the fulfilment of the law*. This synthesis is nothing short of a hallmark of the Deuteronomic preaching, and explicitly characterizes love as a force of the will. Hence it is

[1] Deut. 4.24; 5.9; 6.15; 29.19; cf. the phrases about 'burning fire', 4.11f., 24; 5.4, 24.
[2] Deut. 5.12–15; 16.1–8.
[3] Deut. 18.15f.; 5.20ff.
[4] Deut. 7.21ff.
[5] Deut. 6.5; 10.12; 11.13; 13.4; 30.6.
[6] Deut. 4.4; 10.20; 11.22; 13.5; 30.20. By contrast *y-d-ʿ* is hardly used at all in the prophetic sense.

perverse to interpret love from the angle of obedience as submission to the law, or obedience from the angle of love as a description, figuratively intended, of interior openness to God's will.[1] Instead love, as the answer to God's act of election, cannot but lead to the unqualified affirmation of his will as this is to be known in the word of the law and the prophets. Hence *the law is not an element of the divine sovereignty alien to love, but a direct proof of love,* since it makes the irrational divine purpose, which is incomprehensible to the natural man, clear and reasonable to all, and gives them the feeling of their superiority to all pagan proclamations of God's will.[2] As a means of fellowship, therefore, the law requires from the man who is dedicated to God unreserved obedience. An antinomian love would be a manifest self-contradiction. Rather love leads to a union of the will with God, so that the Deuteronomistic association of love and obedience is best rendered by the word of Jesus in John's gospel: 'If you love me, you will keep my commandments.'[3]

Love, however, *also acts as a safeguard against every kind of externalist legality or casuistic legalism.* Because its very nature demands that it go far beyond all legal requirements, staking a man's whole being without reservation for God's cause, it can never regard individual commandments as anything more than *practical guidance in concrete cases—* guidance which it accepts thankfully, but without anxiety or casuistic striving after perfect performance.[4] In this context the lawgiver is able to illuminate the inner connection between the love relationship of God and Man, and the keeping of the law, from a new angle by linking the law with the *exclusive* character of love. It is *the out-and-out struggle against the worship of idols* which largely gives his legal pronouncements meaning and purpose. As a means of keeping Israel wholly within the domain of the God who watches over her with jealous love, and of preserving in separation from heathenism and in the development of her special character the status destined for her by God, the keeping of the law was bound to lead directly to the profession of sincere dedication to Yahweh.

It is on this basis that *the linking of love with the fear of God,* a combination which clearly causes the Deuteronomist no difficulty, is to be understood. It is the association, which we encountered earlier, of

---

[1] Cf. the telling refutation of these interpretations in Breit, *op. cit.,* pp. 156f.
[2] Deut. 4.6ff.; 30.11ff.
[3] John 14.15.
[4] Cf. on this subject vol. I, pp. 93f.

fear with respect for the divine ordinances for human life which leads him to adopt this expression, too, quite unreflectingly, in order to describe the right attitude to the will of God.[1] To fear Yahweh, to keep his commandments, or to walk in his ways, have here almost become synonyms. Therefore fear and love can be used in the same breath, as descriptions of right conduct toward God, conduct which includes the loyal worship of Yahweh in compliance with his will for the cult.[2] *The requirement of love is thus nothing other than a new clarification and a deeper understanding of the old commandment to fear God.* In this connection it is highly significant that the recapitulation of the Decalogue in Deut. 5 as the fundamental law of the divine covenant, which is surrounded by the awe-inspiring majesty of Yahweh as by a flame of fire, is followed by the commandment to love in Deut. 6.4f. in order, as it were, to point out the real meaning of the covenant law and the root of obedience to it. And because *this love is characterized as gratitude toward the abundantly generous Lord of the nation*,[3] the fear of God associated with it completely loses the element of terror which assails men faced by the alien and sinister grip of the divine power. Instead it serves to separate love once for all from any false familiarity or religious eroticism by fixing the eyes of the worshipper on the majesty of the divine lawgiver, and calling to mind the terrifying anger of God toward his enemies. Confronted by the reality of the Lord of wrath and punishment, no God-Man relationship can endure which claims the name of love, and yet ultimately revolves round the human ego, using God for the satisfaction of its own needs.

It is significant that such a full and resounding proclamation of love toward God, aware of its educational mission, and devoting itself with enthusiasm to the training of the nation,[4] *as good as stops short at the Exile.* This reveals more than mere external coincidence. *Together with the change in the bases of existence brought about by the catastrophe there is also plainly a change in the inner presuppositions upon which the proclamation of the commandment of love had hitherto operated.* The starting-point for this proclamation had, in fact, been the proof

---

[1] Deut. 4.10; 5.26; 6.24; 8.6; 10.12; 14.23; 17.19; 28.58; 31.13.

[2] Deut. 10.12, 20; 13.4f.

[3] Deut. 7.6ff.; 8.5ff.; 11.1ff.

[4] Breit (*op. cit.*, p. 164) has called attention to the frequent use of the root *l-m-d* in Deuteronomy, and the value attaching to the instruction of children: Deut. 4.10; 6.7, 20ff.; 11.19f.; 29.28; 30.2; 32.46. In the Deuteronomic redaction of earlier traditions love toward God is inculcated in several passages: Ex. 20.6; Josh. 22.5; 23.11; I Kings 3.3.

of Yahweh's love visible and available to all. It was there before men's eyes in the existence of the nation, even though that existence might be seriously endangered; and both accusation and attempt at renewal could point to that concrete reality as the tangible evidence that God's purpose was one of love. That men have rejected the proffered hand of the God who has revealed himself is the prophets' reproach to the people; that they should take that hand even now is the exhortation of the lawgivers. In each case the thought revolves round Israel's election by Yahweh's jealous love; and in the light of that, Israel's existence is seen as a well-hedged garden, full of beauty and purpose and harmony. What matters is to strive to preserve this, even if the world at large has to be forgotten in the process. This view of Israel's relationship with God was, however, completely invalidated by the execution of judgment in the disintegration of the nation and the State. Its clarity and reasonableness gave way to the sinister darkness of the rejection of God's people; its pointing to the God of revelation was exchanged for the quest for the hidden God. Hence conduct based on the blessed certainty of the experience of God's love inevitably gave way to trembling obeisance before his consuming holiness; and this called for new assurances that the link with God would remain whatever happened. On all sides piety found itself forced into a combative position which made love for God seem a state of rest in the God-Man relationship which was no longer attainable. In this condition of struggle, however, the battle-cry of faith acquired decisive importance for the shaping of the personal relationship with God. It could no longer be a question of giving out spontaneously the grace of God which one received. What was called for was a deliberate act of will to take one's stand on the divine promise, a bold venture even in the teeth of appearances, a high tension and concentration of the spirit, which must close its eyes to the hypnotic influence of earthly powers, and acknowledge the will of God as the sole power in the universe, despite the fact that neither experience nor feeling were able any longer to break through to contact with it. Only on this basis was it possible to tolerate the dissolution, both external and internal, of the bond of national unity— external because of the surrender of Israel's special position among the nations and her dispersion among the heathen, internal because of the division of the people of Yahweh into those loyal and those hostile to him. Only on this basis, too, could men rise above the daily vexation of the heathen world empire; for the believer reached out beyond the riddle of the present toward a new divine revelation, and resolutely postponed to the future the consummation even of the individual relationship with God. True love for God, however, seems feasible only when the great saving act of Yahweh shall have restored his people, and once more made divine love their joyful possession. In that day Yahweh will circumcise their hearts, so that they can love their God with all their heart and all their soul.[1]

4. THE PERSONAL RELATIONSHIP WITH GOD IN THE POST-EXILIC PERIOD

1. The whole outward situation of the pious in the exilic and post-exilic periods compels him to take the watchword of faith as his guide toward a new basis for his personal relationship with God. But this growing attitude of faith by no means simply corresponds to the prophetic conception; instead, as a result of its pronounced connection with the Law, it takes on a special form, which may best be described as *faith-obedience*. There can be no doubt that here the activity of the prophet *Ezekiel* was especially influential. For bound up with the gracious offer of his God to the exiles, opening up to them the possibility of a new life under the protection of Yahweh, was a definite insistence upon the Law,[2] in which the life-creating will of God[3] is revealed, and the form of worship for the exiled congregation sketched out. With iron logic the prophet leads those who believe his word on to unconditional surrender to the norm of the Law, and teaches them *to make by the obedient ordering of their lives a practical confession of their faith* in divine retribution and in Israel's future. That in doing so he was far from expecting the future salvation to come as the fruit of the obedience to the Law shown by the community which he had trained may be seen from two facts: first, that he bases the divine plan of salvation exclusively on Yahweh's purpose of sanctifying his Name, which has been profaned,[4] and secondly, that he sees the perfect communion of will between God and Man as established by Yahweh's miraculous new creation of the human heart.[5] The first transfers the bringing in of the messianic

[1] Deut. 30.6.
[2] Ezek. 18.
[3] Ezek. 20.11, 21; cf. Lev. 18.5.
[4] Ezek. 36.21–23, 32; and cf. the frequent motive-clause: 'that they may know that I am Yahweh'.
[5] Ezek. 36.26f., which is echoed in 11.19f.

salvation to the necessary accomplishment of God's will in the world which he has created; the second provides the indicative assurance on which is based the imperative exhortation: 'Get yourselves a new heart and a new spirit!'[1] Here, too, Man works out his own salvation with fear and trembling, because it is God who works both the willing and the achievement. In this context the sharp stress on the divine holiness in its transcendent majesty is of especial value in making obedience to the prophet's exhortation an expression of faith in the God who, for all his distant exaltedness, is yet near at hand and effective in operation.

The start thus made on orienting faith in the direction of obedience to the Law—a development which gave the infant community in exile the backbone of its existence, and guarded it against absorption into the heathen environment—received a new stimulus when *the Priestly Law was included among the normative bases of the community*. The more deeply the sovereign favour of the covenant-making, and the necessity of faithful assent, was thus impressed upon those who had been called into the covenant,[2] the more inseparably was this personal turning to God bound up with willing fulfilment of the covenant obligations, in which the earthly existence of the people of God became concrete reality. Here, too, therefore, acknowledgment in faith of God's exclusive sovereignty constitutes the nerve of the subjection of life to the ordinances of the Law, and it is in unbreakable loyalty to that Law that it proves itself.

How strongly this faith-obedience determined the piety of Judaism may be seen clearly enough from the *Psalms*. It is not only in an explicitly didactic poem, such as Ps. 119, that faithful waiting upon God's judgment and salvation is portrayed as the model attitude of the pious devotee of the Law;[3] a psalm of confidence, such as Ps. 4, also associates the bringing of righteous offerings directly with trust in Yahweh (v. 6).[4] In the song of thanksgiving for deliverance from grave peril prominence is given to the trust in Yahweh which this redemption has newly kindled, while at the same time obedience to the Law is mentioned as the natural expression of gratitude.[5] In the petitionary psalm against the tyranny of the godless the pious are seen not only as those who call upon Yahweh alone as the rock of

[1] Ezek. 18.31.
[2] Cf. pp. 288f. above.
[3] Ps. 119.43, 74, 81, 123, 147.
[4] Likewise Ps. 16.
[5] Ps. 40.4f., 9.

their refuge,[1] but also as the righteous, that is to say, those who respond to the covenant relationship, and who allow themselves to be taught out of Yahweh's law.[2] Alphabetic psalms, loosely linking as they do statements of religious experience with devout petitions, present a good cross-section of the piety of the community; and this leaves no doubt that faithful and humble waiting upon God is to be the fundamental attitude of the pious. At the same time, however, the implementation of this attitude is described as a matter of course in the Deuteronomic phrase 'keeping the covenant and the testimonies'.[3] The writer of a psalm of innocence, who boasts of his impeccable legal righteousness, describes people like himself as 'those who seek refuge at Yahweh's right hand'.[4] It is true that the root '-m-n now becomes less prominent as a term for faith, giving way to more striking expressions for the bond between the believer and God; though ne'eman may be used to denote cleaving fast to God or to his covenant, reinforced by the image of the steadfastness of the heart.[5] Nevertheless b-ṭ-ḥ and ḥ-s-h are the predominant expressions for trust, understood in the sense of faith[6]—a spiritual attitude which meets with sympathy even in the later wisdom teaching.[7] The fact that the pious, both in the Psalms and in the wisdom teaching, can quite generally be described as the man who trusts in God[8] means that the universal validity of the attitude of faith for Man's total relation to God has now been given shorthand expression—a situation in which, however, the conventional nature of the usage will have contributed to weakening the original meaning.

This should warn us not to write off the piety of Judaism, in so far as it emphasizes the keeping of the Law, as no more than holiness through works. Where the venture of faith so fundamentally determines the whole God-Man relationship, the shaping of life by the Law is equipped with strong safeguards against the danger of externalism, and constantly leads men back from mere keeping of the commandments to ultimate personal decision. Significant in this context is the central importance of faith in the book of Jonah, where

[1] Ps. 94.22.
[2] Ps. 94.12, 15, 21.
[3] Ps. 25.3, 5, 21 and 10; Ps. 33.20–22.
[4] Ps. 17.7; cf. 26.1.
[5] Ps. 78.8, 37; Neh. 9.8, the latter being patently a reminiscence of Gen. 15.6.
[6] Pss. 13.6; 22.5, etc. In parallelism with the root '-m-n: Pss. 26.1, 3; 78.22; 37.3; parallel to the fear of God: Pss. 40.4; 56.4f., 12. For ḥ-s-h cf. Pss. 17.7; 118.8f.
[7] Prov. 3.5.
[8] Pss. 32.10; 125.1; Prov. 16.10; 28.25; 29.25; cf. Jer. 17.7.

the word *he'ᵉmin* is used to describe right acceptance of the prophetic preaching as faith in God (3.5ff.). The consequence of this faith is both penitent self-abasement in fasting and prayer, and also the turning away from all iniquity by both small and great, even to the king upon his throne. In this example of the readiness of the heathen to believe, to which God responds with his forgiveness, the narrator sets before his contemporaries personal relationship with God as the heart of all piety.[1] This largeness of conception in the requirement of faith should be borne in mind as we go on to examine its limitations.

For what has been said so far by no means implies that in this form of faith-obedience all the riches of the prophetic watchword of faith have been preserved. Instead we must be careful not to overlook *a certain abridgment* of the latter, which consists principally in a lack of that *breadth of vision*, which kept in view God's dealings beyond Israel with the whole Gentile world, and was thus enabled not to over-estimate the importance of the community of Zion but to grasp its role of service in the divine world plan. Now, however, thought tends to revolve entirely round the holy people, and is in danger of making them and their exaltation into indispensable presuppositions of God's universal dominion.[2]

To the narrow, restricted sphere within which the service of God was carried on corresponded all too easily *a narrow and anxiety-ridden working out of this service*. The more rigorous the logic with which the Law was regarded as the means of creating the community and bringing it to perfection, the more necessary was it that all independent thought and action be excluded in favour of faithfulness to the Law even in its minutest detail. There was *no new goal of conduct* beyond the path marked out so exactly, but only a more and more precise fashioning of life within the prescribed limits.

Vis-à-vis God these two factors led to an oscillation between two conditions: on the one hand *claims were put forward* for a reward from God for obedience, this reward being regarded as indispensable confirmation of a man's righteousness; on the other we find a school-boyish anxiety-state, a *compulsive self-inspection* which did not attain to the maturity of unconditional faith and trust.

---

[1] H. Bardtke would prefer to see in this book a picture of the gradual spread of a resurrection movement ('Der Erweckungsglaube in der exilisch-nachexilischen Literatur des AT', *Eissfeldt-Festschrift*, 1958, pp. 21ff.).

[2] For the effect of this abridgment on the future hope, cf. vol. I, pp. 485ff. On the restriction of the salvation-hope to Judah, which goes hand in hand with this, cf. L. Rost, *Israel bei den Propheten*, 1927, pp. 129f.

Vis-à-vis fellow human beings, however, the effects of this attitude showed themselves in a *harsh separation of the pious from the godless*, which in part was dictated by the anxiety of the faithful adherent of the Law at the thought of possible contamination from his opponent's obliviousness of God, and in part was inspired by the self-satisfaction which checked its own piety and that of its enemies against quite external standards. In such circumstances the urge to ever stricter segregation and to callous rejection of the sinner was bound to become deeply rooted, and to endanger both the sincerity and the spontaneity of the life of the community.

II. It was therefore all the more important that in addition to faith-obedience, which provided the type of faith necessary for the formation of the community, *other forms of the disposition of faith* emerged to shape the individual's relationship with God. Thus equally with the faith which impelled men to practical ordering of the present there remained a lively *faith directed toward God's new creation*, as men worked out the implications of the message both of Deutero-Isaiah and of Ezekiel. The natural expression of this faith was an attitude of patient endurance which, despite the oppressions of the present, held fast to the truth of the prophetic hope. Endurance of this kind is referred to in the penitential prayer of the community,[1] and the fact that its longings all remain unfulfilled is explained by the hypothesis of unfaithfulness toward Yahweh, which holds up the realization of his promises. As an addition to the Third Servant Song shows, the Servant of the Lord, who was brought from humiliation to exaltation,[2] stands as a pattern of unshaken endurance. Thus in the fearful break-up of the old national glory men sought a firm foothold in undismayed hope, and in silent waiting upon the God who does not cast off for ever, nor afflict for pleasure, but is good to them that wait for him.[3] Men liked to lose themselves in the consolation which the final fulfilment of the promises would bring to all who wait for Yahweh.[4] Contemplation of the nation's history, which for the Psalmists is a favourite method of convincing themselves of the

---

[1] Isa. 59.9, 11; Ps. 130.5, 7.
[2] Isa. 50.10.
[3] Lam. 3.21, 24–27; cf. Ps. 123.2–4. In the wider sense the numerous references in the psalms of lamentation to Yahweh's glorious redemption ought to be counted under this head, for they often express clearly the notion of waiting upon Yahweh, even though the actual phrase may not be used: cf. Pss. 12.6; 14.7; 22.28f.; 86.9f.; 102.14, 16, 23.
[4] Isa. 30.18; 25.9; Ps. 126.

election, preservation and final exaltation of the people of God, also serves to strengthen this belief in ultimate salvation.[1] Similarly apocalyptic exhorts the impatient student of its calculations to endurance, so that he may be able to attain to the eschatological blessedness.[2]

It is precisely the instance last mentioned which brings out most clearly the danger which threatened this faith in eschatological salvation. Having no support in an assurance that God was near and effective in the present, it was unable to stand on its own feet in the daily life of history. All too readily it was driven to impatient rebellion against God's providence by the riddle of events,[3] either attempting to wrest their secret from them by constantly renewed calculations,[4] or undertaking to force the arrival of the longed-for freedom and dominion by its own efforts, as happened in the groups of post-exilic enthusiasts,[5] and in Jewish Zealotism. It was therefore vitally important that this looking for a God who was to prepare the way for his kingdom by a convulsion of world history possessed in faith-obedience a kind of buttress which anchored it firmly to the tasks of the present, and protected it against unhealthy emotionalism.

III. It was easier to keep the balance between these two types of faith pulling in opposite directions because of *the belief in salvation which concentrated on God's guidance of the individual life*. This third type was certainly not in exclusive opposition to the practical concern with conduct which marked the devotee of the Law, yet it formed a distinctive contrast to it. It may be described as *linking the act of faith with decisive abstention from all willing or action of one's own*, in order that one's personal existence might be placed completely within the sovereign action of God. Here *faith is quite overwhelmingly a matter of resting, being still, and waiting*,[6] in a determination to renounce earthly methods in order to give God's action room to operate, and so to enable his promise of salvation in the covenant to be realized in the way known and possible to him alone. In the inner recollection and concentration on the one real power in the world, the will of God,

[1] Pss. 44.2–4; 47.4f.; 77.6, 15–21; 80.9–12; 102.29; 103.7; 105; 106; 114; 135.4, 8–14; 136.10–24; 147.19f.; 148.14.

[2] Dan. 12.12.

[3] Cf., e.g., the impatience with which redemption is awaited in Ps. 79.

[4] Dan. 9.25–27; 12.7, 11, 12.

[5] Neh. 6.10–14.

[6] Pss. 42.6, 12; 43.5; 119.147; 131.3. This attitude is given especially pregnant expression in Ps. 62(2), 6 by the use of *dāmam lᵉ*, to be silent, to wait silently for, and in Ps. 42 by the comparison of waiting to the longing of the thirsting hart.

which this brings, the pious, however, already experiences the whole reality of fellowship with God; and in face of this the How and When of his external destiny becomes of secondary importance. Thus he can calmly renounce all those ingredients of power which otherwise are of crucial significance for the course of events—outstanding ability, rich possessions, power and influence. Indeed, he can recognize these as obstacles to the communion with God achieved by faith, and warn others against them.[1] By contrast he experiences the condition of faith as a *source of power and life*,[2] indeed, as the introduction into a state of *blessedness which infinitely surpasses all earthly goods*; and this frequently bursts forth in brilliant songs of rejoicing and genuine joy in God.[3] Here, too, the worst enemy of all, namely the doubt which arises in a man's own breast, is overcome by the adventurous certainty of faith's Nevertheless, which is triumphantly conscious of the divine nearness.[4] This joy in God is distinguished from any kind of mystical union not only by the fact that it is quite consciously understood as a fullness of personal life, but also by the sobriety with which the writers continue to accept the full reality of suffering and the oppressive enigma of life. In fact, it is precisely those who are of a broken heart and a shattered spirit who can be certain of God's nearness.[5]

This realization of the personal relationship with God in faithful endurance varied in profundity, but at the same time it is quite exceptionally widely distributed throughout the whole literature of prayer,[6] and also made its mark on the wisdom teaching. Furthermore, in *the Chronicler's history-writing* it found distinctive employment as a *principle of historical interpretation*. His highly exaggerated doctrine of retribution is focused not so much on pious works in themselves as on the interior attitude of men to the God of Israel, the outstanding criterion of which he finds in their readiness or incapacity for enduring God's testing of their trust. Again and again he manages to explain the decisive turning-points in Israel's fortunes in terms of the failure or the vindication of her leaders when faced with the require-

[1] Prov. 3.5; Jer. 17.5, 7; Prov. 20.22; 28.25; 29.25; Pss. 31.7, 15; 37.7, 14–16; 62.10f.

[2] Pss. 31.25; 84.13, cf. 6; 119.93, 149, 154. *he'emīn* appears to be used in the same sense in Ps. 116.10, but the text is ambiguous.

[3] Pss. 16.2, 9ff.; 17.15; 32.11; 37.4; 63.4; 73.25–28; 92.5.

[4] Cf. the exultant conclusion of many petitionary psalms, e.g.: 6.9ff.; 13.6; 22.23ff.; 28.6f.; 73.23ff., *et al.*

[5] Pss. 34.19; 51.19.

[6] Cf. the instructive statistics in Bertholet, *Biblische Theologie des AT* II, p. 238.

ment of unreserved trust in God's covenant promise.[1] The test of the genuineness of the act of faith is here the thoroughgoing renunciation of all foreign aid, even to the extent of refusing to collaborate in any way with the brother-state of Northern Israel. The deficiencies of this religiously based schematic presentation of history are obvious. They are not only the result of a total divorce from real history, to which violence is done by the construction put upon it, but above all they are rooted in a mechanical and external correspondence between faith and God's blessing on Man's outward circumstances. And yet this attempt, carried out with very inadequate methods, to illuminate the history of the nation from the angle of individual faith is a deeply impressive testimony to the serious determination which is resolved to the utmost to base the whole of earthly existence, without recourse to any human aid whatever, on that divine promise which it is the business of faith to grasp, and on that promise alone. That this faith is portrayed as '*the* formative factor of history, pure and simple'[2] is of fundamental importance for the whole attitude to the nation's future; because that humble self-naughting and self-abasement before the utterly sovereign God, which in the mirror of the past can be seen to be the basis of the condition of faith,[3] becomes by an extraordinary paradox the surest way to experience the hidden God's miraculous guidance of history. Here emerges once more, even if weakened and distorted, that *relation of faith to world history* which had once been so powerfully proclaimed by the prophets, and which again and again in critical moments gave the Jewish community the strength to maintain itself between superior powers, and saved it from becoming stunted within the narrowness of its party conflicts. The most impressive monument to the continuing force of this contemplation of history in the light of faith is the book of Daniel, in which at the same time the link between faith and obedience to the Law has become indissoluble.

iv. In such ways as these the individual's relationship with God discovered within faith room to live and breathe. At the same time, however, other indications reveal how the profoundest uncertainties of faith, those which arise as the result of the sin which cuts off from God, were exercising the thinking of the pious, and leading them to

---

[1] I Chron. 5.20; II Chron. 13.14; 14.8ff.; 18.31; 20.1ff.; 24.24; 25.10ff.; 32.20f., and cf. G. von Rad, *Das Geschichtsbild des chronistischen Werkes*, 1930, pp. 15ff.

[2] Von Rad, *op. cit.*, p. 16.

[3] II Chron. 7.14; 12.6, 7, 12; 30.11; 33.12, 23; 34.27.

the conclusion that God's forgiveness was the only means by which real fellowship with him could be made possible. *At this point trust in God becomes a genuine belief in justification.* Thus in Ps. 38 'waiting upon Yahweh' is clearly not only the expectation of divine deliverance from sickness and persecution, but just as strongly the hope of absolution from guilt, the burden of which is threatening to crush the suppliant.[1] In the same way Ps. 143 combines longing for Yahweh with the conviction that it is impossible to stand before his face as righteous. Hence the goodness for which the Psalmist yearns must bestow, in addition to outward deliverance, and indeed as its necessary precondition, gracious dispensation from just judgment on the sinner, and guidance by God's spirit in the right path.[2] For the singer of Ps. 32 trust in Yahweh's favour is linked even more exclusively with the forgiveness of sin and guilt, in which the true saving work of God is accomplished. For the deepest distress of all consists in the wall of separation erected between Man and God by unconfessed and unforgiven guilt; and the sole purpose of God's visitation is to bring about humble and unqualified acknowledgment of sin as the precondition of his forgiveness. Out of this experience, however, grows an *assurance of salvation* which can trust in Yahweh's grace in any tribulation that may come. The *ḥesed* which surrounds those who trust in Yahweh (v. 10) thus denotes in a genuinely prophetic sense the unmerited mercy of God.[3] Correspondingly, hope goes far beyond mere preservation in the face of earthly misfortune to a life of permanent fellowship with the God who justifies the sinner, so that he now becomes as the pious, the righteous, the upright in heart, with whom the godless can be contrasted (vv. 6, 10). Here the confidence of faith comprehends with joyful certainty that the new condition into which God's forgiveness transposes men is already present; in Ps. 130, on the other hand, that which liberates the sinner from the bondage of his guilt is seen to be patient waiting for God's word of absolution, in complete assurance that it will come. This knowledge of God as the one who alone has power to forgive *links faith intimately with the fear of God.* For if forgiveness is a matter of the free word of pardon, which nothing can extort, which human reason cannot hope to understand, and by which God discontinues the legal proceedings which otherwise are the only valid way of dealing with

---

[1] Ps. 38.5, 10, 16, 19.
[2] Ps. 143.2, 6, 8, 10.
[3] Cf. vol. I, pp. 237ff.

the situation (v. 3); and if by so doing he discloses to those under sentence of death an irrational, purely miraculous power of love; then manifestly Man has fallen completely and unconditionally into the hands of the Holy One, and been delivered up to him. But this can only produce the profoundest agitation, the quaking in the inmost soul before the mystery of God's will, in which life and death, ultimate rejection and acceptance, confront the suppliant, and demand his unconditional surrender. 'Thou hast staked all on forgiveness, that men may fear thee' (v. 4)—in this paradoxical proposition the Psalmist can sum up the divine will to save, and in so doing conveys with unequalled effectiveness the exalted nature of his God, who precisely in his limitless condescension reveals the incomprehensible mystery of his being in all its divine majesty. Hence the fear which is learned from God's power to forgive can also find its fulfilment in the faith which, in the form of silent waiting, stakes its whole existence on the decision of this God (vv. 5f.). Moreover, because the concluding strophe transfers the personal attitude of the suppliant to the people of God as a whole, who must reach out with all their soul after this redemption from all iniquity, it points to *a final act of God*, by which alone all guilt will be blotted out, and a new life opened up in God's mercy. Thus belief in justification builds a bridge across to the eschatological hope, thrusting directly into the heart of the messianic salvation as envisaged in the loftiest promises of the prophets.[1] An echo of this attitude, which is motivated by faith's severest problem, and which one cannot fail to recognize even where the actual word faith is not explicitly mentioned,[2] is found in the communal prayer of Micah 7.7ff., which begins with an expression of faithful waiting upon Yahweh, and closes with praise of the God of forgiveness, who in spite of Israel's sin makes good his promise to the patriarchs, because he rejoices in showing mercy.

v. In contrast to this rich potential for differentiation with which the concept of faith is employed in the post-exilic community, the scarcity which characterizes *statements about love for God* is extremely striking. In by far the greater number of instances it is no longer Yahweh toward whom love is directed, but his Name,[3] or his salvation,[4] or his law and his commandments and testimonies.[5] This

[1] Jer. 31.31ff.; Ezek. 36.26ff.; Isa. 53.
[2] Cf. Pss. 25.11; 51; 65.4; 86.5; 103.3; Prov. 28.13.
[3] Isa. 56.6; Pss. 5.12; 69.37; 119.132.
[4] Pss. 40.17; 70.5.
[5] Ps. 119.47f., 97, 113, 119, 127, 159, 163, 165, 167.

association of love with the divine Name affords a parallel phenomenon to a series of similar statements in which the Name as an
object of cultic worship occurs in conjunction with verbs of thanking,
praising, blessing, and reverencing.[1] In all these instances the personal
character of the deity, which is so sharply brought out in the concept
of the Name, acts as an effectual corrective against the tendency of
the cultus to attach most importance to the performance of its rituals,
and preserves in the worshipper a sense of coming personally before
Yahweh. But in so far as the Name sums up the revelatory activities
of the divine nature, gradually becoming a representative of the God
beyond the universe who would otherwise remain in oblivion, the
cultic veneration of the Name of God also reveals the influence of
God's heightened transcendence and unapproachableness as this had impressed
itself upon the consciousness of the people as a result of Priestly
instruction. It is true that in individual passages the direct personal
relationship with God breaks through still, as when 'seeking refuge in
Yahweh' is mentioned in parallelism with love for his Name,[2] or when
the placing of heartfelt thanksgiving above all sacrifice emphasizes
the directness of men's association with God.[3] On the other hand,
the parallelism in the Law psalm, 119, with love for the Law and
testimonies of Yahweh is a clear sign that *the directness of the relationship
with God is becoming less important* than obedience to the records of his
revelation. Similarly in the case of the Gentile proselytes, whose
acceptance into the community was commanded by the prophetic
torah of Isa. 56.1–8, love for the Name of Yahweh is identified with
the zealous fulfilment of the cultic laws, in particular the commandment relating to the sabbath. Even more colourless is the use of '-*h-b*
with the redemption or salvation of Yahweh as its object in Ps. 40.17,
where the translation 'long for' is perfectly adequate. Likewise the
love for the hypostatized Wisdom in Prov. 8.17, 21 no longer evinces
the direct force of feeling, but rather the cooler tone of teachable
devotion.

Where, however, readiness to love has Yahweh as its immediate
object, adherence to the traditional language, in particular that of
Deuteronomy, appears frequently to be standard practice.[4] The

---

[1] Cf. vol. I, pp. 207f.; and pp. 42f. above.
[2] Ps. 5.12.
[3] Ps. 69.37.
[4] The description of the pious as those who love Yahweh and keep his commandments (Neh. 1.5; Dan. 9.4) is definitely a formula based upon Deut. 5.10; 7.9.

pious are sometimes described as *'ōhᵃbē yhwh*, 'lovers of Yahweh',[1] but this stereotyped expression rarely carries the full content of the love relationship. Instead it appears to be synonymous with 'to fear Yahweh and to call upon him'.[2] Nevertheless in Ps. 97.10 something of the exclusive quality of genuine love still comes through, since it seems to be inseparably connected with a clear-cut avoidance of all that is hostile to God.[3] A liturgical prayer like Ps. 31 can use its closing exhortation to the pious to set emphatically before them the call to love God. This is worth noting, because this psalm, precisely on account of its 'lack of originality',[4] may give us a good impression of the average piety of the community, and the material in which it was expressed. The opening of Ps. 116, and the clause added in front of v. 2 of Ps. 18, which makes the assertion of love for God the opening of the whole psalm, should also be noted.[5] Nor can there be any doubt that in the testimonies to the blessings of fellowship with God[6] a submission to God is expressed which may without hesitation be described as love. In Ps. 73.25 there is, in fact, a negative assertion—*'immᵉkā lō' ḥāpaṣtī bā'āreṣ*, 'there is nothing upon earth that I desire besides thee'—which would seem to be properly included as an example of its positive counterpart, the self-forgetful relationship of love.[7] But this only makes it all the more significant that in such passages love is not actually mentioned. It therefore remains true that while, out of loyalty to traditional forms of expression, love for God is certainly referred to here and there in religious language, the phrase is nowhere so comprehensive a description of the personal relationship with God as it was in the pre-exilic period, or as it was still possible for it to be in the faith and confidence which obtained even after the Exile. It is clear that God's hiddenness, even in revelation, and his world-transcending majesty, have now come to loom too large in the religious field of vision for any attitude such as the

[1] Pss. 97.10; 145.20; cf. Deut. 5.10; Ex. 20.6; Judg. 5.31.

[2] Ps. 145.20 and 18f. The description of Abraham as *'ōhēb yhwh* in Isa. 41.8 seems already to bear the weaker sense of 'friend'.

[3] 'You who love Yahweh, hate evil!' Nevertheless, recent scholarship has mostly preferred to adopt a slight emendation of the text, and read: 'Yahweh loves those who hate evil', which fits more easily into the context.

[4] Bertholet, *Die heilige Schrift des AT*⁴ II, *ad loc.*

[5] Even if the text of Ps. 116.1 originally ran differently (so Gunkel, *ad loc.*), the present reading would still be valuable as evidence for the later period.

[6] Cf. pp. 306f. above.

[7] As G. Winter ('Die Liebe zu Gott im AT', *ZAW* 9, 1889, p. 245) quite rightly pointed out. Nevertheless, to try to find here a mystical absorption into the being of God, and a consequent escape from the world, is to break a false trail.

surrender of total love, which is predominantly tuned to the nearness and sensible nature of the divine reality, to be able to control the religious relationship.

VI. In later Judaism *fear* forms the basis of the individual's relationship with God. Nevertheless this is a matter not so much of numinous awe as of a rationally justified anxiety in face of the omnipresent and omniscient divine judge, who watches strictly over the fulfilment of his law, and promises his reward only to impeccable obedience. In the early period the fear of God was something focused on the overwhelming divine exaltedness. In the religion of the Law it has lost this orientation, and is now concerned with the preservation of a man's ego in face of the divine wrath. The more comprehensively the doctrine of retribution dominated the whole of religious thought, the more strongly was fear bound to determine the individual's relationship with God.

The inheritance of the past, however, continued to have its effect, in that faith and love were also retained as constituents of the condition of piety. *Faith* especially plays a great part in the description of a right piety. As early as the Wisdom of Solomon it is mentioned as a precondition of knowing the truth,[1] and in IV Maccabees it gives the strength to endure martyrdom. In Philo it is the noblest virtue, 'the work of a great and Olympian reason',[2] while the Rabbinic exegesis of the exodus from Egypt and of the crossing of the Sea of Reeds breaks into a hymn in praise of faith which has been described as the Jewish counterpart of Heb. 11.[3] The language of such passages, however, is distinguished from earlier ways of talking about faith first of all by the *introduction of a strongly intellectual element*. Acknowledgment of the uniqueness and omnipotence of the Creator God, and of the righteousness of his retribution, plays an extremely important part in this, and brings it into close relation with practical wisdom. In rabbinic teaching, on the other hand, it is the association of faith with obedience to the Law which gives it a new character; here it becomes identical with *willingness to assume the burden of God's sovereignty*. Hence as the basic attitude toward God, decisive for the service of the Law, it can be described, in accordance with Hab. 2.4, as the one command necessary for salvation.[4] 'Faithful' and 'righteous' become synony-

[1] Wisd. 3.9.
[2] *Rer. Div. Her.* 93, quoted in H. W. Heidland, *Die Anrechnung des Glaubens zur Gerechtigkeit*, 1936, p. 93.
[3] G. F. Moore, *Judaism* I, 1927, p. 136.
[4] Mak. 23b in Heidland, *op. cit.*, p. 93.

mous terms, for faith and submission to God can be equated with observance of the Law. No wonder, then, that faith, too, falls under the dominion of the doctrine of merit, and has the same meritorious-ness ascribed to it as to pious works. There can, however, never be any idea that the merit acquired by works might be called in question on the basis of faith, because the condition of faith is valued so highly precisely as a means to loyalty toward the Law, so that '*qua* merit, faith and works are of a kind'.[1] The difference between this concept of faith and the understanding of faith in the Old and New Testa-ments is seen at its most striking in the praise of Abraham as the hero of faith, the one who precisely by virtue of being a man of faith has fulfilled the work which God rewards in him and in his descendants.[2]

Love for God, too, now receives its special stamp from its connection with the Law. The taking over of the twin concepts 'to fear and to love' from the extremely influential Deuteronomic writings ensured that religious language would continue to use it and pay attention to it.[3] Nevertheless, as a result of the connection of love with impec-cable obedience to the Law, its content became no different from that of fear. Hence it could no longer point to the immediacy of the God-Man relationship, and still less could it serve as a comprehensive term for this relationship. However, the association of fear with the con-stant presence of the God of judgment and his threatening wrath prevented a simple equation of the two expressions, even where there was still a failure to recognize them as different motives for conduct. Love became predominantly linked with the optimistic view which regarded the fulfilment of the Law as possible, and so pushed the idea of judgment into the background.

A change began to come about after there had been a psychological deepening of both concepts, as a result of which they were seen as dis-positions of the heart, and strictly as motives for conduct, to be distin-guished from mere pious behaviour (Testaments of the Twelve Patriarchs; Psalms of Solomon). Here, too, greater emphasis was laid on the sincerity of the disposition of love: ἀγαπᾶν ἐν ἀληθείᾳ.[4] The earliest reflection on the differences between the two motives is found

[1] Heidland, *op. cit.*, p. 90.
[2] Cf. pp. 463f. below.
[3] Cf. the excellent monograph on this subject by R. Sander: *Furcht und Liebe im palästinischen Judentum*, 1935. Also A. Büchler, *Studies in Sin and Atonement in the Rabbinic Literature of the First Century* (Jews College Publications 11), 1928, pp. 119ff.
[4] Ps. Sol. 10.3; 14.1.

in the rabbinism of the first century.[1] *Fear and love* are now recognized as *two different types of piety*, which can be understood as coexisting, but can never be brought together in a unified view. Before long fear is characterized as the lower stage of piety, because it produces obedience only from compulsion and desire for reward, while love keeps the Torah for its own sake, without thinking of any egoistic purpose. But because the genuineness of piety is seen not in the mental attitude but in the doing of the Law, even the keeping of the Law from fear cannot be held worthy of reproach. Soon, too, a right coexistence of fear and love in the heart of Man is regarded as the normal attitude toward God, fear seeming necessary to guard one from contempt for the Law, while love helps one to overcome the weariness, indeed hatred, inspired by its oppressive burden and compulsion. The essence of the Jewish religion of the Law may therefore be seen as a regulation of the God-Man relationship which exhausts itself in endless casuistry, and leaves the heart empty; which because of its exact knowledge of the heart of Man strives to incorporate even the lower motive as necessary, and yet at the same time seeks to restrain and combat unbridled desire for reward with the motive of love. It is impossible to find clearer evidence of the lack of a unified religious attitude. The fact that Jesus and his Apostles had recourse to the Old Testament in their description of the right attitude toward God witnesses plainly to the fact that in them the inner schizophrenia of Jewish piety had been overcome, and that the liberation of Man for willing surrender to God had once more emerged into the light of day.

---

[1] Especially clearly in Tractate Sotah of the Mishna.

XXII

THE EFFECT OF PIETY ON CONDUCT
(Old Testament morality)

I. THE NORMS OF MORAL CONDUCT[1]

As LITTLE AS ANY other major civilized religion does that
of Israel know of morality apart from religion. On the
contrary, we would expect from our knowledge of the
Israelite view of God that here above all the derivation of moral
conduct from the all-ruling will of God would be pursued with
especial vigour; and, as we turn the pages of the Old Testament, this
expectation is completely confirmed. From the earliest to the latest
period it is God's demand, which comes vested with absolute
authority, which is the strongest and the dominating motive of human
conduct. The power of the good rests entirely on the recognition of
God as the One who is good. Of moral behaviour for the sake of an
abstract good there is none.

Nevertheless, even within a morality so strongly determined by
religious factors, importance still attaches to the *acknowledgment of such
norms* as possess a certain independent validity for the control of conduct, and do not require the citation of a divine command to support
them in every instance. This means that there is a sphere in which
human behaviour is subjected to an unconditional Ought, because
this is felt to be something absolutely valid in itself. Generally speaking, this is certainly true wherever morality is based on a fairly highly
developed national life; and the point at which a general moral consciousness emerges is, of course, *popular morality*.

---

[1] Cf. P. van Imschoot, *Théologie de l'Ancien Testament* II, 1956, ch. 3: Les devoirs
de l'homme; C. Ryder Smith, *The Bible Doctrine of Man*, 1951.

1. *The importance of popular morality*

Out of the life of the community, in close connection with the particular character and talents of the people, with their historical experience and the influence of their environment, not forgetting also their religious life and thought, is formed a complex of rules and instructions which in its totality constitutes the basis of the community and the precondition of membership, and is thus binding upon every individual within that society. The awareness of such a norm, obligatory upon all, and deriving its power of conviction, and its authority, from the sheer givenness of the community and the nation as the indisputable foundation of all life, is voiced in Israel in those expressive words for socially unacceptable behaviour: *nᵉbālā bᵉyiśro'ēl* and *kēn lō' yēʿāśeh*, 'folly in Israel' and 'one ought not so to do'.[1] At the same time there is an expression here of pride in the distinctive character of Israel compared with her neighbours, to whom she knew herself to be superior, in sexual morality in particular. To the same complex, however, belong all those rules of conduct which proceed from the natural impulses of community and self-preservation, such as the pronounced sense of solidarity in the family and the tribe. Thus, the building up of the family with numerous offspring is of equal obligation on both man and woman, and in a crisis makes even bizarre measures seem justifiable, or at least excusable.[2] The cohesion of the kin-group not only prompts men to rally spontaneously to the cause of a brother, or to protect the family honour, if necessary by violence;[3] it not only binds the woman to her husband's family even after his death, and even at the cost of giving up her honour or her homeland;[4] it also shows itself in the finer forms of consideration toward the father, and honour to the mother;[5] in the form of love for one's children it leads even women to heroic self-denial;[6] and wherever possible it seeks to support those related by blood.[7] But men know themselves to be bound also to a wider circle,

[1] Gen. 34.7; Josh. 7.15; Judg. 19.23f., 30; 20.6, 10; II Sam. 13.12; Jer. 29.23. The expression is adopted in the teaching of the Law: Deut. 22.21. Cf. also Gen. 29.26, and for a positive formulation, Deut. 25.9. Also cf. pp. 236f. above.

[2] Gen. 16.2; 19.32; 30.3, 9; 38.26.

[3] Gen. 13.8ff.; 14.14; 37.22, 29; 34.25ff.; II Sam. 13.20ff.

[4] Gen. 38.13ff.; Ruth 1.16f.

[5] Gen. 9.22ff.; 27.41; 35.22; 44.30ff.; 50.15; II Sam. 16.21f.; I Kings 2.19; Ex. 20.12.

[6] II Sam. 21.10.

[7] Gen. 24.49; 29.10; Ex. 2.11; Judg. 11.6ff.; 20.12f.; II Sam. 19.13; cf. also Judg. 6.15, 34; II Kings 4.13 (reading *ʿammī*).

in upholding the covenant of friendship,[1] and in risking their lives for the national community, whether it be in peril from hostile armies[2] or from some other threat;[3] and at such times all private feuds have to take second place.[4] This social bond results in a conservative retention of traditional morals and forms of law. The inheritance of one's fathers is regarded as sacred, and men are not to be inveigled into alienating it for gain.[5] Society protects the institution of blood-revenge, and only very gradually suffers it to be replaced by objective processes of law. *But popular morality also goes beyond these things to positive moral requirements.* Thus men strive to ensure incorruptibility in a judge,[6] and condemn breach of faith in any form, from simple cheating to assassination, even where the latter hides itself behind justifiable revenge for the blood of a kinsman.[7] Indeed, it is also quite generally regarded as wrong to requite good with evil;[8] and praise is given to the magnanimous conduct of the man who cannot be diverted even by injustice from doing good to his neighbour.[9]

Moreover, this recognition of obligatory norms of conduct in early Israel does not stop at the limits of the nation, but goes beyond them to the self-evident conviction that *certain fundamental ordinances are binding on outsiders also.* This does not apply only to those groups with which one is brought into closer association by covenant and con-tractual relationships, which inevitably presuppose loyalty to agree-ments and the sacrosanctity of oaths.[10] Even where no security has been taken in dealings with neighbouring peoples, the validity of the most general basic moral principles is assumed, and any breach of them is regarded as a sign of the special depravity of the nation in question. Above all there is the obligation of guest-friendship, on which the foreigner must be able to rely, even if it means risking one's own life, or indeed the honour of one's family.[11] Certain requirements of modesty and *pietas* are felt by all nations to be binding;[12] hence even

[1] I Sam. 18.1–4; 19.2–7; 20.8 ('a covenant of Yahweh'); II Sam. 9.1; 21.7.
[2] Judg. 3.27f.; 5.2, 9, 18, 23; 7.23f.; I Sam. 11.7; II Sam. 10.12, etc.
[3] Judg. 21.1ff.; II Sam. 2.26ff.; 24.17.
[4] II Sam. 1.18ff.
[5] I Kings 21.3.
[6] I Sam. 12.1ff.; cf. Ex. 23.1–3, 7–9.
[7] Gen. 31.26ff.; II Sam. 3.28ff.; I Kings 2.5.
[8] I Sam. 25.21.
[9] I Sam. 24.18; Ex. 23.4–6.
[10] Gen. 21.23ff.; 26.28ff.; 31.44, 49ff.; II Sam. 21.
[11] Gen. 18.3ff.; 19.1, 6ff.; Judg. 19.23.
[12] Gen. 9.23; 18.20f.; 20.9.

a foreign people may be a righteous people, preserving the fear of God.[1] Unnecessary cruelty, even toward enemies, is abominable.[2] Abuse of confidence is regarded as wickedness and folly, both in the relationship of servant and master, and in general dealings.[3] Sympathy with the weak is also assumed to exist in foreigners, and violation of it is seen as harsh injustice.[4] In dealings with aliens men try to repay good with good, and indeed expect gross ingratitude to be visited with sure punishment.[5] To show unselfishness toward foreigners is highly praiseworthy,[6] and in his intercession for a foreign city Abraham exhibits behaviour which is plainly regarded as exemplary.[7] Likewise men are prepared to recognize magnanimity, even when it is shown by those who belong to another nation.[8]

II. *The influence of the concept of God on popular morality*

In all these matters Israel was essentially on a level with the more developed nations of the ancient world. She upheld the ethics of a healthy, unspoiled, agricultural people, and thus shows that her moral consciousness was rooted in the basic facts of human life as given in Nature. But at various extremely important points it is possible to detect *a raising of the level*, which is *by no means self-evident*, and which is indisputably religiously conditioned, since it reveals the influence of the God-Man relationship established in the covenant. In the first place we have to remember the *quite new stress which was bound to be laid on ethical norms*, in so far as they were understood as expressing the will of the one divine Lord, who claimed to bring into subjection to himself the whole of human life in all its aspects. Because they were backed by the one absolute authority, these basic principles of human social life were lifted out of the sphere of the merely relative binding force which obtained within the framework and the limits of a particular historical situation, and acquired a share in the timeless and unconditioned quality of the holy. Now it was no longer possible to evade uncomfortable obligations at the solicitation of more com-

---

[1] Gen. 20.4, 11.
[2] Gen. 49.6; cf. 34.30.
[3] Gen. 39.8; 44.4f., 9.
[4] Ex. 2.6; Gen. 19.5ff.; Judg. 19.22ff.
[5] II Sam. 10.2; I Sam. 8.9ff.; 12.7, 13ff.; Judg. 9.16.
[6] Gen. 14.23ff.
[7] Gen. 18.23ff.
[8] Gen. 33. It has already been pointed out at pp. 232ff. above that here a great deal is bound up with the nomad's sense of solidarity.

pelling interests. It was precisely the concrete demand of the narrowest circle of the individual's life which laid hold on him with all the seriousness of a responsibility before God, and which gave the performance of his duty, even in the most humble setting, the nobility of an act of worship. The weight and impressiveness which was bound to attend moral demands in such circumstances may be seen from the formula in which they now frequently occur. Indeed, it is part of the unique nature of the Israelite legal tradition that the technical juristic formulation of casuistic law is constantly being interrupted by *categorical divine commands and prohibitions*, in which the laying down of a human punishment is replaced by the authoritative demand of the divine Lord.[1] And because these apodeictic utterances come together in series,[2] their conciseness, concentrated force, and impressive sequence, as well as the iron ring of the similar individual clauses, convey a powerful sense of the absolute validity of the will standing behind them.

At the same time, however, there are clear signs in these demands, which derive originally from the sacral sphere, of *the tendency toward unification of the ethical norms*. The great, simple, fundamental outlines of moral conduct must be drawn in a few lapidary propositions. Hence these collections go far beyond the domain of casuistic law, and combine with legal both moral and religious requirements. This effort reaches its climax in the Decalogue, where, by partially renouncing external homogeneity of construction, and by leaving out the concrete detail of particular transgressions and the allocation of punishment, the range of the prohibitions is stretched as far as it will go. In this way the individual clauses acquire the significance of general principles for all similar cases, and at the same time allow the moral content to stand out with a heightening of its pregnant and absolute quality. Implicit in the actual selection made from the whole multiplicity of legal and moral prescriptions is the unspoken *conviction of an essential unity behind all moral demands*; and by making an attempt to describe this in terms of the basic principles cited, it contains a critique of the mass of rules for living which had been sanctioned hitherto, and which had grown up as a result of Nature and historical accident. Moreover, inasmuch as the will of God emerges as the

---

[1] On this subject cf. the impressive exposition of A. Alt, *Die Ursprünge des israelitischen Rechts*, 1934, pp. 33ff.

[2] Ex. 20.2–17; 21.12, 15–17; Lev. 18.7ff.; 20.2, 9–13, 15f., 20–27; Deut. 27.15–26.

supreme norm behind all particular requirements, the desired unity of the moral sphere shifts in essence to the personal activity of the covenant God.

In addition to this surehanded selection of essential elements from the traditional popular ethic the moral effect of the new knowledge of God makes itself felt just as much in the *correction and expansion of older legal outlooks.* The norms given in the Book of the Covenant (Ex. 20–23) reveal, when compared with related law-books of the ancient Near East, radical alterations in legal practice.[1] In the evaluation of offences against property, in the treatment of slaves, in the fixing of punishment for indirect offences, and in the rejection of punishment by mutilation, the value of human life is recognized as incomparably greater than all material values. The dominant feature throughout is respect for the rights of everything that has a human face; and this means that views which predominate universally elsewhere have been abandoned, and new principles introduced into legal practice. Ultimately this is possible only because of a profundity of insight hitherto undreamt of into *the nobility of Man,* which is now recognized as a binding consideration for moral conduct. Hence in Israel even the rights of the lowliest foreigner are placed under the protection of God; and if he is also dependent, without full legal rights, to oppress him is like oppressing the widow and orphan, a transgression worthy of punishment, which calls forth God's avenging retribution.[2] The knowledge of God as one who confronts men in personal encounter, and calls them into his service, leads to an awareness of the distinctive position of Man as compared with all the rest of animate Nature, and assures him of his worth as a responsible, personal 'I', with all the obligations that derive from this.[3]

Similar conclusions may be drawn from the patriarchal sagas, which certainly do not give us a picture of spotless saints, and which yet allow us to discern the ideal of the pious man as this was already a living reality in the barbarous times of the Judges and the early monarchy. The peaceableness and unselfishness which stand out in a figure like Abraham, the honour and sincerity for lack of which misfortune dogs the hard life story of Jacob, the forgivingness and

---

[1] Cf. vol. I, pp. 77ff.
[2] Ex. 22.21 (MT 20); 23.9, 12.
[3] This naturally applies even where this awareness has not yet been exalted into a theologically important formula by the concept of Man as the image of God: cf. pp. 118f. above.

placability which are accentuated in Joseph, are not natural, popular virtues, but are learned only from those who are seen to be Yahweh's chosen, and to walk with him. How, in particular, placability and refusal to satisfy the impulse of revenge prevail as a result of men's vision of Yahweh, and in opposition to popular morality, is vividly illustrated by the story of David.[1] The showing of *ḥesed*, faithful love, toward the person who is bound to oneself by a covenant, even when human self-interest counsels different behaviour, is described as *ḥesed* *'elōhīm*, faithful love such as God desires, and himself displays.[2] Likewise, the ruler is urged to restrain blood-revenge, when its implementation would mean more than just the punishment of the killer, and would, in fact, prejudice the continuance of the family, as a work well pleasing to God;[3] and the showing of forgiveness to someone who has grievously offended, instead of exacting one's rights inexorably and in full, is felt to correspond truly to the attitude of God himself.[4] Thus, as men are influenced by their experience of the rule of the covenant God over his people, *new moral norms* are added to those already in existence, and indicate new paths for conduct, which run counter to popular morality and the satisfaction of selfish desires. Indeed, the whole way in which the Yahwist primal history in Genesis can describe the judgment of God on the moral corruption of mankind, and the Elohist patriarchal sagas recognize the righteousness of a foreign people and the existence of ethical obligations unconnected with membership of one's own nation,[5] makes it clear that the powerful experience of the moral will of God in the history of one's own people opens men's eyes to the fact that *moral norms hold good in the history of mankind as a whole*; and this leads them to grasp the unconditional character of the ethical demand as an order of human life unrestricted by national boundaries.

III. *Weaknesses in the validity of the moral norms*

The picture so far drawn presupposes a struggle for the profounder comprehension of the ethical norms. It should therefore occasion no surprise that at points in the early Israelite tradition it becomes apparent that that struggle was denied full success, and that popular

[1] I Sam. 24.7, 11, 19f.; 25.31ff.
[2] I Sam. 20.14; II Sam. 9.3.
[3] II Sam. 14.6ff.
[4] II Sam. 14.14.
[5] Gen. 20.4; 39.9.

morality refused to accept the progressive influence of the divine revelation.

(a) It is in place here to observe that *many areas of popular life were still outside the control of the moral norms*. In these areas conduct was left to the free discretion of the individual, and was often governed solely by natural impulse. Thus *the sexual morality of the man* was still very largely uncontrolled. It is true that he was forbidden to encroach upon his neighbour's marriage; but polygamy was still open to him,[1] and concubinage with slave-women or with those captured in war was quite usual.[2] Nor, apparently as a result of Canaanite influence, was intercourse with prostitutes felt to be repugnant.[3] Similarly, *behaviour toward foreigners*, especially if an open or latent state of war prevailed, was largely left to the caprice of the individual. The assassination of political opponents can be glorified;[4] guile, and robbery with violence, are attributed to the tribes of Dan and Benjamin as titles of honour.[5] It is taken for granted that war against dangerous or treacherous enemies should be conducted without quarter of any kind.[6] Lying is a perfectly proper weapon, when one is in a position of weakness *vis-à-vis* the foreigner, and does not render one unworthy of divine protection,[7] while even theft is regarded in such cases as justifiable.[8] If we wish to consider such cases objectively, we certainly ought to remember that behaviour toward one's enemies is one of those ethical problems which even in Christian ethics have given rise, and still do give rise, to the most varied interpretations. Hence the co-existence of the kind of moral behaviour toward foreigners mentioned earlier,[9] and the amorality to be observed in the present passages is rooted entirely in the difficulty of the practical situation, and is not a sign of especial depravity in moral understanding.[10]

---

[1] Gen. 4.19; 21.10; 22.24; 30.3ff.; Deut. 21.15; 22.19; I Sam. 1.2, 6; 25.43.
[2] Ex. 21.8ff.; Deut. 21.10ff.
[3] Gen. 38.21.
[4] Judg. 3.15ff.; 4.18ff.
[5] Gen. 49.17, 27.
[6] II Sam. 8.2; 11.1; I Kings 11.15f.; II Kings 3.25. Cf. by contrast Deut. 20.19f.
[7] Gen. 12.13; 20.2; 26.7; Ex. 1.19; cf. a similar case as late as Jer. 38.24ff.
[8] Ex. 3.22; 11.2; 12.35f.
[9] Cf. pp. 318f., 321 above.
[10] What gives offence here is really much more the admixture of the religious element, the fact that God requires such morally questionable conduct, or intervenes to protect the guilty from punishment. For such comment as is necessary cf. what has already been said in vol. I, pp. 282ff.

(*b*) The position is different as regards a series of *institutions*, hallowed by morality and law, *on which the moral driving-force of the concept of God, observable elsewhere, seems to have no effect*. The polygamous form of marriage sorts ill with the evaluation of the woman as a personality whom God has called to responsibility just as much as he has the man. Both the acquisition of a wife by payment of a marriage-price, and the recognition of the man as alone having the right to divorce, imply the permanently inferior position of women, and doubtless contribute to the fact that the personal worth of the woman is easily forgotten in favour of the attitude which sees her as a thing and as the chattel of the man. The moral requirement of guest-friendship is stronger than respect for the personal value of the woman, or for one's obligations toward one's own children;[1] the duty of levirate marriage overrides the prohibitions both of unchastity and of incest.[2] In striking contrast, moreover, to the high value set on human life which is such a prominent feature of the covenant law is the custom of the ban, whereby one's opponent, together with his wife and child, is dedicated to total destruction. The fact that such institutions, which undoubtedly contradict the moral tendencies discernible elsewhere within the Yahweh covenant, come under the protection of the covenant God, gives expression to an imbalance which at first seems somewhat surprising. Yet we are dealing with a state of affairs which could not but arise where the national order required by God was not imposed on the people as a complete, logically constructed system, breaking ruthlessly with the past, but was to develop as an organic formation, growing naturally in the given soil of history. Because of the fact that election came to a nation in its natural condition, and called it to fellowship with God in the distinctive character which it had evolved as a result of history, that nation brought with it into the covenant relationship all the details of its life, including the slow growth of its morality and custom, its special social structure, and its natural relationships of obligation and dependence. Hence it was unavoidable that such bonds and obligations, which derived their right to exist not from the worship of Yahweh, but from the social life which had grown up naturally in the past, should, equally with all the rest, be included within the mighty authority of God, who had uttered his Yea to the nation as a whole. No more in this nation than in any healthy people was it possible to

[1] Gen. 19.6ff.; Judg. 19.24f.
[2] Gen. 38.14, 26.

assimilate the heterogeneous elements successfully to the moral goals of the covenant God by any other method than a constant and continuing process of creating and transforming law and custom under the permanent influence of a living awareness of God. It was by God's continual self-communication, both in the guidance of history and in the word of his messengers, that men were given *a powerful impulse to strive for a new self-understanding, and therewith also for a new understanding of moral obligation.* The incongruity, therefore, which we have described, between the inheritance of the past and the new destiny of the people does not point to a closed condition of fossilization, but to *a 'Not yet'*, a condition open to the forces of progress, and one which has, in fact, undergone considerable change. That such forces were already at work in early Israel may be clearly seen from a comparison of the Yahwist and Elohist series of sagas in Genesis. The refinement of moral judgment in the Elohist, which has frequently been remarked, and which may be seen in his omission of gross sexual immorality, his stricter condemnation of lying and stealing, and his more lively sense of the value of the wife,[1] points to the struggle of a more mature morality with the cruder views of the earlier period, a struggle which was the result of a sharpening of the conscience through a more profound experience of God.[2]

(*c*) Bound up with the situation which we have described is the fact that moral consciousness *had not yet succeeded in formulating a unified principle of moral conduct.* It is still a matter of a multiplicity of commands for directing the life of the people of God, though there may also be signs already of that striving after unity mentioned earlier.[3] This is especially marked in the conjunction of cultic and moral commandments, which both in the Decalogue, and in the Book of the Covenant,[4] and in the Shechemite Twelve Commandments,[5] are unthinkingly combined in a single whole of uniform binding force, without any sense of qualitative distinction. The particular majesty of the moral order is obviously still unrecognized.

(*d*) Finally, *there is still a danger that the binding force of the moral norms may be misunderstood as heteronomous.* A positive commandment does not

---

[1] Cf., e.g., Gen. 20 with Gen. 12, and again with Gen. 31.32. On the whole subject cf. A. Weiser, *Religion und Sittlichkeit der Genesis in ihrem Verhältnis zur alttestamentlichen Religionsgeschichte*, 1928, pp. 70ff.

[2] Cf. Gen. 39.9.

[3] Cf. pp. 320f. above.

[4] Ex. 20.22–23.19.

[5] Deut. 27.15ff.

ask for the inner agreement or disagreement of the person addressed, but compels his obedience by an authority which leaves no room for argument. It is true that there is not a complete absence at this stage of that deeper understanding which recognizes the inherent goodness of the will of God. The God who demands is also known in his covenant-making as the God who gives,[1] and the people are aware that the bond between them and God is like that between a son and his father (Ex. 4.22). But the decisive factor in the authority of the commandments is not that God deals with his people as a father but that he imposes his will on them as a ruler; and, generally speaking, when inward responsiveness to this sovereign will, enthusiasm for its greatness, and awareness of its power to form the personality, are lacking, then its command can be felt only as the coercion of an alien law.

The state of affairs mentioned earlier (in para. (b) above), namely that the binding authority of the national community, present in those ordinances of life which had hitherto been accepted as self-evident, was now transferred to the deity, could also have a very similar effect. It was not possible at a moment's notice to harmonize with God's nature and dominion, as this had become known through his act of revelation, something which had derived its justification from the given concrete condition of the people, and give it a meaning derived from its new context. On the contrary, it was bound to be accepted purely as a norm which was not open to argument, and which received its formal authority from the majesty of the divine lawgiver. In this way submission to the commandment incorporated a strongly impersonal element; and where obedience is unable to become the expression of a consciously personal life, it easily tends toward external legality, and never arrives at an understanding of the inward binding force of the moral order.

IV. *The effect of the prophetic movement*

(a) With the new total understanding of the will of Yahweh, on which prophecy built up its message, the struggle in the moral sphere also became more profound and far-reaching. Here first of all *the linking of God's absoluteness with his moral will*, a connection which forced itself upon the prophets with the impact of a new experience of the divine reality, was an influential element. This is most strikingly

---

[1] Cf. p. 368 below.

to be seen in Isaiah's favourite term for God, $k^e d\bar{o}\check{s} \ yi\acute{s}ro'\bar{e}l$, the Holy One of Israel, which combines the moral perfection of the divine nature with his world-transcending majesty, and thus teaches men to understand the sovereign divine will inwardly as the authority of the good, and to make it their own.[1] But even where the moral nature of the power behind the universe is not given such pregnant formulation, nevertheless the prophetic preaching of the holy, personal will of God, who summons all the members of the nation to renounce their sinful self-will, and to place themselves without reserve at the disposal of the claims of the divine will, reveals the nature of the covenant God in all its purity and integrity. Whether Hosea and Jeremiah are portraying this God as questing love, or Amos is hammering home his inexorable will for righteousness, or Deutero-Isaiah is praising, in compelling verses full of power and fire, his absolving mercy as the ultimate basis of the perfect eschatological salvation, in each case the whole history of the nation is presented as caused and carried through by the power of an ethical will, compared with which nothing on earth can be considered to have any power at all.

One further result of this, however, is that *the authority of the moral norms is more inwardly based than hitherto*. It is now rooted in the nature of God as the One who is good, and may therefore properly require from those to whom it is addressed inner understanding and willing agreement. And this all the more because its inculcation by the prophets is not bound up with the creation of new content; it is the well-known ethical demands of the covenant law which are adopted.[2] Attention to the tradition-circles, with which the prophets were associated in just the same way as they themselves passed on what they had received to their disciples, has led more recent scholarship to abandon the unhistorical conception of them as pursuing a revolutionary, lone mission, and to evaluate without prejudice their dependence on the stock of earlier religious material.[3] The ordering of human life by the covenant God now no longer appeals to fear in face of the power of the lawgiver, but to a conscience inwardly convinced of the justice of the good. And so in the prophets the question of obedience to the ethical norms becomes the question of the whole personal attitude to the will of God as revealed in its moral majesty.

---

[1] Cf. vol. I, pp. 279f.
[2] Cf. the earlier remarks on this subject in vol. I, pp. 361f.
[3] Cf., e.g., N. W. Porteous, 'The basis of the ethical teaching of the prophets', *Studies in Old Testament Prophecy presented to T. H. Robinson*, 1950, pp. 143ff.

Here an external submission to particular stipulations can no longer suffice. Instead, men must move on to an *affirmation of the command-ment, proceeding from intimate conviction*, and expressing itself in love, faithfulness, and knowledge of God,[1] in humility and thankfulness,[2] in faith and trust,[3] as a unified total spiritual attitude. This frees the law completely from the danger of being misunderstood as an alien, coercive standard, and exalts it into guidance accepted into one's own being, bound up with one's own best powers, and leading to the realization of the highest values. This *overcoming of heteronomy* is most clearly put into words by Jeremiah and Ezekiel, when they contrast the people of God of the age of salvation with the men of their own day.[4] The law written on the heart gives concrete reality to the full unity of will between God and Man, and renders superfluous any further instruction or exhortation from without; the new heart and the new spirit, which by the indwelling of God's spirit take the divine life wholly into themselves, make the keeping of the divine command-ments the natural outcome of that inner communion with God which thinks and acts from God's angle.

(*b*) With the recognition, however, that the ultimate personal decision involved in the God-Man relationship cannot be made any-where except on the moral level, because it is here that unqualified commitment of the whole person is required, goes the further fact that now *the special character of the moral norms by contrast with the cultic* is plainly perceived by the prophets, and given the most clear-cut expression. In their fight against the falsification of the covenant relationship they came face to face again and again with the appalling fact that cultic performance was used as a welcome means of keeping on the right side of the law precisely where men wished to evade the subjection of their *whole* life to God's demands. The egoistic self-will which sought to strip off the solidarity and readiness for sacrifice required of the covenant people as a burdensome fetter well under-stood how to construct a glittering façade of outward worship, behind which inner alienation from genuine fellowship with God, and efforts to get control of the divine by material and magical means, could luxuriate undisturbed.[5] Here the moral norm proved itself the touch-

---

[1] Hos. 4.1.
[2] Micah 6.8; Isa. 1.2, 4, etc.
[3] Isa. 7.9; 28.16; 29.13; 30.15; Zeph. 3.2, etc.
[4] Jer. 31.31–34; Ezek. 36.26f.
[5] Cf. vol. I, pp. 46f. and 364f.

stone of a right attitude to God, on the basis of which alone could cultic activity acquire legitimation and value. And just as God's divinity could no longer be conceived without moral perfection as the expression of his inmost nature, so in human worship the test of morality took the central place, and all other activity could claim only secondary importance. In this way the majesty of the moral order was made clear, not by derivation from the abstract idea of the Good, which might then be proclaimed as a universal law, but by rooting it in the nature of God himself, thus transforming the heteronomy of the moral norm not into autonomy but into theonomy.

(c) There now occurs an *important shift within the moral norms themselves*. Emphasis is laid on points quite different from those previously stressed, and, in conjunction with this, areas of conduct so far overlooked are brought within the realm of moral obligation. *Much less value is attached to warlike virtues*; the self-assertion of the sinful nation can no longer be regarded as the absolute purpose of God. The path of external expansion, along which national leaders seek to drive their people, is utterly condemned by the prophets as open rebellion against Yahweh, who desires instead, now that his judgments are going forth through the world, self-abasement and obedient submission. This makes it impossible to justify on the ground of the holy war the suspension of basic ethical principles which would otherwise obtain. Although a deeper understanding of God's nature had at one time led to a new justification of the ban in terms of the concepts of judgment and retribution,[1] this institution became less and less a matter of obligation as the secularizing of the monarchy turned war from a sacred activity into an enterprise of human expediency. Indeed, insight into the seriousness of Israel's offence prompted a grim distortion of its original meaning, whereby it became the punishment ordained for the people of God themselves, which the God of the whole world would cause his ministers to carry out.[2]

In these circumstances there was bound to be less and less justification for the warlike spirit in religion and ethics. Only in a very qualified way did military boldness, and the courageous hazarding of life and limb against the enemies of the land, retain moral value.[3] Where the nation is promised redemption from its enemies, it is God alone who casts down the oppressor of his people, thus by his own

[1] Cf. vol. I, pp. 139ff.
[2] Zeph. 1.7; Ezek. 9.1ff.; 16.40; 21.23ff.; 23.46f.
[3] Cf., e.g., Isa. 28.6; Micah 4.13; 5.7.

power excluding all human glory and boasting.[1] Consequently *the emphasis laid on the internal building up of the national community is all the greater*. In the old popular ethic unconditional support for one's 'neighbour' (*rēaʿ*), that is, for the member of the people of Yahweh, who as such stood in an indissoluble association with all other members, already formed one of the main pillars of social morality. Now the sense, which the prophets mediated, of being overwhelmed by the immediate divine presence led to a deepened conception of the duties which that national bond willed by God laid on all who belonged to the nation. In face of the drugging of the social conscience among large groups of the population, who failed to see, beyond the rich and glittering conditions of life in the towns, the oppressed situation of the Israelite peasantry, and who allowed the growing power of the monarchy to blind their eyes to the danger of a mounting proletarianization of the lower strata of society, the prophets called men to take seriously once more the holy will of God, who did not allow the rights of even the poorest member of the community of Yahweh to be bought up by the glamour of superficial cultural development. That which the men of commerce and the owners of the vast estates, who profited from the economic revolution, fought against as the burdensome restraint of outmoded customs was precisely what the prophets taught men *to understand as the foundation of the national existence, rooted in the divine nature*, and the thing for which even the greatest sacrifices of material culture and political influence must be made. For the purpose of Israel's election was *a personal fellowship between God and people*, in which material goods could never outweigh the value of a free human life. Therefore Yahweh as the true shepherd of the flock himself takes up the cause of his people,[2] who have been deserted by the shepherds set over them, and delivers up to destruction those who in their pride despise his will, and abandon justice and equity and practical charity toward the poor and dispossessed among their fellow countrymen, because they regard themselves as the true representatives of the nation. Indeed, in his sovereign direction of history it is precisely the *misera plebs* whom he champions; and policies which, in a false striving after power, and a futile posturing on the international stage, use the deprived as the cheap material of their ambition are bound to shatter against the will of the Lord of the

[1] Isa. 7.7ff.; 10.12, 16ff., 33; 17.12ff.; 18.5f.; 37.29, 33ff.; Jer. 25.15ff.; 46ff.; Ezek. 25ff.

[2] Isa. 14.30, 32.

world.[1] Thus it was that the prophets, in the light of the menacing realities of international politics, into which Israel was allowing herself to be drawn, recognized in social aid and concern a divine concept of universal validity. Furthermore, because Yahweh's behaviour toward his people was understood in a new way as forgiving love and compassion, transcending all legal categories, *a warmer inwardness and a more personal goodwill* issued also in gentleness shown to the poor for his sake, overcoming the hard, retributive character and the coarsely utilitarian standpoint of peasant ethics, and deepening men's obligations toward their neighbour into a relationship of person to person and man to man.

Within this approach to social morality *the so-called passive virtues* take on quite new force in the determination of individual conduct. No longer do a proud sense of independence, and enthusiasm for war, knightly daring and self-confident contempt for one's opponent form the dominant ideal of moral conduct, but humility and self-restraint, patience and love of peace, which best reflect inward solidarity with one's fellow countrymen. Because national disasters are no longer felt as intolerable evil, but as divine judgment, the purpose of which is to educate and perfect, and which God desires men to endure without protest, increasing value is set upon readiness to suffer, and sympathy with the sufferer. It is the arrogant men of power whom judgment threatens; those who wait patiently in suffering have the divine help in which to rejoice. Hence sympathy with the oppressed, and concern for those who have fallen victim to the new conditions, became a principal virtue in a man's relationship with his neighbour. The old popular ethic, in which national self-assertion was felt to have the force of a religious obligation, and in which, therefore, activist qualities were given the foremost place, gave way on the prophetic side, as a concomitant of a completely altered assessment of the world situation, to an *ethic of suffering*. In its orientation toward the maintenance of the people of God this ethic was indeed wholly at one with the previous attitude, but it subjected the behaviour designed to achieve this goal to quite different norms. In the figure of the 'ebed yhwh in Deutero-Isaiah, a figure which admittedly was intended in the first place not as an ethical model but simply as a quite incomparable redeemer figure, the conduct of the pious in the practical details of life was given a new point of focus in this towering monument to the quality of willingness to suffer, with its associated virtues

[1] Isa. 14.30, 32; 28.12ff.; 30.15ff.

of quiet obedience, humble renunciation of self-assertion, and constant endurance under the burden laid upon one. From this starting-point the way was opened up for an evaluation of suffering no longer in purely negative terms, as a threat to life, or a restriction of it, but as a divinely ordained calling, and as active service for God's people. Testimony to this is to be found not only in the early comment on the Servant Songs at Isa. 50.10, and in the attempt to interpret the Servant as Israel at 49.3, but also in the shepherd parable of Zech. 11ff., and in the victory over suffering in the closing strophe of Ps. 22. *The God who suffers for the sake of men,* who was known to Hosea and Jeremiah, *is now balanced by the man who suffers in the service and commission of God,* as Jeremiah set him before the eyes of his people in the real-life example of his own vocation, even before the prophet of the Exile gave him eternally valid form in the innocent suffering of the Servant of God.

(*d*) No less significant than this reshaping of the content of morality is *the enlargement of the area of the moral norms* which took place in connection with the prophetic preaching. It is true that in their instructions the prophets, too, think primarily of social behaviour within Israel, not of the dealings of man with man as such. It is first and foremost the dominion of the will of God in Israel which is the great goal for which they strive. But here again they are driven further by the incomparable greatness of the God made known to them, which caused them to understand the judgment and redemption of the people of God only as acts embracing all mankind, and which made the entry of the nations into God's kingdom the goal of universal history,[1] to a self-evident extension of ethical obligation to humanity as a whole. Even though this happens quite unreflectingly and without systematic elaboration, it elevates the old conviction that basic rules obtain even outside Israel into the *understanding of a universal ethical will of God,* which gives the moral norms established within his covenant people validity for the whole world. This is not to say that the concept of an 'absolute Good', or a moral cosmic law, or anything of that sort, had occurred to the spiritual leaders. Such idealist abstractions conflict too violently with the dynamic of the sovereign divine will, since that will does not allow the Good to be understood otherwise than as its own sovereign institution. No more was it the ethical tradition of the extra-biblical wisdom teaching

---

[1] Cf. vol. I, pp. 377ff., 384ff.

which provided the impetus for the prophets' conception of a universal ethic.[1] Even though they may have had direct access to that tradition, or, as is more probable, were acquainted with its leading ideas through the Israelite wisdom teachers, yet their own interests pointed in a quite different direction. The ethical norms which they proclaim have little to do with the dispassionate ethics of practical affairs as found in the wisdom teaching, but everything to do with the passionate will to righteousness of their God. In their social goals they stand in such sharp contrast to the economic thinking of the ancient Near East[2] that there was virtually nothing to their purpose to be borrowed from the Egyptian and Babylonian teachers. Hence they do not appeal to a *consensus gentium* to establish the validity of ethical laws, even though they impartially acknowledge ethical insight in the heathen; instead they see the teachable subjection of the nations to the will of the covenant God as the one and only way to the setting up of a universal moral law. Precisely because they are destined to be subjects of this overlord, the nations must learn his will; indeed, even at this stage, their ripeness for judgment is seen to be due to their lapse from conduct pleasing to him. That which calls down divine retribution is not their hostility to the people of his choice, but the arrogance and malicious joy with which they overstep the bounds of the task of punishment laid upon them, the inhuman lust for destruction with which the conquerors devastate the lands they have overcome, the insatiable greed of the nations, and their exploitation of lies and deceit.[3] A share in the salvation of the eschaton cannot be given to non-Israelite humanity on any other terms than the abandonment of their proud self-assertion, and their consent to instruction in the divine law revealed in Israel.[4] The fact that the prophets can mention in the same breath with these other crimes the sorcery and enchantments of the nations[5] shows that the point of view which dominates their assessment is the Gentiles' resistance to the will of the cosmic Lord, not the infringement of an autonomous morality. Hence the fraternal and peaceable attitude of the nations united in the future kingdom of God likewise derives from

---

[1] A direct connection is assumed by N. W. Porteous, *art. cit.*, a more indirect one by O. S. Rankin, *Israel's Wisdom Literature*, 1936, p. 14.

[2] Cf. W. Eichrodt, *Was sagt das AT zum sozialen Leben?* 1948, pp. 17ff.

[3] Isa. 10.5ff.; Amos 1.3ff.; 2.1ff.; Micah 4.11ff.; Nahum 3.1, 4; Zeph. 2.13ff.; Hab. 1.1–3; 2.5–15; Ezek. 28.1–19; 31.10ff.; Isa. 47.6–8.

[4] Isa. 2.2–4; 45.14ff., 18ff.; Zech. 8.20ff.

[5] Nahum 3.4; Isa. 47.9–12.

their new attitude to the God of the whole world, whom they worship with one heart and soul, and to whom they bring their offerings.[1]

Thus the eschatological vision of the cosmic Lord, advancing steadily toward the establishment of his dominion, drives prophetic thinking on to the unity and universality of the morality required by God, which is binding on all who bear the face of Man.

(e) That which, in the course of the prophetic struggle for the sovereignty of God over his people, showed itself in the provision of a more profound rationale of the norms of righteous conduct, and in their purification and consolidation, also exerted, without much effort on the part of the prophets themselves, penetrating *effects on the ethical thinking* of their nation. This may be seen most clearly at the point where God's demand impinged upon the ordinances of the nation's life as their determining factor, namely in the Law. It is true that this influence cannot be traced in a continuous legal development—something which by the very nature of our sources is incapable of demonstration—but it can be proved at certain striking turning-points such as are constituted by the Deuteronomic Law and the Priestly collection of laws. At the same time, however, it must be clearly understood from the start that the insight bequeathed by the prophets here inevitably took on new forms; for that which the prophets saw in the light of the coming end, when the old divine covenant was to be done away in order to make room for God's new world, the authors of these laws were bound to set in the context of a continuing covenant relationship, and thus to see it in different colours, like light at a different angle of refraction. Hence they were unable to give full effect in practice to the great pioneering approaches to the universality of the moral norms which had been given them in the prophetic perspective of history. The static quality in the divine order established for eternity in the covenant with Israel led to *disregard of the heathen*, so long as they had not become members of the covenant.[2] The validity of moral obligation extended only to those foreigners living within the immediate sphere of the people of God, who were to an ever greater degree incorporated into the community, though that obligation then attached as much responsibility to dealings with them as with fellow citizens.[3] Nor were the teachers of the

[1] Isa. 18.7; 19.21ff.; Zeph. 3.9f.
[2] Deut. 23.2ff.; 14.21; 23.21.
[3] Deut. 10.18f. (cf. 5.14; 14.28f.; 16.10f., 13f.; 24.14, 17, 19–21; 26.11; 29.9ff.; 31.12); Ezek. 14.7; 47.22f.; Lev. 19.34. On the metamorphosis of the resident

Law any better able to give effect to the mutually exclusive opposition in which, for the prophets, the cultus stood to moral and social conduct, when the nation appealed to its cultic performance as a way of evading their demands. When it was a question of leading the people of Yahweh back to right service of God, *the cultus, as the form of the life of the holy community, could not remain a thing indifferent.* Inevitably, as the strongest bulwark against heathen immorality and idolatry,[1] it became a criterion of really loyal service of God,[2] and claimed equal importance with social duties. The prophetic polemic has yet another effect, in that, in Deuteronomy at least, the sacramental significance of the cultic action recedes in importance compared with its confessional character as a witness to the fact that the worshipper belongs exclusively to Yahweh; and even in the Priestly Law it undergoes some weakening in the limitation of the atoning power of sacrifice.[3] At the same time any misguided attempt to make cultic activity independent is blocked by linking it inwardly with readiness for personal sacrifice in the service of one's neighbour, either, as in Deuteronomy, by combining the cultic festivals and dues with socio-ethical obligations,[4] or, as in the Priestly Code, by using the ideal of holiness to unite moral and cultic purity in one concept.

This effort to make all norms of conduct partake of the lofty nature of moral obligation, and thus to prevent their separating out into spheres of life of differing value, was completed by *the strong pressure for a unified basis to the whole legal system.* Thus Deuteronomy names as the foundation commandment, which gives all individual commandments their meaning, *the requirement to love God,* and thus teaches men to recognize and affirm the will of God, which is at work in the ordering of worship and of social life, as unitary in the act by which it both seeks and creates fellowship. And because in the process moral action is rooted in the utterly personal direction of the will, the heteronomy of the legal demand is overcome, and the ground cut away from under

---

alien into the proselyte, as this takes place in P, thus opening to the foreigner fellowship with the God of Israel in the cult, cf. Ex. 12.48f.; Lev. 24.22; Num. 9.14; 15.14, 26.

[1] Cf. Lev. 18ff.

[2] Cf. ch. XXI, p. 297 above. We are not speaking here of the misconception of the cultus as an especially meritorious work of piety, or as a sacrificial procedure with coercive power over the deity. Critics are for the most part blind to the enormous importance of the cultus for the preservation of the nation.

[3] Cf. vol. I, p. 368 and p. 161, n. 6.

[4] Cf. vol. I, pp. 91f.

any mechanical casuistry in the treatment of individual legal regulations.

Furthermore, just as the concern of the prophets is fulfilled in this *derivation of moral action from personal decision*, so it is in that unification of all socio-ethical demands by which the Priestly lawgiver in the Holiness Code robs legal formalism of any power in the matter of a man's relation to his neighbour, and thus gives the bond with one's brother man all-embracing relevance. The command to love in Lev. 19.18, 34 summarizes both *the never-ending task and the meaningful unity of moral obligation*, and once more opens up the way to action in moral freedom. Thus essential elements of the prophetic understanding are firmly incorporated into Israelite legal teaching in as simple and easily comprehensible a form as possible.

It is, therefore, only to be expected that *a refining and deepening of ethical understanding* should also be discernible in the separate descriptions of moral behaviour. It is well known how emphatically in the Deuteronomic Law expression is given to consideration for the weaker and socially underprivileged section of the people,[1] and how closely this is bound up with a thoroughgoing concentration on the divine purpose of blessing. The laws relating to war and to the king[2] in their turn point to a weakening of the tendency to ascribe autonomous validity to the political sphere, in order that now the resources of the nation, which the political entity had been able to enlist in the service of its own egoistic ends, may be concentrated all the more effectively on the establishment of the theocracy. The king is to find his calling in the disinterested championship of the law of God. The nation, in faith that the almighty Lord stands behind the ethical norms, is to surrender its own absolute value, and to conduct its wars not with the cruelty of those who are afraid for their existence, but only with a concern to ward off anything of a heathenish nature, which might jeopardize its attachment to Yahweh. Likewise, it is now possible to abolish, even in trials for high treason, where it had hitherto been customary, the practice of extending the punishment of the guilty party to his children,[3] and thus to match juristic retribution completely to the basic principle of personal responsibility.

How decisively the harshnesses and severities of the early Israelite ethic were overcome in the outlook of the Priestly lawgiver by a

[1] Cf. vol. I, p. 92, nn. 1 and 2.
[2] Deut. 20 and 17.14–20.
[3] Cf. vol. I, p. 78, n. 3.

finely developed sense of responsibility and obligation may be seen from the well-known treatment of the patriarchal stories in P, where everything offensive has been omitted or adjusted. The strict marriage laws[1] likewise reveal a more careful safeguarding of this most important department of human life. The forcefulness with which this deepened understanding of the ethical norms was conveyed to the people in priestly circles may best be illustrated by a priestly liturgy such as Ps. 15. That which is here impressed upon the visitor to the sanctuary as the duty of those who rightly worship Yahweh does not stop at a number of external actions, but penetrates into the depths of the mental attitude, setting out in the practical details of everyday life what love toward one's neighbour is. Nevertheless, the Priestly lawgivers were not blind to the fact that the natural environment within which human life develops is important for free moral conduct of this kind. In their struggle to ensure, by means of strict land laws, that every member of the nation should be free from enslavement by a capitalist economic system[2] there is no mistaking their watchful sense of responsibility for the independent existence of every citizen, or the significance of their thus accepting one of the major points in the fight of the prophets.

v. *The norms in the community of the Law*

(*a*) The fact that in this way the prophets' new experience of God did not fail to have its effect on the ethical thinking of their contemporaries and their immediate successors, but left behind it profound traces, specifically in the legal organization of the nation's life, ensured its own continuance within the community of the Law. In the event, throughout the whole succeeding period, however great its deviations from the prophetic line may have been here and there, certain of the *bedrock elements of ethical conviction* which the prophets had emphasized with such immense force remained with their validity unshaken, and kept men's moral understanding open to fertilization from the world of prophetic thought.

First and foremost among these is *the knowledge that ethical regulation of conduct is of unique importance for the service of God*. The basic principles on which a moral life is to be led are inalienable components of the will of God, on the realization of which Israel's existence depends. There is no longer any real danger that these basic principles will be

---

[1] Lev. 18 and 20; but also already in Deut. 24.1ff.
[2] Lev. 25.

imperilled by that overvaluation of the cultus against which the prophets had waged so bitter a struggle.

Equally firm is *the conviction that God declares himself faithful to this will of his by guaranteeing blessing and life to those who follow it*, and, on the other hand, pursuing with his curse those who despise it. The assurance that fulfilment of the moral commands implied success in laying the foundation of a happy life could certainly be challenged, but never made a matter for serious doubt. On this basis rest the clarity, firmness and energy which characterize the moral conduct of the Jewish community, giving it its inner superiority over the ethics of heathenism.

Finally, the recognition that truly moral action is not exhausted in the external observance of incidental prescriptions, but presupposes *an interior affirmation of the divine will*, remains a living reality. The personal character of the ethical act, though often obscured, is always preserved.

Thus it was possible for *the sense of moral responsibility to develop strongly* in every sphere of life, once the judgment of the Exile, and its evaluation by prophets and teachers, had forced the post-exilic community to face the full seriousness of the fact of divine retribution, and in God's offer of favour had shown it the way to shape its life afresh. It is true that an ethos of the nation evolved no further; henceforth the nation existed only in the form of the religious congregation, and was obliged with few exceptions to endure passively whatever happened in the political sphere without itself being able to affect the course of events. The result was that within the limited range available ethical consideration and assessment of the various departments of life became all the more intensive. One element in this process which should not be overlooked is the comprehensive *repair of the deficiencies of early Israelite morality*. Thus, with regard to the sexual laxity of indigenous popular morals, there was an effective restriction of unbridled freedom, and a refinement of moral sensitivity, even in the case of the husband. Just as Deuteronomy had already made divorce more difficult,[1] and Malachi had protested against its irresponsible use in the new cultic community,[2] so, too, the fight against offences of sexual laxity takes up a great deal of space in the

[1] Deut. 24.1ff.
[2] Mal. 2.13–16. The interpretation of this difficult passage in terms of the divorce of Jewish wives in favour of alliances with the politically influential families of the semi-pagan people of the land still seems to me the most probable.

writings of the wisdom teachers.[1] It is true that warnings against adultery also form a constantly recurring topic in wisdom teaching outside Israel; but the sense that it was precisely this which distinguished them from the heathen and their depravities, as well as the need for defence against the infiltration of pagan immorality, especially in the Diaspora, made the sexual morals of Judaism more serious and more relentlessly strict. Fornication and sexual impurity are felt to be the worst form of depravity, an attitude which is still influential in the New Testament. The poet of Job wishes the pious man to be wittingly pure, even from lustful thoughts.[2] Ben Sira gives a general condemnation of divorce, except where the shrewishness and wilfulness of the wife make the marriage intolerable.[3] All the higher, therefore, is the value set upon raising a family, and the duty of building it up. One result of this is that the woman is now valued as an independent personality, a development which to a great extent holds in check other views of an opposite tendency. When the Israelite teacher exalts the clever, silent, well-behaved woman as the worthy object of a man's choice, he is valuing her not simply as a helpmeet for the man, but as a human being of his own stamp.[4] And by attaching more importance to her piety than to her outward attractions,[5] and thus basing marriage on agreement in the highest matter of all, he accords her the worth of a personality in the fullest sense. If nothing like this is to be found anywhere else in the wisdom of the ancient Near East, then credit can only go to the Jewish belief in the Creator God, before whom man and woman stand in equal responsibility.

Equally striking is the abundance in Israelite wisdom of sayings relating to the duties of children toward their parents. These are indeed not entirely absent from the pagan literature;[6] but when one compares this handful of references with the insistent and unwearied exhortation of the Israelite wisdom teachers, then it is permissible to ask whether it is not the God of the Fifth Commandment, who as the

---

[1] Prov. 2.16–19; 5; 6.24–35; 7.5–27; 23.27f.; 29.3; 30.20; 31.3; Job 31.1, 9; Or. Sib. II.259, 280–283; III.594–600; Wisd. 3.13, 16; 4.6; 14.23f.; II Enoch 10.4; 24.2; Jub. 20.4; 30.8, etc.

[2] Job 31.1; cf. Ecclus 9.5.

[3] Ecclus 7.19, 26; cf. 25.26.

[4] Prov. 19.14; 31.10ff.; Ecclus 26.1f., 13–15; 36.28f.

[5] Prov. 31.30.

[6] There are one or two passages to be found in the Egyptian wisdom book of Ani, and about the same number in the Babylonian proverbs.

father of his people is the pattern of all fatherhood, who has here opened men's eyes to the especial importance of piety toward parents.[1]

Also worthy of attention is the refinement of men's views about lying and deceit. It is not only the bare-faced lie which is condemned,[2] but also calumny and double-dealing, scandalmongering and over-hasty condemnation, hypocrisy and the concealment of sin.[3] The fact that in later Judaism ἁπλότης, in the sense of 'simplicity and sheer straightforwardness of conduct',[4] emerges as a much-used basic concept of ethics, and that the exclusion of all double-mindedness and duplicity is seen as a capital requirement of genuine morality,[5] is the expression of a matured understanding and incorruptible respect for the duty of truthfulness, such as ancient Israel had never known.

These points, and others which there is no need to enumerate in detail here, illustrate the way in which *the demands of morality became wider in scope and more profound in insight*, as it probed into the various expressions of temperament and character, and directed attention to the inner processes involved in the shaping of men's behaviour toward their neighbours. Here the old fundamental commands are internalized, and developed in all their aspects, and the full range of their relevance is made clear by thorough training.

(*b*) It is in line with this watchful and responsive readiness for ethical education in every department of life that *the cultic statutes also are brought within the sphere of ethical obligation* as means to the God-willed ordering and building up of the life of the community. The Deuteronomic outlook[6] persists in full force in the prophets Haggai and Zechariah, for whom the building of the Temple is valued essentially as an act of faith and confession, in which the congregation finds the right response to God's pardon, and by standing together in solidarity fights for its right to exist in its own way *vis-à-vis* the Persian government. It is because of his sure understanding that any threat to

---

[1] Prov. 1.8; 4.1; 6.20; 10.1; 15.5, 20; 17.21, 25; 19.26; 20.20; 23.22, 24; 28.7, 24; 29.3; 30.11, 17; Ecclus 3.1–16; 7.27; 22.4f.; Tobit 4.3; 10.7; Aristeas 228; 238; Phokylides 8.

[2] Prov. 6.17ff.; 12.19, etc.; Ecclus 15.8; 20.24f.; 41.17.

[3] Prov. 4.24; 6.12ff.; 16.27f.; 26.23ff.; Ecclus 5.14; 7.14; 8.19; 9.18; 11.7; 18.19; 19.7; 20.6–8; 22.22; 26.5ff.; 28.13ff.; II Enoch 42.12; Test. Dan 4; 5; 6; Test. Gad 5, etc.; Pirke Aboth I.18.

[4] Bousset-Gressmann, *Religion des Judentums*[3], p. 418; cf. also C. Edlund, *Das Auge der Einfalt*, 1952.

[5] I Macc. 2.37, 60; III Macc. 3.21; I Enoch 91.4; Test. Benj. 6; Test. Reub. 4; Test. Levi 13; Test. Iss. 3–5.

[6] Cf. p. 335 above.

the cultic congregation is also a threat to the survival of the people of God that Malachi fights for sacrificial worship and for the ordinances of the priesthood just as resolutely as for loyalty to the faith and for brotherly conduct. Here, too, it is possible for the overvaluation of a cultic practice such as fasting to be flatly rejected in order to inculcate all the more emphatically the indissoluble bond between right worship on the one hand and righteousness, compassion and loyalty on the other.[1] Religious practice is led back from external activity to inner agreement with the will of God.

Nor does it in any way imply disregard for the majesty of the moral demand, if Ezra's life-work results in the cultic law being very decidedly set alongside the moral. The nation is here provided with the outward form of its life, in which, after the end of its existence as a political state, it is given the possibility of a life of its own, determined in every aspect by the thought of the sovereignty of God; and this means that the cultus becomes an act of loyalty toward the historical task which God has appointed for them. It has already been pointed out[2] how indissoluble is the link between faith and morals in the cultic forms of expression. There is no question of setting bounds to the control of morality over the shaping of life; on the contrary, the legal constitution of the people of God itself incorporated strong moral impulses, in that it directed the energies of a compact religious fellowship into conduct, and by requiring proof of faith in deeds set itself against fantastic speculation such as threatened from apocalyptic currents of thought.

(c) That it was in no way inevitable for the cultic constitution of the Jewish congregation to lead in principle to an impairment of moral clarity is shown by the powerful reinforcement which the authority of the moral norms received from later Jewish *ideas of resurrection and judgment to come*. Becoming prominent first of all during the serious crisis of the Maccabean revolt as the highly significant metaphysical background to decisions passionately held and equally passionately contested,[3] recollection of the Judge of the world exercised an ever-increasing influence on moral attitudes. In fact, it extended the relevance of the demands of morality even beyond death, and thus was bound to make each individual aware of the

---

[1] Zech. 7; Isa. 58.1–12.
[2] Cf. vol. I, pp. 419ff.
[3] Dan. 12. On the stages by which this expectation was arrived at cf. ch. XXIV below.

infinite importance of the personal position which he chose to adopt.[1]
It both stirred men to reckless sacrifice of their lives for the law of
God and deepened the seriousness of moral decision in daily life. At
the same time it reinforced *the universal reference of ethical thinking*, as
this had already become manifest in the eschatological vision of the
prophets, and in the priestly proclamation of the cosmic God and his
Law.

(*d*) The first *threat to moral understanding* invades the community of
the Law at the point where *the ideal of the holy congregation* is no longer
thought of as the directional indication for her historical task in the
present, nor as an exhortation to be prepared for the consummation
which God himself is to bring about, but as *the condition to be established
by men, with the help of the legal system*, a condition in which the divine
purposes for the world will already have been realized. The possibility
of such a deviation was undoubtedly already implicit in the priestly
understanding of the world and of God, in so far as the static quality
of the eternal divine order could easily be perverted into the im-
mobility and self-sufficiency of a legally regulated situation, as soon
as men lost sight of the infinity of the task set by the Law, and of the
limitations of human action. In Ezekiel, the inflexible seriousness
attaching to fulfilment of the Law still stands in living tension with
the new creation expected from God,[2] just as, in the priestly teaching
of the law, turning in faith to the God who gives so abundantly still
forms the healthy counterpoise to overvaluation of one's own
activity.[3] But in the appendix to the book of Ezekiel the first signs of
movement in another direction become discernible.[4] Here, in sensible
distinction from the prophetic future hope, which looks for everything from Yahweh's intervention, there is the description of a cultic
community built up by human loyalty to the law, a community
which then enters into the very blessings of the paradisal age of
salvation. The peculiar correlation between the maturing of the community from human imperfection to God-pleasing holiness, as a
result of strict legal training, and the transformation of the earth into
Paradise ascribes a value to the Priestly theocracy of Jerusalem which

[1] I Enoch 1.7, 9; 27.4; 47.3, etc.; Wisd. 2.22–3.8; Jub. 5.12; Ps. Sol. 3.10, 12;
14.3, 6; 15.12f.; Test. Benj. 10; Test. Levi 4; Or. Sib. IV.40ff., 180ff.; II (4)
Esdras 5.42; 14.35; Apoc. Bar. 50.4; 54.21; 83.7; IV Macc. 9.8f.; 12.19; 16.25;
18.5; Pirke Aboth II.15; III.1, 17; IV.22.
[2] Cf. pp. 301ff. above.
[3] Cf. vol. I, pp. 421f., 431f., and ch. XXI, pp. 302f. above.
[4] Ezek. 43–48.

makes it appear an ultimate goal of God's government of the world. If this is compared with Zechariah's view of the hierarchical system of the Zion community, for all his recognition of its irreplaceable value, as an interim arrangement, waiting for God's consummation,[1] the difference in attitude is clear. And the specifically Priestly trait of contemplating simultaneously both the future and the present sovereignty of God in the cultic songs of praise[2] could only intensify the process here already in train, namely the transference of the messianic character to the congregation. The exultation of the hymn at the glory of God's eternal kingdom and of its ruler, in which future fulfilment is transposed into a present divine order,[3] was easily pressed into the service of this overvaluation of the humanly attainable community structure. In the same way the promises of a priestly nation of mediators in the age of salvation[4] simply afforded new nourishment to this self-conceit so soon as the element of contrast in the prophetic eschatology was eliminated, and men had forgotten the gulf between Man and the absolute perfection of the transcendent, universal God, that perfection of which the Priestly world-view could speak so strikingly.

This dangerous abridgment of the original priestly attitude received support from the epigones of prophecy as a result of their readoption of a nationalist and particularist hope into the picture of the future. The world sovereignty of Israel, and the world status of the Jewish congregation, became the two sides of the final perfection, and provided common ground for the various religious tendencies of the post-exilic period.

As regards the validity of the ethical norms, however, this meant *narrowing* the earlier view *in a particularist sense*. Two reasons made relentless segregation from the heathen environment seem the natural thing in ethical matters also: first, a community intent on holiness was bound to be anxiety-ridden about contamination by anything heathen, because their whole future depended on perfect fulfilment

---

[1] Zech. 3.6–10; 6.11ff. Like Procksch (*Kleine prophetische Schriften nach dem Exil*, 1916, pp. 39ff.), I consider that the interpretation of this passage in terms of Zerubbabel, which can only be secured at the cost of hazardous conjecture, is mistaken, and that a reference to a hoped-for messianic ruler after Zerubbabel's disappearance is more in accordance with the evidence: cf. my study, 'Vom Symbol zum Typos. Ein Beitrag zur Sacharja-Exegese', *TZ* 13, 1957, pp. 509ff.

[2] Cf. vol. I, pp. 429f., 487.

[3] Pss. 93; 96; 97; 99; 46; 76.

[4] Isa. 61.6–9; 45.14; 19.23; Zech. 2.14f.; 8.23.

of the Law; secondly, God's consummation was restricted to the community of the Law, while the nations were primarily objects of judgment.[1] It is true that in the earlier part of the period voices were raised in support of a freer and more understanding attitude toward the heathen. The beautiful stories of Ruth and Jonah mirror the universalist approach of the prophets and of the circles influenced by them; and an evaluation of pagan worship such as that expressed in Mal. 1.11 succeeds in formulating the universality of God's kingdom in the very cult-terminology of the priesthood in a way that cannot be surpassed. The apocalypse of Isa. 24-27, too, can proclaim judgment and salvation as embracing the whole world.

But the particularist tendency, which acquired its driving force from the absolute status accorded to the congregation, was the stronger, and it was this which became dominant in later Judaism. Here unbridled lust for revenge is directed against the heathen;[2] men like to describe their extermination in the past as God's ordinance for the future as well,[3] and this message is proclaimed by the prophets.[4] Toward the heathen there are no moral obligations; men are to turn away from them with contempt,[5] faithlessness and deceit, cruelty and violence are permitted, in fact enjoined.[6] And those who accord the heathen equal status with Israelites in the community, and despise her law, are with equal severity excluded from the scope of moral obligation.[7] It is a testimony to the vigour with which this separation was enforced that even a man like Ben Sirach, who represents a piety to which extremes of any kind are abhorrent, adopts the same attitude.

(e) The segregation thus achieved was given its special character by the increasingly self-conscious *concentration of all life on the Law*. From the time of the reform of Ezra onwards the Law constitutes the rigidly defined norm of all conduct. The way to this consummation

---

[1] Ezra 9f.; Neh. 13.1-3, 28f.

[2] Pss. 79.12; 137; 149.7; Lam. 4.21; I Enoch 84.6; Ecclus 33.1ff.; 36.16ff.

[3] Josh. 10.28ff.; 11.10ff.; Num. 31.14ff.; Jub. 30.5f., 17f., 23; 35.15; 37.13, 17ff.; 38.2, 12ff.; Test. Judah 9.

[4] Isa. 34.5-17; 65f.; Zech. 9.11-11.3; 12.1ff.; 14.1ff.; Obad. 15ff.; Ps. Sol. 17.24, 34; Jub. 31.17, 20; 35.14f.

[5] Ecclus 50.25f.; Jub. 22.16; 23.24; 29.11; Ps. Sol. 1.1; 2.1f.; 34; 7.2; I Enoch 89f.; Wisd. 12.10f.; 13.1; Judith 12.2; Add. to Esther 3.26ff.

[6] Esther *passim*; Judith 8.35; 9.2ff.; 10.12f.; 11.5ff., 11ff.; 16.18; I Macc. 5; 10.84.

[7] II Chron. 13.10ff.; 25.7ff.; Pss. 28.4f.; 31.18f.; Ecclus 12.3-5; 25.7; Tobit 4.17; 14.7; Ps. Sol. 2.10ff.; 4.1ff.; 8.8ff., etc.; 14.23ff.

had been well prepared by the Law-oriented history-writing, in which the whole past of the people was judged by the criterion of fulfilment of the Law. What the Deuteronomistic redaction of the older historical sources had tried to hammer into the consciousness of the nation, and the Priestly epitome of the primal history had effectively presented through its impressive system of epochs, was now influentially continued by the historical work of the Chronicler. Here conformity to the Law, fixed in written form,[1] down to the very last detail, is stressed as the criterion of conduct pleasing to God, and history is remoulded with the greatest freedom to illustrate this thesis. But the Law was not only proclaimed as the sole standard for public conduct; now private piety, too, began to find in it the only guiding rule for God-pleasing action. A significant pointer to this is the fact that the use of the word *berīt* in the sense of the Law, in which Deuteronomy had led the way,[2] now becomes regular practice in the Psalms[3] to designate the content of the duties of the pious. The growing intensity of this concentration on the Law can be seen particularly in the development of ethical exhortation in the wisdom teaching. In the earlier period[4] its criteria had included the experience of others, one's own insight, and the will of the deity, but the Law of Yahweh is nowhere explicitly mentioned. In the wisdom Psalms,[5] however, the situation is very different. With the exception of Ps. 49 references to the Law of Yahweh as the norm of conduct are found in increasing measure; as in the wisdom writings of later Judaism[6] the bond between the Law and wisdom teaching is an accomplished fact. Indeed, in these writings the Law of Moses is nothing less than the incarnation of Wisdom, conceived as an hypostasis,[7] so that the advantage of Israelite as compared with heathen wisdom teaching consists in the knowledge of the Law as the content of all wisdom.[8] Hence in the end precise and regular study of the Torah, and laborious fulfilment of the Law, of which the 'Sayings of the Fathers'

[1] Cf. the expression *kakkātūb battōrā*, II Chron. 23.18; 25.4; 30.5, 18; 31.3; 35.12, 26; Ezra 3.2, 4.
[2] Cf. vol. I, pp. 53ff., and II Chron. 6.11; 34.32.
[3] Pss. 25.10, 14; 44.18; 50.16; 78.10, 37; 103.18; cf. also Isa. 56.4, 6.
[4] The representatives of this period are Proverbs, Job and Ecclesiastes.
[5] Pss. 1; 19B; 37; 49; 94; 111; 112; 119.
[6] Ecclesiasticus, Baruch, Tobit, Wisdom of Solomon, IV Maccabees, Pirḳe Aboth.
[7] Ecclus 24.23ff.; Bar. 4.1.
[8] On this subject cf. J. Fichtner, *Die altorientalische Weisheit in ihrer israelitisch-jüdischen Ausprägung*, 1933, pp. 79ff.

in the Mishna is the classic exposition, were bound to become the substance of human life.

The inevitable result, where all conduct was thus determined by 'the book of the commandments of God, the Law that endureth for ever',[1] was to weaken the basing of conduct on freedom of decision, and to endanger it by a *rigid heteronomy*. The belief, which became a living force precisely in the post-exilic period, in the personal guidance of the Spirit,[2] according to which the word from the past became living direction for the present through the Spirit of God,[3] did indeed afford some help against such externalization. And the greater religious profundity which marks the later stages of the wisdom teaching meant that the direct reference of all conduct to God by understanding it as the outcome of personal surrender was never completely forgotten. On the other hand, however, the collapse of unified moral obligation into innumerable external rules is clearly discernible in the *lack of a firm orientation* of moral consciousness. The fact that the commandments, in the form of a legal system, describe the behaviour required of Man makes all of them of equal value, and robs conduct of the secure organization that springs from a unified basic attitude. This fission of the ethical norm, leading to an anxiety-ridden subservience to formula, is symptomatically expressed in the constant desire for a 'greatest commandment', a commandment which is identified differently according to the circumstances of different periods. Zeal for a perfect cultus in the Chronicler, or in particular for the hallowing of the Sabbath in the earlier post-exilic period, is later replaced by the especially high value attached to alms-giving in Ben Sirach, or to the burial of compatriots in Tobit, or to fasting in Judith. Uncertainty with regard to the multiplicity of requirements plainly results in the search for one area in which the whole force of the personality can be committed.[4]

It is obvious enough that the longed-for security was not to be obtained by such arbitrary selection of single actions. Hence there developed a tendency to make a *precise record of good deeds*, in order to

---

[1] Bar. 4.1.

[2] Pss. 51.13; 143.10; Job 32.8ff., 18; cf. pp. 6of. above.

[3] Isa. 59.21; Zech. 1.6; 4.6; 7.12; Neh. 9.20, 30.

[4] The goal which the later synagogue were pursuing, with their question about the 'great commandment', was above all to comprehend the multiplicity of the commandments in their ultimate unity, without, however, thereby succeeding in overcoming the heteronomy which was rooted in the impossible immensity of their number. Cf. Matt. 22.36ff., and Strack-Billerbeck, *Kommentar zum NT* I, pp. 907ff.

ensure that one was, in fact, fulfilling the Law. A feature which is so marked in a representative of the ruling classes of the Jewish community like Nehemiah, who in his memoirs makes especial note of every proof of his own faithful fulfilment of the Law,[1] may also be regarded as typical of a more widespread attitude to the ethical command.[2]

Where the letter of the Law was regarded as defining the sphere of ethical obligation, there was the possibility of attempting to overcome in yet another way the uncertainty whether one had perfectly fulfilled the will of God, namely by emphasizing and practising as *works of especial merit* those that were not explicitly required in the Law. The Jewish scribes described these collectively as $g^e m\bar{\imath} l\bar{u}t\ h^a s\bar{a} d\bar{\imath}m$, 'repayment of love', or 'works of love', and included under this head the visiting of the sick, giving shelter to strangers, equipping poor couples at the start of their married life, sharing in the expense of weddings and funerals, consoling mourners, and so on. Such works, with the study of the Torah, and worship, form the three pillars on which the world rests,[3] and, together with almsgiving, equal in weight all the commandments of the Torah.[4] Even by themselves they are of more value than almsgiving. It is clear that by setting such value on works of supererogation the unity of ethical obligation was shattered, and its seriousness and majesty thus imperilled.

In all these blunders of a service of the Law doomed to heteronomy we see the effects of an unfree attitude to the individual commandment; and it was this same attitude which drove men to a *casuistic treatment* of moral demands. Though the influence of popular proverbial wisdom, with its more casual arrangement of exhortations and counsels, as much as the linking of ethics to the Law, may have contributed to the lack of rigid collation and systematization, the decisive factor in a contrary direction was the effort to secure an assured state of perfection in the community organized according to the Law. Because of this, no individual command, once it had become part of the Law, could be unimportant. It was therefore not enough

---

[1] Neh. 5.19; 13.14, 22, 31.
[2] Cf. Pss. 17.4f.; 18.21–25; 35.13f.; 109.4f.; 119.11, 14, 30f., 51ff., 97ff. D. Rössler, *Gesetz und Geschichte in der spätjudischen Apokalyptik* (Wissenschaftliche Monographien zum A. und NT 3), 1960, has emphasized that in apocalyptic value continues to attach to the Law as the charter of election.
[3] Aboth I.2, traditionally ascribed to Simon the Just.
[4] Tosefta Pea 1.19; cf. H. L. Strack, *Einleitung in Talmud und Midrasch*[5], 1921, pp. 26ff., 74ff.

to make clear the great, fundamental guiding-lines of life; even the smallest detail must be so ordered that no gap remained in the tightly organized system, and no uncertainty weighed upon the man who willingly devoted himself to punctilious obedience to the Law. Hence the most pressing business of the scribe inevitably became that of providing each pious soul with ready-made rules for conduct by a complete treatment of all possible cases, and thus making him a member of service to a community which was striving to achieve holiness. As a result of the hair-splitting casuistry which flourished in this soil, and which preferred to build a double or triple fence of duties round the Law, rather than to leave open the possibility of even one breach of its restrictions, there was bound to be an increase both in the multitude of individual requirements and also of the already existent impossibility of obtaining a clear overall view of them, with all the evil consequences which this involved, while at the same time the fact that it was out of the question to fulfil its demands more than ever undermined respect for the Law. This, however, is something which this ethical attitude shares with every casuistical ethic. Now the art of pliable interpretation of the Law was added to the means of lightening the no longer bearable load; and because this art was able to show a way out in disputed cases it made the scribe the master of men's consciences, and imported into the service of the Law a hypocrisy in which the sense of the absolute claims of the moral demand perished.[1]

The fact that, for all this, the Jewish attitude to the ethical norms, taking it all in all, cannot be described as simply one of heteronomy and nationalist particularism, of disunity and relativism, must be attributed to the continuing effect of the new foundation given to moral conduct by the prophets. By taking the prophetic as well as the legal writings into the canon, the community of the Law ensured that its thinking would be constantly cross-fertilized by a thoroughgoing theonomy. Alongside the great mainstream of the ethic of the Law the currents of prophetic thought flow on, and prevent a total silting up by external legalism. Here, too, therefore, as in other spheres, a deep inner fragmentation is the characteristic mark of the Jewish community. As regards the past this derives from the crucial misunderstanding of God's covenant as a complete system to be set up by

---

[1] Perhaps the Tractate Sabbath of the Mishna supplies the best illustration of how real worship of God is bound to be stifled under the heaping-up of detailed commands, from which the spirit has fled.

men within the empirical and contingent situation; but it also points forward into the future, to a creative new foundation of moral thinking and action, to be laid by transposing men into a new total relationship with God, in which the work of grace present in the establishment of the Old Covenant was to come to fulfilment.[1]

2. THE GOODS OF MORAL CONDUCT

i. *The goods within the sphere of natural existence*

Just as important for the development of morality as the norms of moral conduct are the goods to the attainment of which that conduct is directed. Where the goods for which men are striving and the norms governing their conduct are heterogeneous, the norms are always in danger of serving only as means to an end, and thereby losing their character of absolute obligation. Only where the goal of action is homogeneous with the norm is there any guarantee of the coherence and strength of ethics.

To a large extent the goods to which action is directed in ancient Israel are *the natural goods of life*, those which are indispensable for the existence of the community. Peace,[2] or at least victorious war,[3] abundance of children,[4] worldly possessions,[5] long life,[6] friendship and love,[7] these are the goods which come to mind both for the individual and the nation, when they think of the fruit of their deeds, and of the blessing of their God; and it is to these goods that the promises and threats at the close of the Law relate, thus plainly reflecting the universally accepted outlook. With a rising standard of culture spiritual, aesthetic, and social values are added to the list, such as wisdom,[8] beauty,[9] honour,[10] and freedom.[11]

---

[1] On the subject-matter of this section cf. E. Sellin, *Israels Güter und Ideale* (Beiträge zur isr. und jüd. Religionsgeschichte, no. 2), 1897.

[2] Gen. 13.8; 21.27ff.; 26.19–31; 33.15f.; Deut. 33.12, 28; Num. 23.9f.; 24.5f.; I Kings 2.32.

[3] Gen. 14.16ff.; 48.22; II Sam. 18.28; Gen. 49.9; Ex. 15.17; Num. 23.24; 24.9, etc.

[4] Gen. 12.2; 13.15; 15.5; 22.17, 20ff.; 24.60; 26.24; 28.3, 14, etc.; Judg. 11.38; I Sam. 1; II Sam. 6.23, etc.

[5] Gen. 24.35; 26.12ff.; 27.28; 30.29f., 43; 49.20; Deut. 33.18f.; I Sam. 22.7.

[6] Gen. 47.9; Ex. 20.12; 23.26; I Sam. 25.29; I Kings 1.31, 34; Gen. 25.8 (P).

[7] I Sam. 18.3; 20.16; II Sam. 1.26; Gen. 24.67; 29.18ff., 32–35; I Sam. 1.8.

[8] Gen. 49.21; Judg. 14; I Sam. 16.18; 25.3, 33; II Sam. 14.1ff., 20; 16.20, 23; 19.28; 20.16, 22; I Kings 3.9. Joseph stands as a model of wisdom in Gen. 37ff.

[9] I Sam. 9.2; 16.18; 17.42; II Sam. 14.25; I Kings 1.6.

[10] Gen. 38.23; 39.21; Judg. 9.54; I Sam. 2.26, 30; 15.30; 18.5, 16, 28; 25.10ff.;

From this evidence it might seem at first sight as though Israelite conduct was governed by a primitive eudaemonism; but the matter takes on another aspect when we consider the directness with which the divine favour is felt in these goods, and correspondingly the divine anger in their absence. It is not material goods, and their enjoyment in and for themselves, which counts as the ultimate goal, but the divine favour of which they are evidence. As *blessings from Yahweh* they witness to the divine giver on whom all life and prosperity depend.[1] The vitality of this outlook, however, is attributable to the fact that the Israelite did not encounter in his God a capricious supreme power, with whom he had somehow to get along, but with whom he could never enjoy any inward relationship, but rather knew himself to be incorporated into a relationship of loyalty and service toward one who by the covenant-making had called his people to himself,[2] and who now bestowed on the life of each individual not only purpose and direction, but also nobility and worth. The matter did not therefore stop at ascribing gratefully to the Creator and Lord of his people the foundations of national existence in general, though the tireless and pronounced emphasis on the divine generosity in this respect, as, for example, when the occupation of the land is explained as a gift of God's favour,[3] already clearly reveals the basic attitude; it went further to those delicate and profound portrayals of the divine generosity in which the writer understands enough to focus on *the personal dealing of God with the individual as the really important element* in the bestowal of his gifts. Thus the Abraham story shows that it is precisely the selfless man, the one who is not striving for his own advantage, for whom God provides with his blessing. Riches obtained

---

31.4; II Sam. 1.10; 3.7f., 36; 6.16, 20; 13.13. For the opposite cf. the contempt in which the *benē beliyyaʿal* are held: Judg. 19.22; 20.13, etc; similar expressions occur in Judg. 9.4; 11.3.

[11] Gen. 49.15; Ex. 19.4; 20.2; 23.27ff.; Judg. 3.15–29; 5.6ff.; 6.13ff.; 9.8ff.; I Sam. 11.6ff.; and the condemnation of the monarchy in I Sam. 8.11–18.

[1] Gen. 49.25f.; 26.12ff., 29; 27.27f.; 39.5; Ex. 23.25; Deut. 28.2ff. The priests are to lay the blessing of Yahweh on the people, Num. 6.23–27; men fight for the possession of the divine blessing, Gen. 27; Num. 23–24; the prosperity of the tribes is regarded as the result of an oracle of blessing, Gen. 49; Deut. 33; in fact, the continued existence of the whole creation is derived from the blessing of the Creator, Gen. 1.22, 28; 2.3.

[2] This connection is emphasized in Num. 23.22; 24.8.

[3] Gen. 12.7; 13.15; 15.7, 18; 24.7; 26.3; 28.13; 48.21; Ex. 20.12; 32.13; 33.1; Num. 14; Deuteronomy is simply a thoroughgoing exploitation of this point of view.

in an underhand way are endangered by God (Gen. 32); and deep humility is often the precondition of blessing, as in the case of Joseph or of the rise of David. Furthermore, both in refusal and in unexpected bounty, this God constantly points men *to himself*,[1] and makes his gifts the means whereby his own are led to enter into his thoughts, and to understand his nature more profoundly.

However, the most clear-cut instance of the link with God as the proper criterion of what was good in life occurred when, for the sake of this God, the nation was required to renounce worldly goods, and to surrender the pleasures of peace or of rich plunder, namely when the law of her divine Lord, or his claim to sovereignty, supervened.[2] No sacrifice could be too heavy when it was a matter of expiating a breach of this obligation, or an infraction of his command.[3] The up-shot of such cases, in keeping with what has already been said, was that, *in the last analysis, the fellowship with God granted in election and covenant-making was felt to be the goal of moral action more important than all individual goods*, the precondition of all good fortune and blessing.[4] This scale of values was still expressed more in an unreflective feeling for life than in clear understanding, and forced its way into consciousness only where circumstances aroused severe conflict. At other times the obvious coherence of external blessings with the covenant attitude to God concealed the threat to the natural unity of life latent within it. And yet there is no doubt that it was from this new feeling for life that earthly goods acquired both a significance beyond that of mere material enjoyment, and also a limitation, as being no more than signs and pledges of a higher meaning in life. Of all the other religions of antiquity only the Persian can show anything similar, and that only during the early period, when the influence of Zoroaster's inspiring call to the service of the one good God was predominant. The process of hardening into legalism, which soon began, stunted the growth of the fruitful seed here planted.

How vitally Israel's opinion of herself was affected by the detach-ment from egoistic possession or enjoyment involved in her relation-ship with God is shown by the fact that the outward fortunes of the nation were vividly *felt as obstructing or furthering the mission entrusted to*

---

[1] Gen. 15.3ff.; 30.2ff.; I Sam. 1, etc. Cf. the phrase used for earthly good fortune of all kinds: 'Yahweh is with him' (Sellin, *op. cit.*, p. 86).

[2] Judg. 5.15ff., 23; I Sam. 11.7; and the custom of the ban.

[3] Josh. 7; I Sam. 14.37ff.; II Sam. 21.

[4] This comes out especially clearly in the early form of the hope of peace: cf. W. Eichrodt, *Die Hoffnung des ewigen Friedens im alten Israel*, 1920, pp. 101ff.

them as God's people. Because her battles and victories were Yahweh's battles and victories, by which he glorified himself in the sight of the nations, Israel's prosperity and good fortune ought to attest the power and graciousness of her God, to the end that the nations might desire the blessings of this God for themselves.[1] Here the close link between the life of the individual and that of the community in ancient Israel was bound to have the effect of exalting even the natural goods of each individual's life into a contribution to the glorification of his God; and conversely, his own misfortunes were the more grievously distressing as lessening the respect shown to his people. That nevertheless the individual's suffering in such cases did not have the effect of challenging men's faith was due to their readiness, at that period still taken for granted, to submit to the liberty of the hidden God, even though they could not keep account of the workings of his governance in detail.[2]

Since accordingly the goods of life could not be separated from their giver as things of value for their own sake, men also acquired at an early stage an eye for *their inherent dangers.* The demonic element in beauty, which blinds the eyes, and seduces men to ungrateful rebellion against the Lord's anointed; the cleverness, which enters the service of vicious revolt, and stirs up the son against the father; the inordinate ambition, which drives men to deeds of blood, and violates their humility before him who alone is exalted, so that with pitiful excuses they hold back from confessing their transgressions; all these are strikingly set before our eyes in such figures as Absalom,[3] Ahithophel,[4] David,[5] Michal,[6] Saul,[7] and others. And when David is portrayed as the companion of those who have come to grief in civil life, and have been expelled from their families,[8] the narrator is plainly alive to the irony of God's governance, by which he causes his most famous king to arise from the ranks of those deprived of their rights, who have forfeited their honour as citizens. We have here a most remarkable expression of *the relativity of goods so highly prized,* and of men's judgment about possessing or losing them.

[1] Gen. 12.2ff.; 26.28; 30.27.
[2] Cf. vol. I, pp. 262f.
[3] II Sam. 14.25; 15.1ff.
[4] II Sam. 16.23.
[5] I Sam. 25.21f., 26.
[6] II Sam. 6.16, 20.
[7] I Sam. 15.30: cf. Gen. 38.23; Judg. 9.54.
[8] I Sam. 22.2.

Thus the high value attaching to natural goods is essentially determined by the fact that in gaining or losing them Man experiences direct contact with God, and with the divine will that guides his destiny. Hence where ancient Israel's unspoilt joy in existence and unsophisticated will to live has the last word materialistic hedonism is found as little as unimaginative satiety. Instead we see bursting forth all the victorious freshness and thrilling power of a religious faith which is able to absorb and to master the manifold tensions of life, with all its heights and depths, because of its firm attachment to the divine Lord who reveals himself in election and covenant-making.

II. *The ascription of relative value to the natural goods compared with the religious goods of God's salvation*

Inevitably a change took place in the ancient Israelite attitude to the goods of life when there was an alteration in the basic religious attitude. This happened as a result of the radical spiritual process usually described as the Canaanization of Israel.[1] The transformation which this involved in the conditions of social and individual life resulted, on the one hand, in the replacing of the old patriarchal simplicity with indulgence and luxury, which also crippled the religious sense of obligation, and on the other in the spread of poverty and distress through wide sections of the nation, who were uprooted from the way of life of the free peasant, and crushed into that of the proletarianized day-labourer and slave for debt—a process which shattered men's naive confidence in divine justice as much as it increased their moral temptations. Moreover, the counter-effect of the moral forces rooted in the covenant relationship was unable to develop, because the impact of the Canaanite conception of God and of their cult practice falsified the covenant concept, and deprived the sovereign will of God of its power.[2] The result is an autonomy of the natural goods of life which ascribes to them absolute value, driving men to unscrupulous greed and acquisitiveness, to the ambitious struggle for power and to political demagogy, with the accompanying collapse of the coherent moral attitude of the covenant people.

Battle against this disruptive process could be joined with success only at the heart of the matter, the departure from the original strict reference of all action to God. Neither revolution, which after the

[1] Cf. vol. I, pp. 45f., 83f., 328f., 463.
[2] Cf. vol. I, pp. 45f.

division of the kingdoms sought again and again to enforce an improvement along external political lines, nor the cultural reaction of the Rechabites, who enjoined as the means of salvation a violent reversal of the disordered outward circumstances of life in a return to primitive simplicity, were able to make any lasting impression, even though political and cultural factors were able to exert considerable influence in the new situation. Hence, right from its first beginnings, the prophetic movement signifies *the call to concentrate on the religious factor*, to focus all activity simply on the reality of God, whose violent and terrifying irruption into history forms the first and most important theme of the prophetic preaching.

In such circumstances, however, the primary task was to bring out with unmistakable clarity *the extremely relative value of all natural goods*. Where the nation threatened to become untrue to its proper definition by selling itself to material enjoyment and honouring in Yahweh merely the giver of the gifts of Nature, the whole danger implicit in earthly prosperity became manifest. In the Elohist's prophetic history-writing outward success bought by treachery to God's cause already appears as grievous guilt; and from accumulation of this springs the sense of a corporate guilt of the nation.[1] Likewise, from Hosea onwards, the keener vision of the prophets sees that with the entry into the rich land of Canaanite civilization sin, like a red thread, runs right through the whole history of the nation,[2] and that the bountiful gifts of Yahweh have only caused arrogance and lack of conscience, violent egoism and forgetfulness of God to run riot. With all the radical reaction of their uncorrupted judgment the prophets therefore proclaim Yahweh's total removal of all earthly goods.

This new attitude toward earthly goods is *not*, however, *to be confused with hostility to civilization*, of the kind cherished by primitive man, *nor with indifference to civilization*, as preached by mysticism. The prophets clearly distinguish themselves from the Rechabites and their rejection of all the goods of civilized life by acknowledging the latter without reserve as gifts of Yahweh.[3] They castigate only the misuse of these gifts in the service of human self-seeking, or as means to the satisfaction of natural instincts in religion. Hence they see the return of God's favour in the age of salvation as going hand in hand with the

---

[1] Cf. vol. I, p. 463.

[2] Hos. 9.10; 10.1; 11.1f.; 12.8f.; Isa. 2.6–8; Jer. 2.7f., 21; 5.7; 7.22ff.; Ezek. 16; 20.27f.

[3] Hos. 2.10f.; 9.2; Isa. 1.19; 28.23ff.; Micah 2.9.

renewed bestowal of these goods.[1] That which separates them from mystics of every observance is the fact that the frustrations of life and the experience of transcendental happiness or ecstasy do not make them indifferent toward earthly goods. For them poverty, for example, is not something indifferent, but a contradiction of Yahweh's beneficent will which calls the pious to do something to remove it. They do not see the natural goods as either harmful in themselves or as unimportant and valueless for the loyal Yahwist; but they certainly do regard them as only of relative value. For they are measured against an absolute value, namely the destiny of Israel to be God's people, among whom God's kingdom is set up and God's will is done. Where earthly goods come into conflict with this supreme value, there they indeed lose all worth of their own, and fall under condemnation.

This point of view was not unknown even in ancient Israel. It was professed wherever the religious demand called for the renunciation of all other values, as, for example, in the holy war. Only the new spiritual situation, however, caused it to be applied so radically that all existence was brought under its exclusive Either-Or. Yet it was also at this point that the whole glory of the good which had been bestowed in election, and which included within itself all other goods, stood out more clearly than ever before. Now, when the goods of Nature and civilization on the one side, and the worth of being God's people on the other, irreconcilably at war, called for decision, it was possible for the pious to understand consciously and clearly not only the absolutely incomparable value but also *the independence and self-sufficiency of the good actualized in fellowship with God.* The higher world of spiritual and moral life in fellowship with God could be seen and grasped as something unique in kind.[2] That this became a reality even for the individual was ensured by the fact that the prophets were able to see the personal dealings of God with his people with a wholly new clarity, and as a result release the individuality of the God-Man relationship.[3] The God who in the word of faith called men to break free from all earthly ties, and to plunge into the adventure of 'mere' faith, that is, of faith dependent simply and solely on his word, and who also revealed his love in order that all the force of human love, 'with all the heart and all the soul', might come to meet him, by so

---

[1] Hos. 2.16f., 23f.; Amos 9.13; Isa. 32.15ff.; Jer. 31.5, 12; Ezek. 36.8ff.
[2] Jer. 9.22f.
[3] Cf. ch. XX, pp. 245ff., and ch. XXI, pp. 280ff. above.

doing also opened up for each individual the possibility of *directing his desire for happiness, detached from the natural goods, to the realization of a fellowship of will with God himself*, a fellowship which, as a liberation of the innermost being for personal action, gave him the experience of a satisfaction far surpassing all earthly enjoyment. The conviction, explicit or implicit, that the ultimate goal of all that it means to be human, and therefore the supreme good, was contained in such a relationship with God, stands behind the whole struggle of the prophets to break through all the material safeguards, behind which men conceal themselves in the presence of God, to a free surrender of the heart to the Lord who knocks so tremendously in judgment and grace. In short, the whole advantage of being the people of God is no longer simply a good to be experienced and realized only by the group as a whole. Now it also opens up to the individual who has become mature enough for personal decision, and who is aware of the fulfilment which it has to offer, an independent value for his own life.

The test and confirmation of this decisive shift in the sense of ethical value lies in *the changed attitude*, which now begins to emerge, *toward the evils of human life*. The predominantly negative assessment of them as expressions of the wrath of God,[1] which was inevitably preoccupied with fending them off in the present and preventing them for the future, was, it is true, not simply eliminated. Instead the truth which it contained was seen in a new perspective, thus opening up the way for a positive assessment. For wherever the ultimate goal of God's dealings with his people, namely the establishment of a true fellowship with them, was clearly recognized, and made the focus of attention, there, too, the whole of history, with its violent variations of fortune, acquired a unified meaning.[2] All its events, above all those which were disastrous and destructive, had to be pressed into the service of the divine purposes. From being isolated expressions of God's anger they now become *means of educating the covenant people*,[3] witnessing, in fact, to the faithfulness of their God,[4] and fitting into a great, universal plan, in accordance with which the Lord of history was accomplishing his salvation.[5] The transposition of this idea from the life of the nation to the life of the individual was not completed by

---

[1] Cf. J. Scharbert, *Der Schmerz im AT* (BBB 8), pp. 102ff., 190ff.
[2] Cf. vol. I, pp. 381–4.
[3] Cf. J. Scharbert, *op. cit.*, pp. 210f.
[4] Amos 4.6–11; Hos. 11.1–7.
[5] Isa. 1.25ff.; 10.5ff.; 14.26; 22.11; 28.16ff., 23ff.; Micah 4.10; Hab. 1.12; Zeph. 3.7; Jer. 4.6ff.; 31.18ff.; Is. 44.24–45.13; 55.8f.

the prophets, but their own lives and sufferings must have given it a most powerful stimulus. The manner in which they themselves bore the evils of their own life—misunderstanding, isolation, threats, danger of death, sickness, and imprisonment—and made them into means for their own purification,[1] or that of the service entrusted to them,[2] had nothing in common with the defensive attitude of the natural man toward suffering, but revealed a victorious power which did not capitulate even in face of the evils of individual life, but was able to incorporate them into God's plan of salvation.

Also leading in the same direction was the recognition, given increasingly clear-cut formulation, that it was precisely *the deprived and wretched* of the nation, the *ᶜaniyyim*, who were the objects of especial divine compassion, indeed *the real kernel of the people of Yahweh*, for whose sake his providential government takes special steps.[3] Here outward misfortune is so little seen any more as the evil decreed by God's anger that those who are stricken by it are rather the objects of Yahweh's especial good pleasure, and may consider themselves the bearers of the nation's future.

This positive evaluation of suffering was given its most profound rationale where its real meaning was revealed as *vicarious endurance on behalf of others*.[4] In the Servant of God as portrayed in the Servant Songs, Israel was shown a life robbed of all external goods, which was yet a life well pleasing to God because in it God's counsel of salvation was fulfilled. And that which the Servant elected by God was the first to achieve in a unique way for the redemption of his people now lifts the sufferings of all the pious on to another plane. Not only in the association of the Servant of God with faithful Israel, which had already been made at an early stage,[5] but also in a Psalm such as 22, the closing section of which brings the consummation of God's sovereignty into direct relation with the sufferings of the righteous, we can see that the transvaluation of the natural goods of life which had here been achieved, not indeed in the great majority, but in certain circles of the disciples of the prophets, was also guiding the life of the individual along new paths. Innocent suffering as a God-

---

[1] Isa. 8.11ff.; Jer. 15.18ff.; 17.9ff.

[2] Hos. 1.2ff.; Isa. 8.16ff.; 20.1ff.; Jer. 16.1ff., 5ff.; 36.1ff.; 37.15ff.; 40.4ff.; Ezek. 24.15ff.

[3] Amos 8.4; Isa. 3.14f.; 10.2; 11.4; 14.32; 29.19; Micah 2.8f.; 3.3; Jer. 22.16; Zeph. 2.3; Ezek. 16.49; Zech. 7.10.

[4] Cf. J. Scharbert, *op. cit.*, pp. 207, 212f.

[5] Isa. 49.3; 50.10.

ordained service, a concept of which we were made aware in our examination of the moral norms, therefore leads, in fact, from natural happiness to the blessedness of fellowship with God as the supreme good. Here that which was already implicit in the opposition between the natural goods and life in God is expressed in absolutely unmistakable terms, namely that the moral norm, as the requirement of the sovereign divine will, is internally consonant with the moral good, the harmony between God and Man, and thus leads to the heights of pure morality.

That the prophetic attitude to the evils of life does not, nevertheless, imply a lasting devaluation of natural goods, or a spiritualization of ordinary living, is shown by the terminology in which *natural and spiritual goods can be combined in a great unity*. One of these terms is *šālōm*, 'well-being', 'peace', which as early as Num. 6.26 is used in the widest sense to include every divine blessing, and which now combines the supreme good of fellowship with God with the blessings of earthly life (Isa. 9.5f.; Jer. 29.11; 33.9; Isa. 48.18; 53.8). The fact that this value can sum up the whole content of the salvation of the messianic age shows the breadth of its conceptual range. The other is *yeša'* (alternatively *yᵉšū'ā* or *tᵉšū'ā*), 'help', 'redemption', 'salvation', which in the crisis of the Exile came to be a summary term for God's redemption and blessing as a whole (Isa. 45.8, 17; 46.13; 49.6, 8; 51.6, 8). Here the universal significance of the divine salvation is also included, inasmuch as the *yᵉšū'ā* is to reach to the ends of the earth. This provides the correlate to the universality of the moral norms, in which the unity of moral obligation is so clearly expressed in the prophetic writings.

A distinctive mediating position between the prophetic and the early Israelite evaluation of the goods of life is that adopted by *the Priestly world-view*. This is akin to the prophetic preaching in the concentrated force with which it opposes the daemonism which deifies the world with commitment to the God of election, and teaches men to see in the privileged position of the covenant people the blessing which far surpasses all earthly gifts, and for the preservation of which all else can be surrendered.[1] At the same time the fact that both the Deuteronomic and the Priestly Law teaching are primarily concerned with ordering the life of a nation which is in the state of enjoying the covenant favour—a concern characteristically different from that of

---

[1] Cf. pp. 334ff. above, and 371ff. below.

the prophets, whose vision of the God who comes in judgment and new creation led them to surrender the old conception of the covenant people—results in an evaluation of earthly goods which is closer to that of early Israel. It is true that in the light of the threat of judgment upon nation and state, now accepted in all its force, their merely relative value is more clearly seen, and more emphatically stressed, than in the period of unbroken national power. Nevertheless this danger remains, more on the periphery, as the limiting situation to be avoided if possible. The goods of this life and the treasures of religion do not stand to one another in a relation of mutual exclusiveness; instead they are combined in that unity of life which was still so vividly felt in ancient Israel, and at the end of the nation's history was sought for with such yearning. In fact, the power and goodness of the covenant God, and the riches of his eternal institution, are to be experienced as the reality governing all life.[1] Hence the goods that sustain and enrich life must once again be linked as closely as possible with the assurance of God by being understood as the gifts of his blessing, and witnesses to a covenant relationship mighty in operation. The Deuteronomic law-teaching succeeds in expressing this directly and vividly by the use of two terms. First, in naḥªlā, 'inheritance', it creates a symbolic word for the inseparable, because God-willed, mutual belonging of land and people;[2] secondly, in its stress on bᵉrākā, 'blessing', familiar from earlier usage,[3] it establishes a comprehensive term for all the precious things of life destined for the people of God united in the covenant, a term which is characteristically different from the inclusive concepts of the prophets mentioned earlier. This makes it impossible for that transmutation of values to occur, as a result of which evils do not call God's nearness in question, but rather strengthen it; instead, even if still understood as means of education for recalling the erring, they inevitably become an obstacle to the full enjoyment of the covenant favour, and thus something to be avoided wherever possible. This in turn prevents the universal significance of the proffered salvation from emerging clearly, so that it either remains concealed altogether, as in the Deuteronomist, or expresses itself, as in P, in the view of Israel as the mediator of blessing to the nations.

---

[1] Cf. vol. I, pp. 52ff.
[2] Deut. 4.21, 38; 12.9; 15.4; 19.10; 20.16; 21.23; 24.4; 25.19; 26.1.
[3] Cf. G. von Rad, *Das Gottesvolk im Deuteronomium*, 1929, pp. 6f.

III. *The unresolved tension between the natural goods*
and the religious good of salvation

(*a*) The attitude toward moral goods championed by the prophets
was strongly echoed in the post-exilic community, where, often for
the first time, it was properly exploited for the benefit of the life of the
individual believer. In a situation where the individual was struggling
for certainty about what the goal of his conduct should be, without
having the life and prosperity of his nation to guarantee that his
efforts were being successful, and where at the same time the external
pressures which burdened the life of the community made a return to
a naive interrelation of blessing and assurance of God impossible, men
readily accepted the prophetic proclamation of fellowship with God
as the supreme good, embracing all others. It deepened conduct
which adhered to the standard of the Law into an experience of the
personal will of God as a force that renewed life, and made it happy.
Here *the relativization of earthly goods* could find expression in the use of
ᶜaniyyim, 'poor' or 'wretched', as a title of honour for the pious, interpreted by the parallel term *ᶜenāwim*, 'meek', meaning those who
persevere in a right attitude of humility toward God as well as toward
men, and who are therefore assured of the divine good pleasure and
salvation.[1] In the assessment of the afflictions which tormented the
pious, however, the idea of *suffering as purification and education* acquired
undreamt-of force. It is in this very period that moving testimonies to
willingness and patience under suffering[2] confirm that undisturbed
fellowship of heart with God was here vividly understood to be
superior to all the other goods of life, and proved by experience to be
genuine. In fact, there was not a complete lack of understanding even
of *the active value* for the whole community *of innocent suffering*, though,
naturally enough, it did not determine a wide range of corporate
piety. Nevertheless, the passages mentioned earlier,[3] to which the
section about the shepherds in Zech. 11–13 should be added, show

---

[1] Cf. A. Rahlfs, "*ᶜani* und *ᶜanāw* in den Psalmen', 1892; G. Marschall, *Die
"Gottlosen" des ersten Psalmbuches*, 1929. Relevant passages include Isa. 41.17; 49.13;
61.1; Pss. 22.27; 69.33; 74.19; 86.1f.; 132.15f.; 146.7f., etc. E. Sachsse ("*ᶜani* als
Ehrenbezeichnung in inschriftlicher Beleuchtung', *Sellin-Festschrift*, 1927, pp. 105ff.)
calls attention to the possibility that this point of view may have had some influence
beyond the borders of Israel.

[2] Pss. 32.8f.; 66.9–12; Lam. 3.27ff.; Job 5.17; 8.20f.; 33.19–28; 36.15, 18–21;
Prov. 3.12; Ecclus 2.5; 4.17–19; 18.13f.; Ps. Sol. 10.1; 13.7ff.; Wisd. 12.2, 20ff.

[3] Cf. pp. 357f. above.

that the way of vicarious suffering was recognized by many as the one indicated for them by God, and was valued as a contribution to the messianic consummation. Thus the paradox that the highest good was to be found in the stripping away of all earthly goods became a living reality, a paradox which could bring consolation when the fate of the nation was considered, and furthermore was a fact of experience in the life of the individual.

But even where men could not rise to this extreme transformation of the popular striving after happiness, the conviction nevertheless made headway among increasing numbers that a higher life, which could not be destroyed by adverse outward fortune, formed the most precious possession of the pious. Quite early the word *ḥayyīm*, 'life', was frequently used in the sense of 'good fortune';[1] now the content of happiness, as something beyond mere physical existence and its goods, was sought in the inner satisfaction of the heart by a fullness of life which flowed from fellowship with God.[2] Thus the wisdom teachers know of a life bestowed by Wisdom, in which the godless cannot share; for the value of this life no earthly good can ever be a substitute,[3] and it gives courage to the pious even in death.[4] Such a life has as its most precious content the good pleasure of God, and peace of conscience,[5] and it can be acquired and kept amid even the greatest disasters of earthly existence. The poem of Job gives overwhelming expression to this conquest of a materialistically conditioned ideal of life by surrender to the will of the Creator for fellowship with his creature.[6]

The awareness of this kind of higher content in life also finds expression in the prayer life of the Jewish congregation,[7] where again and again the longing for God himself, and for his favour, breaks through all outward distresses. This good of Man's fellowship with God has been given pregnant voice in the phrase 'to see God's face', words which can apply not only to community worship, shared with

---

[1] W. von Baudissin, 'Atl. *ḥayyīm* "Leben" in der Bedeutung für "Glück" ', *Sachau-Festschrift*, 1915, pp. 143ff.

[2] E. Schmitt also draws attention to this higher life in his thorough examination, *Leben in den Weisheitsbüchern Job, Sprüche, und Jesus Sirach*, 1954, pp. 181ff.

[3] Prov. 8.35f.; 10.2, 11; 11.4; 13.12, 14; 14.27.

[4] Prov. 11.4, 7; 14.32.

[5] Prov. 3.21–27; 8.35; 10.9, 29; 11.3–8, 27; 12.2; 13.6; 14.22; 18.10; 28.1.

[6] Cf. ch. XXIII, §6, pp. 489ff. below.

[7] Cf. pp. 499f. below.

all the faithful,[1] but also to the individual's search for God.[2] In seeing the face of God men experience the highest good fortune, from which flow unshakable joy, deep security, and inward satisfaction. In the dark valley, in the challenge posed by the good fortune of the godless, in chastisement at God's hand, these may well be overshadowed; but again and again they break through. Indeed, the triumphant assurance of this all-surpassing value not only proves itself the source of peace and joy in every struggle, and an inexhaustible fount of happiness,[3] it also convinces those who are filled with it of *the indestructibility of the possession given to them*, even in face of the bound set to all earthly things by death. The life which is known to the singer of Ps. 16 is not merely the pleasant lot which has fallen to him in his earthly pilgrimage, and which surpasses all purely terrestrial goods; it reaches its climax only in everlasting joy before the face of God.[4] Likewise the poet of the seventy-third Psalm by divine illumination experiences the self-disclosure of the inconceivable greatness of God as a communication of supraterrestrial life, which removes from the man who is favoured with it even the horror of death. Because the eternal God is his portion, not even the glory of heaven, much less any earthly good, can turn his gaze away from this supreme fullness of life. The wisdom teacher of Ps. 49 also takes refuge from the transitoriness of earthly happiness in the permanence of fellowship with God. The *hope of resurrection*, as this was developed later, however, shifts the true good into a world beyond, and knows of a transcendent life on a new plane of existence, which is wholly steeped in God's light,[5] and is comparable to the life of the angels.[6] The terms 'glory', 'life', and 'light', which are frequently used to sum up this transcendent good of salvation, show that we are here concerned with the essential content of all blessedness, and therefore with something which cannot be further defined. And the fact that these concepts are predominantly employed in a universally oriented salvation-hope means that here the world-embracing scope of the prophetic idea of salvation lives on.[7]

[1] Pss. 27.4; 42.3; 63.3; 84.3.
[2] Pss. 11.7; 17.15; Isa. 38.11; Job 33.26. On this point cf. pp. 35ff. above, and for the literature p. 35, n. 5.
[3] Pss. 16.5; 17.15; 63.4.
[4] Ps. 16.11; cf. ch. XXIV, p. 524 below.
[5] Dan. 12.3; I Enoch 58.3; 108.11–14; II Enoch 66.7; Wisd. 3.7; Ps. Sol. 3.12: cf. P. Volz, *Die Eschatologie der jüdischen Gemeinde*, 1934, pp. 362ff.; H. Bietenhard, *Die himmlische Welt in Urchristentum und Spätjudentum*, 1951, pp. 180ff.
[6] I Enoch 51.4f.; 104.4, 6; Wisd. 5.5; Apoc. Bar. 51.10, 12.
[7] Cf. P. Volz, *op. cit.*, pp. 358f.

(*b*) Nevertheless, the fact cannot be ignored that *the line we have traced is far from the only one*, or even the most pronounced, within the community of the Law. It is constantly accompanied by that other line, which starts from *the Priestly interpretation of the covenant relationship*, and which is characterized by the organic synthesis of earthly blessing and the supreme gift of salvation. This line, too, was of decisive help to the community in its whole ethical attitude in the days when it was slowly establishing itself. For the assurance that possession of the land and all other basic necessities of life were included in the new covenant favour gave unshakeable backing to that astonishingly tough self-assertion, even in desperate situations, by which the community won the right to live in the ancient homeland. And the fact that the blessing was tied to the fellowship of the 'brethren' meant that it was precisely the vision of the hoped-for good which brought out the readiness of the members of the community to help each other, and so contributed to the overcoming of individual egoism. This set up a strong barrier to any mood of escapism from the world, any solitary religion revelling in mystic intimacy with God, any exaggeration of religious individuality into individualism. A community controlled in this way was protected from disintegrating into a world-renouncing sect; it was kept stable by its confession of the God who utters his Yea to the creaturely existence of his elect, and honours it with his promises.

Yet there was a threat to ethical clarity in thought and action in the fact that it proved impossible to unite in fruitful tension the opposite poles in this system of moulding the will. Instead, because each of them worked in one-sided isolation, the result was a series of involuted and stunted ethical developments, which obscured the ethical goal. This applies especially to the weakening, or even total exclusion, of the prophetic pole. The ever more thoroughgoing orientation of conduct in accordance with the Law easily led to the introduction of an *impersonal factor* into that walking with God which was recognized as the noblest good; and this factor did not allow men to open themselves freely to God's operation. Just as expressions of love for God were directed more and more toward mediators, such as God's Name, salvation, or Law,[1] so, in men's zeal for the Law, the Law itself as an objective entity became much more directly the highest good than the giver of the Law, who was thought of as utterly transcendent. *Life with God is now life under the Law*, and the more this

[1] Cf. ch. XXI, pp. 310f. above.

conception was carried out to the letter and down to the last detail, the more did all interest centre on Man's conduct, driving the personal self-communication of God into the background. The Law now acquires its highest value as that which makes right human conduct possible, as a source of supreme wisdom, and as a means to the mastery of life—the qualities for which it is praised in Ps. 119, for example, and in the later wisdom writings.

This weakening of the fellowship with God proclaimed by the prophets resulted in an ideal of human life which was at first only unconscious, and outwardly barely noticeable; but it was bound to have disastrous effects once men accepted *the equation of the eternal kingdom of God with the empirical community*.[1] In such circumstances it could not be long before the natural conditions necessary to the community's existence, and even more the outward privileges befitting her worth, were once more given heightened value as goals of inward behaviour. All the earthly goods which bring respect and influence to a human community now sprang back with full force into men's mental landscape as elements indispensable to any condition pleasing to God, and therefore approved by him. Given such a spiritual attitude, both the nationalist-particularist predictions of the future, with their visions of power, riches and prosperity for the perfected Zion community, and the outlook of the wisdom teaching, with its ideal of a life of affluence and security, embellished with every kind of earthly joy, and well protected from any danger that might threaten, could be accepted and appropriated as an apposite description of the good fortune due to the pious. This was all the more so, when a short-winded doctrine of retribution was no longer able to conceive of a life with God which lacked confirmation of the divine good pleasure in the form of the visible and tangible goods of life, and indeed felt the deprivation of them as impugning the justice of God. In such a context the inclusion of the goods of moral action in the concept of life had a totally this-worldly meaning.[2] Nor was the gradual spread of belief in resurrection able to effect any change in principle; for the other world was conceived simply in the forms of this, only with a heightening of its happiness,[3] and even the new life of the pious comes to mean no more than an especially long duration

[1] Cf. pp. 342ff. above.

[2] Prov. 4.13, 22; 7.2; 9.6; 12.28, etc.; Ecclus 31.14f.; Tobit 4.10; 12.9f.; 14.10f.; Bar. 3.14.

[3] Ps. Sol. 9.5; 14.10; I Enoch 62.14–16; cf. vol. I, pp. 488ff., and Volz, *op. cit.*, pp. 387ff.

for their earthly sojourn.[1] So, too, the specifically national goods of freedom and power, a large population and a glorious Jerusalem with its Temple, bulk very large.[2] Against this line of thought, working from the premiss of a religious community, the scepticism of Koheleth, who argued from an individualist standpoint, was impotent.

Thus the burdening of piety with inferior elements also had its effect in the matter of the goods of moral conduct, and ensured that no proper comprehension of the dominant goal of all ethical action was ever attained. The conception of the divine covenant as a relationship of works overlaid the understanding of it as a relation of grace, and restricted its eternal validity to the granting of national and cultic goods in earthly conditions. Hence those lines of thought which pointed to a universal, other-worldly good were never strongly developed, and only maintained themselves at all with much difficulty alongside others as a part of the traditional stock of concepts. The logical conclusion of this process could only be their complete atrophy within a system fenced in on every side, and ossified, unless by the irruption of a new reality of God the substance of true fellowship with God were once more to be made manifest in the midst of earthly conditions.

3. THE MOTIVES OF MORAL CONDUCT

I. *Natural motives within the divine covenant*

Human conduct is always and everywhere determined by the conflict between Ought and Is, between absolute obligation on the one hand and the will to preserve life and to shape it in an egoistic way on the other. Even if the Ought is felt with very varying force, it is always there, and provides motives for action which derive from a higher dimension, existing independently of the life of the individual. Whether this Ought is experienced by primitive Man in the form of terror of the taboo or among civilized peoples is thought of as based on the will of a god; whether it extends to certain basic obligations only or weaves the whole of life into a system of requirements; all this makes no difference whatever to the fact of its existence or to its qualitative distinction from all other stimuli of the will. Its significance, however, lies in this, that by an unconditional obligation it makes Man conscious of the limitation of his own will, and thus of the

---

[1] I Enoch 5.9; 10.17; 25.6; Jub. 23.27–29; Aboth II.7.
[2] Cf. Volz, *op. cit.*, pp. 368ff.

necessity of decision and responsibility, whereby his existence as a personal 'I' is established. For the motivation of moral conduct, therefore, the most important question is that of the relation in which this unconditional Ought stands to the natural impulses of his will, and whether, and along what lines, it evokes a moral action.

There is no reason to expect that in Israel, any more than in any other people, *the natural social instinct* will not stimulate men to moral action; and that it did, in fact, do so is illustrated in many ways by early tradition. That which furthers the prosperity of the family, or of its larger context, the clan, that which is of service to the tribe and the tribal league, is felt as an impulse to action to which the egoistic interests of the individual must take second place.[1] In friendship, the moral motive shifts from the tie of heredity to freely established obligation, and exempts this even from those rules of intercourse established by contract or custom, which obtain beyond the limits of the nation, and by which exchange and mutual help between neighbouring peoples are made possible.[2] In addition to rational expediency a general feeling for humanity may also be at work here, such as awakes in a highly developed international culture, and finds expression in the practical teaching of the wise, who are, of course, also the most-travelled people.[3]

However strong the stimulus of these motivations of moral action may have been, they are by no means far-reaching enough to bring all the circumstances of life within a system of morality. In large areas of conduct natural egoism remains the dominant motive;[4] elsewhere it is able to overpower moral motives which are accepted in other contexts. Thus the bond between the tribes is constantly being broken by the egoism of the individual tribe,[5] and the solidarity of the tribe may be made use of to protect the criminal who would otherwise be held in execration.[6] Blood revenge more than once runs counter to the higher interests of the national community, and degenerates into cruel brutality against which no protection is possible.[7] On the other side, the motives of the natural social instinct easily fall under the

---

[1] Cf. pp. 317f. above.
[2] Cf. pp. 318f. above.
[3] Cf. H. Gressmann, *Israels Spruchweisheit im Zusammenhang der Weltliteratur*, 1925; W. Baumgartner, *Israelitische und altorientalische Weisheit*, 1933.
[4] Cf. pp. 322ff. above.
[5] Judg. 8.1ff.; 12.1ff.; 18.16ff.
[6] Judg. 20.12f.
[7] II Sam. 3.27 and I Kings 2.5; II Sam. 4.2ff. (?); 21.4ff.

control of prudential expediency, for which even personal relations become means to the attainment of practical ends. This happens especially where the established forms of social organization, such as the monarchy, bureaucracy, priesthood, or prophetic guild, put the dignity and prosperity of their own group above the interests of the nation.[1]

Into this world of rational motivations for moral conduct, however, the institution of the divine covenant on Sinai, and also, though not in a way which we can any longer clearly understand, the religiously controlled migration of the Hebrew tribes associated with the name of Abraham, introduced in principle that *absolute Ought* which, *as the will of the God of election*, laid claim to regulate the whole of life. On the one hand this meant *a powerful reinforcement of the natural motives of conduct*, inasmuch as Yahweh, as protector of the life both of the nation and the individual, removed a man's natural obligation toward his neighbour from the sphere of human discretion, and incorporated it into the basic ordinances of his covenant, vested with unconditional authority. Just as the natural cohesion of the tribes acquired indestructible solidity only through the summons to common sacrifice under Yahweh's banner, so the categorical command of God released a stimulus of the will which resulted in a new conscientiousness in the conduct of members both of the family and of the nation toward one another. For responsibility to the absolute will of God attached immense seriousness to men's duties toward their neighbours, and this seriousness made itself felt not only in a widening and deepening of the range of these duties, but also in their formulation and clear compilation.[2] On the other hand, the natural motives were subjected to a *healthy restriction* of their validity. It was quite possible for the religious demand to clash with them, and when it did, then it alone was decisive. Where popular morality gave free rein to blood revenge, or to vindictive retribution against one's enemies, it is awareness of responsibility before God, focused on his will to redeem, which leads to the overcoming of these natural impulses.[3] Thus the natural egoism of family and nation is broken on this authority which drives men forward to true moral conduct,[4] and awakens a new striving for ever more complete regulation of life along the basic lines of

[1] Cf. vol. I, pp. 328ff., 434f., 439f., 449ff.
[2] Cf. vol. I, pp. 77ff.; also pp. 319ff. above.
[3] Cf. pp. 321ff. above.
[4] Cf. also II Sam. 21; Ex. 32.27ff.

the God-willed community. It is this attitude of the pious which the Old Testament describes as the 'fear of God'.[1]

Two shortcomings are generally held responsible for the fact that the fear of God achieved a dominating position among the moral motives of ancient Israel. The first is that it made conduct more emphatically 'a conscious striving for one's own advantage',[2] with the consequent intrusion of eudaemonism into the moral decision; the second, that the will of God, as an alien coercive principle, made action in moral freedom impossible. This would, however, only be correct if the fear of God implied an enforced subjection to a despotic will, which stood in no inward relationship with the nation, but only moved those dependent upon it by the prospect of reward or punishment. But this, in the light of what has already been said about the fear of God, and the valuation of natural goods,[3] is a complete distortion of the facts. Before the divine demand comes the divine gift, by which God gives himself to his people to be their own God, and opens to them access to his own life. The sense of being called to be the people of God makes the inward association with God, consciously understood as such, the highest good, and places it above all calculation of reward or punishment, with the result that the affirmation of absolute obligation becomes a response on the part of Man to the prevenient goodness of his God. Only this can lead to that enthusiastic championing of Yahweh's unqualified claim to sovereignty against friend and foe, and without reference to egoistic good or bad fortune, which is precisely the attitude so vividly attested in the earliest poetry.

At the same time this is not to deny that God's reward and punishment are spoken of as related to men's behaviour. The early Israelite period, of course, knows nothing of the sort of meticulous calculation of divine retribution in the life of the individual which becomes visible in Judaism; but the occasional mentions of God's blessing as bound up with right conduct[4] are thoroughly unreflective in character, nothing other than vivid expressions of the assurance of God's personal dealing in which he allows the individual to experience him as the loyal and kindly One. Furthermore, the connection of the laws with threats and promises corresponds, in so far as it goes back to the

---

[1] Cf. ch. XXI, pp. 271ff. above.
[2] H. Schultz, op. cit., pp. 15, 18.
[3] Cf. ch. XXI, pp. 268ff., and pp. 350ff. above.
[4] Gen. 26.5; Ex. 15.25, 26b; 19.5, 8.

early period,[1] to the conviction that seed and harvest are co-ordinated in accordance with God's will in the moral life as well, and that the Lawgiver stands surety for the fruitfulness of conduct in keeping with his rules.[2] That, where the personal character of the God-Man relationship succumbed to a contractual interpretation, a calculating attitude and a desire for reward could replace conduct which sprang from the experience of fellowship with God, is obvious, and something of which the old story-tellers were already keenly aware.[3] But to say that this describes the average level of conduct in Israel is to be blind to the generally high level of her assurance of God.

The answer to the second complaint against the religious motive in the morality of Israel's early period is implicit in what has already been said. It is precisely the knowledge of what God is to his people, and what he does for them, which prevents the growth of a blind and forced obedience, and affords the possibility of free decision. Again it is difficult to demonstrate in detail in which spheres this possibility was realized, and so to make clear where there was any falling short.[4] Nevertheless it can hardly be disputed that the whole nature of God's self-communication was pressing in this direction, and, what is more, was understood to be doing so. The very form of the divine covenant created especially favourable conditions not only for the understanding of God's prevenient grace but also for the insight that right conduct toward one's neighbour was inseparable from the receiving of this grace. As a member of the covenant people each citizen was given an incontestable dignity; and therefore the pressure to treat him as a person, and not as an impersonal means to an end, was not some new and incomprehensible addition to the gift of election, but was manifestly a logical consequence already implicit in the gift itself, and as such identical with the giving and demanding will of God. The fact that the unreflective spontaneity of the early period meant that these connections, implicit in the actual situation, were not conceptually formulated in no way detracts from their reality.

Even if the fear of God cannot be rated the compulsion of an alien law in its role as a stimulus to moral conduct, yet such an evaluation would apply more readily to its equally powerful influence in the

[1] Ex. 20.5–7, 12; Josh. 24.19f.; cf. vol. I, p. 457, nn. 1–3.
[2] Cf. vol. I, p. 242, and the similar state of affairs as regards Jesus' use of the categories of reward and punishment.
[3] Gen. 28.20ff.
[4] On this point cf. p. 326 above.

sphere of cultic duties. Even though in ancient times the cult as the natural means of expression of religious faith and of the religious feeling of the community was felt to be a direct necessity in a way quite foreign to the man of today, yet the meaning of any particular ordinance is frequently no longer clear,[1] and it is therefore all the more likely, at the point where it comes into conflict with the moral commandment, to act as an alien coercive principle.[2] Here, however, we have to take into account the force of the conception of God as personal, as a result of which even the morally indifferent sacral sphere is subordinated to the great concept of personal service. Certainly the will of God may not be 'reasonable' and rationally explicable, but neither is it felt to be a tyranny of chance caprice.[3]

It must also, of course, be remembered that the degree to which the people were sensitive to the impact of the presence and intervention of the divine sovereign was not the same at all periods, nor was its effect the same on all sections of the nation. At the same time the religious influences of the surrounding culture were continually weakening and disrupting the specifically Israelite assurance of God. Hence even in the early period other tendencies were active alongside those controlled by the divine covenant and its operations, even if they were not always the dominant ones.

Matters changed when, with the overvaluation of the cultic side of religion in the period of the monarchy, there was a danger that the close connection between worship and morality would be lost, and when the degradation of the concept of God to the naturalistic level under Canaanite influence made the cultus seem the proper way of access to God, and to a share in his vital power. The weakening of the personal element in the concept of God in favour of the veneration of the impersonal force of Nature debased the unconditional Ought into an act of expediency, with the help of which men hoped to enlist the divine power in their own service; and this separation of the giver from the gift made the eudaemonistic motive predominant. Moreover, at the same time men were delivered up to the mystery of the life of Nature, which by its caprice in giving or withholding left them in the dark about its real direction, and therefore drove them into

---

[1] Cf., e.g., the purification rites and food laws.

[2] As in the cases of the ban, or the unbreakable nature of a vow, even where the life of a human being is endangered: Judg. 11.30ff.; I Sam. 14.24, 38ff. For the quasi-material contagious and destructive power of the holy cf. Num. 16.10ff., 35; 17.1ff.; I Sam. 21.5f.

[3] Cf. vol. I, pp. 260f., 272ff.

slavish subjection to an alien norm. The result was that they lost both the explanation of the inner meaning of the divine claim in the act of the covenant God, and also the indissoluble link between cultic and moral action in the fact that both were exercises of free decision in keeping with the nature of the covenant.

II. *The re-establishment of theonomy*

Because it was in the midst of an overwhelming experience of the numinous terribleness and incomparable cosmic exaltation of the God of Israel that men recovered the definition of the picture of God in personal terms, the consequence was that in the preaching of the prophets the unconditional Ought which radiated from the will of God into human life was also lit by the gleam of the fire of judgment. This divine encounter, at whose demand for decision each individual must pause, could not be evaded by impersonal works, nor shut out of ordinary life by transferring it to the magico-sacral sphere, where it could be made subservient to the will of men. All these pious camouflages of the divine reality are here exposed as enmity toward God, and judged. The advent of the universal Lord to sit in judgment on his people forces men to become aware of the unconditional nature of their obligation toward him in the most radical way.

We need at this point do no more than remind ourselves by referring to previous discussion[1] how this supremely moral motivation was purified of all the elements with which a magico-mystical religiosity had obscured and disfigured it, and how from this *a new recognition of the absolute majesty of the moral demand* took its rise. Wherever men acted from a sense of responsibility toward the holy God as proclaimed by the prophets, the cultus as a sacrificial procedure[2] became intrinsically unviable, and could take its place alongside moral conduct only as a testimony of faith in God's promise, of worshipful obeisance in the face of his majesty, and of loyalty toward his community.

It is an important development that *fresh exposition and clarification* of the central motive of the fear of God, by applying it to the various relationships of personal life, now vividly grasped in all their complexity, establishes more clearly and firmly that moral conduct is the commitment of one's own person. The free act of obedience is now

[1] Cf. vol. I, pp. 360ff., and pp. 326ff. above.
[2] Cf. vol. I, p. 100, n. 2.

seen as the practice of love, of the knowledge of God, of humility, of faith, of gratitude—in short as the fruit of a release of all the forces that form the personality;[1] and as such it stands in conscious opposition to all impersonal works, all external legalist conduct, all attempts to reduce life to the fulfilment of the requirements of the law, understood in their literal sense.

It is well known how strong was the influence of this inner development of religious motivation on the understanding of the law, causing it to be seen as an exemplary witness to the will of God, and a multiple exposition of his basically unified commandment.[2] *The Deuteronomic teaching of the Law* is skilled in bringing home to its hearers by pastoral exhortation this turning of the heart to God in humility and love, gratitude and trust,[3] and in making it fruitful for their understanding of the keeping of the law as a new attitude of the will. Again, by the derivation of the whole law from the command to love, the basic demand of the divine will for the surrender of the whole person to the divine Thou was brought within the comprehension of the simplest citizen. In this way even the commandment whose meaning is not immediately transparent—apart from the fact that it comes from the sovereign will of God, and is therefore valid as such—can still touch heart and conscience, because it derives from the counsel of the love of God, who has ordered all things for the sake of his people's salvation, and who accepts no keeping of the commandment just for the commandment's sake, desiring rather to see in each fulfilment of the law the living effect of a single-minded profession of love for God.

Thus *the moral demands*, too, are emphatically included in the prevenient act of God's love, inasmuch as they are seen to be *the obvious logical consequence of his beneficent will revealed in the covenant-making*. Just as he has made the whole nation to be his inheritance, *naḥⁱlā*, so the land, the means by which he wills to bestow the gift of his blessing, also is his heritage. As such it is removed from the grasp of egoistic avarice, and every Israelite as a member of the community has an equal title to it. In this order of equality the citizens may not look upon each other as anything but brothers, for whom there can be no question of depriving any individual of his rights, and who are also bound by their solidarity to the weak, the stranger, the widow, and

---

[1] Cf. vol. I, pp. 357f.
[2] Cf. vol. I, pp. 92ff.
[3] Deut. 6.10ff.; 7.7; 8.2f., 12ff., 17f.; 9.4ff.; 10.21; —6.5; 10.12; 11.13; 13.4; 30.6; —5.6, 10; 7.6ff.; 8.5ff.; 11.1ff.; 26; —1.23; 7.17ff.; 8.3; 9.23.

the orphan, who likewise share in God's blessing. In this way a state of affairs which already effectively obtained in the early period is now expressed clearly, in concepts which everyone can understand, and the stimulus to the will afforded by the natural cohesion of the nation is elevated into the sphere of religious responsibility.

The priestly law-teaching in the Holiness Code links submission to the unconditional will of God with conduct toward one's neighbour, along more markedly individualist lines, by teaching men to understand the faultless regulation of life in accordance with God's commandment as a *forming of human nature after the pattern of the divine*. The holy God wills not only to separate his elect out of the world for his service by sanctifying them—separation being the normal meaning of holiness, when predicated of Man—but also to see the immaculate purity of his own nature, that which separates him from the sinful impurity of human living, reflected in a holy people.[1] This signifies an *advance from a fellowship of will with God to a fellowship of nature*, thus transposing the ultimate motive of moral action into the desire to be modelled on the pattern of the divine, the only way in which Man can be fully incorporated into the divine world. This undoubtedly removes the last possibility of a conflict between the human and the divine will, and guarantees the unity and freedom of moral conduct. It is true that such a concentration on the unchangeable perfection of the divine nature is not so explicitly personal in character as the prophetic and Deuteronomic meditation on the divine act of love in election, even though the Priestly law-teacher is thinking not of a timeless idea but of that perfection of nature revealed by God's manifestation of himself in history. But because Yahweh's purpose of sanctification is understood as a moulding of man in accordance with his own image, and is therefore bound up as closely as can be with his purpose in creation, this divine Ought places the individual, independently of the existence of his people, under an absolute obligation, and by an affinity of nature with God teaches him the infinite value of life.

In this vision of God as simultaneously Creator and Redeemer there is a suggestion of *a universalist motif*, which is prevented from having its full effect only by the segregation of the community from the world around by the Law. In the case of the prophetic preaching, however, the close connection between the categorical divine imperative and the universal relevance of this Ought is unmistakable.

[1] Lev. 19.3, 11ff., 15ff.; cf. vol. I, pp. 277f.

In fact, the transcendent glory of God and his world-controlling power cannot be thought of in separation from the Lord of Israel and of the nations, who draws near to judgment; and it is the former aspect which supplies the resultant stimulus to the will with the confidence that, in carrying out its concrete task in a limited situation, it is realizing a universally valid law, and co-operating in the building of a world-wide kingdom. This gives morality, along with freedom of decision and liberation from purely immanent ends, a universal validity, rooted not in an abstraction which hardly touches the question of concrete duty, but in the reality of a higher will, which takes in all the individual instances of moral obligation, and combines them into a unity.

III. *The corruption of moral motivation by materialism and disunity*

Once the soil of the nation's soul had been broken up by the ploughing of the Exile the seed sown by the prophets and the teachers of the law found more chance to 'take root downward, and bear fruit upward' than had been possible in the chauvinism of the eighth and seventh centuries; and the leaders in the restoration of the Jerusalem community based their actions decisively on the unconditional Ought of the divine will. Moreover, the hard lot of the community, their struggle against enemies within and without, forced them to keep on renewing their efforts for clarity in moral decisions. How strongly in this process fear of God and obedience to the Law became linked with one another has already been described.[1] The prophetic regulation of all action by the unconditional demand of God, which had to be affirmed in personal commitment, combined with the practical requirements of the situation as a whole to focus the moral will on the Law as the direct proclamation of the will of God. The more decisively, however, the reconstruction of the Temple community was based on the Law, and the more strongly men's faith was controlled by the transcendent majesty of the Holy One, thus causing them to look for media of his presence, the higher was the value set upon the Law bound to become, with a resultant *identification of loyalty to its decrees with loyalty toward God.* Faithfulness to the Law now becomes the key motive of God-centred conduct; love for God consists in love for the Law;[2] trust in the Law appears

---

[1] Cf. pp. 344ff., and ch. XXI, pp. 301ff. above.
[2] Pss. 119; 19B.

in parallel with trust in God;[1] and from the second century BC onwards faith is understood as the steadfast confession of faith in the Jewish community, with its teachings and regulations based on the Law.[2]

How powerfully the motive of obedience to the Law dominated ethical thinking, and gradually excluded other motives, is illustrated especially clearly by a development observable in the wisdom literature.[3] Originally instruction for life, of an international character, its earliest examples in Israel exhibit the same predominance of considerations of expediency in motivation as do non-Israelite writings of the same genre. This may be appropriate enough, so far as the rules of practical cleverness are concerned; but it imports into the moral exhortations an element which was bound to be disastrous for the unconditional character of the ethical demand. Even the hint of a religious tone, more marked in some passages than in others, remains for the most part dominated by the idea of reward from God. Only rarely is the bare fact that God's will has commanded such and such a thing mentioned as sufficient reason for human conduct.[4] Nevertheless, the Israelite wisdom teaching is saved from lapsing into a superficial eudaemonism by the fact that it still knows of *a personal God-Man relationship*, and more and more clearly it roots the conduct of the wise in this. In thinking about God the wise is animated not only by fear and humility (this much even the heathen wisdom teachers understand) but he is to find strength to walk the way of life in trusting God.[5] And the fact that in the later sections of the Book of Proverbs, and in the book of Job, acknowledgment of the Holy One, and the fear of God, have already become the major tenets of wisdom means that God's claim to be accorded unique and supreme worth has been given precedence over the skilful calculation of what is expedient. Thus it comes about that in the Prologue of Job we find a sharp condemnation of a calculating piety. With the increasing influence of Law-piety on the wisdom teaching this concentration on the absolute will of God becomes more securely established. In that the counsels and exhortations of the wise become

[1] Cf. E. Kautzsch, *Die Apokryphen und Pseudepigraphen des AT* I, 1900, Sir. 36.3; 35.24a: p. 394.

[2] I Enoch 61.4; 63.5ff.; Judith 14.10; Test. Dan 6; Jub. 17.17f.; 18.16; 19.8f.; Wisd. 3.14; II Macc. 7.40; IV Macc. 16.22.

[3] Cf. p. 345 above.

[4] Cf. the Proverbs of Ani, in A. Erman, *Die Literatur der Ägypter*, p. 295, and Babylonian proverbs in *AOT*, pp. 291ff., nos. 70f. Also Prov. 14.2; 16.6; Ecclus 15.1; 19.20.

[5] Prov. 22.19; 28.25; Ps. 37.5.

identical with the demand of the Law,[1] there is more and more a conscious awareness of the fact that the divine 'Thou shalt' is an absolute, which cannot be further explained, or derived from any other source. For where the absolute command constitutes the fundamental basis of human living, something beyond the scope of discussion, the moral requirement cannot be justified by any calculation of results or considerations of expediency. It is thus ultimately identical with the supereme value, so that the peace afforded by the fear of God compensates men for all outward possessions,[2] and the joy of the pious consists in obedience to the Law.[3] Indeed, as the central stimulus of the will, the Law can cancel even the strongest natural motives, those of self-preservation and mother-love, and can inspire men to die joyfully, as we see so impressively described in the martyr stories of IV Maccabees.

That this central position, which faithfulness to the Law enjoyed among the stimuli of the will, had its shadow-side is clear enough, and, after what has already been said, need only be indicated briefly. The Law as a secondary court of appeal concealed within itself the danger of obstructing direct contact with the will of God, as this made itself known not only in demand and judgment but also in forgiveness and redemption. Living inner exchange with a divine Thou was forcibly supplanted by the dead authority of an impersonal entity, behind which both the infinite majesty and the love, seeking fellowship with Man, of him to whom the Law should have borne witness, was all too easily hidden. Hence, by being tied to the letter of the Law, the infinite range of moral obligation was enclosed within narrow limits; and outside these egoism could luxuriate undisturbed.[4] Because absolutely equal value was ascribed to all the commandments, as a result of an inability to develop the requirements of the Law organically out of the nature of the Lawgiver, an alien legalism was imposed upon moral decision;[5] and the inanimate rigidity and harshness attaching to such a coercive regulation of all life weakened men's capacity to be open to unforeseen cases of moral obligation, and to be led by the Spirit to undertake new tasks.

The most dangerous weakness in the motive of loyalty to the Law,

---

[1] Ecclus 7.31; 28.7; 29.1, 9; 35.23; Tobit 1.6; 4.5; 6.13; 7.11; Wisd. 9.8.
[2] Ps. 40.8f.; Tobit 4.21; Ecclus 1.11f.; Test. Iss. 3–5.
[3] Pss. 1; 19.8ff.; 119.105ff.; Ecclus 32.10ff.
[4] Cf. pp. 344 and 347f. above.
[5] Cf. pp. 345f. above.

however, lay in the fact that it was unable to prevent *the admixture of other motives*. For the line of development which we have been tracing is not the only one in the spiritual constitution of the Jewish community, nor even, indeed, in those writings that witness to it. Instead it is frequently frustrated by a worldly expediency of moral conduct which continually threatens to obscure the unconditional character of moral obligation. Various factors combined to produce this result. Into the old conviction that the covenant law was the basis of the prosperity of the covenant people because it maintained and safeguarded their life—a view which Ezekiel had so energetically championed[1]—intruded the immediate necessities of the concrete situation of the returned exiles in Jerusalem. Here it was not a question whether life was to be more, or less, successful and fortunate, but to whom finally the possession of the land and the control of its constitution was to fall—to the prophetic party, who had blazoned the validity of the Law on their banners, or to the half-heathen mixed population, together with the apostates from the former's own ranks who were fraternizing with them. It is understandable that in such a situation their gaining control of the land, and the enjoyment of its blessings, should be bound up with loyalty to the Law; and this must be borne in mind when evaluating the relevant evidence from this period.[2]

To this, moreover, the post-exilic community added the burning concern of faith with Yahweh's this-worldly retribution in the life of the individual. For them faith in God's righteousness, and the ability to make sense of the course of events in the world as the working out of divine providence, were at hazard in the question whether or not the intervention of God to reward and punish could be demonstrated in the good or evil fortune of the individual. And this all the more so, the less power men had of holding on to the eschatological hope, and the more decidedly they believed that they could perceive in the empirical community and its sacred ordinances the ultimate goal of history. In such circumstances the earthly reward for loyalty to the Law was bound to acquire enormous importance, and the belief that it could be verified in experience was able to become a basic dogma of piety.[3] But no one noticed that in the process God had become the

---

[1] Cf. pp. 301ff. above.

[2] Isa. 57.13b; 58.12, 14; 65.9f., 13, 21ff.; Ps. 37.3, 11, 22, 29, 34.

[3] So in Proverbs (1.19, 31ff.; 2.21f.; 3.31ff., etc.), many Psalms (37; 39; 49; 73; 128), and in the speeches of the friends in the Book of Job.

servant of human pretensions, someone whom one could exhort to fulfil his promises, and whose sovereign will was subordinated to Man's idea of the good. When to this was added the postulate current in the wisdom teaching, namely that of the comprehensibility of God's commandment, and of the rational character of the cosmic process, the way was opened for a utilitarian world-view in which eudae-monistic motives had attained independence and dominating in-fluence. No longer was there any defence against intruding into piety calculations of merit and reward, and seeing in the good fortune of the individual and of the nation the purpose of the divine Ought, an imperative which in itself was simply not open to discussion. God's dealings were understood one-sidedly in terms of judgment and retribution, by which he guaranteed to the pious man the fruit of his works;[1] and rigid concentration on his will and sovereignty, in which at the same time the supreme value is contained, takes second-place to the craving for earthly happiness.

All this was by no means necessarily a question of material goods only. Rather, under the influence of the wisdom teaching, one spiritual good became extremely influential as a motive of conduct, namely the satisfaction inherent in the possession of wisdom itself, a satisfaction which proceeded from a feeling of superiority to the foolish and ungodly, and from the confidence of being able to master life.[2] The changeover from profane and cosmic wisdom to the ethical teaching of the Law affected this not at all. Instead, pride in one's knowledge, and authority as a teacher, are also among the strongest and most prominent motives even of conduct focused on the Law. Where Greek thought, with its unimpaired confidence in the possi-bility of putting into practice what was known to be right, influenced the Jewish teachers, this delight in the ethical formation of life for its own sake is expressed in an emphasis on the virtues, possession of which is a mark of the perfect man, and under the influence of which sensual impulses are mastered, and men attain complete indepen-

---

[1] In the hope of redemption: Isa. 66.12; Zech. 9.11–11.3; 12.1ff.; 14.1ff.; Obad. 15ff.; Dan. 2.44; 4.14ff.; 7.27; in personal experience: Pss. 17; 26; 59, et al.; cf. Neh. 5.19; 13.14, 22, 31. Similar ideas in later Judaism: Ecclus 3.31; 12.2; 17.23; Tobit 4.14; 12.9; I Enoch 91.3; Jub. 20.9; Judith 13.20; Pss. Sol. 5.18; 9.5, etc. For the righteousness of God as revealed in purely mechanical retribution: Chronicles, Jubilees, II Maccabees, Psalms of Solomon, Pirḳe Aboth, etc. Against such a preponderance the occasional demands for disinterestedness in moral con-duct are unable to make any headway: cf. Bousset, op. cit., pp. 415f.

[2] Ps. 119.98ff.; Job 32.8ff.; Prov. 8.1ff.; Wisd. 8.10ff.; 9.16ff.

dence of all the seductions and threats of earthly power.[1] That this involved a by no means unimportant distortion of the central motive of theonomous morality is shown by the bitter conflict in which Jesus found himself on precisely this point with the teachers of his time

This state of affairs was not essentially altered by the gradual spread of belief in resurrection and eternal judgment. This did indeed mean that here and there men's eyes were directed more forcibly to the divine Judge,[2] and that, in face of the justice of the universal Lord, piercing to the utmost depths of the soul, anxiety whether one would be able to stand before him did shake that all too easy satisfaction with one's own loyalty to the Law, of which men loved to boast.[3] But alongside the good of salvation, in this way more definitely spiritualized, the goods of material happiness also assert their right to a place;[4] and thus the concept of reward and punishment, even though now concentrated on the world beyond, is able, as it did earlier, to weaken the truly moral motives, and render them ineffective. Hence in the field of moral motivation also the ethic of the Jewish community affords the same picture of disunity and fragmentation, which we have already encountered in the sphere of the ethical norms and the moral goods.

It is the loftiness of the obligation, the spirituality of the central good, the unconditional character of the Ought, and the perfect unity of these three aspects of moral conduct in the divine Thou as known in the gift of his favour, which give the ethics of the Old Testament their unique inner greatness. But they also raise the further question how, when the goal of life is pitched so high, human failure is to be recognized and assessed. And this confronts us with the problem of sin.

---

[1] Wisd. 8.7; IV Macc. 1.6, 18; 5.23f.; 5.4, 10, 22; 7.9.

[2] Cf. pp. 341f. above.

[3] II(4) Esdras presents a shattering picture of the doubts which such thoughts aroused in the more deeply gifted souls.

[4] Cf. pp. 363ff. above.

XXIII

SIN AND FORGIVENESS

I. THE NATURE OF SIN[1]

1. One can speak of sin in the proper sense of the word only where there is the feeling that an unconditional Ought is being contravened; and therefore insight into the real seriousness of sin is inseparably bound up with the greater or lesser degree of clarity with which men are consciously aware of this unconditional quality of moral obligation. Consequently, it is easy to appreciate that, although an understanding of that which we call sin is found in all religions, its importance for religious life and thought nevertheless varies to an extraordinary extent, and that only in a few religions is it possible for the effort to conquer sin to become a central concern.

In Israel both the high level of the content, and the compelling force of the claim to validity, which characterize the divinely appointed norms of life lead us to expect that here men's failure with regard to them, and the struggle to eliminate this, will play an important role. The nature of sin in the Old Testament is, in fact, already very clearly characterized by *the various terms* used to denote it. And from these it does not emerge as primarily misfortune, or evil chance, or anything of that kind, even though this element is not entirely lacking, but as conduct contrary to the norm.

The root *ḥ-ṭ-'*, which is the one most frequently used to designate both sinful conduct, the sin itself (*ḥaṭṭā't, ḥēṭ', ḥᵃṭā'ā* or *ḥaṭṭā'ā*), and the sinner (*ḥaṭṭā'*, found only in the feminine singular and in the plural), has as its original meaning 'go astray', 'miss the mark', a univocal and easily understandable expression for the formal aspect of the concept of sin, presenting it as a failure with regard to the norm, an offence against a commandment or prohibition. Hence, alongside

---

[1] Cf. C. Ryder Smith, *The Biblical Doctrine of Sin*, 1953.

the religious usage, the word is also extensively applied as a legal concept in the sense of 'crime' or 'misdemeanour'.[1] The incorporation of the word into the religious sphere is exactly in keeping with the importance of superior norms for the religious life of Israel. Similarly, the description of sin by the root '-w-h, used almost entirely in the substantive form 'āwōn, derives from a verb of motion meaning 'bend', 'veer', 'go aside from the right way'. Always implicit in the use of this word, moreover, is the agent's awareness of the culpability of his action, so that the formal aspect is here already supplemented by one of moral content. The root p-š-' mostly has an active sense, and both as a verb and as the noun peša' characterizes sin as 'rebellion' or 'revolt'. Finally, a distinctive nuance is imported into the concept of sin by the verb šāgāh and the associated noun šegāgā, in so far as the emphasis here is on the aspect of 'error', unintended transgression.

Clearly contained in all these terms is *the unifying basic conception of action contrary to the norm*. This can be seen, however, to be continually qualified in one direction or the other, according as the emphasis is to be placed in particular on the action itself, or on the accompanying psychic process. The structural affinity between this view and that of juristic thinking is obvious, and points back to the juristic element present in the foundation of Israel's relationship with God in the berīt.[2] The use of such very common juristic concepts as ṣaddīk and rāšā'[3] to describe the moral ideal illuminates the same situation from a different angle.

In view of the marked predominance of the formal term ḥ-ṭ-' in linguistic usage, especially of the pre-prophetic period, one might be inclined to the opinion that the Israelite concept of sin was primarily concerned with establishing an objective offence, which then has to be made good by an equally objective act of reparation. And it so happens that various instances can be adduced in which all *the emphasis falls on the objective offence*, while the sinful will of the person involved manifestly plays no part. To this category belong such cases as the outrage which brings a curse on the whole land, even though its inhabitants are not responsible for any part of the act itself, or the

---

[1] Deut. 19.15ff.; 21.22; 22.26; II Kings 18.14; Isa. 29.21; Gen. 40.1; 41.9, etc.; cf. G. Quell, 'Die Sünde im AT', *TWNT* I, pp. 267ff.

[2] Cf. vol. I, pp. 36–39.

[3] ṣaddīk, 'righteous', refers primarily to the man who is vindicated by the judgment of the court, rāšā', 'evildoer', to the man who is found guilty.

unwitting adultery which lays on them guilt punishable by death,[1] or the undiscovered murder which brings with it the threat of revenge for the shedding of innocent blood,[2] or a breach of the vow of the ban by a compatriot which, passing undetected, has placed the whole community under the curse of God,[3] or an accidental homicide which has polluted the land.[4] It is a common view that an unwitting ritual offence involves punishable guilt, even to the extent of the death penalty.[5] Related to this seems to be the idea that even a curse incurred quite unjustifiably in perfect innocence is dangerous to the person concerned, or to his family, so long as it is not lifted by a blessing, or turned back on the curser by punishing him.[6] In all these cases the decisive factor is the objective offence, with no reference to the element of volition.[7]

Such views clearly present us with *the after-effects of a dynamistic system of thought*, in which sin is seen as the transgression of the commandment of an alien power which reacts automatically against it, or has the effect of contagious matter, which threatens with destruction even the person who comes into contact with it unconsciously. These ideas are indeed well known to us from the spiritual history of Babylonia, Egypt and Greece, and reveal once again the natural soil of Israelite religiosity, which has been encountered in other contexts.[8]

Here, then, the supreme norm of action is the inviolability of the tabu, which means that the essential thing about sin can only be the objective fact of the sinful action, and that reflection makes no attempt to go beyond this to consider the personal attitude of the agent; but *assessment in moralistic and juridical terms* brings a new element into consideration. Because the old taboo laws were in-

[1] Gen. 20.3ff.; 26.10.
[2] Deut. 21.1–9, which despite its late date undoubtedly witnesses to an age-old ritual.
[3] Josh. 7.11.
[4] Ex. 21.12ff.; Num. 35.31ff. In the same way the violation of a married woman is a capital crime, regardless of whether the offender knew that the woman was married or not: Deut. 22.22ff.
[5] I Sam. 14.43ff.; Lev. 4; 5.1–6, 14–19.
[6] This conception must be the explanation of the shocking testamentary disposition of David, I Kings 2.8ff.; cf. II Sam. 16.5–13. Similarly also II Sam. 21.3.
[7] Num. 22.34 can hardly be included under this head, since vv. 22 and 32 assume a deliberate offence by Balaam, which brings down upon him the threatening of Yahweh's angel. His confession, 'I have sinned' (v. 34), therefore refers to the obstinacy with which he persisted on his wrong journey, even though he should have taken warning from the behaviour of his beast.
[8] Cf. especially the remarks on the cultus, vol. I, pp. 98–101.

corporated into the new legal system established by the *bᵉrît*,[1] they were necessarily understood as the will of the divine lawgiver, and their obligatory character acquired a markedly personal quality. Transgression of the Law was saved from a purely formalist, juristic objectivity, in which attention is paid only to the factual failure in performance, and interest is confined to reparation by a corresponding equivalent, by the unconditional authority of the covenant God, which claimed the right to shape the life of the covenant people, and in increasing measure subjected one sphere after another to itself. The old outlooks were now slowly but inevitably annulled. Behind custom and usage, cultic and moral law, became visible the personal sovereign will, with which all sinful action came into conflict. It has already been noted[2] how powerfully this determined the whole development of legal life, as regards both its gradual permeation by religion and the process of moral internalization. Similarly, we have been able to show elsewhere how the continuing influence in the cultus of belief in *mana* and magic was overcome by giving the rituals concerned new meaning.[3] As far as the understanding of sin was concerned, this process meant that sin was comprehended as a *conscious and responsible act*, by which Man rebelled against the unconditional authority of God in order to decide for himself what way he should take, and to make God's gifts serve his own ego. Thus it comes about that there is a multiplication of terms stressing the wrong attitude of the will in the sinful action.[4] This inevitably did much to counteract the tendency to objectivize sin by weakening the element of personal responsibility; for now the decisive feature was *the conflicting directions of two wills, the divine and the human*, and this conflict could only be resolved by dealings between two persons. Thus even in the early period of Israel's history we see a surprisingly sure grasp of the development of sin in Man, indicating a high level

---

[1] Cf. vol. I, pp. 134ff., 162ff.

[2] Cf. vol. I, pp. 84ff.

[3] Cf. vol. I, pp. 115ff., 121ff., 124ff., 133ff., 142f., 151, 154f., 158–62. The significance of this increased prominence of the divine 'I', and of his personal relation with men, for the religious attitude and for ethical behaviour has already been demonstrated in chs. XX–XXII.

[4] Cf., e.g., two words particularly close in meaning to *p-s-ʿ*, viz. *m-r-d* and *m-r-ḥ*, 'to be rebellious', *m-ʿ-l*, 'to act undutifully', the Piel and Hiphil of the root *š-ḥ-t*, 'to corrupt', *m-ʾ-s*, 'to despise', *g-ʿ-l*, 'to abhor', *p-r-r* I in the Hiphil, 'to break, make of no effect', *lō' š-m-ʿ*, 'not to listen', *šānēʾ*, 'to hate'; also the nouns *ḥāmās*, 'violence', *tōʿēbā*, 'abomination', *rᵉmiyyā* II and *mirmā*, 'deceit', *zimmā*, 'sensual depravity', *'āwen*, 'wickedness, falsehood', *šeḳer*, 'lie', *ʿawlā* and *ʿāwel*, 'perversion', etc.

of understanding of the volitional element in the sinner's conduct. I Sam. 17–20 describes with great sensitivity the gradual growth of jealousy in King Saul, by which he is increasingly blinded, finally falling under the sway of an evil power which derives him to insane and atrocious actions.[1] And throughout the centuries the mastery with which, in Gen. 3, the growth of sin is described, from the first external stimulus, through covetousness, mistrust, and rebellion, to the final eruption in the act of disobedience, has aroused boundless admiration.

In view of this securely established assessment of sin as transgression deriving from the responsible will of Man instances to the contrary may be understood as simply relics from the inheritance of the past, retained with a tenacious persistence. The adjustment of these elements to the situation created by the divine covenant-making was not achieved without difficulty. Nevertheless, *objective guilt is now regarded in a new light*, inasmuch as it is seen in the perspective of what God is doing to establish his holy people. The world of sinister and maleficent power, from contact with which contagion and pollution proceed even without the will of the agent, now becomes the world of alien divine powers hostile to Yahweh; and from this Yahweh's people must at all times keep themselves strictly apart in order not to endanger their belonging to the holy God. Inasmuch as this makes the ritual commandments weapons in the struggle for the exclusive worship of Yahweh, it is easily understandable that the infringement of them by even a single member affects the nation as a whole, and disturbs its relationship with God, if care is not taken to punish the transgressor. And the same applies to a moral offence, where the offender remains unknown. For here again objective guilt is firmly rooted in the obligation incumbent upon the whole nation to watch that the writ of the sovereign divine will shall run everywhere without restriction, and so no longer bears any sort of magical character. The punishment of unwitting offences against the moral norm, however, is patently justified by something far transcending the old dynamistic anxiety about pollution, namely the basic principle of all national law, that where objective damage has been caused atonement is required. In all these cases the thinking is strictly based on the nation as a whole and its needs.

---

[1] J. Köberle (*Sünde und Gnade*, 1905, p. 51) rightly emphasizes that only the particular attacks of raving anger, but not the king's steadily increasing jealousy, and the actions that stem from it, are ascribed to the evil spirit sent from Yahweh.

Nevertheless, there are certainly many instances where the older ways of thought still retain their influence, as, for example, when the doom of sin is seen working itself out in the impersonal transmission of curse-laden impurity, in particular in ritual transgressions,[1] and in those two offences distinguished as capital crimes by age-old tabooistic ideas, murder and adultery.[2] But the law restricts the application of such ideas in practice by a rational assessment of damage, which sets the well-understood interests of the community above the old views of the contagious power of sin, and thus protects the unintentional or unwitting crime from an all too severe retribution.[3] This tendency can be shown to have existed also outside Israel; but faith in God's rule as bringing salvation to his people gave it encouragement which should not be underestimated.[4] And where the old compulsions retained their ancestral power, it was the will of this God which would not allow them to operate in unmitigated harshness, but either by a direct warning to the person in danger[5] or by instituting the means of atonement,[6] nullified the sinister power of the world of dynamistic forces. The degree to which, despite all this, these forces were still able to stunt the concept of sin was no longer sufficient to endanger the decisive importance of personal guilt,

---

[1] Cf. vol. I, pp. 158f.

[2] Cf. the check placed on this by the right of asylum in cases of unintentional homicide (Ex. 21.12ff.; Deut. 19.1ff.), a crime which, according to Num. 35.32f., may not be commuted by the payment of ransom, since to do so would pollute the land. Cf. further the severe punishment of adultery, without any attempt to ascertain whether the offence was committed knowingly or in ignorance: Deut. 22.22ff.

[3] This may be seen particularly clearly in the case of the goring ox (Ex. 21.28ff.), where, although the old view of the maleficent power of the offence still asserts itself in the stoning of the guilty animal, on the other hand the punishment of the owner can no longer be enforced. Rationalization has gone farther in the Code of Hammurabi, in which, according to § 250, the animal, too, is allowed to live. Cf. also Ex. 22.1, where the killing of a burglar is free from guilt; Ex. 21.18f., where unpremeditated bodily injury goes unpunished, though here, too, rationalization has gone farther in the Code of Hammurabi, inasmuch as §§ 206–8 stipulate that monetary compensation shall suffice, even when death has been the outcome of a brawl; Num. 15.22ff., which give the regulations for offences committed by mistake ($\check{s}^e g \bar{a} g \bar{a}$).

[4] The clearest example of this influence is the rejection of indirect talion on the basic principle that normally punishment should not be extended to the children of the offender: cf. vol. I, pp. 77f.

[5] Gen. 20.6f.; according to I Sam. 14.45 an indemnity may be paid in cases of unwitting transgression.

[6] The expiatory effect of purification rites derives not from their material quality, but from the saving will of the covenant God who institutes them.

any more than men's awareness of occasionally incomprehensible anger on the part of Yahweh was able to cast doubt on the moral nature of his will.[1]

But it is also clear how exclusively *the power of resistance to dynamistic and moralistic weakenings of the concept of sin rests on the constantly renewed conviction of God's presence and self-attestation.* Violent conflicts were therefore bound to break out, once familiarity with the Canaanite environment had for many caused that assurance to crumble, and had directed religious thinking along naturalistic paths. Here the one-sided development by which the covenant obligations became no more than rigidly stipulated performances prepared the way for a false moralism in the evaluation of sin. Furthermore, the elements of an impersonal, dynamistic conception of the sphere of divine power and of its infringement which remained from the pre-Mosaic period were able, when combined with the elaborate development of the cultus, to influence religious thinking once more in the direction of tabooism. For where the God-Man relationship was distorted into one of objective works, there, too, magico-sacrificial lines of thought revived, and located the destructiveness of sin less in the offence against the divine person than in the encroachment on the sphere of divine power, the quasi-material holiness of which could be restored by automatically effective means of atonement.

II. It was against the inroads of these ideas that *the defensive battle of the prophets* was fought. The whole secret of their influence was that they had been gripped by a powerful divine will, which subjected the whole of life to its unconditional demand, and allowed no one to evade its call to decision. To the extent to which the prophets succeeded in turning the gaze of their contemporaries toward the divine Lord drawing near to judgment they also destroyed the objectification which rendered sin harmless by believing that it could be expiated by some equivalent reparation, and made men aware of the real seriousness of the injury to the personal relationship between God and Man. This God had shown himself in the history of his people as holy love, unwearying faithfulness, righteousness calling

---

[1] Cf. vol. I, pp. 260f. The punishment of sin by a compulsion to sin, sent by God, and the whole problem of hardening, which Hempel would like to include in this context (*Ethos des AT*, 1938, p. 54), is not really relevant here (cf. vol. I, pp. 376f., 380f.). The judgment decreed on the heathen for their transgression of God's will likewise has nothing to do with objective guilt, for such threats of judgment rest on the assumption that certain moral norms are known to, and valid for, all nations. On the subject of collective guilt cf. further pp. 428ff., 435ff. below.

for the response of trust, compassionate kindness; but at the same time he had solicited from men their personal consent to his offer, their unreserved self-surrender, and their willing obedience. For him no material performance, be it ever so great, could be a substitute for the living movement of the heart, expressing in love, faith, knowledge of God, and gratitude, a personal assent to his claim. Because the will of God was in this way relevant to the totality of human personal life, *individual offences* against this will *could not be regarded atomistically*, listed in the rubric as objective failures of a more, or less, serious degree, to be made good after the manner of legal restitution, or, like tabooistic pollutions, cancelled by the use of sacral techniques of expiation. Instead, the individual actions, as affronts to the divine will, point to a perverted direction of the human will. *Behind the sin stands sin, in the sense of a wrong condition of human nature*, since that nature has turned aside from its only proper goal in God. The prophets describe this condition of human nature sometimes as ingratitude (Amos), or as inner aversion and hostility (Hosea), as arrogance and self-exaltation (Isaiah), or as a deep-seated falsity (Jeremiah). But they all point in the same direction, namely toward an alienation from God which, because it is a voluntary abandonment of Yahweh, breaks the bond between God and Man, and can therefore be nothing other than a disruption and destruction of the divine order.

There can be no doubt that this conception of sin stands in a direct line with that of ancient Israel. At the same time *it has been deepened and broadened by the insight into the full richness of the divine nature, and by the new unfolding of human individuality*. The majesty of God, which fills the whole world, and which the prophets so passionately proclaim, leaves the sinner no possibility of flight, and for the first time makes his responsibility quite inescapable. While the partisans of things foreign found adequate reason for not taking Yahweh's demands any too seriously in the fact that the sphere of his power was so limited when compared with that of the gods of the world-empires, the prophets proclaimed the overthrow of all gods by the enthronement of the One who alone is exalted, and whose judgment no man can escape, though he flee to the ends of the world.[1] Furthermore, by teaching men to understand the rule of this universal God as the dealing of the most personal kind of love and loyalty, and thus providing a rationale of his commandments which created an internal

[1] Amos 9.1ff.; Isa. 2.10f., 19, 21.

obligation, they swept away the deceptive mist which the confusion of Yahweh with the baalistic forces of Nature had spread over the picture of God. The prophets have turns of phrase in abundance with which to throw light on sin as a turning away of the will from the only Lord of all life. They accuse Israel of forgetting and deserting Yahweh, of wishing to know nothing of him, of not troubling herself about him, of not listening to him, of wandering far from him, of being untrue to him, and of rebelling against him. By the same token they avoid those expressions which shift the question into the juristic sphere, in that they hardly cite the laws at all, nor do they speak of the covenant.[1] This is the ultimate explanation why the whole weight of their accusation falls on the transgression of moral commands, where the perversion of personal decision becomes most grossly visible.[2] Compared with failure at this decisive point, all cultic activity becomes valueless, because it has lost its meaning. Only where it expresses the personal surrender of the whole man to God can it keep its place in a worship which is entirely controlled by the personal quality of the God-Man relationship. All mechanistic and magical elements in the cultus are now recognized as a contradiction of God's nature, and as an outrageous attempt to make the deity serviceable to oneself without any personal commitment or regard for the demand and appeal of the divine Thou. Hence the cutting antitheses which contrast the denial of Yahweh in the falsity of the cult with moral profession of the service of this God.

As a result of such insights *moral judgment was refined*, and sin was recognized even where no codified legal regulation could ever serve to prove it. Thus we find the prophets sharpening the consciences of their people by their reproaches against the luxury and self-indulgence, the pleasure-seeking and utterly lascivious impulses, of the upper class.[3] The same applies to their biting criticism of the faithless political intrigues with which Israel, like the rest of the Syrian minor states attempted to lie their way between the great powers.[4] In all this they discern the symptoms of the same contempt for the divine majesty, the same autocratic and high-handed attitude, as in the breaking of the covenant ordinances without a qualm.

[1] Cf. vol. I, pp. 51f.
[2] Cf. vol. I, pp. 362f.
[3] Amos 2.12; 3.15; 4.1ff.; 6.4ff.; Hos. 4.4ff., 13ff.; 7.5; Isa. 5.11, 22; 28.7f., etc.
[4] Hos. 5.11, 13; 7.8f.; 8.8f.; 9.3; 10.5f.; 11.5; 13.2; Isa. 17.3; 28.15; 29.15f.; 30.2ff., 16; 31.1ff.; Jer. 2.14ff.; 9.2; Ezek. 17.12ff.

Where sin is shifted so clearly and completely into the interior
life of Man, and where its most diverse expressions are recognized as
the fruits of a single tree, it also becomes impossible to conceal any
longer *the compulsive character of the apostasy*. Despite all warnings,
despite all the lessons of history, despite the daily experience of the
destructive effect which rejection of God has on life both inwardly
and outwardly, the prophets see their people continuing on the way
to perdition. Before them rises *the enigma of an ineradicable tendency to
sin*, which takes possession of men with compelling power and drives
them along its own road. The Yahwist had already recognized this
inner proclivity toward evil as a deep-rooted condition of Man;[1]
now the prophets point to it again and again. To Hosea this perverted
direction of the will in his people seemed an alien vital principle; a
rūaḥ zᵉnūnim, a spirit of harlotry, must have taken possession of
them.[2] Hence, despite all the unwearying faithfulness with which his
God pursues them, he regards their conversion as impossible, unless
by that same God a miracle is wrought. Isaiah sees his countrymen
tearing each other to pieces in fratricidal strife, and they seem to him
men crazed in mind.[3] But Jeremiah is the one who ponders most over
the riddle of the hypnotic force with which men are attracted by evil,
even though, as a result, they find themselves in the deepest distress,
and indeed cannot go on living without the narcotic of sinful pleasure.[4] He compares the enslaving power which leaves his people no
more free will to the irresistible force of the mating drive in animals
in season, their zeal in safeguarding and cosseting injustice to the
water stored cool in the cisterns, the evil habitus which has become
second nature to them, and which is impervious to all exhortation,
to the colour of the Ethiopian or the markings of the leopard.[5] The
heart of Man appears to him an impenetrable abyss, full of gruesome
riddles, the sight of which kills all hope.[6] For it never occurs to him
to off-load this sinister compulsion on to a non-human power; Man
deliberately hardens himself against the impulses of the good, and
his enmity toward God must, as *šᵉrirūt lēb*, hardness of heart, call
down judgment upon him.[7] Ezekiel likewise portrays the madness of

[1] Gen. 6.5; 8.21.
[2] Hos. 4.12; 5.4.
[3] Isa. 9.18; cf. also 5.18.
[4] Jer. 2.25.
[5] Jer. 2.23f.; 6.7; 13.23, cf. 6.16f.
[6] Jer. 17.9.
[7] Jer. 3.17; 4.4; 9.25.

stiff-necked persistence in sin,[1] as a result of which Israel has sunk even lower than Sodom, and has become a *bēt mᵉrî*, a rebellious house, which opposes a heart of stone to every appeal and exhortation of her God.[2]

This ruthless diagnosis of the sinful constitution of Man, however, makes his situation hopeless. Of all the evils which oppress him sin is now recognized as the most serious, and the breaking of its spell becomes *the most important question in life*. Such an assessment of the situation, moreover, disposes of the attempt of the Law to create a world of righteousness and holiness. Indeed, the whole history of the nation showed how little the Law could prevent rebellion against God's will, but instead inevitably exposed the real depth of hostility to God.[3] *The only course now left open was to turn one's eyes to the eschatological new creation of God's people*, which would be able to heal the irremediable rift between Man and God.[4]

III. This radical quality in the prophetic assessment of sin, which had its effect even on the teaching of the Law,[5] also left its stamp on *the views of the post-exilic community*. Both their consideration of the past, as this was given classic expression in the Deuteronomistic history-writing, and their behaviour in the tasks and struggles of the present, for which our principal sources of information are the post-exilic prophetic writings,[6] witness to *their awareness that sinful opposition to God is a spiritual and personal thing*, as different from external infringement of the law as it is from magical and involuntary pollution.[7] The priestly Holiness Code, which understands sin as a violation of the community relationship which Yahweh has bestowed in the covenant making, concentrates totally on the divine holiness, that is, that perfection of the nature of God to which the sanctification of the people must correspond. Because Man is confronted by the claim of the holy God to sovereignty, he becomes aware of his sin as a violation of holiness, which means, however, a personal opposi-

---

[1] Ezek. 16.48, 51ff.; 23.11.
[2] Ezek. 36.26.
[3] Cf. pp. 396f., 416ff., and 480f. below.
[4] Cf. pp. 457ff. below.
[5] Cf. Deut. 10.16; 30.6.
[6] Isa. 56–66; Haggai; Zechariah; Malachi.
[7] Cf. also the emphasis on the pure or the upright heart: Prov. 4.23; Ps. 73.1, 13, and the testing of the heart in God's presence: Pss. 11.5f.; 17.3; 94.11; 139.23f.; also the prayer for a pure heart and a steadfast spirit: Pss. 51.12; 57.8; 78.37; 108.1; 112.7.

tion to the will of God.[1] How the danger, which emerged with the re-establishment of the cultus, of externalizing the moral judgment was seen and resisted is shown by the verdict passed on customs of fasting,[2] and also by the stress on the inner relationship with God as the really decisive element in cultic action, that which gives it its soul.[3] This is why it is possible for Haggai and Zechariah to bring the act of rebuilding the Temple home to the people as a profession of their faith. That at the same time men fought with equal seriousness against the rejection of God's demand in every sphere, and kept their eyes open as keenly for the temptations present even in the little details of daily life, is shown by that *broadening and deepening of moral obligation* of which we have already had occasion to speak.[4] With such high demands on men to prove themselves, the sense of enslavement to one's own sinful nature could not possibly remain dormant. It finds expression again and again, either in the prayers of the congregation or in the prophetic promise that the effectual power of sin in the community would be overcome,[5] or in the striving of the individual for the assurance of God's favour.[6] If, for all its satisfaction at the progress so far made, the community under its priestly leaders was nevertheless regarded not as the goal of the promised redemption but solely as an interim stage, which would find its fulfilment only in a new people of God with the messianic ruler at their head,[7] then this was certainly due in great part to the longing for the complete abolition of that ineradicable tendency to evil which threatened men's fellowship with God; and this abolition, as an important component part of God's new world, left its stamp on the future hope.[8]

Other factors, however, are already discernible *in the assessment of sin.* Thus the schematism of the Deuteronomic view of history was unable to give full effect to the inwardness, and the profoundly penetrating knowledge of the human soul, which had characterized the prophetic preaching. Its tendency to see *idolatry as really the supreme sin of previous*

---

[1] On this subject cf. the thorough investigation by A. Quast, *Analyse des Sündenbewusstseins Israels nach dem Heiligkeitsgesetz* (Diss. Göttingen: typescript), 1956.

[2] Isa. 58; Zech. 7f.

[3] Mal. 1.6ff.; 2.1ff.

[4] Cf. pp. 338ff. above.

[5] Isa. 59.4, 9–15; 64.11ff.; Ps. 90.8; Zech. 5.7ff.

[6] Job 14.4; 15.14; Ps. 51.7.

[7] Zech. 3.8–10; 6.9ff.

[8] Cf. vol. I, pp. 504ff.

generations, and therefore to make it responsible for the annihilating wrath of God, diverts attention one-sidedly to an outstanding instance of cultic deviation, and so encourages the tendency to be content with the punctilious performance of individual objective acts. Moreover, in the effort to present the righteous retribution of Yahweh as tangibly as possible by correlating sin and punishment there undoubtedly lay the danger of returning to *an atomistic view of individual offences*, thus overlooking both the deep-lying root and the indivisible coherence of the sinful process. The laudatory expressions in many psalms about the singer's own immaculate fulfilment of the Law, and his certainty of reward from God, point to a similar weakening of the sense of sin.[1] The history-writing of the Chronicler, with its exaggerated mechanism of retribution, reveals a not inconsiderable increase in this danger, even though we may grant that his living understanding of the adventure of faith meant that he was still able to preserve the element of personal decision in the case of sin as in other matters.

A weakened and superficial version of the prophetic understanding of sin was here preparing the way, sometimes more, sometimes less obviously, for a more marked and rapid development once *the establishment of the holy community* was accepted in religious thinking *as the goal of God's sovereignty, attainable by Man's performance*, and as the precondition of a change in the world-order.[2] It is true that even now the conquest of sin remained the principal question of both individual and national life, but the crisis of enslavement to sin no longer appeared impossible of resolution. Instead a way out was indicated in the effort to fulfil the Law. Certainly the tendency to sin is felt as a heavy burden; and in *the doctrine of the evil impulse* innate in Man insight into the fact that every man is the prisoner of sin was, from the time of Ben Sirach onwards, given striking expression.[3] Just as Adam had an evil heart, and therefore sinned, so, too, his descendants.[4] But this impulse is not invincible; Man both ought, and is able, to master it, and the Law has, in fact, been given him as a means of salvation, so that in free choice he may be able to take his place on the side of the good. Thus Judaism never acknowledged a *servum arbitrium*, and on this point refused to be a disciple of the prophets. Indeed, for the establishment of the holy community every-

---

[1] Pss. 17; 18.22ff.; 26; 59, *et al.*
[2] Cf. pp. 342ff. above, and vol. I, pp. 169f., 485f.
[3] Ecclus 15.14; 17.31; 21.11; 37.3; cf. Tract. Kidd. 30b.
[4] II(4) Esd. 3.21, 26; 4.30f.; 7.48.

thing depended on *the possibility of a free decision of the will*, and to ensure this the existence of a good impulse in Man, which gave him the power to resist the evil impulse, was also taught.[1] So it came about that *sinlessness* was held to be entirely possible, and was expressly affirmed of certain saints of the past, such as the patriarchs, and Elijah, and Hezekiah. And even though, as a rule, every man submits once to the evil impulse, yet in the righteous there are at most only a few sins to be found, and these do not, in fact, essentially challenge their righteousness.

The relativism which was here being applied to the opposition to God implicit in the fact of sin was carried further by the *differentiation between individual sins*, which went with legal casuistry. By extension from the Old Testament distinction between sins 'with a high hand' and sins of inadvertence, idolatry, unchastity, and the shedding of blood were now explicitly emphasized as truly mortal sins. This meant a lightening of the heavy load laid on men by the thoroughgoing legal view, for which absolutely any deviation from the Law was sin, but only by lessening the importance of sin. Here we can see the weakness of the legalistic ideal, which can be maintained only by inconsistency, and which obscures the sinfully conditioned quality of human nature, and the personal and spiritual character of this conditioning, by the externalization which thinks to register the existence of enmity toward God in the phenomenon of the illegal act. It is obvious that this provided a favourable soil for *the cultivation of a self-righteous, perfectionist conceit*, by virtue of which the 'righteous' separated themselves from the 'sinners', and branded them with the severest condemnation. A piety determined by such influences was bound to reject the call to repentance of the Baptist or of Jesus. Indeed, the mood of penitence which had once dominated the post-exilic community was no longer able to penetrate into the depths of self-understanding, but was taken more in the sense of an outward duty of devotion, the performance of which could even be reckoned to one for merit. It therefore became possible to face the reality of sin only where confrontation with the new divine revelation in Christ caused men to recognize the defilement of their own nature, yet where at the same time surrender to the love which in Christ was seen to be redemptive gave them courage to confess their own forlorn condition.

[1] Test. Asher 1; cf. also F. Weber, *Jüdische Theologie*[2], p. 230.

2. THE UNIVERSALITY OF SIN

1. Both the direction of conduct by the divine ordinance of the Law, and the tendency to regard sin as an isolated, responsible act, seem to encourage an optimistic assessment of the possibility of avoiding sin altogether. And, in fact, men did recognize a kind of conduct which could be described as *ṣaddîḳ*, righteous, *tām* or *tāmîm*, perfect, faultless, *yāšār*, upright, or *sār mēraʿ*, far from evil.[1] Even though there may be no need to take such praise literally in the case of Noah, who was a hero of the primaeval period,[2] yet the situation is quite different with the Job of the old folk-story, for here we have the outline picture of a popular ideal. Whether nevertheless even he is thought of as sinless in the strict sense may be doubted.

Least of all can the term *ṣaddîḳ* be adduced as evidence for such a conception. For 'righteous' is a relational concept, expressing the condition of righteousness within a particular relation of fellowship, not a general state of virtue. But such being in the right in one's relationship with God does not, to Israelite thinking, in any way rule out sin, so long at any rate as this sin does not issue in insolent arrogance, but leads to humble submission to God's punishment, or alternatively to readiness to make use of the means of atonement provided by God. It is precisely the latter which is emphasized by Job (1.5). *Tāmîm*, 'complete', 'undamaged', must have derived from the language of sacrifice, where it denotes the unblemished condition of the sacrificial animal. Transferred from this sphere to the moral and religious behaviour of men, it means conduct pleasing to God, the concrete content of which is once again determined solely by the existing relation of fellowship with him. The contrast with damage or detriment to original value, which is implicit in the concept, seems here to refer first and foremost to the undivided affection of the heart,[3] as is suggested by the use of the substantive *tōm* for single-mindedness and innocence. Closely akin is *yāšār*, which stresses the honesty of the heart that moves straightforwardly toward its goal. Finally, where 'keeping far from evil' implies more than just watchful avoidance of particular evil actions, it means opposition to

[1] Gen. 6.9; 7.1; Job. 1.1.

[2] The same applies to Enoch, Gen. 5.24, whose 'walking with God' is certainly to be understood in P's usual sense as perfect righteousness, even though the meaning of the phrase may originally have referred rather to his initiation into the divine mysteries.

[3] Cf. Deut. 18.13.

that God-forgetful contempt of the divine commands which marks the flagrant sinner.

The Old Testament expressions may be far from the arrogance which is confident of fulfilling God's will to perfection, but they are equally strangers to that exaggerated sense of sin which detects opposition to God in every human action. That Man really can walk in piety and perfectness before Yahweh is taken for granted. The difference between the pious and the sinners, the *ṣaddīkīm* and the *reša'īm*, the *benē 'awlā*, or the *ḥaṭṭā'īm*, the *'īš yāšār* and the *nābāl*,[1] rests on the fact that there is such a thing as *an overall orientation of life which is pleasing to God*. This certainly does not consist in impeccable perfection, but it is fundamentally different from an autocratic contempt for divine authority. Hence it is already possible in the earlier psalms for men to expect retribution proportionate to the righteousness and purity of hands of the worshipper.[2]

At the same time, however, the Israelite remains sober enough to perceive the sins of even the most eminent figures of his nation, and to speak openly about them. Neither with David nor Moses nor the patriarchs does he give in to the temptation to describe them as sinless saints. Indeed, *the deep sense of the infinite gulf between the all-powerful God and impotent Man*, which is characteristic of Semitic religion in general, Israel prefers to transpose into a contrast between the God whose eye penetrates to every hidden thing and Man who rubs along, obtuse and limited;[3] and from this springs a humble readiness to see even incomprehensible visitations as righteous punishment for *hitherto overlooked or forgotten sin*. Thus David does not dare to restrain the cursing Shimei by violence, because he cannot deny that there may be justification for a divine punishment, even though in this specific case he feels himself to be innocent.[4] For the same reason the people receive the coming of the man of God with anxious terror, for fear that he may bring hitherto overlooked and unpunished sin to God's remembrance.[5] And in the opening chapters of the Yahwist's primal history the conviction is made explicit that the sinful character of the human race calls for *permanent expiation*, if it is not to bring down a new annihilating judgment like that of the

---

[1] I Sam. 25.3, 25f.; II Sam. 3.33f.
[2] Ps. 18.21 (vv. 22–28 may be an elaboration of this verse, added at a later date).
[3] II Sam. 14.14, 17.
[4] II Sam. 16.10ff.; cf. I Kings 17.18; Gen. 44.16.
[5] I Kings 17.18; I Sam. 16.4.

Deluge; from the time of Noah's great sacrifice a means of atonement is given to Man, by which a favourable relationship with God can be maintained.[1] The statement which goes farthest in this direction is that in which the Yahwist narrator describes *the sinful quality attaching to human nature in general* as confirmed by the word of God himself.[2] That this opinion does not, moreover, represent something absolutely unique in Israel is shown by the whole complex of the Yahwist primal history; for this sombre vista of human development has been composed by the collation of stories which plainly were often told and widely disseminated. With this should be compared the way in which, in Babylonian religion, confession of sin is extended into an avowal of the sinfulness of the human race in general, as when the worshipper includes in his own self-humiliation the words: 'Men, all of them who are named with names, which of them knows anything of himself? Which has not sinned flagrantly? Which not done evil?'[3] Such admissions, which seem never to be very far from the Semitic mind, and which are plainly intensified by the desire to stress one's own worthiness in the presence of the deity as strongly as possible, in Israel acquired special point, for, when applied to the nation which had been adopted into a covenant with God, their inevitable effect was to destroy any presumptuous self-confidence. This can be clearly detected in the conviction, which emerged ever more plainly during the monarchical period, that a corporate national guilt weighed upon Israel, and threatened her very existence,[4] a conviction which in its turn certainly contributed to strengthening the serious view taken of the sin attaching to each individual.

II. Prophecy took over these insights and deepened them. On the one hand, under the impact of their call experiences, the prophets expanded the tendency to sin present here and now in each individual human being into a *sinful condition of the whole people*, running right back through their whole history to God's fundamental act of election.[5] This not only unites the present as intimately as possible

---

[1] Gen. 8.20f.; cf. O. Procksch, *Genesis*[2, 3], 1924, *ad loc.*; W. Zimmerli, *I Mose* 1–11. *Die Urgeschichte* II, 1943, pp. 75f.; G. von Rad, *Genesis*, 1961, pp. 118f.

[2] Gen. 8.21.

[3] Cf. H. Zimmern, *Babylonische Hymnen und Gebete in Auswahl* (Der Alte Orient VII.3), 1905, p. 18, and also J. Hehn, *Hymnen und Gebete an Marduk* (Beiträge zur Assyriologie V.3), 1905, no. 21.

[4] Cf. vol. I, pp. 462ff.

[5] Cf. vol. I, pp. 376f.

with the past, bringing out its hidden, underlying fixation, and delivering it up to divine judgment; it also strips each individual sinful action of all contingent circumstances, and allows it to be seen in the full import of its guilt as a reinforcement of the corporate anti-God attitude of the nation, thus convicting men of a *common involvement of all its members* in the transgression of the divine will. What is more, there is also a vision of *all mankind as associated in sin*, inasmuch as the prophetic proclamation of judgment reproaches the Gentile world as well with thoroughgoing rebellion against God's will, and so calls it to account, together with Israel, before his universal assize.[1] Here sin is seen as the power which even removes the distinction between the people of God and the nations of the world, thus revealing the whole of mankind as a unity in its failure and guilt before God.

Even though the knowledge of the universality of sin was in this way transformed from the assumption that it was a *condition* which, however well established, could yet be removed by the decision and act of the individual, to the recognition of it as *active opposition* to God, in which all share, yet there was not always and everywhere an equal precision in spelling out the implications of this for the individual, and for his position *vis-à-vis* God. Here the decisive turning-point was the knowledge which burst upon Isaiah as part of his call. For at this moment a pious man saw himself set in such opposition to his God that his own impurity accused him in face of the One who was pure without spot; and because this impurity was understood as *fully responsible opposition to the holy God*, it devoted him irretrievably to destruction.[2] This leads to an intensification of the concept of sin which renders any natural fellowship between the true, pure, and immaculate nature of God and the world of the creature, sunk in sin and guilt, impossible, and delivers the whole earthly order up to death. Here, too, it is no longer possible to draw a line between the community of the relatively righteous, segregating itself from the rest of the world by the covenant law, and the sinners. Even the former are pointed to a new act of God, by which he opens up for them access to himself.

---

[1] Cf. vol. I, pp. 377ff.

[2] Isa. 6.5. The attempts to make the impurity here disclosed mean no more than the imperfection of Man *qua* creature, as a result of which the unveiled vision of God is death to him, come to grief on the expiatory ritual and pronouncement of absolution in vv. 6f.

While there is no other instance of so radical a confession of sin,[1] the judgment of Jeremiah and Ezekiel on the people as a whole may be understood as an *echo of this merciless exposure* of Man's revolt against God. It is not simply that the charges of Jeremiah portray the wickedness of Israel as a corporate guilt from which no one is excepted[2]—a reproach which is undoubtedly more than just an instance of conventional prophetic style. Rather it is the fact that the hope of salvation in both these prophets shows that they cannot envisage any liberation from sin, and from its evil consequences, without an *inner transformation of the natural condition of Man*. This, however, makes the existence of a divine covenant, by which a people of God is separated from the Gentile world, an example of God's patience; for it is now clear that God is in the position not of having to reward a covenant partner who is faithful but of bearing with one who is unfaithful for the sake of his own promises or of his Name, that is to say, out of loyalty to his own plan of salvation (so Ezekiel), or out of unmerited love and compassion (so Jeremiah).[3]

III. It is a testimony to the striking power of this declaration that it was also adopted by the priestly teaching of the law, despite the fact that the motivations of this teaching were in general tuned to a quite different wavelength. It is indeed one of the basic ideas of the Deuteronomic paraenesis to impress upon the nation how completely unmerited is the gracious guidance which Yahweh has given them, and to open their eyes to the fact that they live by the patience of God.[4] Similarly, the exhortation to circumcise the heart, which causes men to look for a divine act of salvation,[5] cuts the ground from under any optimistic self-approval. The Deuteronomistic history-writing carries these lines of thought even further by setting the whole history of the nation under the long-suffering forgiveness of God, without which the sinful people could never have continued to exist. Here all pride is silenced by the realization that there is no man who has not sinned.[6] But even earlier than this the redactor to whom we are indebted for the interweaving of the Yahwist and Elohist accounts of history was already aiming by his arrangement

---

[1] Isa. 8.11f.; Jer. 15.19; 17.14, have to do with particular offences in the conduct of the prophetic calling.
[2] E.g. Jer. 8.6; 5.5; 9.13; 16.12, etc.
[3] Cf. pp. 480ff. below.
[4] Cf. Deut. 9.1ff., *et al.*
[5] Deut. 10.16; 30.6; cf. Ezek. 18.31.
[6] I Kings 8, 46.

of the patriarchal narrative at nothing less than describing how the relationship of the fathers to God was constantly threatened by sin and unfaithfulness, and so glorifying God's patience with his elect. On this point his lead was later to be followed by the redactor of the whole Pentateuch.

The experiences of the Exile prepared a soil in which this pessimistic critique of the human heart could take irremovable root. The confessions of sin in both corporate and individual prayers take it for granted that there are no exceptions to the tendency to sin.[1] The wisdom teachers, who seek to help the God-fearing to shape their lives aright, can state as a fundamental proposition of their knowledge of Man, that no one can vouch for the purity of his own heart, since from what is unclean nothing clean can come.[2] In P the gearing of sacrificial worship wholesale to the task of atonement also trains the individual to acknowledge his sin, and to feel that its expiation is his central concern.

This extension of prophetic thought is, however, distinguished from its source by the tendency to make *the universality of sin a contingency* which Man must register as a fact in order to come to terms with it somehow or other, a condition just like any other characteristic which he discovers in himself, and so to forget the concrete actuality which alone gave this prophetic doctrine its whole weight. For it was only because universal sinfulness was understood by them as an act of turning away from God, and therefore burdened with full responsibility, that their assessment took on its appalling seriousness, its power of condemnation which there was no escaping. Where on the contrary universal sinfulness was taken to refer to an inborn quality, there of necessity the sense of responsibility for it was weakened. Indeed, the temptation could arise to shift the responsibility from oneself altogether, and by a disastrous inversion to make the sinful natural condition an excuse when confronted by the demands of God's will—something which did, in fact, eventually happen.[3] The old categories, according to which sin was regarded as pollution or as morbid matter, are manifestly still at work here, at least to the extent that the prophetic indictment, though accepted, was misunderstood, and therefore was unable to hammer home either the

---

[1] Pss. 130.3; 143.2; Neh. 9; Isa. 59.11ff.; 64.5f.
[2] Prov. 20.9; Job 4.17; 15.14ff.; 25.4, cf. Ecclus 8.5; Eccles 7.20.
[3] Job 7.1ff., 17–21; 14.1–6. Cf. pp. 477ff. below.

profundity of the doom of sin or the real greatness of the divine redemption.

This same misunderstanding even made it possible in later Judaism for men to admit the universality of sin, often in the strongest terms,[1] and yet at the same time to *set up sinlessness as an attainable goal*, illustrating the truth of this assertion from the pious of the past. By concentrating as regards the concept of sin on the Law, and by insisting on freedom of will and decision in respect of the individual commandment, universal sinfulness was made to appear a rule to which there were nevertheless many and important exceptions;[2] and the deep seriousness of the fact that the perverted direction of the will was rooted in the nature of Man, and that it kept alive inner rebellion against God even where outwardly the Law was impeccably fulfilled, was concealed. It was now possible, on the basis of the idea of merit, for even a relative righteousness to lay claim to God's good pleasure; and therefore creaturely sinfulness—a fact readily enough conceded —was no longer able to lead men to unreserved surrender to the grace of God, but was seen instead as a weakness to be gradually overcome, and as something for which satisfaction could be made to the divine righteousness by all kinds of means of expiation. That at the same time there are extant utterances of the scribes which approximate to the prophetic line, and which point to the desperate situation of all human nature, even in the great men of the past, and to the impossibility of standing before the judgment of God, only shows that men were unable to escape from the inheritance of the past, even when they could no longer bring its concern to bear in undiluted form.

3. THE ORIGIN OF SIN[3]

I. In Israel the nature of sin was seen unambiguously as conscious rebellion against God's order; and this order was not something far above the individual human life, some impersonal, rather abstract cosmic law, but the norm, valid here and now, of the covenant on which the existence of the nation rested, and as such it affected men in their individual actions, and directed their moral will to the need

---

[1] Shemoth rabba 31: 'There is no man who has not sinned'; Wayyikra rabba 14: 'Even though a man were the most pious of the pious, yet he must be guilty in *one* direction.' Cf. I Enoch 81.5; II(4) Esd. 7.68f.; 8.35; 9.36.

[2] Cf. pp. 391ff. above.

[3] Cf. A. M. Dubarlé, *Le péché original dans l'Écriture*, 1958, pp. 39ff.; E. F. Sutcliffe, *Providence and Suffering in the Old and New Testaments*, 1955, pp. 39ff.

for constantly renewed decision in concrete situations. In such circumstances *the question of the origin of sin is forced into the background* by the concentration on the individual act in which sin is manifested, and on the practical consequences which result from this. Thus it comes about that when the Old Testament speaks of sin *the chief emphasis* unquestionably *falls on its current concrete expression.* Because in their experience the covenant-making had been the beginning of the nation's existence, men's thinking revolved round the question of responsible behaviour in the context of this institution, and reflection on the origin of the conflict between God and Man became of very peripheral importance. The opening chapters of the Priestly primal history in Gen. 1–11 seem to suggest that the ancient traditions had had something to tell of the antiquity of the world, and of its gradual degeneration; at any rate, the gradual reduction in the length of life in the Sethite genealogy of Gen. 5 is certainly to be interpreted in this sense, and is a feature to which there are counterparts in other Golden Age sagas of the ancient world.[1] But only one Old Testament writer has the ability to tell of *a decisive turning-point, by which the history of mankind became a history of sin,* and that is the Yahwist, the same man whose work supplies the most decided statement about the universality of sin.[2] And quite clearly it was just this keen eye for the universality of sin which forced him to ponder the question, how this perverse sinfulness began. For after the covenant people had come, in the course of their historical experience, to believe in their one God as also the one Lord of Nature,[3] and this belief had taken shape in the affirmation of God as Creator, the problem posed by the monstrous fact of the sinful opposition of the human creature to the will of this Creator could no longer be evaded. The man who knew how to tell of the Flood and of the Tower of Babel found himself confronted by the riddle of the rebellion which sin constituted within the creation of the good God. How he tackled this problem, and formulated it, is one of the most marvellous things in all the mighty series of epic narratives which he left to posterity.

[1] Cf. Josephus, *Ant.* I.3.9 (quoted in A. Dillmann, *Die Genesis,* 1892, p. 108). Similarly II(4) Esd. 5.50ff. That the present form of the Sethite list in P means by the decreasing life-span to suggest increasing sin, in much the same way as we find in Prov. 10.27, is made quite certain by the fact that the list is linked with the Flood story; but this cannot be taken as evidence for the views of the earlier period.

[2] This point has also been strongly emphasized by J. Scharbert, *Solidarität in Segen und Fluch im AT und in seiner Umwelt* (BBB 14), pp. 161ff.

[3] Cf. pp. 98ff. above.

It does not follow that there is any need to question the view that *the narrative of the Fall of Adam in Gen.* 3 may in some sense rightly be described as an 'aetiological myth'. It is clear from the curses that one aim is to portray the origin of conditions which obtain in the present; and this is done in the language of myth, such as is well known to us from the paradise stories of other nations.[1] This situation, however, is no obstacle to a recognition of the profound significance of the faith-concept disguised in this peculiar clothing. Another context in which we have learned to know myth as the language of faith is that of the eschatological hope, where it serves to express the fact of the perfected sovereignty of God, something no longer conceivable in terms of our experience, but unqualifiedly certain to faith none the less.[2] In the same way we find in the biblical primal history a truly prophetic interpretation of the world in which the myth has become something completely different from what it is among heathen nations. Now it is a means of expression for those truths of faith which there is no method of comprehending in conceptual language. Only the substantial content of these truths, therefore, not the vesture in which they are clothed, is decisive for their significance in the world of biblical thought.[3]

At the same time, however, it is essential to realize that the prophetic interpretation of the world given in the primal history deals not with timeless truths, but with *actual events*. What has here to be stated by the imperfect means of the myth is a matter of real processes, of happenings by which the present shape of the world has been determined. This results in a second difficulty for our understanding, inasmuch as these processes are related in the language of historical record, while, in fact, any 'record' of the creation, the Fall, and suchlike, is finally beyond the reach of our historical science. Nevertheless, exactly the same problem arises with regard to the eschatological consummation, which is also concerned with a real event, though there can never be any possibility of incorporating this event into a historical survey. That the biblical authors were unconscious of these barriers—insurmountable to our thinking—between historical record and those events which explain and consummate the

[1] On the use of the term 'myth' cf. vol. I, p. 461, n. 4, and pp. 473ff.; also *Die Hoffnung des ewigen Friedens*, p. 63, n. 1.

[2] Cf. vol. I, pp. 378, 500f.

[3] J. Pedersen ('The Fall of Man', *Interpretationes S. Mowinckel missae*, 1955, pp. 162ff.) provides a comparison of the biblical narrative with similar ideas in the ancient East, though there are more conclusions to be drawn than he has indicated.

meaning of history is obvious. But it would be a sign of exceptional blindness (such as could pass for a responsible attitude only in the Age of Reason) to set aside their statements on the latter subject as unimportant simply on the grounds that our epistemological categories were alien to them. The qualitative otherness, at any rate, of the world before the Fall and after the divine act of redemption was clear to their eyes, and for this very reason they seized upon the myth as their means of expression. But the man whose only alternatives are an annalistic or a psychological understanding of the biblical evidence will here stand before locked doors.[1] At any rate, for a Christian faith which has been schooled in the Bible one of its most certain insights is that in the relationship between God and Man a real event takes place at all times, but equally that this event cannot be grasped and presented by the methods of historical investigation—though this does not mean that it evaporates into a timeless truth of thought. The unshakeable foundation which proves this event to be real is the resurrection of Jesus. Whether one prefers to call this event 'primal history',[2] or 'transcendental history',[3] or 'faith-history', or to use some other designation, or whether one rejects all these terms as misleading, is, when compared with the clear fact involved, a complete side-issue.

What then is the point of the 'aetiological myth' of Gen. 3, when it is evaluated on the above-mentioned assumptions? In the story various facts are strung together one after another which, to a superficial examination, seem to be of equal value—the toil and trouble of mankind, and the fact that the serpent crawls on its belly, the perversion of the fellowship between man and woman into a master-and-slave relationship, and the enmity between Man and beast. And yet, if we meditate more deeply on this story, and at the same time assess it as part of the total complex of the mighty composition of the Yahwist's primal history, it will be impossible to overlook the fact that the dominant aetiology in the story is not concerned with the individual circumstances as such. The truth is rather that

---

[1] Cf., e.g., L. Köhler, *Old Testament Theology*, ET, 1957, pp. 178f., 250, n. 144. Fortunately the author shows elsewhere that he is capable of other approaches, cf. pp. 212f. and 219f.

[2] German 'Urgeschichte'. So M. Kähler, P. Althaus, K. Barth, E. Brunner, R. Bultmann. For more precise references to the literature cf. P. Althaus, *Grundriss der Dogmatik*, 1936, ch. 8.

[3] German 'Übergeschichte'. So E. Wobbermin, *Geschichte und Historie in der Religionswissenschaft*, 1911.

the masterly portrayal of the seduction and its consequences stresses *one* point as the central focus of all the rest, namely that *the cause of all evil, the reason for a distortion in the order of creation, was alienation from God.* Of fundamental importance here is the intimate connection which the narrator is able to make between the immediate concrete fact of sin and its determinative effect on history. The deep psychological understanding and shattering truthfulness to life which dominate the picture of the first estrangement of Man from God seek as their ultimate effect not the reader's or hearer's admiring assent to the refinement of the psychological characterization, but his terrified admission that here lives flesh of his flesh, from which he cannot dissociate himself as supposedly unconcerned. But the effect has not been exhausted once the reader is successfully convinced of *the solidarity with which all men are bound together in sin.* There is also a relentless description of *the consequences of this first conscious rejection of God in the disturbance of the very foundations of human existence, indeed, of Man's own psychical constitution,* in that the abandonment of Man to the sufferings of life in all their manifold forms is explained by his expulsion from God's fellowship, and the inward destruction of the creature originally held in the will of God is displayed in his enslavement to the power of those sinful impulses which drive him on irresistibly through fratricide and the shedding of blood to the wickedness of a generation on whom the divine judgment of the Deluge falls.

If one allows oneself to be guided by this all-controlling 'aetiology' —and it requires an exceptionally unreceptive attitude toward the whole spirit of the narrative to avoid it—then the various elements mentioned at the beginning supply of themselves the proper hierarchy of value, in which the serpent's eating the dust moves to the edge, the perversion of the original lot of Man to the centre, of the picture of a disturbed creation. Indeed, through the childlike language of that ancient feeling for Nature there shines a deeper meaning, which allows us to see in the humiliation of the serpent the degradation of all creatures, and in the struggle between Man and serpent the disturbed harmony of their common life. For all *the individual features ultimately derive from the total fact of Man's existence out of Paradise,* which shows him to be cut off from the divine source of life, and therefore in every circumstance of his existence at odds with his original destiny.[1]

[1] It is highly probable that the Yahwist's masterful control of the ancient

It thus becomes apparent that certain *questions which have been vigorously debated, such as that of the relation of the serpent to Satan,*[1] *or of death as the wages of sin,* possess absolutely none of that importance for the meaning of the whole which has often been found in them. Things are, however, not so simple that, once we have referred to 3.1, according to which the serpent is one of the beasts of the field, and gone on if necessary to recall the widely disseminated folk-belief that the serpent is in league with evil spirits, no more need be said. One must have a very poor eye for the double meaning, observable in other instances as well, of many statements in this remarkable chapter not to notice that one of the most effective technical skills of the narrator consists precisely in his ability to illustrate the ambiguity and half-truth, the refined camouflage and seductive appeal of evil.[2] Thus the superhuman informedness about the tree of knowledge, and the demonic hostility toward God, which burst out in the serpent's words, are an unmistakable sign that a deliberate anti-God power is here at work; and the interpretation of this figure by the Church in terms of Satan was an absolutely correct intuition of its real character, even though the development of the actual Satan concept may belong to a much later period.[3] The reason, however, why the narrator purposely hides the sinister antagonist of God behind the harmless form of the animal is that he is aware of the inexplicable and enigmatic quality of this being, and knows all too well the danger of allowing preoccupation with him to obscure the thing that really matters. Of his own will the seducing power remains

mythical elements of the Paradise tradition goes much farther still, and that he is consciously using them as images for the deepest realities. Thus it is already true that for him the fashioning of the woman out of the rib of the man is no longer just an unsatisfactory anatomical experiment, but expresses the fact that the sexes are inwardly designed for one another; the serpent is no longer the remarkable beast of the field, but signifies the power of evil; the mortal enmity between it and the man signifies the moral struggle which henceforward is laid upon Man, and in which generation after generation wears itself out maintaining the ultimate link with the higher world, but for all its efforts is unable to bring the destructive power of evil under control. All this, however, could only be demonstrated clearly by a detailed analysis of the whole narrative; and since it is not essential to our main contention here, the matter may be left.

[1] The idea that the whole interpretation of the narrative in terms of the 'Fall' depends on the equation of the serpent with Satan (so L. Köhler, *op. cit.*, pp. 175ff.) is completely erroneous.

[2] Quell (*TWNT* I, p. 284) is properly sensitive to this. Cf. also G. von Rad, *Genesis*, p. 87.

[3] Cf. pp. 205ff. above.

in the dark. *The riddle—whence does demonic evil spring?—must remain a riddle*, if evil is not to be misrepresented as harmless. But the two essential statements on the subject are made utterly clear: evil does not come from God, and it is subject to God's power.

Again, the question about *the doom of death as a consequence of sin* is of set purpose treated ambiguously. Clearly, the reason which God gives for his commandment is meant to be taken in the sense that death will be the immediate result of eating the fruit, though it does not exclude a possible reference to the doom of being sold into the power of death. This explains why the serpent can, apparently with justice, call in question the truth of the threat, and yet be then exposed as a subtle deceiver, because the power of death does, in fact, work its will on Man in pain and torment. Thus *it is not indeed the simple fact of dying which is here proclaimed as the punishment of sin*[1] *but the enslavement of all life to the hostile powers of death*—suffering, pain, toil, struggle—by which it is worn out before its time.[2] But with the mention of the tree of life another prospect is hinted at, even if only guardedly and in passing, which might have been opened up to a man who had matured in fellowship with God.

The more clearly the limited importance of the subsidiary questions is recognized, the more sharply does it emerge where the meaning and value of our story are to be sought. It speaks of a decisive event, by which God's plan for Man in his creation was frustrated, and human history came to be stamped with the brand of enmity toward God.[3] *This event has the character of a 'Fall', that is, of a falling out of the line of development willed by God*, and, as the subsequent narrative shows, exerts a determining influence on the spiritual attitude of all men. The teaching of the Church on the subject of original sin has rightly fixed on this passage to show that the real

[1] On the theological significance of including death in the original God-Man relationship, cf. P. Althaus, 'Die Gestalt dieser Welt und die Sünde', *Zeitschrift für system. Theologie*, 1931, pp. 319ff.

[2] This is also the view of Ps. 90.7f., where it is not death as such, but the swift passing of life, which is seen as the punishment of God's wrath. Nor do we find anywhere else any observation to the effect that death as such is the punishment of sin; it is simply the natural lot of Man, which one hopes to arrive at when 'old and full of days' (Gen. 25.8). On grief at the doom of death, and its intensification in view of the fact that death breaks the God-Man relationship cf. ch. XXIV, pp. 501ff. below.

[3] On the consequences of this event for the Christian understanding of Time, cf., in addition to the literature cited in n. 2, p. 403 above, K. Barth, *Church Dogmatics* I-2, ET, 1956, pp. 45ff.

seriousness of enslavement to sin consists in the fact that sin is not simply an 'occasional act . . . always arising out of the wrong decision of the moment, but . . . a perverted tendency of our nature'.[1] The Yahwist narrator does little or nothing to develop this idea dogmatically, because, like all good story-tellers, he leaves it to the reader to draw his conclusions; but his whole composition hammers the message home inescapably, and his distinctive hand is clearly to be seen in God's judgment of the evil character of human nature in Gen. 6.5 and 8.21.[2]

It is, of course, true that assent to this interpretation of the origin of evil is possible only to those who also admit the rightness of the biblical view of the bond uniting the generations. The Bible does not regard this as simply a biological fact with no effect on the world of the spirit, as contemporary science for the most part does, but sees in the physical association of the human race the influence of the reality of a common spiritual world, the most striking observable evidence for which is the inheritance of the total spiritual condition, the character. In the Old Testament this conception is strikingly noticeable in the fact that the prophets bring not only their own contemporaries before God's judgment, and denounce them for their rebellion, but also see them linked with all previous generations in a unitary entity, for which the sins of the fathers are also the sins of those now alive, and will be required of them, while at the same time the fact that the sinful condition of the present generation has resulted from the perverted direction of an earlier one in no sense does away with the responsibility of the former group.[3] And just as, in the prophets, the nation is considered as a single community bound together in spiritual solidarity, so also at bottom is the whole human race, when the evil which reigns within it leads to its being collected as a unitary entity before the judgment-seat of God.[4] This prophetic conception, however, already exists in prototype in the Yahwist, and is that which makes possible his distinctive interpretation of the phenomenon of universal human sin as the solidarity and concrete

[1] E. Brunner, *Man in Revolt*, ET, 1939, p. 145.
[2] An appeal to the statement about the righteousness of Noah is not a valid argument in the other direction, once we consider what was said earlier about the relativity of sinlessness, and bear in mind at the same time the fixity of the forms imposed by tradition on saga material.
[3] On this subject cf. the remarks of J. Hempel, *Das Ethos des AT*, pp. 43f., and W. Eichrodt, 'Heilserfahrung und Zeitverständnis im AT', *TZ* 12, 1956, pp. 103ff.
[4] Cf. vol. I, pp. 376ff.

actuality of a perverted basic attitude of human nature, the pattern and explanation alike of which are to be found in a primal decision. The Old Testament no more provides a theoretical account of this participation of each individual in a common spiritual world than it does of any other matter. A basis in reality for this distinctive mode of human existence may be observed only in that bond which links a man indissolubly with all other beings, namely his creatureliness, by which is signified the fact that his whole life is carried by the power of God's spirit.[1] But if it is the divine spirit which creates the physical and psychical cohesion of the life of the human race in all its members, by virtue of which its first decision becomes the decision of all, it is also the word of revelation which makes men clearly aware of this state of affairs, by drawing God's destiny for Man, and Man's offence against that destiny, into the light, and revealing his opposition to God as the united struggle of all human beings ever since they first rejected their origin. Thus the interpretation of the doom of sin given in the Fall story rests wholly on belief in an indissoluble bond linking the individual human being and the human race as a whole to God, a bond which cannot be done away even by sin, and which for the first time makes God Lord of mankind in the full sense. Biological existence in begetting and procreation is not an autonomous process of natural law, working itself out only in matter, but the outward expression of an inner community of the human race, rooted in the living power of God.

II. It is also a theologically significant fact that the profound conception of Gen. 3 not only is never explicitly referred to in the rest of the Old Testament, but only seldom finds even an echo in its thought. Above all, *prophetism* seemingly passes it over without attention. This is, however, to some extent explicable as a result of the prophets' immmediate task. For them, all the emphasis in their proclamation of judgment had to fall on the capacity of their hearers to decide and to act, since it was their sense of responsibility which they wished to shake into life. They knew themselves to be the messengers of the God who was at that very moment calling his people to account, and setting them before the decisive choice; and all their efforts had to be directed to making their contemporaries understand the immediate threat under which they were living. In such a situation it was hardly possible that they should feel it necessary to look backward to the origin of sin.

[1] Cf. pp. 47ff. above.

Nevertheless, when the prophets reflect on men's *compulsion to act in a way hostile to God* we find them led to use expressions which echo Gen. 3. Thus, for example, they characterize Israel's sin as closely akin to the behaviour of her first tribal father, Jacob, in order by this 'family likeness' to illuminate both the rebellion and the necessity of punishment which run through the nation's whole history, as well as the greatness of the divine mercy.[1] And when Jeremiah ponders the riddle of the irresistible proclivity to evil which he finds in his people,[2] he is led to use categories from Nature, now comparing the constant outbreaks of wickedness with the way in which a well keeps its water fresh and cool,[3] now, more explicitly still, using the black colour of the Ethiopian, and the spots of the leopard, as images for the inward growth by which the evil will is intertwined with the whole nature.[4] And in the painful struggle with his own resistance to God's will he is driven so far as to acknowledge the desperate corruption of the heart, a mystery of unintelligible horror from which he can flee only to the God who knows all, and who even for such a heart has power to heal.[5] Similarly Ezekiel can speak of a stony heart which makes any conversion impossible, unless God himself transforms it into a heart of flesh.[6] Nowhere, however, any more than with other aspects of the prophetic understanding, do we reach the stage of systematic exposition of this theme, resulting from reflection on an original decision of the human race.

Such reflection is even less to be expected in the *Priestly law-teaching*, for what matters here is first and foremost the awakening of moral energy for the purpose of fulfilling the concrete divine demand. The narrator of the Priestly primal history has made no attempt to develop the hints of his source on the gradual increase of corruption in the human race, but simply stresses the climactic point of this corruption by linking the Sethite genealogy with the story of the Flood. The statement about the guiltlessness of Noah may no more be taken as a dogmatic absolute than the assumption of continuing human transgression, expressed in the setting up of the rainbow as a sign of peace, and in the giving of a law for the protection of human life, may be elaborated into a theory of original sin. God's mercy,

[1] Hos. 12.3, 4; Isa. 43.27.
[2] Jer. 3.17; 9.13; 16.12; 2.21, 23ff.; 5.22, 24f.; 8.6f., etc.
[3] Jer. 6.7.
[4] Jer. 13.23.
[5] Jer. 17.9f., 12–14.
[6] Ezek. 36.26.

guaranteed in the covenant sign, goes hand in hand with the seriousness of his judgment, of which the sending of the Deluge at the beginning of the world's history is an unmistakable testimony to all
generations. Elsewhere, however, the ideas which dominate priestly
thinking are the goodness of the world which God has made, and the
irreversible nature of its ordinances;[1] and even the subordination of
the whole cultus to the idea of atonement, while it certainly reckons
with the universality of sin, yet allows it to remain in the class of
momentary transgressions of the Law, and says nothing about its
origin.[2]

III. It is all the more remarkable, therefore, that *in the post-exilic
community understanding of the Yahwist's concern should be manifestly on the
increase*. Alongside the protestations of guiltlessness of the Psalms of
innocence, and the oath of purity in *Job*,[3] stand such shattering confessions as *Ps. 51 and many passages in the book of Job*, which approach or
even equal the Yahwist's profound acknowledgment of sin. Less
weight obviously attaches to those statements which see Man's earthy
origin, and the impurity and frailty of his nature which stem from
this, as the reason for his failure in face of the spotless holiness of God.[4]
Here sin certainly serves to admonish men to be humble, and to give
up their demands upon God, but it is in no sense personal guilt, and
is therefore regarded rather as a reason why God should be patient
with men.[5] More profound are those passages which seek in the
psychosomatic link between each individual and his sinful forefathers
the reason why a man cannot stand before the divine purity and
perfection.[6] 'From the unclean no one clean can come';[7] in this
pregnant saying the unbreakable law of original sin is given terse and
striking expression. Nevertheless, both here and in a passage from the
Psalter like Ps. 143.2, in the thought of the ineluctable universality of
sin the sense of its concrete actuality has been lost, so that now it
seems more of a pardonable misfortune. Ps. 51, however, is quite

---

[1] Cf. vol. I, pp. 412ff., 428f.
[2] This is true even of a statement like I Kings 8.46, which sounds like an
absolute principle, but which, in fact, merely represents the experience of the effort
involved in keeping the Law.
[3] Pss. 17; 26; 59; 18.21–27; Job 31.
[4] Job 4.17–21; 25.4–6.
[5] In the same way the confession of universal human sinfulness in the Babylonian
prayer to Marduk, mentioned earlier (p. 396), constitutes a reason why the god
should hear the petition.
[6] Job. 14.4; 15.14–16.
[7] Job 14.4.

different. Here the worshipper is driven by the heavy guilt which burdens him, and moves him to confession, to stress without reserve the ultimate reason for his action, the perverted fundamental orientation of his heart. Moreover, he expresses this as an insight disclosed to him by God himself: 'I was brought forth in iniquity, and in sin did my mother conceive me.' This sin is not a matter of occasional deviation from the right way, but of *the consistent outcome of the natural tendency of his being*, which is already planted in him by the inheritance passed on to him at his birth. Here we have such a clear confession of original sin—though, at the same time, this is understood not as an easement but an enlargement of the responsibility laid upon Man—that the spiritual affinity with Gen. 3 is incontestable,[1] whether the worshipper himself was conscious of this at the time or not. Only when he has confessed this ultimate background to his deed, a confession which certainly did not come easily to him, does he feel that God's requirement of unreserved sincerity has been fulfilled, and that he can now proceed to ask for forgiveness. In Ps. 130.3 we find a similar confession of the coercive, but inexcusable universality of sin; but this, because of its brevity, does not possess the same far-reaching importance. On the other hand, Ps. 90.7–9 associates the sorrowful fate of human transience so inseparably with the opposition between the holy God and sinful Man that we cannot rule out the possibility that the interpretation of human destiny in the Yahwist primal history may have provided the background for these verses. What was once Man's bliss—to walk in God's light—has become his terror, because this light now penetrates to the most hidden things, and pitilessly strips Man naked to appear in all his enmity toward God before the eye of his Judge (v. 8). In Prov. 20.9 expression is given, quite out of context, to the impossibility of making oneself pure from sin. This may perhaps suggest that such ideas gradually hardened, at least in certain circles within Judaism, into axioms of faith.

In fact, the link between a man's own sin and the sin of Adam and Eve was generally acknowledged in *later Judaism*, and maintained in various forms. The descendants of the first human beings inherited from them not only the doom of death, but also the tendency to sin, whether the beginning of that sin was traced to Eve[2] or whether it

[1] There is no need here to go into the exegetical wriggles used to evade this insight. They condemn themselves by their artificiality.
[2] Ecclus 24.25; Apoc. Mos. 10; 32; Apoc. Bar. 48.42.

was held that the evil heart from which Adam's sin proceeded had
developed in all who were born of him.[1] But this explanation of
universal depravity in terms of the first Fall seldom exerted its full
effect on the understanding of sin. Because the evil impulse was considered part of the endowment of Man at his creation,[2] Adam's fall
was certainly a succumbing to temptation which opened the door for
death and every kind of misfortune to enter the world; but there was
no need to talk of a compulsion to sin, because in the Law the Creator
had, in fact, provided the means of counteracting the evil tendency,[3]
a means so effective indeed that the wisdom which proceeded from it
was able to rescue even Adam from his fall.[4] Another expedient
known in this period was to carry the impulse to sin back as far as the
angels, in whose fall Man was involved,[5] or to the demons, as a result
of whose seductions idolatry came into existence.[6] There is here an
effort to get to know how sin originated—the one thing which in
Gen. 3 was rejected—and this means that men are on the way to
making the riddle of demonic evil rationalistically comprehensible,
and thus to depriving it of its ultimate seriousness. The role which
Satan now plays as seducer[7] allows the individual to oppose the
impulse to sin with his own freedom of decision, and to hope that the
good will may be strong enough to overcome the tempter. Only in
II(4) Esdras is the utterly hopeless inevitability of the doom of sin,
and therefore of the divine wrath, recognized in view of the alliance
of the whole human race in sinful rebellion against God; and accordingly doubt as to the possibility of escaping the judgment is screwed
to the highest pitch. Nevertheless, even here there is no trace of that
logical derivation of sin from the perverted direction of the will,
acknowledged as an expression of one's own intimate nature, by
which alone the profoundest insight into the nature of the power of sin
can be attained. Man of his own free decision turns to sin;[8] each man
in turn becomes his own Adam.[9] Only in face of the redeeming act of

---

[1] II(4) Esd. 3.21f., 26; 4.30f.; 7.48ff., 118.
[2] Ecclus 15.14; 37.3; II(4) Esd. 3.21; 4.4; 7.48; Pesikt. 38b–39a (ed. Buber);
Vit. Ad. 19.
[3] Cf. p. 392 above.
[4] Wisd. 10.1.
[5] I Enoch 10.4ff.; 64.1ff.; Mart. Isa. 5.3; Vit. Ad. 12ff.; Jub. 4.22; 5.1ff.
[6] Jub. 11.4f.; 15.31; on the view of heathen gods as demons cf. vol. I, p. 227.
[7] Wisd. 2.24; Vit. Ad. 12ff.
[8] II(4) Esd. 8.56.
[9] Apoc. Bar. 54.15, 19.

Christ was it possible for the deepest understanding of sin to co-exist with the assurance of redemption.

4. THE CONSEQUENCES OF SIN

I. *Guilt*

(*a*) Purely semantically, guilt as an objective effect of sin, consisting in *liability to punishment at the hands of God*, is not for the most part distinguished from sin by a special term, but the same word is used for both. This is true of the most commonly used term *'āwōn*; in addition the root *ḥ-ṭ-'* is also occasionally employed.[1] The special word for 'guilt' which does exist, namely *'āšām, 'ašmā*, is very little used in this sense;[2] instead it has become predominantly a term for the act of restitution. The fact that the root *r-š-'*, as a result of its forensic importance,[3] is also a favourite usage for referring to religious guilt, shows once again the significance of legal language for religious terminology.

These indications make it clear that the Hebrew had no particular interest in making a sharp conceptual distinction between sin and guilt. This may be due to the fact that the language still reflects the influence of the earliest stage of religious thought, when, as a result of the material conception of sin, guilt meant the sentence which was immediately passed on the offender, while the subjective sense of guilt played no part. We have already discussed in detail how this stage overlapped with the early Israelite period.[4] Here the incidence of punishment and offence was simultaneous, because the latter immediately placed men under the dominion of the demonic powers, or transferred to the offender the contagious morbid matter from the sphere of the taboo.

Nevertheless, at a very early period, and not in Israel alone, this forced involvement in objective guilt, which derives from the world of dynamistic conceptions, was already *breaking up under the impact of rationalistic thought*, and that certainly as a result of the legal life of civilized communities. Thus rational considerations are brought to

---

[1] Cf. the use of the verb to denote a permanent condition of guilt, Gen. 43.9; 44.32; also the noun *ḥaṭā'ā*, Gen. 20.9.

[2] Gen. 26.10; Jer. 51.5; Ps. 68.22 and Amos 8.14 (the text here is, however, uncertain); Ps. 69.6.

[3] Cf. p. 381, n. 3 above.

[4] Cf. pp. 381ff. above.

bear on the exaction of blood-revenge, inasmuch as the determining factor now becomes not simply the cry for vengeance of the blood that has been shed, but also the necessity of making reparation for the damage done, even if only in the negative way of inflicting damage on the enemy clan; and here retribution according to the principle of the exact equivalent, the talion, is the rule.[1] Thus the primary interest of the State, the protection of society, leads to numerous breaches in the principle of automatic involvement in guilt, characteristic of the dynamistic world-view, so that manslaughter is now distinguished from murder, assault from adultery, and indirect from direct culpability; and milder treatment is meted out accordingly.[2]

(b) *The tendency discernible in these developments now receives effective encouragement from the Yahwist faith.* The law becomes an expression of God's sovereignty over his people, and the protection of the community therefore an overriding divine requirement. The effort to protect the life of the citizens both against the excessive penalties resulting from deeply rooted taboo fears and against the individual and the clan who take the law without restraint into their own hands now acquires a powerful ally. The divine Lord extends his protection to each member of his people—he certainly has no interest in allowing the host of his worshippers to be decimated by exaggerated claims for restitution. His will yet further restricts blood revenge, and breaks the spell of dynamistically based fear.[3] His categorical demand, which provides the legal system with its rationale in the form of a single transcendental authority, makes every infringement of the law guilt against God, and thus excludes from the consideration of guilt the dark demonic powers. Furthermore, the fact that the law is applied to the individual, and imposes upon him a personal responsibility which cannot be shifted on to the family or clan, trains him to grasp the idea of personal guilt, which is fundamentally different from any kind of impersonal involvement, and from falling victim to the realm of sinister 'power'. Here the difference between Israel's approach to morality and that of the other civilizations of the ancient Near East emerges clearly. In the latter the dominating fear of demons was able to keep the curse-like quality of guilt much more strongly alive. Guilt

---

[1] The opposite of this may be seen in the unbridled thirst for revenge of Lamech and the Kenites (Gen. 4.23f.).

[2] On this point cf. the instructive remarks of J. Hempel, *Das Ethos des AT*, pp. 55ff., where, too, the parallels from ancient Near Eastern law are set out *in extenso*.

[3] II Sam. 14.13f.

is regarded primarily as the spell and bond laid upon a man by the realm of power which he has unwittingly injured, and its impersonal character is shown by the practice of praying to the most diverse gods to lift the spell and break the chain.[1] Where, however, the guilt is seen as attaching to an injury done to a deity, there the large number of gods, and their mutually conflicting wills, make it impossible to settle the question of culpability cleanly. Not only do men flee from the anger of one god to the possibly more gracious attitude of one or more others, thus escaping personal responsibility, but the uncertainty about the true will of the gods makes any clarity as to the offence impossible, and the frequent complaint of human ignorance of the concrete divine will is sometimes heightened into a reproach that the gods deliberately conceal their will from Man, or even worse, that they reveal to him what is false, and deliberately teach him all evil.[2]

From such blasphemies the pious Israelite was preserved not only by his strong sense of the meaning of election and of the covenant, namely the creation of a holy people, but also by his clear knowledge of the will of God, which, far removed from all caprice or malice, had shown itself a reliable guide for the shaping of the nation's life.[3] In the covenant statutes men possessed a revelation of that will which there was no misunderstanding, and the regularly recurring covenant festival[4] deeply impressed on them the privilege of being certain as Yahweh's people of the divine will for fellowship with men. The later law-teaching was right to see this as the especial respect in which Israel was superior to other nations, and to summon her to rejoice proudly on this score.[5] From this root grew Israel's capacity for not going to pieces over some enigmatic act of God, attributing it to his decision in the consciousness that his was a higher justice, superior to all human wishes.[6]

Where the concept of guilt in this way acquired its special character from the clear dealings of one person with another, it was possible for

[1] Cf. H. Zimmern, *Babylonische Hymnen und Gebete in Auswahl*, 1905, pp. 18f., 23ff.; A. Falkenstein and W. von Soden, *Sumerische und akkadische Hymnen und Gebete*, 1953, pp. 305, 321f., 328.

[2] Cf. B. Meissner, *Babylonien und Assyrien* II, 1925, p. 432.

[3] Cf. vol. I, pp. 36ff., 242ff.

[4] Cf. Deut. 27.14ff.; 31.10ff., and A. Alt, *Die Ursprünge des israelitischen Rechts*, pp. 63ff.

[5] Deut. 4.6ff., 32ff.; cf. Jer. 2.13, 31f.; Ezek. 20.11.

[6] Cf. vol. I, pp. 260ff., 276.

a *living sense of guilt* to grow which was no longer dependent on the prior infliction of a penalty. In this connection it may be significant that the designation of sin which was chosen as the common term for guilt was precisely the one which implied the element of a perverted attitude, namely *ʿāwōn*.[1] And even though on many occasions, especially where national guilt was involved, the existence of sin was only recognized from the fact of punishment,[2] yet the sense of responsibility was so sharpened that men were keen to make reparation even in unintentional cultic offences without waiting for punishment to fall.[3] Furthermore, the belief that Yahweh would punish, even when no human avenger of the guilt was to be feared, was deeply rooted in the conviction of the divine righteousness, which stands by the demands of the covenant.[4] Even when he does not intervene at once, there is no question of his forgetting; either he keeps the guilt by him, tied up in a bag,[5] or written in a book,[6] or he waits until its measure is completely filled.[7] When his punishment of wickedness in high places was proclaimed, this, too, was bound to have the effect of sharpening the conscience of the whole nation.[8] Thus Israel became well acquainted with the punishment of an evil conscience, which outruns the external penalty, and knew how to portray it in striking terms.[9] When fallen Man hides himself in order to elude God's gaze, when David's heart smites him after committing crime, these turns of phrase express eloquently the understanding of guilt as the disturbance of a personal relationship of trust. Hence when the king breaks down at the prophet's sentence, which sets before his eyes the naked truth of the outrage which he has committed, the words which burst forth from him are a confession of sin: 'I have sinned against Yahweh.'[10]

Thus it is the living experience of God's personal dealings with the men whom he has chosen which in early Israel brings out in ever

[1] Gen. 4.13; 15.16; 19.15; Ex. 20.5; 34.7; I Sam. 25.24; II Sam. 3.8; II Kings 7.9, etc.; vb. *ʿāwāh* II Sam. 24.17.

[2] II Sam. 21.1; I Sam. 14.37ff.

[3] Job 1.5.

[4] Cf. vol. I, pp. 242ff.

[5] Hos. 13.12.

[6] Hos. 7.2; Ps. 90.8. Despite the relatively late attestation the imagery can without hesitation be regarded as ancient.

[7] Gen. 15.16.

[8] I Sam. 15.23ff.; II Sam. 12.10ff.; 24.11ff.; I Kings 21.19.

[9] Gen. 3; I Sam. 15.13; 24.6; II Sam. 24.10. Cf. also the Jacob story, which is well aware what it is to be burdened by guilt.

[10] II Sam. 12.13.

sharper relief *the personal element in the concept of guilt*, and thus trains men in a truly moral attitude, which is ready consciously to take responsibility upon itself. It is true that at the same time the original magical ways of thought are far from completely excluded, and indeed sometimes prevail with terrifying harshness;[1] but they have been driven from their dominating position. The breaking of their power has been given its most beautiful expression in the words with which King David resists the involvement of the innocent in his own guilt, and claims the full responsibility for himself: 'Lo, I have sinned, and I have done wickedly; but these sheep, what have they done?'[2]

(c) To this dominance of the personal God-Man relationship in the concept of guilt *the struggle of the prophets* made an important contribution. Their central concern may be summed up by saying that they wish to make their people stand in responsibility before the personal God, who rejects all those objective works which are offered to him in place of personal surrender, and breaks in pieces any material guarantee of his protection which is meant to act as a substitute for a living relationship of the heart. Therefore the purpose of their condemnation of the nation's sin must be to awaken the sense of personal guilt toward the divine Thou, in order that the coming judgment may not be understood as blind fate, or worse still as proof of the impotence of the god of Israel in face of the world powers. Here, first of all, *the individualizing effect of the prophetic preaching*[3] took on great importance. Because by their concrete demands the prophets confronted each individual member of the nation with a decision, they ruled out the possibility of evasion by appeal to the force of circumstances, or to the guilt of the community as a whole. Indeed, that involvement of the individual in the corporate guilt which they laid so heavily on the conscience of the people inevitably had quite the opposite effect, namely to give the personal guilt of the individual its full seriousness by revealing it as an active participation in, and intensification of, the corporate anti-God attitude. The way in which priests and prophets, kings and leading politicians, and the upper class in general, are denounced and made responsible for the back-

[1] E.g. when the descendants of Saul are made to answer for the guilt of the head of the family (II Sam. 21), or in David's testamentary instructions for dealing with those who have sinned against him (I Kings 2). Cf. also the remarks on pp. 381ff. above.

[2] II Sam. 24.17.

[3] Cf. vol. I, pp. 356–60.

sliding of the people,[1] and then in turn the damage done by such leaders is presented to the common people as brought upon themselves by their own indifference and forgetfulness of God,[2] intensifies the responsibility of the individual by directing his attention to the whole. This heightening of guilt by the combination of the sin of the individual with the enmity toward God of the community as a whole was felt, and given classic expression, by Isaiah in the words: 'I am a man of unclean lips, and I dwell in the midst of a people of unclean lips!' (6.5). At the same time, moreover, the sinful total direction of the will, which underlies the individual acts, is understood as a living guilt which excludes a man from fellowship with God.[3]

To make the conscience more sensitive to guilt was also the aim of the prophets' passionate *fight against the godless cult*, which, either by the objective nature of its performance or by the offer of mystical union with the deity, threatened to abolish the personal relationship of obedience.[4] Once the crucial seriousness of Yahweh's moral demand had been established, the completely personal guilt of offences against one's brethren was bound to make objective guilt seem insignificant.

The personal element in guilt, and the *comprehensive nature of culpability* are given their typical expression in the *imagery* with which the prophets illustrate the alienation of their people from God. First and foremost, it is by depicting the rebellion as adultery, or as a failure in filial piety, that they transpose this opposition to God into the conscious life of the will, and characterize it as a threat to Man's total relationship with God. In this way they break through the positions in which men entrench themselves behind the correct performance of religious duties, and bring to light the fact that the trespass on which guilt is based is the revolt of the inmost will from God. Similarly, when the insurrection of the creature against his Creator, the servant against his master, or the subject against his king, is used as an image for Israel's behaviour toward her God, then once again it is the intentional breach of a personal relationship which is the distinguishing mark of the guilt which results from such conduct.

(*d*) The effectiveness of the prophets' deepening of the sense of guilt may be seen from *the popular priestly instruction on the duties of a*

[1] Amos 6.1; Hos. 4.8; 5.1; 6.9f.; Isa. 1.10ff.; 3.12, 14; 28.7ff.; Micah 3.1ff., 5, 9f.; Jer. 2.8; 22.1ff., 13, 17; 28.15; Ezek. 13.4ff., 10; 14.9ff.; 34.1ff.
[2] Hos. 4.12f.; 7.3; 8.4, 12f.; Isa. 29.13f.; 30.9ff.; Micah 2.11; Jer. 5.12f., 31.
[3] Cf. p. 397 above.
[4] Cf. vol. I, pp. 363–7.

visitor to the sanctuary.[1] The unbreakable requirement of his God, as here presented to the pious worshipper, calls on him to pay strict attention to the moral quality of his actions, his false words or evil thoughts, and guides his self-examination toward offences of the will. We have already seen[2] how in this connection the cult preaching, the vow, and the recitation of the prescriptions of the law by the congregation, all helped to keep alive the sense that in every aspect of conduct the determining factor was a man's relation to the righteous and holy God. And because the individual was in this way trained to test himself against the claim to sovereignty of the holy God, he experienced his self-assertion as personal guilt which delivered him up to divine punishment.[3] Again, it was precisely in this context, when a man felt himself in a special way a member of a great community, that it was inevitably borne in upon him that his actions had effects beyond the narrow circle of his own individual life, thus educating him in conscious responsibility. Finally, the irrational commandments relating to purity, which were the most influential in suppressing the subjective element in the sense of guilt, were now drawn into the sphere of responsible conduct toward the community, and infringement of them, as a culpable disregard of one's duty to society, was able to evoke a genuine feeling of guilt.

(e) On the other hand, it was also in this sector that *certain limits* were set to a thoroughgoing treatment of the concept of guilt in moral terms. The need to expiate even unintentional offences was always liable to become the jumping-off point for that impersonal view of guilt which regarded it as an external pollution, with no thought for the inner involvement of the person of the agent. The extent to which such lines of thought were able to influence the sense of guilt plainly depended on the liveliness of the sense of obligation toward the personal God. *In the post-exilic period,* however, the threat from this direction was at first successfully averted. Although ritual separation came to be of great importance for the community, so that desecration of the sabbath now counted as a serious crime,[4] and questions of fasting and of cultic purity evoked sharp conflicts,[5] there is no sign of an objectification of guilt. Personal responsibility is still strictly safe-

---

[1] Pss. 15; 24.3–6.
[2] Cf. vol. I, pp. 419ff.
[3] This has been strikingly brought out by A. Quast, *Analyse des Sündenbewusstseins Israels nach dem Heiligkeitsgesetz,* 1956.
[4] Isa. 56.4, 6; Jer. 17.19ff.; Ezek. 20.12, 16, 19, 21; 22.8, 26.
[5] Isa. 58; Zech. 7f.; Hag. 2.11ff.

guarded. Indeed, that training in the Law which Ezekiel had so
purposefully introduced located enmity toward God wholly within
the knowledge and will of the agent. Again, both in the threats and
exhortations of the law-teaching, and in the lamentation psalms of
the grievously afflicted, we find phrases which catch vividly that
rebellion of the will to which the divine punishment was the response.[1]
Still more do the penitential psalms reveal the desire to submit the
ego without reserve to God's indictment.

Nevertheless, in a different quarter there are the first signs of *a
weakening of the sense of guilt*. The increasingly exclusive concentration
of piety on the Law directed men's attention more strongly to the
individual trespass and its avoidance than to the basic corruption of
the will.[2] In such circumstances it was possible for an *optimistic and
rationalistic view of sin* to gain ground, which differed from the prophets
as to the possibility of doing good and thus standing immaculate
before God, in that while certainly accepting Man's natural state of
sinfulness it excluded this from the scope of conscious responsibility as
merely a deficiency in his equipment, and thus deprived it of its
significance for the recognition of guilt.[3] This meant that the subjection of life in all its aspects to the wrath of God became incomprehensible. All the emphasis fell on the doing of the Law, which
was sufficient of itself to overcome the doom of guilt without any need
in addition for a unique divine act of redemption, transcending all
analogy. In this connection it is important to note *the introduction of
juristic categories* into Israel's thought about the divine act of salvation.
This had already begun with Deutero-Isaiah's downright statements
that no valid bill of divorcement against the rejected wife Israel
existed, that the divine *gō'ēl*, or redeemer, was not exempt from some
kind of obligation to pay the ransom of his people from slavery, that
indeed a real injustice had been done to him by the fact that those
who belonged to him had been enslaved without compensation to
himself, and that a calculation of the guilt accumulated in the past
showed that the penalty had already amounted to far more than the
required measure.[4] Some of this, of course, is simply the product of
lyrical exuberance on the part of the bringer of comfort, and is provided with certain correctives, if his preaching is considered as a

[1] Lev. 26.14ff., 40f.; Deut. 28.15, 46; 29.18ff.; 30.15ff.; Lam. 5.16.
[2] Cf. p. 392 above.
[3] Cf. pp. 399f. above, and 477f. below.
[4] Isa. 50.1; 43.3; 49.26; 60.16; 52.3–5; 40.2; cf. Lam. 4.22.

whole; but it was possible for it to be taken very literally by those who were waiting for the fulfilment of the great promises, and who could use it to limit their responsibility for the oppressive punishment that had befallen them. The songs of lamentation also show clearly enough how men were inclined to qualify the extent of their personal culpability by *a side-glance at the cruelty of the enemy and the guilt of their fathers*.[1] It is in keeping with this that, in the use of the image of God's fatherhood, the thought of the overwhelming power of Yahweh's love, in which alone men can confidently place their trust—the aspect still dominant in Hosea and Jeremiah—is less prominent than the idea of him as creator and ruler.[2] If we also take into account *the schematism of the doctrine of retribution* as found in the history-writing of the Deuteronomistic school and of the Chronicler,[3] then the lines of development become clear which were to lead to a weakening of the idea of guilt as a totality embracing the whole person, a weakening that had the most serious consequences.

The tendencies we have just mentioned were emphasized in *later Judaism*. The insight that sin does not simply result in an objective penalty, but has its real sting in the personal guilt which burdens the individual with his own responsibility before God is consistently maintained. It is expressed above all in those touching penitential prayers of which the literature of later Judaism has left us not a few. Here the sense of guilt toward God, and of turning directly to him, are powerfully attested, pre-eminently in the Prayers of Manasses and of Azarias.[4] Moreover, in general the great part which the concept of conversion plays in the religious life of Judaism[5] speaks clearly enough of the vitality of a sense of guilt which knows itself to have failed God, and which does not attempt to compensate for this fact by any kind of objective performance or material guarantee.

It will, however, be readily appreciated precisely for this reason that Judaism could no longer maintain that radical seriousness of the concept of guilt by which the whole of life is regarded as coming under judgment. The innate tendency to sin had already been

---

[1] Lam. 1.21f.; 2.20ff.; 3.34–36, 59ff.; 4.13, 21f.; 5.7; Isa. 63.18f.; 64.11; Ps. 79.8.
[2] Deut. 32.6; Mal. 1.6; 2.10; Isa. 64.7; 45.9ff.
[3] Cf. p. 392 above.
[4] Cf. also the prayer of Esther and Mordecai in the additions to Esther; Tobit 3.1–6, 11–15; Judith 9.1–14; III Macc. 2.2–20; 6.2–15.
[5] Cf. §5 of this chapter, pp. 470ff. below; also A. Büchler, *Studies in Sin and Atonement in the Rabbinic Literature of the First Century* (Jews College Publications No. 11), pp. 212ff., and 270ff.

removed as a contingency of creaturehood from the sphere of conscious responsibility; now, in the doctrine of the evil impulse,[1] it was
described as a natural endowment implanted by God, and thus God
was made ultimately responsible for Man's sinful desires. It is in turn
this natural endowment which cannot but move the Creator to
sympathy with his creature, and thus induce him to provide a remedy
for this weakness, namely the Law. This reduces the guilt of Man to
neglect of the defence provided against the temptations that beset
him, and makes it proportionate to the greatness of the commandment, the transgression of which is in question, just as, conversely, a
successful struggle means a corresponding increase in merit. *The linking of guilt with the particular transgression of the Law*, a step to which
legalist piety by its very nature had always been prone, now for the
first time becomes the decisive principle, and results in an increasing
loss of understanding for Man's total culpability as a being with a
sinful nature resistant to the divine holiness. What is more, because
the idea of merit attaches to obedient observance of the Law, guilt
loses the character of irreparable damage, and becomes something
which can, in fact, be counterbalanced by the necessary number of
meritorious works. The incorruptible divine judgment is still proclaimed with intense seriousness, now indeed heightened by the
prospect of retribution in the world to come; but the purpose of this is
now to secure performance of enough of God's demand to enable
distributive justice,[2] after weighing reward against punishment, to
bring the balance down on the side of reward. *Thus juristic thinking
triumphs over the religious condition of personal relationship.* The dividing-
wall which it is essential to pull down is no longer the state of inward
alienation from God, but the outward falling short of his demands.
Thus even conversion can become a good work, which frees from
guilt,[3] and conversely the guilt of the godless and the heathen is no
longer expiable, so that the pious thinks himself entitled to meet them
with righteous revulsion and hatred.

But the attempt to ease the burden of guilt-feelings in these ways
could bring no real relief. Instead it revenged itself by the *uncertainty*
which attaches to all human arithmetic. Side by side with the proud
sense of being able to ward off guilt by strict obedience to the Law
there inevitably arises the doubt whether what has been done is really

---

[1] Cf. pp. 392f. above.
[2] Cf. vol. I, pp. 248f.
[3] Cf. p. 474 below.

enough in face of God's incorruptible holiness. Thus those who seek protection from God's wrath under wholly inadequate coverings find themselves all the more the slaves of the sense of guilt; and the Law becomes a taskmaster from whose tyranny men can be freed only by the One who disclosed the full depth of their guilt, but also took the curse of the Law upon himself.[1]

II. *Punishment*

(*a*) Where guilt was understood as a forced involvement in the sphere of destructive power, punishment could be one of two things. It might be a *consequence inevitable in the nature of the morbid sinful matter*, and working upon the one infected by it, or it could be the *protective measure of the community*, averting the contagion from itself. To achieve this it was necessary either to get rid of the sinner altogether, by solemn execration or by capital punishment, or in less serious cases to render the contagion harmless by the necessary purifications and incantations. Traces of this conception persist principally in the ceremonies of ritual purification for objective offences,[2] in the execution of the ban by burning,[3] in the expiation of an unsolved murder by purificatory sacrifice,[4] in the extermination of an undiscovered sinner by a written curse,[5] and in many formal turns of legal language, as, for instance, when it is said that the polluted land vomits forth its inhabitants,[6] or that the nation must put away the evil from the midst of it,[7] or that the sinner shall be 'cut off' from his people.[8]

Limits have already been set to the predominance of this conception of punishment in the civilizations of the ancient Near East by the *community's need for security*. The effect of this factor is to avert serious harm by calculating the claims of the injured party on a rational basis, and then enforcing satisfaction, rather than to afford

[1] Gal. 3.13.
[2] Cf. vol. I, pp. 133–6.
[3] Josh. 7.25.
[4] Deut. 21.1ff.
[5] Zech. 5.1ff.
[6] Lev. 18.25–28; 20.22.
[7] Deut. 13.6; 17.7, 12, etc.
[8] Lev. 19.8; 20.17; Num. 9.13; 15.30f. The remarks of K. Koch, 'Gibt es ein Vergeltungsdogma im AT?' *ZTK* 52, 1955, pp. 1–42, tend toward the view that the sin works the hurt of its author by a kind of natural law. The evidence adduced, however, is not sufficient to cast doubt on the existence of belief in a retributive intervention of God. Cf. F. Horst, 'Recht und Religion im Bereich des AT', *EvTh* 16, 1956, pp. 71ff.

the unlimited protection of the law to a retribution compounded in equal parts of unbridled thirst for revenge and immemorial fear of the curse. As early as the Code of Hammurabi and the Old Assyrian Laws this rational balancing and limitation of punishment can be seen at work precisely in the case of those offences most heavily laden with ancient taboo conceptions;[1] and in the Hittite Law the rationalization of punishment is carried to its extreme, for here all transgressions seem to be assessed on the basis of an enquiry to estimate the damage. The attitude of Israelite law here differs characteristically from the ancient Near Eastern parallels, in that while, as in the Hittite Law, the death penalty is no longer imposed for offences against property, by contrast for the crimes of murder and lust a generally stricter judgment prevails, which still betrays traces of its dynamistic origin.[2]

This difference is all the more strikingly apparent in those cases where *the punishment is regarded as the deity's vengeance on crime*. This, too, was a conception widespread in the national religions of Israel's neighbours. Its effect was to convert punishment into the reaction of a personal will to the infringement of its commands; and it had the further consequence of giving new significance to the old taboo regulations as the gods' own prescriptions for right intercourse with them.[3] The divine judgments with which the law-collections are prefaced show how far this conception of punishment penetrated into the legal sphere. First of all, however, it was not possible for this personal element in punishment to have its full influence, because the gods themselves were not thought of in strictly personal terms, but remained in the category of personified natural forces. Secondly, legal life had been to a large extent removed from the sacral sphere, and the law, even when ascribed as in the Code of Hammurabi to the sun-god, is seen primarily as the work and will of the king, so that infringement of it cannot be described as sin against God. Furthermore, when a man was convinced that he was the object of divine punishment, then in addition to praying for forgiveness and release he could always have recourse to magical practices, and by incantations, sacrifices, and lustrations try to bring pressure to bear on the maleficent divine will. This expedient was encouraged by the uncertainty mentioned earlier about the real will of the gods, which is thought of

[1] Cf. pp. 382f., 413 above.
[2] Cf. vol. I, pp. 77–82.
[3] Cf. A. van Selms, *De babylonische termini voor zonde*, 1933, pp. 89ff.

not only as divided against itself but also as unfavourable to Man. Where none the less it is taken seriously, and binds men to certain actions by a kind of contract, there it is always possible to remove the punishment by works of merit, in particular by rich sacrifices.[1]

Inevitably, the transformation of the old conceptions of punishment in Israel, with her *knowledge of the personal covenant God, and of his clear, unmistakable will,* was incomparably more pronounced than was possible to her neighbours with their knowledge of God. Just as, in Israel, the sense of guilt markedly reflected men's awareness of having offended a personal divine will, so, too, this awareness was bound to give a special cast to the conception of punishment. How terrifyingly punishment was felt as the personal action of the offended God of Israel is shown by the references to Yahweh's anger, which intervenes with fearful jealousy against any contempt shown to him.[2] And yet punishment cannot be understood either as the brutal blow of an offended being or as the unbridled revenge of a wrathful one, because in some way or other it is incorporated into the covenant relationship, within which men have learned to know the normative will of God. Thus it comes about both that the punishments obtaining in civil law are acknowledged without further ado as established by God, whose purpose of justice is made effective in their execution,[3] and also that there is never any question in Israel of a gradual removal of the secular law from the religious sphere such as occurred in neighbouring civilizations.[4]

It was in keeping both with the living juristic element in the terms of the covenant, and with the basically rational character of Israelite thought, that men sought to elucidate Yahweh's judicial activity by means of the fundamental principles of human retributive punishment. Above all it was by applying the *maxims of the talion*[5] that they tried to illustrate God's irreproachable righteousness. The sinner is punished in the thing by which he sinned. The woman receives a curse on her sexual life, because she has experienced the sexual distinction in forbidden ways; she becomes a slave of the man whose decision she was able to influence in accordance with her own will. The monument to the unity and greatness of the human race, the Tower of Babel, becomes the monument to its disintegration and

[1] Cf. A. van Selms, *op. cit.,* pp. 102ff.
[2] Cf. vol. I, pp. 258ff.
[3] Cf. vol. I, pp. 74f.
[4] Cf. vol. I, pp. 92f.
[5] Gen. 9.5ff.; Ex. 21.12–14, 23–25.

impotence. King Adonizedek of Jerusalem meets the same fate as he had devised for seventy other kings,[1] and so on. Underlying all such instances there is undoubtedly a profound thought, namely that *offence and punishment ought to correspond to one another*, and thus make plain that retribution is not simply something external and capricious, but is based on the nature of the case in question. At the same time a cold, juristic formalism is avoided. This may be seen most clearly in the rejection of indirect talion, a practice still very much alive outside Israel.[2] From being a merely natural phenomenon, whereby the punishment reveals the inevitable natural consequence of the morbid sinful matter, *the correspondence has now become moral*, something based on the righteous purpose of the God of retribution. Even where turns of speech are still influenced by the impersonal outlook, according to which sin punishes itself, the polluted land vomits forth its inhabitants, the sowing of the wind reaps the whirlwind,[3] this is already serving to provide concrete imagery for the recognition that Yahweh punishes sin by a power of destruction inherent within it, so creating a just requital. The suspicion is, in fact, awakening that there exist *laws of the spiritual world*, in accordance with which sin must work to undo and destroy its perpetrator. Once again it is the great psychologist of Gen. 3 who has given this insight classic expression by making bitter enmity between seducer and seduced proceed from fellowship in rebellion against God. Another phenomenon well known to the Israelite is the fact that the punishment of sin may consist in the sinner's loss of his freewill, so that he falls prey to a compulsion to go on sinning—a process brought out, for example, in the story of Saul.[4] Often it is explicitly emphasized that God himself has decreed this surrender to the sinful compulsion, that, in fact, he *punishes sin with sin*, the consequence of which is then inevitable catastrophe.[5] Thus clear

---

[1] Judg. 1.7 (MT Adonibezek); cf. I Kings 21.19; II Sam. 12.10; 15.23, 26, 33.
[2] Cf. vol. I, p. 78.
[3] Hos. 8.7.
[4] I Sam. 17–20, on which cf. p. 384 above. Cf. further Ex. 7.23; 8.11, 28; 9.7, 35.
[5] Ex. 10.20, 27 (E); I Sam. 2.25; Judg. 9.23f.; Deut. 2.30; Josh. 11.20; I Kings 12.15. It is plainly a misunderstanding of the Old Testament view to do as does J. Hempel (*Das Ethos des AT*, p. 54) and try to find here a formal theocentric view of sin, on which the human factor is of no significance compared with the all-determining will of God in history, and God as the omnipotent becomes also the author of sin. God's sovereign freedom to punish sin with sin if he wishes, and in that way to bring it to judgment, is quite another matter from the immoral practices of the Babylonian and Greek gods, who make false revelations to men in order to deceive them to their ruin. On this subject cf. also vol. I, pp. 262f.

lines of development can be traced from a more external and juristic, talion type of retribution to a profound correspondence between guilt and punishment, one based, that is to say, on the nature of sin as a turning away from the divine source of life.

In all this it has already become clear that the rational categories of covenant law, effectively as they encouraged reflection on God's punitive action, were unable to *cover it with juristic definitions of punishment*, since these would have meant doing away with a living reaction of the divine personality. Even in his punitive intervention against human disobedience the personal God still asserts his sovereign freedom. He may equally well choose to annihilate quickly, or to wait patiently to store up the punishment,[1] to be harsh and strict or to show a forgiving clemency.[2] Again, where men maintain a lively sense of the numinous terribleness which surrounds the divine holiness,[3] they are inwardly ready to find even the harshest punishment neither meaningless nor cruel, but in keeping with the aweful divine majesty. This openness to the mystery of the divine nature certainly has something to do with the fact that in Israel juristic moralism, which bases culpability on a refusal to carry out one's contractual obligations, and thinks that the resulting liability to punishment can be removed by voluntary works of supererogation, was again and again successfully averted. Finally, the real seriousness of God's punishment was further safeguarded by the fact that the use of magical pressure to escape from God's visitation was completely ruled out. The will of Yahweh as the utterly unique and supreme power, effective in all events, was too firmly impressed on religious thinking to allow of any attempt at going over his head to other powers in order to evade punishment. Where God has not himself laid down definite methods of expiation, and attached his pardon to them, there is no human means of making reparation for an offence against him. It must be left to his sovereign penalty.[4]

Nevertheless, however little men might think it permissible to prescribe a measure for the divine vengeance, yet on *the meaning and purpose of punishment* they were clear, and sure of their ground. If Yahweh's righteousness and faithful love found their goal in the

[1] Num. 16.25ff.; Ex. 32.34.
[2] I Sam. 6.19, etc., and Gen. 18.22ff.; 20.6; Num. 14.18–20; II Sam. 7.14, cf. Ps. 89.31ff.
[3] Cf. vol. I, pp. 275ff.
[4] Cf. I Sam. 2.25.

maintenance of the divine covenant, then his punitive visitation must serve the same end. The judgment of divine wrath is not the meaningless raging of a force of Nature, but is ultimately concerned with *protecting the ordinances of God* through which salvation is to be mediated to men.[1] Parallel with this, however, is the fact that divine election remains independent of human self-interest, and implies no natural tie between God and his people. To guard against such a misunderstanding God's punishment may even rise to the pitch of destroying the national entity altogether.[2] And yet this does not invalidate the general rule that *punishment* occurs *in the service of the constructive and saving will of God*, and has an inherent tendency to convict the sinner inwardly of his sin. Hence value is laid on the fact that the one who has fallen under judgment 'gives Yahweh the glory'[3] by confessing his transgression, and acknowledging the righteousness of the punishment which has come upon him. That Yahweh's punitive action is aimed, not only in the case of the nation but also in that of the individual, at effecting an inner purification and education, is shown by the story of Balaam, whom God punishes first by allowing him to give rein to his perverted will, and then by compelling him to travel the way on which his self-will has entered right to the end.[4] A similar sensitive understanding for the positive value of punishment is disclosed in the Joseph story, when the sons of Jacob are led by the chastisement which falls to their lot to acknowledge the wrong done to their brother.

An obstacle to this deepening of the juristic conception of retribution is to be found not only in *the equation of conscious and unconscious offences*[5] but also in the transfer from human to divine legal practice of the doctrine of *collective liability*. That for the sin of the individual not only he himself but also his family and clan—and, if he occupies an exalted position, then also his tribe and his nation—must be liable is a view understandable on the basis of the strong collective sense of the

---

[1] The instances of God's inexplicable wrath are not under consideration here, since they do not come within the category of punishment: cf. the remarks in vol. I, pp. 258ff.

[2] I Kings 19.17ff.

[3] Josh. 7.19, cf. Job 4f.; Jer. 13.15f. F. Horst has shown that in all probability this fixed association of confession and doxology was a naturalized legal practice, which occurs elsewhere in the ancient world ('Die Doxologien im Amosbuch', *ZAW* 1929, pp. 45ff.).

[4] Num. 22.34f.

[5] Cf. pp. 381f. above.

early period. It finds its most striking expression in the custom of blood revenge, and also lives on in the practice of selling the members of a family into slavery for debt. In accordance with this principle the Israelite army suffers a reverse because an individual has laid hands on enemy property devoted to the ban.[1] On account of Saul's deed of blood, and Ahab's worship of Baal, a famine comes upon the people; for David's census they are smitten with the plague.[2] Along with the man guilty of high treason his whole family suffers,[3] and the cursing of the evildoer brings punishment also upon his descendants.[4]

It is therefore all the more remarkable that, even at a time when there was still a very strong natural feeling for the solidarity created by social bonds, *individual retribution was explicitly made a basic principle of the practice of law*.[5] This presupposes that *in general* the full liability of the whole group to punishment was not assumed even for the case of divine retribution; and, in fact, many statements do point to the fact that God himself prefers not to have to impose this harsh penalty. Thus he sends a warning to the man who may unconsciously plunge both himself and his people into serious guilt;[6] he breaks the vicious circle of blood revenge, which otherwise would rage ruthlessly for ever.[7] With him the righteousness of a few weighs so heavily that for their sake he spares the sinful city, instead of conversely

[1] Josh. 7.

[2] II Sam. 21; I Kings 17.18; II Sam. 24.

[3] II Kings 9.26; Josh. 7.24; cf. Isa. 14.21; Ps. 109.14.

[4] Gen. 9.22ff.; II Sam. 3.28f.; I Sam. 2.31ff. It would be short-sighted to discover in this close connection of the individual with the community simply evidence of a low level of moral thinking. The responsibility which falls on the criminal is considerably intensified if he is convinced that his action has a decisive effect upon the whole circle in which he lives. And the members of family or clan are far more seriously induced to watch over each other, and to bring the erring back to the right path, if they know that they will all be held responsible together for the offence of a fellow member of the group. Modern individualism, which is for the most part the sole assumption behind condemnations of collective liability, by contrast means a loosening of the obligations that bind men to each other, and a dissolution of powerful moral motives, which often enough are replaced by nothing more than irresponsibility. On the other hand, however, it cannot be denied that at this stage the right relationship between the community and the individual person has not yet been discovered; and that moral consciousness cannot come to full maturity where it is kept in a state of compulsive dependence upon the social group. It is at this point that the impersonal conception of guilt and punishment, which obscures the activity of the personal God in the living I-Thou relationship, constantly intrudes itself. Cf. ch. XX above.

[5] Cf. vol. I, p. 78, n. 3.

[6] Gen. 20.6.

[7] II Sam. 14.6ff., 13f.

dragging down the few into the ruin of the whole;[1] and in the end he rescues the one righteous man from the mass which has fallen to destruction.[2] Again, where the individual is ready to take upon himself the responsibility for his act, in order to turn away judgment from those not implicated, there Yahweh is ready to forgive.[3] The utterly inexorable claim of the holy God to sole authority is driven home to men by the decree that the fire of wrath shall carry off not only the criminal himself but also his family to the fourth generation; but the benevolence of the same God is made clear even more emphatically by the fact that it is to the thousandth generation that he desires to reward good.[4] Even though, because of Manasseh, Israel can no longer be forgiven,[5] yet for David's sake God wishes to go on pardoning, and not to abandon his people in the future.[6] It therefore becomes clear that *from an early stage there was a sense of the inadequacy of collective liability*, because it did not fully express the righteous purpose of God, which tended rather in a different direction.

Thus the experience that God deals with men in ways that go far beyond the scope of impersonal liability to punishment paved the way for an understanding of the deficiencies of solidarity thinking in this context. But the individualizing force of the divine will also made itself felt in the ability to *differentiate sins according to the greater or less severity of punishment which they merited*. It is true that there are no theoretically unforgivable sins, for even in the case of offences for which, humanly speaking, the penalty was death, God's sovereignty was allowed a free hand.[7] Also moral transgressions are more lightly judged than cultic ones, inasmuch as the latter are products of an irreverent contempt for God's majesty, and as such admit of no reparation,[8] whereas infringements of social justice can be atoned

[1] Gen. 18.24–32. The ascription of a late date to this passage overlooks the fact that it is not concerned with the post-exilic doctrine of individual retribution, but with the ancient view of collective liability, with the sole difference that the customary reckoning is turned upside down, and that instead of the sin of the few making the whole group culpable the righteousness of the few avails for the salvation of the whole.

[2] Gen. 19.15ff.

[3] II Sam. 24.17.

[4] Ex. 20.6.

[5] II Kings 21.10–15; 23.26; 24.3ff.; Jer. 15.4.

[6] I Kings 11.12, 36; 15.4; II Kings 8.19; 19.34; 20.6; Isa. 37.35; 55.3; II Chron. 21.7.

[7] Cf., e.g., David's reprieve, II Sam. 12.13.

[8] I Sam. 2.25.

for time after time by restitution. Hence the threat of the judgment of hardening, by which Yahweh himself makes conversion and redemption impossible. In such cases a man's total attitude plays a part in determining the assessment of his individual offence, in so far as presumption and arrogance are major factors taken into account. But *the basic direction of the human will stands out as the really decisive factor even more* in the picture of that contradictory figure, the sinner who nevertheless remains the blessed of Yahweh—as, for example, in the cases of David and Jacob. Although unconscious and unintentionally incurred guilt may not go unpunished, it is always understood that there is still a consistent inner orientation of thought and action, even in a man who has fallen into many sinful acts; and the conviction is very much alive that God's punitive retribution does not heedlessly disregard this. To ensure, however, that God's grace is not tied to human merit, there is the effectual corrective of the simultaneous and equally vivid conviction that God is especially strict in judging those who stand closest to him. A relatively trifling offence is regarded as adequate explanation for the fact that Moses and Aaron did not reach the Promised Land; and Saul's rejection was always felt as a deviation from the general pattern of divine goodness and long-suffering, an event in which men recognized with terror Yahweh's inexorable calling to account.

In all these instances the outstanding fact is *the vividness with which men were aware of God's punishment as the operation of a personal relationship between God and Man.* As such it resisted schematization, and made analogies from human legal practice valid only as subordinate aids to clarify the just correspondence of guilt and punishment.

(*b*) This resistance to any objective conception of punishment, and to any attempt to codify it on legalistic lines, was deepened and strengthened by *the work of the prophets.* God's drawing near in judgment might indeed be portrayed in the colours of a natural catastrophe, such as thunder, storm, or earthquake, or be compared to beasts tearing their prey,[1] but for all the crushing weight and merciless severity of the event so described the divine I behind the impersonal process of Nature was never concealed or even obscured. It is not only that, alongside these similes, the concrete personal images of Father or Husband, Vinegrower or Architect, and so on, occur with equal emphasis;[2] the prophetic words of threatening and

[1] Cf. pp. 16ff. above.
[2] Cf. vol. I, p. 380.

punishment also exert their strongest influence by virtue of the fact that they thrill through and through with the breathtaking nearness of the almighty Lord, from whom there is no escape.[1] Similarly, by the form of address which they use in the overwhelming majority of cases, namely the plural 'you', the prophets individualize the 'thou' of legal and liturgical language, and confront each separate person with the punitive action of God. And the hot anger which moves God's hand to punish, and which forces prophetic speech into such bold anthropomorphisms, rules out any idea of an impersonal cosmic law or cold force of Destiny.

In the same way the prophets make it their business to convey to men that punishment is the annulment of a wholly personal relationship between God and Man, thus replacing an external consonance of transgression and retribution with *an inner correspondence*, and enabling them for the first time to understand, and inwardly affirm, punishment as the necessary consequence of sin. The breach of a relationship of trust so personal as that of marriage can result only in the divorce of the wife; for here the inner alienation both becomes externally visible and is worked out to its logical conclusion. The man who, when all natural supports are reeling, refuses to find his foothold on the rock of the promise cannot but stagger, slip, and fall.[2] Deliberate disregard of divine truth, habitual failure to listen to God's warning, inevitably lead to that deadness in regard to God's operations which at the decisive moment notices nothing, but in a stupor, asleep, or drunk, lurches irremediably toward the approaching disaster.[3] Against such a background even the more external correspondences acquire a moral necessity which transcends all formal juristic logic. That the misuse of natural goods to serve a voluptuous luxury ends in deprivation of the most primitive means of existence;[4] that the banditry which seizes its brother's holding makes itself landless;[5] that contempt for the special status intended by God for Israel among the nations, displayed in unworthy toadying to the great powers, is revenged by her sinking to the position of a despised slave;[6] these, and similar apt correspondences, become the signs of an indissoluble inner coherence, in which guilt and punishment go

---

[1] Cf. vol. I, pp. 349ff.
[2] Isa. 7.9; 8.12ff.
[3] Isa. 28.11f.; 29.9ff.; 6.9f.
[4] Amos 4.1ff.; Isa. 5.11ff.
[5] Isa. 5.8f.; Micah 2.1ff., 8ff.
[6] Jer. 2.11, 14ff.

together as an infringement of that divine purpose that embraces and sustains the whole of life.

Ultimately, however, that which makes this complex of guilt and punishment a compelling necessity is *the opposition*, revealed in sin, *between Man's conduct and God's nature*. The Holy One of Israel, whose transcendence is revealed in the fact that he carries out his personal moral will whatever the resistance, is bound to answer rebellion against himself with a punitive judgment which will reveal to the whole world how impotent sin is in fighting against him. The divine love that woos a return of love from Man must make it plain that to reject God's love is to forfeit the only salvation. In this way punishment is cleared of any suspicion that its severity is a matter of mere chance, dependent upon caprice or malice, and is rooted instead in the essential nature of God's revelation.

Because, moreover, the prophets experience the coming of the God whose ambassadors they are as a jeopardizing of the whole present state of the world,[1] they can no longer regard individual acts of divine punishment as isolated judicial sentences of limited scope. Instead they recognize in them a consistent divine activity, pointing to the final, annihilating revelation of his wrath.[2] Thus *punishment becomes first and foremost a definitive execution of judgment*, bringing into the light of day God's radical opposition to sin, as a result of which he is bound to reject sinful humanity. It is obvious that on such a view the element of education and purification can no longer be predominant. The prophets are indeed aware of this purpose of punishment, but they detect it almost entirely in the events of the past.[3] It is precisely because God's earlier blows did not succeed in their purpose of calling the nation to conversion that there is now nothing to look for but the penalty of total destruction. Significant of the increasing hopelessness with which any idea of averting the calamity is regarded is the change in the use of the image of the smelter; in Isaiah this is still accompanied by the vision of a new Jerusalem, but in Jeremiah and Ezekiel it illustrates by contrast the inevitability of destruction.[4] Even where the concept of the 'remnant' seems to leave open the possibility that salvation may come out of

---

[1] Cf. vol. I, p. 345ff.
[2] Cf. vol. I, pp. 267f., 464ff.
[3] Amos 4.6ff.; Hos. 2.4ff.; 7; 8; 11.1ff.; 3f.; Isa. 9.7ff., cf. 1.2, 5, 9; Jer. 2.30; 4.1; 5.3, 12ff.; 6.16f.; 9.6; 18.1ff.; Ezek. 16.47; 23.11, 35; Isa. 42.24; 48.10.
[4] Isa. 1.21–26; Jer. 6.27ff.; Ezek. 22.17ff.

punishment, the 'perhaps' of Amos reveals its utter uncertainty,[1] while in Isaiah the fact that the reality of the remnant depends entirely on faith makes its use as a way of escape from the doom of judgment impossible.[2] The attempts, therefore, which are constantly made to rationalize the prophets' preaching of disaster into a pedagogic and utilitarian device indicate a complete misunderstanding, which disregards the prophets' basic attitude.[3] For them the purpose of punishment was entirely theocentric, and had nothing to do with Man. It would certainly be wrong to conclude from this that their call to conversion was not seriously meant. Far from justifying an inactive despair, these preachers of judgment summoned men to a new effort to achieve righteousness before God—not in the belief that men could in this way create a better world, and thus buy off the judgment of God, but because they were convinced that the requirement of conversion, regardless of whether conversion was still possible for the whole nation or not, had to be taken seriously, and would bestow upon the individual a new relationship with his God. This does not mean that the punishment had ceased to be a judgment subjecting the whole world to the wrath of God, and had instead become no more than a way through to salvation. There is no abatement of its severity; for men it really is darkness and not light. But its purpose lies expressly in the revelation to all the world of the exclusive power and greatness, the holiness, and the sole deity of Yahweh.[4] From this viewpoint all limited, educative punishment is a matter of merely relative importance, standing only in parenthesis to the penalty of annihilation. Thus the promises made to the individual who is faithful to Yahweh are very modest, barely more than that he will escape from the catastrophe with his life.[5] Nor do the prophets claim any special fate for themselves. Equally, however, the hope of salvation which these same prophets proclaim is not based on any idea of the nation's serving its sentence; this, too, is exclusively linked with God and with his sovereign will.[6]

---

[1] Amos 5.15.

[2] Isa. 7.3, cf. 28.16.

[3] For the latest attempt cf. L. Köhler, *Theologie des AT*, 1936, pp. 212f. ([3]1953; ET, pp. 221ff.). In opposition to this view J. Hempel rightly describes the message of the prophets as 'non-pedagogic, and fatal to any conception of the prophets as well-meaning preachers of repentance' (*Ethos des AT*, p. 110).

[4] Isa. 2.11, 17; 5.16; Ezek. 6.14; 7.27; 12.16, 20; 25.7, 11, 17, etc.

[5] Isa. 8.18; 22.20, 23; Jer. 45; Ezek. 14.12ff.

[6] Cf. §5 below.

This expectation of the coming judgment of wrath also explains why the prophets pay no attention to *the problem of the collective liability of the community*, in which no exception is made for the individual. In view of the indisputable importance of prophetism for the development of religious individuality,[1] one might have thought that a detailed treatment of this question would be an indispensable requirement in their work. Nevertheless, it is quite obvious that the prophets themselves did not feel this necessity; and the decisive reason was their conviction that every member of the nation was involved in the mountainous corporate guilt.

There can be no doubt that the prophets, just as much as the pious of earlier generations, acknowledge very different degrees of guilt, as their especially severe reproaches of the upper classes testify. Hence they also take for granted that Yahweh's punishment may work out very differently in individual cases, though they look for a particularly strict judgment on those who have been favoured by God.[2] But confronted by this total account to which Yahweh is calling his people they know no one, not even themselves, who is free from guilt, and they therefore see all as justly dragged down to destruction. Whether in these circumstances the punishment is bound to be felt more severely by one than by another is not to them a matter of decisive importance; for on the one hand they would not dream of using rationalistic legal theories to restrict God's freedom to pass what sentence he likes,[3] and on the other, a visitation which transcends every measure of guilt comes under the heading of evil, and this can never be made palatable to rationalistic thinking by any schematization of retribution. Thus Jeremiah turns shuddering from the fact that God's anger does not spare even the children in the streets,[4] but he sees the greatness of the disaster as fully justified none the less by the deep corruption of all classes of the people. For the same reason even the supposed individualist among the prophets, Ezekiel, speaks of the righteous being carried off with the godless, just as, in a forest fire, green and dry trees go up in flames together;[5] and when his proclamation of the punishment of Jerusalem is countered by the objection that in that event the pious and the godless are

---

[1] Cf. pp. 245ff. above.

[2] Amos 3.1f.; Isa. 5.1ff.; Jer. 5.4f.

[3] Even the correspondence between guilt and punishment, on which they like to lay such stress, does not at any rate have this meaning: cf. p. 432 above.

[4] Jer. 6.11.

[5] Ezek. 21.3, 9.

to suffer the same fate, which is surely unjust, he describes the wickedness of the city as so great that even the saga-heroes of perfect
righteousness, men like Noah, Daniel, and Job, would barely be able
to rescue their own lives from such an environment—a comment
which, of course, implies an annihilating judgment on his contemporaries, who were far removed from such perfection.[1] Nevertheless,
with a fierce irony, he envisages the preservation of a certain number
of the inhabitants in the destruction of the city—not, however,
because by their piety they had extorted from God a just reward, but
so that, as an example of the city's corruption, they may make the
severity of the punitive judgment on Jerusalem comprehensible to
the exiles.[2] Even the popular jibe against belief in the solidarity in
guilt of the whole nation, both past and present, as proclaimed by
the prophets, a jibe which with deliberate one-sidedness lays the
blame for the misfortunes of the present generation on the fathers,
at first goes unrefuted. If the reference to it in the book of Jeremiah
can be attributed to the prophet himself,[3] then all that he would have
said on the subject is that the grievous oppression of corporate
punishment, which gave rise to such bitter scepticism about God's
justice, and which indeed throughout history has produced the same
effect, was, in fact, unavoidable in the present, but in the new age
would be lifted from mankind, together with so many other imperfections of this sinful world-era.[4] Only when, as happened with
Ezekiel, the jibe became an obstacle to the pastoral work of the
prophet, do we find it combated.[5] Yet even here this is not done by
merely denying the underlying truth. Instead, that truth is accepted,
and in the light of it a new deal from Yahweh for the present generation is proclaimed, in that his grace, which desires not the death of a
sinner, will make possible a new beginning which cannot be jeopardized by the natural coherence of the generations in sin. In this way
the most serious scandal about corporate liability to punishment,
namely that it no longer left any hope of conversion and new life

[1] Ezek. 14.12ff.

[2] Ezek. 14.21ff. It is only possible to see in these passages a prediction of the
rescue of the righteous, if no notice is taken of the strong undertone of irony.

[3] Jer. 31.29f. P. Volz would like to make this passage dependent upon Ezekiel's
remarks about divine retribution, but it is difficult to make this fit.

[4] In that case, however, the proverb must have been displaced to its present
position from another setting, since it is, in fact, manifestly superfluous in view of
the following promise of salvation. It might therefore be easier to assume a later
interpolation by another hand.

[5] Ezek. 18; cf. pp. 250ff. above.

even for the pious, was in practice abolished, without, however, denying that these same pious might be involved in every kind of evil. It is first and foremost a question of relationship with God; and the life which he bestows finds its significance less in the enjoyment of earthly good fortune than in that of being reckoned among the host of those who trust confidently in the final redemption of the new people of God, and who wait steadfastly for this goal. The reference to the coming purificatory judgment, which is to prepare the community for the eschatological consummation,[1] gave great prominence in this context to corporate responsibility.

(c) Thus the lines were laid down, along which the prophetic conception of punishment could exercise its influence upon *the community of the Law*.[2] Once men had experienced, in the return from exile, the end of the judgment of wrath proclaimed by the prophets, and the renewal of God's favour, the radical interpretation of punishment in terms of a final reckoning with sinful mankind was naturally bound either to recede completely into the background or to be strongly modified by limiting it to the judgment of the heathen. In its place comes to the fore the individual retribution so impressively proclaimed by Ezekiel, and now given a special stamp by the orientation of all life in accordance with the Law. In the teaching of the Law emphasis naturally fell much more on those isolated acts of punishment by which offences were put right and expiated, and thus the stability of the national life sustained, than on the discovery of the corporate guilt underlying the transgression, a guilt which placed the whole of life under the wrath of God. The resultant overall direction of the moral will received strong support from the priestly conspectus of God's action in the world; for on this view the eternal order stabilized in the Law meant the realization of the sovereignty of God, and the safeguarding and implementation of this order in the teeth of all obstacles became the most important theme of world-history.[3] Here *punishment* acquires its primary importance *as the way to restore the situation willed by God* but jeopardized by human crime. In addition to demonstrating the inviolability of God's sovereign power *its most important purpose* lay in *educating men in obedient submission* and conformity to his cosmic order. There could be no

---

[1] Ezek. 20.33ff.
[2] Cf. J. Lindblom, 'Die Vergeltung Gottes im Buch Hiob', *In piam memoriam Bulmerincq*, 1938, pp. 94ff.
[3] Cf. vol. I, pp. 427f.

more talk of judgment abrogating the covenant; on the contrary, God's supremacy was demonstrated precisely in the fact that he puts down human rebellion without suffering the eternal validity of his covenant order to be violated.[1] In such circumstances, however, individual punishment became meaningful precisely because its significance was limited, and did not demand to be expanded into a sentence on the whole world. Belief in a universal state of sinfulness, which might have pointed in this direction, was worsted by the opposite interpretation.[2] There was still, however, a vivid sense of a penal bond between the present and the past, of sharing the punishment due to the forefathers;[3] though here, too, there was a developing tendency to see this involvement, which contradicted the claims of the individual retribution theory, as grounds for excuse before God, rather to deduce from it the radical conclusions of the prophets.[4] Moreover, the possibility of turning to Yahweh at any time, and thus escaping the sentence, is the constant background of penitent confession.

So far as the life of the individual was concerned, the *emphasis on educative punishment* was bound to become a powerful incentive to strive after purposeful fulfilment of the Law. Indeed, the Deuteronomistic and Chronistic historical works devoted themselves, with a strong pedagogic intention, to the task of setting before the eyes of their people the unwearying, inexorable strictness of the covenant God, as seen in Yahweh's retribution in the past, and of exhorting them to take their punishment to heart. It was precisely in punishment that men now recognized the revelation of God's faithful love, which wounds and binds up, which punishes in order to be able again to have mercy.[5] The primary duty of the one who was being punished, therefore, was to confess his sin; and conversely, to refuse to do this, and thus to make fruitless God's warning and corrective chastisement, was a serious offence.[6] Indeed, there is so little doubt that God's purpose in punishing is to come to Man's help that punishment can be explained in terms of his righteousness;[7] and

---

[1] Judg. 2.11ff.; Deut. 4.31.
[2] Cf. pp. 396ff. above, and 477ff. below.
[3] Ezra 9.7; Neh. 9.33ff.; Lam. 5.7; Isa. 63.17.
[4] Lam. 5.20f.; Isa. 63.17ff.
[5] Micah 7.9, 18f.; Job 5.17f.; Pss. 6.2, 9; 118.18.
[6] Cf. the reiterated attempts of Job's friends to induce him to enter into God's plan for his education, and also Pss. 32.3–5; 38.19; 39.2ff., 10.
[7] Cf. vol. I, p. 249.

even the sinner has at least one righteous deed to his credit, if he bows himself penitently under the divine judgment. No little contribution was made to the dissemination of this idea by the fact that it was a particular favourite with the *Wisdom teaching*; since their own mission was to educate, it must have seemed a very natural thing to them to consider God's will from this standpoint as well. In addition, it provided an excellent means of making God's providence comprehensible to rationalistic thinking.[1]

The idea of punishment as *restitution and reparation*, which had also been current at an earlier period, was less prominent in post-exilic thinking on the subject. For the prophets it had been impossible to look at the matter in this way, for to them sin, considered not as a matter of isolated acts but rather as operative through a total attitude, was clearly something for which there could be no human reparation, just as the nature of sin as a personal turning away from God made the juristic concept of restitution of damage seem wholly inappropriate. In other circles, however, where sin was considered primarily as an individual transgression of the Law, the conception of punishment as reparation, an idea current in legal contexts, could take on a new lease of life. Deutero-Isaiah already echoes reflections of this kind when, for example, the guilt of Jerusalem is regarded as paid for, *nirṣā*,[2] or allusion is made to Yahweh's unpaid compensation, to which he is strictly entitled,[3] or the metaphor of selling into slavery for debt is used to describe Israel's punishment.[4] In Deutero-Isaiah all this is still metaphorical, and only meant to portray the greatness of God's clemency in familiar categories; but in the teaching of the Law the indemnity is given a concrete identity as when the laying waste of the land during the years of exile becomes a reparation for the neglect of the year of jubilee,[5] or when forgetfulness of God in times of abundance is balanced by the deprivations of extreme want.[6] Similarly the wisdom literature, in accordance with the doctrine of retribution, threatens the adulterer with the rape of his own wife, and the field of the fraudulent landowner refuses to bear him crops.[7] In these instances may be seen the beginnings of a *materialistic inter-*

[1] Cf. Job. 5.17; 32–37; Prov. 3.12.
[2] Isa. 40.2; cf. Lam. 4.22.
[3] Isa. 52.2, 5.
[4] Isa. 43.3f.; 45.13; 50.1b, and, in general, the description of Yahweh as *gōʾēl*.
[5] Lev. 26.43, cf. 35.
[6] Deut. 28.47f.
[7] Job 31.9ff., 38ff.

pretation of punishment, which can be distinguished from comparable prophetic statements[1] by the fact that attention is no longer focused so exclusively on punishment as the action of God, but that a more immanent retributive righteousness is envisaged, in keeping with the underlying principles of legal thought. The more exclusively piety was concentrated on the Law,[2] the greater became the danger that such materialism would weaken the personal element in punishment, and encapsulate God's retribution in juristic categories.

Moreover, as a result of this development there was inevitably an increasing temptation to regard external misfortune as punishment from which one could conclude with certainty that the person affected had committed some offence. This was particularly so where the *theory of individual retribution,* as the only possible way of explaining the evil in the world, had become a method of theodicy.[3] This principle inevitably raised *doubts about* the notion of *collective liability,* which was seen as a threat to the immaculate divine righteousness. Thus men felt compelled, in the teeth of the evidence, to assert that God's wrath was visited only on manifest transgressors of the Law, and that in all disasters the righteous were spared. According to the view expressed in the later additions to the Deuteronomic paraenesis it is no longer the whole people, but the covenant-breaker alone, who is to be extirpated by God from every tribe;[4] and the interpretation of suffering on the basis of this theory of punishment emerges in the book of Job as the chief opponent of a living faith in God. It is clear not only that this means a weakening of Man's direct relationship with God by the interposition of a theory elevated to the status of a cosmic law, but also that men's eye for reality is becoming clouded, and a crabbed insistence on the principle of individual retribution is taking the place of a living experience of God.

A number of elements in the situation, however, had the effect of retarding this development, and preventing it from reaching its logical conclusion. First, under the impact of the split between those faithful to the Law and those who despised it, a dividing-line which ran right through the community, *the sense of a corporate guilt* in which even the pious knew himself to be involved remained a living reality;[5]

---

[1] Amos 6.7f.; Hos. 10.13f.; Isa. 5.8f., 13, etc.
[2] Cf. pp. 344ff. and 310ff. above.
[3] Cf. §6 below.
[4] Deut. 29.20.
[5] Cf. Ezra 9.6ff.; Neh. 9.30f., 33ff.

and the mood of penitence which permeated cultic life, and which in the Priestly Code subsumed all offerings under the dominant concept of atonement, constantly impressed on the community that it was an organic unity even in the eyes of God, and kept awareness of this fact alive in the matter of liability to punishment as well. Again, because the prospect of the great day of judgment on the heathen was combined with the expectation of a strict purificatory judgment on the community itself,[1] Yahweh's future reckoning with his people also became a menacing possibility of rejection for each individual, and made it difficult to rest complacently on one's own righteousness. This meant, too, that a door was always kept open for the recognition that *punishment was a matter of God's personal dealings with men*. Thus not only did the liturgical confessions of sin on fast-days exert pressure to bring men to a humble acknowledgment in personal penitence of the righteousness of punishment,[2] but the individual prayers of lamentation also were capable of a depth and immediacy in the confession of guilt which witnesses vividly to encounter in punishment with the personal God.[3]

In later Judaism further impetus was given to this line of development by the great tribulation under Antiochus Epiphanes, and by the enlargement of the expected judgment on to a cosmic scale. Despite the strength of the tendency to individualism the idea continually prevails that the nation as a whole is responsible for the actions of its members, and therefore must also as a community bear God's punishment.[4] Indeed, it is thought of as corporately liable even for the sin of preceding and earlier generations.[5] There is also renewed understanding of the prophetic concept of God's final reckoning with men.[6] Moreover, belief in resurrection is well adapted to set vividly before the soul of the pious his complete defencelessness in face of the divine punishment imposed by the all-seeing Judge of the universe; and, what is more, condemnation, because of the thought of eternity which is now linked with it, takes on a particularly frightful aspect.

Here, too, however, the mainstream of religious thinking was running in a different direction. We have already seen how the threat of radical judgment was lifted from the destiny of the nation

---

[1] Zech. 5.1ff.; Isa. 65.11ff.; Mal. 3.2ff., 19ff.
[2] Joel 2.12f.; Jonah 3.10; Ps. 85.9ff.
[3] Pss. 32; 51.
[4] Jub. 30.15; II Macc. 5.17f.; 7.18, 32; Ps. Sol. 2.3, 7; 8.26; 18.4f.
[5] I Esd. 8.76; Tobit 3.3; Judith 7.28; Bar. 3.8.
[6] Cf. vol. I, pp. 470f.

as a whole.[1] But when the subject under consideration was the fate of the individual, belief in retribution led by a logical development to a *one-sided emphasis on the separate sinful act* and its punishment, in comparison with which the relation between divine retribution and a man's total attitude to life occupied less and less attention. This resulted on the one hand in a petty calculation of the exact correspondence between sin and punishment, in which a penal tariff was set up for all possible sins on the basic principle of 'measure for measure'.[2] The same misconception of God's righteousness, expressed also in the idea of a divine ledger where the transgressions and fulfilments of the Law by each human being were entered in detail, now condemned the God-Man relationship to imprisonment in juristic categories, and thus robbed punishment of its connection with the free and personal action of divine grace. On the other hand, by this time *every evil* had become *a punishment* from which one could deduce with certainty the sin of the person involved. Among the unpleasing phenomena which resulted from this belief were the harshness of judgment based on this kind of reasoning toward those who were suffering, and the artificial assumptions used to maintain it, which did not shrink even from ascribing sin to the child in his mother's womb.[3]

The realities of life caused serious embarrassment to this view of punishment; and one favourite device for escaping from it was *to refer everything to retribution in the world to come*. Thus the sufferings of the righteous could be understood as expiation of their venial sins, securing for them an unimpaired enjoyment of blessedness, while conversely the freedom from punishment of the godless in this world made it possible to punish them with the utmost rigour in the world to come.[4] The problem posed by the death of the righteous, which as the heaviest punishment for sin should really have befallen the godless, was resolved by saying that it was intended to produce hardening in the ungodly, and therefore necessarily carried with it a double reward for the righteous as compensation from God. In the circumstances it naturally had to be maintained that it was possible for the truly righteous to enter Paradise direct without dying, since a stringent ethical individualism could not tolerate the idea of death as an

---

[1] Cf. vol. I, p. 471.
[2] E.g. Tract. Sabbath 32b–33a. Cf. F. Weber, *Jüdische Theologie*[2], pp. 244f.
[3] John 9.2; cf. Midrash Rabba on Ruth 3.13.
[4] Beresh. rabba 33.

integral part of a history of sin beginning from Adam. Thus the effect of the prophetic conception of punishment, as regards both God's saving activity and Man's utterly lost condition, was blocked by the optimistic rationalism which could not allow God to have his own say in the matter.

5. THE REMOVAL OF SIN

(a) The nature of forgiveness[1]

1. When we come to answer the question how sin is to be done away, naturally the same basic distinction applies as figured so largely in our definitions of the concepts of sin, guilt, and punishment. According as the effective influence is that of the age-old primitive conceptions of impersonal numinous power or that of a clear theistic faith, so the balance will come down more heavily on the side of mechanical *purification* or of personally conditioned *forgiveness of sins*. For Israel, moreover, throughout the period of her existence as such, the domination of the world of dynamistic concepts belonged to the past, because faith in the covenant God had given her religious thinking a fixed point of reference; and therefore the first-mentioned possibility could never be more than a matter of relics from an earlier phase, the survival of which illuminates the real seriousness of the spiritual decision with which the irruption of the new reality of God again and again confronted the people of Yahweh.

(a) Such relics are to be found above all, as has already been described,[2] in the sphere of ritual and of the oldest national law. Here the removal of sin is accomplished by purely external procedures, which act *ex opere operato* to carry away the morbid sinful matter. Sometimes this is washed away by special water of purification;[3] sometimes it is burnt away in the fire,[4] or a substance endued with power, such as blood, overcomes the weakening of the character of holiness through sin;[5] sometimes an animal carries it away,[6] or there may in the end be nothing for it but to exterminate the sinner from

---

[1] An exhaustive survey of all the OT passages dealing with expiation and forgiveness is to be found in S. Herner, *Sühne und Vergebung in Israel* (Bulletin de la Société Royale des Lettres de Lund, 1941–2, III), 1942.

[2] Cf. pp. 381f. and 423f. above, and also vol. I, pp. 133ff.

[3] Lev. 14.5; Num. 8.7; 19.9.

[4] Num. 31.22f.; and in a symbolic sense Isa. 6.6.

[5] Especially Lev. 16.14–19; Deut. 21.1ff.

[6] Lev. 14.7, 53; 16.21f.

the community.[1] Here *the word 'atonement'* acquires the meaning of the material removal of a harmful medium of power.

In the Old Testament passages relating to atonement, however, this sense is no longer present. Here in every case it is the disturbed relationship with the personal covenant God which is to be restored by the removal of sin. But without the willing agreement of this God such restoration is unthinkable. In dealing with him there can be no question of coercion by the mechanical methods of magic, for his terrifying otherness, which punishes without fail any attempt by Man to put pressure upon him, is one of the basic facts of his revelation.[2] Where therefore the old purification rites are employed in his worship, they can only remain meaningful if understood as means ordained by God himself for the removal of sin; and they thus acquire their effective power no longer by a quality inherent in themselves, but because this effect has been bestowed on them by God. It has already been explained that in the process their original meaning was obliterated, and frequently transformed by incorporation into new patterns of thought.[3]

In this way *the concept of atonement acquires an eminently personal quality*. Expiation is not a removal of sin independent of the forgiveness of the sin, but constitutes *one method of forgiveness*;[4] and it is precisely in the crucial sphere of sacrificial atonement, where the attempt has so often been made to prove the existence of mechanistic and magical modes of operation, that this can be most clearly illustrated. It was shown earlier that the original meaning of the proper technical term for making atonement, *kipper*, offers no support whatever for such an interpretation.[5] The verb may well be a denominative form from *kōper*, 'money paid in expiation for a life which is forfeit', and designate the provision of such money. This would then link up quite simply with the declarative meaning 'to regard as expiation, to accept or recognize as such', and so with the more general sense, 'to make or grant expiation, to grant forgiveness, to forgive'.[6] The most important question raised by such a description of making atonement is this: does it imply that Man offers a perfor-

---

[1] Josh. 7.25; Deut. 13.6, etc.

[2] Cf. the section on God's holiness, vol. I, pp. 270ff.

[3] Cf. vol. I, pp. 133ff., 158ff.

[4] Cf. A. Büchler, *Studies in Sin and Atonement in the Rabbinic Literature of the First Century*, pp. 375ff.

[5] Cf. vol. I, p. 162.

[6] This follows the explanation given by J. Herrmann, *TWNT* III, pp. 302ff.

mance to God from his own resources, by which he can blot out guilt, and, so to speak, buy off God's anger? Or is such an atoning act part of God's free forgiveness, by which he restores fellowship with the sinner? Now, it may be that traces can be detected of an objective value in the atoning act performed in God's presence. In the first place the gradual limitation of the class of offences which can be expiated by sacrifice to such as have been committed through mistake or inadvertence[1] might suggest the conjecture that on the older view, which desired to make expiation in the same way even for more serious offences, the sacrifice was believed to have objective value for God. But the passages commonly adduced in support of this argument provide no reliable information. Thus the fact that the guilt of the house of Eli is described as too great to be expiated by sacrifice[2] points only to *certain limitations of sacrificial atonement*, which are apparently bound up with the fact that the offence is one of open contempt for Yahweh; there is no definite statement about the way in which expiatory sacrifice is effective. Again, when David invites Saul to let Yahweh smell the savour of an offering, in case the implacable jealousy and hostility toward David which have come over the king should be sent by God,[3] then, if the passage does indeed refer to expiatory sacrifice,[4] this still by no means excludes that personal self-abasement and submission to God's sovereign rights for which the sacrifice elsewhere serves as an expression. The same applies to the atoning sacrifice made by David during the plague visitation,[5] a sacrifice made, after all, on the orders of the prophet, and thus at the indirect command of Yahweh himself. On the other side, however, one might point with more reason to the atonement effected by Aaron's incense offering,[6] an instance in which the efficacy of the holy altar fire and of the person of the priest as the effectual cause are as much stressed as the intervention of Yahweh in causing the plague is played down. Whether this means that an old popular view is reflected in the Priestly narrative, or, as is more probable, that we have here speculation about the atoning efficacy of the holy fire, significant for the latest strata of the Priestly writing, may be left

[1] Cf. vol. I, p. 161.
[2] I Sam. 3.14.
[3] I Sam. 26.19.
[4] This is disputed by J. Herrmann, *op. cit.*, on other grounds.
[5] II Sam. 24.17ff.
[6] Num. 17.11f.

undecided. But nowhere else in the Old Testament is it possible to point a similar statement.

For this reason all the greater emphasis is sometimes laid on the style and manner in which the Priestly law speaks of making atonement. The stereotyped formula at the conclusion of each set of instructions—'the priest shall make atonement' for the transgressor by carrying out the sacrifice[1]— might indeed be understood as referring to a human action effectual in itself, in which everything depends on the correct fulfilment of the ritual, but not on the forgiving will of God.[2] And yet such a conception directly contradicts the fundamental conviction of the Priestly law that all sacrificial actions derive their legitimacy from being established by God himself. Consequently the whole priestly institution of atonement is to be regarded as the gracious creation of the covenant God, who bestows upon his congregation the possibility of expiating all those things that call for expiation, and of assuring themselves, through these visible signs, of his forgiving grace and enduring clemency.[3] If, moreover, one takes into consideration the fact that atoning sacrifice is accompanied by confession of sin and by prayer, elements which, even if not explicitly mentioned every time, nevertheless correspond to the general conviction of the necessity of contrition and repentance on the part of Man,[4] then it becomes quite impossible to agree with any view that turns the Priestly atonement sacrifice into an objective purification; instead it can only be regarded as *a means employed by God's purpose of forgiveness* for the healing of infringements of the covenant.[5] That men's readiness to substitute material satisfaction for personal acceptance of responsibility attaches especially easily to the formal institution of the atonement sacrifice is indisputable; but that is not sufficient reason for regarding such a lapse as an inseparable epiphenomenon, indeed, as an inherent characteristic of the atonement sacrifice. How strenuously Priestly circles in particular were on their guard against this distortion of the atonement offering is shown by the limiting of expiable offences—perhaps under prophetic influence—to sins of inadvertence. Furthermore, it was precisely from the Priestly side that it had already been emphatically

[1] Lev. 4.20, 26, 35; 5.6, 13, 16, 18, 26, etc.
[2] So L. Köhler, *op. cit.*, pp. 213f., *et al.*
[3] Cf. vol. I, p. 162.
[4] Cf. vol. I, p. 160, n. 3.
[5] Cf. A. Quast, *Analyse des Sündenbewusstseins Israels nach dem Heiligkeitsgesetz*, pp. 23f., 63f.

explained in the early period that sins committed in blatant contempt for the will of God could not be expiated by any sacrifice, the reason clearly being that the subjective precondition of atonement was lacking.[1] This obviously implies a continuing and vivid awareness that it is not within Man's power to set clearly defined limits to the effectiveness of sacrificial atonement; on the contrary, this is always something reserved to God's free decision. We shall search the Priestly law in vain for a theory of atonement in the strict sense. Even where the offering of the life contained in the blood is stressed as the crucial atonement offering,[2] the emphasis is simply on the gracious willingness of Yahweh to accept this gift as expiatory, and no exact correspondence with the punishment incurred is in mind. Thus the gaze of the offerer remains directed toward God; and the offering of a pure, innocent life for the one which has become guilty serves to drive home afresh again and again the life-destroying power of sin, which, were it not for atonement, would inevitably deliver the sinner into the annihilating wrath of God.[3]

How closely in Israelite thinking atonement and forgiveness belong together, and how little there was felt to be any essential opposition between them, is vividly illustrated by the conclusion of the Job story.[4] On a one-sided view, interested only in God's personal action in forgiveness, the pardon granted to the friends of Job would be sufficiently motivated by the intercession of the man of God. In fact, however, the three friends receive the specific command to make an exceptionally rich atoning sacrifice, manifestly because this, as a 'token of recognition of the sovereignty of God',[5] attests their penitent submission to his verdict. Moreover, the fact that this sacrifice only acquires its atoning power as a result of Job's intercession serves not only to humble the self-righteous friends before the just man whom they had condemned as a sinner, but indicates the restricted nature of the atoning efficacy of sacrifice, which is not enough in itself, but requires the vicarious intervention of a man of God in order to find favour in God's sight.[6] Precisely because this passage comes from the old folk-

---

[1] I Sam. 3.14.

[2] Notably Lev. 17.11.

[3] On the relation between Israelite and heathen, in particular Babylonian, sacrificial atonement cf. vol. I, pp. 163ff.

[4] Job 42.8f.

[5] L. Köhler, *op. cit.*, p. 215, in a happy deviation from the view which he maintains elsewhere, that sacrifice is an attempt by Man at self-redemption.

[6] On the subject of intercession, cf. further below.

story of pious Job, its ascription of only relative value to the atoning sacrifice may be taken as early Israelite, thus providing a valuable piece of evidence for the close association of expiation with personal forgiveness. The same situation may be seen in the case of Samuel's atoning sacrifice.[1]

Conversely it is of great interest to see how unhesitatingly the prophets make use of cultic expressions and actions connected with atonement, when they are speaking of God's forgiveness. For an Isaiah the experience of pardon takes the form of a purification by the seraph in direct imitation of cultic practice, without, however, casting doubt for one moment on the personal nature of Yahweh's dealings with him.[2] For Ezekiel, too, when he speaks of Yahweh's atoning action on Israel's behalf,[3] the visible signs of expiation apparently play their part alongside God's forgiveness, just as he, too, uses the cultic ritual of purification as an image for the removal of the sinful guilt of the past.[4] Jeremiah employs both the cultic expressions *kipper* and *māḥāh*, when he prays Yahweh to refuse forgiveness to his enemies;[5] the implication here may well be of a refusal to recognize the cultic acts of expiation by which his opponents sought to protect themselves from God's vengeance. Similarly Isaiah rules out the possibility of making atonement for Israel's guilt.[6] In prophetic thought, too, therefore, the idea of atonement rites as media of forgiveness is current in all writers, and no opposition is felt to exist between the two, so long as the ritual remains subordinate to God's will to forgive. First and foremost, however, the prophets as the messengers of judgment have to proclaim the complete ineffectiveness of all atonement procedures in face of Israel's irremediable breach of covenant; and to this their polemic against the godless cult bears witness.

(*b*) On the other hand, they are less antagonistic to another method of expiation, by which guilt may be removed, namely *interceding with God* on behalf of the sinful nation.[7] Intercession itself is no less open than other atoning actions to the ever-present danger

---

[1] I Sam. 7.9.
[2] Isa. 6.6, cf. Num. 31.22f.
[3] Ezek. 16.63.
[4] Ezek. 36.25.
[5] Jer. 18.23.
[6] Isa. 22.14.
[7] Cf. P. A. H. de Boer, 'De Vorbede in het Oude Testament', *Oudtestamentische Studien* III, 1943, and F. Hesse, *Die Fürbitte im AT*, 1951.

of degenerating into an instance of objectively effective power, since a familiar figure in this context is the man who is skilled in divine things, and who intervenes with his liberating word on behalf of those stricken by curse or spell—the difference being, however, that in such cases the word exercises a coercive effect because it is spoken by a man endowed with power, and is not directed to a divine will that is absolutely supreme. The borderline between true intercession and the demonic exercise of power cannot be unambiguously defined from without by conceptual thinking. Hence even in expressly theistic religions it is almost impossible to avoid imperceptibly crossing this line; and even in the Old Testament individual words of blessing and prayer, taken purely as they stand, sometimes seem to fall outside the proper limits of intercourse in prayer with the sovereign Lord of the nation, full of fearful majesty and holiness.[1] Nevertheless, in such cases, where interest in the miraculous power of the intercessor endangers the genuine attitude of prayer, the conviction that even the most outstanding man of God is always subject to the will of the divine majesty, and that the hearing of his prayer is strictly the gift of God's free condescension, still underlies all else as the narrator's implicit presupposition, and the unseen corrective when at any given time the limit is overstepped. Furthermore, the way in which the intercession of an Abraham, a Moses, or a Samuel is described[2] unambiguously subordinates their petition to God's saving dealings with his people, so that both in the acceptance and the refusal of the request the divine plan which dominates history comes to fulfilment. This does not mean, however, that prayer sinks to a meaningless expression of the emotional life of the pious soul. On the contrary, it remains *a real interaction of Man with God and God with Man* in which vital and forceful effect is given to the mystery of men's genuine fellowship with the majestic will by which all things are ordered and controlled. Here the man called and illuminated by God strives with the divine will which is not yet manifest, and on the basis of the revelation already received presses forward to a new revelation of the divine thought, confident that in so doing he is in accord with the profoundest intention of the God who calls, and that, whether his prayer is heard or refused, he will receive the gift of a new communion with the will of that God who, supreme though he be, yet does

---

[1] I Kings 13.6; II Kings 4.16; 13.17.
[2] Gen. 18.23ff.; 20.7; Ex. 32.11–14, 32; 34.8f.; Num. 14.13–19; I Sam. 7.8f.; 12.19, 23; 15.11.

not work without Man. Moreover, both because and in so far as this
will has made itself known as mercy and pardon, intercessory prayer
may take it at its word even when it comes to men in the guise of
judgment. Indeed, it is precisely in this that the distinctive power of
the intercessor lies, namely that as a result of his deeper understanding of the revealed will of God he dares to assert his prerogative with
the confidence of one who is intimate with God, and with the vehemence of his own longing that God's salvation shall be fully realized.
In the process the rights of his own life disappear so completely from
his field of vision that any hardship and mortification he personally
may experience are forgotten, indeed his own existence is offered for
the redemption of the one threatened by the wrath of God. Thus when
the ancient Israelite narrators make Abraham strive with God for the
life of the righteous, or see Moses stake his own life for the election of
his people, or portray Samuel as a loyal advocate of the erring,
despite the ingratitude which he has experienced, they are showing
us *intercession as a complete turning of Man to God, a becoming one with the
will of God to the point of self-sacrifice*, and therefore as something to
which God ascribes atoning value sufficient for the removal of guilt.
On the other hand, such atonement is not a work with its own intrinsic value. It derives its meaning and its effective power from the
fact that it is at bottom a reflection of God's will in a human soul—
which is the reason why, in the New Testament, prayer of this kind is
ascribed to the operation of the Holy Spirit.[1] Hence God himself can
summon men to intercession, and promise to hear it.[2] But even where
he rejects the actual request[3] he does not leave any doubt that the end
which it most deeply desires, the realization of God's plan of salvation
despite human sin, will be achieved; and in this way he confirms the
inward rightness of the petitioner.

Since God's elective action is primarily concerned with the nation,
it is only natural that this should also be the predominant subject of
intercession. This, however, in no way excludes *intercessory prayer on
behalf of individuals*, though the latter may, of course, enjoy a direct
relationship with God as well.[4] As Abraham prayed for Abimelech,
and Moses for Miriam,[5] so other seers and priests, when asked for

[1] Rom. 15.30; Phil. 1.19; Eph. 6.18f.
[2] Gen. 20.7; Job 42.8.
[3] Ex. 32.32; I Sam. 15.11.
[4] Cf. pp. 238f., 241f. above.
[5] Gen. 20.7; Num. 12.13.

their prayers, may have brought their aid to bear for the individual. The picture sketched for us by the Israelite storytellers of the pastoral relationship existing between wide circles of the nation and the *nᵉbî'îm* makes it plain that the exercise of intercession was one of the things for which it was understood that the individual could call on the services of the man of God.[1] Here it was precisely the fact that miracle-working was combined with prayer which ruled out the magical element, otherwise very easily attached to such narratives, by establishing that the miraculous succour was due to the personal intervention of Yahweh. Only in the case of Elijah is the help secured by intercession indicated as also implying divine forgiveness;[2] but the tendency to see God's punishing hand in outward disasters inevitably meant that his forgiveness was thought of as playing some part in outward deliverance.

Since the atoning efficacy of intercession was wholly a function of the intercessor's living intercourse with God in personal self-surrender, it is understandable that *high value* should be *set upon it by the prophets.* The earlier period, precisely because of these interior demands of intercessory prayer, had as a matter of course looked for the great intercessors among the great exponents and champions of the Yahwist faith; and the prophets, too, as men admitted to Yahweh's counsels, and as messengers standing in his presence, consciously accept this as one of their tasks. Thus Amos seeks by intercession to halt the threat of the divine anger, until God's own deliberate decision forbids him to do so;[3] the king makes his request to Isaiah for this service in a critical hour;[4] and Jeremiah can appeal to the fact that he has continually prayed even for his enemies[5]—as the king and the military commanders indirectly testify[6]—until God himself closes his mouth.[7] Ezekiel, too, can cite it as an obvious sign of the genuine prophet that he should step into the breach before God on behalf of his people,[8] and he expects the other leaders of the nation to understand that precisely the same duty falls on them[9]—indeed, in

---

[1] I Kings 17.20f.; II Kings 4.33; 6.17.
[2] I Kings 17.18.
[3] Amos 7.1–6.
[4] II Kings 19.4.
[5] Jer. 15.11.
[6] Jer. 37.3; 42.2.
[7] Jer. 7.16; 11.14; 14.11; 15.1.
[8] Ezek. 13.5.
[9] Ezek. 22.30.

his view, one of the causes of the ineluctable catastrophe was the fact that such intercession was nowhere to be found. This also, however, brings out with complete clarity the limitation of intercession. So far as atoning efficacy is concerned, even this remains dependent on Yahweh's free will to forgive, and can be regarded only as a means subservient to that forgiveness.

(c) Both concepts, that of expiatory sacrifice and that of atoning intercession, are memorably combined when, in *the Suffering Servant of God in Isa.* 53,[1] the vicarious suffering of the righteous is seen as the supreme means employed by absolving grace. It is no accident that the sacrifice of life by which the Servant of Yahweh makes many righteous is described as *'āšām*, a guilt-offering; and the introduction of the communal penitential liturgy form (53.1–6), and the comparison with the lamb, the animal most frequently used for sacrifice (53.7), also bring us into the sphere of the atonement offering. In this way marked prominence is given to the great conception of vicarious self-sacrifice, which in this offering becomes a living reality. Moreover, the appropriation of this offering by faith in its God-willed power to atone is a personal matter in a way quite different from that of the cultic atonement sacrifice, inasmuch as it presupposes union in conscious self-surrender with the one who has become the sacrificial lamb. Indeed, it is this which gives the offering made by the Servant of God its unique character, that it is a self-offering made deliberately of his own free will; and this is especially stressed by the fact that it involves his intervening on behalf of sinners in intercession. It had long ago been realized that intercession involved the surrender of one's own right to life in favour of God's cause; but this feature is now intensified by the acceptance of a whole lifetime of nothing but contempt and misunderstanding, even to the point of dying the death of one branded by God as an evildoer, and therefore in total incognito—a fate which utterly eliminates any trace of self-seeking or self-exaltation. Because, however, this means the attainment of complete identification with the divine will, such intercession becomes powerful to atone for many, and results in the accomplishment of that 'blessed exchange' of *mūsār* and *šālōm*, punishment and salvation, by which the sinners become righteous. Thus in the suffering of his servant God proffers the means of forgiveness, in which the atoning efficacy of sacrifice and of intercession are united

[1] Cf. W. Zimmerli, *The Servant of God*, 1957; E. F. Sutcliffe, *Providence and Suffering in the Old and New Testaments*, 1955, pp. 97ff.

at the deepest level of meaning, and brought to unique effectiveness. Here the exact opposite of all mechanical and magical methods of cleansing from sin is seen in its purest form. At the same time, because it is linked with the final consummation, forgiveness is included in the goal of the ultimate establishment of God's sovereignty, and is recognized as its crucial precondition.

II. Just as the mechanical putting away of sin by magic excludes forgiveness as a free act of God, so *a legalistic understanding of guilt and punishment* narrows and externalizes it. Where punishment is regarded as compensation fitted to the offence, and may possibly even be circumvented by voluntary works of supererogation, *forgiveness* is comprehensible *only as reduction or total remission of punishment.* In this way God's action is bound up with his right to compensation, calculable by Man, and loses its personal character. The most important thing about forgiveness is no longer that an angered God has turned back to his worshipper, but that men have been released from a penal sentence. And even this demonstration of favour can no longer be sought with absolute seriousness, when it can be bought with works of merit. This is the position most frequently adopted in the religions of civilized nations from India to the Near East, even though instances of transition to a personal attitude are not altogether lacking.[1]

(*a*) In Israel the high value set on the covenant statutes, with their threats and promises, as the authoritative description of God's demands undoubtedly provided a starting-point for a similar evaluation of forgiveness to that obtaining elsewhere. At the periods in which waves of foreign influence closed over the nation, whether during the phase of Canaanization after the conquest or that of syncretistic control by foreigners in the time of the Omrid dynasty and the Assyrian overlordship, coinciding as it did with an unhealthy exaggeration of the cultic impulse in the religion of Yahweh, exceptionally favourable conditions were in each case created for a materialistic conception of forgiveness as either a remission of merited punishment or a business deal between partners of equal status.[2] Confidence in Yahweh's loyalty to the covenant led men to bank unscrupulously on his reducing their punishment simply because this was one of his obligations as the covenant God; and this dulled their feeling both for the seriousness of guilt and for the nature of forgiveness.

[1] For examples of these cf. below.
[2] Cf. vol. I, pp. 45f.

There can, however, be no question that such an attitude contradicted the whole basic conception of the Yahwist faith, and was
possible only because this had been obscured. For it was integral to
that conception that the covenant should be understood as the gracious act of the divine Lord, whose passionate concern was to separate
and sanctify his people, and who was therefore ready to avenge with
fearful jealousy any infringement of the order of national life which
he had established. This reality of Yahweh's anger and holiness,
experienced in shattering acts of power, glossed his kindness and
righteousness in a way which left no doubt that God was utterly in
earnest in his demands, and drove home his unconditional freedom to
impose or remit punishment as he pleased, without thereby affecting
men's general certainty as to the consistent character of divine
retribution in its main outline. Here there was no room for an easy
confidence that the God who described himself in the revelation of
his name as 'merciful and gracious, slow to anger, and abounding in
steadfast love and faithfulness'[1] would forgive 'because that is his job'.
Just as, in their wrestlings with guilt and punishment the sense of
being set before the personal God burst upon men again and again,
so they experienced his remission of punishment as a *free act of the
divine Lord,* in which each time *the mystery of his approach to men in a
desire for fellowship with them* made itself known afresh. Hence it was
no more possible to estimate in advance the manner of his forgiveness,
however confidently one might hope for it, than it had been to prescribe the measure of his punishment.[2] In each individual instance
he is seen to be the sovereign Lord even in his loyalty and righteousness—as when he allows Abraham to return from Egypt unpunished
despite his transgression, or repays his lack of faith simultaneously
with the gift of an heir and with severe disappointment in the matter
of Hagar's child; or when he confirms Jacob in the birthright which
he has obtained by fraud, though only by the way of deep affliction
and humiliation; or when he convicts Joseph's brethren of their
crime in the very process of miraculously rescuing them from death
by famine; or when he refuses the forgiveness for which Moses asks,
and yet proves himself the redeemer of his people, who by a marvellous intricacy of operation makes punishment a means of pardon; or
when he delivers David, who has become involved in serious guilt,
from the doom that threatens him, yet makes him taste the fearful

[1] Ex. 34.6.
[2] Cf. pp. 426ff. above.

effects of his sin throughout the whole course of his life. However much men may like to try to elucidate the wisdom and righteousness of divine retribution by analogy from the principle of correspondence obtaining in legal matters,[1] they succeed not at all in making a rigid and formal law out of God's action. The complex reality constantly outstrips their short-winded and artificial calculations, and confronts them with the autonomy of the divine Thou, who moves through startling transformations from punishment to forgiveness.

(*b*) In most cases, however, *the content of this forgiveness* comprises the restoration of external good fortune—health, honour, possessions —or defence against external damage from enemies, crop failure, childlessness, early death, and so on.[2] This unquestionably gives rise to the danger of substituting the material goods of life for God's restoration of favour to Man in personal relationship; but this danger did not, in fact, result in a distortion of the understanding of forgiveness in this particular direction, and the reason for this was in part Israel's *distinctive evaluation of earthly goods* as the outward sign in which one vividly and directly experiences God's dealings with his servants.[3] Because men's gaze is turned from the gain and loss of these goods directly to the divine Lord, and because they feel in them the reality of his rule and judgment, forgiveness, too, even though it is experienced primarily in the restoration of earthly position, yet remains wholly the expression of a free pardon, receiving the guilty back into that relationship of service which obtained before.

For the same reason *the reality of divine forgiveness did not in all circumstances have to be proved by earthly blessings.* If God received the sinner back into favour, one might expect the natural outcome of this to be a change in his earthly fortunes; but the two things were not understood as simply identical. God's pardon was valuable and meaningful in itself, as is shown with increasing clarity by the fact that men could speak of forgiveness which did not just do away with the punishment, but went hand in hand with it, as in the descriptions of Jacob's fortunes or of the affliction of David because of his crime against Uriah.[4] In Isaiah's preaching this insight has deepened into a conviction that God can only reopen fellowship with himself to the sinner by making him live through the abyss of judgment, and in this

---

[1] II Sam. 12.10, pressed even farther in the later additions, vv. 11f.
[2] II Sam. 15.25ff.; 16.10ff.; Pss. 25.18; 38; 39.9ff.; 40.12–14; 107.17ff.
[3] Cf. pp. 350ff. above.
[4] II Sam. 12.13f.; cf. further Ex. 34.6; Num. 14.8.

strange and paradoxical action intertwining punishment and forgiveness as closely as possible.[1] In Zephaniah it is those who have been plundered of all earthly goods, and who have matured to humility, on whom the light of God's pardon and favour rises.[2] The new thing proclaimed by Deutero-Isaiah is that God's good pleasure rests precisely on those who are set forth before the whole world as the victims of severe punishment, and gives them the strength for a bold act of faith in which they prove themselves before that same world to be, in fact, the ones who are borne by his pardoning love.[3] Similarly Ezekiel promises the divine forgiveness precisely to those who think themselves bound to succumb to the full weight of the punishment of the exile, and with that forgiveness the strength for new life.[4] Moreover, according to Jeremiah's letter to the exiles, Yahweh causes himself to be found by those who believe themselves banished not merely from his sanctuary but from his very self.[5] In such passages quite clearly the natural organic unity in which God's favour is matched by vigour and prosperity in one's earthly life, a correspondence which early Israel still upheld without question,[6] has now been abandoned. The shattering revelation of the divine Judge has replaced it with the paradoxical unity, conceivable only in faith, of judgment and grace, a unity for which the harmony of the natural order is something to be recovered only in the imminent new creation of God.

Lacking this eschatological outlook, and focused instead on the saving presence of God in the midst of a purified covenant people, *the Priestly interpretation of history* calls men to affirm in faith the gift of the divine favour in the teeth of the fact that the very existence of the tiny cultic community is continually endangered in the maelstrom of international history; and this, too, breaks the mutual entailment between God's good pleasure and outward human success.[7] By proclaiming that the eternal divine covenant still subsists, and that the sun of divine forgiveness still shines, at a time which an observer judging by outward circumstances would have felt compelled to describe rather as a time of divine wrath, the Priestly stratum bears

[1] Cf. the remarks on faith in Isaiah, pp. 279ff. above.
[2] Zeph. 3.11ff.
[3] Cf. pp. 286f. above.
[4] Ezek. 18.
[5] Jer. 29.12–14.
[6] Cf. pp. 350ff. above.
[7] Cf. vol. I, pp. 431f.

its own decisive witness to God's act of pardon as a redemption and a blessing fundamentally independent of the conditions of men's earthly life.

Correspondingly it is not only in the context of the prosperity of the nation as a whole that outward good fortune comes to be measured against an absolute value, namely the destiny of Israel to be the community of God, and itself adjudged to have only relative value,[1] but this relativization is increasingly applied to the life of the individual.[2] Where, moreover, *communion with the will of God is grasped as the ultimate goal of all desire for salvation*, there, too, the removal of guilt by forgiveness is understood as entirely a matter of God's personal dealing with Man, and as something which is not exhausted by remission of punishment, but includes as its most important content readmission to fellowship with him.

III. If it is in the thought of the prophets that this can most obviously be seen to be true, the reason is that with them *forgiveness is increasingly viewed in an eschatological perspective*. Just as they see sin and guilt agglomerated into a corporate burden on the human race, calling for a final and absolute purification in judgment and punishment, so, too, forgiveness, for all that they indeed reckon with such a thing as an individual divine act at important crises of history,[3] strikes them overwhelmingly as God's concluding act, intimately bound up with the irruption of the new age. If this is sometimes overlooked, then the expressions for forgiveness which the prophets adopt from common usage are partly to blame for the mistake, in so far as their primary reference is to a *temporally limited and repeatable individual act*. Whether forgiveness is described as the wiping out of a record of guilt,[4] the abolition and removal of a burden,[5] the covering or taking far away of a guilt that cries out accusingly for vengeance,[6] or the passing over of such,[7] a ransom from slavery,[8] or the healing of a mortal sickness,[9] or whether it is rendered with *s-l-ḥ*, without the use

---

[1] Cf. pp. 351ff. above.

[2] Cf. pp. 355ff., 360ff. above.

[3] Amos 7.2f., 5f.; Isa. 1.18; Jer. 5.1; 36.3; Ezek. 18.22.

[4] *māḥāh*: Isa. 43.25; 44.22; Jer. 18.23; Pss. 51.3, 11; 109.14; Neh. 3.37.

[5] Micah 7.18; Pss. 32.1; 85.3.

[6] Pss. 32.1; 85.3; 103.12; Isa. 38.17; Neh. 3.37.

[7] Amos 7.8; 8.2; Micah 7.18.

[8] Isa. 44.22, and the description of God as the *gōʾēl* in Ps. 103.4 and Deutero-Isaiah.

[9] Hos. 14.5; Isa. 1.6; Jer. 8.22; 17.14; Pss. 103.3; 107.17, 20.

of concrete imagery, as a passing over, an exercise of forbearance,[1] all these are originally connected with the idea of the remission on a particular occasion of guilt that has accrued, and the restoration thereby of the earlier relationship until new guilt makes new forgiveness necessary. When the offer of forgiveness was thus broken up into separate acts, it was impossible for men to become clearly aware that this particular demonstration of God's favour was the one of supreme and central importance. Certainly they breathed more easily when a guilt resting on the nation had been eradicated by Yahweh's forgiveness, and a right relationship with God thus established. The threat to national existence constituted by God's anger was vividly felt, and men were all the more joyfully ready therefore to take the proof of his favour in visible acts of salvation as the occasion for a general amnesty in which the pardoning action of God was imitated by Man.[2] *nōśē' 'āwōn*, 'he who takes away guilt', gradually became a stock epithet of Yahweh.[3] But even though the forgiveness of sins was felt to be an important component part of divine grace, it yet shared this status with the whole abundance of other goods of salvation in which the demonstration of God's favour was experienced with equal certainty, whether these were the material gifts of earthly blessings or the religious goods of Law and monarchy, priestly and prophetic guidance.

This equality of status was bound to change once guilt was recognized as the doom of truly monstrous enormity which threatened Man's whole existence, and was driving him toward annihilating judgment. Now *forgiveness was acknowledged as the central act of succour* without which all other goods lost their value. Without it the change from doom to salvation, in which God would turn back to his people, was unthinkable. Thus the prophets, when they depict the contrite conversion of their people, and their prayer to be readmitted to fellowship with God, put in their mouths first and foremost an entreaty for forgiveness,[4] making this an indispensable precondition of salvation, indeed the real nerve of God's new creative action. Correspondingly, God's promise of salvation gives the place of

---

[1] Amos 7.2; Jer. 5.1, 7; 31.34; 33.8; 36.3; Deut. 29.19; I Kings 8.34, 36, 50; II Kings 5.18; 24.4; Isa. 55.7; Pss. 25.11; 103.3, etc. On this subject cf. the thorough study of the history of the concept in J. J. Stamm, *Erlösen und Vergeben im AT*, 1940.

[2] I Sam. 11.13; 14.45.

[3] Ex. 34.6f.; Num. 14.18.

[4] Hos. 14.3; Jer. 3.21ff.; 14.7, 20f.; 31.18f.

honour to the gift of pardon;[1] this forms the threshold of the new age in which the creation returns to its original state.[2] But even where it is not mentioned in so many words—for example, in the pictures of salvation in Amos, Isaiah, or Zephaniah—it is still necessarily implied by the fact that the prophetic word of judgment concentrates wholly on the destruction of the fellowship between God and Man wrought by sin; and it would be stupid formalism to deduce from this a proof that for these prophets forgiveness was only of secondary importance. Rather, just as certainly as they envisage salvation not merely as external restoration but as involving a personal act by God in which he turns to men afresh, so here, too, they are in effect speaking of God's act of pardon. Hence the epigones of the prophetic movement came to connect the full manifestation of God's favour with the removal of the sin which separated Man from God by divine forgiveness, sought in penitence and conversion.[3]

The *central importance for salvation* which forgiveness came to have in prophetic thought was not without its effect even where eschatological renewal was not so closely bound up with it. Thus *in priestly thought* forgiveness as an individual act remains at the very heart of the matter, corresponding as it does to the transposition of the great day of Yahweh's judgment into his continual judgment at all times, by which he maintains the order which he himself has established.[4] Nevertheless the growing importance of the concept of atonement for the cultus as a whole pointed to a divine act of pardon which, by appointing the means of atonement, provided the prerequisite condition for the continuance of the covenant, and so was experienced as the basis of the community of God. Similarly, the justification for the idea at the heart of the Deuteronomistic preaching of the eternal covenant was belief in God's readiness to forgive, which calls the transgressor to lay hold in penitence of the proffered grace, and which also subordinates even the severest punishment to the purpose of conversion and to the pardon which this makes possible.[5] The Deu-

---

[1] Hos. 14.5; Jer. 3.22; 4.1; 31.20; Isa. 43.25; 44.22.

[2] Hos. 14.5ff.; Jer. 31.34; Isa. 53.4f.; Ezek. 36.25ff.; 16.63.

[3] Zech. 1.3; Mal. 3.7; Isa. 59.2, 15f., 20; Zech. 12.10–13.1; Jer. 33.8; 50.20. In view of this fact it is simply incomprehensible that anyone can venture such an opinion as the following: On the whole the Old Testament revelation 'speaks only occasionally of forgiveness and certainly does not put it as the centre of its scheme of salvation' (L. Köhler, *op. cit.*, p. 218).

[4] Cf. vol. I, pp. 428f.

[5] Cf. the introductory speeches in Deuteronomy, and especially ch. 30, together with Lev. 26.40ff.

teronomistic history-writing, too, not only speaks of God's over-looking and forgiving of sin as constantly renewed for David's sake,[1] but praises the Temple as the memorial of Yahweh's gracious turning to his people, the place where in faithful prayer she may at all times find access to his forgiveness.[2] Thus the covenant is funda-mentally a work of prevenient grace, grace which, because it knows the sinful nature of the people, offers them redemption and salvation in the form of forgiveness.

IV. (a) The faith of the Jewish congregation was determined at bottom by this urgent necessity of forgiveness as the central act of divine succour for its outward and inward needs. This fact finds its purest expression in the Psalms, where the longing for God and his redemption is focused wholly on the forgiveness of sin, in their prayers for which men wait in humility, but also in unqualified trust in God's unfathomable mercy.[3] The growing assurance of salvation in these texts, rising as it does from profound inward desolation at the desperate condition of mankind in the presence of the holy God to self-commitment in faith to the decision of this same God, who judges in order to redeem, is the echo in the post-exilic community of the prophetic preaching. And the more profound their understanding of the miracle of forgiveness, the more urgently do men reach out to the ultimate act of redemption, by which the curse of guilt is completely done away, and the messianic salvation thereby actualized.

Alongside this vital striving after the central good of salvation, however, there are signs of a marked deviation toward conceptions of forgiveness hitherto successfully averted. A weakened understanding of *the place of sacrificial atonement* in men's relationship to the divine Lord may be seen first of all in the *search for new safeguards* against the baleful effect of unintentional offences. The voluminous redactions and additions to the Priestly law betray the effort to elaborate the Priestly system of expiatory rites, and to systematize it. In addition to the many lesser elaborations the most outstanding testimony to these efforts is certainly the development of the age-old rituals for the purification of the sanctuary and the congregation into the impressive festival of the great Day of Atonement in Lev. 16. Also worth men-tioning in this connection is the cultic scheme in the appendix to the

---

[1] I Kings 11.12f., 34f.; 15.4; II Kings 8.19; 20.5f.
[2] I Kings 8.33ff.
[3] Cf. pp. 309ff. above, where a list of the relevant passages will also be found.

book of Ezekiel,[1] in which is to be found a remarkably independent reorganization of divine worship in the light of the concept of atonement as something ordained by Yahweh, providing safeguards even against future offences. The rooting of atonement in the gracious will of God is still indeed maintained, but the accumulation and systematizing of rites expresses a dangerous tendency to provide an additional guarantee of the effectiveness of the atoning rituals by increasing the number and size of the cultic offerings, whereas the really decisive factor, God's promise, no longer seems to suffice. This is why post-exilic prophecy still has to voice its protest against the conception of sacrifice as a human performance which is of value to God.[2] This intensifies into an exclusive opposition, when sacrifice threatens to become a danger to a right attitude of heart. Both the prophets and some of the Psalmists stress that the thing which matters, as opposed to all the regimentation of cultic sacrificial procedures, is the right of God's majesty to forgive, for this, far more than any sacrificial ordinances, can give the individual the assurance of pardon right in his own heart,[3] and they accordingly use the ritual only as an image of the personal dealings of God with the soul.[4] Such voices maintained loud and clear the warning that sacrifices were not to be regarded as anything more than signs and pledges which pointed men to the really decisive factor, God's activity of reconciliation.

From another angle, the fact that atoning efficacy was now attributed to all sacrifices helped to obliterate the originally highly varied content of sacrificial worship, and to make it the great work of obedience in line with other demonstrations of loyalty to the Law. Thus God's gracious gift of reconciliation, proffered in the sacrament, gave way to Man's pious action, looking for recognition from God, and the great concept of intercession in the sacrifice is lost. The result is that sacrifice is given equal status with other works of obedience.[5]
It is readily understandable that in such circumstances insight into the idea of the vicarious suffering of the redeemer also remained confined to small circles. The note of Isa. 53 still echoes in the shepherd parable of Zech. 11.13, though the detailed references of the latter are veiled in even thicker darkness. The great penitential

[1] Ezek. 43–46.
[2] Mal. 1.10f.; Ps. 50.7ff.
[3] Pss. 40.7f.; 51.18ff.; 69.31f., and the polemical utterances of Ps. 50 on this subject.
[4] Pss. 51.4, 9, 19; 119.108; 141.2.
[5] Cf. the more extensive discussion of this subject in vol. I, pp. 166ff.

lament of Zech. 12.10ff. at any rate strikes the same chord as Isa.
53.1–6, so that here, too, the background may be the atoning death
of the shepherd sent by God. The closing section of Ps. 22, which
links the victory of the kingdom of God with the suffering of the
righteous and his redemption, shows even more clearly that it was
precisely in the severe persecutions to which the pious circles of the
community were from time to time exposed that awareness of the
atoning significance of suffering was not lost. When, however, this
was applied to every suffering of the pious, as happened in later
Judaism,[1] a change in the concept occurs, inasmuch as suffering is
now valued as a work of obedience which God places to one's credit,
without any idea that it ought to result in an inner transformation of
the sinner. Furthermore, it is not possible for the individual to have
confidence for himself on the grounds of his own suffering, since this
avails rather for the nation as a whole. It would seem nevertheless
that the deeper conception of the vicarious suffering of the redeemer
was also handed on in this later period.[2]

(b) Just as the new attitude of Judaism to atoning sacrifice made
direct encounter with God in forgiveness uncertain, so the same is
true of its *evaluation of intercession*. The fact that it is now bound up
with the office of High Priest,[3] who has direct access to God among
the heavenly servants of Yahweh, means that the personal authority
of the intercessor is already being subordinated to that of the office.
This is partly due to the feeling that the transcendent God is inaccessible to any man not specially legitimated; and the same applies all
the more to the transfer of intercession to the angels. Just as, in
Michael, the nation has a mighty representative in heaven, whose
voice prevails on their behalf, so, too, the individual pious possess in
seven angels especially appointed for the purpose,[4] among whom
Raphael is particularly mentioned by name,[5] interceding helpers
who bring their prayers before God. From the championship of an
angel intercessor one may even hope for the rescue of an evildoer
from the annihilating divine judgment.[6]

---

[1] II Macc. 7.37f.; IV Macc. 6.28; further passages in Bousset-Gressmann,
op. cit., p. 198.
[2] So J. Jeremias, 'Erlöser und Erlösung im Spätjudentum und Urchristentum',
Deutsche Theologie II, 1929, pp. 106ff. But cf. also Bousset-Gressmann, *op. cit.*, p. 198.
[3] Zech. 3.7; Baba bathra 147b; but cf. still Nehemiah's intercession, Neh. 1.6ff.
[4] Tobit 12.15.
[5] Tobit 3.16; 12.15.
[6] Job 33.23ff.; Test. Dan 6.

As an operation in the transcendent world intercession is here removed from the domain of Man, who is no longer considered capable of direct dealings with God; but the earlier line is to some extent resumed when, after the destruction of the Temple, the great Rabbis are credited with the same powers of intercession as were formerly attributed to the High Priest.[1] In the stories of these mighty men of prayer, however, there are definite traces of a magical and coercive effect,[2] so that prayer comes close to being a spell, and as a result incapable of serving as a means of expression for confident and faithful converse with God. Thus even these seeming parallels to prophetic intercession reveal the immense inner gulf between them and the combination of childlike realism and fear and trembling in the utterance of the heart which lives in the assurance of the presence of the holy God.

(c) The absolute transcendence of a remote Godhead thus makes forgiveness more markedly dependent on the performance of Man; and similarly the free gift of divine love is more and more concealed behind the *legalistic categories* in which a law-oriented piety contemplates God's activity. The more the divine righteousness was crushed into the schema of a rationalistic theory of retribution, the more one-sidedly was forgiveness understood as remission of sentence, and linked inseparably with the establishing of good fortune in this life. This meant that there was no longer the capacity to accept the paradoxical interrelation of punishment and forgiveness. Outward suffering could be accepted positively as a dispensation of divine grace only on the assumption that it was educative punishment.[3] Martyrdom, of course, constituted an exception to this rule, being made meaningful as the attainment of surplus merit.

Indeed, the emergence of the concept of merit, in which the optimism of a legalist piety reached its climax,[4] now completely obscured the incomparable glory of God's forgiveness, from which in any case the most precious jewel, God's free turning to Man in grace, had been broken off. Once the ideal of a community faithful to the Law, which would have merited the coming of God's new world, no longer seemed impossible of realization, the enjoyment of God's favour by the pious of the past was also ascribed to their spotless legal righteous-

[1] Yoma 53b.
[2] Cf. F. Weber, *Jüdische Theologie*², pp. 299f., and p. 262, n. 1 above.
[3] Cf. p. 437f. above.
[4] Cf. pp. 347f. above.

ness, and the promises made to them were understood as the reward of their works. Especially instructive in this respect is the evaluation of Abraham.[1] God's covenant with him had already at an early stage become important as a strong reason for confidence in salvation, though here God's loving faithfulness was still the predominant feature.[2] In later Judaism, however, he became the great saint and fulfiller of the Law, the man who walked before God without sin, and thus earned such merit that it sufficed to provide atonement for all his descendants.[3] Above all it was by the sacrifice of Isaac that he had a just claim on God's retributive reward;[4] but his faith, too, in marked opposition to the Genesis narrative, was interpreted as a meritorious work.[5] And just as Abraham's merit dictated the course of the whole history of Israel with its miraculous power, and filled his children with confidence that their prayers would be heard, and that they would be safe in the hour of death and judgment, so, too, the patriarchs availed as the righteous for whose sake the world was made[6] and God's glory would finally be revealed.

In a similar way, moreover, Abraham's seed, too, were granted the possibility of atoning for their own sins and for those of others by their merits. In works of charity, study of the Law, and almsgiving, they had means of performing atoning works which were of equal importance with sacrifice, and which therefore made the deprivation of this seem none too grievous a fate.[7]

Thus at the very heart of the desire for salvation we find once again that inner disintegration of the structure of the Jewish faith which continually confronts us in this specific context of the individual God-Man relationship. As religious life was ever more strongly dominated by legal righteousness, and the message of the free gift of God's favour was heavily muffled, the individual's assurance of salvation was subjected to the severest strain, and finally came to a dead end in the utter helplessness of II(4) Esdras and Paul the Pharisee.

---

[1] Cf. on this subject O. Schmitz, 'Abraham im Spätjudentum und Urchristentum', *Aus Schrift und Geschichte (Schlatter-Festschrift)*, 1922, pp. 99ff.

[2] Micah 7.20; Ps. 105.8f., 42.

[3] Ecclus 44.19ff. Cf. Strack-Billerbeck, *Kommentar zum NT* I, pp. 117ff.

[4] I Macc. 2.52. Hence the great popularity of this particular motif in the synagogue paintings, e.g. at Doura-Europos and Beth Alpha: cf. A. Reifenberg, *Denkmäler der jüdischen Antike*, 1937, pl. 40 and 47.

[5] Cf. H. W. Heidland, *Die Anrechnung des Glaubens zur Gerechtigkeit*, 1936, pp. 101f.

[6] Apoc. Bar. 21.24f.

[7] Cf. pp. 347f. above.

(b) *The preconditions of forgiveness*

Forgiveness cannot be thought of as God's personal dealing with men for the restoration of fellowship unless *Man is personally committed to this action on the part of his God.* What might be possible in the case of magical purification or legalistically conceived remission of punishment is unthinkable when it is a matter of the return of the God who has been injured by Man. Here Man must be involved in his most inward self, if there is to be a real renewal of fellowship. Thus it was common knowledge in Israel at all periods that one could not merely hope and pray for pardon, but must humble oneself before God, acknowledge one's unrighteousness, and have an earnest will to turn away from sin. David's behaviour when confronted by Nathan's demand for penitence is described in these terms, and a later writer can relate as much even of Ahab.[1] In the liturgy for the day of fasting, and in the sacrificial laws, penitence and confession of sin form the natural accompaniment to prayer for forgiveness,[2] and the same practice is confirmed by the penitential psalms, both individual and corporate, a psalm-form the age of which is no longer seriously doubted by anyone.[3] There are many expressions for this action on the part of Man: to seek Yahweh (*bikkēš*),[4] or search for him (*d-r-š*),[5] to humble onself before him (*nikna*ʿ),[6] to direct one's heart to Yahweh (*hēkin lēb 'el-*),[7] to soften one's heart (*rak lēbāb*),[8] to confess oneself to Yahweh (*hōdā 'et-šēm yhwh*),[9] to lay to heart (*hēšîb 'el-libbō*).[10] The same meaning attaches to such outward forms as weeping and lamentation, fasting, rending one's clothes, girding one's loins with the penitential garment of sackcloth, sleeping on the ground, sprinkling oneself with ashes,[11] and so on. The prophets fiercely denounce the reduction of these actions to a mere mechanical formality in which there is no real involvement of the heart;[12] but the Priestly liturgy,

---

[1] II Sam. 12; I Kings 21.27ff.
[2] Joel 2.12–14; Lev. 5.5; 16.21; Num. 5.7, cf. I Sam. 7.5f.; Job 42.8.
[3] Pss. 25.7; 32.5; 38.19; 41.5; 51.6ff.; 65.4; 130.3f.; Lam. 3.40ff.
[4] II Sam. 12.16; 21.1; Hos. 5.6, 15; Zeph. 2.3.
[5] Amos 5.4, 6; Hos. 10.12; Isa. 55.6.
[6] I Kings 21.29; II Kings 22.19; Lev. 26.41; II Chron. 7.14; 12.6f., etc.
[7] I Sam. 7.3.
[8] II Kings 22.19.
[9] I Kings 8.33, 35.
[10] I Kings 8.47; Isa. 46.8; Deut. 4.39.
[11] II Sam. 12.16; I Kings 21.27.
[12] Amos 5.5; Hos. 7.14; Isa. 1.10ff.; 29.13; 58.5; Jer. 14.12.

too, contains its warning against such tendencies.[1] At the same time numerous new expressions are developed to describe really genuine turning to God, either characterizing it as a conscious moral action—to seek the good, to hate the evil and love the good,[2] to cease to do evil, and learn to do good,[3] to be ready to obey,[4] to amend one's ways and one's doings[5]—or stressing the necessity of a changed inner attitude—to incline one's heart to Yahweh,[6] to make oneself a new heart,[7] to circumcise oneself for Yahweh, and remove the foreskin of the heart,[8] to break up one's fallow ground.[9] Various metaphorical phrases from cultic language point in the same direction: to wash one's heart from evil,[10] to wash and purify oneself.[11] The abundance of such expressions shows how extraordinarily strongly Israel felt forgiveness as implying a summons to personal openness, and thus confirms from a new angle what was said earlier about God's personal dealing with men in the act of pardon.

It was the word *šūb*, turn,[12] however, which summed up all these descriptions of the right human attitude to God's saving action in a single pregnant phrase. The metaphor was an especially suitable one, for not only did it describe the required behaviour as a real act—'to make a turn'—and so preserve the strong personal impact, it also included both the negative element of turning away from the direction taken hitherto and the positive element of turning towards, and so, when combined with the prepositions *min*, *'el-*, and *le-*, allowed the rich content of all the many other idioms to be reproduced tersely yet unmistakably. Thus it came to be used intensively in the prophetic preaching, whereas previously it had occurred only in isolated in-

[1] Joel 2.12f.
[2] Amos 5.14f.
[3] Isa. 1.17, cf. Pss. 34.15; 37.27.
[4] Isa. 1.19.
[5] Jer. 7.3; 26.13.
[6] Josh. 24.23.
[7] Ezek. 18.31.
[8] Jer. 4.4; similarly Deut. 10.16.
[9] Hos. 10.12; Jer. 4.3.
[10] Jer. 4.14.
[11] Isa. 1.16; cf. the description of Yahweh's action in the same terms, Ezek. 36.25.
[12] On the subject of this word, and the content covered by it, cf. the exhaustive monograph of E. K. Dietrich, *Die Umkehr (Bekehrung und Busse) im AT und im Judentum*, 1936. Also William L. Holladay, *The Root Šubh in the Old Testament with particular reference to its usages in Covenant texts*, 1958. On the traditio-historical and form-critical place of the concept of 'conversion' cf. H. W. Wolff, 'Das Thema "Umkehr" in der alttestamentlichen Prophetie', *ZTK* 51, 1948, pp. 129ff.

stances;[1] and the way in which it is used provides an instructive insight into the Old Testament conception of Man's turning to the forgiving God.

That the concept of turning was already current at the beginning of the prophetic period in Israel is shown by the fact that Amos uses it without further explanation in his reproachful survey of the nation's past.[2] What Yahweh wanted to achieve through punishment was the conversion of the apostate, in order that the broken fellowship might be re-established. But neither Amos, nor Isaiah, who is also acquainted with the concept, make much use of the term in their preaching, the obvious reason being that, in view of the imminence of judgment, and the hardening of the people, the possibility of conversion no longer had any considerable part to play. Even the prophetic name, *šeʾār yāšūb*, lays greater emphasis on the divine threat than on the promise of salvation; for it sets a sharply defined limit to the validity of the belief that membership of the chosen people implies membership of the remnant who will be spared in the coming universal catastrophe by insisting on conversion as an indispensable requirement, and so in effect pronouncing sentence on any assumption that a future for the nation as such was assured. For Hosea alone among the eighth-century prophets is the concept of conversion of major importance;[3] but here, too, hopelessness predominates when the prophet considers the present, in which there is no evidence of anything better than superficial and hasty decisions[4] which set no real term to the impenitence of the past.[5] This is why the one invitation to conversion lays the stress on the radical seriousness of a complete turning.[6] Only when the inconceivable mercy of God accomplishes a new thing, does the hope of a genuine conversion, responding to God's forgiveness, break through fully.[7]

It is striking, nevertheless, that it should be in Hosea, and after him only in Jeremiah, that conversion becomes a theme of the prophetic preaching. This is entirely in keeping with the fact that the divine love which seeks and woos a return of love from Man is such a

---

[1] Josh. 24.23; I Kings 18.37; I Sam. 7.3.
[2] Amos 4.6, 8ff., 11.
[3] Cf. G. Fohrer, 'Umkehr und Erlösung beim Propheten Hosea', *TZ* 11, 1955, pp. 161ff.
[4] Hos. 6.1ff.
[5] Hos. 5.4; 7.10; 11.4f.
[6] Hos. 10.12.
[7] Hos. 14.2ff., cf. 3.5.

prominent feature of the message of these two men. Here the whole pathos of the prophetic preaching falls on the earnestness with which God wills to redeem, so that judgment is ultimately seen as an *opus alienum* to God, and is thus fundamentally distinguished from the coercion of Fate or the action of blind caprice.[1] Because, however, this knowledge of God goes hand in hand with a deepened knowledge of sin, the victory of divine love becomes a problem for the prophet which never relaxes its hold on his spirit, and compels him to carry the concept of conversion through to its logical conclusion. Here it is Jeremiah who, guided by the fact that conversion was a necessity in his own case, has achieved the deepest insights into the tortuous ways in which men will, and then again refuse, to be converted, and, by laying bare the fine threads of hidden motive in the soul, has brought to nought all the efforts men make to justify themselves on frivolous grounds in the face of the prophetic accusation. At the same time, however, he sets most emphatically before the eyes of his people the unexhausted possibilities of the divine mercy. In his preaching of conversion, by illuminating the word *šūb* in all its meanings—turning away, turning back, inward conversion and renewal—like so many different colours of the rainbow, he drives home to his hearers that the real and ultimate demand of the divine Lord is that the heart of Man should decide for God; and thus, even when he is addressing the nation, he directs his strongest appeal to the individual—a fact which is betrayed quite involuntarily by the incorporation of the word *'īš*, 'each one', into his collective address.[2] Yet even though for this reason he can sometimes describe the purpose of all prophetic activity as simply exhortation to conversion,[3] he by no means regards this as a possibility of redemption which will remain open to men for ever. Fond as he is of affirming the possibility of conversion on the ground of God's nature, and of giving it reality in moving language,[4] his knowledge of the compulsion to sin makes him just as clearly deny the possibility on the ground of Man's. Thus by far the most frequent mention of conversion is in connection with men's refusal to be converted in past and present, and the picture of its realization bears a wholly eschatological character.[5] Finally, *the deepest mystery of true conversion* is revealed in the fact that it is *solely the work of God*, who

---

[1] Cf. vol. I, pp. 252ff.
[2] Jer. 25.5; 26.3; 36.3, 7.
[3] Jer. 23.14, 22; 25.4f.; 26.3; 35.15; 36.3, 7.
[4] Jer. 3.21ff.; 31.18ff.
[5] Jer. 3.19–4.4; 31.18–20; 24.7.

makes the new heart in which inward obstinacy is overcome by obedient receptiveness,[1] just as the prophet has experienced within himself, and continually requests for himself.[2] In contrast, however, to the expression of a similar thought in an earlier period,[3] this is no longer concerned with a particular historical decision brought about by God, but with the eschatological event of forgiveness in which salvation is consummated,[4] and is thus rooted in its subjective aspect as well in the divine purpose of forgiveness.

This message finds its strongest echo in Deutero-Isaiah, who has indeed been subjected to the same revelation of God's nature of love. In face of the imminent grace of pardon, which wins the heart of the blind and deaf Servant by its overwhelming demonstration of love, the negative element in conversion, that of turning away from evil ways, as in Hosea almost entirely disappears in order to make room for living turning to God,[5] a process which finds its universal climax in the vision of the turning of the Gentile world.[6] A lapse into purely passive blessedness is, however, ruled out by the fact that the favoured one is summoned to serve, and bear witness to, his God; and it is only his acceptance of this challenge which decides whether the man has allowed himself to be inwardly overcome by God's mercy or whether by refusal he is excluding himself from salvation.[7] Conversion, it is true, is not made a condition of redemption; but, as in Jesus' parable of the beggar without a wedding-garment, it cannot be considered real without the free and conscious Yes of the one who has been favoured. It is the attempt to elicit this Yes which constitutes the hidden tension within the jubilation of the gospel of redemption preached by this prophet.[8]

It was of fundamental importance for the Israelite understanding of conversion that there were two sides to the prophetic preaching on the subject. The prophets made it dependent upon the prevenient operation of God's favour, thus teaching men to understand *forgiveness* from this angle also *as the free action of the divine majesty*; but at the same time they did not jettison all human activity in conversion, but

[1] Jer. 24.7; in 31.31ff. the word *šūb* does not occur, but the substance is identical.
[2] Jer. 15.19; 17.14.
[3] I Kings 18.37, where God turns the heart of the people back to himself.
[4] Cf. pp. 457ff. above.
[5] Isa. 44.22; 43.23; 53.1–6; 55.7; cf. 55.3, 6.
[6] Isa. 45.22.
[7] Isa. 41.9, 26f.; 42.19; 43.10, 12, 21; 44.8, 21, 26; 45.23–25; 48.6, 17ff.
[8] Cf. especially the way in which the prophet frequently breaks into words of rebuke or penitence: 42.18ff.; 43.22ff.; 45.9ff.; 48.1ff.

emphasized the total character, embracing a man's whole being, of turning to God in conscious decision, and so defined *forgiveness as a liberation for personal fellowship* which reached far beyond either objective purification or legalistic remission of punishment. The fact that they insisted strongly on both these aspects, despite the tension existing between them, also proved decisive for the requirement of conversion, and impinged upon the life of the congregation in the form of practical guidance.

For, since both *the Priestly law-teaching* and *the prophecy of an Ezekiel* and his disciples strove to reconstruct the community on the basis of the Law, the conversion of the individual necessarily came into close connection with the keeping of the Law. In the concrete circumstances of Babylonia and Jerusalem, in the midst of a heathen environment, and without the framework of the nation-state to protect and support their life, conversion had to prove its genuineness by its active character, fulfilling all the practical requirements for the continued existence of a holy community in cultic separation from the impurity of heathenism, and in social solidarity in face of the anxieties which threatened that existence. For this purpose training in the Law was indispensable, and Ezekiel did not hesitate to introduce the exiles to this discipline of the will, by using the individual commandments to indicate the boundary-stones of right conduct,[1] and by making the demand for conversion mean primarily that men should *turn away* from all offences hateful to God, such as idolatry and infringement of their moral fellowship with him.[2] In the same way both the popular instruction of the Deuteronomic school and the Priestly Code focused conversion on concrete commands, prescriptions, and rights,[3] contempt for which had called down all the disasters of the past, and the strict observance of which was therefore essential in order to prove the seriousness of the new change.

This quite definitely does not mean, however, that the total reality of conversion was fragmented into a series of separate pious actions. Instead men remain vividly aware of the new interior attitude as an organic whole, so that they speak for the most part in comprehensive language of turning away from evil ways, from godlessness, from breaking faith, and from sins;[4] and the new heart and the new spirit,

---

[1] Ezek. 18; 33.10ff.
[2] Ezek. 14.6; cf. 11.18; 20.7; 18.21, 27, 30; 33.14f.
[3] Deut. 4.3, 9f.; 30.2, 10; II Kings 17.13; Lev. 26.40, 43.
[4] I Kings 8.33, 35, 47; Ezekiel *passim*.

or the circumcising of the foreskin of the heart, are seen as the central reality of conversion.[1] Thus, too, it is not human action which brings about forgiveness; everything man does is still encompassed and sustained by the free grace of God, which has promised the transformation of the heart,[2] and is to be besought in prayer and confession of sin for the gift of pardon.[3] Furthermore, conversion and the necessity of continuing to bear God's punishment are not mutually exclusive.[4] Finally, conversion frequently retains the character of an eschatological event.[5]

Linking conversion in this way to the obedient shaping of men's lives under the guidance of the Law does not therefore clash with the prophetic preaching, though it is true that under the pressure of the task imposed by the Law *a certain shift of emphasis* occurs. In fact, even the earlier prophets did on occasion refer emphatically to the basic commandments of the Law in connection with their demand for conversion, Jeremiah even including cultic obligations.[6] It is therefore somewhat difficult to speak of a new type of conversion,[7] simply because greater stress is laid upon the concrete covenant duties, even though one may readily admit that this development involves *definite dangers*. The latter are, however, only realized when new factors come into play.[8]

The first of these new factors was *the thoroughgoing organization of all piety by the Law*. The effect of this was to make it difficult for men to turn directly to God, since their whole attention was directed to an impersonal, intermediate tribunal. In such circumstances a breach of faithfulness to God was felt rather as a defection from the Law of Yahweh,[9] and likewise conversion was accomplished by turning back to the Law.[10] It may even have as its sole content, to judge from one extreme instance, a cultic act such as the celebration of the Passover in accordance with the regulations.[11] Nevertheless, the fact

---

[1] Ezek. 18.31; Deut. 10.16.
[2] Ezek. 11.19; 36.26ff.; Deut. 30.6.
[3] I Kings 8.33, 35, 47; Judg. 10.10; Lev. 26.40.
[4] Lev. 26.41.
[5] Deut. 4.30; 30.2, 10; Lev. 26.40ff.; Ezek. 36.25ff.; 11.19; 37.24.
[6] Hos. 4.1f.; Isa. 1.17; Jer. 7.5f., cf. 6.16ff.
[7] So E. K. Dietrich, *op. cit.*, p. 138 and elsewhere.
[8] Cf. E. Sjöberg, *Gott und die Sünder im palästinischen Judentum* (BWANT IV.27), 1939.
[9] II Chron. 12.1.
[10] Neh. 9.29.
[11] II Chron. 30.6, 9.

that conversion can be portrayed as it is in Jonah 3.8, 10 is significant for this period, since here both Man's direct relationship with God, and the ethical content of his response to God's call, are brought to life precisely by the fact that the situation is transferred to the heathen world. Within Judaism there is no difference in importance between seeking God and the zealous study of the Law.[1] Here the danger is that conversion will lose its living point of reference in the divine Thou, and thus become misunderstood as a means ready to Man's hand for dictating his relationship with God.

This development was assisted also by the *incorporation* of conversion *into the Jewish theory of retribution*. This is brought out especially vividly in the speeches of Job's friends, who recommend conversion to the great sufferer as the unfailing method of turning away God's punishment, and of recovering all one's lost good fortune.[2] Conversion thus commends itself to the calculations of self-interest as the surest way to escape punishment and calamity; the pious, and therefore clever, man makes use of this constantly available possibility, and is in this way able to win God over to his side. Here almost all sight of God's converting grace has been lost. It is this same incorporation into an all-too-human schematism which makes the picture of conversion in the Chronicler's work so unlifelike and conventional.

Finally, *the splitting of the Jewish community into the violently feuding factions of 'pious' and 'godless'* was bound to weaken any really profound understanding of what it means to turn to God in penitence. Where neither misfortune nor visitation could shake the self-righteous confidence that one belonged to the pious, conversion was inevitably seen rather as something for the godless, of which the righteous had no more need. Thus in reply to Malachi's call to conversion they chant the astonished question: 'How shall we return?'[3] And it is perfectly obvious that the self-righteous attitude of many Psalmists no longer leaves any room for the necessity of their own conversion.[4]

In the early days, however, these various factors were slow to make themselves felt in the Jewish community, and could not conceal the fact that there were still living witnesses to *the inward conversion of the*

---

[1] Ps. 119.2, 10.

[2] Job 8.6f.; 11.15ff.; 22.20ff.

[3] Mal. 3.7.

[4] Pss. 17; 18.22ff.; 26; 59, etc.; cf. Isa. 58.2f. In later Judaism it is primarily the godless and sinners to whom the requirement of conversion applies (I Enoch 50.2, 4; Wisd. 12.10); by contrast the pious patriarchs have no need of it (Prayer of Manasses 8; Ecclus 14.1f.; Jub. 35.5f.).

heart in prayer and confession of sin. Post-exilic prophecy leaves no doubt that on Man's side an inner turning of the whole being away from sin, and a sincere turning to the personal God, are the indispensable pre-requisites of the forgiveness of sins, and carries on the fight against both externalism and narrow-minded particularism.[1] Undoubtedly, too, there was an understanding of the fact that genuine conversion was made possible by God's grace,[2] and the universalist conception still echoes strongly.[3] In the literature of worship such mighty peni-tential psalms as 32, 38, 51, 130, 143 stand out above the level of their surroundings by virtue of the depth and purity of their turning to God, and witness not merely by the fact that they were written at all, but also by their use as favourite formularies of prayer, to the vitality of a genuine concept of conversion in the community of the Law.

Even in *the later period* there is not a complete absence of evidence of this kind, though, in proportion to the *hardening of the legalist ideal*, it cannot be said to burst forth any longer with its original potency.[4] The orientation of conversion toward the Law is in any case clearly on the increase,[5] with the result that the thought of turning directly to God recedes still more into the background. It is true that even now men know of conversion brought about by God himself, but the idea of merit intrudes disturbingly; hence the result, even at best, is only a synergistic doctrine of salvation. For by conversion Man accomplishes a work which brings God's reward in its train. Not only does it serve as a shield against God's punishment even in respect of retribution in the world to come; its atoning power is so great that it can cancel a judicial decision of God himself, even indeed a com-mandment of the Torah, and transform deliberate sins into merits.[6] No wonder that even the redemption of the nation, nay, the very redemption of the world, was thought to be dependent upon it, inasmuch as, when individual sins and merits were atomistically calculated, the conversion of one individual could be enough to make the scales turn favourably. How enormously the idea of human per-formance predominated in all this is shown also by the inclusion of

---

[1] Zech. 1.3–6, cf. 7.7ff.; Isa. 59.20; Mal. 2.6; 3.7; Jonah 3.8, 10; Joel 2.12f.
[2] Job 33.14ff., 17; 36.10.
[3] Jonah, Isa. 56.6f.
[4] So pre-eminently Ecclus; Dan. 9.4–19; 4.24; II(4) Esdras; in addition Tobit 3.2f.; 13.6; 14.6; Ps. Sol. 9.6f.; Apoc. Mos. 25.32; Prayer of Manasses; Jub. 1.19ff.; 5.2, 19; 36.5.
[5] Thus, e.g., in Orac. Sib.; Wisd. Sol.; Apoc. Bar.; II(4) Esdras.
[6] Cf. Dietrich, *op. cit.*, pp. 407f.

Torah study or suffering and death in the system as means of expiation, even if these did not always degenerate into such practices of
penitential self-torture as are related of Adam or of Eleazar ben
Durdaiah.[1]

In this context the superficiality which resulted from this worship
of the Law may be seen also in *the weakening of men's understanding of the
total character of conversion.* The casuistry of Rabbinic law-teaching
robbed it of a unified goal; and overloading with innumerable
detailed demands led inevitably to the attempt to ease the radical
demand, that of conversion, by evasion of the Law.[2] It is true that the
seriousness of conversion was heightened by the thought of retribution
in the world to come; on it now depended no longer merely one's
temporal, but also one's eternal salvation—and in the world to come
there would be no further opportunity for conversion. But even here
alleviations find their way in, either by assuming an opportunity for
conversion during the Messianic judgment or by distinguishing the
perfectly righteous from the real *ba^{c}alē t^{e}šūbā*, who unless they were
converted would be lost, or by separating yet another class, that of the
mediocre, those for whom transgression and merit held the scales
evenly balanced, and envisaging in their case a sentence of restricted
duration. Even though the last-named view is attested only at a late
period,[3] and did not go uncontradicted, it yet shows along what lines
legalistic piety was compelled to forge its way, if it wished to avoid
being oppressed by the prophetic demand for conversion. In such
circumstances it is possible for judgment to fall all the harder, of
course, on the heathen. For them there is no conversion, since God
has destined them for Hell, with the exception of those who have
attached themselves to Judaism as proselytes.[4] Alongside all this,
however, the expression of universalist views is still occasionally to be
found.[5]

(c) The motives of forgiveness

1. The confidence with which the pious Israelite has recourse to
God's forgiveness is based first and foremost on the fact that God's
revelation has itself made known to him the principles which motivate

---

[1] Vit. Ad. 5f.; Aboda Zara 17a.
[2] Cf. Dietrich, *op. cit.*, pp. 395ff.
[3] In Akiba and other scribes.
[4] Cf. Dietrich, *op. cit.*, pp. 395ff.
[5] Wisd. 11.23; 12.20; Tobit 13.11; 14.6; Test. Zeb. 9. For the eschatological
conversion of the heathen, cf. Strack-Billerbeck, *op. cit.* III, p. 150; I, p. 362.

divine action. In the redemption from Egypt, and the subsequent covenant-making, he learns to recognize God's will for fellowship with men, which reaches out its hand to his chosen ones even across sin and unfaithfulness, and helps them to strive against sin, to extirpate iniquity, and to return to truer allegiance. The part played here by *God's goodness, experienced as readiness to succour, in keeping with the covenant which he has made,* has already been described.[1] To this *ḥesed yhwh,* on which men can rely in every distress, it belongs also to forgive transgressions, and so to ensure that the covenant relationship is not destroyed by them.[2] For this reason the story of the wilderness wanderings can tell again and again how Yahweh allows himself to be talked round from anger to favour, because he stands in a special relationship to Israel. Indeed, God himself provides the means by which an offence can be expiated; and even if he does not allow it to go unpunished, yet he uses the punishment to restore the covenant relationship. It is on the basis of this knowledge of the fundamental orientation of God's attitude that the Israelite dares to entreat his God for forgiveness; and throughout every epoch of Israel's history confidence in this motive of divine action remains constant.[3]

Belief that one is justified in assuming this same motivation lies behind *the appeal to God as Father and Shepherd.* For God's election of Israel means that he has adopted her, and so indeed become the Father of his people; and this position is seen to be the foundation both of his claim to obedience from his son[4] and of the son's confidence in his Father's loving concern,[5] a concern which is held with increasing emphasis to include the bestowal of pardon.[6] And in the same sense men speak of God's office of Shepherd, in virtue of which he affords protection and help to the 'sheep of his pasture', despite their errant ways, and does not allow himself to be separated from them for ever.[7]

Another form in which confidence in God's absolving covenant loyalty finds expression is the appeal to *the promise which Yahweh swore to the patriarchs,* that he would multiply their descendants, and give

---

[1] Cf. vol. I, pp. 232ff.
[2] Num. 14.18–20; Ex. 32.11ff.; 34.6f.; II Sam. 24.14, 17.
[3] Cf. Isa. 64.9; Pss. 25.10f.; 80; 103.18; 106.45; 111.7–9, etc.
[4] Isa. 1.4; 30.1, 9; Deut. 14.1; Isa. 45.9–11; Mal. 1.6; 2.10.
[5] Ex. 4.22; Num. 11.12; Deut. 32.6, 18; Isa. 64.7; Mal. 3.17.
[6] Deut. 8.5; Prov. 3.12; Hos. 11.1ff.; Jer. 3.19; 31.20.
[7] Pss. 74.1; 77.21; 78.52, 71; 79.13; 80.2; 107.41; Micah 4.6ff.; Zeph. 3.13, 19; Jer. 31.10; Ezek. 34.12ff., 23; 37.23f.

them the land of Canaan for their possession. By thus extending the
thread of the covenant back into the past,[1] new light is thrown on the
consistency with which God carries out his work. The way in which,
despite their weakness and their failures, he bore with the fathers,
becomes the pattern for his dealings with his people and with his
godly ones. The promise to the patriarchs is seen as the decisive
guarantee that God has bound himself to the people of his choice; and
when faith is growing anxious about the fate of the disobedient nation,
it takes heart from his faithfulness to the word once given to the
fathers.[2] Indeed, the later period regards appeal to the divine
covenant made with the patriarchs as nothing less than the 'most
effective of all methods of ensuring that prayer is heard'.[3] It is because
he has inherited this conception of God as motivated by loyalty to the
covenant that Deutero-Isaiah is justified in comforting those who
despair of God's help by saying that in Yahweh's eyes no writ of
divorce against his rejected wife Israel exists, but rather that God, as
the faithful 'redeemer', will ransom his people from slavery. Thus a
wide range of passages bears witness to the idea that the primary
motivation of forgiveness is God's will to fellowship as revealed in the
covenant, thus giving rich content to faith in his covenant faithfulness.

It should, however, be noted that *God's freedom in the matter of
punishment and forgiveness* is not prejudiced by this confident appeal to
his self-commitment. No support whatever is given to the notion that
Man can exert any kind of pressure on his decision. His action may
frustrate human expectations; but men are ready to adapt themselves, and to accept without murmuring even the puzzling destiny
which causes an innocent man, perhaps one of the great in Israel, to
die the death of the wicked. The combination of a living sense of
God's majesty with confidence in his covenant promise leads men to
deliver themselves into his hands, and to leave the decision to him.[4]

A threat to this attitude arises, however, when the idea of God's
covenant faithfulness is elaborated to mean that, once this close
association with his people has been entered into, *God's honour is im-*

---

[1] Cf. vol. I, pp. 49ff.
[2] Cf. God's words of blessing in Genesis, and the appeal to the God of the
fathers in Ex. 2.24; 3.6, 15f.; 4.5; 32.13; Josh. 18.3; 21.44; I Kings 18.36f.; II
Kings 13.23; Deut. 4.31, 37; 7.8, 12; 8.18; 9.5, 27; 13.18; 29.12; Ex. 6.3–5(P);
Lev. 26.42; Micah 7.20; Ps. 105.9; Isa. 41.8; 51.2; II Chron. 30.6; Neh. 9.7.
[3] Bousset-Gressmann, *op. cit.*, p. 362. Cf. the copious list of passages cited in n. 1
of the same page.
[4] I Sam. 3.18; II Sam. 10.12; 16.10ff.

perilled if the nation falls victim to the annihilating retribution of his anger. From one point of view this is the highest affirmation it is possible to make about election as a motive for God's intervention. Over and above the voluntary self-commitment which awakens confidence in God's goodness and loyalty a motive for his forgiveness is here found in his own nature, which would suffer damage and derogation if Israel's enemies were able to triumph. For with Israel's misfortune dishonour falls on God's name, and with her destruction Yahweh's name, too, would be exterminated from the world.[1] Thus men can pray God to give his own name the honour which is its due before the whole world by pardoning and succouring Israel.[2]

It is clear that *this appeal to God's name contains elements of widely differing value*. On the one hand it expresses a living sense of the unconditional character of God's sovereign will, which tolerates no infringement, and of the inviolability of his historical self-communication to mankind, which, once revelation has taken place, can then not be suspended or effaced without adverse effect upon God himself. On the other hand, the all too naïve identification of the historical existence of the nation Israel with the realization of the concept of the kingdom of God involves the danger that inadvertently the earthly interests of the nation may become confused with God's purpose in revelation, thus prejudicing the sovereign freedom of his forgiveness. Also this danger inevitably made itself felt all the more strongly, the more the Israelite conception of God was corrupted in other respects by the infiltration of heathen elements—a matter on which the polemic of the prophets supplies us with authentic information. Only where the idea of God's honour was purified from the dross of false notions in the crucible of judgment could it give rise to that theocentric rationale of forgiveness which is found in later usage.

II. If Israel's particular experience of God led her to explain the forgiveness of sins in terms of God's goodness, at the same time this is combined in a number of passages with *a universal human idea of God as inclined to overlook and pardon*. This view starts from the frailty and briefness of creaturely life, and sees in the misery and trouble of human existence reason sufficient to awaken compassion in God, as a result of which he can be moved to remit punishment.[3] Indeed,

---

[1] Pss. 74.10, 18; 83.3, 19; 92.9f.; 109.27; 143.11f.; Josh 7.9.

[2] Pss. 138.5; 115.1.

[3] II Sam. 14.14; Pss. 103.14–16; 78.38f.; 89.47–49; 143.2; 144.3f.; possibly also Ps. 39.5–7, 12–14, though the text here is uncertain. At a later period, Eccles 8.6–8; Ecclus 18.8–12; Apoc. Bar. 48.12ff.

because the fact that men, despite all their good intentions, exhibit so many faults and failings is due very largely to their earthly limitations,[1] to punish them for such things seems cruel, and incompatible with God's way of thinking.[2]

This view, which manifestly goes back to a very early period, is the product of a way of looking at things which stands in a certain tension with that other assessment of the sad lot of human life which, as deepened by the prophets, sees it as witnessing to the wrath of God justly punishing the anti-God attitude of Man.[3] We have already seen[4] that behind these two views stand two differing approaches to the question of sin, the one regarding it as a habitual condition, the other as a decision implemented in act. Because sin is, in fact, both of these things, the one view cannot be played off against the other; rather it is only by upholding both that any apposite comment on the actual human situation can be made. It is, however, essential that mature conviction of God's fatherly goodness which is the product of his historical self-communication—a conviction which also sees God's relationship to the creature as such in the light of this historical instituting of fellowship with Man[5]—should remain aware of the basis on which it rests, and not, in an all-too-human self-pity at God's dealings with his creature, make demands which contradict the utterly desperate condition of Man when faced with God's judgment. If not, then sin would be rendered harmless by regarding its inherence in the human condition more as a sentence of Fate than as the just consequence of an actual decision taken against God's will, and it would thus come to be evaluated as a ground of excuse for Man and as a right demand upon God. Because this view starts from the fact of human misery as a reality in isolation, and not from the eternal glory of God, it inevitably ends up by composing a picture of God as it thinks he should be, a picture in which pardoning goodness forms a characteristic of the Creator and Sustainer which is taken for granted. That such a picture of the deity is bound to disintegrate under the burden of any exceptional human distress is a constantly recurring experience in the history of belief in God.

The poet of Job was undoubtedly on the way to postulating just such a non-historical, unconditional divine goodness, for this attribute

[1] Job 4.17–21.
[2] Job 7.1ff., 17–21; 14.1–6.
[3] Ps. 90.5–9; Isa. 40.6ff.; possibly also Ps. 39.12, cf. Duhm *ad loc.*
[4] Cf. pp. 398ff. and 410ff. above.
[5] Cf. vol. I, p. 239.

strikes reason as an evidently necessary correlate of the distressful reality of life.[1] Ps. 103 and kindred passages also verge on this view. And yet it never quite becomes a fact. In the end the poet of Job sharply rejects such a demand for God's commiseration by making all human claims fall dumb before the *revealed reality* of the wondrous and mysterious God for whose sake even the world and its enigmas can be affirmed.[2] And the Psalmist lays such stress on the forgiveness of sins as a product of God's inconceivable mercy so gloriously brought to light in the history of the chosen people that the lament over the transience of Man can be understood not as introducing a new motive for forgiveness, but only as emphasizing the proof of God's fatherly love which in all its greatness condescends to so wretched a creature. Hence, too, the everlastingness of the divine grace bestowed upon the members of the covenant is seen as the conclusive conquest of all the pessimism which might have prevailed, had attention been focused on the rapid passing of human life. To encounter this gracious God, and his eternal merciful will, it is worth while to have lived.

Nevertheless the attitude to human frailty apparent here is clearly distinct from that of the prophets. Set in the context of the eternal divine will for mankind, as a part of his order, which never allows men to escape the awareness of their state of dependence and of being left to the divine mercy, the lot of transience is no longer the goad which arouses a longing for this imperfect creation to be changed into God's perfect world, but the givenness of the human condition, which is accepted into the association between Creator and creature, and above the imperfections of which Man is lifted by the vision of the present grace of God. Because this affirms as a real datum the God-Man relationship, into which, despite his creaturely weakness, Man is inducted by God's covenant-making, real force is undoubtedly given to an important concern of belief in revelation. At the same time, however, it is clear that the only thing which keeps at bay the danger of a lapse into superficial talk of God's fatherly goodness is the fact that this has not meant the silencing of the other view, which looks from human transience into the abyss of divine wrath, wrath which sets unacknowledged sin in the light of its countenance, and

---

[1] This explains why the relevant passages meet with such approval from all supporters of a 'natural theology'; cf., e.g., the remarks of B. Duhm on the 'magnificent and daring ideas' of Job 7.21, in his commentary *ad loc.*

[2] Cf. pp. 489ff. below.

thus causes all human glory to pass away with as little trace as the grass of the field. For this insight there can be no peace of mind in the present experience of God, but only recourse to the promise that God's act of pardon will overcome by a new creation even the compulsion to sin inherent in Man's corporal nature, and so establish full fellowship with his creature.

III. From this starting-point, however, the way was opened up for the first time. to the profoundest statements concerning the motivational basis for God's forgiveness, namely those which speak of *his honour and his love*. In each case the argument works backwards from God's action to his nature. In the first instance it is more of a logical extension on the basis of principles discernible in the divine activity hitherto; in the second it rests on an inner conviction as to the strongest force in God's nature, but one for which there is no further rational derivation of any sort.

The statements about God's injured honour, which he must for his own sake restore, are connected with that popular conception of his faithful love which regards the perfect fulfilment of the covenant obligations as the real mark of the nature of the covenant God, and therefore sees his honour as endangered where such fulfilment is in doubt, and is exposed to attack and denial by the godless.[1] Here, alongside other, strongly anthropomorphic conceptions, the conviction that *constancy and sureness of purpose mark God's actions* is already at work; and in the prophets, who like to contrast God's faithfulness and Man's unfaithfulness, it is elaborated to dominate their whole view of history. Their confidence that God's sovereignty will ultimately be implemented despite all obstacles rests essentially on the assurance that God cannot be untrue to himself, since he, as distinct from all the capricious gods of the heathen, has his plan of salvation, by the revelation of which he has expressed his unshakeable determination to subject the whole world to his own purposes. This assurance finds its most impressive expression in the theology of history of an Isaiah, or in Deutero-Isaiah's revelation of God as glorifying himself by bringing Israel home from Exile. Isaiah ascribes the bringing in of the new age to God's *ḳin'ā*, his jealousy, in which is summed up his will to assert himself and to implement his own nature.[2] In Ezekiel the same thought is rendered by the formal expressions: 'for the sake of my (holy) Name', or 'that ye may know that I am Yahweh'. Not for

[1] Cf. pp. 476f. above.
[2] Isa. 9.6.

Israel's sake, but to sanctify his great Name,[1] which has been dishonoured in the sight of the nations, is the miracle of the sanctification and renewal of the rejected people performed. In this way all assurance of salvation is derived with unqualified rigour from God's faithfulness to himself. As regards the thought of the covenant, which Israel has so shamefully broken, this can no longer afford any kind of ground for hope, but can only reinforce the certainty of annihilating judgment.[2] If hope still exists at all, it is solely because God's honour requires that he sanctify his name before all the world, that is to say, because his will to reveal himself[3] cannot capitulate in face of human resistance, and thus prove itself impotent, but demands to be recognized in all its worshipful holiness and to be adored by a community which surrenders itself to him. In this way the appeal to God's self-assertion is dissociated from a mere sensitive national pride, which confuses God's honour with Israel's, and desires his intervention on account of the mockery of the neighbouring peoples. It is not a matter of the respect accorded to Israel, but of the *justification of the claim of revelation*. It is in the same sense that Deutero-Isaiah proclaims God's unbending determination to stand up for his honour, and by redeeming the rejected people to bring to light the fact that he alone is God, in contrast to all the gods of men.[4] This motive for God's mercy to Israel is also adopted in the poems of corporate and individual lamentation,[5] in that, even in cases of individual distress, the justification of God's honour before the whole world is asserted as the purpose of his succour.

In these instances it is the supraterrestrial power of God's *self-assertion* which ensures the establishment of his sovereignty by conquering even the curse of guilt. Where the same certainty is created by inner conviction it is the supraterrestrial power of God's *self-communication* which is responsible. God's purpose of fellowship, revealing itself in the covenant-making, is recognized precisely in its exclusiveness as the absolutely inexplicable and inconceivable miracle of his love; and therefore, when God cleaves to the people of his election, even though they have become guilty, this is revealed as the *triumph of this love*. The way in which this message endowed the preaching of Hosea and of Jeremiah with its special character, and was

[1] Ezek. 36.22f.
[2] Expressed most forcefully in the parables of Ezek. 16 and 23.
[3] On the connection between Name and revelation cf. pp. 40ff. above.
[4] Isa. 42.8; 48.9, 11; 52.5f.
[5] Pss. 79.9; 102.16; 138.5; 57.6, 12.

adopted and given a distinctive stamp in both the Deuteronomic law-teaching and Deutero-Isaiah's Book of Consolation, has already been described in detail.[1] At first it was undoubtedly concerned with the election and redemption of the nation as a whole. But that it also brought confidence and hope to the life of the individual is shown by the new definition of the God-Man relationship as a loving surrender[2] in which each member of the covenant people allows himself to be caught up by the stream of love as it seeks to penetrate the whole of life within the divine covenant. Only to the man who in this way 'knows' Yahweh[3] is disclosed all the richness of the revelation of love, which as the power of forgiveness is already manifested in the present by the maintenance of the covenant despite all human faithlessness, but proves its miraculous power all the more through and beyond the frightful punishment of wrath in the new creation of a community where small and great alike experience forgiveness as an inner renewal for the most intimate fellowship of love with the divine Lord.

This rationale of divine forgiveness breaks completely with any assurance that can be arrived at by reason, and thus corresponds exactly to revelation's character of irrational miracle, recognized only by inner conviction of its truth. That is why the explanation of love in terms of God's holiness, that is to say, in terms of the mystery of his being as God, as we find it in Hosea, indicating as it does the limits of our understanding, is the only possible statement of the origin of this spring of love.

How strongly the motive of love determined belief in forgiveness is shown not only by the incorporation of the concept of ḥesed, which was originally of quite a different stamp, namely the conditional faithfulness of love to its obligations, into the unconditional quality of the spontaneous demonstration of love,[4] but also by the way in which this divine love is related to the individual, a feature which emerges in the literature of worship.[5] Indeed, in the Jewish community men were able to see in this unfathomable goodness Yahweh's attitude to the whole creation, and to praise the deep fervour of his election love toward Israel precisely in times of severe visitation.[6] Nevertheless, the direct conviction of God's purpose of love was

[1] Cf. vol. I, pp. 250ff.
[2] Cf. pp. 290ff. above.
[3] Cf. pp. 291ff. above.
[4] Cf. vol. I, pp. 236ff.
[5] Cf. vol. I, p. 257.
[6] Cf. vol. I, pp. 238f. and 257f.

severely restricted as the concept of God gradually stiffened into one of transcendent exaltedness, in which the divine nature exists simply in and for itself, and only engages in intercourse with the world of earth through hypostases; nor was it able to assert itself any longer with its original force in face of the dominating concept of the universal Judge. Hosea and Jeremiah had known the suffering love of God, which strives for its people with a self-sacrifice which consumes even its messengers; and the Servant of God in Isa. 53 had pointed to an ultimate realization of this insight. But both the abstract monism of the Jewish picture of God, and the subordination of the sovereign freedom of his mercy to the Torah,[1] remain impervious to this profoundest revelation of the concept of divine love.

6. SIN AND EVIL[2]

1. In Israel sin and evil are not inseparably connected one with the other. The popular conception of evil as a blow from God, and a revelation of his wrath,[3] was never systematized into a watertight entailment making every evil a punishment of sin. Men were unprejudiced enough to accept many different kinds of misfortune as concomitants of the nature of the universe, which, of course, there was no point in discussing further; and under such one could only bow oneself humbly, since the mysterious greatness of God was bound to be in the right as compared with short-sighted Man. Furthermore, the predominance of the sense of collective existence, finding its satisfaction in the life of the national community, allowed no man to advance individual claims to special consideration for the small circle of his own life.[4] Thus it came about that suffering in individual lives did not lead men to challenge belief in God's universal providence, whereas severe national misfortune much more quickly gave rise to sceptical questioning of his righteousness.[5]

A change in this spiritual situation became visible for the first time in the period of Jeremiah.[6] Here, in the problem of the prosperity of the godless, we encounter the claim that in the life of the individual as

---

[1] Cf. F. Weber, *op. cit.*, pp. 157ff.
[2] Cf. J. A. Sanders, *Suffering as Divine Discipline in the Old Testament and Post-biblical Judaism*, 1955.
[3] Cf. on this point vol. I, pp. 258ff.
[4] Cf. pp. 175f. and 237ff. above.
[5] Cf. pp. 239f. above.
[6] Cf. pp. 246ff. above.

well the shaping of a man's fate must be carried out in accordance with the principles of righteous retribution;[1] and the fact that the proverb referring to the absurdity of the popular collective attitude occurs in two places—'The fathers have eaten sour grapes, but the children's teeth are set on edge'[2]—illustrates the force of the reaction which had broken out against the inadequacy of the hitherto accepted view of evil.

At the same time, however, it is significant for the spiritual attitude of Old Testament piety that its principal exponents made no attempt to resolve these tormenting new questions by a theoretical reconciliation of God's wise providence with the puzzling reality of the world, and thus to create something which the Platonic-Stoic world-view was accustomed to treat as an important point in its doctrine of providence, namely a theodicy.[3]

In Jeremiah such problems very definitely take second place to the sufferings and tasks which are demanded of a messenger of God in the storms of the contemporary situation (12.1ff.). It is in these that he must determine for himself, if he is to remain God's mouthpiece, what ultimately he feels to be the supreme content of life, that which far surpasses all else (15.10–21). For the rest, challenges of this kind must, if one looks at the approaching break-up of this world-era, and the new order of things promised by God, seem in the end of peripheral importance (31.29f.). But if for Jeremiah the vision of Yahweh's great breaking down and building anew, in the heart of which the prophet was standing, laid the question to rest, Ezekiel in the same situation uses the demand of his contemporaries for individual retribution as the perfect weapon for beating back attacks on the divine governance, and for awakening a new understanding of Yahweh's intentions. The self-righteous defiance which objects to the heralding of Jerusalem's fall on the grounds that the holy city, or at least the pious within her, merited preferential treatment he shatters by pointing out that in God's righteous judgment there could as little be a transfer of righteousness as that transfer of guilt against which they were rebelling. Nevertheless, God would all the same make an exception in this case by preserving a whole band of fugitives, not, however, because they would have any claim to preservation, but to

[1] Jer. 12.1ff.
[2] Jer. 31.29; Ezek. 18.2.
[3] What follows should be read in conjunction with my earlier remarks on this question in the essay 'Vorsehungsglaube und Theodizee im AT' (*Procksch-Festschrift*, 1934, pp. 6off.).

display them as a living proof to the exiles that the city was indeed ripe for judgment—a scathing, ironic defence of the freedom of the divine Lord and Judge (14.12ff.). But the cynical sceptics who tried to make fun of the prophetic teaching on the culpability of the whole nation before Yahweh by making out that disaster was a punishment of the guiltless for the sins of their fathers (18.2) he confronts, just as he does the desperate pious, who under the frightful pressure of the gigantic national guilt see nothing ahead of them except death or exile, and who have lost all strength to go on living (33.10), with the gracious offer of his God: 'As I live, says the Lord God, I have no pleasure in the death of the wicked, but that the wicked turn from his way and live' (33.11; cf. 18.23, 32).

For this is the major premise, on the basis of which the statements in Ezek. 18 and 33.10ff., so often misunderstood, must be interpreted. With the utmost possible weight and emphasis divine judgment is here linked with the personal decision of the individual; and any transfer of guilt from father to son is denied. This does not mean that a new theory is being put forward, which is to explain God's dealings in every single instance, but simply that in a crisis of faith help is being given to meet the contemporary situation, and *to strengthen men for a new effort in their lives*.[1] Ezekiel is not denying a connection between a man's own fate and the guilt of his fathers; in the situation of the exiles this was only too patent, and in other passages the prophet indeed speaks quite automatically of the collective retribution affecting all members of the nation (20; 21.3, 9; 16 and 23). What he contests is that God has here spoken his last word, and that the lament of 33.10—'Our transgressions and our sins are upon us, and we waste away because of them; how then can we live?'—is justified, countering it with the divine will to redeem and bless all those who allow themselves to be called to the act of moral obedience. Moreover, by laying all the emphasis on the turning of the will, in which the whole course of a man's life is summed up, to or away from God he reveals a divine Lord who is interested not in a calculable sum of works, but in a personal relationship of service and faithfulness. Even though the style may be pedantic, and the sober lawyer's tone recall legal docu-

[1] The present writer thus dissents from the eschatological interpretation, as supported by Bertholet and Herrmann, and believes that J. Köberle and others must be right, when they take the text to refer to a divine retribution constantly at work. To what extent he would again differ from these exegetes as well, and come closer to the views of the first-named, may be seen from what follows. Cf. in addition W. Eichrodt, *Der Prophet Hesekiel* (ATD 22.1), 1959, pp. 143ff.

ments, neither of these features should be allowed to conceal the fact that we have here not a theological theory but one of the first proclamations of salvation capable of speaking to mockers and despairing alike about a God who is something more than justice inexorable in punishment, namely goodness, setting things to rights. This proclamation gives the individual *room to step out beyond the natural involvement of the generations in sin to personal decision for the divine Lord*, the same Lord as in the great vision of the Valley of Dry Bones (ch. 37), where to those who despair that they are as good as dead (37.11) he promises the divine power which will revive them to newness of life.

In this way Ezekiel avoids the path of fruitless argument, which thinks it can overcome crises of faith by working out clever theories about God's actions, and instead brings to his contemporaries the call of their God to new and courageous action in his service. The doctrine of individual retribution, however, constitutes the thought-form in which is clothed the conviction that such service will not be in vain. Finally, because it is designed for a period with fixed limits in the eschatological world-consummation, preceded by purifying judgment (20.35ff., 38; 13.9; 34.22), it does, in fact, find its full meaning only in the equipping of the nation for Yahweh's final redemption.[1]

11. It will be seen, therefore, that the charge often brought against Ezekiel, namely that he set up an abstract retribution theory, and was thus to blame for the unrealistic dogmatic explanation of the world current in Judaism, is quite untenable. There are certainly connections here, but they may well be much less direct than is commonly supposed, and in any case are not sufficient by themselves to explain the characteristic reapplication of Ezekiel's lapidary propositions in the sense which the dogmatics of later Judaism gave to them. To reach that point a new element had to be introduced, and this is to be found in the gradual predominance after the Exile of the priestly view of the world and of life. The more thoroughly was history subjected to God's sovereignty as revealed in the Law, the more completely was religious thought and effort directed to obediently shaping the present in accordance with the norm of the eternal laws of God's kingdom, and so much the less was an explicitly eschatological attitude able to become determinative for piety. But with this change in the tone of religious consciousness the necessity of making the present meaningful as the working out of divine pro-

---

[1] Here lies the element of truth in the eschatological interpretation of the relevant sections.

vidence, and that even—and particularly—in the life of the individual, inevitably awoke with undreamed-of force. As a means to this end the old belief in retribution, which spoke of the good fortune of the pious and the misfortune of the godless, acquired immense importance, for it alone seemed to secure the reality of the living God as the moral power ruling the world. And indeed it did offer a rational, schematic explanation of the world which satisfied the claims of moral thinking educated on the Law. No wonder, then, that it became a central proposition of faith in God, which could never be surrendered, a dogma in the strict sense; and that to question it meant cutting the nerve and heart of all living piety.[1] And the greater the burden on the Jewish community, and the threat to its assurance of God, created by external pressure and internal disruption, the more zealously did religious thought seek with the help of this dogma to construct a position proof against any storm that might blow, a position from which all scepticism about divine providence could be beaten back and refuted. It was in this way that the striving for a true theodicy made its appearance in Judaism. The results of this effort became ominously noticeable in more than one direction. In men's belief about God the righteousness that brings salvation was replaced by the impartial distribution of reward and punishment in accordance with the rule of the Law, *iustitia distributiva* —a deplorable narrowing of outlook. As regards their view of history, the old historical tradition, with its reverence in face of God's inconceivable majesty, was no longer tolerated, and was rationalized by introducing a mechanical retribution, as a comparison of the Chronicler's work with the books of Kings especially makes clear. As for the hope of redemption, where the future consummation was slyly transformed into an ideal situation brought about by human exertions, Israelite world-sovereignty with an abundance of natural and material goods here regained a permanent place as a particularly striking proof of righteous retribution.[2] And in the prayer life the so-called Psalms of innocence,[3] which make God's impartial retribution a reason why their prayer should be heard, most of all betray the injurious effect on piety of calculations of merit and reward. Above all, however, the justification of God which the dogma of retribution

---

[1] Especially in Proverbs (1.19, 31ff.; 2.21f.; 3.33ff., etc.), many Psalms (37; 39; 49; 73; 128), and in the speeches of the friends in Job.

[2] Isa. 66.12; Zech. 9.11–11.3; 12.1ff.; 14.1ff.; Obad. 15ff.; Dan. 2.44; 4.14f.; 7.27.

[3] Pss. 17; 26; 59, *et al.*; cf. Neh. 5.19; 13.14, 22, 31.

attempted proved least convincing just where it was most urgently needed, namely in the case of the misfortunes of the pious. Even though the ideas of testing and education, of ultimate compensation, or of all the more certain blessing for one's children, might serve to quieten many of the queries of the doubting, yet such consolations were contradicted by the extreme severity of the visitation, and in their place came the strong temptation to argue from the inexplicable fate of one's fellow countryman to his guilt—reasoning typically portrayed in the book of Job, and seemingly to be found also in many Psalms.[1] Such experiences were bound to plunge the upright believer into the most serious temptations, and to threaten him with complete bewilderment about God. At this precise juncture, however, the strength of genuine belief in God proved itself by the way in which it saw through the gimcrack of human attempts to justify God, rejected all the creations of theodicy, and sought the answer to the problem of faith rather in God himself than in clever theorizing.

III. This breakthrough from the God of rational abstraction to the living God of revelation was accomplished in three directions, the first of which was conscious *attachment to the prophetic message of the God who comes*.[2] Even though the groups who maintained the genuine eschatological attitude were only small, yet it was precisely in these circles that the message of Deutero-Isaiah about the vicarious suffering of the servant of God was preserved, and applied to men's own lives. It is not only the pericope in Deutero-Zechariah about the vicarious suffering of the good Shepherd[3] which shows a continuing living understanding for the fact that it is precisely the man who stands closest to God who must pass through great suffering if he is to become the right tool in God's hand for the building of his kingdom. Men dared to see their own personal sufferings also in the light of the eschatological consummation, as, for example, in Ps. 22, where the closing section (vv. 23–32) interprets suffering in a manner quite outside the schematism of retribution, as a building-stone for the completion of the kingdom of God. It is the fact that God finds in the suffering of his faithful ones the most effective means of establishing his sovereignty over mankind which gives this poet, even in the midst of the dark night of his affliction, the profound consolation which

---

[1] Pss. 7.4ff.; 35.11, 19; 41.7f.; 69.5, 22; 70.3f., etc.
[2] On this point cf. the remarks at pp. 106f. and 354ff. above, and in vol. I, pp. 345ff.
[3] Zech. 11.4–14; 13.7–9; 12.10ff. Cf. O. Procksch, *Die kleinen prophetischen Schriften nach dem Exil*, 1916, pp. 107ff.

helps him over his abandonment by God, and enables him to find the victorious answer to the crippling questions of doubt as to the meaning of suffering.

In this instance it was the vision of the God who comes which thrusts theodicy out of its place; but for other harassed people the fetters of human theory were broken by *escape to the direct experience of God's nearness*. The poet of Ps. 73 has described for us most movingly how he suffered under the daily contradition between his experience of life and the assertion of righteous divine retribution, and laboured to resolve the tormenting riddle in some way or other (73.16). But despite all his ponderings no attempt at theodicy could satisfy him. In the end he broke free, in a quite different way, from the error of trying to compute God's retribution, namely when, by direct divine illumination,[1] his eyes were opened to that wherein the miracle of true fellowship with God really consists: not in any earthly gift whatsoever, be it never so great and glorious, but in the personal self-disclosure of God, who is inconceivably great, as himself the faithfulness that sustains and the communication of a supraterrestrial life that bestows on even the most wretched of human lives an incomparable inner value not to be endangered even by death. In face of this priceless possession how the good fortune of the ungodly, to all seeming so incomprehensible, shrivelled to a delusive nothing!—especially when, at his latter end, the terror of death brings the experience of being utterly forgotten by God! With a shout of real jubilation the Psalmist after such an experience casts himself anew into the arms of his God, confident of having found an answer to the riddle of life far superior to all the expedients of human reason.

The only other texts comparable to this experience of the presence of God as the true and indestructible content of life are the confession of Jeremiah (Jer. 15.15–21) and the song of thanksgiving in Ps. 16.[2] Yet we may see in these proof that again and again men arose in Israel who found the way out of the cul-de-sac of theodicy back to God himself, and thus preserved for true belief its royal status as the direct experience of reality, unprejudiced by any ambiguous aids.

The third protest against the attempt to construct a theodicy on the basis of a rationalistic theory of retribution found its backing in

---

[1] This is certainly the sense in which v. 17 should be interpreted; cf. pp. 522f. below.

[2] The dialogue section of the book of Job (ch. 3–21) strives toward this, without however attaining it. Pss. 17.15 and 63.4 come at least very close.

the *belief in God as Creator*. The classic witness here is Job 38–41.[1] The answer here offered to the preceding question of God's righteous providence, which has been so passionately debated, provides—as indeed, after Job's bitter struggle against his friends' attempts at theodicy, was only to be expected—no sort of rational solution. The retreat from the moral world to the creation, and to the power, greatness, and wisdom of God visible therein, absolutely does not imply an argument from this evidence to a cosmic Mind which, both in Nature and in human life, has ordered all things for the attainment of rational goals, even though not always, it may be, in a way accessible to human calculation. Instead, and obviously quite intentionally, those works of creation are cited which witness to the Creator as the incomprehensibly miraculous, the one whose governance can no longer be organized into a system of rational goals. The marvellous structure of the cosmos, with its mysterious forces of fearful power for blessing or destruction, is something the management of which can certainly not be fathomed in terms of human utilitarian calculation; the wild animals, whose nature and impulses exclude them from all rational interpretation, yet manifestly stand under the good pleasure of God. This picture would be misunderstood, however, were it not also noticed that it desires to proclaim more than just the bewildering incomprehensibility of God's universal design, which causes the questioner to lay his hand upon his mouth, and to prostrate himself in the dust.[2] The Creator's freedom, so strongly emphasized, is no cruel caprice, no malicious joke, doing no more than hurl Man down into the sense of his own nothingness;[3] it also includes a mysterious inner association of the Creator with his creature, by virtue of which Man feels himself claimed and moved in his innermost self by God's governance, even when he does not understand it. Through the whole panorama runs a thrill of exulting adoration

[1] We may disregard the question whether these chapters contain the solution of the problem of Job originally intended by the poet, or whether the dialogue section does not, in fact, point in a different direction, since this is not directly relevant to our present concern.

[2] The first to put his finger firmly on this point was R. Otto (*The Idea of the Holy*, ET [1923], 1959, pp. 93ff.), but B. Duhm had already pointed the way in his commentary. Cf. W. Vischer, *Hiob, ein Zeuge Jesu Christi*, 1934. M. Sekine, too, draws attention to the positive meaning of the belief in Creation in the book of Job, though with the concept of new creation, making Job appear as the 'restored primal Man', he may well be intruding an alien idea ('Schöpfung und Erlösung im Buch Hiob', *Eissfeldt-Festschrift*, 1958, pp. 213ff.).

[3] This is how it appears to the Indian view of Nature, and also frequently to that of modern Man.

and amazement,[1] which is only possible because Man senses and feels, within the enigmatic, something infinitely valuable in which he himself, as creature of this Creator, is included. This inner conviction of a creating power which, as the sheerly miraculous, is able to persuade men of its higher right, and to quiet all the questionings of doubt, is the real content of the speeches of God, and the devastating refutation of all rational theodicy. With this may be compared only the change which takes place in the soul of the singer of Ps. 139, where anxiety-ridden flight from the inescapable God gives place to adoring contemplation of his wisdom and care, and the relationship of Man to his Creator, rooted in the creation itself, convinces him of a new kind of fellowship with God (vv. 13ff.).

In all this, however, one thing should not be overlooked, namely that something has to be presupposed in order to make it possible for Man to become thus in tune with the marvellous melody of the works of creation. This something is the word of the Creator to his creature. That God himself speaks, and guides men to a true understanding of his wonders in creation, is by no means self-evident—at any rate, most certainly not in the Wisdom literature, to which of course, Job also belongs. To explain the introduction of God as absolutely nothing more than a poetic device to underline the lesson of the book would be to draw the sting of the work in a quite impermissible way. On the contrary, it is an essential part of Job's satisfaction that he is allowed to see God, and is considered worthy to be addressed by him (42.5f.). The poet therefore conceives the interpretation of the creation which he is presenting not as a mental concept which any reflective person could grasp in view of the greatness and beauty of Nature; rather is it integral to his conception that the Creator does not remain dumb, but speaks to his creature. This means, however, that the mysterious problem of suffering can only be overcome on the basis not of rational human thought, but of the category of revelation, that which is sheer miracle and of which the origin can never be traced. From this it follows that any theodicy whatever has become intrinsically impossible. *Even the concept of creation is an affirmation of faith*, possible only because the Creator has first spoken; and it reveals not a rational world-order which can be made clear to everyone but a direct confrontation with the presence of the miraculous and mysterious God, to whose hidden abysses suffering, too, belongs. For the sake of this God the world with all its

[1] Duhm, somewhat inexactly, terms this 'enthusiasm'.

enigmas, even suffering, can be affirmed; for by speaking he comes out of his hiddenness, and enters into a positive moral relationship with his creature. He is still none the less surrounded with miracle and mystery; but as the one who offers himself in fellowship he makes both these things perceptible and comprehensible even to the creature as goods of infinite value in which may be found the stilling of all longings.

Thus it is that these chapters of the book of Job, which seem to disregard so studiously the distinctive stock in trade of Israel's religion, in fact point back to their unexpressed but indispensable background in the revelation-history of the covenant people. For only Israel knows the Creator who reveals himself in the Word, but can never be known from the world, since he is not a Demiurge, a First Cause in the series of the natural process, like the artificer-gods of heathenism, nor the ultimate ground of being underlying human spirituality, as in the Platonic-Stoic philosophy, but the sovereign Lord of the world, who accomplishes the creation as the utterly free decision of his will, subject only to its own internal norm. The revelatory utterance in which he draws near to Man points back to, as it is ultimately grounded in, that other utterance which, as the word of creation, called the world out of nothingness into being. Thus Gen. 1 is seen to be the ultimate base on which rest the affirmations of the book of Job, affirmations which for their part, like a finger raised in warning, bid us beware of misunderstanding the account of creation as though its intention were to present a rational cosmic Mind immanent in human reason. In this account the rational purposefulness and design of the cosmos play a very different part from that which they did in Job, and betray a markedly different sense of the world and of life;[1] even so they are still not a bridge leading men to grasp the concept of a Creator, but are in their turn entirely dependent on faith in the absolute Lord of the World. And it is in the absolute miracle of the word of creation, by which the universe is raised out of nothing, that the fact of his lordship is concentrated. In both Job and Genesis the affirmations about the Creator witness to a theology of origins which is qualitatively different from the deistic concept of God as *prima causa*; for they see the relation of Creator to creature in the form of a *creatio ex nihilo*, something which is not to be understood simply as an initial decision, but as a direct and constantly renewed divine shaping and control. In both texts

[1] Cf. pp. 158f. above.

there is the complete antithesis of any conception of the world which argues back from the harmony of the cosmos comprehensible by the intellect of Man to rationality in the laws that rule it, and to perfection in the giver of those laws. Hence in both texts we find also the decisive objection to theodicy, namely that this, for all that it purports to justify the Lord of the world, in fact sets him on the same level as the world, and makes him an object of knowledge.

This also enables us to see in the right light the extension, which occurs from time to time in later Judaism, of the covenant concept to cover God's relation to the world. As early as Deutero-Isaiah the relationship of the Creator to his creatures has moved into the sphere of the covenant, inasmuch as Yahweh's 'righteousness', that is, his covenant goodness, loyalty, and succour, are described as the way in which the ruler of the universe operates.[1] It is precisely by bestowing on his people the Servant of God as covenant mediator,[2] and by granting her the perfect salvation in the form of the covenant,[3] that he causes his light to shine forth over the nations of the earth, and leads them to submit voluntarily to the new divine order,[4] but at the same time brings about the cosmic renewal and transfiguration.[5] That which in Deutero-Isaiah is wholly bathed in eschatological light acquires a strong present reference in the hymns in praise of Yahweh's kingship,[6] where not only the nations but the whole of Nature is seen as dominated by the righteousness of God. Indeed, it is generally true that God's rule in Nature and in the world of men are mutually associated in the closest possible way.[7] Thus it comes about that the creation by itself can be understood as the basis of a relation of fellowship, inasmuch as the divine covenant faithfulness (*ḥesed*) in the form of world-embracing goodness binds together Creator and creature.[8] All these affirmations reveal a synoptic view of creation and history, in which confidence in the practical proof of Yahweh as the true God afforded by history finds reinforcement

---

[1] Isa. 42.6; 45.8, 24; 51.5f. Cf. God's covenant with mankind, or with the earth: Gen. 9.9ff., 13.
[2] Isa. 42.6; 49.8.
[3] Isa. 54.10; 55.3; 61.8.
[4] Isa. 42.1–4; 45.22; 49.6; 51.5; 55.3–5.
[5] Isa. 40.3f.; 41.18ff.; 43.19ff.; 55.13; 60.13, 19f.
[6] Pss. 93; 96; 97; 99.
[7] Pss. 65.5ff.; 89A; 135.6f.; 136.4ff.; 146.6f.; 147; 148; cf. Jer. 33.19–26.
[8] Cf. vol. I, p. 239, and also G. von Rad, 'Das theologische Problem des alttestamentlichen Schöpfungsglaubens', BZAW 66, 1936, pp. 138ff. (ET in *The Problem of the Hexateuch*, 1966).

and backing from the visualizing of his creative power and greatness. Here again, however, it is possible to do this not because the regularity and purposefulness of the natural process are optimistically transferred on to history, in order to rescue its teleology, but because God is already known as the One whose creative word called Nature into existence as a totality adapted to include personal life, and who in this natural order gives himself to be known by men for the same as he claims to be in history, namely the sovereign Lord.

The fight against any attempt to construct a theodicy on the basis of belief in creation was to be waged once more, and with rigorous logic, this time by the writer of the little book Koheleth (Ecclesiastes, the Preacher). Against the self-confident wisdom teaching, which took on a new lease of life in the Hellenistic period as a result of an acquaintance with Greek philosophy, and presumed to initiate men into God's counsels and to resolve the enigmas of the world,[1] there came out to battle a man intimately acquainted with the thought of the wise, and himself a member of their circle (12.9). In constantly fresh turns of thought he made his sallies against the claim of wisdom to supremacy, in order to destroy its false prestige, and to confront it with the fact that One higher than the wise had appointed bounds that it was not to pass. For wisdom, too, bears the mark of all earthly things. In itself it possesses no absolute value, nor can it mediate such; when measured by the highest goal, it is vain. Knowledge of this fact, however, grows from being plunged in the creative power of God, whose absolute freedom works itself out in a predestination which is opaque to Man (6.10; 9.1), but is nevertheless not an impersonal Fate, but a personally determined action which has revealed itself to men as such. There is no doubt that the Preacher has modelled his view of life on the creation story in Genesis.[2] Hence he knows that the Creator has made everything beautiful in its time, and has put eternity in Man's heart, thus binding him inwardly to himself. This, too, is why joy can be praised as the first of the Creator's gifts,[3] wisdom can be recognized as a high good within its limits,[4] and Man can be encouraged to faithful labour.[5] It may indeed be true

[1] Prov. 8.1ff.; Wisd. 7.14, 17ff.; 8.8; 9.16ff. Cf. R. Gordis, *Koheleth, the Man and his World*, 1951, which, however, overestimates the heterodoxy of the Preacher.
[2] This has been very finely demonstrated in detail by Hertzberg in his commentary (*Der Prediger übersetzt und erklärt*, 1932, pp. 37ff.).
[3] 2.24; 3.1–8, 22; 8.15; 9.7; 10.19; 11.9.
[4] 2.13f., 26; 4.13; 7.4f., 11f.; 9.16ff., etc.
[5] 9.10; 11.6.

that the treasures of the life of Old Testament faith are, on the whole, no longer open to this wise man. But his teaching remains none the less, the genuine product of the Old Testament knowledge of God, and remains a faithful guardian of that divine otherness which cannot be absorbed into any human system. For, 'whatever God does endures for ever', and, 'God has made it so, in order that men should fear before him' (3.14).

All these three ways were products of a faith which drew from the fullness of Old Testament revelation in order to overcome the challenge which sprang from the riddle of suffering; but none of them was able to point out the right direction for Jewish piety. The attempt at theodicy with the help of the retribution theory remained dominant, corresponding to the restriction of God's acts of grace by the norm of the Law,[1] and inevitably therefore it made use of every technique for this kind of human justification of God, in order to bring the incomprehensibilities of the present world situation into a harmonious equilibrium which human reason could grasp. But far from actually arriving at such an equilibrium, the attempt only caused the burden of the problem to fall back on reflective thought, and made it impossible for the tormenting struggle for a liberating answer ever to find rest. II (4) Esdras is indeed the most eloquent witness to this continuing perplexity. Within the tranquillity of various small groups those answers of faith which were based on the reality of God as revealed could go on having their effect. But the conquering power implicit in them could only be made successfully the effective substance of the community's faith where the reality of God's love entered the life of men in such overwhelming power that it broke through the wall of legalism, and was able to awaken a conviction of fellowship with God which embraced past, present, and future, and in face of which the puzzling question of suffering lost its fatal power. Only in the New Testament community are the assurance of the coming Kingdom of God, based on the victory of Jesus Christ, and the security in fellowship with the exalted Lord, in whom the whole cosmos possesses its origin and its central meaning, so strong and all-embracing that the problem of the evil in the world loses its importance, and gives way to that joyful confidence which considers 'that the sufferings of this present time are not worth comparing with the glory that is to be revealed to us' (Rom. 8.18).

[1] Cf. pp. 441ff. above.

XXIV

THE INDESTRUCTIBILITY OF THE
INDIVIDUAL'S RELATIONSHIP
WITH GOD
(Immortality)[1]

1. Our previous discussion of the world of the dead and of beliefs about the dead[2] will already have demonstrated the close affinity which exists on this subject between Israelite and Babylonian views, and made clear the strict separation of the land of the dead from the world of the living, in which Yahweh wills to rule. Even though it is taken for granted that Yahweh's power of control extends to Sheol, this does not alter the fact that death is felt to be the ultimate bound, which excludes not only from earthly life but also from enjoyment of fellowship with God. Nevertheless, this seemingly wholly negative attitude of the world of Israel's faith to death by no means exhausts what there is to be said about the assessment of death in Old Testament belief. Quite apart from the change in outlook which takes place within the compass of the Old Testament scriptures, there are a number of points to be mentioned even for the early Israelite period, which give the Israelite attitude to death a character different from that of the outlook of the most closely related non-Israelite peoples,

---

[1] On the subject of this section cf. A. Lods, *La croyance à la vie future et le culte des morts dans l'antiquité israélite* (2 vols), 1902; J. Lindblom, *Das ewige Leben. Eine Studie über die Entstehung der religiösen Lebensidee im NT*, 1914; F. Nötscher, *Altorientalischer und alttestamentlicher Auferstehungsglauben*, 1926; also L. Dürr, *Die Wertung des Lebens im AT und im antiken Orient*, 1926; G. Quell, *Die Auffassung des Todes in Israel*, 1925; E. F. Sutcliffe, *The Old Testament and the Future Life*, 1946; A. T. Nikolainen, 'Der Auferstehungsglaube I', *Annales Academiae Scientiarum Fennicae*, series B, vol. XLIX.3, 1944, pp. 1–206; O. Schilling, *Der Jenseitsgedanke im AT*, 1951; R. Martin-Achard, *De la mort à la résurrection d'après l'Ancien Testament*, 1956.

[2] Cf. pp. 210ff. above.

and which form the indispensable precondition for the change which was to occur later.

Once again we see the effect of the distinctive stamp given to the God-Man relationship by the covenant-making. The experience of God's will directed toward the nation in the covenant gave Israel's understanding of life a distinctive character which could not be without its effect on their view of death. First, their conception of the dependence of life upon God is quite different from that of heathenism. Pagan Man, too, knew that earthly life sprang from the world of the divine, and always had need of that divine source of life which alone is not subject to death, if it were to come successfully through the dangers that threatened it. But the mystery of life asserts its independent status *vis-à-vis* the world of the gods; it is at bottom the great magic, which the gods have mastered in order by the food and drink of life to keep death far from them. Man can contemplate making use of this magic, should he succeed in breaking through the barriers which separate him from it. Thus Gilgamesh hopes at the end of his odyssey to escape the doom of death with the help of the herb of life; and it is well known what unwearying efforts the Egyptians made to secure the way to divine life with the help of magic. The Adonis mysteries allow us to assume the same for Canaanite religion, where the Baals were worshipped as the givers of life *par excellence*.

By contrast, Yahweh reveals himself as the One who is free, who has control over the life of his worshippers, and from whom no one imagines that they can wrest the secret of life. Something of the sort may still echo in the old myths of the Tree of Life in the Paradise garden, and of the angelic marriages; but the imagery has long since been made to serve the purpose of illustrating vividly the exalted nature of the universal Judge, who in his righteous governance prescribes the course of earthly life for his creatures. But Yahweh's unrestricted lordship, by virtue of which he as the only possessor of the spirit of life holds sway over the existence of his creatures,[1] acquires its distinctive character from the relationship which he has established between himself and the people of his choice. That life is a gift bestowed by God, over which Man cannot of his own resources exercise control, is a truth sealed by the fact that life is called to God's service, and obliged to take its constant orientation from

[1] Cf. pp. 47ff. above, and vol. I, pp. 213f.; also Deut. 5.30; 30.20; I Sam. 17.26; II Kings 19.4; Pss. 36.10; 42.3; 104.29f.; Job 34.14f.; Jer. 2.13; 17.13.

his will.[1] Life is only rightly understood as God's gift when it becomes Man's answer to God's call. But it is at this very moment that it also becomes full of promise.

This view of life is undoubtedly most clearly illustrated by the prophets. The only guarantee of life is the word which God speaks to his people; outside of this death reigns. On the nation's attitude to the word of God pronounced in the Law and in the prophetic message depends therefore the decision about its existence. But the individual, too, acquires his significance within the community only because God's word calls him to action, and so brings the disintegrated forces of the personality into unity with God's will, and thus to life.[2] Where, on the contrary, the individual evades the claim of God's word, there he falls prey to enslavement by his impulses, and thus to self-destruction.[3] Only in willing submission to the word which God addresses to Man is the continuing existence of personality ensured, that is to say, true life can flow only from God's self-communication. It can never be guaranteed by the powers of the psyche, determined as these are by Nature, or by an indestructible soul-substance; and it can just as little result from drawing near to the divine sphere of life by cultic or material means. For this reason the Deuteronomic law-teaching, in turning the prophetic preaching into common currency, attempted a new variation on the connection between life and God's word, not only by imbuing the hearing of the word of the Law with all the seriousness of a decision for life or for death,[4] but even more generally by describing the word proclaimed by Moses as the medium of life,[5] and by placing the powerful life-giving effect of the word of God on a par with the physical maintenance of life by food.[6] Called to identify his will with the will of God, Man would

---

[1] On this point cf. the earlier remarks about the claim laid to the whole of life by God's sovereign will: vol. I, pp. 92f., 209f., 222f., 292ff., 301; and above, pp. 243f., 320f., 350ff.

[2] Cf. vol. I, pp. 358f., 360f., and above pp. 245f., 351ff.

[3] Given its most violent expression by Jeremiah in the second chapter of his book: cf. 2.8, 13, 20, 23–25, 31, 33f. Telling formulations of what it means to live in attention to God's word are also to be found in Ezekiel: cf. Ezek. 3.18ff.; 14.13ff. with specific reference to the prophetic word; 18.1ff.; 20.11, 13, 21 to the word of the Law. Also relevant here is the message of faith in Isaiah and Hab. 2.4, in both of which life is promised to the man who allows himself to be seized by the word of God: cf. pp. 279ff. above.

[4] Deut. 30.15ff.

[5] Deut. 32.47.

[6] Deut. 8.3.

come to know, as he realized this fellowship in practice, liberation to true life, in which the enjoyment of earthly goods was bound up as closely as possible with the inner freedom and independence of the man who sees his existence incorporated into a higher order, and thus made meaningful.[1] But this distinctive understanding of life as deriving from the word of God, which calls Man as a genuine partner to responsibility, and thus gives him true personhood, runs, even if not formulated so exactly, much farther back into the Old Testament witness. As early as the nabistic movement, we find right at the heart of the struggle of the *n*^e*bī'īm* a new summons to the nation to the service of God, even at the cost of a renunciation of material goods, since in this way alone could life acquire its meaning.[2] When God's word is rare in the land, poverty and insecurity invade life.[3] Finally, by basing the whole structure of the national life on the word of God in the law, where the divine promises and threats set in motion forces of life and death, the same conviction that fullness of life is to be found only in the fellowship bestowed by God is ultimately implied, even if not as yet fixed in conceptual form.[4] The result is to rule out any possibility of living life in one's own power, but at the same time to guarantee the call to a life that is meaningful.

The fullness of life which transcends merely empirical living, and which is granted to the man who is bound to God's word and who perseveres in his service, is, of course, known all the more to *the piety of the Psalms* from the earliest to the latest period. It outweighs by far all the riches of life which proceed from the natural earthly goods, such as abundant harvests, a flourishing host of children, long life, honour, and respect,[5] and is the real good of life, which alone be-

---

[1] It is quite impermissible to treat the Deuteronomic concept of life as if it implied no more than temporal extension and animal vitality. What the law-teacher has to say about freedom from anxiety, about pride in the purposeful order and development of the national life, about deliverance from the spell of poly-theistic materialism, involvement in magic, and demonic seduction (7.17ff.; 8.2ff.; 4.6–8; 4.15ff.; 21.1–9; 13.2ff.), shows clearly enough that he is aware throughout of being concerned with life of a higher order, whose 'distinctive character lies beyond the empirical process', that is, in a meaning guaranteed by God. This means that for Deuteronomy, as for the prophetic preaching, to limit the OT concept of life to a long and fortunate earthly existence, as Bultmann does (*TWNT* II, p. 853), is untenable.

[2] Cf. vol. I, pp. 320f., 326f., 328.

[3] I Sam. 3.1.

[4] Cf. pp. 71ff., 245f., 249ff. above.

[5] Pss. 4.8; 16.5ff.; 17.14f.; 23; 36.10; 42.5; 51.14; 63.4; 73.23ff.; 84.11.

stows upon God's other gifts their true meaning, and their right position within the whole scope of existence.[1]

Even the *wisdom teaching*, which takes such emphatic account of retribution in this world, knows that gaining or losing life is a matter of something higher than the earthly goods acquired by human cleverness, namely the striving for right wisdom in living.[2] This knowledge leads men to an existence with a full spiritual and moral content, in that it recognizes as the distinguishing marks of true life the being preserved by God's discipline, and the practice of the righteousness which he values.[3] Even if in this concept of the content of life direct relationship with God is enfeebled by the fact that the authority of Wisdom is given precedence,[4] nevertheless here, too, incorporation into a higher order clearly remains the fundamental prerequisite of all true life, and a sovereign will its only security, a security removed alike from Man's discretion and control.

II. When life was understood in this light men's *inward attitude to death* was bound to differ from the outlook prevailing in the rest of the ancient Near East, whatever the manifest affinities between the two conceptual systems. In Israel there could be no question of battering against the unyielding bounds of death on the pretext that it left unsatisfied Man's hunger for happiness, or interposed its veto to his striving after the infinite or his lust for life. Life is absolutely not a self-contained, mysterious power, access to which is open to those with the necessary knowledge, but is utterly and completely tied to God. Death, therefore, is no cruel enemy, whose terrifying sovereign power hurls men from the realm of life, and against which they seek defence in magic and spells. It is simply the end of life, determined by God, and to be as readily accepted at his decision as the gift of life itself.[5] Thus, where the Old Testament tells of the death of the pious, we find a tranquil submission, indeed, a strict sobriety, which accepts death as the totally final, and thus comes to terms with it. There are neither attempts to overcome the mystery of death by mythopoeic fantasies, by bold analogical reasoning from the life of Nature, or by rituals of power, nor palliations of death's final decree by efforts to maintain a link with the departed. Whatever of

[1] Cf. pp. 361f. above.
[2] Cf. pp. 361ff. above.
[3] Prov. 8.35; 10.11; 12.2; 13.14.
[4] On this point cf. pp. 80ff. above.
[5] For this absolute resignation cf. David's words in II Sam. 12.23; also Ps. 89.49; Job 7.9.

such is still present in traces of feeding the dead, or enquiring from them, is placed under strict interdict by unconditional attachment to Yahweh.[1]

(a) It would be perverse to ascribe this simply to the obtuseness of the Bedouin mind, reckoning only with naked reality, and naïvely realistic in its thinking—a picture which is felt to be very modern, and is therefore projected on to the early Israelite. The nomad knows quite enough about necromancy and all the magic connected with the dead.[2] One might more reasonably point to the sense of collective life, for which it is primarily the continuing life of the tribe or clan which matters; but though this is indeed a disposition which makes death easier to accept, it does not really explain the striking renunciation of the will to live in face of it. We should instead remember *the intensive relation of the whole of life to God*, in virtue of which *men's attitude to death* also *concentrates on God's dealings with Man*. This happens in two ways. On the one hand the God-Man relationship gives life a content which means that, when it has completed its course, it has become 'ripe' for ending in death. Here the manner of speaking which was customary in the ancient East far beyond the borders of Israel,[3] namely that the departed died 'in a good old age', 'old and full of days',[4] acquires a new meaning. Over and above the natural satisfaction that the whole course of life has been covered undisturbed, it expresses a fullness in the quality of life, which has been earned in intimate association with the God who calls men to fellowship with himself. This corroborates the observations made earlier on the subject of the new meaning of life understood in terms of God's word. On the basis of this new meaning death can be comprehended as a right and logical conclusion.[5]

(b) Alongside this peaceful conformity with God's order, however, there is yet another attitude to death, echoes of which can be detected even in early Israel, and which as time goes on becomes more and more the dominating melody. This is *lamentation over death* as the

[1] Cf. pp. 215ff. above.
[2] Cf. J. J. Hess, *Von den Beduinen des inneren Arabiens*, 1938, pp. 164ff.; A. Musil, *Arabia Petraea* III, 1908, pp. 449ff.; J. Goldziher, *Muhammedanische Studien* I, 1889, pp. 231ff.
[3] Cf. L. Dürr, *op. cit.*, pp. 13ff. (cf. p. 496, n. 1 above).
[4] Gen. 15.15; 25.8; 35.29; Judg. 8.32; Job 42.17; I Chron. 23.1; 29.28.
[5] G. von Rad has given a very fine exposition of this in his essay 'Alttestamentliche Glaubensaussagen vom Leben und vom Tod', *Allgemeine Evangelische Lutherische Kirchenzeitung*, 1938, cols. 826ff., which contains some excellent comments on the problem of death.

deepest and most painful disturbance of the condition of life established by God. As early as the time of David there are occasional outbreaks of lament at the tragic fate of Man, who is 'like water spilt on the ground, which cannot be gathered up again'.[1] If the righteous is carried off by an 'evil, early death', then this may well wring from men the dismayed and sorrowful cry of 'Why?'[2] Similarly the storyteller, in the last duties of love shown to the dead, portrays the mute resistance to the heart-rending brutality of the doom of death, which can move to gentleness even contemporaries accustomed to harsh retribution.[3] Nevertheless, in the earlier period this lament is mostly repressed by the resignation with which the individual is wont to accept his lot. Only as individuality awakens to more vigorous life does the need for unrestrained expression of mourning over the mortality of the human race increase, and make itself heard in the Psalms, the wisdom writings, and the utterances of the prophets.[4]

Such passages express *a universal human feeling* in face of the senseless breaking off of hopeful life similar to that encountered in the lamentations of Babylonia and Egypt.[5] But *in Israel* men shrink from this threat to life *all the more* because of the unqualified way in which death, even in this fearful guise, is understood as a decision of that same God who, by calling them into fellowship with himself, has opened up to them the possibility of a truly meaningful life. Precisely because men have learned to know this God as the giver of life, his No to life shakes them to the very roots of their being. Moreover, for the loyal member of the covenant community the evasion of ascribing death's power to carry off all indiscriminately to the demons or to the magic of evil men is completely blocked by his rigorous adherence to the will of God as the only determining causality. Thus the pious man on whom death suddenly falls is faced with the contradiction between the destining of his life to the glory and praise of God, and its abandonment by that very same God to the 'land of no return', where one is for ever shut out from God's work and God's community. Indeed, by means of illness, perils of war, imprisonment, sin, and so on, the power of the world of death even reaches right into this life, and menaces the earthly existence which is nevertheless thankfully

---

[1] II Sam. 14.14.
[2] II Sam. 3.33.
[3] II Sam. 21.10.
[4] Ps. 103.15f.; Job 14.1f.; Isa. 40.6f.
[5] Cf. M. Jastrow, *Die Religion Babyloniens und Assyriens* II.1, p. 127; *AOT*, pp. 26ff.; 28f.; 287ff.

received and highly valued as the destiny appointed for men by God, the Lord of life.[1] Hence the impressive laments of the prayers in which the sick person presents this contradiction to his God: 'For Sheol cannot thank thee, death cannot praise thee' (Isa. 38.18); 'Is thy steadfast love declared in the grave, or thy faithfulness in Abaddon?' (Ps. 88.11 MT 12); 'Save my life . . . for in death there is no remembrance of thee; in Sheol who can give thee praise?' (Ps. 6.4f. MT 6f.).[2] Such a situation is bound constantly to reawaken that *trembling awe before the numinous mystery* which plays so great a part in the Old Testament God-Man relationship. The dominating importance, however, of the will to fellowship revealed in the covenant relationship comes to light in the fact that submission to the unapproachable majesty and terrifying otherness of the Holy One imports no submoral traits into the picture of God, but with the tension brings also the strength to cleave unswervingly to the will of God as fundamentally salvific in purpose.[3] Indeed, it is worth noting that because of this confidence in God's will to fellowship the indiscriminate committal of the human race to death is adduced as a *reason for God's forbearance* with the weakness and sin of his worshippers.[4] And even where men are not blind to the darker side of this particular argument there is still a remarkable childlike confidence which flees from its terror at the universal doom of death to the fatherly care of God shown in a short reprieve of life, and there finds an adequate substitute.

(c) The sense of *the harshness of the doom of death* as the final separation from God is, however, incomparably more profound when the rending of the God-Man relationship by death is explained in terms of just that quality in God's nature which the covenant-making impressed so ineffaceably on the national conscience, namely *his implacable opposition to sin*. By seeing the delivering up of human life to the hostile forces of death as the result of a divine sentence stemming from mankind's decisive turning away from God, in which we all share, the Yahwist narrator[5] gives the doom of death for the first time its full bitterness. Responsibility for the disruption of fellowship with God by death now falls back upon Man. It is he himself who by

[1] Cf. Ch. Barth, *Die Errettung vom Tode in den individuellen Klage- und Dankliedern des AT* (Diss. Basel), 1947.
[2] Cf. also Pss. 28.1; 30.10; 88.6, 11; 115.17; Isa. 38.11.
[3] Cf. vol. I, pp. 259ff., 274ff.
[4] Cf. pp. 477f. above.
[5] Cf. pp. 402ff. above.

the consciously affirmed, anti-God quality of his own nature has incurred that fundamental disturbance of his whole existence which leaves him a prey to life's suffering, and separates him from God. But though this intensifies the problem of death, it also raises the fateful decision to close life in death from the incomprehensible to the perspicuous, since this is now the reaction of God's righteousness in keeping with his revelation in the covenant, and demonstrates itself as such in the conviction of men's consciences. All the greater now appears the sustaining mercy of the covenant God, all the more humbly now does Man bow himself beneath the judgment executed in death. But he has something wherewith to compensate for the wrath of God revealed in the transience of his own life. This is God's call to service, giving his servants the right to ask for a new demonstration of favour in the manifestation of his glory from him who has been the refuge of his people from of old, so that the work of their hands may achieve some continuing stay.[1] From this it may be seen that it was the grace of God in the election of his people which gave them the power to look into the ultimate abyss of the riddle of death without thereby being hurled into hopeless scepticism.

III. All the more profound then must the challenge have been, when not merely the individual but *the chosen people itself was given up to destruction*. The preaching of the prophets proclaimed this frightful destiny to their contemporaries as the outcome of Yahweh's final reckoning with his people. No wonder that men fought against such a bleak prospect with every means at their command. Indeed, it would seem that at this juncture even the idea of resurrection was to be found in men's mouths as one of the cheap grounds for comfort by which they might parry the seriousness of the prophets' threat. At any rate, the interpretation of Hos. 6.1f. in this sense is, despite many objections,[2] still the most probable.[3] It is true that in the national

[1] Ps. 90. The separation of vv. 1 and 13–17 from the rest of the psalm, as argued by Duhm and others, is dictated by the aesthetic sense of modern Man, and does the poem an injustice by removing the distinctive tension which exists between the doom of death and belief in election, and which has here been given characteristic expression.
[2] A list of these has been compiled by Nötscher, *op. cit.* (cf. p. 496, n. 1 above), pp. 138ff.
[3] On this subject cf. especially W. von Baudissin, *Adonis und Esmun*, 1911, pp. 403ff.; then E. Sellin, 'Die alttestamentliche Hoffnung auf Auferstehung und ewiges Leben', *NKZ*, 1919, pp. 241ff.; A. Weiser, *Das Buch der zwölf kleinen Propheten* I² (ATD 24), 1956, p. 57; T. H. Robinson and F. Horst, *Die zwölf kleinen Propheten* (HAT I.14), 1938, p. 25.

lamentation which Hosea puts into the mouth of his contemporaries the prophet's own demands seem very largely to be acknowledged as just. The speakers praise conversion, and wish to strive for a real knowledge of God; indeed, they are prepared to renounce all the other expedients they have tried, and to throw the whole destiny of the nation on Yahweh's mercy. And yet, and yet—another note also sounds through this penitential liturgy. The words, 'he has torn, that he may heal us; he has stricken, and he will bind us up', bear the stamp of an all-too-ready confidence, an all-too-assured taking things for granted. And v. 2 indicates the source of the strength of this confidence that they will win life from Yahweh. The reviving after two days, and the raising up on the third day, do not correspond directly to the situation of the people, which is by no means dead, but only sore wounded and disabled. It is therefore probable that this image of rising from the dead, which is alien to the genuine Yahwist faith, should be connected with the world of thought of the cult songs of the dying and rising gods, and of the resuscitation ceremonies of their worshippers, which enjoyed great popularity in Egypt, Syria, and Babylonia, and which also found devotees in Israel during the later monarchy.[1] That the third day was the customary terminus, on which the resurrection of the god who had descended to the underworld was celebrated with great jubilation, is known to us at least from the cults of Attis and Osiris. Moreover, the real purpose of the cultic and magical procedures is to transfer the divine vital power, which rises again from death, to the worshippers of the god. Hence by putting into the mouth of the suppliants expressions which derive from the resurrection cults the prophet presents them as remaining entirely within the realm of Nature mysticism, and as transferring to Yahweh the ideas and concepts there current. And by doing just this he makes it clear in what respect their confession is lacking—not in the moral intentions of Man, but in the true living power of God! The god upon whom these penitents call is not the Lord of the Covenant, who has cast the covenant-breakers far from him, and can

[1] Ezek. 8.14; Zech. 12.11; Isa. 17.10. Cf. the form of the lament for the dead in I Kings 22.24 (LXX); Jer. 22.18; 34.5, which seems to be imitating the style of the lament for Adonis. Cf. W. Baumgartner, 'Der Auferstehungsglaube im alten Orient', *Zum Alten Testament und seiner Umwelt*, 1959, pp. 124ff. On the other hand, there are no valid pieces of evidence for the thesis of various English and Scandinavian scholars (cf. vol. I, p. 437, n. 2) that Israel adopted the ancient Near Eastern belief that the king, as the incarnation of the dying and rising god, mediated the conquest of the forces of death in the cultic drama—a point that was clearly perceived by A. Bentzen, *King and Messiah*, ET, 1955.

give them new life only through the inconceivable miracle of his love, which eludes all human calculation; it is the god who, like the forces of Nature, reveals himself in a regular cycle, and who revives and establishes by the same necessity with which he punishes and destroys. All that matters is to restore contact with the lost deity by proclaiming oneself his true worshipper, and then the blessings are released automatically, just as—a significant analogy from the life of Nature—after a time of drought the return of the rains awakens new life from the dead earth.

But this is not the conversion which the prophet requires, for it lacks that full understanding of *hesed* which befits the covenant relationship, and which takes seriously the God of history. Hence this turning to God is as valueless as the swiftly passing morning clouds, which dissolve in the heat of the day, or as the dew, which is quickly consumed by the scorching sun (v. 4).

In this way the message of the prophets draws a sharp boundary-line against all resurrection concepts derived from analogy with Nature, in order that the seriousness of its proclamation of judgment may stand unimpaired.[1] Hence, when the resurrection of the nation from the grave of exile is promised for the first time, all such comparisons from the life of Nature are rejected, and the incomparable miracle is ascribed directly to the divine spirit of life. Indeed, the impression is given that Ezekiel himself, to whom we are indebted for *the mighty vision of the Valley of Dry Bones*,[2] felt strongly the monstrous, unnatural quality of a resurrection, and at first held back from it in revulsion.[3] Only the definite command of his God to summon by his prophetic word the power of that divine breath which throughout the world calls forth new life[4] to an unheard-of deed of wonder leads him to experience the divine will which bursts even the gates of death.

This meant that the desperate lament of the exiles, who in their deportation had experienced the death of the nation as a fearful

---

[1] Sellin's conjecture that 13.14 should be inserted between 14.5a and 5b, and the whole understood as a promise, giving us a prediction of Israel's return from a state of death, is attractive; but it may be doubted whether it should be adopted, since no convincing reason can be adduced for so decisive a rearrangement of the text.

[2] Ezek. 37.

[3] The emphasis on the utter dryness of the bones is undoubtedly meant to stress the incredibility of the event, and the hopelessness of the situation, viewed from a human standpoint. The evasive answer to Yahweh's question (v. 3) indicates how far, till that moment, any such conjecture had been from the prophet's mind.

[4] Cf. pp. 47ff. above.

reality, and had seen this, in accordance with ancient Man's sense of life, as the annihilation of all hope, was now answered by God in a way which reawakened their totally extinguished will to live. God's faithfulness to his plan of salvation, which faith had hitherto stead-fastly maintained in face of the doom of death, is not imperilled even if he abandons his people to suffering and death, because he is the God of wonders, who executes judgment, the God who can recall to life even from the tomb. But faith in this faithfulness must also pass through the crisis of death in order that its confidence may be placed uniquely and alone in the miraculous living power of its God, and that it may cast no more sidelong, yearning glances at earthly security. Only in this way can it fully comprehend the rich content of God's offer of life in the covenant-making.[1]

In Ezekiel's vision the new life of the nation rested wholly on the life-creating word of his God, which the prophet was commissioned to utter. So, too, with *Deutero-Isaiah*. At the very beginning of his book of consolation the existence of the people of God is derived from the word; and, by contrast with the unspeakable sadness evoked by the vision of death's limitless dominion over mankind, firm ground is thereby indicated, on which hope can still find a foothold even in face of the withering and fading of Israelite national glory.[2] 'The word of our God will stand for ever' (v. 8). In this word, which in the promise of judgment and salvation moves inexorably toward its own realiza-tion, the prophet recognizes the irrefragable loyalty of God's will to

---

[1] The precision of Ezekiel's description of the process of resurrection does not allow us to conclude, with Sellin, Nötscher, and O. Schilling (*op. cit.*, p. 496, n. 1 and p. 504, n. 3 above), that the idea of the raising of the dead was at that time familiar and much discussed in exilic circles. In other passages, too, the prophet is inclined to minutiae in his descriptions; moreover, here the idea of clothing the new hope for the revival of Israel in the image of new life breathed into dead bones came to him from the constant refrain of the doubters: 'Our bones are dried up, and our hope is lost; we are clean cut off' (37.11). The exiles think of themselves as already laid in the grave, applying to the doom of banishment the same image which had earlier been used for severe sickness or danger of death. That is why the interpretation of the vision, keeping still to the terms of the imagery, can speak of the opening of the graves, and the bringing up of those buried within, in order to hold out a prospect of restoration for the nation. It may have been precisely the hopelessness universally regarded as attaching to the fate of the buried which stimulated the prophet to depict the utterly inconceivable miraculous power of his God in the imagery of the individual resurrection of the dead, in order to illustrate as drastically as possible his own conviction that for God nothing is impossible. But the facility with which he returns from this image to the restoration of the nation shows quite clearly that at that period an individual resurrection of the dead was not seriously discussed.

[2] Isa. 40.6-8.

fellowship, which first took historical form in the election of Abraham,[1] and which is to attain its goal in the redemption of the exiles to a new life on an earth returned to the harmony of Paradise. In his picture of the great turning-point in the national destiny he does not pursue further the idea of resurrection from the dead; but the passage through the darkness of death is for him the heart of God's saving work in the case of *one* figure, namely the Servant of God in Isa. 53. In that the messianic redeemer is not spared descent even into this deepest darkness of human suffering, indeed, that he has affirmed it as an expression of God's wrath on sinners, and has vicariously taken it upon himself, the greatness of God's work of salvation is for the first time fully revealed to the prophet. Because death, as the punishment of sin, is overcome by the offering of the Servant's own life, a new fellowship between God and sinners is made possible, since by the atonement here wrought the godless are justified. The reference is admittedly first and foremost to a new people of God in a new world of God, and not to resurrection or immortality. It is no accident that one is constantly faced with the problem that the resurrection of the Servant himself is nowhere explicitly stated. And yet the passage seizes on the decisive aspect of the conquest of death, namely the point at which, in the character of the judgment of divine wrath, it pronounces men guilty, and rejects them from fellowship with God. Even though the prophet says nothing more about the death or survival of those who are inwardly one with the Servant, and therefore pardoned, yet he has stripped death of its terror, because its sting has been broken by the expiation of sin.[2] In this way a concern with the achievement of salvation opens up a vision of the breaking of the power of death which inevitably exercised a continuing influence in the succeeding period.

---

[1] Matters are less clear in the case of the counterpart figure to the Servant, namely the one who occurs in the Shepherd parable of Zech. 11–13. Nevertheless it would seem that here, too, it is the martyr's death of the good Shepherd (13.7–9) and his restoration and glorification by God (12.8) which evokes the great penitential lament (12.10) from the nation which had rewarded him with ingratitude, and which therefore leads to a return to Yahweh, which forms the precondition for the absolution and pardon of the messianic age (13.1). Cf. O. Procksch, *Die kleinen prophetischen Schriften der nachexilischen Zeit* (EAT 6), 1916, pp. 108ff., 112ff.; K. Elliger, *Das Buch der zwölf kleinen Propheten* II³ (ATD 25), 1956, pp. 171f., 176. H. Junker, in commenting on Zech. 12, speaks more cautiously of a messianic motif akin to that of Isa. 53 (*Die Hg. Schrift des AT*, ed. Feldmann and Herkenne, VIII.3.II, pp. 181f.).

[2] Isa. 41.8f.

IV. As a result, *the idea that death might be overcome even in the case of the individual* came, so far as we can tell, to be at home in Israel's faith *in two different ways*. On the one hand, more precise elaboration was given to *the conquest of death as an eschatological event*. The lines along which this development took place are barely perceptible to us, because the literary evidence is extraordinarily sparse. For this reason the possibility cannot be ruled out *a priori* that foreign influences, in one form or another, may also have had their effect Nevertheless our first task must be to understand the distinctively Jewish form of the belief, and its relation to earlier groups of Old Testament concepts. In this connection, it is no accident that the extant passages which do speak of a resurrection even of the individual believer manifestly come from times of great crisis. Both *the little apocalypse of Isa.* 24-27 and *the book of Daniel* are the product of periods when severe tribulation was having a profoundly convulsive impact, the former from the time when 'the birth-pangs of a new era created an age of neurotic anxiety'[1] after the victorious career of Alexander the Great, and the setting up of the kingdoms of the Diadochi, the latter from the period of intense persecution under Antiochus Epiphanes. Both strive for certainty and clarity with regard to God's universal plan, and find comfort in the vision of the final victory of the kingdom of God over all the powers of the world. The link here created between redemption from a critical historical situation and the great changeover into the new age is entirely in tune with the historical perspective of prophecy, where the particular historical decision of the moment is also seen as closely connected with the last act of the great world drama. In that God reveals himself as king of the universe, and both in the annihilation of his enemies and in the new creation of a perfect world makes visible to the eyes of all the final realization of his purpose in the shaping of history, the looked-for consummation is demonstrably *eschatological history* even in these late visions of hope. But the great act of judgment which leads up to the turning-point of the ages grows constantly more unlimited in scope, and draws into its sphere the heavenly as well as the earthly world, the dead as well as the living. Thus, together with the 'kings of the earth upon earth' 'the host of the high ones on high' are struck by God's retribution,[2] and to fail or to pass the test in the great final

---

[1] O. Procksch, *Jesaja* I, 1930, p. 344.
[2] Isa. 24.21.

conflict against the power of evil means punishment or reward beyond death.[1]

And yet it is *not primarily the idea of retribution* which leads to the postulate of a resurrection of the dead.[2] At least in the Isaiah apocalypse *hope of a revelation of God's glory plays an incomparably more important part.* This can already be seen in the promise, which goes far beyond the resurrection of the dead, namely that death will be destroyed for ever.[3] Taken in conjunction with the great royal banquet which Yahweh prepares for all nations on the holy mountain, this clearly signifies the return of humanity to full, unclouded fellowship with God, who, with the advent of his world-wide dominion, expels all the destructive powers of death in order to communicate to men his unrestricted fullness of life. To faith's grasp of this glorious goal of God's universal consummation a decisive contribution was undoubtedly made by the strong development of individuality in the religious life of the community.[4] Where the individual was confronted so strongly with the demand for self-sacrifice on behalf of God's sovereignty on earth, and given such decisive importance in the great struggle between the anti-God powers and the people of God, his personal existence could no longer be allowed to disappear behind the continued life of the nation. Precisely because men felt death so profoundly as a senseless breaking off of life, and regarded it as a rending of the God-Man relationship bound up with God's curse on sin, the abolition of death was now bound to become also a major and indispensable feature in the establishment of God's perfect sovereignty.

An inevitable consequence of this was the inclusion in the picture of *a recall of those who had gone to their deaths in God's cause.* And here it was precisely the fate of the suffering Messiah, who was led to new life through the darkness of death, which was able to provide an enduring stimulus. Just as endowment with the spirit was now extended from the messianic king and the other instruments of God's rule to every member of the people of God,[5] so, too, the latter now gained a share in redemption from the doom of death. *The reinterpre-*

---

[1] Dan. 12.2f.

[2] This is, none the less, the commonest assumption: cf., e.g., J. Pedersen, 'Wisdom and Immortality', *Wisdom in Israel and the Ancient Near East* (*VT*, Suppl. III, presented to H. H. Rowley), 1955, p. 245.

[3] Isa. 25.8.

[4] Cf. pp. 249ff., 256ff. above.

[5] Cf. pp. 58f. above.

tation of the Servant of God in Deutero-Isaiah in terms of the nation, a process which seems indeed to have begun fairly early, certainly helped to prepare the way for such hopes. Thus the Isaiah apocalypse also links the resurrection of those members of the people of God carried off by death with the final achievement of the messianic salvation, expressing this apparently as a desire of the prophet brought before God in prayer.[1] Here again it is *not so much the question of the moral ordering of the world which drives men to such a prayer*—there is no judgment of the dead—as *suffering under the limitless dominion of death*, which threatens to give the lie to God's universal design, and to destroy the hope of the coming salvation.[2] The prophet who, despite this assault on his faith, which he recognizes as Yahweh's discipline, holds fast to the divine promise, can no longer conceive of his God's victory as complete, unless Yahweh's dead, that is, those who have died in his service, are snatched from the kingdom of the dead, and brought back to fellowship with their God. The God who in the end calls his people, outwardly subject to the world-powers, to full enjoyment of his life in his kingdom, also overturns the land of the shades. Thus the hope of the full victory of the living God over all the powers of death, and of complete fellowship with him, issues in the vision of eschatological resurrection.

The idea of the return of the dead to living fellowship with God is expressed in a very similar way in the hymn of praise with which, in Ps. 22, a sufferer who has passed through the deepest night of pain concludes his passionate lament and prayer. When his conviction that God will listen to him overflows in vv. 28–31 of his poem, and he hears not only the nations right to the ends of the earth, but also the dead, joining with him in the great song of praise offered to the God who leads men to glory through suffering, *it is clear that he is developing ideas concerning the messianic achievement of salvation* which had been touched upon in the song of the Suffering Servant of God. Here, too, features which at first attached only to the figure of the individual Chosen One are now transferred to the suffering community, inasmuch as it is not vicarious suffering in the strict sense, but rather the suffering of steadfast faithfulness in God's service, which is assigned to all the pious as the most effective method for the building

---

[1] Isa. 26.19, in the attractive interpretation of O. Procksch, *op. cit.* By transposing certain verses W. Kessler understands this as a promise of the prophet (*Gott geht es um das Ganze. Jes. 55–56 und Jes. 24–27* [BAT 19], 1960, pp. 154ff.).

[2] Isa. 26.18.

of the kingdom of God. Just as the note appended to the Third Servant Song is already a call to men to show the same readiness for suffering as that displayed by the Servant of God,[1] so the pious of the Jewish community take heart from the fact that in their paths of pain divine thoughts of salvation are hidden. Hence they see the victory of their cause as pledge and first instalment of the irruption of God's sovereignty into all the world.[2] Moreover, the fact that in the return of mankind to its God, which the hymn in praise of the divine redeemer sings in anticipation of the age of salvation, the resurrection of the dead is a fixed element shows how strongly, at the date of our Psalm, this idea had already become linked with faith in God. In contrast to that sharp separation between Yahweh and the world of the dead which in earlier times had figured in petitionary psalms,[3] here *the full revelation of God's victory over all hostile powers is seen in the homage which those who have fallen asleep pay to Yahweh because of his redeeming act of power*. Once again, therefore, it is not a calculating belief in retribution, but an exuberant conviction of the living power of God, which bursts open the gates of the underworld.[4] And the fact that the resurrection of the dead here finds both its basis and its content in gratitude and praise establishes a firm contrast between the derivation of the new life from God's will to fellowship as expressed in his word and any kind of magical or mystical communication of life.

The belief in resurrection attested by the book of Daniel[5] is clearly both much more strongly developed and indeed already a fixed dogma. Not only the pious, but also the godless are to awake to life from death. Whether this means that a universal resurrection is already envisaged is questionable. The text speaks only of 'many', so that, in fact, the thought is more probably of a limited number, among whom, in accordance with the whole thought-content of the book, must be included first and foremost those who take part in the great eschatological battle.[6] To all further questions, as, for example, whether all

---

[1] Isa. 50.10.

[2] This disposes of all attempts, such as those made by Duhm, Löhr *et al.*, to explain the concluding section of our Psalm as an independent poem or a later addition.

[3] Cf. p. 503 above.

[4] This is also borne out by the silence concerning any judgment of the dead; the only thought seems to be of a revival of those who had already been proved faithful in their earthly life.

[5] Dan. 12.1–3.

[6] Cf. Dan. 11.22, 33.

Israel is affected by the resurrection or only a selected part, whether the heathen, too, are envisaged, and if so in what proportion, no answer can be deduced from these terse sentences. But the most probable explanation of a brevity which is at no pains to give more exact information is that a developed belief in resurrection already existed in wide circles, and that the author therefore had no need to say more on the subject than that which was especially close to his heart.[1]

His particular interest, however, plainly lay in *the carrying out of divine retribution even on the departed*. In the varying lot which befalls each after the resurrection, and which irrevocably determines his state for all time, each receives the fruit of his deeds. Again, the author concerns himself no further with the actual circumstances of blessedness or damnation for those who are raised; and therefore all conclusions about a supraterrestrial heavenly kingdom to which the pious are destined, or a hell of torments for the godless, remain conjectures which it is impossible to establish more firmly.[2] It is enough that *in their fate the whole seriousness of historical decision for or against God is to be made visible*. The apocalyptists, however, show themselves incomparably more interested in *the destiny of a select group* of the risen than in that of the generality. These are the *maśkilīm*, the wise, who have led many to righteousness. According to 11.33 this refers to the teachers of the people, who by their interpretation of the will of God in this last tribulation have strengthened the faith of many, and have thus equipped them for courageous endurance. Some of them, indeed, seem even to have suffered martyrdom. One would not go far wrong to think of people like the author of the book of Daniel himself, a man who knew that he had been favoured in a special way with superhuman understanding. By their instruction these men have helped many to righteousness, that is, to conduct in accordance with the covenant, steadfast against all seductions, and cleaving fast to the God of the fathers. Hence they are to be transfigured with heavenly splendour, that is, to receive a share in the divine glory. Once again we may detect *the transfer to the faithful of a distinction originally proper to the Messiah*, for, as we remarked earlier, in later Judaism the

---

[1] Nötscher (*op. cit.*, p. 166) disagrees.

[2] On the glory of light which surrounds the wise cf. below. It is incorrect to refer Isa. 66.24 to the fate of the ungodly; the passage is not concerned with those who have been raised from the dead, but with the desecration of the corpses of those who have been smitten by Yahweh.

Messiah is the possessor of the divine glory.[1] If the Son of Man, who according to Dan. 7.14 is clothed with power and glory and royal dominion, is interpreted in terms of the people of the saints of the Most High,[2] then the endowment of the scribes with the divine δόξα hardly calls for any special additional explanation.[3] The comparison of their δόξα with the splendour of the firmament or the light of the stars may suggest that, as an aristocratic *élite*, they receive a special degree of that divine glory shared by all the rest of the redeemed. The whole conception of the divine *kābōd* streaming out over the new earth is fundamentally different from the idea of the astral religions that mortal men are translated to places among the constellations.

It is significant that this form of the resurrection hope is not extended to the nation as a whole, but only to a greater or lesser number of its members. It thus retains its special reference to the individual, just as indeed it corresponds to the individualizing demand for retribution. In the forefront, however, stand those who have been brought safely through the great tribulation, and in whom God's providence has preserved for itself a people to inherit the eschatological salvation.[4] *This proves that the resurrection hope is still completely ancillary; the fundamental feature of the Old Testament hope, that history should issue in the consummation of God's sovereignty, and the establishment of his kingdom over Israel, has not been replaced by an other-worldly good of salvation for the righteous individual, divorced from all relation to things earthly.* For such a hope, however, focused as it was on the consummation of history, it was essential that in the establishment of the divine community those also should have their part who in the decisive crisis had fought in the front line. As they had witnessed to the living God right to the end, without thought for their own mortal danger, so that same God would not complete his kingdom without them. The conviction, amid the seemingly hopeless distresses of the time of

[1] Cf. p. 34 above.
[2] Dan. 7.27.
[3] There is no reason to think that a reminiscence of the translation of Enoch and Elijah is involved, nor to assume a mode of existence different from the kingdom of God established on earth, such as translation to a place among the stars or to a supraterrestrial kingdom (as against Sellin, *op. cit.*, pp. 261ff., and Nötscher, *op. cit.*, p. 164). A connection with fire as the special element of Ahura Mazda (so Bertholet, 'Zur Frage des Verhältnisses von persischem und jüdischem Auferstehungsglauben', *Festschrift für C. Andreas*, 1916, p. 57, and *American Journal of Theology* XX, p. 28) is even more completely outside the scope of Old Testament thought.
[4] Dan. 12.1. On the subject of this *providentia specialis* cf. pp. 176f. above.

persecution, that one was set in the last decisive moments before the final victory of the cause of God, and would receive from him the reward of either eternal acceptance or rejection, filled the historical moment with a final, absolute importance, and gave each individual combatant the sense of taking part with his whole existence in the world process now hastening to its goal. *Here the prophetic view of history*[1] *at last finds its full application to the life of the individual.*

As one surveys the picture of the eschatological resurrection hope, in so far as this is developed within the Old Testament, one receives the impression of a concept of faith which has not yet been elaborated or fixed in a dogmatic form, but is still elastic and bound up with the actual struggle for assurance of God. In the forefront stands the simple statement that death cannot for ever cut off loyal Yahwists who have fallen asleep from association with God, but must let them go free after Yahweh's final victory over his enemies. On the other hand, nothing precise is stated either about the nature and manner of this resurrection or about the form of resurrection existence—whether, for example, it is to be completely earthly or one of transfigured corporeity. This much only is clear, that *the raising of the dead takes place in a way consonant with Israelite ideas of the human condition after death.* The dead 'awake',[2] just as beforehand they slept in the dust of the earth;[3] and consequently they return to life in their total humanity, even supplied with a body. Just as death did not bring about a separation of soul and body,[4] but rather delivered both to a shadow existence, so resurrection cannot relate, for example, solely to a transfigured spirit. Even the expression 'to rise' speaks, in fact, for the idea of coming forth from the grave or from the underworld. But there is a complete *lack of any more elaborate descriptions of this process; interest attaches wholly to full re-entry into a life of fellowship with God.* The Daniel passage is unique in laying stress on the share in the divine light-glory, an image which is in any case entirely in keeping with the conception of God's new world as a revelation of the divine *kābōd.* Undoubtedly the text opens up the possibility of pursuing further speculations, but in the period with which we are concerned no use was made of this opening.

---

[1] Cf. vol. I, pp. 382ff.

[2] Isa. 26.19; Dan. 12.2.

[3] Dan. 12.2; Pss. 22.30 (emended); 13.4; Nahum 3.18; Jer. 51.39, 57; Job 3.13; 14.12.

[4] Cf. pp. 214f. above.

In view of this simple form of the hope, and the close connection of its main concerns with those of earlier Old Testament expectations about the future, *there are clearly great difficulties in assuming extra-Israelite influence*. We have already seen that there is no borrowing from pagan life-mysticism, which finds its most characteristic expression in the cult of the dying and rising gods. One further point which should be made in this connection is that even when, in the later period, there is explicit indulgence in reflection on the life-force which brings about the constantly repeated rejuvenation of Nature, and on its speculative connection with Man's lot, namely in the book of Job, such a belief in life and immortality, deriving possibly from analogy with Nature, is expressly rejected.[1] The disinclination of the Yahweh religion for all Nature mysticism thus remained constant from the earliest to the latest periods.

At first there seems to be a better prospect of proving *influence from Persian resurrection beliefs*, for the inner structure of this founder-religion is incomparably more closely akin to that of the Yahweh faith than were those of the heathen Nature religions, an affinity which was also acknowledged by the friendly attitude of the Jewish community toward the religious views of their Persian overlords, who themselves worshipped the God of Heaven. In addition, actual borrowings can be incontestably proved, notably the connection of the demon Asmodeus (Tobit 3.8) with the Persian Aeshma Deva.

And yet, at least in our era, the divergences between Persian and Jewish resurrection beliefs are too great to make mutual influence probable.[2] To begin with, the whole conception of human existence after death is totally different. The Persian view, according to which the separation of soul and body takes place immediately after death, the soul migrating into the other world, while the body is exposed to destruction by wild beasts, is irreconcilable with the Jewish ideas mentioned earlier. Moreover, for the Persians the differing lot of

---

[1] Job 7.9f., 21; 10.21; 14.7ff., 18ff.; 16.22.

[2] Among those who have expressed themselves against Persian influence are: J. T. Addison, *Life Beyond Death in the Beliefs of Mankind*, 1933, p. 135; A. Carnoy, *La Religion de l'Iran* (Histoire des Religions, ed. M. Brillant and R. Aigrain, 2.IV), p. 258; J. Duchesne-Guillemin, *Ormazd et Ahriman*, 1953, p. 83. A mediating position is adopted by R. Martin-Achard, who would wish to describe the Persian faith as an 'indirect medium of revelation' (*op. cit.*, p. 154). Similarly L. Rost ('Alttestamentliche Wurzeln der ersten Auferstehung', *In memoriam Ernst Lohmeyer*, 1951, pp. 67ff.), who regards Persian influence as probable in the specific case of the double resurrection to bliss or woe, but otherwise stresses the OT roots of resurrection belief.

good and evil begins at once after death, in that the soul during the time until the general resurrection already comes to enjoy bliss or damnation in a preliminary way. Here, therefore, the primary concern is righteous retribution, while in Judaism this definitely is of less importance than the idea of God's complete victory over all the forces of death. Correspondingly, resurrection in the Persian religion is from the start bound up as closely as possible with the universal judgment, and strictly speaking is only for the purpose of enabling this to be perfectly carried out. In Judaism the idea of judgment makes only gradual headway; and in Daniel, where its influence is seen in the varying lot of the righteous and the ungodly, it is still not organically united with the general world-judgment portrayed in ch. 7, a fact which would be quite incomprehensible if there had really been direct borrowing from the Persian. Furthermore, in Judaism the Messiah is not directly involved in the resurrection, whereas among the Persians it is he who has to perform the raising of the dead.

Very striking, too, is the limitation of the resurrection in Jewish faith to a limited number of qualified people, while in the Zoroastrian religion from the very beginning it extended to all men. Here we see the effect of the different starting-point of the hope, which in Judaism did not lie in a systematic completion of the doctrine of retribution, but in the conception of life as God's free decision, by which he destines Man to fellowship with himself, and in the assurance of a final, unrestricted implementation of his life-creating will, which cannot be permanently limited even by death.

v. As these differences indicate, the idea that the eschatological resurrection hope, in the form attested in the Old Testament, was influenced by Persian conceptions can be shown by any reasonably detailed comparison to be inadmissible; and the same applies all the more to the *second way* in which men arrived at an assurance of the conquest of death by the individual namely their *realization that in direct encounter with God life acquires an indestructible content.* We may call this the way of faith-realism. This way was, however, open only to those who had previously been engaged in a severe struggle for assurance, and had been compelled in desperate distress to acknowledge the inadequacy of all human answers to the problem of God. *The poet of Job* depicts this distress for us in all its profundity, when he sets the patient hero before our eyes, stripped of all earthly goods and turned into a beggar, brought near to death by incurable sickness, and now compelled to undergo the shattering of all those supports which in other cases the individual finds in the fellowship of believers. He is made to experience the dogma of retribution—the scrupulous application of which to the individual was meant precisely to safeguard belief against the challenges which threatened it from the enigmatic course of events[1]—as an impassable prison wall, which not only leaves him alone with himself, and so makes it impossible for him to find comfort where his fathers found it, in the hope of a consummation of the divine community, but also delivers him up to inner self-destruction, because it blocks his every access to God, and in face of death proves him a God-rejected sinner. He finds that the pressure of his friends' exhortations to repentance disfigures the God whom he had hitherto served into a diabolical caricature, whose grinning mask reveals no more than a grisly will to destruction. But all his previous experience of his God makes it impossible for him now to curse that God wildly, and dismiss him for ever, even though he very nearly gives in to this temptation.[2] It is as if he were invisibly held by God; he cannot break away from him. That which, in earlier days, he had himself encountered of God's truth, love, and righteousness proves itself stronger than all the logical demonstrations of his friends, and of his own heart. Timidly at first, then ever more surely, the realization comes to him that the God against whom he had so desperately fought is not the true God; that behind the hostile will which dashes him to the ground, hurls his integrity in the mire, and abandons him to death, must stand another God, whom even his friends do not know, whom indeed they wrong with their clever techniques of disputation, since by these they in fact only conceal the truth, and mercilessly lead the innocent to the slaughter.[3] And by turning from the friends to God himself, who in former days has thought on his worshipper and pardoned his sin,[4] who as the Creator surely cannot disown his own handiwork,[5] who as the God of truth cannot be deceived, and as the Righteous One helps the oppressed to his right,[6] he dares in the teeth of all appearance to do the unbelievable, the audacious thing, and to hammer at the door of his God in order to summon him to his aid as Judge against the demonic god

[1] Cf. pp. 486ff. above.
[2] Job 7.11ff., 19f.; 9.15ff., 22f., 29–31; 10.13–17.
[3] Job 13.7ff.,; 19.2ff., 21f., 28f.
[4] Job 7.8, 20f.
[5] Job 10.8–12; 14.7ff., 15.
[6] Job 13.9ff.; 16.18–17.9; 23.7.

with whom he has to strive.[1] But he does not pray for his restoration. His outward lot, to which in a short time death will in any case put an end, has become a thing indifferent to him when compared with the deepest and only decisive question of his life—whether the almighty God truly wishes to establish a personal relationship with little Man, and to acknowledge it. Here neither the riddle of suffering, nor the problem of retribution, but the question of God is central. Here, too, *it is death who is shown to be the real enemy*, the one who inexorably tears away every link with God, and now, as he stands menacing before Job, condemns to absolute hopelessness every possibility of making certain of God. For the way out which Nature seems to suggest in the revival of plant life, namely that Man may yet be brought back by God from the realm of the dead, he cannot in strict sobriety accept as a human postulate without God's own promise to confirm it.[2] Only one possibility remains open, namely that yet before his death, indeed, it may be only in the very moment of that death,[3] God in person will come to meet him, and show himself in face of all human offences as witness, surety, and redeemer, who for all his inconceivable power remains bound in a personal relationship with his creature. Because Job longs for this alone, and finally with marvellous confidence avows himself loyal to this God, he has grasped that the vision of God (of which the language of prayer also speaks as the highest happiness[4]) is in the most literal sense the proper content of life. In faith he has accepted the word of God, the word of justification which God speaks to us, as in itself the essence of life and of blessedness even for the individual believer; and in comparison with this, death has no more terror, and the suffering of life is no longer a temptation. In so doing he has not, as he is often misunderstood to have done, satisfied the needs of his religious and moral self by an intellectual postulate,[5] but from his experience of the divine will to fellowship he has thrown himself on the breast of God, who cannot deny himself and become a demon; that is to say, he in

[1] Job 16.21.
[2] Job 14.7–12, 13–20.
[3] The passage which, apart from 16.18–17.9, is crucial here, namely 19.23ff., has come down to us in a very corrupt state, and cannot be wholly satisfactorily restored, despite all the attempts at repair. But that it does not refer to resurrection and eternal life in the ordinary sense should be beyond question, in view of the train of thought in the passages that precede and follow, especially their contemplation of the doom of death (vv. 21, 23–26, 24.24; 30.23).
[4] Cf. pp. 361f. above.
[5] So Duhm, Sellin and others.

his own particular situation has taken seriously the ancient Israelite faith that everywhere where God calls to men, life in the fullest sense is to be found. The fact, moreover, that in this hour when God reveals himself to him, the individual, he can endure joyfully despite the approach of death, signifies a triumph over death, and an assurance of the victory of life, which had hitherto been denied to early Israel. These things cannot be neatly 'deduced' from various premisses, even though it is quite true that definite prior spiritual conditions are necessary for them. They can only be known as the mystery of faith, which encounters God and is saved.

It is in the nature of the case that the poet of Job should not have succeeded in setting out at all clearly the achievement of this solution of the problem of God. God's confirmation of the certainty of faith cannot be presented like a play; it can attest its truth only inwardly in the heart of the hearer. Moreover, the appearance of God at the end of the book does not fulfil the expectations of Job's faith developed in the first part, but leads off along a different track.[1]

No one has ever known better than the poet of Job how to formulate from the depths of experience the only real assurance of life which there can be for the Old Testament believer, namely that which is given in the encounter with God and with his liberating word. But others, too, struck out along the path he took; and that which he could indicate only gropingly, fumbling for the right words, found in them clearer and less ambiguous expression. Closest to him undoubtedly stands *the poet of Ps.* 73, who likewise experienced the most serious threat to his assurance of God in a desperate struggle with the Jewish doctrine of retribution. His lot was, however, easier than that of Job, in that he had not lost contact with the *dōr bāneykā* the generation of God's children. It would have struck him as a betrayal of the great community of God, if he had, on the basis of the limited sphere of his own life, been willing to dare to call God's faithfulness in question.[2] Nevertheless, he faces the bankruptcy of all clever theories about God's providence; they are bound to come to grief on the fact that the way of God with his community is completely

---

[1] We agree with the view, put forward and convincingly argued in particular by Sellin, that not only the Elihu speeches but also the concluding section of the book is an independent composition, which stands in no more than a very loose relation to the line of thought developed in ch. 1–31. Whether the same author has attempted different solutions, or whether different authors are to be assumed, is to be answered, at least for the Elihu speeches, in the latter sense.

[2] Ps. 73.15.

hidden.[1] What finally brings rest to his deeply agitated heart is no new edition of the old retribution doctrine, but a more profound vision of that in which human life is truly grounded, and from which it derives its value. Decisive on this point is the picture of his own good fortune, contrasted with the fate of the godless, at the end of the psalm.[2] If here he is not speaking of long life and good days for himself, but, in fact, accepts the possibility of a lamentable end, for which only something much higher can console him, then the *' aḥᵃrît*, the end of the godless, which has taught him something so great,[3] must also consist in more than mere outward ruin. In their case, too, it is Man's relationship with God which is meant. It is the fact that God expends no more thought on them when their hour of death has come, but dismisses them from his mind like a worthless dream-image, so that then they truly stand in terror before nothingness, which makes their situation, outwardly so secure, a slippery ground on which a fearful fall constantly threatens for those caught in the toils of baseless illusion.[4] Conversely, he who even now goes through life at God's right hand has set his foot on an indestructible ground. In all trials and tribulations he knows what it is to be with God, to be held by his hand, and to be guided by his counsel, and thus his life has a content which cannot be endangered by any outward event. *God himself has become his portion. This is the bold image with which he dares to describe it, and thus, too, it continues to be*—this is the enlightening, all-irradiating certainty—*when body and soul go down into death*, and the whole man is given up to destruction. As to *how* this can happen, the only word at his disposal is the well-known term for being translated, *l-ḳ-ḥ;*[5] God's 'counsel', which guides his life, also has its possibilities for leading him even beyond death into the divine light-glory. That the example of Enoch and Elijah, however, does not exactly correspond to that which he expects for himself, but rather is used to suggest a new possibility, is shown precisely by the sober account which he takes of death. What is involved here is not a vaulting over the doom of death, nor can he ask for the splendour and glory of a heavenly life. 'Whom have I in heaven beside thee?'—thus, with one gesture of the hand, he brushes aside all the glories and mysteries of

---

[1] Ps. 73.16, 21f.
[2] Rightly pointed out by R. Kittel in his exposition.
[3] Ps. 73.17.
[4] Ps. 73.18–20.
[5] Gen. 5.24; II Kings 2.9.

the other world after which late Jewish apocalyptic reached out in its craving for knowledge. For him the decisive point is that his fellowship with the God in whose company he has lived his life here on earth, and in whose love all his longings have found their rest, cannot be done away by anything.

It is no more possible here than in the case of Job to speak of a belief in resurrection. And yet this psalm speaks even more clearly of a continuing conscious life of the human self which God has considered worthy of his fellowship; but it does so in such a way as to burst the limited potential of all previous conceptions. *še'ēr* and *lēbāb*, flesh and heart—here unquestionably poetic diction, used in place of the more customary *bāśār* and *nepeš*, body and soul, to describe the whole man in his earthly corporeity—may fall prey to death. Nevertheless, the man has not fallen out of his association with God; his real 'I' remains *'im yhwh*, with, or in the presence of, God. Not, however, in such a way as if, by a natural process, an eternal part of the man was separated from his earthly and transient parts; there is no admixture here of any sort of Greek belief in the soul. *On the contrary, all the emphasis is laid on God's holding, leading, and carrying away, and thus on God's Yes to the life of his worshipper.* And that this Yes of God's has a once for all validity, and for this very reason prepares for the pious a fate different from that of the godless; nay more, that in this very Yes or No of God to the life of Man, and not in any outward circumstances of that life, is taken the real decision about his life, which for the believer signifies ultimate security, for the unbeliever irretrievable abandonment; this is the conviction of faith which causes death to lose its power as the destroyer of the God-Man relationship.

The classic simplicity of this answer to the problem of death lies in its absolute concentration on that which the worshipper has realized to be life in the full sense. A watchful eye on judgment in the next world, or reflection on the eschatological resurrection, are both therefore poles apart from this approach. Here we are not strictly concerned with the postulate of a belief in retribution, even though it must certainly have been the pressure from this direction which helped to push the psalmist's thoughts to the decisive point. Basically it is simply *the acquiring of a clear vision for the reality of a religious life*, as a result of which all calculating, demanding, or postulating falls away as foolishness. The Psalmist describes this attainment of clear-sightedness very beautifully as an entering into the holy counsels or mysteries of God.[1] He is therefore aware that there is nothing which he has given himself; he has received his certainty as a gift by the opening of his eyes to God's mysterious action. And what he now sees, after 'the cataract has been cut away', is basically, as in the case of Job, only a new dimension of the ancient faith of Israel, that Man lives by God's call.

Only on one other occasion does this confident expectation of a 'taking up' recur without the hope either being carried a stage farther or being based on new principles. For Ps. 49.16f. treats this conquest of death by the believer so one-sidedly in terms of the contrast with the irremediable death of the worldly, who brag about their wealth, that it is never really made explicit that this certainty is inwardly rooted in the gracious word of God. One may therefore wonder whether, as a result of the marvellous experience of Ps. 73, a doctrine distinguishing between the fate of good and bad had already come into existence, which in limited circles of the pious had been elevated into a dogma of the higher wisdom, and was now arrogantly contrasted with the folly of the great mass of men. Furthermore, the association of the taking up with ransoming from Sheol[2] intrudes an alien note, inasmuch as the world of the dead here appears as an independent power which can assert its claims even in dealings with Yahweh. Nevertheless, in view of the bad state of preservation of the text throughout the psalm, which makes the whole character of its train of thought doubtful, and indeed even makes it possible to excise the crucial verse 15 as a gloss,[3] one should be chary of drawing too far-reaching conclusions.

---

[1] The unusual nature of the expression in v. 17 does not, however, justify such arbitrary emendations of the text as that adopted by Gunkel, when he changes *miḳdᵉšē* to *mišpᵉṭē* or *mōḳᵉšē*. Apart from the somewhat distant comparison with the μυστήρια θεοῦ in Wisd. 2.22, the obvious passage that comes to mind is Ps. 25.14: 'The secret of Yahweh is for those who fear him.' Even if, with Gunkel, the render-ing 'trustful intimacy, friendship', is preferred for *sōd*, the idea is still of a knowledge which is not open to everyone, but is accessible only in the interior converse of God with his elect. Thus the *miḳdāšīm* of Ps. 73 are clearly holy places into which the profane cannot enter, areas of God's dealings with men which are open only to the one who humbly seeks refuge in Yahweh. A. Weiser would prefer to read the singular, with the LXX, and has in mind 'an encounter with his God that was brought about by the theophany, assumed to have taken place in the cult of the Covenant Festival' (*The Psalms*, 1962, p. 511). He sees here a reference to a special revelation of God, by which a new faith-understanding was given to the psalmist.

[2] Cf. J. J. Stamm, *Erlösen und Vergeben*, 1940, pp. 16f.

[3] So Gunkel *ad loc.* Ch. Barth, *op. cit.*, p. 160, however, provides good grounds for disagreeing with this conclusion, though he refuses all the same to find here any

On the other hand, in *Ps. 16* speaks a spiritual kinsman of the worshipper of Ps. 73, even though in his language he hardly has any point of contact with the latter, and is led by quite a different route to the faith that conquers death. If in Ps. 73 it is the need for God which leads the writer down into new depths of understanding, here it is the poet's *overwhelming bliss in God* which drives him to bold utterances of heaven-storming confidence. The manner in which this worshipper describes the happiness of his life in the present[1] is characteristic of his attitude to life as a whole. Because of this inward happiness, that which God apportions him, whatever it may be, disposes his heart to praise and thanks. This is not a question of pieces of especial good fortune, regarded as outward gifts of God, but of the living intercourse of the heart with its God, who in counsel and advice gives himself to be experienced as a living helper by the one who has opened his heart to him. That moreover, which, in the present constitutes for him the content of life and the essence of all good, he knows to be allotted to him in the future also as his abiding portion.[2] Step by step the praise rises right up to the level of sheer exultation, as he sees the limits which otherwise are set to all earthly well-being yield before the happiness of fellowship with God. His whole manhood, described in its inward and outward existence as heart, liver,[3] and flesh, rejoices over this in its feeling of God-given security. For Sheol and the grave can no longer terrify him; he has gained a path of life shown him by God, who leads him to a joy that satisfies utterly before God's face, to pleasures such as only God's right hand can impart.

Here once again we stand before *a conquest of death which proceeds from a profoundly inward knowledge of what life really is.* This worshipper, too, bothers himself no further about the state of the blessed in the other world; apocalyptic knowledge about the courts of heaven, and their glory, interests him not at all. His whole and sole concern is a life before the face of God, in that fullness of joy which wells from completely unclouded fellowship with him. It is because he knows of

---

hope of something beyond an earthly life. A different view is taken by J. Fichtner, *Die altorientalische Weisheit in ihrer israelitisch-jüdischen Ausprägung,* 1933, p. 68; J. J. Stamm, *op. cit.*; A. Weiser, *The Psalms,* pp. 389f.

[1] Ps. 16.6–8.
[2] Ps. 16.9–11.
[3] *kᵉbēdi* is certainly to be read in v. 9 instead of *kᵉbōdi*, providing a term for the feelings to parallel those for willing and thinking: cf. p. 146 above.

the reality and happiness of such a life that he dares to defy death. The God who has revealed himself to him as the one who gives new form to this life does not allow his devout worshipper to be snatched away from him by death and the grave, but sets him for ever before his face. How this happens, whether he is to be spared the death of body and soul by a translation, or whether, as is more probable, that death is unable to encroach upon his real 'I', which belongs simply to God, there is no unambiguous statement. Far more important than any 'How' is the reality of God, affirming that it is indeed so; and this alone is decisive.

In view of the profound unity in these hymns of praise between their understanding of life and their overcoming of death the doubts expressed as to whether their scope is really so far-reaching cannot be allowed to prevail.[1] The man who finds here reference to nothing more than preservation from the evil of an early death externalizes the joy of the psalmist, which has its roots in the depths of the inner life, in a most intolerable way, and degrades the three concluding verses into a remarkably empty piece of phrase-making. If the singer really wished to say no more than that he would go his way secure in God's protection, then he could have stopped at v. 8, or at most have added a vow of thanksgiving. It is clear, however, that in the concluding section the supreme goal is named for the first time, the goal toward which his whole life strives, the pleasant lot in which, both now and in the past, his heart has always rejoiced.

The common factor linking all these witnesses to the conquest of death in the life of the individual is that their certainty is built on the gift of fellowship with God here and now. Because God has spoken to Man, and still speaks, he is therefore lifted out of the compulsion of mortality, and sees before him the path of life. No eternal substance in Man asserts itself against death, no attribute of his spiritual being bestowed upon him at his creation assures him of immortality; but like the concept of person itself[2] the survival of the person is only to be comprehended *in actu Dei*. 'Where, however, or with whom, God speaks, whether in wrath or in grace, the same is certainly immortal. The Person of the God who speaks, and the Word of God show that we are creatures

---

[1] Ch. Barth, *op. cit.*, pp. 153f. The argument that in this as in other passages no conclusion is reached as to what is really to be understood by eternal life in the beyond applies a false yardstick to the utterances of the psalm, takes no account of the starting-point or the real concerns of the poet. The same applies to A. Weiser, *The Psalms*, p. 177f.

[2] Cf. vol. I, p. 360.

with whom God wills to speak even unto eternity and in an immortal manner.'[1]

VI. From the second century onwards evidences multiply that *the concept of eternity has been accepted into the community's life of faith.* Even though it was never able to enjoy universal recognition, it was still felt by the religiously most vital section of the community to be the indispensable final note in their assurance of salvation, and gave their faith an even greater sense of superiority to the religious thinking of heathenism. The passion with which it is used in II Maccabees in controversy with the heathen oppressors shows how men's sense of the unconditional character of God's demand is now linked indissolubly with the assurance of eternal election or rejection even for the individual.[2]

And yet this dogmatic hardening brought with it a not inconsiderable change in this concept of faith, as a result of which its direct origin in God's word of election was loosened and obscured, while other, pseudo-religious explanations began to play a part. The two lines which we saw leading up to the personal hope of immortality, the eschatological and the faith-realistic, were not combined for their mutual reinforcement; instead they became, frequently misunderstood and coarsened, the starting-points for speculative elaborations on the hope of the conquest of death. The critical point in all this was not the wandering off into fantasy, which heaped up contradictory statements about the conquest of death by the faithful, and was unable to give any kind of coherent notion of the time of the resurrection, the place of a future life, whether the call to a new life was to be for all or only for some, how judgment was to be held and retribution executed.[3] But on the one hand, especially in Palestinian Judaism, direct assurance of God was replaced by an intellectual theorem, dictated by the human need for retribution, which found its basis in very human ideas of the way in which God's righteousness ought to reward and punish, and liked to have the bitterness and difficulty of the service which he desired richly recompensed with eternal life and

[1] Luther (Weimar), *Works*, vol. 43, p. 481, quoted in E. Brunner, *Man in Revolt*, p. 468.

[2] Cf. L. Rost, 'Alttestamentliche Wurzeln der ersten Auferstehung', *In memoriam Ernst Lohmeyer*, 1951, pp. 67ff.; G. Molin, 'Entwicklung und Motive der Auferstehungshoffnung vom AT bis zur rabbinischen Zeit', *Judaica* IX, 1953, pp. 225ff.; H. J. Kraus, art. 'Auferstehung', *RGG*[3] I, pp. 692f.

[3] For the individual features of the variegated picture cf. the systematic compilations in Bousset-Gressmann, *op. cit.*, pp. 269ff.; P. Volz, *Die Eschatologie der jüdischen Gemeinde im neutestamentlichen Zeitalter*, 1934, §§ 37ff., pp. 229ff.

happiness.[1] On the other hand, a substitute was found for God's decision as the sole guarantee of the conquest of death, by equipping Man with an immortal soul, thus building into human nature a solid insurance against the annihilating judgment of death which at once betrays its alien origin by the contrast which it affords to the Old Testament conceptions of the nature of Man. There can be no doubt that these lines of thought from Hellenistic philosophy of a Stoic-Platonist stamp found their way into the community through the mediation of Hellenistic Judaism; and by combining the doctrines of the pre-existence of the soul, of the continuing life of the spirit, which welcomes death as a release from the burdens of the flesh, of the passing of the pious almost by a law of nature from earthly life to a state of blessedness, and of the ungodly to a state of torment, a hope of immortality was fashioned which was markedly alien to the faith of the Old Testament.[2] Moreover, in both cases there was a pressing danger that the hoped-for life after death would not be understood as new life in the true sense, life which derives its quality from undisturbed fellowship with God, but would offer no more than a life of earthly bliss, conceived sometimes in more material, sometimes in more spiritual terms, only going on for ever. Only where there is an emphasis on the sinlessness of the new life, and on the complete transformation of its quality by the dissolution of all the conditions of existence on earth,[3] is a barrier set up against the secularizing of the hope of eternity in the service of human self-interest.

The way in which the hope of eternity thus slips back into the constructions of human expediency, which conceal the only sufficient reason for such a hope, namely the nature of God's self-communication, shows how questionable it is to see in the overcoming of a 'this-worldly fixation' simply the removal of an obstructive limitation, which had only been allowed to develop as a result of an inferior feeling for life.[4] It is certainly true that in the restriction of the God-

---

[1] II Macc. 7.9, 36.

[2] In addition to the Wisdom of Solomon, Jubilees, I Enoch, and IV Maccabees, it was Philo above all who was responsible for the marked prominence of this substitution of a philosophical belief in immortality for the original belief in resurrection. Even Josephus betrays this influence in many of his remarks about immortality.

[3] Cf. the abolition of the evil impulse in the messianic age (Strack-Billerbeck, *Kommentar zum NT* IV, pp. 479f.; F. Weber, *Jüdische Theologie*[2], pp. 399f.), and the utterance of Rab in *Berakoth* 17a, quoted in Strack-Billerbeck, *op. cit.* I, p. 890.

[4] This, in essence, is the view of F. Baumgärtel, *Die Eigenart der alttestamentlichen Frömmigkeit*, 1932, pp. 36ff. and 103ff.

Man relationship to earthly life lurk certain temptations which have a disadvantageous effect on piety. On the other hand, however, we should not overlook the danger in transcending the bounds of death by those speculations with which high-handed Man seeks to break down a door that is barred to him. The enormous variety of beliefs about the other world in heathen religions, even in their highest forms, can be condemned, on the basis of the Christian understanding of God, as nothing more than disobedience to God and an escape from his holiness, and thus as holding no promise. Indeed, the influences from this quarter which have affected Christian belief in eternity have only too seriously falsified and corrupted its original form. By contrast, the obedience with which the faith of Israel rejected every solution of the riddle of death which was not legitimated by God's revelation displays an inner greatness which could well serve Christians as a serious exhortation and warning. Barring the way to the dangers of utilitarianism and eudaemonism, of speculative theodicy and theories of retribution, stands that training in ultimate seriousness and concentrated energy in the fulfilment of God's demands in this world which was effective precisely because of this limitation. 'Here there was no question of relativizing the problem of God's relation to the world and to Man for the sake of a possible future. There was no other world to provide men with a constant temptation to put off, or deny importance to, everything that disquieted them. Instead there was no evading the necessity to take both the earth and Man seriously in the context of God.'[1] We have already seen[2] how new resources were constantly developed to ward off such dangers successfully. Furthermore, it was precisely along these lines that the faith of the Old Testament was enabled, even where God's power to redeem was revealed in all its richness, to establish a chaste and sober concept of eternity, based on personal relationship with God, and to be content with that.

This form of the hope did not, however, find the counterpart to its own essential nature in the mortality belief of later Judaism, but in the New Testament hope, which, because of its absolute connection with the act of God in Christ, rejected all extraneous supports for the concept of eternity. In the death and resurrection of Christ death has already been brought to nought, and the bond uniting the believer to the God revealed in Christ enables him here and now to

[1] G. von Rad, *op. cit.*, col. 834.
[2] Cf. pp. 350ff., 366ff., and 488ff. above.

pass from death to life.[1] This being taken up into the life of Christ is not however accomplished as a mystical or magical process, but is a new direction for human life, apprehended in conscious decision,[2] and placing life and death completely at the service of the Lord.[3] The conquest of death which this brings with it does not, however, signify a state, but a movement, never completed on earth, which requires the old man continually to die afresh,[4] and finds its blessedness in the hope offered and guaranteed by the Gospel.[5] Here for the first time both the lines of the Old Testament hope of eternity, the eschatological and the faith-realistic, combine. The conquest of death prepared for the individual by God stems from the life of fellowship with God apprehended in the present, but is completed through and beyond death in that perfect world to which the resurrection of Christ points as an earnest and a pledge.

[1] John 5.24; 6.50; 11.25f.; cf. II Tim. 2.18.
[2] Rom. 6.11ff.; 8.2–4.
[3] Rom. 14.7–9.
[4] Rom. 8.13; II Cor. 4.7–12; 5.14f.; John 21.19.
[5] Rom. 5.2; 8.24f.; Col. 1.27; Titus 3.7; I John 3.3.

INDEX OF SUBJECTS

Figures in italic refer to sections on the subject in question; superior figures refer to footnotes

INDEX OF MODERN AUTHORS

INDEX OF BIBLICAL PASSAGES

OLD TESTAMENT

545

29	248	52.29 f.	137	3.14	48, 50, 56
29.11	358			3.18 ff.	498
29.12–14	456	*Lamentations*		3.22	56
29.23	317	1.11	138	4.14	138, 252
31	253	1.16	138	6.9	37
31.5	355	1.19	138	6.14	434
31.10	475	1.20	145	7.27	434
31.12	355	1.21 f.	421	8.1	56, 251
31.14	138	2.11	145 f.	8.3	50
31.18 ff.	356, 458, 468	2.19	143	8.4	33
31.20	145, 459, 475	2.20 ff.	421	8.14	505
31.22	104, 162	3.6	95	9.1	19
31.25	134	3.13	145	9.1 ff.	172, 329
31.29	484	3.17	139	9.2	197 f.
31.29 f.	436, 484	3.21 ff.	305	9.2 ff.	199
31.31 ff.	58, 310, 328	3.25	139	9.3	33
31.33 f.	295	3.27	177	9.5	19
31.34	458 f.	3.27 ff.	360	10	194, 202
31.35 f.	157	3.34 ff.	421	10.4	33
32.17	159	3.37 f.	176	10.5	204
33.8	458 f.	3.38	108	10.6 f.	204
33.9	358	3.40 ff.	465	10.18 f.	33
33.19–26	493	3.58	138	11.1	50
33.20	159	3.59 ff.	421	11.5	48, 132
33.22	196	4.13	421	11.16	251
33.25	160	4.16	38	11.18	470
34.5	505	4.20	47	11.19	59, 133, 144,
35.15	468	4.21	344		471
36.1 ff.	357	4.21 f.	421	11.19 f.	301
36.3	457 f., 468	4.22	439	11.24	50
36.7	468	5.7	438, 421	12.9	251
37.3	451	5.16	420	12.16	434
37.9	138	5.20 f.	438	12.20	434
37.15 ff.	357			13.3	132 f.
38.24 ff.	323	*Ezekiel*		13.4 ff.	418
39.16	77	1	193, 202	13.5	451
39.18	286	1.3	56	13.9	486
40.4 ff.	357	1.5 ff.	93	13.10	418
42.2	451	1.13	204	14.1	251
42.20	138	1.15–21	32, 194	14.6	470
43.6	137	1.23 f.	32	14.7	334
43.10	172	1.24	204	14.9 ff.	418
45	434	1.26	21	14.12 ff.	434, 436, 485
45.5	131	1.26 f.	21	14.13 ff.	498
46 ff.	330	1.28	18, 20, 32	14.21 ff.	436
48.36	145	2.1 ff.	18	16	354, 481, 485
49.20	183	2.2	48, 50	16.40	329
50.20	459	2.4 ff.	73	16.47	433
50.45	183	3.1 ff.	73	16.48	390
51.5	413	3.10	19	16.49	357
51.11	133	3.12	50	16.51 ff.	390
51.39	515	3.12 ff.	18	16.63	448, 459
51.57	515	3.13	20	17.12 ff.	388

APOCRYPHA AND PSEUDEPIGRAPHA OF THE OLD TESTAMENT

NEW TESTAMENT